WESTMAR COLLEGE LIBRARY!

W9-BXA-132

A POLITICAL HISTORY
OF GHANA
1850–1928

Oxford University Press, Amen House, London E.C.4

GLASGOW NEW YORK TORONTO MELBOURNE WELLINGTON
BOMBAY CALCUTTA MADRAS KARACHI LAHORE DACCA
CAPE TOWN SALISBURY NAIROBI IBADAN ACCRA
KUALA LUMPUR HONG KONG

A POLITICAL HISTORY OF

GHANA

The Rise of Gold Coast Nationalism
1850—1928

BY

DAVID KIMBLE

OXFORD
AT THE CLARENDON PRESS
1963

DT
511
.K42
1963

966.7
K49

© *Oxford University Press 1963*

56681

PRINTED IN GREAT BRITAIN

HELEN

PREFACE

'KNOWLEDGE is like the baobab tree; one man's arms cannot encompass it.' Certainly this study would have been impossible without the extended help of Helen Kimble. It is customary for an author to thank his wife; I continue to have more cause than most.

My debt to the existing literature is acknowledged in footnotes, but two publications deserve special mention: Martin Wight's *The Gold Coast Legislative Council* (London, 1947), which first aroused my political curiosity; and, in a different vein, the *Report of the Commission of Enquiry into Disturbances in the Gold Coast, 1948*, which offered the first key to the unexpected riots which preceded my arrival in Accra.

Perhaps 1948 was an ideal time to commence a first-hand study of African nationalism, though it might not have seemed so to those politically conscious Africans who suspected that the Colonial Office had sent me to explain how difficult self-government really was, or to the colonial officials who temporarily succeeded in persuading the Vice-Chancellor of Oxford University that I was 'too closely associated with the nationalist movement'. Truly one year as a long-range extra-mural tutor from Oxford and thirteen years as Director of Extra-Mural Studies in Ghana provided an ideal opportunity for the friendships, travel, and research which made this book possible.

Throughout this period I have been accumulating a formidable debt of gratitude to people in many walks of life.

First of all, to Thomas Hodgkin, who as Secretary of the Oxford University Delegacy for Extra-Mural Studies pitchforked me into the midst of Gold Coast life and politics, and whose unrivalled knowledge of nationalist Africa today has provided a constant inspiration and stimulus.

Second in point of time, to David Williams, editor of *West Africa*, who encouraged me to record and analyse my impressions of the political scene in the form of articles for his weekly journal. It was not long before I looked further, back to the 1930's, for the origins of the contemporary unrest, a search that eventually led me back as far as 1850.

Next, to my former colleagues in the University of Ghana, some of whom may have forgotten that they ever helped me:

Dennis Austin, Rev. Professor Christian Baeta, Paul Bertelsen, Harry Bevin, Professor Ernest Boateng, Lalage Bown, Professor Kofi Busia, Dr. Douglas Coombs, Dr. J. C. de Graft Johnson, Modjabeng Dowuona, Professor St. Clair Drake, Professor John Fage, Dr. Thomas Hilton, Soas Jones-Quartey, Rev. Professor Noel King, Professor John Lewis, Joe Price, Margaret Priestley, Frank Roberts, Ivor Wilks, Jack Woolley, and the late Rev. Dr. Sidney Williamson; and especially Edgar Metcalfe and Dr. William Tordoff, for their many detailed comments.

David Balme, the first Principal, and his successor, Dr. R. H. Stoughton, for their consistent encouragement.

Kwesi Mensah, my secretary, for his willingness to type fast and almost faultlessly at any hour of the day or night; and all the other members of the Institute of Extra-Mural Studies who often found me more preoccupied than they had a right to expect.

To my many Ghanaian friends, who never ceased to surprise me by their unfailing generosity:

Sir Henly Coussey, George Grant, T. Hutton Mills jun., Magnus J. Sampson, and W. E. G. Sekyi, now all 'of blessed memory'.

I. K. Agyeman, Kofi Antubam, F. Awoonor Williams, F. L. Bartels, J. H. Braimah, John Buckman, S. Bus-Kwofie sen., A. Casely Hayford, K. A. Gbedemah, K. G. Konuah, Sir Arku Korsah, A. A. Y. Kyerematen, Nene Mate Kole, Sir Leslie M'Carthy, M. A. Ribeiro, and the Tolon-Na; and especially Dr. J. B. Danquah, Dr. J. W. de Graft Johnson, and W. S. Kwesi Johnston, for their valuable documents and notes.

To several of the modern wandering scholars, notably Dr. G. W. Carpenter, Professor P. Curtin, Rev. A. G. Fraser, Professor G. S. Graham, L. B. Greaves, my brother Professor G. H. T. Kimble, Rev. C. Kingsley Williams, Professor R. Lystad, Professor D. McCall, Professor I. Neustadt, P. M. Sherlock, and Rev. Dr. B. G. M. Sundkler, whose visits to Achimota and Legon provided brief encounters of value; Rev. Dr. H. Debrunner, for the loan of early Mission records and pamphlets; and especially Professor James Coleman and Professor David Apter, who were able to open up new fields of research and analysis in West Africa.

In substance, this book is the dissertation for which I was awarded the degree of Ph.D. in the University of London. I am indebted to Professor Kenneth Robinson and Professor Donald G. Macrae of that University for their helpful comments.

There are many other people, especially in Ghana, who have furnished me with manuscripts and memories; they have not been forgotten, but much of their material has yet to be used, when (as I hope) this political history is carried forward in a second volume, extending probably up to 1948.

DAVID KIMBLE

The University College, Dar es Salaam
July 1962

CONTENTS

LIST OF MAPS

PLATES

INTRODUCTION

THE idea of nationalism is one that tends to elude accurate definition.[1] There is something to be said for A. Cobban's view: 'To attempt a definition of the nation, or even more of the concept of national self-determination, at this point, would be to prejudge the whole issue of our study.'[2] Nevertheless, it is relevant to note that the word 'nation' is commonly defined in subjective terms; for example, as a group of people who feel themselves to be a nation. Ernest Renan, in a famous nineteenth-century address, *Qu'est-ce qu'une nation?*, described it as 'a spiritual principle'.[3] It has even been said that 'The only way to decide whether an individual belongs to one nation rather than another is to ask him'.[4]

The study of nationalism is in danger of being divided into watertight compartments. The modern nation-state based on popular sovereignty was a Western invention, derived perhaps ultimately from Rousseau and given popular currency through the French and American Revolutions.[5] On the other hand, increasing attention is being paid to 'colonial' or even 'African' nationalism, almost as a species *sui generis*. Yet the emergent nations of Africa owe much of the strength of their demand for political self-determination to ideas from overseas, many of which were transmitted during the nineteenth century as imperial expansion took place in competitive, nationalist terms.[6] African nationalism, although it may be precipitated by the domination of alien European powers, is not otherwise fundamentally different in kind from nationalism elsewhere.

National sentiment—the sense of 'belonging'—is more likely to develop in the presence of certain objective factors, of which the most important are a national homeland and a common language and culture. National feeling may further be reinforced by a common ancestry, or shared traditions of origin; by religious beliefs held in common; and by the physical advantages of economic interdependence and ease of communications. Nevertheless, the subjective idea of nationhood may exist in the absence of one or more of these elements. The Swiss lack a common language, the citizens of the United States have no common ancestry, religion divides the Belgians, while Pakistan is not even a single entity on the map. It would be difficult to say that any one

[1] See, for example, the introductory 'Note on the Use of Words' such as nation, nationality, nationalism, in the Royal Institute of International Affairs Study Group Report on *Nationalism* (Oxford, 1939). [2] *National Self-Determination* (Oxford, 1945), p. 5.

[3] *Discours et conférences* (Paris, 1887), p. 277.

[4] W. B. Pillsbury, *The Psychology of Nationality and Internationalism* (New York, 1919), p. 267.

[5] Cf. H. Kohn, *The Idea of Nationalism* (New York, 1945), p. 3: 'Nationalism is inconceivable without the ideas of popular sovereignty preceding.'

[6] Cf. the stimulating discussion by H. Kohn of the relationship between *Nationalism and Imperialism in the Hither East* (London, 1932), ch. iv.

of these factors is essential, though the presence of each may make an important contribution to national unity.

Here, however, we must with Sir Ernest Barker distinguish further between 'the sense of nationality'—when the members of a group are 'aware of their peculiar nationality as a fact or a feeling which distinguishes them from other nations'—and the 'passion of nationalism'—when the members are 'seized by the idea of nationality as the one cardinal principle on which their life ... ought to be organised and developed'.[1] The distinction is particularly relevant to a study of colonial nationalism, which seems to depend upon a few key leaders—an active *élite*—inspired by such a passion, and seeking to communicate it to an ever-widening circle.

This book is not intended to be an analytical account, but rather an historical case-study of nationalism as it developed in one African colonial territory. It would therefore be inappropriate to squander preliminary pages on niceties of definition. A comprehensive rather than a restrictive approach is required, which will permit consideration of all the various threads which have gone to make up a complex pattern in the Gold Coast. J. S. Coleman's rigorous definition of nationalism is the most helpful yet published;[2] he tends, however, to stress its political objectives, whereas a wider frame of reference is sometimes useful. Here, therefore, nationalism is taken to include (*a*) opposition to alien control, (*b*) the consciousness of belonging to a particular African nation (actual or potential), to Africa in general, or to the Negro race, (*c*) pride in the nation's culture, traditions, institutions, and achievements, (*d*) awareness of common political rights and responsibilities, (*e*) an articulate demand for a self-governing nation-state, and especially (*f*) all forms of persuasion, agitation, and concerted action through which such sentiments are expressed or encouraged.

In this wider sense, nationalism may include many different kinds of organized protest, which may be couched in tribal, religious, economic, cultural, or racial terms; at one moment it may be the voice of the Chiefs and landowners, at another the ratepayers or the intelligentsia. With T. L. Hodgkin, we may extend the word 'nationalist' to cover 'any organisation or group that explicitly asserts the rights, claims and aspirations of a given African society (from the level of the language-group to that of "Pan-Africa") in opposition to European authority, whatever its institutional form and objectives'.[3] All these activities are, however, likely to find their most enduring outlet in the political demand for self-government. Gradually the nation comes to be regarded as the ideal political unit to replace what has been called 'the multi-cellular tissue of tribalism'.[4] Even if we refuse to accept what J. E.

[1] *National Character and the Factors in its Formation* (London, 1927), pp. 116–17.
[2] *Nigeria: Background to Nationalism* (Los Angeles, 1958), p. 425.
[3] *Nationalism in Colonial Africa* (London, 1956), p. 23.
[4] Margery Perham, 'The British Problem in Africa', in *Foreign Affairs* (London, 1951), vol. xxix.

Powell calls the unproved 'colony-equals-nation' assumption,[1] we cannot refuse to recognize the social and political consequences of that assumption. The history of the Gold Coast can only be fully interpreted in the light of the rise of nationalism.

.   .   .   .

The name Gold Coast has been retained throughout.[2] The reason is partly that it occurs so often in quotation, but also that it is a useful reminder of the contrast between the colonial territory and the independent nation. The name Ghana, although officially introduced only in 1957, is now often applied retrospectively to all phases of the country's history. In fact, the attempt to attribute Gold Coast origins to the ancient empire of Ghana, and the suggested change of name, form an interesting minor aspect of nationalist thought, and can be traced back further than is often supposed. The initial stimulus may have come from European historians, but African writers soon made 'the Ghana hypothesis' their own.[3]

As early as 1887, A. B. Ellis, in his book on *The Tshi-Speaking Peoples*, quoted a traditional account of the migration of the Akan peoples from the interior: 'In the beginning, the Fantis, Ashantis, Gamans, and all people speaking our language, lived in a far country, beyond Salagha. There was not much bush there. The land was flat, and covered with grass, and the people had plenty of cows and sheep.' The story tells how the Fulas, 'of a red colour', who had Muslim connexions, came and made the black people their slaves, until they fled into the thick forest. There they built many towns and villages, and gradually expanded southwards. 'No one was living in the forest country, and thus, after many years always coming downwards, they reached the sea. And when they saw the sea, with the waves leaping, and the white foam hissing and frothing on the beach, they thought it was all boiling water, and they were much afraid.'[4] Ellis suggested that the forest people of the Gold

---

[1] 'Nationalism', in *World Perspectives* (London, 1956).

[2] 'The Gold Coast' initially referred only to the coastal Forts and Settlements, and later to the Colony south of Ashanti; eventually it acquired a much wider application. The area discussed in this book, and generically referred to as the Gold Coast, is the territorial entity created by the Imperial Orders in Council of 1901, i.e. including Ashanti and the Northern Territories, but excluding the British mandated area of Togoland (which was administered with the Gold Coast only from 1919 onwards, though it now forms a part of the State of Ghana). Where the name is used in a more restricted sense, this will be clear from the context.

[3] In what follows, the various versions of the theory are quoted for their political and psychological interest, and no attempt has been made to sift opinions from facts. The connexion between the ancient and the modern Ghana is still largely a matter for controversy and research; a useful summary of the limited evidence available is given by J. D. Fage, 'Ancient Ghana: A Review of the Evidence', in *Transactions of the Historical Society of Ghana* (Achimota, 1957), vol. iii, pt. 2.

[4] A. B. Ellis, *The Tshi-Speaking Peoples of the Gold Coast of West Africa* (London, 1887), pp. 331–4. It is a pity that Ellis did not give the source of this graphic account, since most of the subsequent African versions of the migration theory spring from educated, rather than traditional, sources.

Coast might originally have come from Wangara, which had belonged to Ghana.[1]

The first Gold Coast writer to claim a definite historical connexion with Ghana was the Rev. J. B. Anaman, at the turn of the century, in his *Gold Coast Guide*. He appears to have drawn mainly upon W. D. Cooley's *The Negroland of the Arabs Examined and Explained* (London, 1841), for his account of an ancient Negro empire called 'Genewa', whose capital was 'Ghanah', probably located 'near the site of the present Timbuctoo'. Anaman gave currency to the view that there had been large-scale population movements out of Ghana, in two directions, one of them towards Benin.

The other forcing a passage through the jungles southward of Genewa, settled itself within the regions of the Kong Mountains, in the district then called by the Arabs, Wangara. To the latter belonged the Ashantis and Fantis, who were then related together as brothers.

The city built by the Fantis was Takyiman, from which, by-and-by, pressed by the growing power of the Ashantis and by severity of famine, they withdrew further southward, till gradually they overspread the whole region now known as Fantiland.[2]

This theory was based on speculation rather than on authentic records, and Anaman in his account does state that this was what was 'believed' to have occurred. But, as Brodie Cruickshank had once remarked in another connexion, 'it was not necessary that such reports should be true in order to their being believed'.[3] The migration theory was taken at its face value by most Gold Coast readers, and the idea of attributing national origins to an ancient and powerful race was bound to have a strong influence.

The first detailed account of the empire of Ghana to be published in English is to be found in the remarkable book *A Tropical Dependency* by Lady Lugard. She pieced together the evidence of medieval Arabic writers, and deduced that the site of Ghana was probably identical with that of the modern Walata. With some certainty, however, she was able to state that around 1067, the date of El Bekri's contemporary account, Ghana was 'the principal black kingdom of the Western Soudan'. She referred to schools and centres of learning, and quoted descriptions of the town as the meeting-place of commercial caravans from all parts of the world, and 'the resort of the learned, the rich, and the pious of all nations'.[4]

Lady Lugard knew Cooley's *Negroland of the Arabs* as 'a learned and most careful examination of the ancient geography of the country'; but she did not pay much attention to the origins of the coastal tribes, and her references to possible migration were not very flattering. Nevertheless, her book was well

[1] J. D. Fage says that Wangara was the source of the gold traded in Ghana, although itself 'just outside the political control of Ghana'. *An Introduction to the History of West Africa* (Cambridge, 1954), p. 20.

[2] J. B. Anaman, *The Gold Coast Guide* (London, 1895, 2nd edn. 1902), pp. 8–9.

[3] Brodie Cruickshank, *Eighteen Years on the Gold Coast of Africa* (London, 1853), vol. i, p. 190.

[4] Lady Lugard, *A Tropical Dependency* (London, 1905), chs. ix–xiii.

received in the Gold Coast, and was in fact used at Achimota during the 1920's as the main textbook for a new history course, which included the story of Ghana, Melle, and Songhai.[1] This aroused keen interest among both students and staff. J. E. K. Aggrey at the time of his death was working on an historical thesis, and his uncompleted notes show that he hoped 'to prove that a number of the Negroes, pure Negroes, who inhabit say the Gold Coast, are a conquering race who trace their lineage to Songhay, to Melle, to Ghana, to Egypt, to Meroe of the Ethiopians'.[2]

It was left to an Englishman, the Rev. W. T. Balmer, to bring the possible connexion with Ghana more fully home to Gold Coast students in *A History of the Akan Peoples*, published in 1926. Following Lady Lugard, he identified Walata as the central city of Ghana; and he took as virtual certainties many of the probable facts which she had cautiously set down. Thus we get for the first time a confident, coherent account of the 'powerful Negro kingdom ... known as Ghana' which 'lasted nearly a thousand years', with 'a tradition that its history goes back much further still, perhaps to 600 B.C.'. Balmer described Ghana's unity in struggles against invading races, as a result of which 'this Negro kingdom was able to extend its rule all over the Western Sudan even to the shores of the Ocean'. More important, he claimed: 'It is very probable that the Fanti, Ashanti, Ahanta and Akan people in general formed part of this ancient Negro kingdom.' Still more attractive was his suggestion that the Negro peoples, partly as a result of their contact with Europeans, might 'recover once again a position of power and influence among the nations of the earth, not only equal to that which they held in the far-off days of the vanished kingdom of Ghana, but one which will far exceed it in all that is worthy of esteem'.[3]

Balmer's glowing account was to prove most influential,[4] especially as it was this that first aroused the interest of the young J. B. Danquah, who was soon to realize the political possibilities of the idea. In his *Akim Abuakwa Handbook*, published in 1928, Danquah the historian was fairly cautious in his references to Ghana, simply stating that 'The Akan Race (Ashanti, Fanti, &c.) claim a historical connection with the ancient Kingdom of Ghana or Khana'. It so happened that Danquah the nationalist was already trying to think of a new name for the Gold Coast, instead of calling it after 'one particular mineral it produces'. At this juncture he suggested 'Akanland', since the Akan language was spoken and Akan tribal states were found 'throughout

---

[1] A. G. Fraser, 'What Achimota Has Done', in *The Gold Coast Review* (Accra, 1927), vol. iii, no. 2.   [2] Quoted by E. W. Smith in his *Aggrey of Africa* (London, 1929), p. 277.

[3] W. T. Balmer, *A History of the Akan Peoples* (London, 1929), pp. 26–28.

[4] Balmer's book was based on his lessons at Mfantsipim between 1907 and 1911. One of his students was J. W. de Graft Johnson, who later published *A Historical Geography of the Gold Coast* (London, 1929). He reproduced the extracts from Anaman already quoted above, and added that the Wangaras and Hausas of the Northern Territories and Northern Ashanti were 'believed to have belonged to the ancient Arab state of Ghanah'. Ibid. pp. 135–40. Cf. *African Glory* (London, 1954), by his nephew, J. C. de Graft Johnson.

the country . . . excepting the Northern Territories and the Ga–Adangbe south-eastern corner on the Coast'.[1] This was of course open to criticism; and even when, a few years later, he suggested 'Akan–Ga' as a possible improvement, *West Africa* commented, 'it would appear that Dr. Danquah's views on nationhood do not extend to the non-Akan population of the Northern Territories'.[2] It was not long after this that Danquah proposed 'New Ghana', instead of Gold Coast, 'which has so much of a taint of the old slavery days'.[3]

There was to be much further historical speculation, and considerable political discussion, before the name of Ghana was eventually adopted, and Kwame Nkrumah, the first African Prime Minister, announced, 'we take pride in the name, not out of romanticism but as an inspiration for the future'.[4]

[1] J. B. Danquah, *The Akim Abuakwa Handbook* (London, 1928), p. 38 n. and App.

[2] Report of a London lecture by Danquah on 'Some Modern Tendencies towards Nationality in the Gold Coast', and editorial comment, *West Africa*, 8 Mar. 1930.

[3] Danquah noted in his 'Diary of a Man about Town', *The Times of West Africa*, 26 Mar. 1934, that this suggestion had already been taken up in 'one or two quarters in the press'.

[4] *Legislative Assembly Debates*, 18 May 1956.

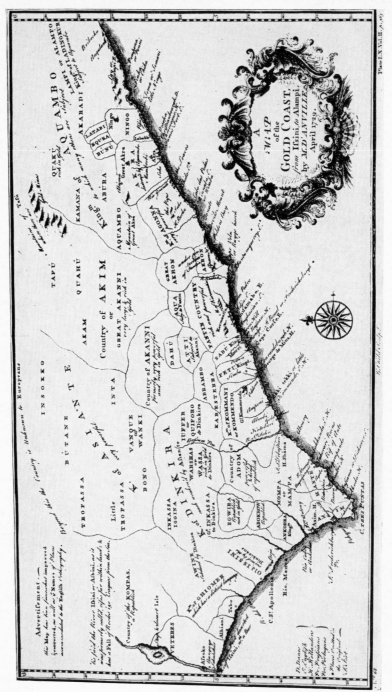

MAP 1. The Gold Coast, 1729—by M. D'Anville.

I

THE ECONOMIC BACKGROUND

Before 1850

FROM the earliest days of European contact, it was in the economic, rather than the social, cultural, or political sphere, that the Gold Coast felt what is so often called the impact of 'the West'.[1] It was trade that first brought white men to the coast of Guinea. The Portuguese, the French, the English, the Dutch, the Swedes, the Danes, and the Brandenburgers came one after the other in search of gold and slaves. In return they brought beads, metalware, and cotton goods; later, fire-arms, spirits, and other products of a more technologically advanced economy.[2] This seaborne export trade fundamentally altered the pattern of internal exchange; formerly, the only long-distance outlet had been northwards across the desert,[3] but now the more enterprising tribes developed trade routes to the coast, along which European goods penetrated back to the interior.

Permanent coastal forts and trading stations were soon built to give continuity to the operations of the merchant fleets, and to protect their stores. Often perched on rocky promontories, they served as a vivid visual reminder of the precarious foothold won by Europeans, who never became a settler community and for centuries remained on the defensive against both the climate and the inhabitants.[4] The merchant adventurers could generally count on the support of their governments, especially where international rivalries were reflected in the competition for African trade; and if they were granted subsidies or monopoly privileges, these were normally subject to Crown or parliamentary control. But the British Government had no direct responsibility for the forts or their administration until well into the nineteenth

---

[1] 'The West' is a convenient term, although not strictly accurate here, since western Europe actually lies due north of the Gold Coast (and of modern Ghana).

[2] J. W. Blake, *Europeans in West Africa, 1450–1560* (London, 1942), vol. i, p. 50, and vol. ii, p. 270 n.

[3] Gold and slaves had been sent across the Sahara from very early times; another important export from the northern hinterland of the Gold Coast was kola nuts, in exchange for which Venetian beads and Tripolitanian silks were sent overland from the Mediterranean. See E. W. Bovill, *The Golden Trade of the Moors* (Oxford, 1958), esp. ch. 22.

[4] The Portuguese, in particular, encountered strong opposition to the construction of their first Gold Coast fort, and were never welcome in the surrounding country. Blake, *Europeans in West Africa*, vol. i, pp. 43–44. K. O. Diké emphasizes that it was the opposition of the Chiefs, rather than the disadvantages of the climate, that kept later merchants from venturing into the interior or seeking territorial conquests; African traders jealously resisted any attempt to usurp their functions as middlemen between the coast and the interior. See his *Trade and Politics in the Niger Delta, 1830–1885* (Oxford, 1956), pp. 6–7.

B

century, when direct control appeared likely to be cheaper and more efficient than large annual grants.[1] Trade remained the main object of Anglo-African relationships, so that when the Gold Coast Settlements were taken over by the Crown for the brief period 1821–8, and more permanently in 1843, it was a case of the flag following trade and not vice versa.

Three and a half centuries of commercial contacts thus preceded the era of alien political control. Throughout this period the initiative came from the European nations, whose need for trading outlets was far greater than that of the African tribes they bargained with. The 'three-cornered trade' between Europe, West Africa, and the West Indies was launched and directed from the physical apex of the triangle. Yet Africans were not unwilling partners in this commerce, even in the slave trade which has since lain so heavily on the conscience of Europe. Its abolition in 1807 was strongly opposed not so much by the London Committee of Merchants (though their agents on the coast demanded and received a compensatory increase in salary[2]) as by the African suppliers of the trade. As the Committee explained to the Treasury in London, Africans were hardly likely to acquiesce in the destruction of a trade 'not inconsistent with their prejudices, their laws, or their notions of morality and religion, and by which alone they have been hitherto accustomed to acquire wealth, and to purchase all the foreign luxuries and conveniences of life'.[3] The abolition of the trade did little to diminish the importance of slavery in the internal economy of the Gold Coast—nor did the British naval patrol succeed in preventing the export of slaves to other European nations, which actually increased after 1807. But there was an immediate and complete change in the character of the Gold Coast's trade with Britain, materially assisted by the effects of the Industrial Revolution.

The task of the abolitionists had been made easier—though the magnitude of their achievement is not lessened—by the changes then taking place in the British economy. Growing industrialization, especially in the cotton industry, was providing an alternative outlet for the capital accumulated in the slave trade; and as it happened both were centred in Lancashire. West Africa came increasingly to be regarded as an important market for British manufacturers; and though it could no longer supply slaves, a substitute export was developed in palm oil. Gradually the old triangular trade was replaced by a two-way steamship traffic, manufactured goods flowing in one direction and primary products and raw materials in the other—a pattern which has persisted up to the present day. A new factor was thus introduced into

[1] The Company of Merchants Trading to Africa had received nearly £800,000 in subsidies between 1750 and 1807. *Report from the Select Committee on Papers relating to the African Forts* (London, 1816), pp. 109–10. Since it had been formed largely to promote the slave trade, its survival after 1807 was anomalous.

[2] E. C. Martin, *The British West African Settlements, 1750–1821* (London, 1927), pp. 150–1.

[3] Letter of 9 Apr. 1812, from the African Committee to the Lords of the Treasury; *1816 Report*, app. no. 11.

Gold Coast economic life—the idea of production expressly designed for the export market.[1]

Hitherto, the long and often disreputable history of European trade had left little mark upon the indigenous economy. Slaves had been assembled purposely for export; but external demand had affected the volume and direction rather than the character of the trade. Other commodities exported, notably gold and ivory, had been generally regarded as a disposable surplus, and little effort had been made to adjust the supply to the market. Imports from Europe were a welcome but by no means indispensable addition to the amenities of traditional life. In simple subsistence societies, trade and exchange normally come into being at the points of contact between them rather than within each separate community.

This, however, is not to suggest that the village, or even the tribe, was ever a self-contained economic unit, isolated from external influences. Although firmly based on subsistence agriculture, an exchange economy seems to ante-date all written records; even the Carthaginians are said to have found the system of 'silent trade' established in West Africa.[2] This was a form of barter; but in the early days of European contacts it was recorded that 'They are very wary people in their bargaining, and will not lose one sparke of gold of any value. They use weights and measures, and are very circumspect in occupying the same.'[3] That is, not only were Gold Coast Africans experienced traders, but they had already brought gold dust, their most durable, portable, and universally acceptable commodity, into something approaching monetary use.[4]

Nevertheless, the limited extent of the money economy and the long period of the international slave trade failed to alter the essential characteristics of the economic system; the basis of subsistence agriculture, the dependence upon slave labour for manual tasks, the primitive methods of inland transport, the limited range of goods produced and of demands to be satisfied, the corporate system of land ownership, and the whole network of social obligations which set limits upon individual acquisition of property. The full impact of Western economic forces, and their stimulus to nationalist thought and activity, were not felt until the pattern of British authority was firmly

---

[1] Between 1827 and 1841 the quantity of palm oil exported from the Gold Coast to Britain rose fairly steadily, from 248 to 2,137 tons, at an average value of about £35 per ton. Total imports from Britain rose from £22,414 to £133,510 in the same period; in 1841 the main imports were:

Cotton piece goods	£73,606	Hardware and cutlery	£5,363
Arms and ammunition	£24,298	Iron and steel	£2,893
Brass and copper goods	£13,343		

Report from the Select Committee on the West Coast of Africa (London, 1842), app. no. 36.

[2] Herodotus, *History*, bk. iv, ch. cxcvi.

[3] Richard Eden's account of John Lok's voyage to Mina, 1554–5. Blake, *Europeans in West Africa*, vol. ii, pp. 343.

[4] It is surprising how many writers describe as 'barter' the trade conducted with gold dust or cowries as a medium of exchange.

established, providing a political framework for more thorough penetration. It was not until the last quarter of the nineteenth century that economic change began to acquire the momentum of a revolution, with the consolidation of imperial rule.

A Sluggish Economy, 1850–74

When the Gold Coast Forts and Settlements were separated from Sierra Leone in 1850, their external trade was not in a very flourishing condition. Palm oil was the major export, but the supply fluctuated considerably, and even in the best years the export figures never approached those from other parts of the West Coast. The trees were not deliberately cultivated; but the gathering, extraction, and transport of the oil required a considerable amount of labour, and the trade seems to have been more widespread throughout the community than the jealously guarded slave traffic had been. The second main export was gold dust; this came mainly from Ashanti, and the supply varied according to political relationships with that power. Other primary products exported included ivory, gum copal, and monkey skins, but these were of relatively minor importance. On the side of imports, textiles headed the list by value; wines and spirits came a close second, followed by gunpowder, guns, hardware, tobacco, and beads.[1] All of these were traditional items in the coast trade, and the very simplicity of the list suggests that there had as yet been little expansion or diversification of the demand for industrial products.

The final supplanting of merchant government by colonial rule had had little effect on the organization of the trade. The independent merchants—who might still be called upon to act as temporary officials and were frequently agitating for a greater voice in the Government—now included a few mulattoes and well-to-do-Africans.[2] They ordered goods 'on consignment' from English shippers—of whom one of the largest was Forster & Smith—received them on credit, and disposed of them from their 'factories' or trading stations, often accepting primary produce in return. Increasingly, however, the merchants were paying out cowries, especially for palm oil; and the growth in oil exports was often attributed to the rapidity with which this currency was coming into general circulation.[3] This was even more significant in its effect on the internal economy, by facilitating what the *Blue Book* of 1850 called

---

[1] See Brodie Cruickshank, *Eighteen Years on the Gold Coast of Africa* (London, 1853), vol. ii, pp. 41–42, and *Copy of the Report of Colonel Ord, the Commissioner appointed to inquire into the Condition of the British Settlements on the West Coast of Africa* (London, 1865), pp. 17–18 and 39.

[2] See Ch. II, pp. 65–66, below.

[3] Andrew Swanzy said that when he had first come to the Coast in 1844, cowries had not been in general circulation; but later, Africans had been much more willing to bring their oil down to the merchants when payment was offered in cowries. *Report from Select Committee on Africa (Western Coast)* (London, 1865), reply to question 4,689. According to the *Gold Coast Colony Blue Book*, 150 tons of cowries were imported in 1850.

'extensive minute transactions', and encouraging the operations of African middlemen and petty traders, whom the European merchants on the coast regarded as a welcome adjunct to their business.[1]

This system was considerably affected by the advent of steam transport. The African Steamship Company commenced a regular service from Liverpool to West Africa during 1852–3. The large exporters continued to ship their own cargoes under sail to the coastal merchants with whom they had long-standing connexions; but the steamers offered a faster, cheaper service to anyone who could pay the freight rates, and were willing to accept produce and deliver merchandise in smaller lots than before. The result was that small-scale business men were enabled to enter the direct import–export trade in increasing numbers, and the credit system became more widespread.[2] Within a few years the steamers were said to have called into existence 'a new class of traders who, satisfied with smaller profits, are by their enterprise and personal exertions doing more to push and extend the trade than was ever attempted by the few monopolists who formerly enjoyed it'.[3] The entry of Africans was encouraged by a few of the smaller Liverpool firms;[4] and this was one of the many crusades into which F. Fitzgerald, the London editor of *The African Times*,[5] flung himself, declaring 'We want a race of *native capitalists* in West Africa . . . and we will do our best to help in the creation.' His own contribution was to set up a special agency to help African traders by buying and selling goods on their behalf via London or Liverpool on a non-profit-making basis.[6]

The wider diffusion of trade and credit throughout the community was reflected in a growing demand for European-type goods; but it also brought an increasing problem of failures and bad debts.[7] The reaction of the English firms was a growing reluctance to ship goods on credit to independent traders; instead, they began to appoint their own paid agents or 'correspondents' on the coast, including a handful of Africans, such as Robert Hutchison, who claimed to be worth £60,000 in 1855.[8] This practice was adopted even by

[1] According to Cruickshank: 'There was not a nook or corner of the land to which the enterprize of some sanguine trader had not led him. Every village had its festoons of Manchester cottons and China silks, hung up upon the walls of the houses, or round the trees in the market-place.' He commented upon 'the peculiar partiality of the natives of the Gold Coast, and, we believe, of Africa generally, for pedling. . . . One is at a loss to conceive where there is any room for buyers among such a nation of pedlers.' *Eighteen Years on the Gold Coast*, vol. ii, pp. 33 and 36.

[2] A. McPhee, *The Economic Revolution in British West Africa* (London, 1926), pp. 71–73.

[3] Letter of 31 Mar. 1857, from Ord (at The Hague) to Labouchere; CO/96/42.

[4] *1865 Report*, evidence of J. A. Tobin, replies to questions 5,333–5 and 5,370–1.

[5] See Ch. V, p. 192 n., below.   [6] *The African Times*, 22 Feb. and 23 May 1868.

[7] The career of an imaginary but typical entrant into the palm oil trade, Mr. Nebuchadnezzar Skate, who declared himself bankrupt after living on credit for 22 months, was lampooned in *The West African Herald*, 24 Oct. and 1 Nov. 1858. My attention was called to these articles—which contain many interesting glimpses of the trading methods of the day—by Dr. C. J. Gertzel.

[8] Letter of 10 Sept. 1855, from R. Hutchison to Secretary of State, enclosed in Dispatch No. 85 of same date, from Connor to Molesworth; CO/96/34.

the Swanzy brothers, who had built up a substantial business by their own exertions in the Gold Coast, but who eventually retired to England to direct operations.[1] The independent African traders continued in business during the 1850's and 1860's;[2] but they were more severely hit than the big firms by the depression in the palm oil trade which followed.

The first major setback to palm oil exports came during 1858–60, with a collective 'hold-up' of supplies in the Krobo area, arising out of a rebellion for which the inhabitants were heavily fined.[3] The collection of the fine was farmed out to Swanzy's, who undertook to pay the Government in cash and recover the fine in palm oil from the Krobos; the quantity of oil due was fixed by contract at a total of 195,000 gallons, or one-third of the total exports for 1857. This did not leave an excessive margin for profit, although it was calculated at a price below the 1s. per gallon then being paid; the main advantage to Swanzy's was that they gained a monopsony of the oil in the richest producing area, other firms being excluded. The agreement was regarded as so valuable that French and Spanish agents offered to take over the collection at a premium; but the only concession was that Hutchison, Swanzy's main African agent, farmed out £3,000 of his contract to Forster & Smith, and a further £750 to an independent African trader, W. Addo.

Any intention the Krobos might have had of paying soon disappeared when market prices began to rise. A remarkably effective hold-up of palm oil lasted for several years;[4] not only did this seriously affect Gold Coast earnings abroad, but the collection of the fine proved a costly fiasco. Although government troops intervened in support of the merchants, and in 1863 the Governor converted the balance of the fine into cowries,[5] the total collected was only about half the original sum. Eventually the British Treasury had to compensate the merchants—except for the unfortunate Addo, who being illiterate had put in his claim too late—to the tune of nearly £3,500.

[1] H. Swanzy, 'A Trading Family in the Nineteenth Century Gold Coast', in *Transactions of the Gold Coast & Togoland Historical Society* (Achimota, 1956), vol. ii, pt. ii.

[2] 'There were merchant princes in those days, when such men as the Hon. Samuel Collins Brew, the Hon. George Blankson, the Hon. James Bannerman, Samuel Ferguson, Esq., the Smiths, the Hansens, and others flourished.' J. E. Casely Hayford, *Gold Coast Native Institutions* (London, 1903), p. 95. He might also have mentioned R. J. Ghartey and F. C. Grant.

[3] A full account of this episode, drawn from Colonial Office correspondence, has been given by Freda Wolfson, 'A Price Agreement on the Gold Coast—the Krobo Oil Boycott, 1858–1866', in *The Economic History Review* (London, 1953), vol. vi, no. 1. She does not, however, mention its early connexion with the poll tax; for details of the origins of this dispute, see Ch. IV, pp. 187–8, below.

[4] Figures of palm oil exports to the United Kingdom reveal the extent of the loss:

1857	.	.	1,870 tons	1861	.	.	1,352 tons
1858	.	.	763	1862	.	.	1,974
1859	.	.	810	1863	.	.	2,213
1860	.	.	843	1864	.	.	4,464

Annual Accounts of Trade and Navigation . . . relating to the Colonies, 1857 to 1864.

[5] The amount still due, £7,750, at the prevailing rate of exchange (2s. 6d. per 'head' of 2,000 cowries), worked out at 124 million shells.

This episode illustrates certain economic trends which were to become increasingly marked: the financial advantages of the big firms as against small traders, their tendencies towards oligopoly and market-sharing agreements, their close association with the Government—which identified the two agencies almost as one in the public mind—and the remarkable solidarity of the African producers when they wished to protest against economic grievances. The fact that the palm oil contract held prices at an artificially low level in the face of a rising market helped to foster a belief that low produce prices were always due to the machinations of the merchants. The vagaries of the world produce market were difficult to understand, especially since the demand for oil was subject to remarkable fluctuations, while gold, the other main export, remained virtually changeless in value.

In fact, the quantity of palm oil exported recovered, soon after the Krobo incident had been settled, and increased for several years. But prices fell again;[1] a severe blow came in 1860 from the Californian discovery of mineral oil, which rapidly supplanted palm oil in many industrial uses, although the economic effects for the Gold Coast were somewhat mitigated by the discovery of palm-kernel oil soon afterwards. External trade continued to decline, and critics in England were able to point to a record low level of imports and exports in 1863, the year when the Government was brought to the brink of war with Ashanti. Nevertheless, a parliamentary inquiry of 1865 somewhat reluctantly confirmed the Government decision not to withdraw from the Settlements.

Throughout this period the most notable efforts to diversify the economy and encourage African enterprise were made by the Basel Mission. As an integral part of their programme they established industrial workshops for the training of locksmiths, blacksmiths, wheelwrights, carpenters, shoemakers, and other artisans;[2] in addition, they maintained their own 'factories', all profits from trading in excess of 5 per cent. being devoted to educational and religious work.[3] The Rev. E. Schrenk, giving evidence in 1865, welcomed the effect of trade in 'enabling the native people to see different European articles which must enlarge their views', and thus provide an incentive to enterprise. But he lamented the fact that cheap imported manufactures tended to oust the products of native industry, remarking that no one along the coast would think of making iron and textiles any longer, although six days' journey into the interior people were still doing so.[4]

Some early experiments in commercial agriculture ran into difficulties of various kinds. During 1837–40 James Swanzy was managing a coffee plantation quite happily on the basis of 'pawned' labour, and was not a little aggrieved by the interference of the visiting British Commissioner, who considered the

---

[1] Five-year average prices for palm oil in the United Kingdom were: 1856–60, £43. 12s. per ton, 1861–5, £37. 4s. per ton. Prices continued to decline, with little interruption, till the end of the century. McPhee, *The Economic Revolution*, p. 33.   [2] *1865 Report*, Schrenk, 3,222.
[3] G. A. Wanner, *Die Basler Handels-Gesellschaft A.G. 1859–1959* (Basel, 1959), ch. 2.
[4] *1865 Report*, Schrenk, 3,295.

system too near slavery.[1] The estate was then bought by the Rev. T. B. Freeman, the Wesleyan General Superintendent, who christened it Beulah and developed there a self-supporting Christian community and agricultural training centre, with some success, until his resignation in 1856.[2] There were other short-lived plantation schemes; a group of Cape Coast traders, for example, brought in an American expert to advise them on the planting of 25,000 cotton bushes, and in 1864 the Basel Mission arranged a shipment to Liverpool of 440 cwt. of cotton grown in the trans-Volta area.[3] All these projects suffered from the shortage of regular labour and the basic lack of transport and marketing facilities.

The Basel missionaries, being the first Europeans to attempt to settle inland, were fully alive to the transport problem. They constructed their own road from Christiansborg to Akropong, in spite of considerable difficulty in raising funds. The first issue of *The African Times* in 1861 published an appeal for assistance on their behalf; and when Schrenk visited England a few years later to collect money for roads he fortified himself with a recommendation from Fitzgerald. After several week's fruitless propaganda, Schrenk was advised to recast his appeal for mission work in general, rather than just for roads, which he did with some success.[4] But in 1865 he sadly told the Select Committee: 'without roads there will be no civilisation . . . our Governors do not understand it—that is the greatest pity.' As an African witness put it, more directly: 'We want a good Governor and plenty of good roads.'[5]

So long as the Gold Coast consisted of a series of isolated coastal settlements, British administrators and merchants had been mainly concerned with the links from east to west between them. The roads were poor or non-existent, and the steamer services of the 1850's had provided the first speedy and regular link between the various seaboard stations. Inland trade, thanks to the tsetse fly, had to rely on the only available beast of burden, 'man, the weakest and most costly of all'.[6] The clearing and maintenance of trade routes to the interior were responsibilities laid directly upon the Chiefs. In 1862, for example, it was announced that the people were to turn out for two or three days every month to work on the roads under their Chiefs and headmen, who would be fined for any failure. The Governor's proclamation was full of worthy sentiments: 'It is not possible for AFRICA to become rich or happy unless the inhabitants have the means of seeing one another easily and of exchanging readily those things which they do not want for things which they do want. Good roads have made the white man what he is.'[7] But so long as

---

[1] *1865 Report*, Andrew Swanzy, 4,813–6.

[2] *The Life and Journals of the Rev. Daniel West*, ed. by T. West (London, 1857), entry for 21 Nov. 1856.

[3] *1865 Report*, Schrenk, 3,217 and 3,220–1, and Andrew Swanzy, 4,827.

[4] *Elias Schrenk, ein Leben im Kampf um Gott*, ed. by S. Schrenk (Stuttgart, 1936), ch. 7.

[5] *1865 Report*, Schrenk, 3,343, and Henry Barnes, 5,812.

[6] *Report on the Economic Agriculture of the Gold Coast* (London, 1890), p. 32.

[7] Proclamation of 27 Jan. 1862, enclosed in Dispatch No. 36 of 9 Apr. 1862, from Andrews to Newcastle; CO/96/57.

African traders brought their own goods down to the coast, the Government took no direct responsibility for improving north–south communications.

In 1870 the editor of *The African Times* urged the construction of main roads to the interior, as channels of civilization.[1] Fitzgerald published his voluminous correspondence with the Colonial Office, and continued the campaign editorially, addressing his remarks particularly to the Fanti Confederation: 'Roads Will Make Kings And Chiefs Rich.'[2] The Governor-in-Chief in Sierra Leone ridiculed these schemes, maintaining that 'Africans, like North American Indians, always walk "in single file" however open the space may be'; he thought that the existing paths would suffice for years to come, provided they were kept open.[3]

The Fanti Confederation leaders, encouraged by Fitzgerald, wrote into their constitution the intention to make 'good and substantial roads' throughout the interior districts, starting with a link between Mankessim, Egimaku, and the coast. They specified a standard width of 15 feet, with deep gutters on either side; and their scheme of 1872 included a generous estimate for roads, one-fifth of the total of £20,000 that they proposed to spend.[4] Whether this sum could have been raised, even with government sanction, is a different matter; but they were at least aware of the need. During the next few years *The Gold Coast Times* took up Fitzgerald's campaign, demanding official action.[5] A deputation of London and Manchester merchants who met the Secretary of State in 1883 raised the question of roads, among other matters, and Lord Derby agreed that a substantial sum from the reserve fund might be applied to this purpose.[6] But the Governor did not, apparently, take the hint.

Apart from government labour employed on the road from Accra to Aburi, maintenance work was left to the Chiefs, who were rewarded at the rate of 10s. per quarter, per mile of road kept clear to a width of 12 feet, or fined for failure.[7] Most of these were in reality little more than bush tracks. The merchants thus had small incentive to venture into the interior, and while they remained on the coast there was no effective demand for good roads; so the vicious circle continued. It has also been argued that so long as traders were liable to atttack from hostile tribes *en route*, it was safer not to establish well-kept roads, but to preserve the possibility of unexpected local detours.[8]

Between 1850 and 1874 there had been little change in the structure of the

[1] Letter of 28 Mar. 1870, from Fitzgerald to Granville; CO/96/86.
[2] *The African Times*, 23 Apr., 23 May, and 23 Aug. 1870.
[3] CO/96/85. Cf. *1865 Report*, Ord. 1,126–9.
[4] Fanti Confederation Constitution of 1871, Articles 8 and 26; CO/96/89. See also Ch. VI, p. 257, below.
[5] For example *The Gold Coast Times*, 23 Feb. 1875, and 25 Jan. 1878. Cf. *The African Times*, 1 Feb. 1879: 'our cry, "Roads, roads, must be made on the Gold Coast" '.
[6] *The Times*, 13 Dec. 1883.
[7] According to Dispatch No. 347 of 12 Nov. 1891, from Hodgson to Knutsford; CO/96/219.
[8] Cf. H. J. Bevin, 'The Gold Coast Economy about 1880', in *Transactions of the Gold Coast & Togoland Historical Society* (Achimota, 1956), vol. ii, pt. ii, p. 78.

economy. Apart from the external stimulus of steam transport, technical progress had scarcely touched the Gold Coast, and individual experiments with new products and techniques proved powerless to divert the well-worn channels of commerce and agriculture. External trade was highly susceptible to the vagaries of world demand for primary products, and the internal market was expanding only very slowly. The Government was directly responsible for the coastal settlements alone, and lacked both the interest and the resources to provide for the economic development of the interior, while African schemes for improvement were generally discouraged as politically dangerous.

The Expansion of Trade, 1874-90

The year 1874 was marked not only by a military campaign which was designed as a final answer to the recurrent invasions from Ashanti and their interference with trade, but also by a clear British decision to remain on the coast and assume fuller responsibility for the Protectorate. This change of policy was brought home to the Chiefs with startling suddenness when an enthusiastic Governor proceeded to abolish both slavery and slave-dealing throughout the Protectorate.[1]

This was a considerable blow to vested interests and established custom in the Gold Coast; it meant that a complete change in economic roles and social stratification had been decreed virtually overnight.[2] It was now clear that imperial rule was not a mere cipher at headquarters, but was going to affect intimate personal and domestic relationships throughout the area under British authority. As in other parts of the world, many of the emancipated slaves remained in so-called 'employment' with their former masters. Nevertheless, a potential labour force was bound gradually to emerge, looking towards the possibilities of wage employment;[3] and in the next generation this was increasingly to be absorbed by the cocoa farms and the mines. Meanwhile, the apparent ease with which the change had been accomplished no doubt encouraged the local Government in its aspirations towards Ashanti and farther north, where the problem of slavery had previously been thought to present an insuperable obstacle to the extension of British rule.

After 1874 the military power of Ashanti no longer formed an effective barrier to direct trade between the coast and the interior, and some enterprising individuals were enabled to explore the inland routes. So far, the only important inland trading centre for European firms had been Akuse, which

---

[1] See Chs. VII, pp. 270–4, and VIII, pp. 302–4 below.

[2] Casely Hayford alleged that it also seriously affected commercial prosperity, by discouraging traders from the interior, who found that their slave carriers deserted on reaching the coast. *Gold Coast Native Institutions*, p. 97.

[3] As early as 1852 an Ordinance provided for the enrolment and regulation of canoemen and hammockmen, and laid down a schedule of payments. But regular employment, except for teachers and clerks, was virtually unknown before 1874.

depended on river transport up the Volta; the Basel Mission also had a few small establishments elsewhere, for example at Anum and Ho, where the missionaries, F. Ramseyer and J. Kühne, and the young French trader, M. J. Bonnat, were captured by the Ashantis in 1869.[1]

Bonnat, undeterred by his four years' detention in Kumasi, returned there in 1875 and became the first European from the coast to penetrate north of Ashanti. After an unsuccessful attempt to reach Salaga overland, he travelled most of the way by canoe up the Volta, arriving there in January 1876, two days in advance of Dr. V. S. Gouldsbury, the Civil Commandant of Accra. Bonnat was very impressed by the importance of Salaga market, where he saw caravans from Timbuktu, Lake Chad, the Niger, and Senegal. He had almost decided to set up a chain of trading stations along the Volta, as a link with the coast, when tempting proposals concerning gold-mining in the south-west turned him to pioneering in that direction.[2] Gouldsbury, who had left baggage, bedding, and servants behind in the race to be the first white man to enter Salaga, also reported favourably on trade possibilities. He travelled through Yeji, Yendi, and Krachi, where he made a treaty guaranteeing freedom of trade and transit between there and the coast.[3]

African merchants, as well as Europeans, were looking towards the trade of the interior. Robert Bannerman, who had travelled to Salaga with Bonnat, soon started to trade there on his own account.[4] *The Gold Coast Times* wrote on 13 August 1881: 'We do not approve of the policy of waiting till the traders of the interior come down to us; we strongly believe that we must first open up the intercourse with them ourselves.' The editor hinted at large profits waiting to be made out of the difference between the low rates charged in the interior and the 'satisfactory prices' obtainable in England for ivory and other products. An increasing number of northern traders began to take advantage of the new opportunities.[5] This trade was as yet a mere trickle compared with the steady stream of more valuable goods flowing in and out of Ashanti by the main route across the River Prah;[6] but the latter was subject to frequent

[1] See Ch. VII, p. 269, below. For an account of the Basel Mission trading station at Akuse, 1877–81, see E. Preiswerk, *Aus den Briefen eines Missionskaufmannes auf der Goldküste* (Basel, 2nd edn. 1882).

[2] J. Gros, *Voyages, aventures et captivité de J. Bonnat chez les Achantis* (Paris, 1884), pp. 252–65.

[3] Treaty of 8 Mar. 1876, signed by King, Fetish Priest and Chiefs of 'Crackey'; *West African Treaties* (London, 1892), African (West) No. 411, pt. iii, Gold Coast, no. 22.

[4] Bannerman Papers, SC 2/63, G.N. Archives.

[5] During the three months Nov. 1881 to Jan. 1882 over 1,600 of them travelled in each direction between Salaga and Accra. They came down with shea butter, leather goods, local cloth, and live-stock, returning with salt, cotton, metalware, and guns. *Further Correspondence regarding Affairs of the Gold Coast* (London, 1882), C. 3386.

[6] During 1881, 49,500 people were recorded as crossing the Prah northwards, and 49,300 southwards, many of them for trading purposes. Gin, rum, salt, brassware, pipes and tobacco, Manchester cotton goods, guns and gunpowder were normally exchanged for gold dust, ivory, monkey skins, sandals, and country-made cloths. Enclosures in Dispatches Nos. 83 and 84 of 18 Mar. 1882, from Rowe to Kimberley; CO/96/138.

interference from the border tribes. The Secretary of State now lent weighty support to the encouragement of trade with the more distant peoples, and during 1881–2 positive efforts were made to open up the routes circumventing Ashanti to the east and to the west.[1]

Although the Colonial Office was at the time firmly opposed to any extension of political authority on the Gold Coast, no objections were raised to this pushing of the 'traders' frontier' northwards.[2] As has been neatly pointed out, 'Refusals to annex are no proof of reluctance to control.'[3] In fact, where British interests could not be protected by the informal methods of commercial expansion, local administrators were only too eager to extend their formal sovereignty. A case in point was the south-east corner of the Gold Coast, where the essential interaction between economic and political imperialism is illustrated by a process that might be called the extension of the 'smugglers' frontier'.

By a treaty made with the Dzelukofes in 1874, the Volta was to be kept open for all lawful traders, and the British were empowered to occupy certain ports on the eastern side of the river.[4] When the frontier was thus extended to Adafia, some of the traders did not welcome British protection, which involved paying customs duties. They moved on a mile beyond the border to Denu, and there established stores for landing duty-free goods, encouraging the local inhabitants to smuggle them into British territory. In 1878 the local Commissioner, Lieutenant A. B. Ellis, attempted to put down smuggling by force, but this led immediately to disturbances, and soon afterwards to fresh treaties ceding further territory along the seaboard to Britain.[5]

Once again the traders repeated their leapfrog progress. Several German merchants established themselves farther to the east, beyond the new British frontier, and eventually petitioned the German Government for protection against interference from the British and the local Chiefs. This request, reaching Berlin when the revival of colonial ambition was at its height, prompted in 1884 the first of a series of treaties and expeditions which were eventually to give the Germans control of Togoland.[6] At one stage in the later

---

[1] For the officially sponsored journeys of Captain R. La T. Lonsdale, see Ch. VII, pp. 276–7, below.

[2] W. K. Hancock's penetrating analysis of the 'traders' frontier' in his *Survey of British Commonwealth Affairs* (London, 1940), has placed all subsequent writers in his debt. Particularly relevant here is his account of the 'underlying identity of process between the "old imperialism" and the "new imperialism" ', between the economic frontier and the frontier of imperial rule. See vol. ii, pt. i, ch. i, section 1. The evolution of the traders' frontier in West Africa is studied in detail in vol. ii, pt. ii, ch. ii.

[3] J. Gallagher and R. Robinson, 'The Imperialism of Free Trade', in *Economic History Review* (London, 1953), vol. vi, no. 1.

[4] Treaty of 22 June 1874; *Affairs of the Gold Coast* (London, 1875), C. 1140.

[5] A. B. Ellis gave his own account of these operations in *A History of the Gold Coast of West Africa* (London, 1893), ch. xxviii. The seaboard of Agbosome and Aflao was ceded under treaties of 2 and 6 Dec. 1879. African (West) No. 411, pt. iii, nos. 25 and 26.

[6] H. Zoller, *Togoland und die Sklavenküste* (Berlin, 1885), and H. Klose, *Togo unter deutscher Flagge* (Berlin, 1899).

bargaining, Britain even offered to give them the vital coastal triangle of land to the east of the Volta, in exchange for certain Pacific islands; but fortunately for the economic development of the Gold Coast, and much to the relief of the interested British Chambers of Commerce, this scheme fell through.[1]

During the 1870's and 1880's the British Government was mainly concerned to restrain the empire-building proclivities of local officials, as witness the mock-petulance of Lord Salisbury's outburst at the Foreign Office: 'Governor R has had no better occupation for his spare time than to annex some place with an unrememberable name, near Dahomey on the lagoon. Really, these proconsuls are insupportable. . . . I have implored the Colonial Office to recall Governor R.'[2] The history of dealings with Ashanti and the surrounding tribes during this period illustrates only too clearly the tension between Colonial Office restraints and the anxiety of local officials to enter into the international scramble for trade, treaties, and territory. Governor Sir William Brandford Griffith, for example, was particularly conscious of the danger to British commercial interests from French and German expansion.[3]

Yet the traders themselves were not always convinced of the advantages of British protection, and often felt that the basic requirements of civilized commerce were simply not being provided by the authorities. Andrew Swanzy, for example, argued that European capital and energy were essential for the development of African commerce; but, he complained, too many officials were ignorant of commercial affairs, were generally opposed to the traders, and considered themselves 'specially appointed to protect the natives against them'.[4] The rising class of African business men had their own problems arising out of the credit system, their traditional obligations, and their lack of experience in dealing with overseas firms.[5] They also suffered, in common with the expatriate merchants, from the lack of any constitutional outlet for their economic grievances during the period 1874–86, when there were no unofficial members of the Legislative Council at all.[6]

At this stage, the protests of the African merchants had not taken on a

[1] See J. L. Garvin, *The Life of Joseph Chamberlain* (London, 1934), vol. iii, chs. lviii, lxi, and lxii.

[2] The episode referred to may have been the cession of Agbosome and Aflao (see n.5, opposite); H. T. Ussher was Lieutenant Governor of the Gold Coast and Lagos at the time, and his name may have been decorously concealed by a change of initial, or simply forgotten. The letter of 12 Nov. 1879, from Salisbury to Lyons, is quoted by Lady G. Cecil, *Life of Robert Marquis of Salisbury* (London, 1932), vol. iv, p. 251.

[3] See Ch. VII, pp. 279–80, below.

[4] A. Swanzy, *Trade on the Gold Coast* (London, 1874).

[5] An interesting brief case-history of the 'losses and crosses' of African merchants is provided by J. E. Ocansey, *African Trading, or The Trials of William Narh Ocansey, of Addah, West Coast of Africa, River Volta* (Liverpool, 1881). This palm oil exporter had his own agents along the coast, but lost £2,000 on the death of one of them. He was the brother of the local Chief, and had to stand surety for the damage when the people plundered a wrecked ship of Swanzy's; as a result of this episode, Ocansey lost 2,000 dollars and his brother, who was poisoned by the people. A final blow was when a Liverpool agent misappropriated the payment he had made for a steam launch.

[6] See Ch. XI, pp. 409–15, below.

strictly nationalist character; they made common cause with the Europeans, often in demanding political representation and attacking government inefficiency or apathy in economic matters. There was frequent friction with the authorities over the vexed question of customs duties; and a steep rise in 1890 helped to precipitate a frontal attack on Brandford Griffith personally and upon the policy of his administration, from virtually the whole trading community.[1]

The 1890's saw a general increase in the scale of trading operations. Larger firms began to reap the advantages of capital and size which have always been particularly important in West Africa, for such reasons as the long period for which stocks must be financed, the constant fluctuations in prices, the need for heavy fixed investment in buildings, warehouses, and transport, and the universal demand for credit.[2] The tendency towards large-scale enterprise was well illustrated by the formation of the Royal Niger Company in 1886, and although the Gold Coast never returned to the chartered company system, the more powerful European concerns were all anxious to consolidate their private trading empires. The development of the Elder Dempster shipping line, under Sir Alfred Jones, provided new opportunities for the export–import trade.[3] But smaller firms were placed at a disadvantage by the formation of the West African shipping ring in 1895, which led to the raising of freight rates, offset only by a rebate system which operated to the benefit of larger concerns.[4]

It was mainly the European firms who grew and prospered under the new system, at the expense of many of the small African traders, who were unaccustomed to partnerships outside the family, or to the impersonal mechanism of the joint-stock company. Lacking reserves of capital, many were driven out of business, and the resulting destruction of the credit system

[1] For details see Ch. VIII, pp. 309–11, below. Some indication of the scale of the European firms is given by the number of signatures from their employees: F. & A. Swanzy, 36; Basel Mission Trading Co., 12; Alex Miller & Co., 10; Fischer & Co., 8; McIver & Co., 8; Fletcher & Hope, 8; Gebs Ter Meulen, 8; Taylor Laughland, 7; Yates Bros. & Shattuck, 6; Pickering & Berthoud, 5; H. B. W. Russell, 4; H. Rottmann jun., 4. The Governor soon afterwards instructed his officials not to 'place themselves under obligations of any kind to the Mercantile Community', and refused to allow commercial men to stay at Aburi sanatorium; he was indignant when the Colonial Office would not countenance this pettiness. The Head of the African Department, however, sympathized with Brandford Griffith, calling the traders 'a very rowdy, hard drinking lot'. Minute of 19 Sept. 1893, by A. W. L. Hemming; CO/96/235.

[2] Cf. P. T. Bauer, *West African Trade* (Cambridge, 1954), pp. 104–6.

[3] E. Baillaud speaks of 'cette superbe flotte, forte de plus de cent navires, qu'il construisait toujours plus grands et toujours plus beaux, alors que les anciens paraissaient suffire largement à assurer le trafic'. *La Politique indigène de l'Angleterre en Afrique Occidentale* (Paris, 1912), p. xxxiii. This author stresses Jones's influence on West African development between 1890 and 1908; he was President of the Liverpool Chamber of Commerce and of its African Section, founded the Bank of British West Africa, and had an active hand in the British Cotton Growing Association, mining and railway schemes, and the Liverpool School of Tropical Medicine. See also A. H. Milner, *Life of Sir Alfred Jones, K.C.M.G.* (London, 1911).

[4] McPhee, *The Economic Revolution*, pp. 95–98.

'threw hundreds of poor people for want of a patron on their own resources and the rich Merchants became poor and in many cases hardly able to live. The poor people then eked out a precarious livelihood by farming, fishing and petty trading.'[1] On the other hand, trade was no longer the only outlet for enterprising Africans; since 1874 the development of the gold-mining industry had not only brought in European capital on an increasing scale, but had also encouraged the rise of a new type of African 'middleman', negotiating concessions between the mining companies and the Chiefs.

Gold-mining and the Land Question

Although the Gold Coast's eponymous mineral was the earliest, and the most enduring attraction for European commerce,[2] it was not until the late nineteenth century that overseas firms were able to undertake direct mining on a permanent basis. Gold was traditionally regarded by the Akans as sacred, and only to be extracted for the well-being of the State.[3] The Portuguese are known to have worked two early mines, at Abrobi and Aboasi; but the former collapsed in 1622, owing to badly-shored tunnels, and the latter in 1636, during an earthquake.[4] These disasters were regarded as supernatural vengeance, and for the next 200 years the European merchants had to obtain gold by barter. The sources were rich enough to provide an economic foundation for the great Akan States in addition to exports valued by a Dutch writer just after 1700 at 7,000 marks (about £220,000) annually.[5] But no attempt was made to improve on the traditional methods of shallow digging and washing, which literally only scratched the surface of the deposits.

The pioneer of the modern mining industry appears to have been Thomas Hughes of Cape Coast, who imported some heavy machinery and commenced working in Western Wassaw; but in 1861, after striking a rich vein, he was forbidden by the Chief to exploit it, and his machinery was destroyed.[6] Public interest in Europe was stirred by the reports of soldiers returning from the Ashanti war in 1874, who proclaimed, 'with a marvellous unanimity of

[1] Report of 30 July 1900, by the President, Accra Town Council; CO/96/362.

[2] Within a few years of their discovery of 'A Mina' (The Mine) in 1471, the Portuguese had built a castle to protect their trade in gold: 'This, as we know, was the first stone building in the region of the Ethiopias of Guinea since the creation of the world', according to D. Pacheco Pereira, the Portuguese explorer, who described the building of the castle in 1482. *Esmeraldo de Situ Orbis* (c. 1505), translated by G. H. T. Kimble (London, 1937). The first English contact with the Gold Coast was when some of Captain Thomas Windham's crew returned to England from a voyage of 1553-4 with 150 lb. of gold dust. T. Astley, *A New General Collection of Voyages and Travels* (London, 1745), vol. i, pp. 141-4.

[3] Eva L. R. Meyerowitz, *The Sacred State of the Akan* (London, 1951), p. 197. Referring to the gold mines, W. Bosman stated that 'the Negroes esteem them Sacred, and consequently take all possible care to keep us from them'. *A New and Accurate Description of the Coast of Guinea* (London, 1705), p. 80.

[4] W. W. Claridge, *A History of the Gold Coast and Ashanti* (London, 1915), vol. i, pp. 86-91.

[5] Bosman, *Description of the Coast of Guinea*, pp. 89-90.

[6] J. A. B. Horton, *West African Countries and Peoples* (London, 1868), p. 265.

iteration, the magic word—Gold'.[1] Ramseyer and Kühne, during their captivity, were more impressed by the brutalities of the court of the Asantehene—or King of Ashanti—than by the 'ostentation and gaudy show' of gold and jewels.[2] But Bonnat took the opportunity to discover what he could about the gold-bearing regions and African methods of working;[3] and on his return to Europe after his pioneer journey to Salaga he was approached by a French mining engineer interested in gold prospecting. As a result, he led yet another expedition, this time up the River Ankobra in 1877, which resulted in the formation of a company to exploit the first actively-worked mining concessions, at Awudua and later at Tarkwa.[4]

The Colonial Office welcomed this new field for European enterprise and for the economic development of the Gold Coast, even though the British possessed no territorial rights beyond the Forts and Settlements.[5] But the Governor was more cautious. He believed that if Europeans were to come in to develop mining successfully, the Government would have to take over the land, since the tribes would never alienate it willingly. They were the 'rightful owners of the soil in the Protectorate', and the Chiefs were unlikely to agree that any change of ownership might be for their own good.[6] Nevertheless, many Chiefs were only too glad to offer valuable concessions to Europeans in return for what appeared to be profitable revenues.[7] This went on to such an extent that by 1879 the Secretary of State began to wonder whether the Tarkwa Chiefs had not disposed of the rights and property of their people in a manner contrary to native custom.[8]

To ask this question was in a way to miss the point. The Government at that time knew little of the detailed customs and procedures regulating land rights and transfers; it seems clear, however, that these were not fixed in a rigid pattern, but were capable of extension and adaptation to changing circumstances.[9] The one almost invariable principle was that of group rather than individual ownership; and this was not infringed by the mining concessions, which did not involve any transfer of ownership from groups to

[1] R. F. Burton and V. L. Cameron, *To the Gold Coast for Gold* (London, 1883), vol. i, p. ix. Cf. 'Gold is there in profusion, and to be had for the seeking'. H. Brackenbury, *The Ashantee War* (London, 1874), vol. ii, p. 351.

[2] F. Ramseyer and J. Kühne, *Four Years in Ashantee* (London, 1875), p. 85.

[3] Gros, *Voyages . . . de J. Bonnat*, pp. 197 and 264–5.

[4] 1879 Report of the African Gold Coast Company; CO/96/129. See also H. Bevin, 'M. J. Bonnat: Trader and Mining Promoter', in *The Economic Bulletin* (Accra, 1960), vol. 4, no. 7.

[5] Minutes of 16 and 18 Apr. 1877, by A. W. L. Hemming; CO/96/122.

[6] Dispatch No. 143 of 29 Sept. 1877, from Freeling to Carnarvon; CO/96/121.

[7] Lord Hailey, while emphasizing the strength of religious feeling concerning land in the Gold Coast, commented rather unkindly that this had not deterred the Chiefs from making concessions on a large scale. *An African Survey* (Oxford, 2nd edn. 1945), p. 834.

[8] Letter of 4 Sept. 1879, from Hicks Beach to African Gold Coast Company; CO/96/126.

[9] To take an example that has nothing to do with European influences, 'among groups of Akan origin settled among the Adangme the matriclan has been replaced by a patrilineal concept in all that affects land'. R. J. H. Pogucki, *Gold Coast Land Tenure*, vol. ii, 'Report on Land Tenure in Adangme Customary Law' (Accra, 1955), p. 43.

individuals.[1] The important question seems to have been whether native custom was being unduly stretched to cover cases to which it was not strictly applicable; or whether a new element was being introduced, within the customary framework, whose economic and social repercussions might tend to disrupt the system as a whole.

Land rights in the Gold Coast, following the usual African pattern, were traditionally held by a group, normally the clan or extended family. Their title might date back to the original settlement of the land, or to the distribution by the Chief of territory acquired in war; but at any moment in time it would be regarded as a trust for all members of the group, including the ancestors, the living and the unborn.[2] The land in fact was a symbol of the continuity of the family, and in this lay a good deal of its religious significance. Although it was a source of wealth—including in this term the means of subsistence—it was not, originally, a commodity to be traded.[3] As Lucy Mair points out with reference to Buganda, the status of a wealthy man could not under such a system be attained by bargaining the use of surplus land in any form of sale or lease.[4]

Any land not already owned by a family would normally fall into the category of 'stool' land;[5] this was held on behalf of the community as a whole by the Chief acting as custodian, and it was available for disposal subject to the consent of his elders.[6] As the Omanhene of Adansi said in 1912:

All land in Adansi is the property of the Adansi people, with the exception of one piece of land which has been given to the Government. The fact of the British having come to the country has made no difference; things are exactly as they were before. There is land attached to my stool and also to the stools of my sub-chiefs, the latter including family land. There is no land in individual ownership. The paramount Chief and sub-chiefs hold the land so long as they are on the stool, as trustees for the

[1] To quote only two authorities: 'in the Customary Law, we find no trace of individual ownership', Casely Hayford, Gold Coast Native Institutions, pp. 46–47; and 'The conception of the actual soil as belonging to individuals . . . was quite unknown and was in fact almost inconceivable', R. S. Rattray, Ashanti Law and Constitution (Oxford, 1929), p. 361.

[2] Cf. R. S. Rattray, Ashanti (Oxford, 1923), p. 216.

[3] This prohibition was particularly strong in Ashanti; cf. Rattray, Ashanti Law and Constitution, p. 349. A. B. Ellis also said that 'On the Gold Coast . . . the sale or purchase of land is unknown', except among Europeans and Anglicized natives. The Yoruba-Speaking Peoples of the Slave Coast (London, 1894), p. 189.

[4] L. P. Mair, Studies in Applied Anthropology (London, 1957), p. 25.

[5] This term (relating to the Chief's stool as the symbol of his authority) appears to be more accurate than 'tribal' land, which according to Casely Hayford had no meaning in customary law. The Truth about the West African Land Question (London, 1913), p. 70. H. C. Belfield made a threefold distinction between tribal, stool, and family land, which has often been repeated; but only the two latter seem to be relevant. Report on the Legislation Governing the Alienation of Native Lands in the Gold Coast Colony and Ashanti: with some observations on the 'Forest Ordinance', 1911 (London, 1912).

[6] The word 'Chief' has here been used in a general sense, to cover all holders of that office with some degree of responsibility for land. In practice, the paramount Chief would be the ultimate authority for the State as a whole, but other Chiefs might be responsible for the disposal and oversight of lands in their own town or village, or attached to their own particular stool.

people. Land belonging to my stool may be disposed of by me with the consent of my elders. If a sub-chief wishes to dispose of land he must inform me, but this is merely formal, I am not in a position to exercise the power of prohibition.[1]

Any of his own people might apply for a grant of unallotted land,[2] and would then become entitled to occupy and use it in perpetuity, subject only to the observance of customary obligations. No regular payment or tribute would be required, although the Chief would probably expect some customary 'drinks' or sheep in consideration of his assent to the transaction. But even this did not involve individual ownership in the English sense, since it would soon enter the category of family land: 'What the head of a family acquires to-day in his own individual right will, in the next generation, be quite indistinguishable from the general ancestral property of which he was a trustee.'[3] Any surplus might be temporarily abandoned, but would remain part of the family holding; only after a long period had elapsed would it revert to the stool—i.e. it would be once more the direct responsibility of the Chief, who could then make any fresh grants required.[4]

There was also distinct provision for the grant of land by the Chief to 'strangers' coming into his territory who wished to settle and work there. The rights so granted were often strictly limited; for example, the stranger's family would be entitled to use the land but not to exercise rights of group ownership, and on his death the agreement might have to be renewed.[5] Sometimes, however, a more permanent grant of land might be made to a whole group of strangers who wished to settle in new territory. Some of the people of Juaben, for example, fled south with their Chiefs after the civil wars that followed Sir Garnet Wolseley's 1874 march to Kumasi, and were given land to settle in; they founded the town of New Juaben, now called Koforidua.[6]

The whole leisurely process of land grants and reversions could only have been evolved in a society where land was abundant and commanded no rent in the economic sense. It was bound to be modified as the pressure of population and the demand for land, for both building and farming purposes, increased. The type of land in demand would not then be abandoned until it

---

[1] *Belfield Report*, p. 97.

[2] The terms 'unoccupied' or 'uncultivated land' are often used, but since such land might already 'belong' to a family, 'unallotted' seems more appropriate here.

[3] Casely Hayford, *Gold Coast Native Institutions*, p. 47.

[4] Lord Hailey, *Native Administration in the British African Territories* (London, 1951), pt. iii, p. 253. These arrangements may be taken as applying fairly generally to people of Akan descent. Among the Gã and Adangme peoples, the head of the kinship group rather than the political Chief would act on their behalf in land matters. In the Northern Territories, landowning kinship groups were represented by a special official, the *Ten'dana*, as distinct from the secular Chief. For some account of the system in the north, see Ch. XII, pp. 487–90, below.

[5] For example, among the Adangme (where there is a noticeable tendency to avoid sales of land to strangers) the children of a deceased stranger must always renew a tenancy. Pogucki, *Gold Coast Land Tenure*, vol. ii, p. 18.

[6] Rattray, *Ashanti Law and Constitution*, p. 176.

reverted to the stool; instead, a family group might allow others the use of its surplus, or even sell it outright.

The system of granting something similar to an English leasehold appears originally to have been the prerogative of the Chief. The grant of land for building forts dates back to the beginning of the European connexion. Annual payments were fixed in gold, according to the 'Notes' jealously guarded by local Chiefs, and complications sometimes arose when these were captured in war.[1] Later, individual merchants and firms were granted land on which to build their houses and stores, in exchange for a percentage levy upon their trade. Their refusal to pay this in 1872 led to some rioting in Cape Coast, and the first recorded boycott of European goods, when some purchases were actually confiscated by the organizers.[2] Such grants of land were not attacked as running contrary to native custom, and they seem to indicate considerable flexibility in assimilating alien economic forces.

Traditionally, however, the most common form of payment for the use of land by strangers seems to have been the *abusa* system, whereby the land-owner received a one-third share of the produce. It is difficult to trace how far back this goes, but it appears to have been well-established by the nineteenth century, when it was certainly applied to grants of family and stool land. An early example arose out of the award of hunting rights, when the landowner would require a portion of the animal killed; and similarly gold-mining agreements were common whereby the owner received a one-third share and the paramount Chief, whether or not he was the owner of the land, had the right to all nuggets found.[3] It is unlikely that *abusa* was ever applied to subsistence farming; but as soon as cash crops began to be cultivated, it provided a ready-made system for granting the use of land to strangers, and eventually the introduction of cocoa brought it into widespread use.[4]

[1] J. Mensah Sarbah, *Fanti National Constitution* (London, 1906), pp. 61–62.

[2] The levy had become a kind of brokerage, amounting to one dollar in thirty-two, on the gold, ivory, or cash received by the merchants. The Cape Coast Chiefs claimed that the custom had been in existence since the coming of the first white men, and there is no record of any specific objections by the merchants until the late nineteenth century. Payments had lapsed when trade was interrupted by the Ashanti war of 1863; when trade eventually began to revive the Chiefs renewed their claim and the merchants refused to continue payment. Disturbances followed, and the merchants' houses were threatened; but the Acting Administrator refused to call out the troops to protect them as he felt that the merchants had provoked the trouble. Letters of 30 Nov. 1872, from Salmon to Harley; CO/96/94.

[3] Casely Hayford, *Gold Coast Native Institutions*, p. 49.

[4] Cf. G. Balandier's reference to 'the utilization of traditional models for new purposes'. 'Social Changes and Social Problems in Negro Africa', in *Africa in the Modern World*, ed. by C. W. Stillman (Chicago, 1955), p. 67. Polly Hill in *The Gold Coast Cocoa Farmer* (Oxford, 1956), quotes the one-third custom as existing in Akim Abuakwa before 1883 (i.e. before commercial cocoa production), and describes how *abusa* became widespread as a convenient means of granting cocoa farming rights to strangers. She also gives the fullest description of the system available. Pogucki states that *abusa* was not customary among the Adangmes and Gãs, who made use of it only to acquire land from Akans when sale was refused, and only for cocoa production, never for food crops. *Gold Coast Land Tenure*, vol. ii, p. 35, and vol. iii, 'Report on Land Tenure in Gã Customary Law' (Accra, 1956), p. 34.

The general economic pressure was towards the commercialization of land quite apart from the direct influence of Europeans. It is therefore not surprising to find that procedures for the sale of land also appear to have become entrenched quite early in customary law. R. J. H. Pogucki, for example, suggests that the principle was of long standing, not only among the Gãs, whose economic development had been strongly influenced by urbanization and European legal concepts, but also among the Adangmes—dating back possibly as far as 1814—the Ewes and other tribes, in addition to the Akans.[1] R. S. Rattray has given details of similar procedure among the Ashantis, though in 1923 he called it a comparatively modern innovation;[2] and nearly all the accounts quote customary phrases which indicate that such sales originated within the framework of traditional religion rather than under outside influence.[3]

Thus transfers of land rights, and even sales of land, were clearly recognized under customary law. The conditions upon which they were made varied according to the use to which the land was to be put, and its relative scarcity, as well as the local customs of the tribe. But almost everywhere provision was made for the 'stranger', a concept which normally covered a person of different tribal origin, although for purposes of land tenure it might simply refer to a member of a different kinship group. Among the Gãs, a distinction might be made between strangers of African origin and non-Africans, but this affected only the procedure, and not the rights which such a stranger could acquire. Thus the alienation of land to Europeans by means of mining concessions could hardly be said to have raised a new principle, or contravened customary law.[4]

But the traditional system could not so easily adapt itself to the vast increase of wealth that could be won from gold-bearing land by the use of modern machinery. The Chief who drove out Thomas Hughes and broke up his machines clearly recognized the problem—although such Luddite

[1] *Gold Coast Land Tenure*, vol. ii, pp. 32–33, and vol. iii, pp. 10–11. Cf. C. K. Meek, *Land Law and Custom in the Colonies* (London, 1946), p. 180.

[2] Rattray, *Ashanti*, pp. 235–7.

[3] For example, in Krobo: 'My ancestors shall not have the right to reclaim, I have parted with the land.' The use of English legal phrases and documents seems to have been a later development, superseding some but not all of the customary procedure. Pogucki, *Gold Coast Land Tenure*, vol. ii, p. 33. According to *The 'Sunlight' Reference Almanac* (Aburi, 1936), pp. 98–99, the *guaha* custom for outright sale of land was of ancient origin, and had been used for the sale of slaves, when 'it was common to see a number of cowries under one's seat to indicate the various slaves bought'. The ritual for land sale included the pouring of libation to the ancestors by the vendor, who would ask them to settle elsewhere, and the ceremonial use of palm leaves.

[4] The term 'alienation' is commonly used to describe the grant of land rights to aliens (i.e. Europeans) under such concessions, and has been retained here. The Lands Bills of 1894–7 were designed partly to protect Africans from such alienation—although, as we have seen, it might be strictly in accordance with customary law. Some confusion was therefore caused when Africans attacked the Lands Bills as an attempt to 'alienate' the lands of the people. They, however, were using the word in the strict sense of a transfer of ownership (to the Government), which was certainly not provided for under customary law.

actions seldom provide a solution to economic difficulties. As soon as overseas prospectors moved in, the mere hint of gold was enough to drive up the bidding for concessions; and although the sums offered in annual payment might have seemed small to Europeans, yet they were well above any revenues previously obtainable from land, or from indigenous methods of mining.[1] Any reluctance of the Chiefs to allow large-scale development was soon overcome by this factor. In addition to the regular sums agreed as rents or royalties, large down-payments were sometimes offered; and in the absence of any clear-cut distinction between the Chief's private expenditure and his outlay as the representative of the State, the wealthy Chief soon began to realize distinct personal advantages.[2]

The development of modern gold-mining thus represents the first serious impact of Western economic forces upon traditional forms of social organization. The entry of European capital was negotiated without necessarily violating customary procedure, and the extent of the problem of land alienation was much exaggerated by officials.[3] But it brought 'big money' into the villages at a time when the range of goods available from abroad was rapidly increasing, and often distorted the age-old system of stool finances. The sudden increase in land values, and hence in the wealth at the disposal of some Chiefs, was to become an increasing source of friction between the traditional authorities and the educated, cash-conscious, politically restless minority.[4] But because the Government stepped in with the Lands Bills of 1894-7 in an attempt to control excessive alienation and facilitate approved expatriate enterprise, the economic frustrations that had been building up erupted first in a political outcry against the British administration rather than against the Chiefs.[5]

It was not only the traditional authorities who profited from this new source of wealth. The services of African lawyers were in constant demand, acting on behalf of the Chiefs and sometimes for the concessionaires. Others were encouraged by the prospect of tempting profits to enter the field directly,

---

[1] By 1912, the usual payment seems to have been £50–£200 'consideration money' per 5 square miles, plus a rent of £10–£12 per annum, rising to £300 once machinery was installed. *Belfield Report*, evidence of F. T. Dove, C. H. Armitage, and C. E. D. O. Rew.

[2] Belfield heard conflicting evidence on this point, which indicated the uncertainty and the local variations of procedure. Some witnesses said that the Chief had no right to dispose of such sums for his personal advantage, and that if he did so it might cause his destoolment. But expenditure for stool purposes was sometimes interpreted to mean the Chief's 'personal maintenance' as well as the liquidation of stool debts, or even anything requisite 'to maintain the dignity of the stool'. Nene Mate Kole of Manya Krobo stated categorically that the King's portion of the consideration money was 'for his own use. Each may spend his share as he likes.' Ibid. evidence, *passim*.

[3] It was estimated in 1900 that the Chiefs had granted mining concessions over an area exceeding that of the Colony itself. This fallacy was exploded by Belfield, who gave statistics of all concessions properly validated; but it has since been repeated by R. L. Buell in 1928, and given still wider currency by Lord Hailey in 1951.

[4] Cf. L. P. Mair, *Native Policies in Africa* (London, 1936), p. 164.

[5] See Ch. IX, 'The A.R.P.S. and the Lands', below, for an account of the agitation.

buying up concessions from the Chiefs and then renegotiating them to European companies. *The Gold Coast Times* on 26 November 1881 urged its readers not to be passive onlookers at the operations of 'our foreign friends' at Tarkwa: 'They only come to benefit themselves alone. . . . The land is ours.' The following year the Gold Coast Native Concession Purchasing Company was formed, with F. C. Grant (proprietor of the newspaper) as chairman, in association with J. F. Amissah, John Sarbah, James Brew, G. E. Eminsang, and J. W. Sey. This combination began to fall apart as soon as difficulties were encountered;[1] but other enterprising groups and individuals continued in the field, to such an extent that their speculative activities became a source of annoyance to the tidy mind of officialdom during the 1890's.[2]

Some Africans tried to form companies to undertake mining directly; for example, Dr. Africanus Horton, in association with Fitzgerald of *The African Times*, attempted to float the Wassaw and Ahanta Gold Mines Syndicate in 1880. But inevitably Africans found it more difficult to raise capital; apart from a few prosperous traders and lawyers, the process of capital accumulation had barely begun, and the idea of investing it in business enterprise was totally new. The extended family was both the repository and the source of funds for its members, and it was not easily to be replaced by the joint-stock company, which would be the first to suffer from any conflict of loyalties that arose. In any case, the legal and institutional framework was lacking; apart from the absence of a capital market for local issues, there was no provision even for the registration of companies in the Gold Coast.[3]

Overseas firms were to some extent handicapped by such local problems, and especially by the difficulties of obtaining a secure title to their concessions, which sometimes led to protracted litigation;[4] but their relative advantages in raising capital and in drawing upon the general commercial facilities of Europe virtually excluded African enterprise from the field. Between 1880 and 1888 the number of companies actively developing concessions in the Tarkwa area rose from three to ten; they were then employing about forty Europeans in addition to their African labour.[5] The rush for concessions had not yet led to a mining boom. Even though the mines were relatively close to the coast, the difficulties of climate and transport were considerable. Nevertheless, prospectors were always willing to listen to tales of more easily won gold farther inland, and some were already looking hopefully towards Ashanti.

To the outside world, Ashanti had long presented a picture of hope, promise, and potential wealth. The first British travellers to Kumasi, early in the

---

[1] *The Gold Coast Times*, 22 Apr. and 30 Sept. 1882.   [2] See Ch. IX, p. 343, below.

[3] Although the English Companies Acts of 1862 and 1867 had been applied to the Gold Coast under the Supreme Court Ordinance of 1876.

[4] The Land Registration Ordinance of 1883 provided for the voluntary recording of instruments affecting land, and the Land Registry Ordinance of 1895 for deeds.

[5] See *Reports relating to Her Majesty's Colonial Possessions* (London, 1889), no. 66; also E. Ashmead, 'Twenty-five Years of Mining', in *The Mining Journal* (London, 1909), pp. 62 ff.

nineteenth century, had returned with glowing accounts of Ashanti gold.[1] While the Asantehene was in power, European prospectors were not welcomed; it was said that his revenues were derived principally from his gold mines, and all nuggets found in Ashanti were his by right.[2] It was thought that the richest deposits lay in the fabulous Kong mountains, which John Duncan had hoped to reach from Cape Coast in 1844.[3] Richard Burton wrote in 1863: 'What the mineral wealth must be there, it is impossible to estimate.'[4] Kong itself lay to the north-west of Ashanti and Techiman, but the mountains were believed to stretch right across the hinterland of the Guinea coast, from Sierra Leone to Lagos.[5] Dr. R. A. Freeman, who accompanied the 1888–9 mission to Gyaman, was not allowed to explore farther towards Kong, to test his theory that the mountains did not exist at all. But he returned convinced that there were few spots either on the coast or in the interior where gold was not to be found.[6] George Ferguson, on his way up to Attabubu in 1890, took special note of small-scale African mining activities, and gave tantalizing reports of nuggets worth £100.[7]

After the British expedition to Kumasi and the removal of Prempeh in 1896, followed by the conclusion of treaties with the hinterland States, the Government hoped to open up this wide new territory. Sir William Maxwell's message to the Legislative Council in 1897—delivered on the same day as the introduction of the Lands Bill—read almost like an open invitation to traders and prospectors to extend their operations to Ashanti.[8] The road to the interior now lay open, and there were well-authenticated reports that parts of it, at least, were paved with gold.[9] Possibilities seemed boundless, and there was a great influx of mining and commercial enterprise into Kumasi.

The most lucrative bargain was struck by the prospector E. A. Cade, who had journeyed through Adansi in 1895, and secured from a group of African concessionaires, including J. P. Brown, J. E. Ellis, and J. E. Biney, a written

---

[1] For example, T. E. Bowdich, who gave vivid details of 'the general blaze of splendour and ostentation'. *Mission from Cape Coast Castle to Ashantee* (London, 1819), p. 35.

[2] Prince Ossoo Ansah's account, published in *The Times*, 29 July 1873.

[3] The Asantehene could not promise that Duncan would be allowed to go beyond Kumasi, so he went to Dahomey, through which he claimed to have reached and crossed the mountains. J. Duncan, *Travels in Western Africa* (London, 1847), 2 vols.

[4] R. F. Burton, *Wanderings in West Africa* (London, 1863), vol. ii, p. 130.

[5] For example, see map in Burton and Cameron, *To the Gold Coast for Gold*, vol. i, frontispiece.

[6] R. A. Freeman, *Travels and Life in Ashanti and Jaman* (London, 1898), pp. 183 and 529.

[7] G. E. Ferguson, *Report on Mission to Atabubu* (London, 1891).

[8] *Legislative Council Minutes*, 10 Mar. 1897.

[9] Freeman claimed to possess a pair of solitaires made of gold 'washed from dust swept up in the streets of Cape Coast'. *Travels and Life in Ashanti and Jaman*, p. 529. He also said that grains of gold could be seen sparkling on the ground in Axim after a shower. Lady Hodgson doubted the truth of this story, so when she visited Axim a woman was sent out to bring a bucketful of dust from the main street—and after washing, an unmistakable rim of gold dust appeared. *The Siege of Kumassi* (London, 1901), pp. 304–8. Eva Meyerowitz has recently claimed to have seen 'stretches of earth, bordering the street, where gold dust sparkled', without even the benefit of rain, in Wassaw Amanfie. *The Sacred State of the Akan*, p. 201.

agreement leasing 100 square miles of land from the Chiefs of Adansi and Bekwai.[1] The Government was at this time unable either to recognize or disallow Cade's negotiations, since they took place in Ashanti; he then returned to England, and in 1897 formed the Ashanti Goldfields Corporation. A fresh agreement was now drawn up, with the Government, as third party, receiving a certain royalty itself and passing on to the Chiefs the sums originally promised to them.[2] Apart from these obligations, the Corporation secured what was virtually an *imperium in imperio*,[3] with the right to undertake mining, trading, rubber and timber extraction, road-making, and town-building. In 1898 the Corporation's first mine, which was to have such a profitable future, was opened at Obuasi by the representative of the Governor.[4] Cade next proposed that his Corporation should take over all the metalliferous, timber, water, and rubber rights of Ashanti, in return for a payment of £5,000 down and a further £500,000 to conclude the deal—the latter sum to be spent on a railway; but this Chamberlain refused, commenting, 'Mr. Cade has a low opinion of my intelligence.'[5]

The local Government, however, displayed more interest in mining developments south of Ashanti, where its responsibilities were of longer standing and easier to enforce. In 1897 there was even an attempt at public enterprise in the mining industry, when Maxwell was authorized to spend £1,000 on a scheme for alluvial gold-mining, complete with imported Chinese miners and prospectors.[6] This was unpopular among Africans,[7] and the sixteen unfortunate immigrants, arriving at Kibi during the rainy season, suffered from malaria and unsuitable food.[8] Undeterred by this minor fiasco, official optimism

---

[1] J. P. Brown had been connected with the Ashanti Exploration Company since 1891. This seems to be a classic case where Africans had recognized economic opportunities, but lacked the capital and technique to develop them. Their original lease was drawn up on 1 Aug. 1895, for a period of 99 years from Mar. 1890. *West African Lands Committee: Minutes of Evidence, &c.* (Colonial Office, 1916), question 4,972 and reply.

[2] The Chiefs of Adansi and Bekwai were thus to receive £100 and £66 annually, while the Government would get a royalty of 3 per cent. on profits, plus a commuted royalty of £500 for each of the first five years. Ibid. This agreement was not affected either by the 1900 Concessions Ordinance or by the 1903 Ashanti Concessions Ordinance.

[3] Sir Francis Fuller, the Chief Commissioner of Ashanti, agreed with E. D. Morel, a member of the West African Lands Committee, that this was an accurate description. Ibid. 4,880.

[4] C. H. Armitage and A. F. Montanaro, *The Ashanti Campaign of 1900* (London, 1901), p. 10. See also *Gold from the Gold Coast* (Chamber of Mines, Accra, 1950).

[5] Letter of 25 Mar. 1899, from Cade to Chamberlain, and his Minute of 13 Apr.; CO/96/352.

[6] The idea of importing Chinese labour had been canvassed for many years: e.g. by Brackenbury in *The Ashantee War*, vol. ii, p. 352; by H. T. Ussher in 1879, on the grounds that it would 'stimulate the lazy African to competition' (CO/96/218); by the District Commissioner at Axim, a suggestion followed up by Colonial Office inquiries at Hong Kong in 1889 (CO/96/203); and by Maxwell himself in a memorandum written on his way to West Africa, on 'Coolie Immigration. Gold Coast', dated 28 Mar. 1895 (CO/96/269).

[7] *The Gold Coast Express*, 20 Oct. 1897, claimed that the project had been condemned everywhere: 'We do not want the "celestials" in West Africa on any account. . . . China is large enough surely for her own people.'

[8] Dispatch No. 495 of 23 Dec. 1897, from Hodgson to Chamberlain; CO/96/300.

soared. A retired Director of Education assured his readers that vast deposits of the precious metal lay in the interior, waiting to be discovered and worked by European energy and enterprise.[1] Experts from the Transvaal visited Tarkwa; and the Annual Report on the Gold Coast for 1898 estimated that £40 million worth of gold could be extracted within ten years. Soon the inevitable boom was well under way, which was to result within three years in the formation of about 400 companies with a total nominal capital of many millions.[2]

The Expanding Network of Communications, 1890–1907

Until the turn of the century there had been no alternative to ill-kept roads except water transport in a few favoured areas.[3] But by the 1890's, with the growing importance of mining, as well as cash crops and timber extraction, there was a new, urgent, demand for efficient transport. At first this was concentrated upon the roads. A vivid description of their inadequacy was published in 1890:

> Except in the immediate vicinity of the largest coast towns there are no 'roads' in the country. The so-called roads are mere foot-paths, 12 to 18 inches broad, with the high bush on either side, tortuous, blocked with fallen trunks, flooded with water in the rainy season, interrupted by bridgeless rivers which must be waded, and crossed by unbridged gullies which must be descended on one side and scrambled up on the other. Even travelling between the principal towns the journey must, in great part, be performed along the beach through heavy sand for want of a highway. Nowhere in the Colony are there to be found roads fit for carriage traffic.[4]

An Inspector of Interior Roads was then appointed, but nothing further was done by Brandford Griffith. The merchants' memorial of 1892 alleged that the natural products of the country lay rotting in enormous quantities, simply because there were no roads to bring them to the coast.[5] This claim was

---

[1] G. Macdonald, *The Gold Coast, Past and Present* (London, 1898), p. 98.

[2] D. A. Sutherland, *The Primitive Uses of Gold and Methods of Gold Mining* (Accra, 1952).

[3] In addition to steamboat services up the lower Volta—and the floating of palm oil casks down river—the development of mining encouraged the use of the Ankobra, where during 1881–2 at least one company was running a steam launch about 30 miles inland to carry machinery and stores. Other, smaller rivers were served by canoes. Bevin, 'The Gold Coast Economy about 1880', in *Transactions*, vol. ii, pt. ii, pp. 77–78.

[4] *Report on the Economic Agriculture of the Gold Coast.*

[5] The few main roads did not penetrate very far inland, and there were no proper cross-country links between them. An official list of 1891 mentioned the following:

1. Shama to Tarkwa—thence to Asankrangwa and Enchi.
2. Elmina to Cape Coast—thence to Jukwa and Mansisu; here the road branched (a) to Sefwi and Gyaman, and (b) through Western Wassaw to Asankrangwa and Enchi.
3. Cape Coast to Prasu.
4. Saltpond to Ajumako, Akim-Swedru, and Insuaim [now Oda].
5. Winneba to Agona-Swedru, Nsaba, and Insuaim.   [*continued overleaf.*]

refuted in detail by the Governor, who went to the length of asking every District Commissioner whether he had seen any produce 'rotting'. But the Secretary of State publicly admitted that he was not altogether satisfied with the Government's record concerning roads;[1] in fact, he had already instructed Brandford Griffith, despite arguments about the difficulties of wheeled traffic, to create a Roads Department without further delay.[2]

In 1894 the Trade Roads Ordinance empowered the Chiefs to call on their people for six days' labour in each quarter, and gave legal sanction to the existing system of fines and payments. But better-quality roads were exceedingly costly to construct as well as to maintain; for example, a four-mile cart road from Axim to the River Ankobra was estimated to cost £500 per mile; it actually cost £7,168, including bridges and a landing pier.[3] Nor was it possible to reduce appreciably the time of cross-country travel by foot and hammock, or of transport by head-carriage and cask-rolling.[4] As *The Gold Coast Chronicle* advocated: 'a few lines of Rail to the interior would do the country more good than roads that cost a large sum of money to keep in a good condition.'[5]

The first, quixotic railway project in the Gold Coast had been the shipment in 1873 of materials for a light tramway from Cape Coast to the River Prah, which failed to materialize in time for Wolseley's expedition; afterwards the Colonial Office could think of no alternative use for the rolling-stock.[6] Fitzgerald of *The African Times* was, of course, not lacking in enthusiasm; in 1879 he announced the formation of the West African Railroad, Tramways and Canal Company, whose paper projects included railways from the River

6. Accra to Nsawam, Kibi, and Abetifi.

7. Accra to Aburi, Akropong, Sra, Odumasi, Kpong, Anum, and Kpeve.

8. Keta to Kpeve.

'Of these roads Nos. 1, 3, 7, and 8 are in good or fair order either wholly or in part'. Dispatch No. 347 of 12 Nov. 1891, from Hodgson to Knutsford; CO/96/219.

---

[1] *Despatch from Governor Sir W. Brandford Griffith, K.C.M.G., forwarding a Memorial from Merchants, Agents, and Traders of the Gold Coast Colony, with his observations and the Secretary of State's Reply* (London, 1893), C. 7225.

[2] Dispatch No. 172 of 12 June 1893, from Ripon to Brandford Griffith; CO/96/233.

[3] Dispatch No. 166 of 7 July 1892, from Brandford Griffith to Knutsford; CO/96/224.

[4] See Tables I and II, opposite. In the towns many government officers travelled in 'go-carts'; but these were unserviceable on bush tracks, where pushing was harder work than carrying. The Governor was told by a trader that it cost him 7s. to 9s., according to the weather, to hire three men to roll American puncheons the 17 miles from Temang to Accra; for butts of palm oil he paid four men 16s. to 20s. Dispatch No. 171 of 12 June 1893, from Brandford Griffith to Ripon; CO/96/234. Nearly twenty years later the system was unchanged: 'Generally speaking three men will undertake to roll two barrels to the coast, the three concentrating their efforts upon a single barrel going uphill, while on the level road or downhill they control the two barrels between them. I met three such men who had rolled two casks for 25 to 30 miles, a work of two days, for which they receive 20/- per cask.' J. H. Harris, *Cocoa Production in West Africa* (London, 1911).

[5] *The Gold Coast Chronicle*, 18 Feb. 1893.

[6] Dispatch No. 371 of 29 Dec. 1873, from Wolseley to Kimberley, and subsequent minutes; CO/96/103 and 107.

Travel and Transport at the Beginning of the Twentieth Century[1]

TABLE I. *Hammock Travel*

Cape Coast to:	Time taken		Cost
	hours	minutes	£ s. d.
Axim . . .	30	30	1 0 0
Dixcove . .	20	0	14 0
Ajua . . .	15	40	12 6
Takoradi . .	13	0	— — —
Sekondi . .	11	40	9 0
Shama . . .	8	0	6 9
Komenda . .	4	45	4 6
Elmina . . .	2	15	2 3
Anomabu . .	4	30	3 6
Saltpond . .	6	0	4 6
Mumford . .	14	10	12 6
Apam . . .	15	25	13 6
Winneba . .	18	15	15 0
Accra . . .	30	55	1 0 0

TABLE II. *Carrier Transport*

Distances in days between towns	Axim	Dixcove	Sekondi	Shama	Elmina	Cape Coast	Saltpond	Winneba	Accra	Prampram	Ada	Keta	Tarkwa	Aburi	Akuse
Axim . .	—	1	2	3	4	4	5	7	8	9	11	14	3	9	11
Dixcove . .	11	—	1	2	3	3	4	6	7	8	10	12	2	8	10
Sekondi . .	2	1	—	1	2	2	3	5	6	7	10	12	2	7	9
Shama. .	3	2	1	—	1	1	2	4	5	6	8	10	2	6	8
Elmina . .	4	3	2	1	—	1	1	3	4	5	7	9	3	5	7
Cape Coast . .	4	3	2	1	1	—	1	3	4	5	7	9	4	5	7
Saltpond .	5	4	3	2	1	1	—	1	3	4	6	8	5	4	6
Winneba .	7	6	5	4	3	3	1	—	1	2	4	6	7	3	5
Accra . .	8	7	6	5	4	4	3	1	—	1	3	4	8	1	3
Prampram .	9	8	7	6	5	5	4	2	1	—	2	3	9	1	3
Ada .	11	10	9	8	7	7	6	4	3	2	—	1	11	3	2
Keta .	14	12	11	10	9	9	8	6	4	3	1	—	13	4	4
Tarkwa . .	3	2	2	3	4	4	5	7	9	9	11	13	—	9	11
Aburi . .	9	8	7	6	5	5	4	3	1	1	3	4	9	—	1
Akuse .	11	10	9	8	7	7	6	5	3	3	2	4	11	1	—

Ankobra to the Wassaw goldfields, and from Elmina to Accra, not to mention a canal from there to the Volta. But the shareholders were not forthcoming, and a few months later he was complaining bitterly of African apathy.[2] With the revival of trade in the early 1880's, further amateur railway proposals were mooted, including one by Africanus Horton, but again nothing came of

[1] *Précis of Information concerning the Colony of the Gold Coast and Ashanti* (London, 1904).
[2] *The African Times*, 1 Apr. and 1 Oct. 1879.

these.[1] In 1890 Brandford Griffith suggested the construction of light railways from the main coast towns into the interior,[2] and the first practical step was taken with a preliminary survey during 1893–4.[3] The British Chambers of

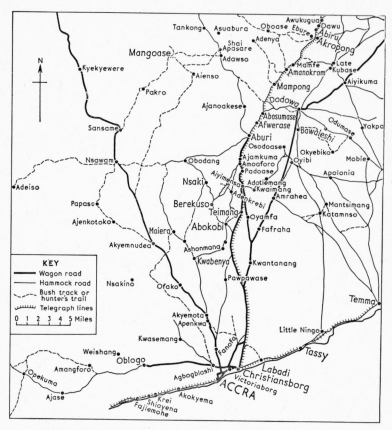

MAP 2A. Communications in the Accra area at the beginning of
the twentieth century.

Commerce renewed their demands for railways, as well as better roads, in West Africa, and several Gold Coast towns urged their own advantages as railway termini in 1895.[4]

This was the formative year for railway policy. In June Lord Ripon received at the Colonial Office a deputation of West African merchants, which in-

The African Times, 2 Jan. 1882; also CO/96/147.
    [2] Dispatch of 10 Nov. 1890, from Brandford Griffith to Knutsford; CO/96/212.
    [3] Report on Survey by Captain J. I. Lang, dated 17 Oct. 1894; CO/96/253.
    [4] For example, Letters from the Accra and Cape Coast Chambers of Commerce, and the Anomabu Public Association, in 1895; CO/96/261 and 263.

cluded J. H. Cheetham of Accra.[1] In August yet another deputation, including merchants, shipowners, and bankers, accompanied by several M.P.s, met a stronger Secretary of State for the Colonies. Characteristically, Joseph

MAP 2B. Communications in the Cape Coast area at the beginning of the twentieth century.

Chamberlain at once declared that if the people of Britain were not willing to invest some of their superfluous wealth in the development of 'their great estate', then he saw no future for such countries, and felt it would have been better never to have gone there.[2] He had already decided that colonial railways should be undertaken by government, rather than private enterprise, in the interests of economy. The first public indication of this new policy was

---

[1] Report of meeting of 25 June 1895, and subsequent Letter of 3 Aug. 1895, from the London Chamber of Commerce to Colonial Office; *Further Correspondence relative to Affairs in Ashanti* (London, 1896), C. 7918.

[2] *The Times*, 24 Aug. 1895; see also *West African Railways* (London, 1895), the deputation's own pamphlet.

given in his brief speech on the Colonial Estimates for 1895,[1] and Governors were circularized accordingly.[2]

Chamberlain's emphasis on the need for direct taxation, at his meeting with the 1898 A.R.P.S. deputation,[3] was prompted mainly by his anxiety to raise funds for railway development. The deputation, taken by surprise, suggested too late that the railways could be developed by private enterprise, and that the Chiefs might provide some labour.[4] Meanwhile the Railway Ordinance of 1898 empowered the Gold Coast Government to acquire land for tracks and stations under the existing Public Lands Ordinance; an authority was also obtained to raise loans in England.[5] Chamberlain considered that loan expenditure on the railways could soon be repaid; and his imagination was fired by the consequent prospects for the mining industry, upon which he enlarged in the House of Commons.[6]

In 1898 the construction of a 3-foot 6-inch gauge, single-line track from Sekondi commenced, reaching Tarkwa in 1901; this substantially lowered the costs of gold production and influenced the mining boom. An Ashanti Railway Ordinance was enacted in 1902, and by the end of that year the line had reached Obuasi; in December 1903 the first train was enthusiastically welcomed in Kumasi. The rapid growth in passenger traffic, and the reduction in transport time and costs, were equally remarkable. In 1904 over 91,000 passengers were carried; while each head-load of 60 lb. could now be sent to or from the coast at a cost of 4s. instead of 26s. 6d., in three days instead of eight.[7]

The rapid development of both mining and railways brought about a considerable inflow of capital, and also encouraged a general increase in imports, which rose by about £1 million annually between 1898 and 1902. Indirectly, too, the mining boom had an important influence upon the ancillary services necessary for economic expansion. The first systematic attempt to survey the country was made largely in order to avoid the constant litigation and confusion over concession boundaries. Up to 1900 surveying had been undertaken piecemeal, on treaty-making expeditions, or along the railway route; but in

---

[1] *Parliamentary Debates*, House of Commons, 22 Aug. 1895.

[2] *Papers relating to the Construction of Railways in Sierra Leone, Lagos, and the Gold Coast* (London, 1904), Cd. 2325.   [3] See Ch. VIII, pp. 311–12, below.

[4] Letter of 18 Aug. 1898, from Ashurst, Morris, Crisp & Co. to Colonial Office; CO/96/333.

[5] Under the General Loan and Inscribed Stock Ordinance of 1898, which provided for a sinking fund. The Railway Loan Ordinance of the same year empowered the Governor so to borrow £220,000 for the Sekondi–Tarkwa line; further sums of £665,000 in 1902, and £360,000 in 1903, were authorized for the completion of the line to Kumasi. The British Government initially provided cheap loans at 2¾ per cent., which gave the railways a good financial start. Later loans had to be raised directly in the London money market, at the prevailing rates, which explains the relative slowness of railway development after the initial impetus during 1898–1903. See McPhee, *The Economic Revolution*, ch. iii, for an account of the progress and the significance of railway development.

[6] *Parliamentary Debates*, House of Commons, 2 Aug. 1899.

[7] *Departmental Reports*, Transport, 1903, and Government Railway, 1904.

that year a Mines Survey Department was created. The first party started work in 1901, and they were joined the following year by a young Captain F. G. Guggisberg. Their task of marking out concessions involved them in creating a skeleton map of the country, by means of a series of accurately surveyed lines,[1] and in 1906 a map of the Colony was produced, showing each district, as well as the proposed boundary with Ashanti.[2] The following year the connexion with the Mines was officially ended, and a new Survey Department was formed, to serve more general needs. During 1907–8 a series of sheets was published, mapping the country as far as 7° N. latitude, i.e. including Kumasi, on a scale of 1/125,000.[3]

Gradually the Government began to extend other minor but important services, and to equip the country—though not yet in any deliberate, planned fashion—with a more efficient network of communications. In 1888, for example, a Post Office Ordinance provided for an inland postal service, to cover the Protectorate as well as the Colony; and a little later postage stamps were introduced for private mail, much to the annoyance of some merchants.[4] By the turn of the century the volume of mail handled was growing rapidly. In 1901 there was an enormous temporary increase, due to the gold-mining boom; in addition to the extra business correspondence, circulars of all kinds were pouring into the country from advertising firms in England.[5] But apart from this peak, the steady expansion continued, as may be seen from the following figures, selected at five-year intervals:

TABLE III.[6]

Year	Post Offices	Items forwarded
1897 . .	34	584,216
1902 . .	41	832,441
1907 . .	61	1,600,617

The history of the telegraph system illustrates the changing emphasis of the Administration. Wolseley's successful field telegraph to Kumasi in 1874 was used for military purposes only.[7] A link between Cape Coast and Accra was

[1] Ibid. Director of Surveys, 1906.

[2] *Map showing the proposed Boundary between Gold Coast Colony and Ashanti. Also the proposed District Boundaries of the Gold Coast Colony* (Accra, 1906).

[3] 'Brief History of the Mines Survey Department, Gold Coast Colony, by Major F. G. Guggisberg, R.E., Director of Surveys', in *Government Gazette*, 3 Aug. 1907. See also Decima Moore and F. G. Guggisberg, *We Two in West Africa* (London, 1909).

[4] The Stamp Ordinance came into effect on 1 Aug. 1890, and a few days later the Governor received telegrams from F. Macan and Miller Bros. protesting against shortages of stamps in Cape Coast (they had deliberately sent in their clerks to buy up the entire stock). Enclosures in Dispatch No. 171 of 12 June 1893, from Brandford Griffith to Ripon; CO/96/234.

[5] *Departmental Reports*, Post and Telegraph, 1902. [6] Ibid. 1897, 1902, and 1907.

[7] Dispatch No. 371 of 29 Dec. 1873, from Wolseley to Kimberley; CO/96/103.

opened in 1887, the Liverpool–Accra submarine cable having come into operation the previous year. In 1889 an Ordinance provided for the construction of telegraph lines over private land, with penalties for damage, and gave the Post Office a monopoly of private telegrams. But it was not until 1894 that a direct line was completed all along the coast, joining Axim–Sekondi–Elmina–Cape Coast–Saltpond–Winneba–Accra–Ada–Keta–Lomé.[1] The telegraph was rapidly developed as a means of internal communication, especially after a permanent line to Kumasi was completed in 1897, the rise in unofficial telegrams being the most noticeable feature:

TABLE IV.[2]

Year	Telegraph Offices	Telegrams	
		Official	Unofficial
1897 . .	26	41,757	42,823
1902 . .	32	117,611	130,466
1907 . .	46	66,039	164,863

By 1907 the system had been extended to Tamale and Wa,[3] thus providing an important unifying link throughout the Gold Coast.

Telephones, being more costly and technically more complicated, were slower to develop, although there was at least one early private experiment in Cape Coast.[4] In 1890 an exchange in Accra linked several government offices,[5] and two years later a line was erected to Aburi, making use of the existing telegraph poles.[6] By 1907 there were only four towns with exchanges, and 111 subscribers, less than half of them being private users.[7]

Meanwhile, the extension of British authority over a much wider area, which was confirmed by the Orders in Council of 1901, bringing Ashanti and the Northern Territories under direct rule or protection,[8] transformed the productive potentialities of the hinterland and widened the area of exchange. Economically speaking, the Gold Coast was fortunate to have a variety of land and natural resources enclosed within its new boundaries. The territory stretched from the fishing villages of the coast, through the gold mines and the rich forest area (the source of palm produce, rubber, kola, timber, and

---

[1] CO/96/135, 175, 181, and 243. Formerly steamers had been the main means of conveying news along the coast. Cf. *The Gold Coast Times* (Cape Coast), 27 Aug. 1881: 'Reports of disturbances at Quittah [Keta] have reached us. By the expected homeward steamer we shall perhaps receive some reliable information respecting them.'

[2] *Departmental Reports*, Post and Telegraph, 1897, 1902, and 1907.

[3] *Government Gazette*, 28 Dec. 1907.

[4] A line between Brew House and Hamilton House, which was not very successful. *The Western Echo*, 24 Apr. 1886.

[5] *Gold Coast Colony Blue Book*, 1890.

[6] Dispatch No. 171 of 12 June 1893, from Brandford Griffith to Ripon; CO/96/234.

[7] *Departmental Reports*, Post and Telegraph, 1907.

[8] See Ch. VIII, pp. 322–4, below.

later cocoa), and across the orchard bush to the fringe of the northern cattle country.[1]

By 1907 modern trade routes had spread right through and across the Gold Coast; they were often deflected by customs posts from crossing the east–west boundaries, but barriers to internal trade were being removed wherever possible. In that year the Governor announced that all caravan tolls between Ashanti and the Colony had been abolished, and that he hoped shortly to do likewise between Ashanti and the Northern Territories: so that, for purposes of trade and finance, the Colony and its dependencies might be 'definitely considered as one country, with absolute freedom of traffic between the various divisions'.[2] The important political advantages of the extension of a system of orderly administration also played their part in bringing the economy, at the beginning of the twentieth century, to the brink of a new phase of development. The *pax Britannica* had been imposed largely to protect commerce; now economic and social development was to lay the foundations of African unity within the shelter of that *pax*.

Cocoa and the Market Economy

Perhaps the most important single development facilitated by the new political and economic structure was the large-scale growth of small-scale cocoa production. Although Tetteh Quarshie is now as firmly associated in Ghana with the introduction of cocoa as the English King Alfred with the burning of the cakes, in fact he was by no means the first to try it out. The Basel Mission imported some cocoa seedlings from Surinam as early as 1858,[3] and certainly had some plants bearing fruit in the 1860's.[4] It seems clear, however, that when Quarshie returned to Mampong-Akwapim from Fernando Po in 1879 with his handful of seeds, his example attracted African imitators as that of the Mission had never done;[5] and since cocoa takes four to five years to come into bearing on virgin land, there may be a direct link with the first recorded export of 121 lb. of cocoa in 1885. No further exports were

[1] The main climatic and vegetational zones in West Africa run from east to west; the penetration of European powers from the coast followed the direction of the pre-existing north–south trade routes, even though it seemed at the time to be determined by haphazard competition for treaties and territory.   [2] Rodger, *Legislative Council Minutes*, 30 Sept. 1907.

[3] Article by Preiswerk-Imholf in *West Africa*, 2 Mar. 1929.

[4] Horton reported in 1868 that the Basel missionaries were attempting to naturalize the Mexican cocoa or chocolate plant: 'They have a few trees growing at Accrapong [Akropong] which have borne very large fruit.' *West African Countries and Peoples*, p. 147.

[5] Thus Tetteh Quarshie may be said to have provided that economic leadership, in Schumpeter's sense, which is a necessary prerequisite of development when new possibilities present themselves. Inventions or innovations are not enough: 'As long as they are not carried into practice, inventions are economically irrelevant.' The main problem for such leadership, especially in an undeveloped society, is 'the reaction of the social environment against one who wishes to do something new'. But cocoa cultivation seems suddenly to have surmounted this obstacle in the last few years of the century, and it seems fair to ascribe the credit for this—rather than the mere introduction of the plant—to Quarshie. See J. A. Schumpeter, *The Theory of Economic Development* (Harvard, 1951 edn.), pp. 74–94.

recorded until 1891, by which time Basel missionaries were selling imported cocoa pods to African growers,[1] and the new government botanical station at Aburi was cultivating and distributing young plants.[2]

Annual totals of cocoa exported crept towards the figure of 13 tons in 1895; but ten years later they had leapt up to more than 5,000 tons, and by 1911, with nearly 40,000 tons, the Gold Coast was the world's leading producer. Between 1902 and 1911 world production and consumption had doubled;[3] but whereas many other growing countries were dependent on European capital and management, the Gold Coast outstripped them all with a spontaneous diffusion of enterprise among African farmers. This was justifiably described before the West African Lands Committee as a unique example of indigenous industry;[4] and the achievement is not lessened by the fact that the Government provided what advice and assistance it could over growing and selling the crop.

In 1898 the Government had introduced a marketing scheme for both coffee and cocoa, advancing money on the produce to the growers, selling it for them in England, and then paying out any balance after expenses had been deducted. This scheme did not last very long, partly owing to criticisms from the West African Trade Association. The European merchants already established on the coast took an increasing interest in cocoa purchasing; during 1901–2 complaints of the prices offered in Accra were heard, especially from farmers several days' journey from the coast. They even asked for a recommencement of official shipments. Sir Matthew Nathan began to fear the total disappearance of the cocoa industry, as had happened with coffee; but when he approached the Accra Chamber of Commerce, they denied the validity of the official figures.[5] The Colonial Office found it impossible to judge whether prices were fair, or whether a ring existed; but the next Governor later criticized the wide margin between the merchants' price of 16s. a load (60 lb.) and the price in England of 50s. a cwt., and initiated some further, unprofitable government shipments. The merchants claimed that no allowance had been made for the normal 20 per cent. loss in weight during transit, and that the failure of the scheme proved they had not been making unfair profits.[6]

It seems, however, that there were cocoa-buying agreements in 1903, 1904, 1905, and 1906–10;[7] the increasing number of buyers had already entered upon the cycle of intensive competition followed by attempted combination

---

[1] *Belfield Report*, evidence of J. P. Brown, p. 108.

[2] A. W. Cardinall, *The Gold Coast, 1931* (Accra, 1932), p. 82.

[3] See *W.A.L.C. Evidence*, p. 381, and cf. Gold Coast export figures, pp. 39 and 52, below. In 1911 the second largest producer was Ecuador, with nearly 39,000 tons.

[4] Ibid. E. D. Morel and W. A. Cadbury, 10,652.

[5] Enclosures and covering Dispatch No. 113 of 17 Mar. 1902, from Nathan to Chamberlain; CO/96/395.

[6] W. H. Grey, *Legislative Council Minutes*, 6 Nov. 1911.

[7] *Report of the [Nowell] Commission on the Marketing of West Africa Cocoa* (London, 1938), Cmd. 5845, historical introduction.

which was to prove so ruinous to the trade in later years.[1] In some areas the farmers combined together in an attempt to obtain better prices; examples were the Larteh Planters' Union and the Dodowah Planters' Company.[2] The main purchasing agents represented the established import–export firms; in 1906 Cadbury's bought their first small consignment direct, and soon set up a local buying organization. They devoted much attention to improving the quality of shipments;[3] and by 1913 it was a common practice to offer differential prices for quality.[4] The improvement of transport facilitated the spread of buying stations farther up country, and this in turn encouraged the diffusion of cocoa growing over a wider area.

The cocoa industry remained in the hands of the small-scale farmer; although there was no legal obstacle to plantation development, few overseas firms were interested, and fewer still able to show results. The failure of one such attempt was blamed on the proximity of neglected 'native plantings';[5] but it is at least possible that the indigenous farmers knew more about the dangers of over-clearing the bush than their more ambitious European neighbours. In any case, cocoa cultivation in the early days was largely a matter of trial and error; and this can be a costly process on a large scale, as more recent experiments in tropical agriculture have shown. A further point in favour of the small plot was the ease with which local inhabitants could apply for grants of land from their own stool. At first, a man would require only as much as he could cultivate with the help of his family, though he might clear new farms from time to time as his skill and capital increased. This did not mean that every farmer produced on a small scale; but even the wealthiest were more likely to have a series of farms, often in different places, in different stages of bearing, than one large-scale holding.

A rather different development in States where there was little land available was the formation of 'companies', who would migrate—sometimes temporarily—to other areas where they could apply for land as 'stranger farmers'. This system originated among the Krobos, and was soon followed elsewhere. In the Larteh area of Akwapim, for example, it is thought that all the land suitable for cocoa had been bought up by about 1900—often being paid for out of profits acquired in the palm oil trade—and thereafter migration by companies was common.[6] Sometimes they would simply be granted the life-interest appropriate to strangers in return for a one-third share of the

---

[1] Cf. W. K. Hancock, *Survey of British Commonwealth Affairs* (London, 1940), vol. ii, pt. ii, pp. 201 and 207.

[2] *W.A.L.C. Evidence*, Cadbury, 10,565 and 10,572.

[3] Some far-sighted Chiefs, notably Nene Mate Kole of Manya Krobo, encouraged better methods of cultivation, and some actually imposed fines for poor quality cocoa. Ibid. 10,579–83.

[4] Ibid. 10,660, 10,531, 10,591, and 10,598–600.

[5] Ibid. A. C. Goff, 11,246–9.

[6] Polly Hill, *Cocoa Research Series*, No. 14, 'The Acquisition of Land by Larteh Cocoa Farmers' (University College of Ghana, 1958).

crop, under the *abusa* system. Increasingly, however, they sought to purchase the land outright, subject to any reversionary conditions imposed by local customary law; it would then be divided between the members according to the size of their contribution, and would be regarded as individual property.[1]

It seems clear that the permanent nature of cocoa farms, as opposed to seasonal and shifting food production, gradually brought about some modification in the system of land tenure, and encouraged the individualization of holdings.[2] Indeed in Ashanti the Chief Commissioner intervened with an executive ruling 'that where a man had properly planted a plantation it should be regarded as his own, so as to give him the fruits of his labour. That was the beginning of individual ownership'.[3] When pressed on this point before the West African Lands Committee he admitted that in fact such a declaration had not received the sanction of customary law.[4] Rattray in 1929 denied that individual ownership of land existed in Ashanti, although he acknowledged the growing tendency to individualization of the right to use land.[5]

The buying system that was growing up also imported a considerable degree of economic individualism into the farmer's handling of his crop and of his land rights. The most common practice was for the buyer to make his contracts at the beginning of the growing season, to ensure that as many farmers as possible would sell their crops to him. Some firms would clinch the bargain by means of a small advance, sufficient to finance the cost of transporting the cocoa; others would pay for the whole crop in advance at an agreed price, and take a chance on future market fluctuations.[6] The need for working capital effectively prevented Africans from entering the buying trade in large numbers; but there were a few established firms—notably Ofori Bros.—and some individuals who had accumulated wealth by trade, inheritance, or perhaps from dealing in concessions. W. H. Grey, the chief agent for Miller's and Swanzy's, said in 1912: 'In every district there are two or three men who have a few thousand pounds' and who would use it for purchasing cocoa, making advances to as many different farmers as they could.[7]

---

[1] Such companies seem to have been fairly common in the cocoa areas, but their history and organization has only recently received detailed attention. In Obomofo-Densua, for example, a company of a dozen Shai people bought nearly 600 acres in 1906 for about £600, and the land was then divided into individually-owned strips. Later subdivision by inheritance and sale produced seventy-five separate farms; but although the company still exists virtually all the cocoa has now been destroyed by swollen shoot. In Togoland migration took place much later; in Jasikan, for example, thirteen companies were found who had purchased land during 1926–8, and twenty-six during 1930–40. Hill, *Cocoa Research Series*: No. 3, 'An Economic Survey of Cocoa Farmers in the Jasikan Area of Trans-Volta Togoland'; No. 9, 'Obomofo-Densua, a Company of Cocoa Farmers'; No. 10, 'Adidiso, a Company of Cocoa Farmers'; and No. 12, 'The Nankese-Shai Company of Cocoa Farmers' (University College of Ghana, 1957–8).

[2] Cf. Meek, *Land Law and Custom*, p. 179.

[3] *Belfield Report*, Fuller, p. 87.   [4] *W.A.L.C. Evidence*, Fuller, 4,743–55.

[5] Rattray, *Ashanti Law and Constitution*, pp. 349–50.

[6] *W.A.L.C. Evidence*, Cadbury, 10,553–6.   [7] Ibid. Grey, 5,456–8.

Although little security was necessary for such loans, since they were re-deemed by delivery of the crop, it did not take the growers long to realize that their farms represented a permanent form of security for the loans increasingly in demand for family or personal reasons. The pledging of property (such as kente cloths or gold ornaments), of persons (under the pawning system), or of land, was already a long-standing custom. In exchange for a loan, nominally free of interest, the debtor would hand over the use of the pledge to the creditor—who could wear the cloth, employ the pawn, or harvest the crops of the farm, without becoming the absolute owner. The cocoa farmer who borrowed in this way might automatically redeem his farm after a given period of time, or after cocoa of a certain value had been produced, in which case the agreement represented a form of lease; but sometimes he might be expected to redeem it by repayment of the loan in cash, which often meant a long delay before he could find either the money or a fresh creditor.[1]

Thus the widespread development of cocoa led indirectly to the creation of a complicated pattern of indebtedness among farmers, which modern research has only just begun to unravel. It seems clear that this cannot be condemned out of hand as a social evil, since lending was widely regarded as a social service, many creditors being relatives or close friends of their debtors, rather than professional moneylenders. The provision of credit for agricultural purposes was generally the least important of the farmer's reasons for borrowing;[2] the net result was some redistribution of the wealth derived from cocoa. The greater part of the profit made, however, seems to have been reinvested; as farmers' incomes rose, they acquired more land and employed more labour, in a 'benign spiral' which was broken only by the severe onset of swollen shoot in the 1940's. Apart from this, there was con-siderable investment in house-building, and in the rising generation, through expenditure on education; and in some areas the cocoa farmers contributed generously to public improvements.[3]

The rise in cocoa incomes was perhaps the most important aspect of the growth of the money economy, which had been proceeding rapidly towards the end of the nineteenth century. Overseas coins had been brought increas-ingly into use; but in 1880 foreign silver dollars, and in 1889 gold dust, were demonetized by Ordinance, and thereafter British silver predominated. A

[1] Hill, *Cocoa Farmer*, chs. v and vi; and *Cocoa Research Series*, No. 15, 'The Pledging of Cocoa Farms: Terms and Conditions in Different Areas of Ghana, with an Appendix on the Causes of Indebtedness.' Pogucki quotes lawsuits as early as the 1850's to show that the practice of pledging land in the Gold Coast is of respectable antiquity; he emphasizes that it is the possession and usufruct—but not the ownership—of the land that passes to the creditor, and therefore the system cannot be described as mortgaging, although English-type mortgages are also found. *Gold Coast Land Tenure*, vol. ii, pp. 36–38.   [2] Hill, *Cocoa Farmer*, pp. 52, 56–57, and 71 n.

[3] During the First World War three bridges were built over the River Densu (at an average cost of £1,200) by the people of Akwapim, then one of the richest cocoa areas; and they spent over £47,000 on contractor-built roads from 1916 to 1926. Hill, *Cocoa Research Series*, No. 14, 'The Acquisition of Land by Larteh Cocoa Farmers'.

need for more specialized banking and remittance services soon grew up in the towns. Money orders had been exchangeable with the United Kingdom from 1870 onwards; in 1881 the Mercantile Association in Cape Coast petitioned the Governor for an internal postal-order system.[1] A Savings Bank Ordinance was enacted in 1887; but wider facilities were needed. Africanus Horton had founded his own Commercial Bank of West Africa, with headquarters in Sierra Leone, in 1882; he had planned to establish branches in Cape Coast, Lagos, and Bathurst, but died the following year.[2] On 6 June 1885 *The Gold Coast News* suggested that the establishment of a commercial bank would be supported by the educated inhabitants. In 1892 two Gold Coast Africans spoke in London on the need for a sound bank: 'In our leading towns are many men of large means, who, having no opportunity for investment, their money becomes unprofitable.'[3] In 1894 the Bank of British West Africa was founded, and given a monopoly of the import of British silver coin;[4] a branch was opened in Accra in 1897, and one in Kumasi eleven years later. Banks, however, never became an important source of credit for Africans; in the relative absence of individual titles to land, would-be borrowers found it difficult to offer adequate security in the European sense, and in any case they often preferred to rely on their personal credit through the traditional system of pledging.

The circulation of British currency increased to such an extent that even before 1900 the West African Governors began to demand a share of the profits on its issue. Chamberlain suggested such a scheme to the Treasury; but the reply came *ex cathedra*: 'My Lords do not view with favour the proposal to take advantage of the predilection of African natives for silver coins as a means for passing an unlimited quantity of Imperial tokens into that continent.'[5] A few years later the Treasury introduced special nickel-bronze coins of the values $1d.$, $\frac{1}{2}d.$, and $\frac{1}{10}d.$, although still refusing to consider any form of profit-sharing.[6] This small change helped considerably to widen the area of internal exchange at a time when the Gold Coast's international trade was increasing beyond all precedent.

Tables V and VI illustrate the remarkable progress, particularly in the export trade, during the period 1898–1907.[7] The more lasting results of the

[1] *The Gold Coast Times*, 21 Jan. 1882.   [2] *The African Times*, 1 Dec. 1882, and 1 Dec. 1883.

[3] G. Acquah Robertson and A. Bruce, *Address to the Balloon Society of Great Britain* (London, 1892).

[4] *Agreement with the Bank of British West Africa, Limited, as to Transaction of the Banking Business of the Government, dated 16th June, 1896* (Accra, 1900).

[5] Letter of June 1899, from Treasury to Colonial Office; African (West) No. 592 (London, 1901).

[6] Africa (West) No. 645 (London, 1903). It was not until 1921 that the West African Currency Board was established, to issue its own coins, and later notes, on behalf of the four Governments. This had been recommended by the *Report of the Departmental Committee appointed to Inquire into Matters affecting the Currency of the British West African Colonies and Protectorates* (London, 1912). For a fuller account, see W. T. Newlyn and D. C. Rowan, *Money and Banking in British Colonial Africa* (Oxford, 1954), ch. ii.

[7] Cf. S. H. Frankel, *Capital Investment in Africa* (London, 1938), especially ch. v, 'Africa Joins the World Economy', giving comparative figures for various African territories.

mining boom can clearly be seen in the steady expansion of gold exports after 1903, at the same time as high cocoa exports were beginning to eclipse the palm oil trade. Improved communications also encouraged the export of other forest products, notably timber; and kola was now being sent south instead of northwards in increasing quantities. Although economic expansion

TABLE V. *Gold Coast External Trade*[1]

(£'000)

Year	Imports c.i.f.	Exports
Average		
1878–82 .	369	401
1883–7 .	423	421
1888–92 .	536	550
1893–7 .	857	820
Annual total		
1898 .	1,102	993
1899 .	1,323	1,112
1900 .	1,295	885
1901 .	1,801	560
1902 .	2,125	774
1903 .	2,083	981
1904 .	2,002	1,340
1905 .	1,486	1,646
1906 .	2,059	1,996
1907 .	2,366	2,642

TABLE VI. *Value of Selected Gold Coast Exports*[2]

(£'000)

Year	Gold	Rubber	Cocoa	Palm oil and kernels	Kola nuts	Lumber
Average						
1893–7 .	83	301	1	266	31	58
Annual total						
1898 .	64	552	10	365	36	110
1899 .	51	556	16	289	57	87
1900 .	38	328	27	336	43	68
1901 .	22	104	43	268	35	55
1902 .	97	87	95	368	37	22
1903 .	255	197	86	251	51	49
1904 .	346	361	200	215	55	54
1905 .	597	324	187	167	60	84
1906 .	822	335	336	206	74	80
1907 .	1,131	333	515	221	79	169

[1] *Gold Coast Colony Blue Books*, 1878 to 1883 and 1886 to 1907. The figures for 1894–5 have, however, been taken from Brandford Griffith's trade summary enclosed in his Dispatch of 10 Nov. 1890, to Knutsford; CO/96/212. All his other figures agree with the *Blue Books*, and it therefore seems likely that the exceptionally high figures originally published had subsequently been corrected.   [2] Ibid. 1893 to 1907.

was geared to the international market, and depended largely upon the growth of expatriate buying and selling organizations, this was not a new factor in the Gold Coast economy. The main difference at the turn of the century was the speeding up of the pace of development, based partly on overseas capital investment in the mines, and partly on the astonishing expansion of cocoa farming. The net effect of all these changes can be summed up as nothing less than an economic revolution.

The Emergence of Employed Labour

As the new export market expanded, and communications improved, African farmers and cocoa buyers began to employ labour on an increasing scale. As soon as holdings increased beyond the size that could be economically worked by one family, hired labourers were required. So long as land remained plentiful, and local people could obtain their own farms for the asking, the labourers would normally come from outside the area. The seasonal nature of cocoa also suited the stranger who wished to preserve his home ties rather than settle permanently in a new area.

The payment of these workers was often arranged by means of an adaptation of the *abusa* system, whereby the labourers received a one-third share of the proceeds when the farm came into bearing. As marketing arrangements became more standardized, however, a new system developed in some areas: the *nkotokuano* labourer received a fixed sum per load for all the cocoa he harvested for his employer.[1] This more nearly resembled the payment of wages on a piecework system; but the growth of wage-earning employment on a significant scale was due mainly to the operation of overseas firms, especially in mining, and to the increase in the number of regular workers required by the Government. During the construction of the first railway, it was reported that men were coming to Sekondi to seek work from many parts of the Colony, and even from farther afield.[2] Some indication of the growing numbers employed in the towns is given by the Census figures, although these cannot be taken as either accurate or exhaustive. In 1891, for example, an attempt was made to classify occupations in sixteen coastal towns,[3] including:

Farmers and agricultural labourers.	.	3,510
Mechanics	.	3,091
Civil servants . . .	.	1,376

The 1911 Census gave figures for twenty-nine Colony towns,[4] which are not necessarily comparable, including:

---

[1] See Hill, *Cocoa Farmer*, chs. i and ii.

[2] Report by District Commissioner, Shama, for the quarter ending 31 Mar. 1898, enclosed in Dispatch No. 330 of 4 Aug. 1898, from Hodgson to Chamberlain; CO/96/319.

[3] *Report on the Census of the Gold Coast Colony for the Year 1891* (London, n.d.).

[4] *Census of the Population, 1911* (Accra, n.d.).

Farmers	.	.	.	.	.	8,802
Labourers	.	.	.	.	.	5,198
Clerks	.	.	.	.	.	2,349
Carpenters	.	.	.	.	.	1,445
Bricklayers and masons.		.	.	.	557
Engine drivers	.	.	.	.	15

The most important labour development during this period—in the gold mines—is not recorded in the Census figures at all. Their ever-growing demand for workers soon brought the wage-earning system within the experience of even the most remote villages of the Northern Territories. This movement was initially welcomed and assisted by government officials; in fact they regarded the scheme for recruitment as a 'labour crusade', opening up great possibilities both for individuals and for the country as a whole, and at first elaborate precautions were taken for the welfare of the workers, although later there were grave abuses.

It was in 1906 that the Chamber of Mines first inquired about the possibilities of recruiting labour from the north. A. E. Watherston, the Chief Commissioner, at once canvassed the idea enthusiastically among the Chiefs, pointing out the advantages to their young men in terms of cash, experience, and new skills gained. The Chiefs, however, were understandably doubtful: the few who had already left their villages had seldom returned; would proper travelling and working conditions be guaranteed, and could the men keep in touch with their homes while away?[1]

As a result, Watherston arranged for a party of twenty to thirty young men, chosen by the Chiefs and accompanied by an official, to visit the mines and see for themselves the work, food, and conditions that would be offered them. He pointed out that they should not be taken to any mine that had the reputation of treating its employees harshly, not so much from a desire to mislead them as because he knew they were 'extremely nervous people'.[2] The party enjoyed their trip,[3] and recruiting started in 1907. The Chief Commissioner was genuinely anxious to get as many young men as possible out of the north before the threatened annual outbreak of cerebro-spinal meningitis, and suggested that head-money should be paid to Chiefs for the men they provided.[4] The mining companies agreed to this, and payment was made through the Secretary for Mines, a government official.[5] By 1909 the mines' demand for labour exceeded 5,000 men a year, and seemed insatiable. Watherston visited Sekondi to discuss travelling facilities personally with the General

[1] Letter of 18 May 1906, from Watherston to Colonial Secretary; 1953 Acc. No. 1290, G.N. Archives. [2] Ibid.

[3] Report by Captain Irvine, enclosed in his Letter of 25 Jan. 1907, to Chief Commissioner; 1953 Acc. No. 1290, G.N. Archives.

[4] Letter of 3 Sept. 1907, from Watherston to Colonial Secretary; 1953 Acc. No. 1292, G.N. Archives.

[5] Letter of 2 Sept. 1909, from Watherston to Commissioners, forwarding head-money received from the Secretary for Mines; 1953 Acc. No. 1296, G.N. Archives.

Manager of the Railways, and also arranged that the men should have some savings left when they returned home.[1]

After a brief post-war slump, the demand for labour increased once more,[2] and the mines became worried about the wastage on the journey south. Inevitably, some of the migrants were attracted by the open-air life on the Ashanti farms that they passed on their way, and this seasonal labour considerably assisted the expansion of the cocoa industry.[3] The mines now sent up their own recruiting agents, but many workers were still supplied by the Chiefs, who were paid 5s. for each man who reported to the District Commissioner, and a further 7s. 6d. on his return after completing a nine months' contract of service. The Regulation of Employment Ordinance of 1921 made desertion (i.e. breach of contract) a penal offence, for which the Chamber of Mines had been pressing for some years. Unfortunately the humane provisions of the original scheme were now entangled with an excess of red tape. One regulation ran: 'Women in number up to 15% of the total may accompany the labourers'; most of the men's wages were compulsorily saved for them until they completed their service.[4] To encourage recruitment, photographs were officially circulated, showing mining labourers 'before' and 'after'.[5] But the Chiefs were increasingly reluctant to send more men, which was not surprising after the appalling mortality in the influenza epidemic of 1918–19; on a conservative estimate, over 25,000 of their people died, mainly women and young persons—i.e. about 6 per cent. of the population of the Northern Territories.[6]

Although the Chief Commissioner, A. Philbrick, had been responsible for helping to draw up the latest post-war scheme, he felt increasing doubts after watching it in operation. In 1923 he pointed out that although no force was exerted, the fact that recruiting was done through the Political Officers, who issued instructions to the Chiefs to find a certain number of men, must

[1] Letter of 1 June 1909, from Watherston to General Manager, G.C. Railways; 1953 Acc. No. 1296, G.N. Archives.

[2] The African labour force reached a peak of 15,000 in 1917, fell to 9,775 in 1920, and averaged just over 10,000 during the years 1922–5. Sutherland, *The Primitive Uses of Gold and Methods of Gold Mining*, app. III. In one year alone 4,636 organized labourers were sent from the Northern Territories to the mines, railways, sisal plantations, and surveys; in addition, of the many thousands of casual labourers who travelled south, 16,816 were counted at one ferry. *Departmental Reports*, Northern Territories, 1922–3.   [3] Ibid. 1913.

[4] Scheme agreed between Government and Chamber of Mines, enclosed in Letter of 14 June 1921, from Chief Commissioner to Commissioner, S. Province; 1953 Acc. No. 1398, Case No. 5/1920, G.N. Archives.

[5] Photographs enclosed in Letter of 22 Nov. 1921, from Chief Commissioner to Provincial Commissioners; ibid.

[6] The figures were officially estimated at about 17,300 in the NE. Province and 7,900 in the NW. Province; but A. W. Cardinall, one of the District Commissioners, pointed out that many of the Chiefs did not count children who had died. The epidemic had not been followed by any large number of suicides, as had happened after the measles outbreak the previous year: 'Grief in this case appears to have been too great and to have rendered people apathetic.' 1953 Acc. No. 1394, G.N. Archives.

necessarily leave the impression that it was by a government order that they were sent down. He thought it extremely probable that the Chiefs exercised a certain amount of compulsion in their natural anxiety to stand well with the Government. He suggested that officials should therefore leave recruiting entirely alone, except to introduce the recruiters to the Chiefs and to assist as at present with the financial arrangements.[1] The Governor readily agreed, being surprised to hear of the current practice, which he considered entirely wrong in principle.[2]

But in 1924 an even more serious problem became apparent, when statistics revealed a very grave death-rate among mining labourers. The Secretary of State instructed that recruitment in the north should cease forthwith,[3] and an eminent physician was sent out to conduct a special inquiry, which revealed some very unsatisfactory conditions in the mining areas. He found the main factors in the high death-rate to be: the prevalence of *ankylostomiasis* (hookworm), the large number of unfit men (especially with T.B.) coming south, unsatisfactory housing conditions at Abbontiakoon, a polluted and insufficient water supply, and inadequate medical arrangements at Tarkwa and Abosso. He urged the compulsory registration of deaths, and a large number of preventive measures, including the preliminary rejection of unfit men, inoculation against pneumonia, the improvement of hospital, medical, and sanitary services, better village planning, and definite encouragement to the men to bring their wives.[4]

The result was the Mining Health Areas Ordinance of 1925; and after some months' interruption, recruiting (by agents of the mines alone) was resumed.[5] In 1927 new and stricter conditions were imposed on the Taquah and Abosso Mines Company;[6] this time the Chief Commissioner insisted that the men should be interviewed by a Political Officer before leaving the north, to make sure that they were really going of their own free will.[7] The mining companies now found that organized recruiting would be so expensive that it was no longer worth their while.[8] So the Administration was relieved of its major responsibility in this field; but the seasonal pattern of migration remained an important characteristic of the Gold Coast labour market, while the annual draining away of so many able-bodied men reduced the prospects of development in the north, and profoundly affected the character of village life there.

[1] Letters of 20 Nov. and 17 Dec. 1923, from Chief Commissioner to Colonial Secretary; 1953 Acc. No. 1398, Case No. 5/1920, G.N. Archives.

[2] Letter of 9 Jan. 1924, from Colonial Secretary to Chief Commissioner; ibid.

[3] Telegram of 5 July 1924, from Colonial Secretary to Chief Commissioner; ibid.

[4] 'Preliminary Report by Sir W. J. Simpson on Investigations regarding the High Death Rate of Mines' Labourers', submitted to Secretary of State in Sept. 1924; ibid.

[5] Letter of 25 Mar. 1925, from Colonial Secretary to Chief Commissioner; ibid.

[6] Letter of 15 Sept. 1927, from Manager, Taquah and Abosso Mines, to Colonial Secretary, referring to a recent interview with the Governor; 1953 Acc. No. 1419, Case No. 6/1925, G.N. Archives.   [7] Letter of 3 Oct. 1927, from Chief Commissioner to Colonial Secretary; ibid.

[8] Letter of 24 Nov. 1927, from Secretary for Mines to Acting Colonial Secretary; ibid.

It is interesting to note that these illiterate workers relied throughout upon the Government to protect their rights. It was not likely that they could easily organize any form of union unrelated to their family and social structure; and trade unions were everywhere slow to develop, even in the more urbanized and industrial centres farther south. The first permanent unions were those of craftsmen, organized somewhat on guild lines.[1] The Gold and Silversmiths' Association, for example, was formed in protest against the Gold Mining Protection Ordinance of 1909; two years later it was reported to be a powerful organization in Accra, ruled by its own Chief and councillors.[2] Another early union was the Gold Coast Carpenters' Association, which was registered under the Companies Ordinance in 1910. There were also other guilds of self-employed workers, including masons, blacksmiths, and coopers; nearly all had elaborate rules concerning apprenticeship, and mutual help at funerals.[3]

More modern types of union organization began to emerge after the war, when a boom in cocoa production, coinciding with an extension of public works programmes, helped to precipitate a serious shortage of labour. During 1920 the Government was able to obtain only a fraction of the number of artisans required, and only 40 per cent. of the necessary unskilled labour.[4] One result of this situation was the formation of an Artisans' and Labourers' Union in Accra, which threatened to call a strike if their demands for increased wages, a seven-hour day, and free hospital treatment were not met. Guggisberg received a deputation at Christiansborg Castle, and promised to put right certain minor grievances, although a pay increase was refused.[5] In 1921 some government artisans did come out on strike against threatened reductions in pay, but to little purpose.[6] The same year the Regulation of Employment Ordinance attempted to bring labour legislation up to date; the Master and Servant Ordinance, which had survived since 1893, was then repealed. In 1924 there was a strike at the Ashanti goldfields at Obuasi, in protest against the introduction of clocks to record working times by means of punched cards.[7]

As yet, however, employed workers represented only a small minority of the working population. This much seems clear from the selective figures published in the 1921 Census, although it should be remembered that they are incomplete, probably inaccurate, and misleading in some respects.

[1] There is, however, a record of an early strike of Cape Coast canoemen in 1896. *The 'Sunlight' Reference Almanac*, p. 13. In 1898 the first Commissioner of the Northern Territories deplored the formation of 'a trade union of a most pernicious kind' among the carriers from the coast, who were able to 'dictate to a helpless Government' the terms on which they would convey loads. CO/96/345. No doubt he exaggerated their strength.

[2] O. Kitching, 'History of Trade Unions in the Gold Coast', a lecture given at Akropong, Ashanti, 1952.

[3] *Census of the Population, 1911*.

[4] Guggisberg, *Legislative Council Debates*, 21 Jan. 1921.

[5] 1953 Acc. No. 1395, Case No. 4/1919, G.N. Archives.

[6] *Departmental Reports*, Public Works, 1921.   [7] *West Africa*, 1924–5.

TABLE VII. *Occupations of Men in 32 Main Towns*[1]

Farmers 21,272	Blacksmiths 825	
Clerks 12,273	Goldsmiths 802	
Fishermen and boatmen . . 9,502	Motor drivers 536	
Carriers and labourers . . 8,870	Teachers 458	
Traders 5,555	Fitters and mechanics . . 347	
Domestic servants . . . 3,243	Printers 120	
Carpenters 2,159	Ministers of Religion . . 66	
Tailors 1,204	Lawyers 50	
Bricklayers and masons . . 1,024	Doctors 7	

This total of 68,313 still did not include the mineworkers, by now perhaps the most significant concentrated labour force (estimated at over 10,000 in 1921), but very isolated in their specially constructed townships.

It will be seen that clerks formed the largest single employed group; they were certainly the most articulate, and during 1918–21 the grievances of those who were civil servants became an important political issue. Owing to their special status and quasi-European habits, they were particularly vulnerable to rises in the cost of living. There seems no reason to doubt their claim that in eight years the purchasing power of the £ had fallen more than 50 per cent.,[2] yet at the beginning of 1919 the salary of the lowest grade still stood at £36 per annum, an amount that had been considered inadequate to meet the cost of living in 1896.[3]

This tendency of wages and salaries to 'stick' for many years at conventional levels, regardless of the cost of living, was not confined to clerical workers. The daily rates paid to general labourers in government employment had risen during the same period, reflecting the increased demand, but the lowest wage remained at 9*d.* per day, although in 1921 some could earn as much as 1*s.* 9*d.*[4] Manual workers were still for the most part unorganized, apart from the few examples already mentioned. The origins of any given group of workers would probably be very mixed, yet tribal and family loyalties still remained their strongest ties, transcending those of common occupational and economic interests. It was not until after the Second World War that trade unions were to become an active force, or to contribute in any significant way towards the nationalist movement.

The Pattern of Exploitation

Although the Gold Coast had made such an impressive economic entry into the twentieth century, there were some Europeans who felt that its natural

[1] In the same towns 47,131 women were recorded as gainfully occupied, including 11,957 'farmers' and 11,613 traders and hawkers, with a further 16,666 engaged in preparing or selling various types of food. Other groups included 1,641 'labourers', 1,678 dressmakers, but only 80 teachers and 20 civil servants. *Census Report 1921 for the Gold Coast Colony, Ashanti, the Northern Territories and the Mandated Area of Togoland* (Accra, 1923).

[2] Petition of 17 Feb. 1920, to Guggisberg from A. Konuah and others. 'Report of Committee of Enquiry on the Native Civil Service', *Sessional Paper No. VII of 1920–21.*

[3] For details of civil service salaries and negotiations during this period, see Ch. II, pp. 101–4, below.   [4] *Gold Coast Colony Blue Books*, 1895 to 1921.

resources and potential markets could be exploited still more efficiently by expatriate enterprise. It was certainly frustrating to see cocoa farms being cleared by the simple experient of cutting down and burning valuable timber and oil-palms; but government attempts to protect the farmers from themselves by means of forest legislation ran into the emotional block set up in African minds by the Lands Bill agitation of 1897–8, and remedial measures were delayed for many years.[1] Sir William Lever, one of the largest buyers of palm produce in the United Kingdom, was appalled by the improvident attitude of farmers and the wasteful local methods of oil extraction.[2] But his attempt to secure monopoly advantages for large-scale processing in the Gold Coast was equally unsuccessful.

In 1910 Lever Bros. had set up kernel-crushing mills at Opobo and Apapa in Nigeria, and two years later they secured the reluctant permission of the Colonial Office to do the same in Sierra Leone.[3] When proposals were made for a local monopoly in the Gold Coast, the Governor, J. J. Thornburn, objected as a matter of principle, with the support of his Executive Council.[4] But the Secretary of State, L. Harcourt, had already signed an agreement, and now produced a draft Bill, instructing the Governor to see it through the Legislative Council. This was designed to encourage capitalists to erect modern machinery for the expression of palm oil, and empowered the Government to grant exclusive rights for the operation of mechanical mills, as well as for the construction of railways, within a circle of 10 miles' radius, over a period of twenty-one years.

Shortly after the Palm Oil Bill was published in the Gold Coast in 1912,[5] one of the European unofficial members of the Legislative Council attacked it in a letter to *The Times*,[6] and an influential storm of protest arose in England.[7] The Chambers of Commerce of Manchester, London, and Liverpool sent a deputation to the Colonial Office, and Harcourt was sharply questioned in the House of Commons.[8] Under pressure, the Secretary of State published the draft Bill, and the relevant correspondence, for the benefit of Parliament.[9] A representative of Lever's was closely examined on the scope and the underlying motives of the proposals before the West African Lands Committee

[1] See Ch. X, pp. 362–6, below.

[2] The age-old process of extracting oil from the fleshy pericarp of the palm nut was by means of boiling and skimming. Since the nineteenth-century discovery that the hard kernel also contained oil, some producers were willing to crack them locally by a laborious manual process, but most of the kernels were exported whole.

[3] C. Wilson, *The History of Unilever* (London, 1954), vol. i, p. 181.

[4] Quoted by R. Gwynne, *Parliamentary Debates*, House of Commons, 12 Aug. 1913.

[5] *Government Gazette*, 17 Aug. 1912.

[6] Letter from Giles Hunt, *The Times*, 12 Sept. 1912.

[7] A letter defending the Bill appeared over the signature of 'Africanus' in *The Times*, 1 Jan. 1913. W. H. Grey said that this had been prompted by the Secretary of State, and might just as well have been signed 'Pro Bono Publico'. *Legislative Council Minutes*, 28 Jan. 1913.

[8] *Parliamentary Debates*, House of Commons, 13 Nov. and 5 Dec. 1912, and 28 and 30 Jan. 1913.   [9] Cd. 6512 (London, 1912), and Cd. 6561 (London, 1913).

then sitting; they were not unduly impressed by his claim that it was 'more or less' a philanthropic scheme.[1]

In view of all this, it is surprising that the Bill was handled rather tactlessly during its passage through the Legislative Council in 1913. At the second reading, vague promises of improvement by the Colonial Secretary did not satisfy those who fundamentally criticized the wisdom of granting a concession to Lever's amounting to about one-tenth of the total palm-growing area.[2] At the committee stage the European and African unofficial members continued to protest strongly against the 'Monopoly Bill', as it was labelled by W. H. Grey, who represented opposing mercantile interests.[3] An adjournment was necessary because of unsatisfactory drafting, and at the very last moment the A.R.P.S. produced a hostile petition, supported by an address from E. J. P. Brown.[4] But their criticisms were virtually ignored and, after a few minor amendments, the Bill was finally passed, against the votes of the unofficial members present.

The controversy was renewed in the House of Commons, where persistent critics objected to the terms of the agreement, which appeared to them as a *fait accompli*.[5] It was alleged that Lever, while a member of the House, had made his arrangements 'behind the Speaker's Chair'.[6] The Secretary of State, however, claimed that the Ordinance was a form of protection for local producers, who were suffering from the competition of large-scale plantations and processing in Liberia, the Cameroons, and the Congo, and that they would not feel any restrictions: 'The only thing the natives are prevented from using is the depericarping machine, and they have never even heard of it.'[7] The most Harcourt would concede was a promise that if any conflict of interest arose between the inhabitants and European concessionaires the interests of the former should prevail.[8] But the storm had been raised to no purpose. By the time the Palm Oil Ordinance was enacted, it was already clear that the experiments in Nigeria and Sierra Leone had proved a financial fiasco. The subsidiary concerned, West African Oils Ltd., lost over £50,000 in 1913, and consequently never took advantage of the exclusive rights secured in the Gold Coast.[9]

The distaste of Lever's for competition was increasingly shared by the large firms already in the West African market. The older concerns, which had been built up on an individualist basis, now sought to protect themselves in turn from the competition of new-comers, whether large or small. Before the First World War 'the whole trading community was honeycombed with under-

[1] *W.A.L.C. Evidence*, L. H. Moseley, 5,202.
[2] *Legislative Council Debates*, 28 Jan. 1913. [3] Ibid. 26 Mar. 1913.
[4] Petition of 30 June 1913, to Governor and Legislative Council from the A.R.P.S.—'for themselves and on behalf of Kings and Chiefs of the Western, Central and Eastern Provinces'; ibid. 4 July 1913.
[5] It was alleged that only £15,000 had been paid by Lever Bros. and that no royalties had been demanded. Sir G. Parker, *Parliamentary Debates*, House of Commons, 31 July 1913.
[6] Gwynne, ibid. 12 Aug. 1913. [7] Harcourt, ibid. 31 July 1913.
[8] Ibid. 12 Aug. 1913. [9] Wilson, *The History of Unilever*, vol. i, pp. 180-3.

standings'.[1] Shortly afterwards a new giant, the African and Eastern Trading Corporation, emerged from the amalgamation of Swanzy's, Miller's, and the African Association (itself the result of a combination of the 1880's). In 1920 Lever's purchased the assets of the Niger Company, and on 2 October *West Africa* pointedly commented: 'The earth is the Lord Leverhulme's and the fulness thereof.' Some Africans regarded these developments with suspicion and increasing alarm. Nana Ofori Atta asked whether the process of amalgamation of large firms 'should not be viewed with grave apprehension'; but he received cold comfort from the Colonial Secretary, who saw no reason for anxiety.[2] Lever's had already begun to negotiate for a merger with the African and Eastern, which was not however achieved until 1929. This produced the United Africa Company—as a subsidiary of Lever Bros.—which unquestionably dominated the whole of the West African market.[3]

It was not surprising that African primary producers, at the opposite economic pole, should come to distrust the operations of such large-scale expatriate enterprise. This was particularly true in the cocoa trade, where the known or suspected collusion between the merchants from time to time over buying prices brought upon them also the blame for world price movements which were beyond their control.[4]

The outbreak of the First World War had meant the closing of the German market, and considerable uncertainty over British prices; the Gold Coast buyers delayed their crop purchases, and prices fell heavily. By the end of 1914 they had risen again a little, but were still only half what they had been a year previously. The farmers, especially in the Central Province, then became reluctant to sell; despite meetings at which government officials tried to explain the market situation, they continued to complain of the price offered, and many preferred to leave the cocoa pods on their trees.[5] Two years later a large percentage of the Ashanti crop was held back when prices fell again, due to the increasing difficulty of securing shipping space and the accumulation of stocks in England.[6] During 1917–18 it was estimated that not more than three-quarters of the total crop was gathered and only half sold.[7] This normal economic reaction by the farmers was the first indication of what were later to become organized hold-ups.

Much resentment was caused by the war-time licensing system, which prevented the farmers from shipping their own cocoa and made them suspect deliberate exploitation. The fact that the largest produce buyers were also the main importers did not improve commercial relations, for rising prices

[1] McPhee, *The Economic Revolution*, p. 74.

[2] *Legislative Council Debates*, 30 Dec. 1920.

[3] Wilson, *The History of Unilever*, vol. i, pp. 304–5. Cf. Hancock, *Survey*, vol. ii, pt. ii, pp. 207–8.

[4] The pre-war buying agreements were continued intermittently between 1910 and 1917, and during 1925–7. *Nowell Report*, historical introduction.

[5] *Departmental Reports*, Central Province, 1914.

[6] Ibid. Ashanti, 1916.   [7] Ibid. Agriculture, 1918.

of consumer goods were also causing considerable hardship; and in 1918 the two matters were linked in a joint attempt by the Chiefs to bring economic grievances to the notice of the Government. They complained, 'Whilst the Gold Coast produce is taken for almost nothing . . . the prices of European Goods have reached such a prohibitive height that one feels most unhappy', and threatened that if no official action were taken, they would themselves have to do something 'to guard our people against such manifest exploitation of the natives' poor resources'.[1] The Governor, at an interview, agreed to assist them by granting cocoa export licences forfeited by firms from enemy countries. He also accepted in principle the idea of an agricultural bank, on condition that proper farmers' associations were formed.[2]

The Aburi–Nsawam Growers' Association, which had been founded in 1914, now made a trial shipment of over 700 bags of cocoa in an attempt to get a better price. At once several other growers' associations were formed with the object of shipping their own cocoa, 'feeling that they had been unmercifully exploited of late by the buyers'.[3] This development aroused bitter opposition from the European firms, and the Chambers of Commerce in London and Liverpool sent a deputation to the Colonial Office to make allegations against the Gold Coast Government. The Governor denied their accuracy, although he realized that it was only natural that the merchants should dislike the granting of licences to farmers instead of to themselves.[4] But he was also aware of the long-term danger to the industry if the growers became so discouraged that they let their farms revert to bush, thus allowing the spread of cocoa diseases.[5]

Once the war ended, export prices started to improve, and a tremendous boom in cocoa took place.[6] This may best be appreciated by studying the dramatic and almost continuous rise in the monthly price per load; for example, the Koforidua price rose steadily from 6s. in October 1918 to 60s. in March 1920.[7] The 'Combine clique', however, were still suspected of profiteering from the 'iniquitous prices' of imports.[8]

When the slump came in the middle of 1920, Guggisberg made personal propaganda tours, and delivered over fifty addresses to large gatherings of Chiefs, councillors, farmers, and cocoa traders in the Colony, urging them to carry on normally.[9] But low prices, averaging 10s. per load, continued throughout 1921, and the Governor's advice was no longer acceptable. To

---

[1] Memorandum of 5 Mar. 1918, to Governor; S.N.A. 692, Case 33/1918, G.N. Archives.
[2] Nana Ofori Atta, *Legislative Council Debates*, 13 Apr. 1938.
[3] *Departmental Reports*, Agriculture, 1918.
[4] Nana Ofori Atta, *Legislative Council Debates*, 13 Apr. 1938.
[5] Clifford, ibid. 25 Oct. 1917.
[6] 'The demand for cocoa and chocolate in Great Britain was unprecedented.' In the United States 'the approaching doom of Abolition' encouraged 'the novel idea of . . . cocoa instead of cocktails'. E. J. Organ, *The Gold Coast Cocoa Industry and its Recent Developments* (Bournville, 1921).   [7] See graph facing p. 50.
[8] *The Gold Coast Independent*, 8 Nov. 1919.
[9] *Legislative Council Debates*, 21 Jan. 1921.

make matters worse, the price rose tantalizingly to around 15*s*. in September and October, but dropped back again for the rest of the main crop season. An estimate of cocoa costs and profits made in Ashanti at this time emphasized the narrow margin to which the farmer was working. At a price of 12*s*. per load, a grower with 5,000 trees might expect to clear £38. 6*s*. for his whole farm in the main season, and £5. 5*s*. for the mid-season crop; his expenses were estimated at 6*s*. 9*d*. per load.[1]

The Akwapim farmers, who had a longer history of cocoa growing, and much more at stake, formed an Association in 1921 which forbade anyone to sell their cocoa at a price lower than 15*s*. a load. This was the first organized attempt to stop cocoa sales, instead of leaving the decision to individual farmers; it was reinforced by the swearing of traditional oaths, and probably the militant group loyalty of the old Asafo companies was diverted into this new form of economic self-defence.[2] The campaign was remarkably successful: 'with very few exceptions, it was impossible to purchase cocoa in any Akwapim village'. A similar combination of farmers organized a hold-up in the Densu valley near Mangoase; and in the District Commissioner's court at Koforidua, a number of persons were fined for interfering with carriers taking cocoa to buyers' stores.[3]

Soon an attempt was made to organize on a wider basis, and a Gold Coast Farmers' Association was formed for the Colony. In January 1922 they sent a deputation to meet the Governor at Nsawam, where questions of price, hold-up, and storage were discussed. Some members appeared determined to burn their cocoa rather than let the merchants have it at the current price of 12*s*. 6*d*. a load. The Agriculture Department recognized this 'attempted combination of farmers' as a sign of awakening, and hoped to guide them into 'proper channels'. Agricultural Officers succeeded in introducing further farmers to the techniques of collective action by starting three more Cocoa Growers' Associations, at Mampong, Bompata, and Tasamanso, and drawing up rules for them. Meanwhile, farmers who had carried over their cocoa into the first quarter of 1922 were fortunate enough to find a much higher price than they would have got earlier, even though some of their crops had by then deteriorated; some farmers even believed that the local hold-up, small as it was, had influenced the European market, and hence the local price.[4] It is unlikely that the majority knew anything about the world market; more probably they regarded the hold-up as a successful method of haggling over the local price.

In 1924 some of the leading Chiefs in the Eastern Province sent a delegation to England to attend the World Cocoa Conference. As a result of their con-

[1] *Departmental Reports*, Ashanti, 1921.
[2] For oath-swearing customs and the Asafo companies, see Ch. III, pp. 127, 142–3 and 156–7n., below.
[3] *Departmental Reports*, Eastern Province, 1921 and Agriculture, 1921 and 1922–3.
[4] Ibid. Agriculture, 1922–3.

PLATE 1

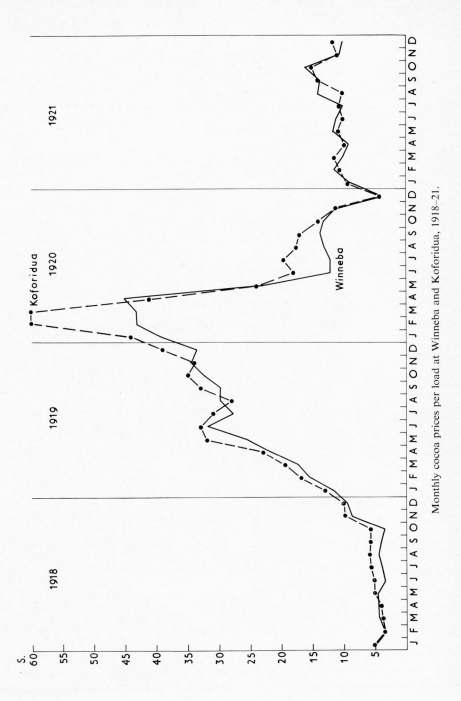

Monthly cocoa prices per load at Winneba and Koforidua, 1918–21.

tacts there, the delegates decided to arrange for the Gold Coast Farmers' Association to ship their own cocoa direct to the United States. Operations were commenced during the 1924–5 season on such a large scale that shipments through the usual firms were seriously reduced. The cocoa was bought on credit at 25s. a load, which was about 5s. in advance of the highest price paid by the European merchants. Thousands of tons were shipped; the majority of farmers received one-quarter to one-third of the full price, the balance being credited to them; only a few were paid immediately in full.[1] Unfortunately the Association's broker misappropriated much of the proceeds and absconded; it was estimated that about £300,000 was lost, and legal proceedings continued up to 1937.[2] This fiasco temporarily put an end to the idea of African farmers organizing their own export of cocoa.

Towards the end of 1928 there was considerable dissatisfaction with the low prices merchants were paying for cocoa, and with the failure to reduce prices of imported food, despite a reduction in customs duties.[3] Although these two grievances arose from different economic causes, together they meant a worsening of the farmers' terms of trade, and inevitably they were regarded as evidence of a concerted policy by the firms. The growing suspicions of the farmers were brought to a head by the formation in 1929 of a pooling agreement between all the principal European merchants concerned in the purchase of West African cocoa. 'The Pool', as it immediately and inimically came to be called, was formed in the face of the slump in world prices of all primary products. It was also the culmination of a long series of informal agreements designed to restrict competition in a highly uncertain trade; and it led directly to the formation of a Gold Coast and Ashanti Cocoa Federation, which organized a remarkably widespread and effective hold-up of cocoa during the 1930–1 season.

Despite the mutual suspicion and intermittent conflicts between the producers and the buyers, and despite the wasteful economics of imperfect competition, cocoa had during this period succeeded in becoming the mainstay of the Gold Coast economy. With the phenomenal increase in the tonnage sent overseas, the cocoa export duty, which had first been imposed in 1916 to finance the building of roads and railways, soon began to yield anything from a quarter to half a million pounds annually, an unforeseen windfall that made a considerable difference to planned economic development during the 1920's.[4]

It is instructive to compare the profitable results of this duty—and of a similar duty imposed on diamonds in 1919, within a few months of their discovery —with the extraordinary story of the palm kernels export duty, introduced

[1] Ibid. Eastern Province and Agriculture, 1924–5.

[2] *West Africa*, 1925 to 1937, *passim*.

[3] *Minutes of 10th Session of the Central Provincial Council*, Akim Oda, 15 Nov. to 3 Dec. 1928.

[4] This was a specific, not an *ad valorem* duty, and varied between $\frac{1}{2}d$. per lb. (1919–22) and $\frac{1}{4}d$. per lb. (1924 onwards).

for very different reasons. During the war a committee appointed by the Secretary of State in London had urged the need to develop the British kernel-crushing industry, so as to be able to compete on better terms with Germany after the war. In order to secure supplies at reasonable prices, the committee proposed that immediately after the war, for a limited period of five years, the British Colonies should introduce a preferential duty of £2 per ton—which could be increased if necessary—on all palm kernels exported to countries outside the Empire.[1]

TABLE VIII. *Cocoa Exports*[2]

Year	Quantity ('000 tons)	Value (£'000)	Yield of export duty (£'000)
1918	66	1,797	131
1919	176	8,279	419
1920	125	10,056	580
1921	133	4,764	622
1922	159	5,841	646
1923	198	6,567	461
1924	223	7,250	368
1925	218	8,222	255
1926	231	9,181	269
1927	210	11,728	245
1928	225	11,230	263

The Governor of the Gold Coast, Sir Hugh Clifford, was a member of this committee in its early stages; but he left England before the report was drawn up, and disagreed thoroughly with its conclusions. When the Secretary of State instructed him in 1916 that a Bill should be introduced,[3] Clifford duly prepared a draft, but argued against it in the strongest possible terms. He said that the palm kernel industry was already almost moribund in the Gold Coast,[4] that the duty would enable the merchants to lower the prices paid, and that consequently the African producer would probably be ruined; if it were necessary 'for imperial reasons' to establish a new industry in Britain, then Parliament should bear the cost.[5] The Secretary of State, however, replied

[1] *Report of the Committee on Edible and Oil Producing Nuts and Seeds in West Africa* (London, 1916), Cd. 8247.

[2] *Gold Coast Colony Blue Books*, 1918 to 1928–9.

[3] Dispatch No. 338 of 1 June 1916, from Bonar Law to Clifford, forwarding copies of the *Report*; G.N. Archives.

[4] Exports of palm kernels had been falling steadily for several years:

1912	.	. 14,628 tons	1914	.	. 5,633 tons
1913	.	. 9,744	1915	.	. 4,064

The Governor attributed this decline almost entirely to the rival attraction of cocoa, which was much easier to produce. Clifford, *Legislative Council Debates*, 28 Oct. 1918.

[5] Dispatch No. 823 of 8 Nov. 1916, from Clifford to Bonar Law; G.N. Archives.

that the legislation was designed ultimately to benefit the West African producers; even if this were not achieved, he felt sure that the Gold Coast would not object to 'some small financial sacrifice'. He suggested that if Nigeria and Sierra Leone, much larger producers of palm kernels, were prepared to accept the proposed duty, it was hardly for the Gold Coast to stand out. The Bill was therefore to be pressed, with minor amendments.[1]

Since the outbreak of the war there had been a growing interest in Britain in the development of imperial resources and of mutual trade.[2] This had led directly to the propaganda of the Empire Resources Development Committee, which unfortunately cannot entirely be regarded as a lunatic fringe, since its views had some influence on the new restrictionist policy. The E.R.D.C. was formed early in 1917, with an ambitious programme which included the setting up of a body of concessionaires to carry on industries in the Colonies. This would not be under direct government control, but would be bound to return a percentage of profit to the British Government—in London, not in the Colony concerned—for reduction of the war debt. 'Think what it would mean', one influential exponent urged, 'if all the products of West Africa, mineral and vegetable, were controlled for the benefit of the Empire as a whole!'[3] A few West Africans, and every champion of theirs in London, could think only too well what it would mean.[4]

Meanwhile, the Balfour Committee on commercial and industrial policy after the war had been discussing, *inter multa alia*, the 1916 proposals for preferential duties on palm kernels, and the general need for regulating Empire exports, in order to give priority to the requirements of Britain and her allies. The policy was endorsed in principle, although it was pointed out that hardship to the producers could only be avoided if most of the supply could be absorbed at reasonable prices.[5] Clifford was still strongly opposed to the principle. In August 1917 he renewed his arguments against the Palm Kernels Export Duty Bill to the Secretary of State;[6] and there was considerable opposition locally, even before the first reading. These objections could not prevail against the influential weight of opinion in England, and in October 1918 the proposal was debated in an atmosphere of suspicion and resentment.

The speech of the Comptroller of Customs, giving the reasons for the Bill,

[1] Quoted by Clifford, *Legislative Council Debates*, 29 Oct. 1918.

[2] For example, *Final Report of the Dominions Royal Commission* (London, 1917), Cd. 8462.

[3] A. Bigland, M.P., 'The Empire's Assets and how to Use Them', in *Journal of the Royal Society of Arts*, vol. lxv, 30 Mar. 1917.

[4] The Gold Coast Aborigines' Rights Protection Society asked the Governor for an assurance of protection against the E.R.D.C.; in London the scheme was attacked by the Anti-Slavery and Aborigines' Protection Society, by the Association of West African Merchants, and by numerous writers in *West Africa*. Clifford assured the Legislative Council that he had studied it 'with almost equal closeness and disapproval'. *Legislative Council Debates*, 2 Nov. 1918.

[5] *Final Report of the Committee on Commercial and Industrial Policy after the War* (London, 1918), Cd. 9035.

[6] 'Despatch from Sir Hugh Clifford to the Secretary of State dealing with the Trade Interests of the Gold Coast Colony', *Sessional Paper No. II of 1917–18*.

has to be read to be believed. Before the war, he declared, Germany had had a monopoly, which was now to be transferred to British hands. Palm kernel crushing was of national importance to Britain: 'It means employment, and employment means men, and men mean bayonets', under the protection of which the people of the Colony could sleep in security. In the last resort, his case was unanswerable. He did not believe that Gold Coast Africans would suffer: 'There is no reason to think they will fare worse at the hands of the British Monopolist . . . than . . . at the hands of the German Monopolist . . . and even if I thought they would lose I would still support the Bill.'[1] The unofficial members riddled this flimsy economic fabric with neat holes. It was pointed out, for example, that Britain could not absorb the whole production of palm kernels; that the burden of the tax would fall wholly on the producer, and not on the consumer; that the costs of marketing were much higher in the Gold Coast than in Nigeria and Sierra Leone, owing to the lack of river transport; and that they should not be compelled to accept the measure 'merely out of consideration for other Colonies'.[2]

The Governor was obviously troubled by the situation. In support of the Bill, he quoted not only the Secretary of State's Dispatches, but also his own very cogent objections, which had prompted them.[3] The second reading was carried by the official majority; but for the first time in the records of the Council, all the unofficial members voted unanimously against a Government Bill.[4] The Colonial Office still would not allow the Bill to be withdrawn, and it had to be brought forward again in October 1919 by the new Governor, F. G. Guggisberg, a few days after his arrival. The Colonial Secretary then argued that since the Imperial Government had placed an embargo on virtually all palm kernel exports to countries outside Britain no duty would be payable, and the Bill would be 'largely nugatory'. He was also able to point to a great increase in local prices, from £10 to £26 per ton, as a result of the removal of price control in England. Guggisberg was in a difficult position; he assured members that he strongly opposed the taxation of local produce on principle, but attempted to win them over by descriptions of front-line fighting, statistics of prisoners of war, and an appeal to their loyalty to the Empire.[5] Eventually the Bill went through at the latest possible moment, on the day when the duty was actually scheduled to come into force.[6]

There was little more that local politicians could do, although J. E. Casely Hayford raised the matter in his speech on behalf of the National Congress

[1] O. Mitchell, *Legislative Council Debates*, 29 Oct. 1918.
[2] Grey and Nana Ofori Atta, ibid.
[3] Clifford, ibid.
[4] Some years earlier the four unofficials had voted against a money Bill, but this was suggested to them by the Governor as a means of recording their protest against certain expenditure already incurred, and not against the Bill itself. *Legislative Council Minutes*, 1 May 1905.
[5] *Legislative Council Debates*, 20 Oct. 1919.
[6] See *Board of Trade Journal*, 11 Aug. 1919.

to officials of the League of Nations Union in London, a year later.[1] Liberal spokesmen in England kept up the attack;[2] and in 1921, during the sittings of the Committee on Trade and Taxation for British West Africa, some influential commercial voices were raised against the duty.[3] The committee reported that there was no justification from the point of view of the Colonies for the retention of the differential duty.[4] But eventually it was 'economic cause and effect rather than moral argument' that defeated the palm kernels policy. The duty was withdrawn in 1922, after it had succeeded only in stimulating alternative sources of supply of palm kernels outside the Empire, and the production of substitute oils and fats for use in industry.[5]

Planned Economic Development, 1919–28

There could scarcely be a greater contrast between the role Guggisberg was forced to play during that first encounter with the Legislative Council, and the progressive economic policy by which he proceeded to make a unique contribution to the history of the Gold Coast. This was the age of paternal administration;[6] much that was achieved through the Governor's personal initiative might not have been politically acceptable a generation later, but he came at a time when the country needed exactly the kind of economic planning and leadership that he was able to give. It would be difficult to find a parallel among colonial Governors of any period for his combination of idealism, moral fervour, and shrewd practical foresight.

Within six weeks of his arrival, Guggisberg announced a Ten-Year Development Plan which would, if all went well, involve a total expenditure of something approaching £25 million.[7] This was no mere expression of post-war optimism. The plan was not so much a statement of the Government's fixed financial intentions as a careful estimate of the cost of the material developments which were considered necessary during the next decade, and which would be carried through provided the funds were available.[8] The Governor proceeded to lay the foundation for the General Reserve Fund which was

[1] Quoted by M. J. Sampson (ed.), *West African Leadership* (Ilfracombe, 1940), p. 44.

[2] For example, *The Economist*, 1 Nov. 1919, and *Parliamentary Debates*, House of Lords, 17 Dec. 1919.

[3] The only strong plea for the duty was made by a manufacturer who had put up a £1 million crushing mill between 1916, when the Edible Nuts Committee reported, and 1919, when the duty was imposed. See *Minutes of Evidence taken before the Committee on Trade and Taxation for British West Africa* (London, 1922).

[4] *Report of a Committee on Trade and Taxation for British West Africa* (London, 1922), Cmd. 1600, p. 64.

[5] For an account of the collapse of the scheme, and a devastating exposure of the 'ju-ju economics' of the E.R.D.C., see Hancock, *Survey*, vol. ii, pt. i, chs. i and ii.

[6] A characteristic aside was recorded in 1919 when Guggisberg told the Gã Mantse and Mantsemei of the proposed new alloy coins, and remarked, with paternal solicitude, 'you will have to be very careful to prevent the babies from swallowing them'. 1953 Acc. No. 1395, Case No. 4/1919, G.N. Archives.

[7] *Legislative Council Debates*, 17 Nov. 1919.   [8] Ibid. 27 Feb. 1922.

eventually transferred to the country's development reserves after the Second World War. He borrowed £4 million in London, so that the total development expenditure for 1920–3 was very close to the original estimate of £6½ million. The post-war depression forced a reduction of £12 million in 1922, which mainly involved dropping the proposed Northern Territories railway. But Guggisberg refused to postpone or cancel other major items, pointing out that only the development of transport could enable the Gold Coast to afford long-desired social and educational advances, and to attract the overseas capital on which further development would depend.[1]

TABLE IX. *Guggisberg's Ten-year Development Plan*[2]

(£'000)

	Original plan 1919	Revised plan 1922	Revised plan 1927
Harbour.	2,000	1,840	3,551
Railways	14,581	6,076	5,948
Roads	1,000	750	1,619
Water supplies . . .	1,790	1,208	634
Town improvements and drainage .	1,850	300	740
Hydraulic and electric works . .	2,000	200	199
Public buildings (including Achimota)	1,100	1,000	2,273
Posts and telegraphs . . .	90	422	336
Maps and surveys	200	120	200
Agriculture and forestry . . .	..	..	252
Takoradi town	..	..	669
Miscellaneous	..	100	225
	£24,611	£12,016	£16,646

The biggest single scheme carried out under the plan was the construction of the deep-water harbour at Takoradi, which eventually cost well over £3 million. Railway extensions were also a major feature, notably the completion of the line from Accra to Kumasi, which had been started in 1909 and left un-finished during the war.[3] Perhaps the most significant transport development was the widespread construction of motor roads. A few cars had been in use since the beginning of the century;[4] but even in 1909, a year after the Motor Traffic Ordinance had come into force 'to protect the public from incompetent

---

[1] For educational plans and progress during the 1920's, see Ch. II, pp. 109–24, below.

[2] Governor's Annual Addresses, *Legislative Council Debates*, 1919 to 1927.

[3] F. D. Hammond, *Report on the Railway System of the Gold Coast* (London, 1922).

[4] The first car was a Gardner-Serpollet, paraffin-fired, steam-driven model, imported in 1902 for the use of Governor Nathan. It remained in use until about 1908, when it was sold to a French trader for £5; he could not persuade it to move, and the Sanitary Department later dropped it into the sea. The first petrol-driven car was imported from France in 1903. For fuller details, see F. G. Guggisberg, 'A Review of the Development of Communications in the Gold Coast in the 20th Century', *Legislative Council Debates*, 3 Mar. 1927.

and careless driving',[1] only eleven cars and sixteen lorries were licensed under it. The main drawback was that heavy lorries tore up the roughly levelled earth roads;[2] they appeared an impossibly costly form of transport, until the introduction of the light Ford chassis, which produced 'a veritable revolution in the transport problems of the Gold Coast'.[3]

Strange as it may seem today, in an age that demands material progress and technical assistance as an essential condition of the imperial relationship, there had been some African criticisms of the new Governor's emphasis on transport improvements. The new Takoradi harbour came in for special attack. There were few who were sufficiently national in outlook to be enthusiastic about the project; and unofficial members of the Legislative Council could not resist this opportunity for a jab at the Government. Guggisberg, however, refused to accept a motion for the deferment of the scheme—presented after the preliminary work had been started—which he said would be 'equivalent to committing political hari-kari'.[4] He could see that this was the only means of increasing the country's external trade on the scale for which he hoped; all the other surf ports were pitifully inadequate, in spite of the breakwater built for Accra during 1907–16.

The opposition to Takoradi harbour was taken up by an A.R.P.S. conference of Chiefs at Cape Coast, who cabled a protest to the Secretary of State; and there was considerable pressure from commercial interests in England for an inquiry into Gold Coast Government expenditure,[5] especially after the report of the Trade and Taxation Committee under Clifford. This concluded, with reference to West Africa generally, that 'the abnormal and, in a measure, the fictitious prosperity' of these Colonies during 1919 and 1920 had led to the work of reconstruction being undertaken 'on too lavish a scale and with too great rapidity'.[6] Guggisberg indignantly denied that such criticisms could be applied to the Gold Coast, and effectively refuted them in detail.[7] He refused to be discouraged by the post-war slump, arguing that even during 1921–2 the trade figures had been higher than ever before, except for the boom year of 1920.[8] By 1924 he was able to point to a revival of trade, with the highest recorded quantity of cocoa exported, and a new peak of revenue (nearly double the 1919 figure) as sufficient justification for his confidence.[9]

[1] *Government Gazette*, 11 Nov. 1907.

[2] Some early experiments had been made with tarred surfaces in 1901. An unexpected snag was that a large number of carriers became incapacitated from sore feet. 'The experiment was then tried of tarring the carriers' feet'. *Departmental Reports*, Transport Department, 1908.

[3] Clifford, *Legislative Council Debates*, 28 Oct. 1918.

[4] Guggisberg, ibid. 27 Feb. 1922.

[5] *West Africa*, 1922, *passim*.   [6] Cmd. 1600, p. 58.

[7] 'Dispatch from the Governor to the Secretary of State No. 558 dated the 17th August, 1922, with reference to the Statements on the Financial Position of the Colony, made in the Report of the Committee on Trade and Taxation for British West Africa', *Sessional Paper No. VII of 1922–23*.

[8] Guggisberg, *Legislative Council Debates*, 27 Feb. 1922.

[9] Ibid. 6 Mar. 1924. For figures of revenue, expenditure, and international trade, 1919–28, see Table X.

It was fortunate for the Gold Coast that Guggisberg's term of office co-incided with years of unparalleled prosperity. With the aid of the cocoa export duty, and the capital assistance of yet another loan of nearly £4¾ million in 1925,[1] he was able to see completed, before the years of depression began, the Accra–Kumasi railway line (1923),[2] the 'finest hospital in Africa' at Korle Bu (1924), the harbour at Takoradi (1928), over 3,000 miles of new motor roads,

TABLE X. *Revenue, Expenditure and International Trade* [3]

Year	Revenue	Expenditure	Year	Imports	Exports
	£	£		£	£
1919	2,601,360	1,781,170	1919	7,946,981	10,814,175
1920	3,721,772	2,856,347	1920	15,152,145	12,352,207
1921 1st qr.	792,489	1,021,647	1921	7,661,324	6,942,197
1921–2	3,016,520	3,285,290	1922	7,900,539	8,335,400
1922–3	3.357,197	2,934,994	1923	8,448,862	8,959,213
1923–4	3,742,834	3,155,124	1924	8,315,234	9,914,937
1924–5	3,971,187	3,828,333	1925	9,782,619	10,890,223
1925–6	4,116,442	4,255,126	1926	10,285,876	12,104,800
1926–7	4,365,321	4,328,159	1927	13,770,542	14,350,355
1927–8	5,217,639	4,714,947	1928	12,200,045	13,824,875

a number of major electricity and water-supply projects—and, of course, the secondary school at Achimota. As the Governor himself said, the real object of the development programme was 'to give us sufficient revenue to carry out the educational and sanitary reforms necessary in this country, and to make that revenue a permanent one'.[4] For the next twenty years the country simply coasted along under the impetus Guggisberg had given.[5]

*   *   *   *   *   *

The extent of economic change during 1850–1928 should not be over-estimated. There had indeed been two periods of intensive, almost revolu-tionary development, 1897–1907, and 1919–27, both of which saw a great increase in the exploitation of primary products and a marked improvement in internal communications.There must have been a considerable rise in the standard of living, both urban and rural, the extent of which can only be guessed at. Nevertheless, the tropical environment remained hostile to human

[1] Guggisberg, *Legislative Council Debates*, 22 Feb. 1926.

[2] After this had been opened, the Omanhene of Cape Coast made a belated request for a new railway based on Cape Coast, which had been commercially overshadowed by Sekondi as the rail terminus. *Memorial from the Omanhene of Cape Coast to His Majesty's Principal Secretary of State for the Colonies* (London, 1923).

[3] *Gold Coast Colony Blue Books*, 1919 to 1928–9.

[4] Guggisberg, *Legislative Council Debates*, 24 Apr. 1925.

[5] To take railways as an example, 233 miles of new track had been built between 1919 and 1927, and 250 miles of prospective lines surveyed, at a total cost of nearly £6 million. No more railway building was carried out until towards the end of the Second World War. F. M. Bourret, *The Gold Coast* (London, 2nd edn. 1952), ch. iii.

endeavour. Endemic diseases—malaria, hookworm, yaws, to name only a few—continued to take their toll of life, and of efficiency in those who survived. Animal and plant pests and diseases were almost as disastrous in their effect upon welfare; the tsetse fly, for example, reigned in the forest, although swollen shoot of cocoa was yet to be discovered. The climate was more comfortable for the insect population than for man; high temperatures and humidity effectively restricted the intensity of work, the concentrated but variable rainy seasons dictated short cropping periods, while the frequent droughts could ruin food production and sometimes endanger human life. Public services such as piped water, drainage, or electricity were rudimentary in the towns and unknown in the villages. Modern advances in medical knowledge could make little impression, with one major hospital and only a handful of government doctors. Agricultural methods were primitive and wasteful of labour, industry was virtually non-existent, and the economy was remarkably vulnerable to the vagaries of the world market. In spite of a certain amount of individual accumulation of wealth, the majority of Africans remained on the margin of subsistence.

These problems have been of less political significance in the Gold Coast than in some 'settler' countries, where the visible disparity of standards of living has offered a ready-made nationalist issue. Economic grievances have not been the most important ones, but the pace of economic progress has to some extent controlled political developments.[1] It is easy to see, however, why the first serious resistance to British authority arose out of proposals for direct taxation in the 1850's,[2] when we remember that the money economy was then only in its infancy. In later years, when educated leaders had visited other countries and seen better conditions of life, demands for economic improvement entered increasingly into political programmes, from the Fanti Confederation to the National Congress of British West Africa.[3] Meanwhile, the African farmer and clerical worker could never be said to be oblivious of their economic interests; demands for higher export prices or for increased wages and salaries became increasingly vocal and were sometimes taken up by organized groups. More important, any threat of alien economic exploitation—especially any transfer of land-ownership—was able to arouse strong national feeling. But perhaps the greatest contribution of economic development to nationalism was the welding together of disparate social, tribal, and political units into one interdependent economy.[4]

[1] Cf. D. E. Apter, 'Some Economic Factors in the Political Development of the Gold Coast', in The Journal of Economic History (New York, 1954), p. 409: 'political democracy, particularly of the British parliamentary sort, cannot be "transplanted" to alien soil if the overwhelming concern of the people is a struggle for basic subsistence'.

[2] See Ch. IV, 'Taxation and Representation, 1850–62', below.

[3] Cf. Casely Hayford on economic development, Ch. XIII, pp. 551–2, below.

[4] Community of economic life, or economic cohesion, was one of the four characteristic features of a nation propounded by Stalin in 1913—the others being community of language, community of territory, and community of 'psychological make-up' or national character. J. Stalin, Marxism and the National and Colonial Question (Moscow, 1940), pp. 5–7.

During the administration of Guggisberg, and largely owing to his fore-sight, the Gold Coast—Colony, Ashanti, and Northern Territories—became an economic unit. The pioneering of the 1890's, in mining, cocoa, exploration, and annexation, began to yield dividends, while the foundations of future development were laid. These were also the foundations on which the later, more militant, national movement was to build. Guggisberg provided the schools from which the next generation of nationalists emerged, the roads along which they travelled, and the harbour from which prospective leaders sailed into a national-minded world. The relative prosperity of the 1920's meant that the slump, when it did come, was felt all the more severely; and the resulting hardship and poverty were inevitably associated with colour consciousness and accusations of imperialist exploitation. Thereafter, econ-omic grievances became increasingly important, while the growing inequali-ties of wealth were eventually to bring about a complete change in the leader-ship, pace, and direction of nationalism. The economic history of the period 1850–1928 thus offers a key not only to contemporary political developments, but also to those of a later period. The background to nationalism would not be complete, however, without a separate study of Western education as the main formative influence upon its leadership.

II

EDUCATION AND AFRICAN LEADERSHIP
1850–1928

THE word 'education' in the Gold Coast has always been used in a rather restricted sense: namely, formal instruction in European-type schools. Those who have been to school are said to be 'educated'; those who have not, are not, whatever their degree of proficiency in their own craft or trade, and whatever the period that has been spent in instructing them, within the complexities of their own family and social system. Although this is not the place for an examination of traditional methods of education, some indication of relative attitudes is given in the following account by an educated Chief:

In the olden days the son of a fisherman spent his mornings by the seashore, swimming in the surf until he became proficient in swimming and diving as in walking and running. With a miniature net he practised casting in imitation of his father . . . The son of the farmer accompanied his father to the farm and gradually acquired the father's lore. He studied when the planting should be carried out, the right times for clearing and growing crops, and when the harvest was ripe and ready for the gathering.

In like manner the girl trod in the footsteps of the mother. Almost as soon as she could walk, she accompanied her mother to the well and to the market, carrying her little waterpot or bundle of market produce . . . As she grew older she took her part in the household offices and was taught apprenticeship by mothering the younger members of the family . . . I may say, then, that the education of the African child by the African system is a preparation and practical training for the life that lies before it.

The kind of education introduced here by our white friends was only literary. Boys' heads were filled with stuff which they did not understand, much less apply . . . As we were taught, so did we teach.[1]

Education, in the European sense, was brought to the Gold Coast not in response to any pre-existing demand, but as an essential part of missionary programmes. Its history goes back almost as far as the European connexion, though less continuously.[2] Several short-lived efforts were made, spread over many centuries, before schools became firmly established. The earliest teachers met with either indifference or active opposition, for the advantages of reading

---

[1] Nana Annor Adjaye, *Nzima Land* (London, 1931), ch. vi.

[2] No full-scale history of education in the Gold Coast has yet been published. F. L. Bartels has written a detailed account of 'Gold Coast Education: its Roots and Growth', covering the period up to 1858, and I am grateful to him for allowing me to read his manuscript. An outline of more modern developments is included in some recent books, e.g. C. G. Wise, *A History of Education in British West Africa* (London, 1956).

and writing, especially in a foreign language, were not so immediately apparent as those of trade, and they were considerably less relevant to the needs of traditional African society.

It was not long, however, before those in closest contact with the European came to attribute his material advantages to the mystique of his education.[1] They also saw that only those Africans who had been to school could hope for employment as teachers, clerks, or even in higher posts. Education thus offered the prospects of a regular salary, increased authority and prestige, possibly the chance of a trip to Europe, and certainly a means of avoiding the manual labour which was traditionally allotted to slaves, but was liable to be demanded by the white man of any illiterate African. Eventually, therefore, Say's law came to operate in the field of education, and the supply—from outside—began to create its own demand. By the twentieth century a widespread pressure for more and better schools had become politically important; and education had become the main agent of social change, as well as the major determinant of social status in the new, semi-Westernized society.

Educated Africans, however, found it increasingly difficult to fit into the traditional order, where religious and secular authority rested with the Chief, where the social hierarchy descended in clearly defined stages, and where status depended on birth and lineage rather than individual qualifications or achievements. Thus there emerged a growing cleavage between the Chiefs and the educated community. This became more acute as some of the politically conscious staked a claim to leadership on a national scale, transcending the local authority of the Chiefs.[2] In this they were discouraged not only by the traditional rulers, but also by British administrators, who sought to uphold the established social order. Nevertheless, it was the educated élite who were destined to become nationalist leaders, and the despised semi-educated group who were to provide their mass support. The development of education in the Gold Coast is therefore an essential background to any study of the rise of nationalism.

The first attempt to found a school may have been made in 1529 by the Portuguese. In that year King João III certainly instructed the Governor of the City of São Jorge (Elmina) to provide reading, writing, and religious teaching for African children,[3] although no records of any such school appear

---

[1] Cf. M. J. Herskovits on the African's belief that 'it has been the ability to read and write that has given the European his controls over man and nature. It is this, therefore, that he seeks for himself and, above all, for his children, so that they will have more adequate control of this power and, to an extent not vouchsafed him, will be enabled to apply it in solving their own problems.' 'Some Contemporary Developments in Sub-Saharan Africa', in *Africa and the Modern World*, ed. by C. W. Stillman (Chicago, 1955), p. 271.

[2] For friction between Chiefs and Christians in Akim Abuakwa in 1887, see Ch. III, pp. 155-6, below. For the conflict between Chiefs and educated 'youngmen' after the First World War, see Chs. X, pp. 389-96, and XII, pp. 469-73, below.

[3] Instructions of 8 Feb. 1529, from King João III to Estêvão da Gama, reproduced by Fr. António Brásio, *Monumenta Missionaria Africana* (Lisbon, 1952), vol. i, p. 502.

to have survived. Various short-lived educational attempts were made by the missionaries who occasionally came to the coast singly or in small groups; but the teaching was in a foreign language, its content was unrelated to the daily problems of village life, and its main purpose was to introduce an alien religion. These efforts often encountered a blank wall of indifference; the Rev. T. Thompson, an Anglican chaplain who started a school in Cape Coast in the 1750's, remarked: 'several of the young Blacks came to me; but Children growing weary of what is no longer a Novelty, and the Parents neglecting to keep them to it, and make them come duly, my hopes were quickly at an end of doing any Good in this Way'.[1]

The Dutch and the Danes, however, had already opened schools in the coastal forts primarily for their mulatto children, and these proved more per-manent, since the fathers at least realized the need for education;[2] they also attracted some children from the surrounding villages. The British authorities re-established a school in Cape Coast in 1766 under the Rev. Philip Quaque, an African who had been educated and ordained in England.[3] With the en-couragement of the Society for the Propagation of the Gospel and the London Committee of Merchants, this survived in spite of many vicissitudes into the colonial era, and it provided the main source of teachers as more schools were opened. Two at least of Quaque's students, John Martin and Joseph Smith, later emerged as leading civic personalities. Another ex-pupil, William de Graft, was indirectly responsible for bringing the Wesleyan Methodist mission-aries to Cape Coast in 1835,[4] and they placed a great emphasis on educational work from the start.

Missionaries of different denominations were soon doggedly establishing schools wherever possible in the face of great difficulties, not the least being the fearful death-rate among Europeans. By 1844 the Wesleyans had schools in eighteen towns, mainly along the western part of the coast, but also

[1] T. Thompson, *An Account of Two Missionary Voyages* (London, 1758); reprinted in facsimile with Introduction and Notes by the S.P.C.K. (London, 1937).

[2] The Dutch started to teach children 'to read, to pray and to live pious lives' in the 1640's at Elmina, but mainly owing to language problems little progress was made. M. Hemmersam, *Reise nach Guinea und Brasilien, 1639–1643* (Nuremberg, 1663), republished in *Reisebeschrei-bungen von deutschen Beamten und Kriegsleuten*, ed. by S. P. L'Honoré Naber (The Hague, 1930), vol. i, section iii, p. 60. The Danish school, at Christiansborg, was founded in 1722. G. Nor-regaard, 'De Danske Etabilissementer Paa Guineakysten', in *Vore Gamle Tropekolonier*, ed. by J. Brøndsted (Copenhagen, 1953), vol. i, p. 568.

[3] Quaque was the only survivor of three boys sent to London by the missionary Thompson; see F. L. Bartels, 'Philip Quaque, 1741–1816', in *Transactions of the Gold Coast & Togoland Historical Society* (Achimota, 1955), vol. i, pt. v. From the days of the Portuguese it had been the custom to educate a few promising boys in Europe.

[4] The British and Foreign Bible Society supplied Bibles to the Governor, to be presented to the boys leaving school. One of them, William de Graft, was sufficiently enterprising not only to found his own study group, but also in 1833 to ask a ship's captain for more Bibles. This request, reaching the Wesleyan Methodist Missionary Society, prompted them to send out the Rev. Joseph Dunwell in 1835. G. G. Findlay and W. W. Holdsworth, *The History of the Wesleyan Methodist Society* (London, 1921), vol. iv, pp. 151 ff.

including Accra, Winneba, and even a short-lived attempt in Kumasi. The Basel Mission had started work in 1828 in Danish Christiansborg, but their main educational effort began in 1843, when they founded a school at Akropong, followed by a catechists' seminary in 1848.[1] The North German (Bremen) missionaries, working across the Volta from 1847 onwards, soon established their first small school at Peki in an area later to come under British influence.[2]

By 1850, when the Gold Coast became a separate Colony, the main educational drive was coming from the two major missionary societies. There must have been over 1,000 pupils, all told, in their schools, although few remained long enough even to get a thorough grounding in the three R's. The Basel Mission alone offered any instruction beyond that level, and it is not surprising that the initial handful of seminary students made their mark in later life; notably Carl Reindorf (pastor and historian), David Asante (evangelist), and George Cleland (merchant and member of the Legislative Council). In addition to this missionary enterprise, the British Government had inherited from the Council of Merchants the semi-official school at Cape Coast. There was no specific commitment or obligation to maintain this, but officials had an interest in maintaining the supply of clerks. Teaching in all the schools was conducted in European languages, although the Basel missionaries had already commenced their intensive linguistic studies of the vernacular.[3]

The main openings for mission-trained Africans lay naturally in the mission field. The brightest boys were trained as teachers, interpreters, catechists, or local preachers, and some of them proceeded to ordination.[4] Others found employment in commerce, or as government clerks and 'writers'. Officials had begun to realize the limitations of the local system, and in 1846 the Governor reported that the results of education were 'not so healthy, vigorous, and permanent as they would be if they were associated with various branches of useful mechanical knowledge'.[5] This criticism was often repeated in subsequent years, without however exerting any noticeable influence on policy. Meanwhile, several of the merchants continued to send their sons to Britain—or sometimes to Sierra Leone—for higher education, and they returned to positions of influence and respect in the community.[6]

[1] W. Schlatter, *Geschichte der Basler Mission, 1815–1915* (Basel, 1916), vol. iii, pp. 16–26; *The Basel Mission Centenary, 1828–1928* (Accra, 1928); and *A Hundred Years, 1848–1948. The Story of the Presbyterian Training College, Akropong* (Accra, 1948).

[2] G. Müller, *Geschichte der Ewe-Mission* (Bremen, 1904), pp. 1–9.

[3] See Ch. XIII, pp. 510–11, below.

[4] Joseph Smith, William de Graft, John Martin, John Hagan, John S. Mills, and George Blankson were all recognized local preachers for the Wesleyans by 1838. Martin was the first African to be ordained as a Wesleyan minister, in 1852; he was followed by J. A. Solomon, T. Laing, and Prince J. Ossoo Ansah, in 1859. The first Africans ordained by the Basel Mission were T. Opoku and A. Clerk (a West Indian), in 1872.

[5] Report by Winniett for 1846, enclosed in his Dispatch of 20 Feb. 1847, to Grey; J. J. Crooks, *Records relating to the Gold Coast Settlements from 1750 to 1874* (Dublin, 1923), p. 308.

[6] In 1788 there had been about fifty mulatto and African children from the Windward and Gold Coasts being educated in Liverpool alone. 524 K. 14, British Museum. A school had been estab-

Africans in the Public Service, 1850–63

When the Crown had taken over the Gold Coast Forts and Settlements from the London Committee of Merchants in 1843, the tradition had been retained of appointing various prominent citizens to public office.[1] Their prospects had depended on their ability and willingness to serve, and it would appear that the question of colour had scarcely been relevant.[2] Thus when the Gold Coast was granted its own Government, independent of Sierra Leone, it was not regarded as anything out of the ordinary that a number of Africans, including several mulattoes, were appointed to key official posts.[3] Such a policy was actively encouraged by Lord Grey, who believed in demonstrating the practical advantages of education.[4]

The outstanding example was James Bannerman, who accepted the post of Civil Commandant at Christiansborg in 1850; this prosperous merchant, the son of a Scottish father and an African mother, had been a Justice of the Peace since 1820. The Governor thought so highly of him that he arranged for Bannerman to take over in his absence; and, when Winniett died at the end of the year, Bannerman became Lieutenant-Governor. A number of influential European and African merchants at once petitioned the Colonial Office to appoint him as Governor, on the grounds that his knowledge of the people, based upon long personal experience, would further the cause of social progress.[5] Although their purpose was partly to prevent the nomination of the unpopular Judicial Assessor, who had previously acted as Governor, the fact that they could so write of Bannerman shows that they were not thinking in terms of colour. The Secretary of State, however, thought that Bannerman

lished at Freetown by the Sierra Leone Company in 1792; the first record of a Gold Coast child being sent there dates from 1795. In 1827 the Church Missionary Society founded a College for teachers and catechists at Fourah Bay, which soon attracted students from other parts of West Africa, including a few from the Gold Coast.

[1] Under the 1829 'Rules for conducting the Affairs of Cape Coast Castle and Accra, and securing the Appointment of fit and proper Persons for the Charge and Management of those Forts', merchants who were British subjects and who had lived on the coast for at least one year were eligible to elect, and to serve as, members of the Council, and to be appointed as magistrates. This did not exclude non-Europeans. Crooks, *Records*, pp. 255–60.

[2] In 1852 it was claimed that educated Africans enjoyed 'all privileges and advantages of the White Merchant Traders'. Dispatch No. 29 of 13 May 1852, from Hill to Pakington; CO/96/25. The following year the Secretary of State affirmed the equality of white and coloured people before the law, warning the Governor against 'implying or seeming to imply that the former have a right to different treatment for similar offences'. Dispatch No. 15 of 7 Mar. 1853, from Newcastle to Hill; ibid.

[3] Mulattoes took a leading part in public life during the nineteenth century, partly because of the educational advantages they had often enjoyed. They have been treated here as Africans rather than Europeans, since they generally thought of themselves as such. The matrilineal system common to most Gold Coast tribes automatically meant that they 'belonged' to their mother's family rather than to their father's.

[4] Minute of 12 Oct. 1850, by Grey; CO/96/19.

[5] Memorial of 21 Dec. 1850, to Secretary of State from merchants and principal natives (including Cruickshank, and Kings of Cape Coast and Anomabu), enclosed in Dispatch No. 90 of 24 Dec. 1850, from Bannerman to Grey; ibid.

was too closely connected with too many of the merchants,[1] and a new-comer, Major S. J. Hill, was eventually given the post.

At the time Bannerman took over the Administration, Joseph Smith—teacher, Wesleyan preacher, and, more recently, merchant—was acting as Colonial Secretary in addition to holding the post of Collector of Customs.[2] Bannerman was already employing his son Edmund as secretary, and he soon made three further African appointments: Charles, his eldest son, to be Acting Commandant of Winneba; Samuel, another son, Acting Commandant of Christiansborg; and George Smith, Commandant of Anomabu. Winniett had apparently decided to make these appointments before he died, but to be on the safe side Bannerman consulted some of the merchants before nominating his own relatives, and they evidently raised no objections.[3]

Other early Governors were similarly colour-blind. As soon as Hill arrived in 1851 he commissioned twelve Justices of the Peace, of whom at least half were Africans: Joseph Smith, Henry Barnes, and the four Commandants already mentioned.[4] He formed such a high opinion of James Hansen, Clerk to the Judicial Assessor, that he commended his request for the post of Colonial Secretary, urging that it was 'most desirable' that this should be held by a permanent resident.[5] Although this enterprising application was not approved in London, Hansen was later promoted Chief Clerk and Cashier at the Treasury, with a salary of £250 per annum.[6] There were other examples of contemporary Africanization—as it would have been called a century later—including the tempting dual office of Collector-General of Customs and the Poll Tax, which was held for a short period by Thomas Hughes.[7] But in practice relationships varied with the Governor who happened to be in office. In 1856, for example, it was alleged that the 'harsh demeanour of Government and contempt for coloured people' was at the root of the disaffection in Cape Coast.[8]

In 1857 Sir Benjamin Pine, anxious to retain secure control of the unsettled eastern districts, replaced the ageing James Bannerman by the Rev. T. B. Freeman, the energetic ex-General Superintendent of the Wesleyan Mission, who was also a man of colour, though not of Gold Coast descent.[9] The Governor deliberately took other opportunities 'to advance the Native Civil Servants', for example by promoting Edmund Bannerman to the post of Civil Commandant of Keta. But Pine's successors did not share his anxiety for the advancement of educated Africans. E. B. Andrews soon put an end to

[1] Minute of 29 Feb. 1851, by Grey; CO/96/19.
[2] Dispatches Nos. 62 of 27 July and 68 of 21 Aug. 1850, from Winniett to Grey; ibid.
[3] Dispatch No. 84 of 16 Dec. 1850, from Bannerman to Grey; ibid.
[4] Dispatch No. 76 of 28 Oct. 1851, from Hill to Grey; CO/96/23.
[5] Dispatch No. 49 of 12 Aug. 1854, from Hill to Newcastle; CO/96/30.
[6] Dispatch No. 62 of 10 July 1857, from B. Pine to Labouchere; CO/96/41.
[7] Confidential Dispatch of 20 Sept. 1856, from Connor to Labouchere; CO/96/38.
[8] Report of 16 May 1856, from Ord to Labouchere; CO/96/40.
[9] Dispatches Nos. 75 of 12 and 83 of 28 Nov. 1857, from B. Pine to Labouchere; CO/96/41.

his experiment in municipal self-government,[1] and resented the fact that the Government was forced to employ even 'a certain amount of native talent'.[2] Two Sierra Leonean doctors, J. Africanus B. Horton and W. B. Davies, after having qualified in Britain, had been posted to the Gold Coast as Assistant Staff Surgeons; but in 1861 the Senior Army Medical Officer reported that they did not possess the confidence of Europeans, nor even of the native community, although their learning and ability were not questioned. It was feared that their association with European officers might lead to manifestations of distrust on either side, and encourage them in 'a defiant deportment, which would seriously demoralize and mar the efficiency' of the Medical Department.[3]

The fall from grace of the Bannerman brothers, owing to various financial and technical misdemeanours, brought to a head the Administration's increasing distrust and suspicion of African officials. In 1861 Edmund Bannerman was accused of embezzling £395 while a magistrate—he confessed after conviction—and was sentenced to seven years' imprisonment with hard labour. Andrews, at one stage, even proposed transportation; but the Colonial Office dismissed this as a wild suggestion.[4] *The West African Herald* (owned and edited by Edmund Bannerman's brother, Charles) took up the issue as one of racial discrimination, in terms that would hardly have been possible ten years earlier: 'Had he been a white man, we are certain the Governor would never sanction these most extraordinary proceedings. There is no need to multiply proofs as to the treatment here adopted towards coloured men and ... white men' (5 October 1861). Soon afterwards Charles Bannerman criticized another judgement, and was himself imprisoned for contempt of court.[5] In 1863, curiously enough, he appeared for the prosecution when a third brother, James Bannerman jun., was convicted of extortion, fined £50, imprisoned for 12 months, and dismissed from the magistracy.[6] Once again deportation was suggested, and turned down by the Colonial Office, although an official noted: 'It would no doubt be a great blessing if not a single Bannerman were left at the G. Coast.'[7] Edmund Bannerman appealed unsuccessfully for commutation of his harsh sentence,[8] but was released on health grounds, and soon began to practise, like his brother Charles, as an 'attorney'.

---

[1] See Ch. IV, pp. 185-7, below.

[2] Dispatch No. 116 of 3 Dec. 1861, from Andrews to Newcastle; CO/96/55.

[3] Letter of 23 Oct. 1861, from Senior Medical Officer to Director General of Army Medical Department, London; this was published over thirty years later in *The Gold Coast People*, 30 June 1893. The correspondent who had unearthed the letter commented: 'If the future historian wishes to know why after Horton and Davies no other natives were trained for the Army or the Civil Service for appointment in Western Africa the above will at least throw a side light on that question.'

[4] Confidential Dispatch of 31 Jan. 1862, from Andrews to Newcastle, and Minutes thereon; CO/96/57.   [5] Dispatch No. 48 of 2 June 1862, from Ross to Newcastle; CO/96/58.

[6] Dispatch No. 80 of 7 Sept. 1863, from R. Pine to Newcastle; CO/96/62.

[7] Minute of 31 Oct. 1863, by G. Barrow; ibid.

[8] Petition of 29 Dec. 1862, from Edmund Bannerman, enclosed in Dispatch No. 8 of 12 Jan. 1863, from R. Pine to Newcastle; CO/96/60.

The Early Attorneys and their Trials, 1863–73

At this time there were no barristers or solicitors in the Gold Coast; but since the institution of the Supreme Court in 1853, legal proceedings had become more formalized, with the result that some educated Africans began to specialize in the presentation of cases. In 1864 a court order was made that these attorneys should take out regular licences. Six or seven did so; and this practice provided the first semi-professional opening of any significance.

The attorneys soon became the subject of controversy. It was claimed locally that 'suitors eagerly avail themselves of the services of these men to conduct their cases for them'.[1] But some of the Chiefs were jealous, especially when their subjects obtained the assistance of advocates to plead against them; Joseph Martin, sent by King Aggery of Cape Coast to give evidence before the 1865 Select Committee in London, criticized 'the employment of attorneys when the natives had better speak for themselves'.[2] Government officials also complained of the erroneous impression that Africans could not take legal proceedings in British courts, even in the most trifling cases, without the advice and assistance of a lawyer.[3]

These were not, of course, qualified lawyers. Nevertheless, they were an important intermediary between the formality of the courts and their illiterate suitors, and they probably attempted to make English legal procedure acceptable to Africans accustomed to more dilatory processes of justice. This naturally excited the impatience of British magistrates, one of whom complained of the waste of time caused by 'an excessive mass of evidence'.[4] In 1865 the licences were discontinued,[5] and the attorneys were forbidden to wear wigs and gowns in court. The following year several of them crossed swords with the magistrates; for using strong language to the Bench, W. C. Finlason (from Jamaica) and Charles Bannerman were prohibited entirely from practising, and the latter was also sentenced to three months' imprisonment. The Administrator, Colonel E. Conran, proceeded to interdict all self-educated attorneys from practising in the courts. Four of them thereupon petitioned in protest,[6] and when the Secretary of State heard about this, he roundly condemned the prohibition as arbitrary and impolitic.[7] Conran was instructed immediately to withdraw it,[8] and attorneys were once again licensed and enrolled in 1867.

[1] Letter of 12 July 1865, from Cape Coast; *The African Times*, 23 Aug. 1865.

[2] *Report from the Select Committee on Africa (Western Coast)* (London, 1865), para 55.

[3] Letter of 26 Aug. 1865, from Acting Colonial Secretary to Acting Chief Justice, enclosed in Dispatch No. 92 of 1 Sept. 1865, from Conran to Cardwell; CO/96/68.

[4] Letter of 3 June 1873, from Chalmers to Pope Hennessy; CO/96/114.

[5] *Government Notice*, 20 June 1865.

[6] Petition of 17 Oct. 1866, from Charles Bartels, G. Blankson jun., H. F. Spilsbury, and W. A. Ward, and covering Dispatch No. 99 of 19 Nov. 1866, from Conran to Blackall; CO/96/72.

[7] Minute of 7 Feb. 1867, by Carnarvon; ibid.

[8] Dispatch No. 72 of 15 Feb. 1867, from Carnarvon to Blackall; ibid.

The new Chief Magistrate, W. A. Parker, was no more kindly disposed towards them. He made certain that Charles Bannerman's petition for reinstatement would be rejected;[1] further, he revived a year-old libel case (taken out by his own landlord) against Finlason, which had been left on the files for lack of evidence, and without hearing any further depositions sentenced him to a fine of £200, which resulted in his temporary imprisonment. But Finlason's appeal was granted in Sierra Leone, where Parker's action was condemned as 'very wrong and without precedent'.[2] Meanwhile, anonymous attacks upon him in *The African Times* would appear to have inflamed his animosity.[3] During 1868 both Edmund and James Bannerman jun. were prohibited from the courts, and were given sentences of six and twelve months respectively for personation, illegal restraint, and extortion.[4] Parker also took the first opportunity to imprison Finlason again, sentencing him to a year and a day with hard labour for using threatening language to a Justice of the Peace who had entered his house without a warrant.[5] Edmund Bannerman wrote to *The African Times* from 'Parker's Bastille—James Fort, Accra', protesting against such sentences, and accusing the Chief Magistrate of behaving 'like a bully' on the Bench.[6]

Although the Executive Council in Sierra Leone ordered Finlason's release, Parker continued on his vindictive career,[7] until the Governor-in-Chief, realizing that he was 'possessed of a species of monomania about a few characterless persons whom he has very injudiciously provoked into hostility',[8] secured his transfer to St. Helena early in 1869, under an official cloud.[9] *The African Times* rejoiced;[10] but the new Chief Magistrate, D. Chalmers, although better fitted for the post, was equally strongly opposed to the African attorneys. He alleged that they lacked the necessary education, and in particular that they exacted excessive fees from suitors, although he could hardly deny that there was a demand for their services. Chalmers was not sorry to find that their licences had lapsed, and took no steps to renew them. In 1870 he forbade

[1] Jan. 1868; CO/96/75.   [2] *The African Times*, 23 May 1868.
[3] For example, 'Justice Without Juries', ibid. 23 Dec. 1867, and a letter signed 'Accra', ibid. 23 Mar. 1868.
[4] The case was prominently reported in *The African Times*, 16 May 1868, under the heading, 'Justice on the Gold Coast'. Another brother, Robert Bannerman, was also sent to prison in the same year.
[5] Letter of 3 June 1868, from F. Fitzgerald, editor of *The African Times*, to the Colonial Office; CO/96/78.   [6] *The African Times*, 23 June 1868.
[7] For example, the case of J. Dodoo, who was dismissed with a caution after he had been remanded in prison for eighty days. Dispatch of 21 Jan. 1869, from Kennedy to Granville; CO/96/79.   [8] Dispatch No. 5 of 14 Jan. 1869, from Kennedy to Granville; ibid.
[9] 'Mr. Parker is wholly unfitted for the office of Law Adviser to the Administrator, and his mode of dealing with the Natives is both mischievous and dangerous to the public peace. I learn . . . that he has adopted the prevailing vice on this Coast—drinking to excess; and that he has been seen under the influence of drink on the "Bench", and on one occasion in a place of "Public Worship" . . . I fear that nothing short of his removal from office can restore peace or confidence at Cape Coast.' Confidential Dispatch of 25 Jan. 1869, from Kennedy to Granville; ibid.
[10] For example, 23 Apr. 1869.

the attorneys to act in civil cases concerning Africans, and in 1873 he was arguing that they should be excluded altogether from all the courts.[1]

Once again more liberal views prevailed in London, and the Secretary of State refused to authorize this. Lord Carnarvon suggested that the attorneys should be required to pass a simple examination before the Chief Magistrate, designed to prove their knowledge of court procedure, and of the broad general principles of civil and criminal law; and that a table of fees should be made public.[2] But the deterioration in personal relationships in the Gold Coast could not so easily be reversed.

It is difficult to sum up the issues involved. It is obvious that the integrity of the public service in Cape Coast of the 1860's had not reached even the standards of Victorian England; and there was an increasing number of cases where financial irregularities were detected, and sometimes punished with extreme severity. These were even used—as by Parker—for settling personal scores. Similar quarrels sometimes arose between Europeans; it was easy for members of the small, English-speaking community to get on one another's nerves in a trying climate. Andrews, for example, was criticized in London for arresting a high-ranking officer 'out of personal feelings under the disguise of public duty'.[3] But all too easily the issue became one of colour, and prejudices were aroused on both sides.

Government and Elementary Education, 1850–1919

It was perhaps inevitable that the few educated Africans should sometimes find themselves at cross purposes with the Administration; and some Europeans seemed unable to control their resentment against African advancement. Yet in fairness to the Government it should be remembered that the development of education had been official policy from the 1850's onwards. This was one of the main objects that the Governor, with the full support of Grey, hoped to secure from the introduction of a poll tax.[4] Encouraged by the Chiefs' initial reception of this, Hill proceeded towards the end of 1852 to pass an Ordinance 'to provide for the better Education of the Inhabitants of Her Majesty's Forts and Settlements on the Gold Coast'. With a touching faith in the improving qualities of the three R's, he included provision for 'the daughters of the better class of Natives whose education has hitherto been sadly neglected, producing in consequence a very low state of morality'.[5]

The Government could not afford to be very ambitious in its plans. But at least the year 1852 marked an official determination to develop education,

[1] Letter of 3 June 1873, from Chalmers to Administrator-in-Chief; CO/96/114.
[2] Dispatch No. 124 of 17 July 1874, from Carnarvon to Officer Administering the Government; ibid.
[3] Minute of 19 Apr. 1862, by Newcastle; CO/96/57.
[4] See Ch. IV, pp. 169 and 173, below.
[5] Dispatch No. 75 of 1 Dec. 1852, from Hill to Pakington; CO/96/25.

even though the officials were less experienced than the missionaries in how it should be done. Up to then, the Basel Mission in the east and the Wesleyans in the west had been shouldering the whole cost of education, except for the Cape Coast Castle school, which was costing the Administration some £100 annually, and the Dutch Government school at Elmina. Four years later the British authorities had managed to open nine more schools, including one for girls at Cape Coast;[1] the official expenditure was now over £700, including £260 from the poll tax receipts.[2]

Meanwhile, missionary education continued to expand, providing more clerks and teachers, and a good many restless young men who did not quite know to what use to put their newly acquired reading and writing. Official statistics for 1858 give some indication of the results achieved by the Wesleyans, over a fairly extensive field, and by the intensive drive of the Basel Mission. At that time the former had twenty-nine day schools, most of them mixed, spread out along the coastal area from Dixcove to Prampram; the total enrolment was some 900 boys and 230 girls. The Basel Mission had thirteen day and four boarding schools, concentrated in the Christiansborg, Aburi, and Akropong districts, where over 250 children were enrolled in separate boys' and girls' schools. In addition, a most rigorous course was provided in the Akropong Training College, which was also the headquarters for the Mission staff of thirty European pastors and teachers.[3] Their most original contribution to Gold Coast education was to develop practical work side by side with book-learning. The Rev. E. Schrenk even put this first before the 1865 Select Committee, when he described the work of his Mission as 'industrial schools or shops, schools, and preaching'.[4]

Africanus Horton, the Sierra Leonean doctor, took a keen interest not only in political movements in the Gold Coast, but also in education, which he considered to be 'fearfully neglected' and declining in quality.[5] H. T. Ussher, the Administrator, was initially polite enough to invite him to draw up a scheme for the establishment of a good school, 'of a higher class than hitherto', which would encourage the Fantis to educate their children.[6] In 1870 Horton published his main suggestions, which included government day schools in Cape Coast, Anomabu, Winneba, and Accra; an Academy for more advanced pupils; the employment of well-trained teachers at liberal salary rates; and the establishment of a Board of Education with its own inspector.[7] Unfortunately

---

[1] The first separate school for girls had been opened in 1821 in Cape Coast Castle, under the charge of the widow of an officer of the Company, who taught mainly needlework. CO/267/54 and 56. A later teacher was a talented mulatto who afterwards became schoolmistress of the first Wesleyan Girls' School. T. B. Freeman, 'Elizabeth Waldron. A Mother in Israel', MS. now at Wesley Girls' High School, Cape Coast.　　　　　　[2] *Gold Coast Colony Blue Book*, 1856.

[3] Ibid. 1858.　　　　　　　　[4] *1865 Report*, evidence of Schrenk, reply to question 3,216.

[5] J. A. B. Horton, *West African Countries and Peoples* (London, 1868), p. 114.

[6] Letter of 21 Apr. 1870, from Ussher to Horton, quoted in his *Letters on the Political Condition of the Gold Coast* (London, 1870), p. 145 n.

[7] Ibid. Letter no. ix, dated 2 May 1870.

Ussher was upset on political grounds by the publication of Horton's *Letters*, and accused him of being the principal schemer behind the Fanti Confederation; he even attempted to have him removed from the Gold Coast.[1] Plans for increased government aid towards education were forgotten; and the Fanti Confederation scheme of 1872 was turned down, including its estimate of £4,000—one-fifth of the proposed budget—to be spent on education.[2] Ironically enough, when token annual grants of £100 to the Basel Mission and £50 to the Wesleyans were introduced by the Government in 1874, the Colonial Office suggested that the inhabitants might 'hereafter be induced to tax themselves for educational purposes'.[3]

In fact, the demand for education was growing rapidly. The merchants were anxious to see a better level of education for boys, in order to fit them more effectively for employment.[4] Those Africans who had themselves been to school realized the advantages to be gained; as one of them wrote, 'let every young man who earns a reasonable income unswervingly aim at, and strain every nerve to procure, a good education for his children'.[5] In 1878 a deputation of 'educated native gentlemen' asked the Lieutenant-Governor for an adequate school in Accra; and the following year the 'scholars' of Elmina—whose traditions of education under the Dutch went back over 200 years—petitioned for a government school in their town.[6] *The African Times* even claimed, with perhaps pardonable exaggeration, that 'A remarkable peculiarity of the West African natives everywhere is a burning desire for education.'[7]

Meanwhile the Wesleyans continued to increase rapidly both the number and the size of their schools. Ussher in 1880 raised their grant to £200; but this disappointed the General Superintendent, who pointed out that the Mission had an enrolment of over 3,000, whereas the Government was spending £300 annually on its own 170 scholars. He now asked for a minimum annual grant of £500, claiming that they could educate ten times their present number of pupils 'without much additional expense'. He also claimed that nineteen out of every twenty Africans employed by the Government had been educated in Wesleyan schools.[8]

The Colonial Office was reluctant to approve increased grants for Mission schools until some means of testing their efficiency could be devised.[9] Ussher favoured the development of secular education, to avoid the problem of inspection and grants. Lord Kimberley, however, did not think a secular system would be the best for 'these ignorant Africans', and he advised the Governor to work through Mission, rather than government schools, giving

---

[1] See Ch. VI, pp. 243–5, below.
[2] Fanti Confederation scheme of 16 Apr. 1872; CO/96/94.
[3] Minute of 1 June 1874, by A. W. L. Hemming; CO/96/111.
[4] *Gold Coast Colony Blue Book*, 1870.   [5] *The Gold Coast Times*, 5 Dec. 1877.
[6] CO/96/124 and 127.   [7] 1 Oct. 1880.
[8] Memorandum of 9 Dec. 1881, by General Superintendent of Wesleyan Missions; CO/96/136.
[9] Dispatch of 8 Mar. 1880, from Hicks Beach to Ussher; CO/96/130.

them aid according to results, but avoiding too much red tape.[1] Largely as the outcome of these discussions, an Education Ordinance was enacted in 1882, and applied generally to British West Africa. This provided for both government-financed schools, and denominational schools which would receive grants-in-aid according to their efficiency.[2] A Board of Education was set up to control and supervise the system, and the Principal of Fourah Bay College, the Rev. M. Sunter, was appointed Inspector of Schools; in practice his time was shared between all the West African Settlements.

The new developments were welcomed by the Cape Coast press;[3] but it was not long before *The Gold Coast Times* complained that the Ordinance was not worth the paper it was written on, and suggested that a compulsory attendance clause should be added, for all children under a certain age. 'We should then', the editor happily concluded, 'have educated people in all classes.'[4] In December 1886 *The Gold Coast Methodist*, with no such Utopian axe to grind, deprecated 'the present illiberal and limping line of procedure'. The missionary societies were understandably impatient with the system of grants; Sunter himself complained that it was unworkable and ridiculously complicated, so that no school was able to qualify, in the proper sense, for aid. Not the slightest advance had been made since the enactment of the Ordinance, and the Gold Coast was, 'educationally speaking, little more than a stagnant pool'.[5] The neglect of girls' education was 'a relic of barbarism'. But Sunter saw clearly the potential role that the Government could play in the building up of a nation: 'Evolution will come from within do as we please; be it our place to guide and control . . . [so] as to weld the various tribes of the Gold Coast Protectorate into one compact mass, a credit to the Colonial Government.'[6]

The Administrator was not impressed: 'Mr. Sunter's remarks . . . are not conceived in that practical shape which would enable the Government to take action upon them.'[7] Sidney Webb, in the Colonial Office, realized that the Gold Coast was 'in a hopeless muddle' over grants-in-aid;[8] and on his

---

[1] Minute of 4 June 1880, by Kimberley; ibid.

[2] The following figures show the number of schools, pupils, and teachers in 1881:

	Schools	Enrolment	Teachers
Government . .	3	507	16
Basel Mission .	47	1,285	79
Wesleyan Mission .	84	3,057	106
Bremen Mission .	4	n.a.	n.a.
Roman Catholic .	1	150	3
	139	c. 5,000	c. 210

Source: CO/96/143.

[3] For example, *The Gold Coast Times*, 20 May 1882.   [4] Ibid. 9 Sept. 1884.

[5] Letter of 28 July 1886, from Sunter to Colonial Office; CO/96/178.

[6] M. Sunter, *General Report on the Schools of the Gold Coast Colony for 1886* (Accra, 1887).

[7] Dispatch No. 218 of 10 June 1887, from White to Holland; CO/96/181.

[8] Minute of 26 Oct. 1887, by S. Webb; CO/96/187.

suggestion new legislation, drafted by Sunter on the basis of Lagos experience, was passed in 1887. The Board of Education was enlarged, and empowered to make its own rules for administering grants-in-aid, which were now to take school attendance figures into consideration. The new Ordinance proved much more workable, and government grants showed a marked rise from merely nominal figures to £1,673 in 1891–2, and £3,400 in 1895–6.[1] The dual structure of goverment and assisted schools was to remain the basis of Gold Coast education for many years.

In 1890 the first Director of Education was appointed, only to withdraw immediately; and his successor, a confirmed alcoholic, resigned in 1893.[2] In spite of this unfortunate beginning, the formation of a department with a regular schedule of inspection facilitated the keeping of continuous, systematic records; so that from this time onwards the outlines of educational development may be traced from official statistics. The expansion made possible by the 1887 Ordinance is illustrated by the following quinquennial figures:[3]

TABLE XI

Year	Government schools	Inspected schools	Total enrolment
1887	2	25	2,799
1892	3	71	6,666
1897	7	111	n.a.
1902	7	117	12,136

At the turn of the century schools of all types in the Gold Coast were still almost entirely Mission-run, to such an extent that Christians were commonly called *sukul-fo*, 'people of the school'.[4] The Government had hardly begun to establish schools inland;[5] and the system of grant aid did not extend beyond the borders of the Colony, as shown by the map opposite, taken from the report of the Education Department for 1902. In 1842 King Kwaku Dua of Ashanti had questioned the Rev. T. B. Freeman concerning the danger that education might make the people rebellious. The missionary assured him that, with a few possible exceptions, education had a tendency to make them more dutiful and obedient;[6] nevertheless, the ruling powers in Ashanti did

[1] F. Wright, 'System of Education in the Gold Coast Colony', in *Board of Education Special Reports on Educational Subjects* (London, 1905), vol. 13, pt. ii.

[2] CO/96/210, 214, and 230.

[3] *Departmental Reports*, Education, 1887, 1892, 1897, and 1902.

[4] H. Belshaw, 'Religious Education in the Gold Coast', in *International Review of Missions* (London, 1945), vol. 34.

[5] Lip-service was paid to the principle. For example, Minute of 10 Feb. 1894, by A. W. L. Hemming: 'It is very desirable to extend education in the interior as well as merely in the Coast towns.' CO/96/242.

[6] T. B. Freeman, *Journal of Various Visits to the Kingdoms of Ashanti, Aku, and Dahomi* (London, 2nd edn. 1844), entry for 4 Jan. 1842.

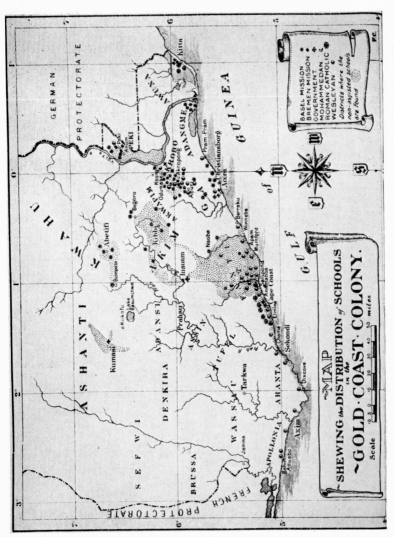

MAP 3. The distribution of schools—a map published in *Departmental Reports*, Education, 1902.

their best to block the progress of education. In 1876 a later Asantehene told the Rev. T. Picot: 'We will not select children for education; for the Ashantee children have better work to do than to sit down all day idly to learn hoy! hoy! hoy! They have to fan their parents, and to do other work, which is much better.'[1] Long after the military expedition of 1896 an Ashanti tradition persisted, particularly among illiterates, that the main point at issue had been a British demand to build a school in Kumasi.[2] Certainly the arrival of missionaries and teachers was the most immediately obvious consequence of Prempeh's removal. Within two years the Basel Mission had opened fourteen schools in Ashanti, with 395 children, and the Wesleyans seven, with 437.[3] But the 1900 rising proved a serious set-back to their work.

The grants paid to schools in the Colony were based on a code which had been in force earlier in England. According to the 1902 Rules of the Gold Coast Board of Education, payments were to be made by results: i.e. 2s. per head for each 'pass' in arithmetic, reading, and writing, and additional amounts for other subjects, these being calculated on a sliding scale based on average attendance. No allowance was made for teachers' salaries; and the Missions complained that this made it difficult, if not impossible, to put certificated teachers in infant schools.[4] In general, the result was that the schools most in need of help received the lowest grants, while many others received none at all, being unable to fulfil the conditions (e.g. as to numbers) for inspection and assistance. Little contribution was made by school fees, which varied considerably; there were none in the government, Roman Catholic, and some Wesleyan schools, while 'the Germans' charged from 1s. to 5s. annually, and the other Wesleyan schools 2s. to 12s.[5]

The system of grant payment encouraged the crowding of half-taught subjects into an ill-regulated curriculum, not to mention the unhealthy suspense surrounding the Inspector's annual visit and perfunctory questioning of the pupils. The annual examinations imposed a fairly rigid pattern upon school life, which progressed from the infant classes through seven elementary standards. The complete course took ten years, but only a small minority remained

---

[1] Letter of 3 May 1876, from Picot, published in *The African Times*, 1 Aug. and 1 Sept. 1876.
[2] R. S. Rattray, *Ashanti Law and Constitution* (Oxford, 1929), p. 222.
[3] *Departmental Reports*, Resident in Ashanti, 1898.
[4] The Methodist Church in 1900 had 100 schools, with 202 teachers and 6,200 pupils, financed as follows:

Government grants .	.	£1,612
Fees . . .	.	475
Church sources	.	1,567
		£3,654

Teachers' salaries amounted to £2,074, an average of only £10 per annum. C. T. Eddy, 'Educational Developments in the Gold Coast since 1900', a lecture given at Achimota, 1952.
[5] Educational survey for *Bell's Weekly Messenger*, enclosed in Dispatch No. 204 of 3 Sept. 1890, from Brandford Griffith to Knutsford; CO/96/211.

so long as this, as can be seen from the following figures for the distribution of pupils in the various classes in 1900:[1]

Infants	St. I	St. II	St. III	St. IV	St. V	St. VI	St. VII
6,293	1,012	831	731	584	426	308	144

From 1903 onwards, pupils were rewarded by the grant of a certificate for passing Standard VII, and this provided some encouragement; between 1904 and 1914, the numbers in Standard VII increased from 1 to 2 per cent. of the total enrolment.

There was no formal training for teachers, except that provided in the Basel Mission Seminary at Akropong, which received a grant-in-aid from 1902 onwards; but a certificate could be obtained by external examination. In 1905 there were only eighty-one certificated teachers,[2] and the schools relied mainly on post-Standard V boys, employed as pupil-teachers under the supervision of the headmaster, who received a bonus if he also managed to get them through their own final school examinations. Little attempt seems to have been made to adapt the method of teaching to local conditions; the syllabus, too, was almost entirely English in origin. Hardly any material was available for even an introduction to local history and geography.[3] The lessons, as might be expected, consisted mainly of repeating and learning by heart set answers to questions. The town schools met in large halls, with several classes in progress at the same time. All this was, of course, modelled upon the 'Lancastrian' or monitorial system common in English charity schools during the nineteenth century, with the important difference that the main medium of instruction was a foreign language. Further, there were no alternative schools available, as in England, for the more fortunate or more gifted pupils, who might expect to reach responsible posts in later life.

The Government was conscious that the schools were attempting too much on the intellectual and literary side, at the expense of practical work. Various suggestions were made for the training of apprentices overseas,[4] but there was little response, and such schemes neglected the basic defects of the schools

[1] *Departmental Reports*, Education, 1901.   [2] Ibid. 1905.

[3] For the teaching of history in schools, see Ch. XIII, pp. 525–8, below. An early 'Map of the Gold Coast—and Inland Countries between and beyond the Prah and Volta' was produced by the Basel Mission. *The Gold Coast News*, 29 Aug. 1885. Hesketh Bell's *Outlines of the Geography of the Gold Coast Colony and Protectorate* (London, 1895), was favourably reviewed in *The Gold Coast Chronicle*, and teachers were sometimes encouraged during their training to draw local sketch-maps. It was several more years before enough survey work had been completed even for a reasonably accurate wall map of the Colony and Ashanti to be published. By 1910 this was reported to be in use in all large schools, 'and pupils are beginning to understand more about the geography of their own country than was formerly the case'. *Departmental Reports*, Education, 1910.

[4] For example, Dispatch No. 259 of 18 July 1894, from Ripon to Brandford Griffith; CO/96/249.

themselves. Even when evening classes were held for Accra and Cape Coast teachers in the principles of technical education, the emphasis was on merely theoretical knowledge, and they were soon closed down as virtually useless.[1] The jails were alleged to provide the best education because they gave an admirable training in crafts, which there was therefore no excuse for neglecting in the schools.[2] Many officials were in sympathy with such criticisms;[3] but no attempt was made to follow the Basel example.

There were still many educational problems to be solved at the beginning of the twentieth century, apart from the ever-present question of finance. The opposition of the Chiefs remained a factor to be reckoned with, especially inland. More serious was the failure of many children to complete their courses, which was attributed partly to the indifference of their parents, and partly to the increasing attraction of paid employment, especially during the mining boom. These premature school-leavers, with 'a smattering of learning, and the arrogance of ignorance', were justifiably accused of bringing the name of scholar into contempt, and spreading distrust of the schools.[4] Complaints of irregular attendance continued for many years, especially as opportunities grew of securing casual employment during school hours, and thus earning something towards the fees.[5]

Some attempt to improve the content of education was made by Sir John Rodger, after he had visited Negro schools in the United States. A combined institution for elementary technical education and the training of teachers was opened in Accra in 1909; and a fixed time was optimistically prescribed for 'hand, eye and industrial training' in all primary schools.[6] This arrangement did not last long; in 1914 the time allotted was drastically reduced, owing to the difficulty experienced in filling it up. The Technical Institute developed only slowly, but the Government Training College—as it came to be called— supplied a long-felt need with its two-year course, even though the students had little general background and, at first, no practice school. The influence of the certificated teachers was soon noticed, and by 1918 nearly every assisted school had at least one qualified teacher, trained either by the Government or by the old Basel seminaries. On the debit side, there was no recognized salary scale for teachers; prospects were poor and the profession was understandably unpopular.[7]

Another important reform was introduced in 1909, when the system of payment by examination results was abolished, and replaced by grants of a varying percentage of the teachers' salaries, calculated according to a general estimate

[1] Dispatch No. 371 of 3 Sept. 1896, from Maxwell to Chamberlain; CO/96/260.

[2] *Departmental Reports*, Education, 1898.

[3] For example, F. M. Hodgson was reported to be 'entirely in agreement . . . that too much attention has been, and is being paid to literary training in this Colony, and not enough to training in useful industries'. Letter of 11 June 1896, from Acting Colonial Secretary to Director of Education; CO/96/286.   [4] *Departmental Reports*, Education, 1901.

[5] Ibid. 1913.   [6] Ibid. 1909.   [7] Ibid. 1914, 1915, and 1918.

of the efficiency and equipment of the school.[1] This had the double benefit of removing the premium on cramming, and encouraging the employment
of better qualified teachers. On the other hand, it also meant that the non-
assisted schools fell further and further behind the standards of the others. Yet
the growing demand for education was stretching the official and Mission network to its limits; there were actually more non-assisted than government and
assisted schools combined, although their average size was much smaller.[2]

The First World War, in many ways a period of national awakening, saw
an intensification of the demand for education. Several attempts were made to
establish new, independent schools, with varying degrees of success. The most
notable was the Accra Royal School, founded in 1915 by J. Kitson Mills; at
first funds were raised by entertainments and subscriptions, but the register of
pupils grew rapidly, and by 1922, when it began to receive regular government
assistance, there were 852 pupils (including 105 girls) paying a total of £431
in fees.[3] The Rev. Mark Hayford, who founded the Accra Baptist School, had
more difficulty in raising capital, and classes were crowded into the lower
part of his family house.[4]

The official system continued its gradual progress, expansion being most
marked during the war years, as the following figures show:

TABLE XII[5]

Year	Government schools	Assisted schools[6]	Total enrolment	Average attendance	Grants-in-aid
					£
1904	7	132	13,955	10,234	4,636
1909	9	155	16,711	11,968	6,387
1914	12	148	20,246	15,152	9,312
1919	19	194	27,318[7]	21,928	6,599

Grants-in-aid, on the other hand, although they were doubled during the
decade 1904–14, remained almost stable (at just over £9,000) during the war
years; and when the Bremen and Basel Mission schools were taken over
during 1917–18, the nominal total of grants actually fell by £3,000, since the
teachers were now paid directly by the Government.[8]

[1] *Departmental Reports*, Education, 1909.

[2] The Education Department records are incomplete, but in 1909 there were estimated to be
211 non-assisted schools, and in 1916, 259 with 12,241 pupils.

[3] *Departmental Reports*, Education, 1922–3.

[4] T. Jesse Jones, *Education in Africa* (New York, 1922), p. 141.

[5] *Departmental Reports*, Education, 1904, 1909, 1914, and 1919.

[6] Figures of 'assisted schools' for 1904 and 1909 include all the schools inspected, whether or
not grants were paid; for 1914 and 1919 (and all subsequent government statistics) they include
only those schools which actually qualified for grants.   [7] This total included 4,600 girls.

[8] All German missionaries were deported in Dec. 1917, and the remaining members of the
Basel Mission early in 1918. The Colonial Secretary argued from the grounds of 'the increasing

The most serious anomaly in the system was the maldistribution of schools between the various regions. This was no doubt historically inevitable. It was only in 1909 that the first government schools had been opened outside the Colony, in Kumasi and Tamale; Sunyani and Gambaga followed in 1912, and two years later a government girls' school was established in Kumasi. The disparity was intensified by what seems to have been a deliberately isolationist policy in the Northern Territories.

The story of education in the north provides many illuminating contrasts with earlier developments in the Colony, and even with Ashanti. No missionaries had arrived before a Protectorate was formally declared in 1901, and thereafter a paternalist administration retained the initiative in educational as in all other matters. A. E. Watherston, Chief Commissioner from 1905 to 1909, was anxious to ensure that the next generation should be 'men of more comprehension, education and less superstition';[1] he sent a few boys down to school in Cape Coast, and encouraged the formation of 'boys' brigades' in Tamale and Gambaga, providing P.T. drill and elementary English lessons, even before the government schools were opened.[2] But educational progress was very slow. One reason was the reluctance of the parents, which was due at least in part to 'the not unnatural fear that when their boys learn to read and write they will not be content to return to live with them again'.[3] More significant, however, was the fact that the Missions were not allowed freely into the north to develop educational and social work as elsewhere.

This policy may perhaps have been influenced by developments in Northern Nigeria, where F. D. Lugard had agreed in 1900 to maintain all the undertakings of the Royal Niger Company, including a pledge not to interfere with the Muslim religion. But, as J. S. Coleman points out, this was not a promise to forbid Christian Missions, nor was it even held to be legally binding. Lugard's main reasons for the exclusion of missionaries were his fears of armed resistance by the Emirs, and his belief that Christian doctrines might upset the traditional order underpinning the system of indirect rule. He did, however, encourage Missions in pagan areas; and two C.M.S. schools were allowed to open in 1903 and 1905 on the specific invitation of the Emirs of Bida and Zaria.[4]

In the Gold Coast Watherston certainly seems to have considered Islam a religion 'eminently suited to the native', which was helping to spread civilization, encouraging 'a much more decent life', and giving an impetus to

brutality with which Germany had prosecuted the war', and the 'notorious' fact that the Mission was 'essentially German in character'. *Legislative Council Debates*, 4 Feb. 1918. Yet only three years later Guggisberg called this step 'the worst blow inflicted by the war in this country'. Ibid. 21 Jan. 1921.

[1] Letter of 7 June 1907, from Watherston to Colonial Secretary; 1953 Acc. No. 1290, G.N. Archives.   [2] 1953 Acc. Nos. 1296 and 1370, Case No. 149/1909, G.N. Archives.

[3] *Departmental Reports*, Northern Territories, 1911.

[4] J. S. Coleman, *Nigeria: Background to Nationalism* (Los Angeles, 1958), pp. 133–6.

trade. He reported approvingly on the work of a Muslim revivalist at Wa: 'A cleanliness and sobriety came over the country in two weeks that years of our administration have failed to produce.'[1] Such an attitude, however, led him to an active hostility to Christian Missions far stronger than Lugard's, though it was considerably less appropriate in a predominantly pagan territory, with nothing to correspond to the powerful Emirates of Northern Nigeria. From the start there was personal antagonism between the missionaries and the Chief Commissioners, who tended to regard Mission schools as competitive with rather than complementary to their own; and, thus handicapped, education in the north fell further and further behind the south.

The White Fathers from Wagadugu managed to get a foot in the back door. They were both fortunate and astute enough to meet the Governor on a visit to the north in 1906, and secured permission to open a station and school at Navrongo, provided that English was the only language taught and that government regulations were complied with.[2] Watherston then seems to have made it his business to be as unhelpful as possible. He refused them permission to work in Wa, because this was the most important Muslim settlement,[3] complained that the White Fathers were 'deceitful and very untrustworthy', and ordered a 'watchful eye' to be kept on them.[4] The Chief Commissioner was especially annoyed that, being French Canadians, they were unable to teach English properly;[5] he was also prejudiced against one of them by the fact that 'His social class is very low'.[6] The Father Superior at Wagadugu was persuaded to arrange a transfer, and at the end of 1907 the White Fathers opened a school and carpentry workshop at Navrongo with twenty-six youths sent by the District Commissioner.[7] When Watherston visited the school, he agreed that the Mission could be of considerable service from an educational point of view, 'if they will only run straight'.[8] He was later willing to recommend that two further stations should be opened, at Lawra and Bawku,[9] but would not allow the White Fathers to start work in Tamale, although in 1909 he privately invited the Basel Mission to open a 'factory' there for training trade apprentices. His point of view was strictly utilitarian; as an afterthought

[1] Letter of 18 May 1906, from Watherston to Colonial Secretary; 1953 Acc. No. 1290, G.N. Archives.

[2] Letter of 3 Feb. 1906, from Watherston to Father Superior at Wagadugu; ibid.

[3] Letter of 1 June 1906, from Watherston to White Fathers; ibid.

[4] Letter of 11 June 1906, from Watherston to Colonial Secretary; ibid.

[5] The Father Superior later claimed that the twenty-three boys being instructed in English 'can generally say in this language all that they want to say, though not always in the same purity of language as Shakespeare would have said'. 1912 Report by Father Morin; 1953 Acc. No. 1346, G.N. Archives.

[6] Letter of 5 July 1907, from Watherston to Colonial Secretary; 1953 Acc. No. 1292, G.N. Archives.

[7] Report by District Commissioner, Navarro, dated 2 Nov. 1909; 1953 Acc. No. 1346, Case No. 81/1905, G.N. Archives.

[8] Letter of 19 Mar. 1908, from Watherston to Colonial Secretary; 1953 Acc. No. 1292, G.N. Archives.   [9] Letter of 30 Mar. 1909, from Watherston to Colonial Secretary; ibid.

he added that as several Africans from the coast attended daily services, and more on Sundays, they would be glad of their own church.[1]

There was no radical change of policy when Watherston died. The next Chief Commissioner, C. H. Armitage, soon had some stormy passages with various Missions. He was dissatisfied with the White Fathers' educational work, which he condemned as a comparative failure, and criticized them for having as their main object 'proselytism'.[2] He also tried to prevent them from opening a nunnery for work among women, until influential Catholics in England intervened.[3] Armitage would really have liked a complete government monopoly of education; but in 1913 he suddenly appeared quite prepared to grant the White Fathers sole control of missionary work down to a line drawn at 9° N., arguing that 'natives who have adopted the Roman Catholic religion are much more amenable and law-abiding than those who have embraced other religious beliefs', and that the establishment of rival Missions would not be conducive to the good of the inhabitants.[4] His apparent volte-face was to be explained not by any increased love for the Catholics but rather by his fears of a Protestant invasion.

The Rev. W. R. Griffin, General Superintendent of the Wesleyan Mission, had visited the Northern Territories in 1911 and asked for a grant of land at Wa, at a peppercorn rent;[5] afterwards he announced the appointment of two missionaries, one for work in Tamale, and the other in Wa.[6] The Chief Commissioner at once declared that the time had not yet arrived for the opening up of the north to further Christian enterprise. He complained of the friction that had been caused by Catholic converts refusing to work either for the Administration or the Chiefs, compared the progress of their schools unfavourably with those of the Government, pointed out that Wa had a considerable Muslim population which it would be unwise to disturb, and suggested darkly that the Wesleyans should first set their own house in order.[7] As a result, the Governor advised them that it would be a mistake to start work in the north.[8]

Armitage was correspondingly annoyed when the Rev. H. G. Martin arrived in Tamale in November 1912, and he made the young missionary feel as unwelcome as possible. Armitage firmly refused to grant either the

[1] Letter of 29 Apr. 1909, from Watherston to Chief Agent, Basel Mission (preceded by telegram); ibid.

[2] Letter of 15 Oct. 1912, from Armitage to Colonial Secretary; 1953 Acc. No. 1299, G.N. Archives.

[3] Letter of 17 July 1912, from Armitage to Colonial Secretary; ibid. Also Letter of 10 Dec. 1912, from Colonial Office to E. H. Freshfield; 1953 Acc. No. 1346, Case No. 81/1905, G.N. Archives.

[4] Letter of 5 Mar. 1913, from Armitage to Colonial Secretary; 1953 Acc. No. 1299, G.N Archives.

[5] Letter of 5 Dec. 1911, from Griffin to Commissioner, NW. Province; 1953 Acc. No. 1379, Case No. 4/1912, G.N. Archives.

[6] Letters of 25 Mar. and 20 May 1912, from Griffin to Acting Chief Commissioner and Governor; ibid.   [7] Letter of 5 June 1912, from Armitage to Governor; ibid.

[8] Letter of 28 Dec. 1912, from Colonial Secretary to Griffin; ibid.

land which the Wesleyans claimed had been agreed by the Acting Chief Commissioner,[1] or the use of any government building for the conduct of services;[2] he lost no opportunity to harass Martin, accusing him of employing government schoolboys in his house and spreading malicious gossip about officials.[3] He even refused to allow any religious instruction to be given to the boys, in or out of school.[4] The Chief Commissioner was, of course, well aware of the disturbing influence of Wesleyan missionaries farther south, where they had encouraged Africans to think for themselves, allowed them to challenge officialdom, and even given them active support in the recent protests against the Forest Bill.[5] He may also have read a recently published book on Northern Nigeria, in which Lugard was quoted as saying: 'the preaching of equality of Europeans and natives, however true from a doctrinal point of view, is apt to be misapplied by people in a low state of development, and interpreted as an abolition of class distinction'.[6]

In March 1913 Armitage received a sharp reprimand from Accra, expressing the Governor's profound regret and extreme displeasure at the language he had used to a missionary body of world-wide repute. The Government had no power to prevent the establishment of a Mission in the Northern Territories, quite apart from the fact that the Secretary of State had already expressed his approval.[7] Unabashed, Armitage claimed that he had merely been obeying 'instructions' from Accra;[8] but the Acting Chief Commissioner, once again left in charge, offered land for a station after all,[9] and Martin was permitted to give religious instruction to government pupils out of school hours, with their parents' consent.

By the time the Chief Commissioner returned from leave, Martin had been replaced by the Rev. J. H. Stormonth, whom Armitage now welcomed warmly 'both as a missionary and a fellow man'. He even increased the area of land to be leased in Tamale.[10] Nevertheless, he managed to offend Stormonth almost immediately, by asking for advance notice of his itinerary when travel-

---

[1] Letter of 3 Feb. 1913, from Armitage to Griffin; 1953 Acc. No. 1379, Case No. 4/1912, G.N. Archives.

[2] Letter of 7 Feb. 1913, from Martin to Commissioner, S. Province; ibid. Case No. 62/1919.

[3] 1953 Acc. No. 1838, Case No. 7/1913, G.N. Archives.

[4] Letters exchanged between Martin and Armitage on 24 Mar. 1913; ibid.

[5] See Ch. X, pp. 362–70, below. The General Superintendent himself had accompanied the 1912 A.R.P.S. deputation to their interview with the Secretary of State; and Armitage had carefully filed a local press report that Griffin had presented Casely Hayford and the other delegates as 'Princes of West Africa' on the platform of a Wesleyan conference at Liverpool, where they had been given 'a grand reception'. The Gold Coast Leader, 24 Aug. 1912, filed in 1953 Acc. No. 1379, Case No. 4/1912, G.N. Archives.

[6] C. W. J. Orr, The Making of Northern Nigeria (London, 1911), p. 263.

[7] Confidential Letter of 12 Mar. 1913, from Acting Colonial Secretary to Armitage; 1953 Acc. No. 1383, Case No. 7/1913, G.N. Archives.

[8] Confidential Letter of 29 Mar. 1913, from Armitage to Colonial Secretary, referring to code telegram he had received in 1912; ibid.

[9] Letter of 30 Apr. 1913, from Acting Chief Commissioner to Martin; 1953 Acc. No. 1379, Case No. 4/1912, G.N. Archives.   [10] Letter of 10 Jan. 1914, from Armitage to Griffin; ibid.

ling—the routine procedure for all officials.[1] Stormonth took strong exception to the implication that his work for God was to be subject to government rules.[2] The Chief Commissioner insisted that he would have to be responsible if anything happened to an unprotected white man wandering into a hostile district;[3] and although the quarrel was patched up, he maintained an absolute refusal to allow Stormonth to enter the NE. Province.[4]

One of Stormonth's accusations was that no attempt had been made to stop the evangelizing efforts of the Muslims.[5] This did not perturb Armitage in the least. He quoted in reply a recent letter from Griffin disclaiming any such intention;[6] and on the outbreak of war with Turkey in 1914, he instructed his officials to explain to the Muslim communities that 'Great Britain is not only the greatest Mohammedan Power in the World but the true and consistent friend of the followers of that Religion.'[7] In view of all this, it is surprising to find Armitage complaining, in the same year, of the lack of educational facilities in the north:

> With the Colony enjoying, in addition to the Education Department, the educational services of the Church Mission Society, the Roman Catholic, Wesleyan, Basel and Bremen Missions, I respectfully submit that a few crumbs from this feast of instruction might well be spared for the children of this Dependency.[8]

His purpose was not, of course, to invite more missionaries, but to secure grants for government schools in each Province, in addition to those already opened at Tamale and Gambaga.

Some senior officials in Accra were apparently unaware of the serious effects of Armitage's policy of exclusion. In 1918, when the Scottish Mission submitted plans to take over the work of the Basel missionaries, the Colonial Secretary was surprised to find that there was no mention of work in the north. He expressed the hope that their operations would soon be extended to the Northern Territories, whose need was at least as great as other parts of the Colony.[9] But the extent of the leeway to be made up may be gauged from

[1] Letter of 12 Jan. 1914, from Armitage to Stormonth; 1953 Acc. No. 1300, G.N. Archives. Cf. Watherston's objection expressed a few years earlier to 'any European wandering about the country at present without the Commissioner knowing something of his movements'. Letter of 3 Sept. 1909, to Colonial Secretary; 1953 Acc. No. 1296, G.N. Archives.

[2] 1953 Acc. No. 1383, Case No. 7/1913, G.N. Archives.

[3] Letter of 20 Feb. 1914, from Armitage to Stormonth; 1953 Acc. No. 1301, G.N. Archives.

[4] Confidential Letter of 7 Apr. 1914, from Armitage to Stormonth; ibid. Armitage also informed Stormonth on another occasion that his proposed preaching tour in Dagomba must be postponed indefinitely, for reasons which he could not at present explain, but 'in the interests of the country that I administer'. Letter of 24 Nov. 1914; 1953 Acc. No. 1302, G.N. Archives.

[5] Letter of 6 Apr. 1914, from Stormonth to Armitage; 1953 Acc. No. 1383, Case No. 7/1913, G.N. Archives.

[6] Letter of 7 Apr. 1914, from Armitage to Stormonth; ibid.

[7] Letter of 7 Nov. 1914, from Armitage to Provincial Commissioners; 1953 Acc. No. 1303, G.N. Archives.

[8] Letter of 27 Feb. 1914, from Armitage to Colonial Secretary; 1953 Acc. No. 1375, Case No. 30/11, G.N. Archives.   [9] Slater, *Legislative Council Debates*, 31 Dec. 1918.

the official statistics for 1919, which reveal only too clearly the differential impact of education upon the Gold Coast:

TABLE XIII[1]

Area	Government schools	Assisted schools	Total schools
Colony:			
Eastern Province	5	114	119
Central Province	3	42	45
Western Province	3	19	22
Ashanti .	4	19	23
Northern Territories	4	—	4
	19	194	213

Secondary Education and African Initiative, 1876–1919

Throughout the greater part of the nineteenth century, nearly all those Africans who had received anything beyond elementary schooling had had to seek it abroad.[2] This gave some foundation to the criticism that they were detached from their own people; some Africans themselves complained that 'the greater part of those educated in England have not turned out as should have been desired', and even concluded that it was 'dangerous' to send children there for education.[3] But without going to these extremes, many were anxiously demanding the development of secondary education in their own country. The Government did not attempt to meet this demand until after the First World War; although some officials were uneasy about the lack of facilities,[4] once more the initiative was first taken by the Missions with the increasing support of educated Africans themselves.

In 1876 the Wesleyans opened the first High School, at Cape Coast; this was designed for boys who had already passed through the primary schools, and included classes in carpentry, printing, and metalwork.[5] The standard of

[1] *Departmental Reports*, Education, 1919.

[2] Most of them were trained in England. A few were sent to school in Freetown, including G. E. Ferguson, T. Hutton Mills, J. E. Casely Hayford, and his elder brother E. J. Hayford, who attended the Wesleyan Boys' High School. Few Gold Coast students were trained at Fourah Bay College during the nineteenth century, probably because it was run by the C.M.S., who had no missionaries in the Gold Coast. The College was affiliated to Durham University in 1876, but only three of its fifty-nine graduates up to 1900 came from the Gold Coast. P. E. H. Hair, 'An Analysis of the Register of Fourah Bay College, 1827–1950', in *Sierra Leone Studies* (Freetown, 1956), N.S., no. 7. Dr. Africanus Horton had been the first to suggest hopefully that Fourah Bay should become the University of Western Africa; *Political Economy of British Western Africa; with the Requirements of the Several Colonies and Settlements (the African View of the Negro's Place in Nature); being an Address to the African-Aid Society* (London, 1865).

[3] *The Gold Coast Times*, 5 Dec. 1877.

[4] For example, Confidential Dispatch of 24 Jan. 1893, from Brandford Griffith to Ripon; CO/96/230.

[5] Advertisements continued to appear for a Basel Mission 'Grammar School' at Christiansborg;

scholarship may not have been very high at first, but the school was destined to survive, after various metamorphoses, as the foundation of the modern system of secondary education.[1] In 1889 it was closed by the Synod owing to lack of funds; but Cape Coast opinion would not acquiesce in this, and J. W. de Graft Johnson sen., with the financial backing of John Sarbah, J. P. Brown, and W. E. Pietersen, succeeded in getting it reopened under the title of the Collegiate School. The Wesleyan Mission resumed control in 1892; soon afterwards the Principal, the Rev. F. Egyir-Asaam, resigned, and founded 'Asaam's Grammar School'.[2] The Mission also applied for government assistance to found 'an Institute for the Higher Education and domestic training of the girls of this Colony' at Aburi. This school, which was opened in 1895, was the first attempt to provide secondary education for girls, and offered 'the advantages of an English training without the disadvantages of long residence in England'; but it did not flourish, and was abandoned for a time.[3]

Progress was still an uphill struggle; but by the beginning of the twentieth century J. Mensah Sarbah and other Cape Coast leaders were becoming increasingly conscious of the need for secondary education on 'national lines'. Partly inspired by memories of the Fanti Confederation, they founded the Mfantsi National Education Fund, with the support of a few Chiefs willing to provide for 'the proper education and technical training of the people still under our stool', by the relatively painless means of contributing 10 per cent. of their rents received under the 1900 Concessions Ordinance.[4] The plan was to establish both primary and secondary schools, to offer 'Queen Victoria scholarships' for liberal and professional studies, and to encourage local literature. Children were to be taught reading and writing in Fante, as well as the history and geography of the Gold Coast, with special reference to indigenous institutions and customs.[5] The scheme, however, was of importance for its aspirations rather than its achievements.

It soon became clear that the Chiefs were not going to be the main source of finance for education; in any case, they had no administrative machinery to run their own schools. The next idea that occurred to Mensah Sarbah and W. E. Sam, after a visit to England in 1903, was to raise money by public

but this was a middle school, which went up to Standard VII only. More advanced training, within a limited field, was provided by the Basel Mission Seminary for pastors and catechists, opened at Abetifi in 1899, in addition to their Akropong Teachers' Seminary.

[1] The first pupils included J. Mensah Sarbah, F. Egyir-Asaam (then W. F. Penny), J. J. Clement, W. Fynn, R. J. Hayfron, B. P. Wood, S. C. Crankson, G. Grant, B. Arthur, and H. Van Hien. Among the early teachers were Kofi Asaam (then Thomas Penny) and E. J. Hayford. *The Gold Coast Leader*, 20 Nov. 1926.   [2] Ibid.

[3] Confidential Dispatch of 21 June 1893, from Brandford Griffith to Ripon; CO/96/234. Also A. E. Southon, *Gold Coast Methodism* (Cape Coast, 1935), p. 131.

[4] The Secretary and Treasurer of the Fund was T. F. E. Jones, and the trustees included the President of the A.R.P.S., W. E. Sam of Tarkwa and J. E. Casely Hayford. The Governor was also invited to act as a trustee, but politely declined, although he was genuinely interested in the scheme. Dispatch No. 228 of 30 May 1902, from Nathan to Chamberlain; CO/96/397.

[5] J. E. Casely Hayford, *Gold Coast Native Institutions* (London, 1903), app. C.

subscription. Prudently limiting their own liability, they floated Fanti Public Schools Ltd., with the professed aim of promoting secondary schools in all the main towns. There was little financial support from the public; but they did succeed in opening another school in Cape Coast in 1905; this was soon amalgamated with the Wesleyan Collegiate School, and took the name of Mfantsipim. When the Rev. W. T. Balmer visited the school on a tour of inspection on behalf of the Mission in 1907, he found only eight boys meeting together to study as best they could with no teachers at all. But he was so impressed by their keenness that he applied for transfer from Sierra Leone, and built up the school into a recognized secondary institution; when he left in 1911 there were ninety-one pupils. Balmer himself has recorded, 'No teacher ever had a keener set of boys to deal with.'[1]

Educated Africans showed similar initiative in Accra by founding the Accra Grammar School, with the Rev. S. R. B. Attoh Ahuma as Principal. This was the first secondary school to receive a government grant, the 'fairly large' sum of £100 in 1906. It soon ran into difficulties over finance and management; the Inspector advised that the large board of control should be reduced in size, and Attoh Ahuma left to become headmaster of a rival concern, the Accra Collegiate School. Attendance fell off at the Grammar School, which consequently had to struggle on as best it could without a grant; by 1914, however, it was well established with 237 boys and 48 girls. The Collegiate School managed to qualify for assistance in 1909 only; but the work could not be maintained at a secondary level, and within two years it was closed.[2] Such were the pitfalls of private enterprise in education, although there were always others to try again.[3]

A firmer start was made by the S.P.G., when they opened a secondary school in Cape Coast in 1910 (this was later known as St. Nicholas Grammar School, and eventually became Adisadel College); the following year it began to receive regular government assistance, although enrolment increased only slowly. Even the small A.M.E. Zion Church felt the urge to found a college, although the first attempt, by Bishop A. Walters in 1912, did not survive for long.[4] The absence of the Government was becoming more noticeable and less easy to justify. By 1913 there were many Africans who felt, in the words of the A.R.P.S., that it was 'much to be deplored that up to the present the Government has not established any Secondary Schools in the Colony.'[5]

---

[1] W. T. Balmer, *A History of the Akan Peoples* (London, 1925), p. 13.

[2] *Departmental Reports*, Education, 1906 to 1914.

[3] Another African independent school which attempted to offer something beyond elementary education was the West African College of Music and Commerce, founded by C. E. Graves of Cape Coast in 1916. This soon announced grandly: 'Children quickly taught to play Mendelssohn, read Shakespeare, write Verses, translate Caesar, correspond in French, report in Shorthand, etc.' *The Gold Coast Nation*, 25 May–1 June 1918.

[4] *Departmental Reports*, Education, 1910 to 1913.

[5] Memorandum of 16 May 1913, from A.R.P.S. to Clifford; J. E. Casely Hayford, *The Truth about the West African Land Question* (London, 1913), app. B.

PLATE 2

a. J. E. Casely Hayford, with his son Archie

b. J. E. K. Aggrey

c. John Sarbah

d. George Ferguson

During the war years unofficial pressure increased in the Legislative Council, where it was emphasized that children still had to go to Freetown, Lagos, or England for higher education.[1] *The Gold Coast Independent* (7 September 1918) asked rhetorically whether the establishment of secondary schools was an official obligation or an act of grace; in any case, progressive readers were urged to take the initiative themselves: 'We have already indicated that we stand for National Institutions, for . . . Heaven helps those who help themselves.'

The Education Department was at least aware of the problem, and reported ponderously, 'there appears to be the prospect of provision being made to enable pupils to obtain, in this Colony, an education more advanced than is possible at the present time'.[2] This did not sound very promising, and early in 1919 a few Africans made a gallant attempt to launch their own Gold Coast National Education Scheme, to establish, maintain or assist secondary education in the Colony, Ashanti, 'and elsewhere when advisable'. At a meeting in Accra at the Native Club it was decided to invite 200 'Founders' each to pay £50 within five years. A board of trustees was appointed, most of them leading figures in the National Congress of British West Africa.[3] To a certain extent, therefore, this abortive movement was associated with the demand for a greater African share in the political leadership and administration of their own country.

' The "educated native" . . . the curse of the West Coast'

Although the Government from 1850 onwards had been increasingly concerned with the development of education, its officials seemed to cherish an increasing distaste for the products of the schools. This dualism of policy, though lamentable, was fully understandable. From the most utilitarian point of view, educated Africans were necessary to assist in the day-to-day business of government; once educated, however, they were no longer so easy to manage, and were apt to challenge authority in unpredictable ways. Even Hill, with his liberal policy concerning education and African promotions, distrusted the so-called 'scholar' class, and complained in 1852 that certain educated natives with no real claims to power were assuming authority over the people and exercising an undue influence with the Chiefs and headmen.[4]

Yet it was inevitable that education should carry with it a claim—even if strictly non-traditional—to enhanced status within the community.[5] There

---

[1] W. H. Grey, *Legislative Council Debates*, 1 Dec. 1914.

[2] *Departmental Reports*, Education, 1918.

[3] The trustees were: T. Hutton Mills and M. C. Hansen (Eastern Province), H. Van Hien and the Rev. G. R. Acquaah (Central Province), and J. E. Casely Hayford and R. J. Hayfron (Western Province). *The Gold Coast Independent*, 29 Mar. 1919.

[4] Dispatch No. 18 of 23 Apr. 1852, from Hill to Grey; CO/96/25.

[5] Cf. 'The idea of power—from the example of the "orders" or regulations emanating from the administration—tends to associate itself with the use of writing.' G. Balandier, 'Social Changes and Social Problems in Negro Africa', in *Africa in the Modern World*, p. 66.

was a steadily increasing minority of Africans who had profited from the best opportunities that were offered locally, together with a few who had managed to secure higher qualifications overseas. Such men naturally tended to assume a position of leadership, especially in Cape Coast and Accra; there were always one or two scoundrels ready to impose upon the gullible, but more often than not the educated leaders identified themselves closely with the interests of their own people. In particular, opposition to government measures was bound to originate with those who could read the relevant documents, although it was sometimes accompanied by misunderstanding of their purport.

This claim to leadership on the part of the educated few therefore irritated government officials, who despised the African for imitating European ways[1]—though he had no other model to follow—and retained something of the romantic ideal of the 'noble savage' in preferring to deal direct with uneducated Chiefs and villagers. To a certain extent, they were justified in their distaste for the many half-educated boys who considered that a few years at school entitled them to the deference of their elders and to exemption from manual labour. The genuine respect accorded to learning in the Gold Coast could easily be misappropriated by those who had scarcely begun to learn.

Here, however, much of the blame must rest with the kind of education offered, which was so largely verbal and literary, designed to produce clerks rather than farmers; while few children had the opportunity to come into contact with scholarly minds, or to acquire the humility that accompanies true learning. The term 'scholar', which aroused so much awe among illiterates, thus came to be used by Europeans in a contemptuous sense of those whose learning was more apparent than real. Unfortunately this contempt was often extended to cover all who were articulate in English, from the barely literate to the well-informed critic.

Thus in 1865 it was the 'scholars' who were particularly blamed for misinterpreting the Select Committee *Report*, and for encouraging a demand for self-government that had not previously existed.[2] Even the most progressive administrators honestly believed that the *Report* was unrealistic, and that the continuance—even the extension—of British influence would be needed for a long time to come. They continued to do all they could to improve the country in the interests of the inhabitants, and were correspondingly resentful when educated Africans began to draw up schemes that showed they would prefer to manage—or mismanage—their own local affairs. This was the key to Conran's stern treatment of King Aggery and his advisers (1865–6), and Ussher's of the Fanti Confederation leaders (1868–70), as well as the official attitude adopted towards the early attorneys. Colour also began to enter

---

[1] Cf. Coleman, *Nigeria*, p. 147: 'any human relationship cast in the model–imitator mold tends towards a superior–inferior stratification of attitudes. It is psychologically difficult for a model to regard an imitator as his equal'.

[2] See Ch. V, pp. 213–14, below.

into abuse of the 'discontented and unprincipled natives, principally mulattoes and semi-educated blacks (who appear to be an evil inseparable from all negro communities)'.[1]

Reports like these from the Gold Coast strongly impressed London officials, who were probably unaware that some of the despised 'scholars'—including Charles Bannerman, one of Conran's chief scapegoats—had been well educated in England. G. Barrow, in an influential Colonial Office memorandum of 1869, attributed all the troubles arising along the West Coast of Africa to the educated natives. In particular *The African Times*, 'to which they are almost the sole subscribers & contributors', was accused of instigating them against the Gold Coast Government:[2] 'There are notorious black sheep at the G. Coast, supported through thick & thin by the Editor of the "African Times" & this gives a black line morally, as well as physically, to that portion of the country.'[3] This attitude sank deep into the official mentality. The use of the word 'black' by Europeans at this time would repay study. It has always been a word with unpleasant associations in English;[4] but it now began to carry overtones that implied moral turpitude in those whose physical colour happened not to be white. Perhaps unconsciously at first, it came to be a term of denigration, in the widest sense, of all Africans. Another unfortunate association of ideas is illustrated by the phrase 'half-caste and half-educated';[5] and so mulattoes often came in for their share of abuse, for example as 'handsome, clever & specious, but ... thoroughly unprincipled'.[6]

Barrow also drew a sharp distinction between the tribes of the interior and the educated Africans in the towns. The implication was that the urbanized group could be dismissed as unrepresentative, and this is a view that has persisted in many parts of Africa right up to the present day.[7] It was only natural that educated Africans should make their homes in the towns, where they

[1] Dispatch No. 32 of 6 Apr. 1868, from Ussher to Kennedy; CO/96/76.

[2] This London-published newspaper continued to demand that the Gold Coast should 'associate educated natives with her Government in Legislative and Consultative bodies'; but this was hardly likely to appeal to the Colonial Office, accompanied as it was by a denunciation of 'Usshers, Parkers ... and such-like official pests'. *The African Times*, 23 Sept. 1869.

[3] Memorandum of 9 Mar. 1869, by Barrow; CO/96/79.

[4] Cf. blackball, blackleg, blackguard, Black Hole of Calcutta, black-hearted, blackmail, blacklist, and even blackwater fever. On the other hand, many Europeans remain blissfully unaware of Rattray's theory that the Gold Coast word *oburoni*, for white man, was derived from the word for white clay; and that, since dust and dirt to an African often look white it meant 'the dirty one'. R. S. Rattray, *Ashanti Proverbs* (Oxford, 1916), pp. 143-4.

[5] For example, Minute of 19 Feb. 1855, by H. Merivale; CO/96/31.

[6] Undated Minute of 1872; CO/96/94.

[7] An American writer has aptly described the role of the leaders or 'agitators' who in such a situation are normally accused by the ruling group of working up a contented people 'to demand a freedom of which they are incapable and which they do not really want'. He points out how 'They discover that, as members of the nationality or class to which they belong, there are limitations placed upon them of which they cannot help becoming conscious, and they react to that consciousness on behalf of the whole group ... It is a customary procedure to try and suppress these leaders, and invariably the result is an increase in the solidarity of the group behind them.' H. A. Miller, *Races, Nations, and Classes* (Philadelphia, 1924), pp. 120-1.

could find the employment for which they had been trained, the higher living standards which they had been led to expect, and the schools which they demanded for their children. This did not mean, however, that they had cast off all tribal allegiance or kinship obligations. Even when the Fanti Chiefs deliberately sought educated advisers and mediators between themselves and the strangers who governed in Cape Coast, this was seized upon as evidence not of the solidarity of educated and traditional groups, but of the evil influence of the former upon the latter.

From this time onwards there was a definite 'Colonial Office attitude' towards educated Africans, which ill became a government whose declared object was to bring education to Africa. In 1869 the Acting Administrator was criticized in London for having made 'rather too much of the "educated natives"' in Accra when they set up their own municipal management committee.[1] The editor of *The African Times* was so indignant at the official attitude towards the leaders of the Fanti Confederation that he wrote to the Colonial Office with a lengthy defence of 'the Educated Native Mercantile Communities', who, he said, spoke the English language, read English periodicals and literature, admired English freedom and institutions, and were 'covetous of full English rights and privileges'.[2] The Secretary of State was not impressed, and eventually decided that it would be better to have 'nothing to do with the "educated natives" as a body'.[3]

Nevertheless, some were ready enough to give their services in an emergency; in 1870, for example, Ussher commended the great bravery of L. Hesse and the brothers Robert and Edmund Bannerman in his expedition against 'the piratical Volloes and Doffoes'.[4] The Gold Coast Rifle Volunteer Corps—which had been founded in 1863 by R. Hutchison—was re-formed in June 1873, and fought against the Ashantis under Captain John Sarbah.[5] This contrasts strangely with the experience of Major W. F. Butler, whose heroic flank attack on Kumasi the following year failed owing to the desertion of many of his reluctant Fanti forces. Something of the explanation can be read between the lines of his published account of the campaign; for example, 'Alternately by bribes, threats, promises, and reproaches, I have succeeded in getting these savages so far.' Again, 'This continent holds the extreme of all that is revolting in man and in nature . . . the African race stands to-day as it stood 3000 years ago; hopeless to man, and cursed by heaven . . . those who know the negro best, like this man-and-brother theory least.'[6] Butler's views

[1] Minute of 9 Oct. 1869; CO/96/81.
[2] Letter of 2 Mar. 1872, from Fitzgerald to Kimberley; CO/96/95.
[3] Minute of 22 Feb. 1873, by Kimberley; CO/96/104.
[4] Dispatch of 22 June 1870, from Ussher to Kennedy; CO/96/85.
[5] J. B. Anaman, *The Gold Coast Guide* (London, 1902 edn.), p. 42. Other volunteer officers were Lieutenants S. H. Brew and Thomas Penny, and Sub-Lieutenants J. P. Brown (Adjutant) and Samuel Bannerman.
[6] W. F. Butler, *Akim-Foo: the History of a Failure* (London, 1875), pp. 19–21 and app. no. 32.

were not typical; but in the general ignorance of African conditions they were bound to have some influence, and to add one more handicap to the difficulties of language, environment, and prejudice faced by the emerging educated group.

Caustic remarks on educated Africans now began to appear with increasing frequency over the initials A. W. L. H. in the Colonial Office records. This was A. W. L. Hemming, who registered the view in 1875 that 'The "educated natives" or "scholars" . . . have always been a thorn in the side of the Govt. of the G. Coast. They have been at the bottom of most of the troubles on the coast for some years past'.[1] During the next twenty years he saw no reason to alter this opinion, which became increasingly influential as he rose to the position of head of the African Department.

On one occasion it was reported that certain Fantis were causing 'stoppages of roads . . . robberies and plunders' in Ashanti; local officials immediately concluded that it was the 'scholars' who were responsible.[2] Hemming was quite ready to believe this, and suggested that the Chiefs should be directed to 'catch' them and send them back into the Protectorate.[3] In 1884 the Governor complained that they were 'an embarrassing and mischievous element in the dealings of the Government with the Natives', responsible for nine-tenths of the local tribal disputes.[4] In London, therefore, the deputation scheme of 1885–7 appeared simply another manifestation of the trouble caused by the 'scholars'; and it was at this time that Hemming registered the scathing comment: 'The "educated native", such as Messrs. Bannerman, Brew &c, is the curse of the West Coast.'[5]

To set against this remote, Olympian judgement, perhaps one should note the testimony of a missionary who saw the educated African for what he was worth in his own humble environment:

At Abassa I had the pleasure of meeting a catechist . . . My good friend was 'passing rich on £20 a year'. I suppose he was the only 'scholar' in that town, but he wielded a mighty influence upon all with whom he came into contact. He was the friend and counsellor of kings and chiefs, and was held in the highest esteem among all men in the villages for many miles round. To such as he, representatives of all ranks of society come to have their domestic, social, and political grievances adjusted.[6]

---

[1] Minute of 6 Feb. 1875, by Hemming; CO/96/115.

[2] Report of 5 July 1883, by Captain Barrow, enclosed in Dispatch No. 295 of 21 Aug. 1883, from Rowe to Derby; CO/96/151.

[3] Minute of 12 Oct. 1883, by Hemming; ibid.

[4] Dispatch No. 422 of 29 Aug. 1884, from Young to Derby; CO/96/159.

[5] Minute of 24 July 1886, by Hemming; CO/96/174. The following year Hemming remarked, in passing, 'all natives are incorrigible liars'. Minute of 23 Feb. 1887; CO/96/179. A letter from the recently qualified barrister, J. Mensah Sarbah, on the jurisdiction of the Chiefs was coldly dismissed: 'he evidently knows nothing of what he writes about'. Minute of 4 Mar. 1887; CO/96/188.

[6] D. Kemp, *Nine Years at the Gold Coast* (London, 1898), pp. 74–75.

Inevitably the 'educated native' cry was raised during the agitation over the Public Lands Bill of 1897. 'Why Blame the Educated?' asked *The Gold Coast Methodist Times* on 30 April 1897. However patriotic, however constitutional their plans, they were always represented as 'discontented upstarts and amateur demagogues'; even if it were granted that every social and political movement originated with the educated class, that was no reason to brand them as criminals. The first A.R.P.S. petition went further than this, and set forth a definite claim to leadership on behalf of educated Africans. It was held that on the strength of the recommendations of the *1865 Report* the Kings, Chiefs, and other inhabitants had sent their sons to be educated in England, 'and to be trained there in the English system of Parliamentary Government and as professional men'. As a result, it was claimed, there was now an educated class capable of leadership: 'These gentlemen, from their education and position, have become the leaders of their fellow countrymen, by whom they are followed, trusted, and beloved.'[1]

There was a tendency sometimes to overlook the relative size of the educated minority; in fact, there could hardly have been as many as 200 Gold Coast Africans at that time who had received a higher education or travelled overseas.[2] But this small group included several men of high calibre, and if their right to leadership was rejected, certainly there was no one else who even claimed to represent the interests of the African population generally. As Casely Hayford put it: 'Does a native cease to be a native when once he is educated?'[3] Mensah Sarbah gave a very clear picture of the inevitable process involved in the creation of public opinion:

for all practical purposes, definite public opinion about the acts of the Government and legislature emanates from the educated classes, and whenever the untaught masses study and examine political questions which directly affect them, such as the Lands Bill of 1897 and the Town Councils Ordinance, they gain a great deal of their knowledge and ideas from what their privileged educated brethren tell them.[4]

The claim to educated leadership was to be repeated many times by Africans, and as frequently challenged by Europeans, during subsequent years.[5] Some

---

[1] *Report of the Proceedings of the Deputation from the Kings and Chiefs of the Western Province of the Gold Coast* (London, 1898).

[2] Some account of the leading educated personalities of the late nineteenth and early twentieth century, and some idea of their numbers, is given by C. F. Hutchison, *The Pen Pictures of Modern Africans and African Celebrities* (London, n.d.), written about 1928; and by M. J. Sampson, *Gold Coast Men of Affairs* (London, 1937).

[3] Published in the Gold Coast press, Sept. 1905, and quoted by Casely Hayford, *The West African Land Question*, p. 3.

[4] J. Mensah Sarbah, *Fanti National Constitution* (London, 1906), p. 239.

[5] For example, Casely Hayford's speech to the National Congress in 1920 (although his claims were strenuously denied by Nana Ofori Atta, as spokesman for the Chiefs); see Ch. X, p. 381, below. Cf. J. W. de Graft Johnson, *Towards Nationhood in West Africa* (London, 1928), p. 50: 'Why should not the educated African, who thoroughly understands his people to a degree nobody else can . . . take the lead in the forward march of progress?' At the same time, he felt it

administrators realized the contradictions inherent in British policy, which, as Sir John Rodger put it in 1909, involved turning out 'black and brown Englishmen' by the score, and 'cursing the finished article when the operation is complete'.[1] He did his best to reform the educational system; but Anglo-Saxon attitudes could not be reversed overnight.[2] As the numbers of the educated grew, so did their grievances, which gave an edge and an urgency to nationalist demands. Educational standards rose slowly, but not as slowly as opportunities, so that this merely intensified social and political frustrations.

Higher Appointments for Africans, 1872–1902

There is evidence that from the 1870's onwards educated Africans were becoming increasingly anxious over their prospects of employment and advancement.[3] Apart from the few attorneys who could make an independent living, and a certain number who had been trained for work in the Missions, the majority of them still looked to government service; but between 1850 and 1872 the numbers of the educated and the competition for employment had grown considerably.

When J. Pope Hennessy discussed the taking over of Elmina in 1872, G. E. Eminsang and other 'Free Burgers' held up the good policy of the Dutch on this matter as an example to the British. Pope Hennessy told them it was his earnest wish to employ educated Africans instead of Europeans as far as possible in every branch of the civil service. They replied that with such a policy the British Government was heartily welcome to Elmina;[4] and soon afterwards Eminsang himself was appointed as Civil Commandant. In Cape Coast the Chiefs and company leaders asked for preference to be given to 'educated Natives fit for Government appointments or employments'. They were particularly anxious about the competition of 'foreigners of their own colour';[5] but officials do not seem to have paid much attention to this distinction.

necessary to record 'a solemn protest against the malicious propaganda about the educated African'. In 1922 the Phelps-Stokes Commission was impressed by 'the small but influential group of educated Natives' in the main Gold Coast towns. 'Their blood-kinship with the Natives of the country marks a vital difference between them and the educated groups of Freetown and Liberia . . . they undoubtedly dominate the thought and action of the Native groups.' Jesse Jones, *Education in Africa*, p. 124.   [1] *The African Mail*, 9 July 1909.

[2] In 1945 Lord Hailey could still remark upon 'the preference for the uneducated over the educated native which is so much more conspicuous in British than in French territories'. *An African Survey* (Oxford, 2nd edn. 1945), p. 258.

[3] Cf. a Memorial of 1869 from the 'Sierra Leone native pastors' effusively thanking Kennedy for his appointment of an African as Chaplain of the Gambia, 'a post not hitherto known in the history of these settlements to have been filled by any in a full capacity except by Europeans'. Quoted by Horton, *Letters on the Political Condition of the Gold Coast*, no. ix. dated 2 May 1870

[4] Dispatch No. 38 of 4 Apr. 1872, from Pope Hennessy to Kimberley; CO/96/92.

[5] Memorial of 4 June 1872, from Chiefs and captains of the companies of Cape Coast to Pope Hennessy, enclosed in his Dispatch No. 93 of 29 Oct. 1872, to Kimberley; CO/96/94.

Lip-service was often paid to the argument that it was both convenient and economical to replace Europeans by suitably qualified Africans. Pope Hennessy wanted to act upon this, and supported Africanus Horton's application to succeed Ussher as Administrator. But his high opinion of the ability and zeal of the doctor—'one of the most useful officers on the Coast of Africa'[1]—did not impress Lord Kimberley, who remarked cuttingly that Horton's own letter was quite sufficient to prove his unfitness.[2] A few months later Horton, as Acting Civil Commandant of Sekondi, was criticized for his handling of a riot; the Secretary of State took this as confirmation of his worst doubts, and remarked, 'I fear except in quite subordinate posts we cannot safely employ natives.'[3] The recent dubious financial practices of the attorneys and others had prejudiced the standing and the prospects even of Africans of such undoubted calibre as Horton.

Nevertheless, as the jurisdiction—and the day-to-day business—of the Government increased, it became necessary to call upon more Africans to fill responsible posts. The Colonial Office was often reluctant to approve the appointment of further Europeans on the grounds of health, as well as economy; and when the post of District Commissioner fell vacant at Sekondi, the Governor was asked whether there was no African official he could recommend.[4] In 1883, of the forty-three 'higher posts' in the Gold Coast, nine were filled by Africans, including seven District Commissioners.[5] Clearly this involved less expense to the Government, for the thirty-four European posts required seventeen further Europeans on the staff as reliefs.[6]

The efficiency of African officials seems to have depended very much on the eye of the beholder. The first Post Office annual report was sent to London in 1885 by E. Rowland Cole,[7] and was received with approval by Sidney Webb, who remarked on the impossibility of obtaining annual reports from the English heads of the Constabulary and Audit Departments.[8] On the other hand, when an African District Commissioner was charged with misconduct, Hemming took it as 'another instance, of which we have already had so many, of the almost universal failure of the natives when placed in offices of trust & in a position of authority'.[9]

[1] Dispatch No. 90 of 24 Oct. 1872, from Pope Hennessy to Kimberley; CO/96/94.
[2] Minute of 22 Nov. 1872, by Kimberley; ibid.
[3] Minute of 21 Feb. 1873, by Kimberley; CO/96/96. By contrast, Ussher, who had been equally strongly criticized by Pope Hennessy for a similar failure in dealing with a riot at Elmina, and whose private life was not above reproach (he had been cited by Eminsang in a divorce case), later returned to the Gold Coast as Governor.   [4] Mar. 1880; CO/96/130.
[5] The five District Commissioners in the Gold Coast proper (excluding the Lagos Settlements) were J. S. Parker at Ada, J. Smith at Saltpond, J. Simons at Sekondi, C. Bartels at Winneba, and H. Vroom at Pram Pram. There were two Revenue and Customs officers: S. Bannerman and J. Hagan.
[6] Dispatch No. 337 of 18 Sept. 1883, from Rowe to Derby, and Minutes thereon; CO/96/151.
[7] Rowland Cole, from Sierra Leone, had been Postmaster since 1870, though his name did not appear in the 1883 list of 'higher posts', above.
[8] Minute of 21 May 1886, by Webb; CO/96/173.
[9] Minute of 18 July 1886, by Hemming; CO/96/174.

The conflicting pulls of family and public loyalty often created difficulties; sometimes African and European standards of expected conduct differed sharply. In 1887 Frans Smith of Sierra Leone was appointed Puisne Judge in the Western Province, and soon occasioned adverse reports. The Administrator complained that Smith's family connexions were prejudicial to his position as a Judge—for example, he was accused of favouring the clients of his barrister brother-in-law, P. Awoonor Renner—and that continual comment was being made by the community generally.[1] Hemming found in this case yet another difficulty in the way of employing Africans in high and responsible places. He pointed out with some justice that the number of educated families was small, and that they often intermarried; 'unfortunately they cannot be trusted to be impartial when dealing with their relatives'.[2] There seemed to be no way out of this; even if Smith could be exchanged for a replacement from some other territory, 'what Colony will put up with a black judge?'[3] But it was noted that the Governor had spoken highly of Smith, so this particular matter was put by.

It should be remembered that it was not only the so-called higher posts which carried enhanced privileges and prestige. Salaried employment was still so rare that even quite humble clerical jobs were keenly sought after; as Coleman says of a later period in Nigeria, the clerk was 'literally and figuratively closest to the European . . . the symbol of power, the object of emulation'.[4] In nineteenth-century Gold Coast society he was almost as noteworthy, and in his collar and tie commanded almost as much outward respect, as the lawyer or the doctor. He appeared to be in touch with, if not a member of, the ruling oligarchy, which had not yet become a rigid hierarchy.

It was not long before even junior civil servants found that political activities were a barrier to advancement. In 1886 T. Hutton Mills, a young clerk in the office of the Queen's Advocate, was dismissed for his part in a riot in Accra. It was alleged that he had shouted, 'We must kill all the white men to-day', and although Hutton Mills claimed that this was an inaccurate version of a remark he had never intended seriously, even an appeal to the Secretary of State failed to secure his reinstatement.[5] The Government seems thereafter to have been determined to make it clear that African civil servants

[1] Confidential Letter of 27 Oct. 1887, from White to Holland; CO/96/183.

[2] The fact that the Governor's son was Acting Queen's Advocate was probably regarded by some Africans as a worthy reward of his filial piety, rather than of his undoubted ability; and it would not have been publicly known that his transfer to the West Indies in 1888 was due to Colonial Office anxiety to avoid any appearance of nepotism. CO/96/188.

[3] Minute of 25 Nov. 1887, by Hemming; CO/96/183. This was hardly a fair comment. One of Smith's parents had been born in West Africa, but otherwise he was officially described as 'to all intents and purposes an English gentleman'. CO/96/340. A problem of accommodation was later created by his desire to live in European quarters, although he was not entitled to European leave.

[4] Coleman, Nigeria, p. 132.

[5] Dispatch No. 29 of 21 Jan. 1887, from Brandford Griffith to Stanhope, and Minutes thereon; CO/96/179.

should not be involved in any kind of public criticism of authority. Another political dismissal soon followed. J. Bright Davies, the Chief Clerk in the Colonial Secretary's office, was suspended for having signed—in company with a great many other inhabitants of Accra—a farewell address to an Assistant Inspector of Police which was alleged to reflect injuriously and libellously on his predecessors in office and the police in general. Bright Davies refused at first to give an explanation for what he later said he thought he could do in his private capacity as a citizen. His dismissal was partly due to the official desire to discredit this theory, but probably more to the fact that he was suspected of being a regular contributor to *The Western Echo*.[1]

The individuals concerned in these two episodes proceeded to make a name for themselves in what were virtually the only professions not controlled by the Government. Bright Davies became a prominent journalist—for some years he was editor of *The Gold Coast Independent*—which meant public esteem, if not a secure income. Hutton Mills went to England to read law, was called to the Bar in 1894, and after his return became a leading politician and member of the Legislative Council.

The legal profession was unique for both the political independence and the unprecedented income it offered to those who succeeded in qualifying.[2] For example, Awoonor Renner in 1888 turned down a senior government appointment on the grounds that he was making £1,000 a year from his private practice.[3] A lawyer's prestige was enhanced not only by this material affluence, but also by the fact that on occasions he could subject members of the ruling race to cross-examination. From this time onwards, it was noticeably the lawyers who took the lead in political movements, protests, deputations, and petitions. Their legal training and drafting ability, the wealth they had to contribute and their leisure to organize proved invaluable assets in the early days of the nationalist movement.

Those civil servants who were reasonably efficient at their work, and were prepared to keep quiet politically, were still sometimes given the opportunity to rise to higher ranks. Brandford Griffith clearly saw the need for training Africans to hold 'superior positions in the service of the Colony', largely on the grounds of economy. As an experiment, he granted George Ekem Ferguson, a young clerk in his office, a year's leave with pay for training in England in 1889.[4] Ferguson became a qualified surveyor, and was subse-

---

[1] Details of this incident are given in CO/96/175.

[2] The first qualified African lawyer to practise in the Gold Coast was J. Renner Maxwell, during 1883-4; he was followed by P. Awoonor Renner in 1884. J. Mensah Sarbah, the first lawyer entirely of Gold Coast descent, qualified in 1887.

[3] Confidential Dispatch of 15 Jan. 1889, from Brandford Griffith to Knutsford; CO/96/200.

[4] The Governor also recommended Ferguson's sister as Postmistress and Telegraph Clerk at Anomabu, in the belief that 'the admission of young ladies who are natives of the Colony to the public service is calculated to have a most useful, beneficial, and moralizing effect generally in the service'. Minute of 15 Apr. 1890, by Brandford Griffith, enclosed in his Dispatch No. 221 of 18 Sept. 1890, to Knutsford; CO/96/211.

quently employed not only in mapping large areas of the Gold Coast, but also in concluding numerous treaties which profoundly altered the shape of the country. His advancement opened the way for a modest extension of overseas training. Brandford Griffith realized that Ferguson's efficiency had more than repaid the expense; and, recalling the ability of other Africans who had qualified as barristers and doctors, he proposed that one four-year government scholarship should be granted annually. The Colonial Office was divided in its reactions. Hemming called the idea premature, and thought that Foreman of Works was the highest to which 'sharp boys' like Ferguson might attain; but the Permanent Under-Secretary approved the Governor's efforts to make use of local talent.[1]

A *cause célèbre* soon arose over the appointment and promotion of government doctors. In 1892 Dr. J. F. Easmon applied for the post of Chief Medical Officer. He came from Sierra Leone, where he had previously failed to secure a similar appointment, on the grounds that an African would be unsuitable. Now he urged that he had been an Assistant Colonial Surgeon since 1880, and had acted as Chief Medical Officer on eight occasions, for a total of four years. On the Governor's strong recommendation, he was appointed.

But evidently all was not well. Some Gãs resented this decision; and in 1894 Dr. B. W. Quartey Papafio went so far as to petition the Secretary of State against Easmon's promotion of another doctor, complaining that there was prejudice against himself and even enclosing testimonials from his own patients. He referred to the general 'antipathy and dislike' of the few Sierra Leone immigrants, and being the only native of the Gold Coast on the medical staff he feared further injustice.[2] An article attacking Easmon was published on 23 June 1894 in *The Gold Coast Chronicle* (partly owned by the Papafio family); and one result of this feud was the foundation by a group of Sierra Leoneans of a rival newspaper in Accra, *The Gold Coast Independent*, in 1895. By an ironic twist of fate, Dr. Easmon was suspended from the position of Chief Medical Officer in 1897, for being too closely associated with the management of *The Independent*, as well as for carrying on private practice, contrary to regulations.[3]

The removal of a Sierra Leonean did not open the way to a Gold Coast appointment. It was not long before another memorial came from Dr. Quartey Papafio, complaining that he had been passed over in favour of a European Chief Medical Officer. The Acting Governor admitted that Quartey Papafio was a very good and careful officer; but it was felt to be undesirable

---

[1] Confidential Dispatch of 24 Jan. 1893, from Brandford Griffith to Ripon, and Minutes thereon; CO/96/230.

[2] Petition of 30 June 1894, to Ripon from Quartey Papafio, forwarded by Brandford Griffith in his Dispatch No. 245 of 24 Aug. 1894; CO/96/247.

[3] Confidential Dispatch of 7 July 1897, from Maxwell to Chamberlain; CO/96/295. Also the voluminous Report of Commissioner of Enquiry *re* conduct of Dr. John Farrell Easmon; CO/96/296.

that the large number of European doctors should be 'under the orders of a native'. A new rule was therefore suggested, that Native Medical Officers should not be considered eligible for promotion beyond the rank of Senior Assistant Colonial Surgeon, and that of the two posts of that rank, one only should be open to them. The Colonial Office agreed in principle, but was reluctant to come out into the open: 'We can always justify a particular case, but an express rule would be open to objection'; there might be criticisms that could not easily be given an entirely satisfactory reply. So, with almost every justification except that of justice, it was decided to tell Quartey Papafio that 'other qualifications than seniority have to be taken into consideration'.[1]

By 1902 it seemed easier to come out frankly. A pamphlet drawn up for the new West African Medical Service stated that applicants must be of 'European' parentage; and an unpublished note makes it clear that this was designed to exclude Africans and Asiatics, not to include 'foreigners' from Europe.[2] A question was raised in the House of Commons concerning British-qualified Indian doctors, but Chamberlain dealt with this in summary fashion; privately, he thought it 'pretty clear to men of ordinary sense that British officers could not have confidence in Indian or native doctors'.[3]

Seven West African medical students at Edinburgh University (including F. V. Nanka-Bruce) had also seen this pamphlet, and persuaded the Dean of their Faculty to take the matter up on their behalf. They complained particularly that since the days of Horton and other African doctors there appeared to have been a complete reversal of policy.[4] A letter from the Colonial Office to Edinburgh closed the issue with a magnificent lack of logic:

there are special difficulties in the way of employing native doctors, even if fully qualified, to attend upon European officers, especially when stationed in the bush or at outstations. Qualified medical men of African parentage, however, although it is not proposed to employ them on the West African Medical Staff, are not excluded from public employment in West Africa.[5]

Exclusion and Frustration, 1897–1920

Before the turn of the century the doors of African opportunity were closing fast. As the complexities of government increased, so the requirements

[1] Dispatch No. 112 of 15 Mar. 1898, from Hodgson to Chamberlain, and Minutes thereon; CO/96/313. Dr. Quartey Papafio retired from government service in 1905. He began to take an active part in politics, and in 1912 was a member of the A.R.P.S. Forest Bill deputation, which suggests a connexion between the frustrated personal ambitions of the intelligentsia and their opposition to the Government on nationalist issues.
[2] Minute of 21 Mar. 1902, by R. L. Antrobus; CO/96/403.
[3] Minute of 29 Apr. 1902, by Chamberlain; ibid.
[4] Letter of 19 Mar. 1902, from Professor Sir William Turner, Edinburgh, to Chamberlain; ibid. The students appear to have been unaware of the appointment of Dr. R. A. Savage, a Nigerian graduate of Edinburgh, as Assistant Colonial Surgeon in 1901; but this was the last African medical appointment for many years.
[5] Letter of 5 May 1902, from Colonial Office to Turner; ibid.

for incoming officers were continually raised. Candidates for the post of District Commissioner had now to be either solicitors or barristers;[1] and we have already seen that legally qualified Africans preferred the higher rewards of private practice. There were few enough Africans who had the necessary experience or qualifications to take charge of a government department, and after Brandford Griffith's time there was a noticeable lack of enthusiasm to create opportunities for them to gain such experience, or to institute training and scholarship schemes.[2] No definite directive was laid down;[3] but the handful of Africans who were already in senior posts gradually dropped out, for various reasons, and no effort was made to find others to replace them.

In 1897, for example, the year of Ferguson's death and Easmon's suspension, a minor peccadillo on the part of Rowland Cole—he had lent money to a subordinate at a rate of interest that appeared 'usurious' to European eyes—led to a severe reprimand, and he did not remain long as Postmaster. The most senior African civil servant, H. Vroom, had earned a C.M.G. for his political services, and had acted for a time as Secretary for Native Affairs, before the office was properly established;[4] but he resigned from government service in 1901, after allegations of his interest in concession-mongering in the Wassaw district.[5] J. A. M'Carthy, from Sierra Leone, was Solicitor-General during the 1890's, and at times acted as Attorney-General; but he was eventually replaced by a European.[6] Over fifty years later, after two world wars, the appointment of African heads of departments was to be hailed as a major innovation.

In the early years of the twentieth century it was becoming easier to recruit Europeans for Gold Coast appointments. Research in tropical medicine, in which Chamberlain took a keen personal interest, laid the foundation for great improvements in health throughout West Africa;[7] the most immediate

[1] *Information regarding the Appointment of the District Commissioners of the Gold Coast Colony* (London, 1898). By 1899 there were only three African District Commissioners: H. Vroom, J. A. Williams, and A. W. Thompson. Dispatch No. 493 of 13 Nov. 1899, from Hodgson to Chamberlain; CO/96/345.

[2] Hodgson considered the Cambridge Senior Local Examination a waste of time and money, and recommended that it should be discontinued owing to the low numbers and quality of the candidates (in 1895 there were two, in 1896 four, and in 1897 three, none of whom passed 'or came near passing'). Confidential Dispatch of 18 June 1898, to Chamberlain; CO/96/317. But this was simply to tighten the vicious circle, and to remove one of the few openings to promotion.

[3] The Chief Commissioner of the Northern Territories, however, urged the Governor to reconsider his decision not to appoint any more Native Officers to the Gold Coast Regiment, since they had done so well in the north. Confidential Letter of 8 Mar. 1902, from Morris to Nathan; 1953 Acc. No. 1289, G.N. Archives.

[4] Confidential Dispatch of 20 Nov. 1895, from Maxwell to Chamberlain; CO/96/262.

[5] Evidence was later given of Vroom's interest in certain concessions made during the 1890's while he was District Commissioner at Tarkwa; e.g. by his cousin, W. E. Pietersen, in the Full Court, Cape Coast, 27 June 1905. P. Awoonor Renner, *Cases in the Courts of the Gold Coast Colony and Nigeria* (London, 1915), vol. i, pt. i.

[6] His son, Sir Leslie M'Carthy, who many years later became a Judge, still remembers this period at the turn of the century for the deliberate policy of replacing Africans by Europeans.

[7] J. L. Garvin, *The Life of Joseph Chamberlain*, vol. iv (London, 1951), ch. 85, 'Tropical Medicine'.

56681

effect was to reduce the death-rate among Europeans, once the causes of malaria were understood. The senior civil service expanded rapidly. There were 274 officers listed in 1908; but only five of these were Africans, and except for Judge Frans Smith (who had managed to retain his appointment since 1887) they were of comparatively junior rank.[1] There was intermittent public criticism of the quality of the European influx. Casely Hayford complained that entrance was not by competitive examination, as for the Indian Civil Service: 'Patronage rules the day at Downing Street.'[2]

It was the curtailment of opportunity for Africans that aroused most un-official comment. The lawyers had never been happy at their exclusion from native tribunals under the Ordinance of 1883. In the Legislative Council Mensah Sarbah argued that the gulf between the Government and the people could be bridged if more use were made of Africans for administrative pur-poses.[3] In 1910 a European unofficial member criticized the abolition of the post of Native Commissioner; the last two, he said, had recently been re-placed by inexperienced Europeans, who had had to be taught their work by clerks and interpreters.[4] Hutton Mills complained the following year of the discrimination against qualified African doctors, which did not exist in South-ern Nigeria and Sierra Leone. The Governor frankly admitted the difficulty caused by European officers, who often objected to being treated by Africans;[5] but Casely Hayford was unwilling to accept such arguments for a policy which he called 'nothing short of a scandal'.[6]

In 1913 the A.R.P.S. presented Sir Hugh Clifford with a memorandum which included the usual plea for 'competent and worthy natives' to be appointed to important administrative positions.[7] They did not anticipate much response to this. As Hutton Mills later publicly admitted: 'Prior to Your Excellency's arrival ... the educated natives, especially the lawyers, were beginning to entertain the fear ... that they were not wanted in the country.'[8] But immediately the tide began, however slowly, to turn. Clifford promised to give Africans an increasing share in the work of the administra-tion.[9] In Ceylon, where he had previously served, all the Crown Counsel, as

[1] The other four were: W. Bannerman, District Postmaster (first appointed 1905); S. H. Brew, Assistant Chief Clerk (1905); Alex Konuah, Sub-Assistant Treasurer (1901); and J. L. Minnow, 3rd Class Supervisor of Customs (1904). *The Gold Coast Civil Service List* (London, 1908).

[2] *Gold Coast Native Institutions*, p. 218. This had been a favourite theme of Fitzgerald: 'A really good administrator, at 2,500 *l.* a year, would be infinitely cheaper for the Coast than one of the wretched class of vicious or pompous humbugs.' *The African Times*, 28 Feb. 1873.

[3] *Legislative Council Minutes*, 2 Sept. 1907. Cf. Maxwell's complaint that 'the European public servants are, with two or three exceptions, wholly ignorant of the native languages and are not therefore in confidential communication with natives of any class'. Confidential Dispatch of 13 June 1895, to Ripon; CO/96/258.   [4] Grey, *Legislative Council Minutes*, 28 Oct. 1910.

[5] Hutton Mills and Thorburn, ibid. 6 Nov. 1911.

[6] *The West African Land Question*, p. 107.

[7] Memorandum of 16 May 1913, from A.R.P.S. to Clifford; ibid. app. B.

[8] *Legislative Council Minutes*, 1 May 1914.

[9] Ibid. 3 Oct. 1913. He also began a lengthy struggle behind the scenes to open the Medical

PLATE 3

a. The Legislative Council in 1907

From left to right, seated: Sir William Brandford Griffith (Chief Justice), Sir John Rodger (Governor), Major H. Bryan (Colonial Secretary).
Standing: A. Willoughby-Osborne (Attorney-General), J. P. Brown, W. C. F. Robertson (Secretary for Native Affairs, Extraordinary Member), C. Riby Williams (Treasurer), Giles Hunt, J. Mensah Sarbah.

b. The Legislative Council in 1919

From left to right, seated: Dr. B. W. Quartey-Papafio, H. M. Lewis (Treasurer), Togbui Sri II (Fia of Awunaga), A. R. Slater (Colonial Secretary), Nana Ofori Atta (Omanhene of Akim Abuakwa), Brigadier-General F. G. Guggisberg (Governor), Nana Amonoo V (Omanhene of Anomabu), R. W. Wilkinson (Acting Attorney-General), E. J. P. Brown, Dr. D. Alexander (Acting Principal Medical Officer), Lt.-Colonel C Harding (Commissioner of Eastern Province).
Standing: C. W. Welman (Acting Clerk of the Legislative Council), J. E. Casely Hayford, J. T. Furley (Secretary for Native Affairs), E. H. D. Nicolls (Director of Public Works), J. L. Atterbury (Acting Commissioner of Central Province), Captain P. Jeffs (Governor's Private Secretary), C. W. Pettit (Secretary for Works), H. E. G. Bartlett (Acting Commissioner of Western Province), J. I. Lauder (Acting Comptroller of Customs), F. Dawbarn.

well as the Solicitor-General, had been natives of the island. Now minor history was made in the Gold Coast when a young Ga lawyer, E. C. Quist, became the first African Crown Counsel in 1914. His experience was not altogether happy, and he soon resigned. The Governor considered that he had performed his duties creditably and fearlessly, but that there were special difficulties in taking responsibility for official prosecutions in a small community.[1] This episode appears to have retarded hopes of direct African appointments to senior posts. At the same time, there was practically no opportunity for them to work their way up from below.

There was by now virtually a complete dichotomy between the higher appointments reserved for Europeans, and the 'Native Subordinate Service', which offered the only openings for Africans. Allegations that there was no room at the top were closely linked with the mounting dissatisfaction over conditions and prospects in the lower ranks of the service. It had once been possible for 'sharp boys' like Vroom and Ferguson to be singled out for special service and the chance of promotion. As the Administration became more hierarchical it became clear that Africans were mainly required for routine duties. There was less opportunity for individual encouragement and more scope for dissatisfaction. The rigid demarcation between clerical and administrative posts was, of course, a tradition adopted from the British civil service, where it reflected existing class distinctions; but this did not make it easier to accept in the Gold Coast, where it appeared as an application of racial discrimination, and thus became politically important.[2]

Frustration and discontent had been building up within the service for some time. Up to 1896, government clerks had been classified in six groups, the maximum salary for each ranging from £18 to £200 per annum. There were only four officers at the top of the scale, however, and more than three-quarters of all the 233 clerks employed were receiving less than £80 per annum. A committee of inquiry then calculated that the lowest possible cost of living for a clerk was about £45 per annum, and recommended a minimum salary of £36 per annum. This was accepted, although it still meant that some educated Africans could not live without running into debt, unless helped by their families.[3] As more and more Europeans came in to fill the higher

---

Department to African doctors; see *Legislative Council Debates*, 2 Nov. 1918. But this battle was not won until Guggisberg's time.

[1] Ibid. Quist's resignation proved no handicap to a long and distinguished career, which eventually brought him to the position of first Speaker of Ghana's National Assembly.

[2] Cf. Coleman, *Nigeria*, p. 156.

[3] Report of Committee dated June 1896, and covering Dispatch No. 281 of 13 July 1896, from Hodgson to Chamberlain; CO/96/275. Some Europeans thought that even this was too high. One of them, in an address to the Royal Colonial Institute, asserted that an African clerk had few expenses, and that 'proportionately' he was really paid a higher salary than the average European official, who had to be 'ready to perform *any* duty at *any* moment, and very often without extra remuneration'. T. H. Hatton Richards (former Assistant Colonial Secretary), *The Gold Coast Colony* (Liverpool, 1897).

appointments, the number of African clerks employed continued to expand—and the new school-leavers had few alternatives to government employment. But their salaries remained static; the lowest grade continued for over twenty years to receive an amount that had been inadequate to meet the cost of living in 1896.

Within a year of his arrival Clifford turned his attention to the problems of the civil service. In 1913 he set up a committee to revise clerical salaries; their report, quickly produced, led to a reorganization of the service and a revision of all salaries—costing an additional £6,000—although the starting rate remained at £36 per annum. The strength of feeling against higher-paid Europeans was illustrated in 1916 by the first independent act of the African unofficial members of the newly enlarged Legislative Council. They all formally declined to support the proposed salary increases for junior European officers, which were based on the report of another committee, and had already been delayed over a year; they also asked for the abolition of existing duty allowances.[1] These were officially regarded as an integral part of a European officer's salary while he was in the Gold Coast, not as a special privilege, and their abolition would have meant a total cut in remuneration of £25,000. Despite all explanations and arguments, the African members still felt that European salaries were excessive; and they resented it when the Colonial Secretary accused them of administering a stab in the back to over-worked civil servants.[2]

In 1918, as a result of petitions from both sections of the service, the European war bonus was increased, and a similar bonus was introduced for 'Native subordinates'; both these payments were approved by the Legislative Council without demur.[3] The Governor realized, however, that grievances still existed, and a Commissioner came out from England to examine all official salaries. As a result, proposals came direct from the Secretary of State for a 10 per cent. war bonus to be paid to African officials; and in anticipation of this, they received one month's advance of salary in January 1919. But there were immediate protests that this was insufficient, and a deputation of clerks asked the Governor for a bonus of 20 per cent. Dissatisfied with his answer, they telegraphed their demand to the Colonial Office, threatening to take extreme measures, which might 'clog the wheels of the administrative machinery'.[4]

This uncompromising attitude might have ruined the clerks' chances, had it not been for some strategic manœuvring by both sides in the Legislative Council. When the motion for a 10 per cent. bonus came up for discussion, Casely Hayford attempted to move that it should be raised to 25 per cent., but was ruled out of order as that would be a financial resolution. Never-

---

[1] Protest of 28 Oct. 1916, by Hutton Mills, Nana Ofori Atta, Nana Amonu V, Togbui Sri, Casely Hayford, and E. J. P. Brown; printed as app. III to the Supply Bill, 1917.

[2] *Legislative Council Debates*, 30 Oct. 1916.   [3] Ibid. 19 Aug. 1918.

[4] Deputation of 8 Feb. to Clifford, and Telegram of 10 Feb. 1919, to Milner; quoted by Colonial Secretary, ibid. 19 Feb. 1919.

theless, he was allowed to speak very much to the point, and the other un-official members strongly urged the necessity for an increase. The Governor heard them sympathetically, promised to telegraph their sentiments to the Secretary of State, and persuaded them to support the original 10 per cent. motion, in token of co-operation.[1] As a result, Lord Milner eventually agreed to a war bonus ranging from 12 to 20 per cent. for the lowest-paid African clerks, which was announced in the Legislative Council in June 1919, amid the exchange of mutual courtesies between officials and unofficials.[2] By the end of the year the African members were only too ready to approve the extension of a war bonus to civil servants earning over £700, who had not previously received it. 'I personally think that every encouragement should be given to the European officials', said Casely Hayford.[3]

All might be sweet reasonableness within the Legislative Council, but it was not so in the civil service, where personal relationships were deteriorating rapidly. In February 1919 a most revealing petition had been sent to the Secretary of State, praying for the recall of the Colonial Secretary, A. R. Slater; it was signed by practically every government clerk in Accra, right up to his Chief Clerk in the Secretariat, F. J. Ribeiro. Slater was particularly disliked because he would not support the demand for a 20 per cent. bonus; it was also alleged that he had on other occasions failed to support the legiti-mate requests of the clerical staff, including a claim for the supply of free false teeth. Significantly, Slater was accused of being 'a Negrophobist' and hence incapable of dealing fairly with questions affecting their interests.[4]

This petition is important not for its result—since it achieved precisely nothing[5]—but for the discontent it revealed within the service. There was a general impression that grievances did not get a fair hearing, combined with frustration over the lack of opportunities for advancement, and jealousy of higher-paid Europeans. *The Gold Coast Independent* alleged that Africans, however highly qualified, were kept out of even acting appointments in order to prevent their access to secret files of 'confidential humbug and untruthful tales'.[6] There was, in fact, almost a complete breakdown of confidence between Africans and Europeans, which even a long-overdue revision of salary scales could do little to remedy.

[1] *Legislative Council Debates*, 19 Feb. 1919.

[2] Ibid. 30 June 1919.

[3] Ibid. 17 Nov. 1919.

[4] Petition of 20 Feb. 1919, to Milner; 'Despatches relating to a Petition from Native Officials in the Gold Coast Praying for the Recall of the Colonial Secretary', *Sessional Paper No. III of 1918–19*.

[5] Clifford found the petition 'more acutely distressing than any local event' during his admini-stration. The Secretary of State commented on the lack of intelligence and sense of responsibility of those who had signed it, and asked for separate reports at the end of six months on the most senior of them. Ibid. It was Slater himself, as Acting Governor, who later forwarded these, and reported the restoration of confidence and normal relations. 'Further Despatches relating to the Petition from Native Officials in the Gold Coast Praying for the Recall of the Colonial Secretary', *Sessional Paper No. I of 1919–20*.

[6] *The Gold Coast Independent*, 26 Apr. 1919.

The war-time and post-war rise in the cost of living was a serious problem for all those urban workers who could not fall back upon the reserves of the subsistence economy. The lower-paid clerical employees were least equipped to stand the strain, and their economic grievances were harder to bear when colour, not efficiency, seemed to be the bar to promotion and greater economic security. A series of petitions and committees during the years 1919–20 indicated the growing urgency of the situation.

In April 1919, for example, Clifford authorized an official inquiry into a complaint against inadequate emoluments and unsatisfactory conditions of service, lodged by 361 African clerks.[1] The committee was also asked 'to make suggestions with a view to satisfying the legitimate aspirations and securing the contentment of the Gold Coast Native Officials'—phraseology which marked a new concern with the psychological welfare of the service. The result was a new salary scheme for African civil servants, which was announced later in the year, after Clifford had left. At last the starting rate for clerks was to be raised, from £36 to £48 per annum, giving them 'a straight run up to £180'; the number of higher clerical appointments was also to be increased from twenty-six to fifty.[2]

Even this did not satisfy the clerks for long; only a few months later they were urgently demanding fresh salary scales—and some immediate relief—to meet the soaring cost of living.[3] F. G. Guggisberg, the new Governor, responded by authorizing an immediate 'temporary' increase in the war bonus;[4] further than that, he set up a new Native Civil Service Committee to reconsider the matter on a much wider basis, including not only salaries but promotion policy. The six members, who included Casely Hayford and M. C. Hansen, set to work in July 1920; unfortunately for the clerks, however, they proved over-enthusiastic advocates, and even a sympathetic Governor found their salary recommendations 'embarrassing in their liberality'.[5] More modest proposals were then made by the Government, but even these were rejected by Winston Churchill, the new Secretary of State, towards the end of 1921; the most he could concede was the incorporation of the war bonus, already being paid, into existing salary scales. This brought the clerks' starting rate, for example, up to £60.[6]

[1] Petition of 31 Dec. 1918, to Clifford; 'Report of a Committee appointed by the Governor to Enquire into the Conditions of Service of Native Officials', *Sessional Paper No. V of 1918–19*.

[2] Colonial Secretary, *Legislative Council Debates*, 17 Nov. 1919. Also 'Despatches relating to the Native Officials' Salary Scheme', *Sessional Paper No. XV of 1918–19*.

[3] Petition of 17 Feb. 1920, to Guggisberg; 'Report of Committee of Enquiry on the Native Civil Service', *Sessional Paper No. VII of 1920–21*.

[4] The increased bonus was paid as from 1 Jan. 1920 to Native Subordinate (pensionable) staff at a rate varying from £12 per annum for 4th Class officers to £36 for Special Class officers; the total cost was £39,000 per annum. Colonial Secretary, *Legislative Council Debates*, 25 May 1920.

[5] Confidential Dispatch of 17 May 1921, from Guggisberg to Churchill; G.N. Archives.

[6] Dispatch of 1 Nov. 1921, from Churchill to Guggisberg; 'African Civil Service', *Sessional Paper No. I of 1922–23*.

The unavoidable publicity in the Gold Coast, and an inexcusable delay over the decision in London, due partly to a ministerial change, made this eventual disappointment even more galling. Here was a ready-made nationalist grievance, which provides a revealing background to the new-style agitation and demands of Casely Hayford's National Congress of British West Africa.[1]

The Post-war Demand for Equal Opportunity

The main business of Guggisberg's Native Civil Service Committee was, however, to advise on the conditions under which Africans should be appointed to the higher posts usually held by Europeans. This was a subject that Clifford had had very much at heart; in 1918 he had assured the Legislative Council that the time would come for extending African opportunities 'far further than is at present possible'.[2] But public opinion was not content to hasten slowly, and the demand for a more liberal policy was increasing, both inside and outside the Legislative Council.

The pressure was intensified by the feeling that Africans deserved a greater share in the administration of their own country, having contributed substantially to the war effort.[3] A correspondent to *The Gold Coast Nation* had asked in 1915: 'What will be the effect on us Natives, as regards our condition, after the War, from the fact of so many Black races fighting alongside with the White? . . . Is there any difference in the Souls of men, who willingly have laid down their lives for the glorious British Empire . . . ? In 1918 the same newspaper urged, among the necessary post-war changes in 'this hoary system of Crown Colony Government', that merit and not colour should be the qualification for higher appointments.[4] *The Gold Coast Independent* attacked the deliberate exclusion of qualified Africans from responsible positions both in government service and in commercial firms. Such discrimination on the grounds of colour, 'for which our Creator alone is responsible', was condemned as contrary to British tradition.[5] The most painful grievances were aired in the Legislative Council, and critical suggestions by Hutton Mills included the appointment of an African as Attorney-General.[6]

The old beliefs in the incapacity of Africans were fading in the face of reality; to take one small example, after eighteen years' insistence on white men as engine-drivers it was now admitted that Africans were replacing them successfully.[7] No doubt the critics underestimated some of the difficulties;

---

[1] See Ch. X, 'The A.R.P.S. and the National Congress', below.

[2] *Legislative Council Debates*, 2 Nov. 1918.

[3] For details of Gold Coast contributions, in arms and men, see Ch. X, p. 376, and Ch. XIII, p. 545 n., below.   [4] *The Gold Coast Nation*, 11 Nov. 1915, and 24–31 Aug. 1918.

[5] *The Gold Coast Independent*, 14 Sept. 1918.

[6] But Clifford took the view that African lawyers should first accept lower-paid appointments and then work their way upwards, instead of claiming to step from lucrative private practice straight into one of the senior government posts. *Legislative Council Debates*, 2 Nov. 1918.

[7] Grey, ibid.

what they felt most keenly was a sense of injustice and inequality of status in that the doors were closed to them. There was a tendency to hark back to the old days and to think that Africans could move straight to the senior posts they had occupied in an earlier, less complex system. As *The Gold Coast Independent* put it: 'every office from that of the Governorship downwards has been held by a black or coloured man . . . No amount of disparaging of their descendants will obliterate the fact.'[1]

Nevertheless, the newspapers were almost pathetically eager in their welcome to two African appointments made by Clifford early in 1919,[2] even though these were not at the most senior level. C. E. Woolhouse Bannerman, a barrister, was made a Police Magistrate, and Dr. C. E. Reindorf became a temporary Medical Officer. Casely Hayford congratulated the Government on this tentative step forward, although he was careful to reserve his hopes for the time 'when even higher posts will be accessible to Natives, and men will be found to fill them', if possible chosen from the ranks of the clerical service, like some early District Commissioners, such as Vroom, Williams, Thompson, and Minnow.[3]

Guggisberg simply added his own characteristic drive to the policy already initiated by Clifford; but his approach captured the public imagination in a way his predecessors had never done. At one of his first meetings with the Legislative Council he had announced, 'Our policy is to employ every suitably qualified native that we can', and urged that improved technical training was essential to progress.[4] The Native Civil Service Committee produced recommendations which were very much in line with Guggisberg's own views on higher appointments, so that there was little difficulty over implementation. They even prepared a draft public statement on policy, containing the following pledges:

The Government desire so to develop the country and so to educate the people that they may gradually replace Europeans in the Higher Appointments . . .

Any Higher Appointment which the Government consider could with no loss of efficiency direct or indirect be held by any African will be thrown open and the vacancy notified in the Government *Gazette* in addition to the newspapers in England.

The draft also included a reference to the proposed reorganization of the educational system; but it was stressed that the qualifications required of Africans could not be lowered without detriment to the country. The scope for exceptional promotion, based on outstanding service or personal qualities, might be tested by acting appointments.[5]

The African members of this committee had promised a minority report

[1] 12 Apr. 1919.

[2] For example, *The Eastern Star*, quoted in *West Africa*, 14 June 1919.

[3] Casely Hayford, *Legislative Council Debates*, 4 July 1919.

[4] Guggisberg, ibid. 17 Nov. 1919.　　　　　[5] *Sessional Paper No. VII of 1920-21.*

on certain matters; but its completion was delayed by Casely Hayford's absence in England on the National Congress deputation.[1] It was no mere coincidence that one of the items in the 1920 Congress petition and memorandum concerned the 'invidious distinctions' in the West African Civil Service. The Congress demanded that discrimination should be avoided and appointments made to depend on merit and not on colour, race, or creed; they also urged that duly qualified and experienced legal men should be admitted to judicial posts, and that the Medical Service should be thrown open to Africans without reservation, since the large African population needed their services, whatever might be the views of Europeans.[2]

Such egalitarian demands had figured prominently from the start of the National Congress. Hutton Mills and Casely Hayford had urged that both Europeans and Africans should submit to the same qualifying examination, on the basis of which all appointments in the civil service should be made.[3] Dr. H. C. Bankole-Bright had spoken out against the unjust treatment of African medical practitioners, and Dr. F. V. Nanka-Bruce had been attacking discrimination ever since his student days in Edinburgh. The Deputy Governor, who attended the inaugural Conference, had summed up their main objects as 'a reform of the Legislative Councils on some electoral basis and to press for the throwing open of higher administrative posts to Natives'.[4] The Congress movement as a whole well illustrates the grievances, ambitions, and wounded self-esteem of those who had long felt themselves denied any proper part in public affairs and administration. It is hardly surprising that Casely Hayford preferred to take their demands to London rather than wait for slow, unspectacular committee wheels to grind out results that so often before had proved unsatisfactory.

But this Governor was in earnest. During 1920 Guggisberg's efforts resulted in the creation of twenty 'special class' appointments for Africans, instead of bringing in more Europeans; and estimates for the next year allotted them a further seventeen such posts. Early in 1921 he outlined to the Legislative Council a progressive programme for the gradual replacement of at least 50 per cent. of existing European staff. This was not only desirable but essential for economy.[5] There had already been considerable retrenchment during the war;[6] the reduced establishment had been able to carry on to meet the

---

[1] Guggisberg, *Legislative Council Debates*, 4 Feb. 1921.   [2] See Ch. X, p. 384, below.

[3] Cf. the article by 'Ex-Governor' in *West Africa*, 15 Mar. 1919, urging the introduction of examinations for entry into the West African Civil Service. He was thinking mainly of European candidates; but a week later the same newspaper published a symposium on 'The West African Civil Servant', in which it was suggested: 'The educated Native is knocking at the door, and we are timorous about opening the portal. Africa is becoming articulate, and telling us things which make us uncomfortable.' Ibid. 22 Mar. 1919.

[4] Dispatch No. 289 of 9 Apr. 1920, from Harper to Milner; 'Correspondence relating to the National Congress of British West Africa', *Sessional Paper No. VII of 1919–20*.

[5] Guggisberg, *Legislative Council Debates*, 21 Jan. 1921.

[6] In Aug. 1914 the European establishment numbered 613 officers. Three years later this had

emergency, but now, with the new Governor's plans for post-war social and economic expansion, more staff were urgently needed. The obvious answer was to employ Africans; and Guggisberg felt that such a policy would in itself do a great deal to develop the country.

The African members of the Legislative Council were not yet willing to take anything on trust. E. J. P. Brown at once asked why the Africans to be promoted to Assistant Colonial Secretary and Assistant Treasurer were to have the word 'Junior' attached to their titles. He demanded 'the opportunity to show that we can be trusted to hold positions of trust', and attacked the tendency of some heads of departments to quote individual failures as a reason for excluding Africans. C. J. Bannerman also criticized the recommendation that an African should get 20 per cent. less pay than a European holding the same post, which he called 'unworthy of this Council . . . unworthy of the English Crown . . . unworthy of anything English'.[1]

The critics were answered by further plans for reform. In June 1921 Guggisberg produced an outline for reorganization into a Senior Service (mainly but not exclusively European), a Junior Service (for pensionable African staff and those appointed to replace Class B Europeans), and a Subordinate Service (including learners, artisans, road overseers, &c.). This was designed to provide 'a definite path of promotion from the lowest to the highest service and to carry out the Government policy for the steady replacement of Europeans by Africans'.[2] Pending the Secretary of State's consideration of this scheme, the 1922 estimates included twenty additional appointments for Africans to hold posts generally classified as European, and it was stated that twenty-one more would be promoted to the senior division of the Junior Service, where formerly Europeans had been employed.[3]

Progress, however, was not yet fast enough to satisfy impatient Africans, nor even the Governor himself, who had foreseen some but not all of the difficulties. The enforced retrenchment of 1922–3 meant a general reduction in staff and prevented many new appointments being made; but by 1924 Guggisberg made it clear that further economy must depend on a settled policy of appointing qualified Africans. He was now willing to employ as many as were available even at the cost of 'a slight loss of efficiency',[4] thus going even further than the 1920 Native Civil Service Committee had proposed.

Once again the question of medical appointments was to provide a test for

been reduced to 521, but with the secondment of others for military service only 430 were actually available for duty, i.e. a reduction of 30 per cent. Clifford, *Legislative Council Debates*, 24 Oct. 1917.

[1] E. J. P. Brown and C. J. Bannerman, ibid. 4 Feb. 1921. The principle became entrenched, despite repeated attacks over the years. Guggisberg held, and his successors reiterated, that 'There are certain conditions of service in this tropical country that justify a slightly higher rate being given to the European'. Ibid.

[2] Memorandum of 23 June 1921, by Guggisberg; G.N. Archives.

[3] Guggisberg, *Legislative Council Debates*, 27 Feb. 1922.

[4] Ibid. 6 Mar. 1924.

official sincerity, in the eyes of public opinion. African doctors had to go abroad to qualify, and on returning had difficulty in obtaining the necessary clinical experience for government service. During 1924, therefore, a new class of Junior African Medical Officers was created, at a salary of £400 per annum; these men would be employed on hospital work until they were considered sufficiently experienced for appointment as full Medical Officers. When this scheme was published,[1] the Gold Coast medical practitioners declared that they were 'aggrieved and humiliated' by it. This was partly explained by the fact that neither of the two African doctors already holding senior appointments was of Gold Coast origin. Even after the Governor had fully explained the reasons for the scheme, early in 1925, and had outlined his long-term ambition for a Gold Coast degree of medicine that should be accepted throughout the world, Casely Hayford objected to the procedure whereby regular appointments were to be left to the discretion of the Director of Medical Services. His speech revealed how deep-rooted were African suspicions: 'until we knocked and knocked and knocked at the time, the West African Medical Staff was a closed door: they did not want us to get in. It was a question whether we were ever going to get in at all.'[2]

The following year the Governor had an opportunity to demonstrate his good faith. The first African to complete his course as a Junior Medical Officer, Dr. E. Tagoe, was posted to Dunkwa; but there were immediate protests from the non-official European community, who organized a hostile petition and even a long-range question in the House of Commons. Guggisberg stood firm, and refused to transfer the doctor; and his handling of the incident was such that E. J. P. Brown publicly congratulated him: 'you have touched the heart of the whole country'.[3]

But there remained the problem of securing sufficient qualified Africans to replace Europeans in other departments. One method was to increase the opportunities for in-service training, which had been intensified since 1919. As far as long-term policy was concerned, the Governor declared that 'we depend entirely on Achimota College and on the secondary system of education that the latter will in due course bring into being throughout the country'.[4]

The Drive of the 1920's

From the start, the keystone of what would now be called Guggisberg's Africanization policy had been the intensive development of educational opportunities. After the financial stringency of the war, the need for making

---

[1] *Gold Coast Gazette*, 2 Aug. 1924.
[2] Guggisberg and Casely Hayford, *Legislative Council Debates*, 3 and 24 Feb. 1925.
[3] Guggisberg and E. J. P. Brown, ibid. 3 and 24 Mar. 1927.
[4] Guggisberg, ibid. 6 Mar. 1924.

up lost ground was urgent.[1] The political accident of the expulsion of the Basel and Bremen missionaries meant that the Government was directly responsible for 60 per cent. of the schools in the country, as compared with about 8 per cent. in 1914;[2] this gave it a much closer control of the educational system than before, with a correspondingly greater chance of reform and development.

The intense African interest in education has already been noticed, with special reference to secondary schools. Clifford declared in 1919: 'Never in the course of my experience of the tropics have I found a place where the people were so avid of education. It is the only country, I fancy, where the schoolboy, without being a prig, is more anxious to go to school than his parents are to send him.'[3] He had already appointed a special committee under D. Kingdon, the Attorney-General, to make recommendations for the educational system;[4] but it was not until Guggisberg's arrival that the opportunity for advance was seized with characteristic energy. The new Governor was especially disappointed that the latest estimates had not made provision for a government secondary school—a project he felt the Colony could not afford to delay. He was even more dismayed at the lamentable state of affairs in education which could be discerned between the lines of the Kingdon report; but there was an urgent need for more far-reaching reforms than they had suggested, for it was the whole system which was to blame.[5]

In an unprecedented statement to the Legislative Council, designed 'to take into our confidence the people of this country', Guggisberg outlined in 1920 a twelve-point policy for education, describing both the immediate steps he proposed to take, and the educational structure that should ultimately emerge. His list of promised reforms showed up by implication the worst defects of the existing system: ill-paid, inefficient teachers; examinations regarded as the object, not just the test, of education; inappropriate textbooks;[6] the lack of practical and industrial work; the neglect of girls' education; and the widespread belief that school stopped at Standard VII. This last point was to be tackled by the establishment of a first-class secondary school, a project which was already taking shape in Guggisberg's mind. But he planned a

---

[1] Guggisberg declared, 'the greatest evil of the war which concerns the progress of the Gold Coast people has been the delay in extending our educational system'. *Legislative Council Debates*, 17 Nov. 1919.   [2] *Departmental Reports*, Education, 1929–30.

[3] Report of speech by Clifford in *West Africa*, 21 June 1919.

[4] 'Report of the Special Committee appointed by His Excellency Sir Hugh Clifford to Report upon and to make such Recommendations as seem desirable in the Educational System of the Gold Coast', *Sessional Paper XVII of 1918–19*.

[5] Guggisberg, *Legislative Council Debates*, 26 Nov. 1919, and 23 Feb. 1920.

[6] This matter had been 'under consideration' since 1889, when the Board of Education had suggested 'the introduction of a Reading Series containing stories and lessons bearing upon life in Africa, and therefore more generally suitable than Nelson's Reading Series which frequently deal with matters wholly unfamiliar to the children of this Colony; but for the present Nelson's Series up to Standard IV is approved for use.' Circular of 7 Sept. 1889, from Board of Education at Accra; CO/96/204. And there the matter had remained.

thorough reorganization, covering infant, primary, and secondary schools, industrial, technical, and clerical education, teacher training, and evening classes for older men. As a preliminary measure the Governor announced that he was forming an Educationists' Committee to consider his proposals in detail. Even before they had reported, the Education Department would be expanded, increasing grants would be paid to assisted schools,[1] a site would be selected for the government secondary school, and the other departments would step up their own training programmes.

These points were to be elaborated and added to by the Governor over succeeding years in his frequent public addresses, memoranda, and directives to committees. On this first occasion he was really thinking aloud, casting his ideas in an habitual numbered sequence that gave them an impressive authority. What was so new, however, was his desire to carry the people with him, by public discussion of his policies in advance, by detailed consideration in committees on which Africans were fully represented, and by insisting on speedy action once decisions had been taken. In educational matters Guggisberg was more impatient than the nationalists, and often forestalled their demands, having a clearer idea of what was wrong. Certainly nothing quite like this had ever been heard in the Legislative Council before. Casely Hayford at once rose to congratulate the Governor on his statement, and for taking the educated community into his confidence;[2] the other unofficial members were left speechless.

Guggisberg was as good as his word. Action followed immediately, and a few days later the Educationists' Committee commenced their daunting task, which was virtually to consider the past, present, and future of education in the Gold Coast.[3] Their terms of reference included a long list of detailed questions, and a request for a programme of action for the periods 1921–2, 1923–5, and 1926–30. The Governor was careful to associate the Chiefs, as far as possible, with his new plans; and Nana Ofori Atta wrote to the Committee urging that 'the student should be imbued with the true ideals of his country . . . to enable him to adapt himself to the customs, manners and institutions of the place to which he belongs'.[4]

The 1920 Educationists' Committee produced a voluminous report, which included an historical survey and detailed recommendations covering the whole range of educational activity. Special attention was paid to the proposed government secondary school, including the selection of the Achimota site,

---

[1] In fact, the grants paid for 1920 were more than treble the total for 1919; see tables on pp. 78, above and 120, below.   [2] *Legislative Council Debates*, 23 Feb. 1920.

[3] The members were: the Director of Education, D. J. Oman (Chairman); Archdeacon G. W. Morrison of Kumasi; J. Spio-Garbrah (the only African member); the Rev. S. J. Gibson; the Rev. A. W. Wilkie; and a secretary appointed from the Education Department.

[4] 'Report of the Educationists' Committee appointed by His Excellency the Governor on 5th March, 1920, to advise the Government on Educational Matters, together with Minutes of the Meetings of the Committee', *Sessional Paper No. IV of 1919–20*.

the house system, the appointment of staff, the general content of secondary education, and the need for a new teacher-training college to be built near by. Many of Guggisberg's other proposals were whole-heartedly endorsed. New salary scales were set out for teachers—women to receive the same as men— and increased rates of grants for assisted schools, conditional upon their payment of the new salaries. It was urged that expenditure on education, in view of its 'supreme importance', should be regarded as a first charge on government revenue; an indication of the new approach was the recommendation that the Director of Education should be given a seat on the Legislative Council— a point that had probably not even occurred to anyone before.

The Committee sounded a new and significant note in regard to religious training: 'It should be our aim to maintain whatever is good in African custom, institution or thought. One inestimable good is the close relation in African thought between religion and the common things of life.'[1] The Governor was thinking along similar lines, and he declared soon afterwards that the dangerous gap between the 'vast masses composing the stools' and the educated communities of the towns could only be closed by 'more and better education', not less.[2] If carried out in the right way, this could be used to strengthen native institutions, as well as to encourage the development of individual character, responsibility, and citizenship.[3]

Guggisberg began to implement some of the Committee's more urgent recommendations even before their report had been printed. During 1921 the Accra Technical School was enlarged, the teacher-training course was extended from two years to three, and infant teaching was reorganized, with special attention to the use of the vernacular; pupil-teaching, which had been condemned as merely 'a means of obtaining cheap labour', was abolished.[4] The first major innovation, however, was the establishment of four Junior Trade Schools in 1922, in widely separated parts of the country—Yendi, Mampong-Ashanti, Asuantsi, and Kibi—with strong support from the local Chiefs. A four-year course was offered to ex-Standard III boys, their work including useful trades—carpentry, bricklaying, and road-making—as well as food-farming and the care of cash crops such as cocoa and palm oil.[5]

All these developments cost money. The annual expenditure on education had risen from £17,000 in 1910 to £56,000 in 1920, and again to nearly £100,000 by 1921–2. But this was only the beginning; the increase had been

---

[1] *Sessional Paper No. IV of 1919–20.*

[2] E. J. P. Brown agreed with the Governor that 'the higher a man's education the more he becomes imbued with race pride, and the less will be the tendency to break away from immemorial customs'. *Legislative Council Debates*, 4 Feb. 1921.

[3] Guggisberg, ibid. 21 Jan. 1921.

[4] *Departmental Reports*, Education, 1921. The rate of pay for pupil teachers in 1920 was £4. 8s. to £8 per annum, with a few fortunate exceptions who received as much as £12, according to the Educationists' Committee.

[5] Memorandum of 18 Feb. 1921, by Guggisberg; Board 252, M.P. 3962, G.N. Archives. Also 'Junior Trade Schools of the Gold Coast Colony', *Sessional Paper VII of 1923–24.*

spent mainly on bigger grants, and higher salaries for more staff. The extension of the system as a whole was yet to come, and might cost up to half a million annually. Such sums were out of the question on current budgets; and this explains the Governor's determination to press on with his Ten-Year Development Plan, which he considered the only means of equipping the country to earn the revenue that would finance the necessary social and economic developments.[1]

Educational progress in the Gold Coast was not proceeding in isolation from the outside world. A welcome stimulus came from the visit of the Phelps-Stokes Commission on Education in Africa, which included among its members J. E. K. Aggrey, a Fanti from Anomabu who had spent twenty-two years studying and teaching in the U.S.A.[2] This inquiry, financed by an American charitable bequest 'for educational purposes in the education of Negroes both in Africa and the United States', and planned in conjunction with missionary bodies, visited the Gold Coast in 1920, and eventually covered most of Africa south of the Sahara. Its importance for the Gold Coast lay not so much in the 1922 survey and recommendations, useful though these were, as in the fact that it focused attention on the needs and problems of African education, and encouraged local administrators to study the experiments that had been made among American Negroes. As a direct result, the Director of Education visited the Southern States, where he was deeply impressed by the kind of work carried on at Hampton and Tuskegee Institutes, especially in industrial training and community projects.[3]

When the Phelps-Stokes report, prepared by T. Jesse Jones, was published, Guggisberg greeted it as 'the book of the century, a combination of sound idealism and practical common sense'.[4] In it he found many of his most cherished principles given wide publicity: for example, rural improvement, girls' education, character training, the pressing need for secondary schools, and especially for the co-operation of the people themselves. Education, it was stressed, must 'conserve what is sound in Native life and transmit the best that civilization and Christianity have to offer'. Small wonder that the Commission found Guggisberg's own plans for the Gold Coast 'among the most significant governmental movements for education observed in Africa'.[5]

An important section of the report was devoted to 'Native leadership'. The Commission urged that African education must cater both for the masses and for the leaders, but that the latter must be trained directly for service to the community. In particular, they criticized the universal tendency to discount African leaders, whether this sprang from a failure in understanding,

---

[1] Guggisberg, *Legislative Council Debates*, 27 Feb. 1922.
[2] For details of Aggrey's remarkable career, see E. W. Smith, *Aggrey of Africa* (London, 1929).
[3] 'Report by the Director of Education on his Visit to Educational Institutions in the United States', *Sessional Paper No. IV of 1922-23*.
[4] Guggisberg, *Legislative Council Debates*, 1 Mar. 1923.
[5] Jesse Jones, *Education in Africa*, chs. i–v *passim*.

I

from antagonism, or from the wrong type of education. The Commission stated, as a new guiding principle, that 'Every people must have some of its own to serve as leaders'; and they added a good word for the 'increasing enthusiasm of Native peoples' for self-determination and 'nationalization', provided this was based on self-respect, rather than on distrust or hostility towards other peoples.[1]

This semi-official recognition of African needs and aspirations was received with mixed feelings in the Gold Coast. In many ways it was balm to African self-respect, and helped to secure support for educational progress. But the report aroused controversy in the United States, where W. E. B. Du Bois attacked it for supporting the Booker T. Washington doctrines of racial co-operation, and for encouraging Negroes to study agriculture, where white men would 'cheat them out of a decent income'. These arguments were later taken up and repeated by *The Gold Coast Leader*, which accused Jesse Jones of attempting 'to make the African fit in with the European's scheme of African exploitation and control'.[2]

The report was closely studied at the Colonial Office, and a second important outside stimulus to development was provided by the formation in 1923 of a permanent Advisory Committee on Native Education in the Tropical African Dependencies. This owed its origin to a memorandum prepared by J. H. Oldham of the International Missionary Council—who had already played a leading part in the planning of the Phelps-Stokes Commission—urging the need for continuity of policy and fuller co-operation between Governments and Missions.[3] Guggisberg saw in this Advisory Committee 'a safeguard against the educational crank', and a guarantee that 'the welfare and progress of the native races will take precedence of all other considerations'.[4] He was also fortified in his resolve to press on with the development of Achimota as the apex of the new educational system—and, indeed, as 'the greatest institution for the higher education of the native races of Africa'. The pupils would, he hoped, be fitted by their education to become leaders in thought and industry: 'in fact we hope to assist in the making of the progressive African'.[5]

Meanwhile Guggisberg had appointed another committee which sat in 1922 to consider the building plans and estimates for Achimota in the light of rising costs and falling revenue.[6] It had already become clear that the provision of new primary schools might have to be restricted; but there was no

---

[1] Jesse Jones, *Education in Africa*, pp. 58–59.

[2] *The Gold Coast Leader*, 24 July 1926. For some indication of Du Bois's racial views and their impact on the Gold Coast, see Ch. XIII, pp. 542–4, below.

[3] 'Educational Policy of the British Government in Africa', in *International Review of Missions* (London, 1925), p. 423.

[4] Its first declaration of policy was contained in *Educational Policy in British Tropical Africa* (London, 1925), Cmd. 2374.

[5] Guggisberg, *Legislative Council Debates*, 1 Mar. 1923, and 6 Mar. 1924.

[6] For details of government revenue and expenditure in the 1920's, see Ch. I, p. 58, above.

question of postponing the plans for the secondary school, although this might be combined with the existing training college, as an economy measure. The committee produced much useful guidance for the future policy of Achimota, with no reservations about the rightness of the Governor's decision: they suggested that the relevant question was not 'can we afford to build?' but 'can we afford not to build?'[1]

The foundation stone of Achimota was laid in March 1924, and soon afterwards the Rev. A. G. Fraser, of Trinity College, Ceylon, was appointed Principal, with the unusual permission of the Secretary of State to choose his own staff. His first choice—which he made a condition of his own acceptance of the post—was Aggrey, who returned from the United States to become Assistant Vice-Principal; and their arrival together in Accra in October (with other members of the staff) was welcomed at formal receptions given by local organisations, including the Ladies' Section of the National Congress.[2] Later they visited Kibi, Cape Coast, Sekondi, Tarkwa, and Kumasi, winning support for an institution that was being criticized in the press for its high cost and its emphasis on African languages and customs.

The staff of Achimota were encouraged to travel widely and to study local institutions before the school was opened. W. E. F. Ward, for example, one of the first assistant housemasters, laid the foundations of a serious study of African music, folk-lore, and stool histories, and later criticized those teachers who were ashamed of what they considered good enough only for illiterates.[3] During the initial years Aggrey's eloquence did much to counter African suspicions of the motives behind Achimota.[4] Guggisberg also had to answer criticisms from the other side that the provision of higher education was deliberately inviting political trouble; he argued that 'the safeguard *against* trouble is the local education of the many . . . rather than the education in Europe of a few'.[5]

Meanwhile Fraser was working out his own detailed plans. He stressed the cardinal principle that a strong body of qualified Africans was required on the staff, to raise the sense of personal dignity and responsibility amongst the boys. He substantially enlarged Guggisberg's original conception to include

[1] 'Interim Report of the Educationists' Committee, 1922, appointed by His Excellency the Governor 23rd May, 1922', *Sessional Paper No. I of 1924–25*; this includes the 'Governor's Memorandum of the 23rd May, 1922, on Secondary Education'.

[2] *The Gold Coast Independent*, 22 Nov. 1924.

[3] W. E. F. Ward, 'Music in the Gold Coast', in *The Gold Coast Review* (Accra, 1927), vol. iii, no. 2; also 'On the Teaching of Music', in *Government Training College Magazine* (Accra, 1927), no. 17. He later drew freely on his careful research into oral traditions for *A History of the Gold Coast* (London, 1948), lamenting the fact that 'traditional history is vanishing from the national memory'. Preface, p. 7.

[4] Cf. a letter from the editor of *The Vox Populi* to Aggrey, dated 4 July 1925: 'Personally I have been a vigorous and blatant critic of Sir Gordon, but I have been constrained by facts to bow and do obeisance to his 'big soul' . . . Hats off to him and ungrudgingly let us offer him our oil of sympathy and petroleum of co-operation.' Smith, *Aggrey of Africa*, ch. xiv, 'The Genesis of Achimota'.   [5] F. G. Guggisberg, *The Keystone* (London, 1924), p. 10.

all ages from kindergarten to pre-matriculation level, right from the start; the Accra Training College was also to be incorporated and, later, university-level classes would be undertaken.[1] The Governor agreed, and at one stage even visualized Achimota as more like a university college than a secondary school;[2] this should have appealed particularly to Casely Hayford, who had been advocating a national university since 1911, a demand reiterated by the National Congress during the 1920's.[3]

The estimated capital cost of Achimota had now risen to over half a million, with an annual recurrent expenditure of £50,000, which would only partly be offset by fees. By 1925 it appeared that the funds could be made available. The unofficial members of the Legislative Council were looking with optimistic faith towards 'that green hill—Achimota';[4] and the Governor, who had every confidence in Fraser, successfully urged the Secretary of State to accept the new proposals.[5] In May the Prince of Wales set the seal of respectability on the project by unveiling a tablet naming the school and college after him.[6]

The following year the first kindergarten pupils were taken into a staff house, while Achimota masters took over responsibility for the Training College in Accra, and for the regular refresher courses for teachers.[7] A by-product of one of these was the formation in 1926 of a central Teachers' Association, under government auspices, to unite several local unions;[8] a full-time secretary was appointed and by the end of the following year there were sixty-two branches.[9] The teachers were beginning to challenge comparison with the clerks as an articulate, educated group of some potential influence. An attempt was also made to interest a wider public in problems of education, through an annual series of conferences held at Achimota and attended by Chiefs, officials, lawyers, teachers, and leading Africans. After the first one a local newspaper commented: 'It is a happy augury that already Achimota is considered as a national institution.'[10]

---

[1] 'Preliminary Report on Achimota School and College by the Rev. A. G. Fraser, Principal', dated 8 Dec. 1924, *Sessional Paper No. XII of 1924–25.*   [2] Guggisberg, *The Keystone*, p. 31.

[3] See Ch. X, pp. 383, and 400–2, and Ch. XIII, p. 530, below.

[4] Casely Hayford, *Legislative Council Debates*, 24 Feb. 1925.

[5] 'Despatch from His Excellency the Governor to the Secretary of State for the Colonies on the System of Education, Cost of Building and Equipment and Annual Cost and Revenue of Achimota School', *Sessional Paper No. IX of 1925–26*; also 'Despatches on the subject of the Cost of Achimota College and School in continuation of Sessional Paper IX 1925–26', *Sessional Paper No. X of 1927–28*. According to Fraser, 'Guggisberg . . . had no special desire for vast buildings . . . But he none the less spent over half a million on their immediate erection, as the only means for securing permanence for Achimota . . . Once committed to so expensive a plant he believed it would be difficult for any future Secretary of State or Governor to starve higher education.' *West Africa*, 30 Jan. 1937.

[6] *Visit of His Royal Highness The Prince of Wales to the Gold Coast Colony, 1925* (Accra, 1925).

[7] *Departmental Reports*, Achimota, 1925–6 and 1926–7.

[8] *Notes of Lectures given at the Teachers' Refresher Course—July 8th–21st, 1926* (Achimota, 1926).   [9] *Departmental Reports*, Education, 1927–8.

[10] Quoted by Smith, *Aggrey of Africa*, p. 268. Cf. *Report of Achimota Educational Conference held on 21st & 22nd December, 1927* (Accra, 1928).

In January 1927, three months before Guggisberg left the Gold Coast, and six months before Aggrey's death, the Prince of Wales' College was formally opened at Achimota; the large crowd on this national occasion included numerous Chiefs and even the former Asantehene, now returned from exile. For the first year there were 60 kindergarten and 60 primary pupils; during 1928–9 upper primary, secondary, and university preliminary classes were added, making a total of 406 pupils, including 55 girls.[1] From the start they were encouraged to undertake social service projects in the neighbourhood, such as running dispensaries and children's clubs, and visiting hospitals.[2]

Fraser secured acceptance of a liberal constitution for Achimota, which had been implicit in his plans from the first. It was no longer to be even a special kind of government department, but the entire management and superintendence were to be handed over to a council, partly official, partly unofficial, including both Europeans and Africans. This he felt to be essential, especially since the death of Aggrey, because

in educational work conducted by one race for another there is great danger of creating an inferiority complex in the pupils ... the cleavage seems permanent and the hostility may become real ... I want Africans who shall appear at least from time to time in the compound and be the equals of any member of the staff. This can be achieved through their presence on the governing body.

Though the staff were largely foreign, people must feel that the school was 'national in spirit and sentiment'.[3]

Guggisberg had not forgotten the needs of the more remote parts of the country; in 1920 he had defined 'the Gold Coast' for educational purposes as the Colony, Ashanti, the Northern Territories, and also 'our part of Togoland'.[4] The north, already the most backward area educationally, had fallen further behind during the war—when the White Fathers had had to close their primary school at Navrongo[5]—and had derived no benefit from Guggisberg's early concentration upon secondary education, since neither such schools nor their pupils were in sight there. At Yendi, however, the first Trade School in the country had been opened in 1922; the Chief Commissioner of the Northern Territories called this 'the biggest thing done in all the 20 years I have been out', because it was at last beginning education at the right end.[6]

Education had hardly begun to contribute to the development of the north. As late as 1924 the average attendance at all five government schools was 261

[1] Slater, *Legislative Council Debates*, 15 Feb. 1929.

[2] *Departmental Reports*, Achimota, 1927–8.

[3] Memorandum of 2 Mar. 1928, by Fraser; 'Despatches on the subject of a proposed Constitution for the Prince of Wales's College and School, Achimota', *Sessional Paper No. XIX of 1928–29*.

[4] *Legislative Council Debates*, 23 Feb. 1920.

[5] Letter of 2 Feb. 1915, from Father Superior to Chief Commissioner; 1953 Acc. No. 1346, Case No. 81/1905, G.N. Archives.

[6] Chief Commissioner's Confidential Diary, 16 July 1921; 1953 Acc. No. 1415, G.N. Archives.

(including seventeen girls), and only five pupils were in Standard VII.[1] The instruction was entirely in English, and in this it was fairly efficient. But the inhibiting effects of such a policy were reflected in the programme of a school concert at Tamale, which included the following items:[2]

Opening song 'You Gentlemen of England'
Song   'Hurrah! Hurrah for England'
Recitation   'Doctor Quack', by Kwaku Dagomba
Song   'Our Home is the Ocean Blue'
Dialogue   'The Wolf and the Lamb', by Iddrusu[3]
'God Save the King'

It was hardly surprising that many Chiefs remained unconvinced of the practical value of sending their sons to school; or that the District Commissioner at Wa, finding that all his schoolboys wanted to be clerks, sent a *cri de cœur* for advice on what else they could do. He foresaw 'a danger of the Protectorate being overrun by an excess of half-educated natives without a means of livelihood as they would consider manual labour beneath their dignity'.[4]

The general feeling of educational despair was summed up by a Provincial Commissioner who wrote: 'We seem to be neglected up here, no one ever comes to inspect the schools and no money is received to buy materials for games.'[5] But Guggisberg, as soon as he began to study the possibilities in the north, rejoiced at the fact that they had not yet had time to make all the mistakes of the south, and at the excellent opportunity to implement the principles set forth by his Educationists' Committee, in what was in effect virgin ground. He was particularly anxious to do nothing that would extend or perpetuate the 'inadequate and inefficient' system then obtaining in the Colony and Ashanti.[6]

The contrast with previous policies was clearly shown in 1924, when Guggisberg held a conference on 'Steps to Co-ordinate the Advancement of Christianity and Education in the Northern Territories'.[7] As a result of this the Governor drew up a personal memorandum, which was to give a new direction

[1] Report on school attendance for quarter ending Mar. 1924; 1953 Acc. No. 1406, Case No. 4/1922, G.N. Archives.

[2] Programme enclosed in Letter of 3 Nov. 1922, from Acting District Commissioner, West Dagomba, to Chief Commissioner; ibid.

[3] This was R. S. Iddrusu, who thirty years later was to become a leading politician in the Northern Territories. He helped to found the Tamale branch of the first political organization during 1948, later became Chairman of the Convention People's Party in the Northern Region, and was elected M.P. for Tamale in 1956.

[4] Letter of 31 July 1922, from Acting District Commissioner, Wa, to Commissioner, N. Province; 1953 Acc. No.1406, Case No. 4/1922, G.N. Archives.

[5] Letter of 20 June 1923, from Commissioner, N. Province, to Director of Education, Accra; 1953 Acc. No. 1409, Case No. 35/1922, G.N. Archives.

[6] Minute of 1 Oct. 1924, by Guggisberg; 1953 Acc. No. 1406, Case No. 4/1922, G.N. Archives.

[7] Conference of 22 Dec. 1924, attended by the Governor, Colonial Secretary, Director of Education, Fraser, and Aggrey; ibid.

to the educational development of the north. The aim was to encourage the Missions as far as possible, but to insist on official approval of their work and on ultimate control of all schools by the Government. A new scheme of organization was proposed, based on Tamale, and linked less rigidly with Accra; and a special post was to be created for a Superintendent of Education, Northern Territories.[1]

During the following year Guggisberg was mainly preoccupied with the fundamental reform of the system in the south, which he considered 'rotten at the core'. To the Legislative Council he enunciated fifteen principles as a guide to reconstruction;[2] and the 1925 Education Ordinance was an attempt to put these into effect.[3] A new Board of Education was set up, with an unofficial majority, including four Africans. There was to be a substantial increase in government assistance to Mission and other schools, with strong incentives for efficiency; primary day schools rated 'good', 'fair', or 'poor' were to receive 80, 55, and 30 per cent. respectively of their African teachers' salaries, and boarding schools up to 90 per cent.[4] Improvements in salary and status for the teaching profession were to be accompanied by the establishment of a central register of qualified teachers. The most controversial clauses prevented the employment of unregistered teachers, which meant that although the Government had no power to close an assisted school directly, many would have to be shut down owing to the lack of qualified staff. In this way it was hoped to get rid of inefficient or positively harmful teaching and to raise the standards of the better schools.[5] Other, complementary measures included the establishment of a uniform Standard VII examination for the whole country, improvements in the school curriculum, a £20,000 grant towards new buildings for the Scottish Mission Training College at Akropong, the lengthening of the standard teacher-training course to four years, and the detailed discussion of problems of vernacular teaching and textbooks.[6]

In 1927, when the new Ordinance came into effect, grants to assisted schools in the Colony, Ashanti, and British Togoland totalled nearly £70,000, more than twice the level of the previous year. At the same time, 136 of the

[1] Memorandum of 23 Feb. 1925, by Guggisberg; ibid.

[2] *Legislative Council Debates*, 3 Feb. 1925.

[3] Following Guggisberg's usual practice, a committee had been set up to consider the drafting of the Ordinance, which included Fraser and representatives of the four main Missions—Wesleyan, Scottish, Roman Catholic, and English Church Mission.

[4] Soon after the Ordinance came into effect the maximum grant was raised to 95 per cent., owing to the heavy burden of the higher rates of pay. But inevitably the non-assisted schools were now unable to afford qualified teachers, and they found it increasingly difficult to raise their standards.

[5] 'Many existing schools are very inadequately staffed and equipped and are doing more harm than good to the people who attend them.' *Departmental Reports*, Education, 1926–7. Cf. the remarks of the District Commissioner at Saltpond: 'The standard . . . is low and until a better teacher is turned out education will be merely a superficial veneer. Many 7th Standard boys do not even make efficient letter writers.' Ibid. Central Province, 1925–6,

[6] Ibid. Education, 1925–6 et seq.

so-called 'bush schools' were closed, either voluntarily or on the advice of Inspectors. This caused widespread discontent and criticism, in the rural areas as well as in the towns;[1] the Manbii Party of Accra complained that the closure had been too precipitate, however worthy the motives.[2] Guggisberg was unwilling to give way on this policy, for he considered that the existing standard of teaching beggared description.[3] He set up yet another committee to consider the problem, but they could find little to recommend beyond the creation of two-year rural training colleges, to speed up the output of teachers.[4]

TABLE XIV. *Educational Statistics, 1920–8* [5]

Year	Government schools	Assisted schools	Total enrolment	Average attendance	Grants paid
					£
1920	19	198	28,580	23,162	23,290
1921	20	214	31,089	26,115	25,921
1922	20	213	33,353	28,045	27,371
1923	21	222	35,408	30,178	30,757
1924	21	215	34,690	30,456	28,626
1925	22	212	32,827	29,573	28,879
1926[6]	17	221	32,461	29,332	32,225
1927	18	234	33,054	29,640	69,738
1928	18	241	34,446	31,858	81,316

Meanwhile separate provision had been made for educational reform in the Northern Territories. The Rev. A. H. Candler had been appointed Superintendent in 1926, and had begun work by touring the country, getting rid of some of the worst teachers, and drawing up detailed proposals for reform.[7]

[1] *Departmental Reports*, Central Province and Eastern Province, 1927–8.

[2] Petition of 19 Nov. 1927, to Governor from Gbese Mantse, W. A. Adjin, G. D. Laryea, and six illiterate supporters; app. A to 'Report and Recommendations of the Committee appointed by His Excellency the Governor in March, 1928, to Consider the Problem Created by the Closure of Inefficient Schools', *Sessional Paper No. XXI of 1928–29*.

[3] Guggisberg, *Legislative Council Debates*, 3 Feb. 1925.

[4] Fraser was a member of this committee, but later attacked the government policy towards non-assisted primary schools, urging that more help and encouragement should be given to them. Otherwise, 'granted the same rate of increase in school accommodation and of children in the classes, we shall see every child in the Gold Coast able to go to school in seven hundred years' time'. *West Africa*, 18 Apr. 1936.

Fraser also advocated substantial grants for Mission secondary schools which could set a high standard, though on a less expensive scale than Achimota. Quoted by Slater, *Legislative Council Debates*, 17 Feb. 1930. St. Nicholas Grammar School had been receiving assistance since 1911, and Mfantsipim since 1923, but no other secondary school had been grant-aided since the war. African-sponsored schools included the Accra High School, founded by the Rev. J. T. Roberts of Sierra Leone in 1923; a compatriot, the Rev. E. F. O'Reilly, established his Educational Institute in 1925.

[5] *Departmental Reports*, Education, 1919 to 1928–9.

[6] The figures for 1926–8 exclude the schools in the Northern Territories, but include those in British Togoland.

[7] Report of 20 Nov. 1927, by Candler; 1953 Acc. No. 1406, Case No. 4/1922, G.N. Archives.

The Northern Territories Education Ordinance of 1927 established a local Board of Education with five government members (including the Chief Commissioner), plus the Superintendent himself, and one representative from each Mission in the north.[1] For the first time, grants were to be paid to Mission schools; the conditions for these and the requirements for all new schools were laid down in general terms. In the following year Fraser travelled to the north and reported very favourably on educational standards, which he attributed largely to the inspiration of Candler.[2] He found, however, that the White Fathers' school at Navrongo, which they had rebuilt, was by far the best, because its centre of interest lay not in the three R's—though these were excellently taught—but in the community life of the pupils.[3]

Even Guggisberg's drive, however, could not correct the regional disparities in education that had grown up over the years. The numerical lead of the Eastern Province was to some extent reduced, partly owing to the greater number of 'bush schools' closed there, and partly to accelerated progress elsewhere. By 1929 the regional distribution of government and assisted primary schools was as follows:

TABLE XV[4]

Area	Number of schools	Change since 1919
Eastern Province . .	101	−18
Central Province . .	51	+6
Western Province . .	25	+3
Colony	177	−9
British Togoland . .	96	n.a.
Ashanti	36	+13
Northern Territories .	5	+1

The north still remained very much the 'poor relation', as far as education was concerned.

Some measure of the general expansion of activity throughout the country under Guggisberg is given by the fact that, excluding the cost of Achimota, the total of government expenditure on education in 1927–8 was approximately three times as great as in 1919.[5] Future plans included the early

[1] In addition to the White Fathers at Navrongo and the Wesleyan Methodists at Tamale, the Catholic Mission from Keta had established a station at Kete Krachi in 1925.

[2] The first Superintendent was gratefully remembered in the north for many years: 'Everyone appreciated the work that was done . . . by Rev. Candler . . . After 1931 there was a decline.' Kabachewura, *Record of the Fifth Session of the Territorial Council*, 1949.

[3] Memorandum of 11 May 1928, by Fraser; 1953 Acc. No. 1409, Case No. 35/22, G.N. Archives.

[4] *Departmental Reports*, Education, 1919 and 1929–30.

[5] According to the *Gold Coast Colony Blue Books*, in 1919 £54,442 was spent on education; in 1927–8 this had risen to £161,610, including £11,809 for the Northern Territories, but excluding £34,101 for Achimota.

establishment of a West African Medical School at Accra;[1] the site was selected by Guggisberg before he left, and a committee was appointed to draw up a detailed scheme.[2] But the final decision fell to a new Governor, A. R. Slater, who saw his main duty simply as 'consolidation'.[3] He claimed that there was no evidence of any real desire on the part of the Gold Coast people for this project, and agreed with the Governors of Nigeria and Sierra Leone that it was premature, as well as too expensive, in view of the recent fall in revenue.[4] No protest was made in the subsequent debate; and his advice was accepted by the Secretary of State.[5] Meanwhile, the Ten-Year Development Plan dropped out of the public eye; and from 1929 onwards the effects of the world slump meant a drastic curtailment of social and economic development.

A similar fate awaited Guggisberg's plan for increased African opportunities in the higher ranks of the civil service. Between 1919 and 1926 twenty-seven Africans were admitted into European appointments (as compared with only one, Woolhouse Bannerman, permanently employed in 1919). In an attempt to ensure continuity of policy, the Governor then announced a detailed programme for the next twenty years, summarized as follows:

TABLE XVI. *Proposed Higher Civil Service Appointments*

Year		European	African	Total
1925–6	.	481	28	509
1926–7	.	496	31	527
1930–1	.	467	76	543
1935–6	.	396	148	544
1945–6	.	319	229	558

Any branch of the Administration was to be open to suitably qualified Africans, except that they could not yet become Judges or Political Officers. The former reservation was made by the Secretary of State; the latter was justified by the argument that Africans had opportunities to serve their

[1] A West African Medical School had first been proposed by Dr. Africanus Horton as early as 1861. *West African Countries and Peoples*, pp. 46–50 n. Cf. Sir Harry Johnston's more recent suggestion in *The African World* 'for a West African University and Medical School at which ten times the present number of Negro doctors might be trained', quoted approvingly by Hutton Mills, *Legislative Council Debates*, 2 Nov. 1918.

[2] *Gold Coast Gazette* (*Extraordinary*), 9 Nov. 1927.

[3] Slater, *Legislative Council Debates*, 1 Mar. 1928.

[4] The revised estimate of revenue for 1928–9 then stood at £3,629,320, a drop of about £1½ million; and a government deficit of about £½ million was expected, after many years of surplus. *Legislative Council Debates*, 15 Feb. 1929.

[5] 'Despatch from the Secretary of State relating to the Proposal to Establish a Medical College in the Gold Coast, together with Regulations and Conditions for the Award of Government Scholarships to African Students for the Purpose of Studying Medicine in the United Kingdom', *Sessional Paper No. XVI of 1930–31.*

country in the Oman Councils of their own States. Both of these exceptions were strongly criticized by the press and in the Legislative Council.[1] But the Governor made a clear statement of principle which went a long way towards meeting the demands for equal opportunity: 'Neither an African nor a European will have any claim to promotion to a Staff Appointment on account of his colour but because he is the best man for the appointment.'[2]

Guggisberg considered this policy essential, on the grounds of both justice and economy; but it was soon abandoned during the slump. During 1930–2 over 250 serving officers were retrenched, including equal numbers of Europeans and Africans,[3] although the economic argument for employing Africans could hardly have lost its force, and there was no return to long-term planning after the emergency was over. It is, of course, easy to criticize Guggisberg's programme in retrospect. Like most long-range forecasts, it took too little account of changing general conditions; the assumption that the senior service would expand by only fifty additional staff over a period of twenty years seems particularly unrealistic, so that even if all the proposed African appointments had been filled, the proportionate increase could not have been achieved. But the policy was carried out neither in the letter nor in the spirit; by 1938 there were still only thirty-one Africans in senior appointments, and in 1948 only ninety-eight out of a total of over 1,300.[4]

This failure has been officially attributed to 'the confident, but unfortunately unfounded, expectation that the opening of Achimota would at once produce an abundance of qualified men'.[5] But Guggisberg's hopes were never so naïve as this; in 1926 he made it clear that an appreciable number of candidates could not be expected from Achimota until at least ten years had elapsed.[6] In fact, after the slump Africans complained that civil service retrenchment had left insufficient vacancies for those coming forward from Achimota. Guggisberg also laid specific responsibility for training upon heads of departments, and there is some evidence that they were not always anxious to hasten the new order of things. Whatever the causes, the fact remains that 'the ambitious and noble vision of Sir Gordon Guggisberg remained an elusive mirage, while the lofty structure which he had designed was destined never to be erected'.[7]

---

[1] J. E. Casely Hayford and K. A. Korsah took every opportunity to demand the reopening of the Political Service to Africans; e.g. in the 'Report of the Select Committee on the Estimates for 1929–30', *Sessional Paper No. XXIII of 1929–30*. But it was not till 1942 that two African Assistant District Commissioners were appointed.

[2] Guggisberg, *Legislative Council Debates*, 22 Feb. 1926.

[3] Slater, ibid. 24 Sept. 1931. In addition, 327 vacancies were left unfilled (180 of them being African posts), and the African police force was reduced by 150. The clerks also had their starting pay reduced from £60 to £48, thus losing their hard-won gain of 1921. Acting Colonial Secretary, *Legislative Council Debates*, 19 June 1930. Cf. p. 104, above.

[4] *Report of the Commission of Enquiry into Disturbances in the Gold Coast, 1948* (London, 1948), Colonial No. 231, para. 124.

[5] 'Report of the Select Committee of the Legislative Council on the Africanization of the Public Service', *Sessional Paper No. I of 1950*, para. 5.

[6] *Legislative Council Debates*, 22 Feb. 1926.   [7] *Sessional Paper No. I of 1950*, para. 5.

As a prospect for the future, however, this imaginative scheme of Africanization was of tremendous importance. For the first time a clear statement of long-term policy replaced annual hopes and promises; and while it could not be held to bind future Governors, at least the general line of advance was laid down, which would make subsequent changes of policy more difficult to explain. The unofficial members of the Legislative Council took it upon themselves to watch the implementation of the policy from year to year; and the promotion of Africans became a duty expected of the Government, instead of a favour occasionally conferred. Resentment against the failure of subsequent administrations to fulfil the hopes and promises of the 1920's became an important nationalist grievance; and the serious nature of the omission later became apparent with the rapid approach of self-government.

Meanwhile, the achievements in the field of education remained, and helped to build up the pressure for African advance. Achimota was the keystone of Guggisberg's plans, and although it was not the only secondary school of importance it continued to set a standard for all the others. As a result, a good many of the political leaders of the 1940's, not to mention the Cabinet Ministers of the 1950's, owed at least part of their education to Achimota; and it was appropriate that the Rev. Fraser was one of Ghana's most honoured guests at the Independence celebrations. Under Guggisberg, the truth of Lord Hailey's remark was amply borne out: 'in Africa education is, and is intended to be, an instrument of change'.[1] But after 1927 it was left to Africans once more to take the initiative. As Casely Hayford said: 'There must be an educational awakening throughout West Africa greater than at any time in African history, and when this pentecost breaks in upon us, we shall begin to tread the sure path to national emancipation.'[2]

[1] *An African Survey*, p. 1207.

[2] Presidential Address, 4th session of the West African National Congress, Lagos, Dec. 1929; M. J. Sampson (ed.), *West African Leadership* (Ilfracombe, 1950), p. 90.

III

SOCIAL CHANGE

THE changes in African society that have preceded or accompanied the development of nationalism are as clear in outline as they are imprecise and unprovable in detail. Statistical data are meagre before the end of the nineteenth century, and even then they are unreliable. There is nothing to set beside the results of modern social surveys and fieldwork in order to compare the structure and dynamics of society a century ago. Contemporary observations abound, but often tell us more about the observer than about the contemporary scene; accounts of even the recent past tend to evoke either a golden age of social stability or a lurid nightmare of primitive stagnation and savagery.[1]

Traditional Social Organization

It is reasonably safe to offer a few broad generalizations about the peoples of the Gold Coast in the pre-colonial era. They lived in a large number of isolated, self-contained societies: isolated by difficulties of transport, by fear of warfare and slave-raiding, by a relatively self-sufficient economy, and by a tightly-knit sense of community and kinship. The unit of social organization varied from the family compound to the widespread Confederacy of States which owed allegiance to the Asantehene or King of Ashanti.

Political patterns in West Africa have been usefully classified into three main types by Daryll Forde.[2] First, there were the small-scale, politically autonomous local communities, whose social world was to be numbered in hundreds. Their isolation was progressively broken down in colonial times. Secondly, he distinguishes 'dispersed tribal societies', without any central organs of government, where a large number of local communities, often extending over a considerable area, were linked to one another through 'traditions of

---

[1] Brodie Cruickshank, for example, wrote in 1853 of the 'very enslaving nature' of native institutions, conjuring up a picture of the Gold Coast in its 'wild and almost primitive state', when dark and cruel superstitions reigned, and where 'the bleeding victim' lay 'prostrate beneath the sacrificial knife'. *Eighteen Years on the Gold Coast of Africa* (London, 1853), vol. i, pp. 306–7, and vol. ii, p. 228. Fifty years later, J. E. Casely Hayford saw in the same distant past 'a system of self-government as perfect and as efficient as the most forward nations of the earth to-day can possibly conceive. A people who could . . . evolve the orderly representative government which obtained in Ashanti and the Gold Coast before the advent of the foreign interloper, are a people to be respected and shown consideration when they proceed to discuss questions of self-government.' *Gold Coast Native Institutions* (London, 1903), pp. 128–9.

[2] 'The Conditions of Social Development in West Africa', in *Civilisations* (Brussels, 1953), vol. ii, no. 4.

kinship and related religious dogmas and social exchanges supporting the moral values of kinship'. This was characteristic of some parts of the Northern Territories. Thirdly, the 'archaic State system'—a politically centralized State, subject to the authority of the Chief[1]—was to be found in various forms almost everywhere among the Akan peoples,[2] notably the Ashantis, and also among some of their neighbours, including the Dagombas and others to the north.

All of these societies had their own clearly defined system of rights and obligations, whether or not this was orientated towards a political Chief. The social relationships of the individual and, more important, his social status were determined largely by lineage, kinship, and age. A man might be born either slave or free; the fact of slavery did not extinguish all his rights, but it did severely limit his social horizons and his economic functions. The matrilineal system of the Akans and others—which has been described perhaps more accurately as one of 'double descent'[3]—was only a special case illustrating the general principle that rights of succession and inheritance were determined according to an elaborate lineage structure.[4]

The most important application of this principle was in the procedure for the selection of a new Chief. The succession was determined within fairly narrow limits. Among the Akan peoples, only the members of one or more royal lineages were eligible; but within these limits (and others set, for example, by ceremonial taboos) there was some scope for choice, usually exercised by the Queen Mother or blood relatives and by the elders on behalf of the people; the succession was not automatic.[5] To take another example, among the patrilineal Dagombas the sons or grandsons of Chiefs were eligible in varying degrees for certain offices; but the final selection was made by the Ya-Na or his divisional Chiefs, and further advances could come by promotion from one rank of Chief to another.[6] Kin-right and selection were thus combined in accession to the highest office.

[1] The State—a social and political entity—does not necessarily coincide with the tribe, an ethnic group. Cf. D. E. Apter, *The Gold Coast in Transition* (Princeton, 1955), p. 88.

[2] The term 'Akan' was originally used for a group of languages, and by extension has come to mean the peoples speaking those languages. The Akan language group (defined, Ch. XIII, p. 509, below) covers most of the peoples of the Colony and Ashanti, except for the Gãs and Adangmes, who inhabit the area in and around Accra, and the Ewes, who live mainly to the east of the Volta and beyond the borders of the former Gold Coast. From about 1928 onwards the use of the word 'Akan' was deliberately cultivated by Africans, to encourage political unity. J. W. de Graft Johnson, for example, defined it as 'A general term applied to the aborigines of Ashanti and the Colony, showing their common ancestry.' *Towards Nationhood in West Africa* (London, 1928), p. 90.

[3] Cf. J. B. Christensen, *Double Descent among the Fanti* (New Haven, 1954).

[4] See J. Mensah Sarbah, *Fanti Customary Laws* (London, 1897), ch. vii, 'Succession and Inheritance'.

[5] Ibid. pp. 19–20. Also R. S. Rattray, *Ashanti Law and Constitution* (Oxford, 1929), p. 85 and *passim*.

[6] A. Duncan-Johnstone and H. A. Blair, *Enquiry into the Constitution and Organisation of the Dagbon Kingdom* (Accra, 1932).

Once 'enstooled', however, the Chief represented in his own person the wisdom of the ancestors, and the collective authority of the people over such important matters as war, land, justice, and orderly government; central to all this was the religious nature of his office. Among the Akans, the Chief was 'the supreme priest of all the gods in his kingdom', with the duty of seeing that all the rituals connected with them were carried out, to protect the welfare of his people. He bore the title *Okomfo Ohene*, Chief of the Priests[1]; and the sacred origin attributed to chieftaincy is well illustrated by the story of Okomfo Anokye and the Golden Stool of Ashanti.[2]

The religious authority of the Chief did not preclude the exercise of certain constitutional safeguards against his misconduct or abuse of power. The ultimate sanction was 'destoolment', or removal from office. Popular pressure could be brought to bear through the semi-military Asafo companies,[3] composed of 'youngmen', i.e. those members of the community not of royal blood nor holding any office connected with the stool; they were entitled to lay complaints against the Chief before the council of elders, with whom the final decision rested. One of the recognized grounds for destoolment was habitual disregard of this council's advice;[4] and the Chief's duty of consultation with the representatives of his people, coupled with the possibility of removing him in the last resort, meant that even if the system did not approach democracy, at least it avoided the dangers of autocracy. It might, more accurately, be called a demosocracy, in the sense of rule by the popular heroes of the people—with the important qualification that loss of popularity often meant loss of office.

For the members of traditional society there was a certain amount of mobility within the limits ascribed by birth. The free-born might be captured and enslaved in warfare, or temporarily 'pawned' into servitude to pay off a debt; while at the other end of the scale the selection of a Chief could be strongly influenced by a man's personal qualities or achievements—his courage in warfare, his wisdom in council, his humility and generosity, or

---

[1] Eva L. R. Meyerowitz, *The Sacred State of the Akan* (London, 1951), p. 68.

[2] See Ch. VII, p. 265, below. The sanctity of the Chief has considerable relevance to modern political developments. In the language of Apter, 'the chieftaincy as a sanctional source, a symbolic referent, an integrational integer, and for sub-ethnic and ethnic definition, represents the orientational base out of which the charismatic authority of Nkrumah, the present prime minister of the Gold Coast, has developed'. *The Gold Coast in Transition*, p. 108.

[3] The Asafo company system has been described by Casely Hayford in *Gold Coast Native Institutions*, ch. ii, and by A. ffoulkes, 'The Company System in Cape Coast Castle', in *Journal of the African Society* (London, 1908), vol. vii, no. 27. A modern American analysis is to be found in Christensen's *Double Descent among the Fanti*, ch. vi. See also p. 141, below.

[4] Other grounds included: cowardice and theft (first offence); adultery, drunkenness and debt (habitual); and general misconduct, which included 'Quarrelsome disposition, being given to brawling, using the hand freely on his servants and courtiers, disloyalty to the Government and any action derogatory to his position'. Letter from the A.R.P.S. to Nathan, published in the *Government Gazette*, 30 Jan. 1904. Cf. J. Mensah Sarbah, *Fanti National Constitution* (London, 1906), pp. 42 ff.

sometimes simply by his impeccable physique.[1] Other offices in the State, including the position of councillor and sometimes even of *Kyiami* ('linguist', or spokesman of the Chief), were allotted with reference to merit as well as to family status. Social obligations were, however, clearly defined and recognized as binding upon every member of the group. The duties—and sometimes tribute—owed to the Chief, in both peace and war; the respect accorded to age; the allotment of tasks on the farm; the special functions of women in the home; the obligations due towards members of the extended family; the appropriate courtesies for each member of the kinship group—all these and many more were rigidly supported by various religious, economic, and physical sanctions enforced either by the social group or by the Chief acting on their behalf.[2] The community was all-important; the individual was bound to conform. The criterion for any action was not individual profit nor even potential social betterment, but whether it had been approved by the ancestors and sanctioned by custom.

The use of the past tense should not mislead us into considering this social order as of mainly historical importance. Indeed, given the paucity of written records, it is only possible to make such generalizations because enough of significance has survived into the present. The study of social change in the Gold Coast, and of its relevance to nationalism, must take into account both the indigenous society and the outside forces that have stimulated change, as well as the actual process of development. We cannot expect the resulting social patterns either to recapture the old or to reproduce the new in its entirety. As M. J. Herskovits has recently put it, there are no 'fresh cultural slates on which a foreign way of life can be newly inscribed. What is taken over is projected against pre-existing patterns, and the result is never identical with the model.'[3]

Societies in Transition

Economic development was the main mediating force whereby the individualist, competitive, acquisitive attitudes and values of the West were introduced into African society. The impact was least, however, during the centuries of pre-colonial coastal trade, greatest during the comparatively short colonial era. The early European traders brought new means to wealth and power: their guns and gunpowder profoundly altered the balance of power among the coastal States with which they came in contact, and contributed significantly to the rise of the interior kingdoms, notably Akwamu and Ashanti.[4] But before the nineteenth century, external trade brought little

[1] Cf. K. A. Busia, *The Position of the Chief in the Modern Political System of Ashanti* (Oxford, 1951), p. 9. [2] Cf. J. B. Danquah, *Obligation in Akan Society* (London, 1950).

[3] 'Some Contemporary Developments in Sub-Saharan Africa', in *Africa in the Modern World*, ed. by C. W. Stillman (Chicago, 1955), p. 278.

[4] This tendency is well illustrated in the new material brought to light by the research of I. G.

disturbance to the social order within these States, and scarcely affected the more loosely-knit societies of the hinterland.

The progressive assumption by the British of jurisdiction and political control brought about a gradual acceleration of the pace of social change. The isolated, autonomous States and tribal societies were brought into a new relationship with a central power, and hence with one another. The super-imposition of external authority seriously weakened the powers of the Chiefs, and the sanctions at their disposal. The prevention of inter-State warfare, for example, deprived them of their main means of gaining new prestige, territory, and wealth, and of providing an outlet for the aggressive impulses of their young men.[1] British interference with traditional judicial systems was initially prompted by humanitarian motives; but the prohibition of some common punishments—such as the chaining, mutilation, or enslavement of prison-ers—deprived the Chiefs of their most important physical sanctions. Europeans also failed to understand the nature of many of the offences punishable by death. African customary law, like English law, aimed to protect society from unscrupulous individuals; but its definition of anti-social acts extended much farther, and there was little concern with protecting the rights of the indi-vidual during the processes of law.

Economic sanctions, especially the control of wealth by the traditional authorities, were also weakened by the creation of new openings for individual trade and enrichment. More important, perhaps, the religious authority of the Chief and his ability to invoke supernatural sanctions were undermined by the introduction of a new religion, Christianity; this offered not only the prestige of association with the ruling race, but also the utilitarian advantage of education, which in turn led to wider economic opportunities.[2]

British protection—and later, direct rule—meant far greater security for the individual. Within his society, he was no longer at the mercy of physical cruelty and exploitation, even when authorized by the Chief; outside, he was protected from molestation by hostile tribes or slave-raiders, and his terri-torial mobility was greatly increased. Some fugitives from traditional justice were thereby enabled to escape and claim refuge with the British; far more important, however, was the fact that many traders were enabled to extend

Wilks into the rise of the Akwamu Empire from 1650. He shows that the direction of expansion was dictated not only by political expediency, but also by the economic attraction of the coastal trade. At first the aim of the Akwamus was to obtain control of the Accra–interior trade routes as a source of revenue from tolls, with which to purchase guns and gunpowder; but economic ascendancy soon led to the conquest of Accra itself, 1677–81, and the emergence of Akwamu as a coastal power. (In 1693 the Akwamus even captured Christiansborg Castle from the Danes, and appointed their own Governor for a year.) 'The Rise of the Akwamu Empire, 1650–1710', in *Transactions of the Historical Society of Ghana* (Achimota, 1957), vol. iii, pt. 2.

[1] Cf. W. Bosman, *A New and Accurate Description of the Coast of Guinea* (London, 1705), p. 70: 'The chief employments of the inhabitants are merchandise, agriculture, and war; to which last they are particularly addicted.'

[2] For detailed consideration of the impact of Christianity, see pp. 151–66, below.

the area of their operations, or to seek new markets farther afield. There was also much greater scope for anti-social individuals to evade traditional obligations within their own community.

The superimposition of external authority which brought these changes did not supplant the rule of the Chiefs. But it led to considerable tension between the Chiefs and the British Government on the one hand, and increasingly between the Chiefs and their subjects on the other.[1] Similarly, the time-honoured relationships between groups and individuals were seriously affected by the economic and political changes of the nineteenth and twentieth centuries, even though these did not mean the complete destruction of the older social order. The expanding economy brought intercommunication and interdependence on an ever-widening scale. The kinship group or extended family began to lose its importance as an economic unit, and hence to some extent its social self-sufficiency; meanwhile, new associations began to emerge, based on common economic, cultural, or political interests, instead of kinship and age-structure.[2]

A radical change of status for a substantial class of people was implied—though not at first strictly enforced—with the abolition of domestic slavery in 1874. This, however, did not present a serious social problem since the ex-slaves were gradually absorbed into the emerging wage economy, and many found new patrons in Christian missionaries anxious to demonstrate the brotherhood of man. More significant was the fact that, as money incomes increased, wealth tended to accumulate in the hands of the younger men, who were more adaptable and more susceptible to outside influences; the introduction of Western education threw emphasis even upon the children. In a society in which respect and high standing had been accorded to age—to such an extent as to make some communities almost a gerontocracy—this reversal of status brought about a widening dichotomy between the generations, which found strong political expression during the twentieth century.[3]

The significance of all these changes, as far as the individual was concerned, might be summed up as a movement towards achieved—as opposed to ascribed—status.[4] It must be remembered, however, that the traditional system allowed certain scope for achievement, as already shown, and that the shift was gradual and partial, not sudden and total. Allied to this was the increasing emphasis upon the role of the individual, and the undermining of communal values and sanctions. Yet, though kinship ties might often be weakened, and

[1] These points are developed more fully in Ch. XII, below.

[2] See pp. 146–50, below.

[3] Cf. G. Balandier's comment: 'The colonial situation involves not only . . . the appearance of new processes of social differentiation; it entails . . . a reorientation of the social structure. In overturning the traditional equilibriums, it lets come to the surface some of the very antagonisms repressed in order to maintain these equilibriums. This is particularly apparent in the relations between sexes and between generations.' 'Social Changes and Social Problems in Negro Africa', in *Africa in the Modern World*, p. 56.

[4] Cf. J. S. Coleman, *Nigeria: Background to Nationalism* (Los Angeles, 1958), p. 96.

new social groupings began to emerge, the tenacity of family and tribal loyalties often considerably modified the pace and direction of economic change; and they certainly had a strong influence upon the development of nationalism in the Gold Coast.[1]

The Nineteenth-Century Conflict of Cultures

The establishment of permanent European administration on the coast brought a new, alien culture-group into close juxtaposition with African society. Even though British officials never became an integral part of the community, they introduced novel economic requirements, political prohibitions, judicial decisions, religious attitudes, and patterns of behaviour; and all these profoundly modified social norms and orientation in the coastal towns, their influence gradually penetrating to the interior.

During the nineteenth century there was some friction at nearly every point of culture-contact; it appeared that Africans had to reject the old entirely if they were to reap the benefits of the new, and since this was virtually impossible the attempt must often have set up severe psychological conflicts. British officials, however, were serenely confident of their civilizing mission, and increasingly attempted to exert their influence beyond the coastal forts. Certain customs, such as human sacrifice, slavery, and pawning, were obviously un-Christian; others, such as the cruel treatment of prisoners, or riotous celebrations that often ended in needless bloodshed, revolted the humanitarianism of Victorian administrators; while the scarcity or total absence of clothing offended their sense of propriety.[2]

There was a great deal of ignorance and misunderstanding about the significance of local beliefs and institutions. The Chief was treated primarily as a secular ruler, whose powers, suitably modified, could be incorporated within a new institutional framework, while fetish practices were expected to wither away, if not actually suppressed. Images of barbarism, bloodshed, and slavery tended to dominate European thinking about Gold Coast society;[3] and many honestly felt that the solution was to suppress all the savage and heathen customs. Then, surely, it would be only a matter of time and suitable Ordinances before superstitions were dispelled, and replaced by more enlightened modes of conduct.

[1] See especially Chs. V, XII, and XIII, below.

[2] In 1872 some British merchants registered a complaint after seeing two young girls parading through Cape Coast, naked and decorated with beads, in celebration of puberty rites. There was considerable argument as to the degree of indecency involved. CO/96/94.

[3] For example, the quotation from Cruickshank, p. 125 n., above. Cf. Winwood Reade, *Savage Africa* (London, 1863), the narrative of a tour through West and Equatorial Africa, 'with notes on the habits of the gorilla; on the existence of unicorns and tailed men . . . on the origin, character and capabilities of the negro and on the future civilisation of Western Africa'. Although generally a fair-minded observer, Reade retained his belief that 'The typical negro is the true savage of Africa . . . unrestrained by moral laws' (pp. 554–5).

Thus, for example, in 1868 the Administrator, H. T. Ussher, enacted the Native Customs Regulation Ordinance, which prohibited entirely the public celebration of the yam custom, and any other processions or festivals involving the firing of guns or drumming, within the town of Cape Coast.[1] A few months later he was out of patience with the 'silly custom' of deer-catching at Winneba, which had led to another disturbance, although forbidden.[2] The Secretary of State dismissed the affair as 'Precisely similar to an Irish faction-fight.'[3] A similar parochial outlook was displayed by F. M. Hodgson in 1896, when he proudly reported that the Head Chief of Srah had formed 'a drum and fife band with English instruments', and that there were several others in nearby towns: 'I am very glad to see this disposition on the part of the natives to abandon their hideous performances on tom-toms, gong-gongs and native horns in favour of music of a more civilised character. It marks an advancement towards enlightenment.'[4]

Sometimes serious difficulties were created by the Government's failure to understand local customs and beliefs, the classic case of course being Hodgson's demand for the Golden Stool of Ashanti, which precipitated the siege of Kumasi Fort in 1900. It was not until after the shock of this conflict that a new Governor, Nathan, was able to acknowledge the difficulties created by past policy, and recognize the existence, especially in Ashanti, of 'A complicated system of administration, hallowed by antiquity and historic precedents, which our ignorance and policy have alike tended to break down, and a deep-rooted superstition which we are unable to understand and from which our presence in the country has detached a portion of the people.'[5]

The majority of Europeans in fact took little interest in African customs and institutions, except to condemn them, or to use them as background material for travellers' tales. There were some exceptions. The Basel missionaries, living and working closely with the people, studied their customs sympathetically, though often with a critical eye.[6] A. B. Ellis, an officer in the 1st West India Regiment, who was also a prolific writer, produced the first two serious studies of Gold Coast peoples in a more detached spirit of inquiry.[7] These contain a wealth of detail about religion, government, customary

[1] In 1880 this Ordinance was applied also to James Town and Christiansborg. In 1892 it was superseded by the Native Customs Ordinance, which prohibited the celebration of the yam custom in the twelve main coastal towns, except with the written permission of the District Commissioner. This annual religious ceremony, properly called *Ahubaw*, was something of the nature of a harvest festival, when prayers were offered to the ancestors; for details of its observance, see Mensah Sarbah, *Fanti National Constitution*, pp. 13–14.

[2] Contrast the official attitude in 1956, when the Governor and the Prime Minister of the Gold Coast attended the Winneba deer-hunt.

[3] Dispatch No. 119 of 20 Apr. 1880, from Ussher to Hicks Beach, and Minute thereon by Kimberley; CO/96/130.

[4] Dispatch No. 386 of 29 Sept. 1896, from Hodgson to Chamberlain; CO/96/277.

[5] Confidential Dispatch of 19 Mar. 1901, from Nathan to Chamberlain; CO/96/378.

[6] See p. 159, below, for details of some of their publications.

[7] A. B. Ellis, *The Tshi-Speaking Peoples of the Gold Coast of West Africa* (London, 1887), and

laws, and folk traditions, and indicate sufficient respect for local culture to make it worth recording for its own sake. Ellis does not seem to have been read by educated Africans.[1] They were unlikely to cherish or cultivate their own customs so long as European manners and institutions were continually held up as a superior example. This assumption had to be questioned before African self-respect could be restored.

The task was a hard one. During the later years of the nineteenth century many Africans were understandably turning away from customs they had been taught to regard as pagan and inferior. At least one was ready to disown his past in terms that Ussher himself could hardly have faulted:

Some of the dances in this colony are certainly so offensive to public decency that we can not understand why they are not suppressed. The time has come for us to get rid of many of the old institutions which come directly into conflict with modern ideas of civilization ... A list should be made of all the customs and institutions which should be abolished.[2]

Many hoped, by earnest cultivation of Western habits and modes of thought, to demonstrate their own level of education and social status; often the imitation was unconscious, simply because the model was there. Europeans had, in fact, become a 'reference group' for patterns of behaviour among those Africans who came in contact with them.[3] E. W. Smith describes lectures (e.g. on 'The Stately Homes of England'), meetings (e.g. of the Society for the Prevention of Cruelty to Animals), and books being read (e.g. Beeton's *Complete Etiquette for English Gentlemen*) during this period, and remarks 'It was undoubtedly an English Kingdom of God that the Cape Coast prophets looked forward to.'[4]

European styles of dress were important as an outward and visible sign of inward and spiritual superiority. The cult of English fashion seems to have begun in the 1820's, with encouragement from Sir Charles Macarthy.[5] When the Rev. T. B. Freeman visited London twenty years later, 'he brought many orders from Christian natives to this country, for English articles of dress and furniture, to a very considerable amount'.[6] In 1868 Dr. Africanus Horton

The Ewe-Speaking Peoples of the Slave Coast of West Africa (London, 1890). Ellis also wrote *West African Sketches* (London, 1881), *The Land of Fetish* (London, 1883), and *The Yoruba-Speaking Peoples of the Slave Coast* (London, 1894). For his historical work, see Ch. XIII, pp. 521–2, below.

[1] Neither Mensah Sarbah nor Casely Hayford mentions Ellis in any of their publications. The ignorance was mutual. Ellis does not betray any awareness of the existence of educated Africans.

[2] *The Gold Coast Express*, 28 Sept. 1897.

[3] Cf. J. C. Mitchell, 'The African Middle Classes in British Central Africa', in *Development of a Middle Class in Tropical and Sub-Tropical Countries* (Brussels, 1956), pp. 222–32; and for reference-group theory, see *Continuities in Social Research*, ed. by R. K. Merton and P. F. Lazarsfeld (Glencoe, 1950). [4] *Aggrey of Africa* (London, 1929), p. 43.

[5] Letter of 16 Sept. 1826, from R. Hutchison; CO/267/93.

[6] *Report from the Select Committee on the West Coast of Africa* (London, 1842), *Part I. Report and Evidence*, reply to question 3,645. Cf. Andrew Swanzy's statement in 1865: 'of recent years ... the natives on that particular coast are more attentive to their domestic comfort; I have shipped chairs and those things.' *Report from the Select Committee on Africa (Western Coast)* (London, 1865), reply to question 4,680.

remarked that although ninety-nine out of a hundred Fantis wore native dress, European costume had come to be especially associated with 'those who are educated and those in a high state of social existence'.[1] Clerks employed in government, in particular, were required to attend at their offices dressed in European clothing;[2] this involved extra expense, but came to be regarded as the hall-mark of a new way of life. Towards the end of the century we find Hodgson writing approvingly that King Mate Kole had discarded native dress, 'by reason of his education and therefore more enlightened ideas', and supporting his application to wear a special uniform on occasions of state.[3]

Those who could afford to encouraged their wives to dress in Victorian style, especially on Sundays; and this had an indirect influence on women's dress in other sections of the community. It was in the 1860's that 'the Kabasrotu (a corruption of "cover shoulder"), a sort of loose jumper for the upper part of the body', had been introduced by R. J. Ghartey of Winneba, for use among the women of his household.[4] This fashion spread; but some extreme reformers were not content with the gradual infiltration of European ideas of decency: 'No woman should be allowed to go through a single street in the country with her breast uncovered!' wrote an angry young man of 1897.[5] Already, dress was an important means by which 'ladies' anxiously sought to distinguish themselves from their unenlightened sisters. As a Wesleyan missionary noted, 'The "lady" wears a European dress, the "woman" only wears cloth'.[6] The Ladies' Mutual Club, founded in Sekondi in 1904, wrote essays on such topics as 'The term Lady', and made an early rule that members who went out in native dress should be fined. After a year or two, however, they relented sufficiently on the question of language to allow members to speak Fante 'at the meetings of the Club once a month, in order to feel at home'.[7]

[1] J. A. B. Horton, *West African Countries and Peoples* (London, 1868), p. 131.

[2] Report of Committee on the Clerical Service, enclosed in Dispatch No. 281 of 13 July 1896, from Hodgson to Chamberlain; CO/96/275.

[3] Dispatch No. 238 of 11 July 1893, from Hodgson to Ripon; CO/96/235. The application was granted, but the Colonial Office lacked Hodgson's earnest moral approach to the matter: 'if the King is to wear this uniform, which seems to be something between that of a Turkish general officer and a superior kind of postman, he certainly ought to have brass spurs on his patent eather boots'. Minute of 15 Aug. 1893; ibid.

In 1899 the Northern Territories administration ordered the following experimental items for sale in government stores: '50 Drawers cheap pairs; 50 Trousers of striped cloth very loose in seat and leg and having strong tapes at waist and ankle; 25 Jumpers of striped cloth'. Unfortunately these were later found to be 'almost unsaleable, as the people infinitely prefer to make up their own attire, which is mostly of the flowing robe description'. Letter of 9 Mar. 1899, from Northcott to Colonial Secretary, and Report on the Northern Territories for the year 1899 by Morris; 1953 Acc. No. 1288, G.N. Archives.

[4] E. J. P. Brown, *Gold Coast and Asianti Reader* (London, 1929), bk. i, pp. 165–6.

[5] *The Gold Coast Express*, 28 Sept. 1897.

[6] D. Kemp, *Nine Years at the Gold Coast* (London, 1898), p. 61.

[7] Report of 11th anniversary of the Club in *The Gold Coast Nation*, 30 Sept. 1915.

It was perhaps the superficial manifestations of the Western way of life that were most readily taken over and consciously imitated during the process of acculturation. It was also these that attracted most controversy and were most earnestly rejected in later years, as cultural nationalism gathered force.[1] Yet deeper and more subtle influences were at work, especially in the schools, the churches, and the market-place. No matter what clothes people wore, what language they spoke, what type of houses they lived in, an alien culture had come to stay in the Gold Coast, and could neither be wholly accepted nor wholly rejected. It was assimilated primarily by educated Africans, and their role in the changing social structure merits closer examination.

The New Élite

Changes in social structure, as opposed to patterns of behaviour, are less documented and more difficult to assess in detail. There is no doubt that economic development led to the enrichment of certain groups and individuals. At first it was the traditional authorities who benefited from the process of land alienation, and to some extent from the growth of cocoa farming. But they had no monopoly of economic opportunities; even in the nineteenth century there were some land speculators and a few professional men earning large incomes, which were later invested in cocoa farming or buying. Increasingly, the wealth from cocoa came into the hands of those whose status was simply that of 'youngmen' in the old society, but who now helped to focus discontent against both the Chiefs and the colonial authorities.[2] It was the professional handful, in particular, who had sufficient wealth and leisure to devote to politics, and from whose ranks the early leadership of the national movement was drawn.

One of the most important means of expressing nationalist grievances was the expensive technique of sending deputations to London. The way in which these were financed is an interesting index of the change in their social and economic backing. In 1865 King Aggery of Cape Coast sent two educated commissioners to appear before the Select Committee; the money for this was borrowed in advance, and in default of payment the guarantors (including one of the commissioners) were imprisoned. Thirty years later, when the Asantehene sent an embassy of eight, consisting mainly of traditional office-bearers, in the vain hope of securing the independence of his kingdom, he levied a special tax throughout Ashanti, since the State coffers were then running low. In 1898, however, the three prosperous merchants sent by the A.R.P.S. to protest against the Lands Bill were probably able to pay their own expenses initially, until these were refunded by the grateful Chiefs. The success of this mission inspired the Chiefs to pay up handsomely in advance

---

[1] For the development of cultural nationalism, see Ch. XIII, pp. 517–28, and 545–6, below.
[2] See Ch. I, pp. 33–37, above, and Ch. XII, p. 471, below.

for a deputation to protest against the 1911 Forest Bill, and £3,000 was available for the merchant, doctor, and two lawyers who appeared before the West African Lands Committee. But in 1920, when the National Congress of British West Africa organized a deputation that forfeited the support of the Chiefs, they had to contribute largely towards their own expenses, and several of the members had their own commercial reasons for visiting London.[1] The technique of organizing mass support and securing a multitude of small subscriptions had not yet been studied.

By the 1920's there was a small but growing group of African business men and traders, who might be regarded as constituting the nucleus of a middle class.[2] But it is risky to apply the analysis appropriate to Western society in the different social situation of the Gold Coast. Complicating factors arise not only from the persistence of traditional patterns and values, but also from the explosive force of Western education. Some writers assume that the end-product of education was the creation of a new class in West Africa. J. S. Coleman, for example, emphasizes the isolation of educated Nigerians, due to their 'Conversion to Christianity, knowledge of and preference for English, imitation of European behaviour, and postschool employment in an urban milieu'; it is doubtful, however, whether these common factors are sufficient to justify his grouping them together as a single class, especially since he makes no reference to their economic interests.[3]

Various attempts have been made to define an African middle class. Some would place it between 'the wealthy aristocracy and the impoverished masses of the old economy',[4] but this hardly seems relevant to the Gold Coast. One writer distinguishes a middle class somewhere in between the lower class of peasants and wage-earning labourers, and the European 'upper class' of officials and entrepreneurs;[5] but it seems unsatisfactory to lump together in theory all Africans engaged, at whatever level, in commerce, teaching, and the civil service, as well as members of the professions. T. L. Hodgkin, however, is careful not to include the infinitesimally small group of lawyers,

[1] Details of these ventures are given in Ch. V, pp. 205–9 and 212, Ch. VII, pp. 285–95, Ch. IX, pp. 349–55, and Ch. X, pp. 368–70 and 385–92, below.

[2] In *The Red Book of West Africa*, compiled by A. Macmillan (London, 1920), a page of portraits of 'some representative native business men of Accra' shows the following faultlessly-dressed gentlemen: E. A. Manyo Plange (Director and Manager, Tropical Traders Ltd.), T. P. Allotey (Managing Director, Gã Trading Co. Ltd.), J. M. Abadoo (Managing Director, Smith & Co.), J. Buckman (Land Surveyor and Architect), A. J. Ocansey (General Merchant), S. O. Akiwumi (Produce Merchant), J. Hansen Sackey (Auctioneer), F. R. C. Lutterodt (Government Photographer), Nmai Dsane (Secretary, Kle Merchandise Co.), M. Larye Sowyah (Chairman and Managing Director, Kle Merchandise Co.), J. A. Pinnock (Managing Director, Mangoase Products Co. Ltd.), and J. B. Kumi (Managing Director, Larteh Planters' Union Ltd.). The same book lists twenty-one African trading firms in Accra (but only one each in Sekondi and Kumasi), and shows some of their imposing buildings.   [3] Coleman, *Nigeria*, p. 115.

[4] International Institute of Differing Civilizations, *Development of a Middle Class in Tropical and Sub-Tropical Countries* (Brussels, 1956), p. 448.

[5] M. L. Kilson, 'Nationalism and Social Classes in British West Africa', in *The Journal of Politics* (Gainesville, 1958), vol. 20, pp. 374–5.

doctors, property owners, and senior civil servants, and defines the middle class as consisting of relatively small-scale entrepreneurs, traders, and the less exalted ranks of the educated salariat. His analysis of their ambiguous status, patterns of consumption, and political and social attitudes, is useful and suggestive.[1]

But it seems clear that the concept of class structure is not particularly helpful in analysing the shifting patterns of African society.[2] Even today, when the process of social differentiation has been carried to considerable lengths, the network of kinship ties, involving obligations towards members of the extended family at all social levels, prevents the formation of rigid class barriers. Gold Coast society in the nineteenth century saw the emergence of a significant educated group, dependent on non-traditional sources of income, who set patterns of social behaviour in the towns, and from time to time exerted a strong political influence upon rural Chiefs. But they do not easily fall within any rigorous definition of a social class. This is true whether one chooses an economic interpretation—such as Max Weber's, in terms of common interest in the possession of goods, opportunities for income and market situation[3]—or whether with J. Schumpeter one defines a class by the purely social criterion that intermarriage prevails among its members.[4]

One is left sharing G. Balandier's doubts whether the new social strata which transforms the traditional African status system can be regarded as classes, in the sense in which modern industrial societies understand them. His study of modern Brazzaville has shown the emergence of some aspects of a middle-class spirit among what he calls the 'educated progressives'.[5] But he concludes that in general 'the maintenance (even at a low level) of the familial economies and the persistence of certain traditional relations between individuals of unequal economic status', as well as the shallowness of modern economic distinctions, and the tendency to unite in opposition to foreign rule, counteract 'the formation of those radically incompatible groups which are the social classes'.[6]

[1] T. L. Hodgkin, 'The African Middle Class', in *Corona* (London, 1956), pp. 86–87.

[2] Even a Soviet scholar has recently admitted that it is not always possible to determine the nature of the class structure emerging from what he calls the 'primaeval community system'. I. I. Potekhin, 'The Origin and Development of National Capital on the Gold Coast'; Lecture, University College of Ghana, Dec. 1957.

[3] Weber offers some applicable generalizations concerning the transition from status to class: 'When the bases of the acquisition and the distribution of goods are relatively stable, stratification by status is favored. Every technological and economic transformation threatens stratification by status and pushes the class situation into the foreground.' He suggests that '"Property" and "lack of property" are ... the basic categories of all class situations'; but West Africa has not yet fully reached this stage. *From Max Weber: Essays in Sociology*, ed. and translated by H. H. Gerth and C. W. Mills (New York, 1946), pp. 180–95.

[4] *Imperialism and Social Classes* (Oxford, 1951), pp. 137–47.

[5] *Sociologie des brazzavilles noires* (Paris, 1955), ch. iv, 'Les problèmes de l'organisation sociale et de la vie politique'.

[6] 'Social Changes and Social Problems in Negro Africa', in *Africa in the Modern World*, pp. 61–63.

The concept of *élites* appears far more relevant to the analysis of changing social structure in West Africa. Here, the definition of S. F. Nadel seems most useful: 'a stratum of the population which, for whatever reason, can claim a position of superiority and hence a corresponding measure of influence over the fate of the community'. He emphasizes that an *élite* must have some degree of corporateness and exclusiveness, forming a more or less self-conscious unit within the society.[1] This enables us to classify the Western-educated group as an *élite* in Gold Coast society, without any assumption as to identity of economic interests or of marriageable status. Still more illuminating is Nadel's discussion of the *élite* as a standard-setting group; the recognition of their superiority tends to be attached not merely to their special advantages, such as the wealth of the rich or the learning of the educated, but is extended to cover their general interests, manners—and, one might add, styles of dress—so that their status is enhanced by being in some respects imitable. Furthermore, the extent of their social influence may depend upon the close personal relations between the members of the *élite* and the rest of the community, and on their readiness or wish to communicate their values to other people. The stronger such links, the greater the power of the *élite* to facilitate or hinder new developments and to make new ideas acceptable to the group at large.[2]

Here we have the key to the tremendous social and political influence of the Gold Coast educated *élite*. They normally remained bound by family obligations (especially where the extended family had raised the funds for educating one or two chosen members) and by personal allegiance to their Chiefs; even if they had moved away from their traditional communities, their enhanced status gave them a strong potential influence there. During the latter half of the nineteenth century many Chiefs anxiously sought the guidance of educated advisers to help them in their new relations with one another, and with an alien central Government beyond the confines of their own States. European administrators, seeing only the gulf that divided the educated few from the illiterate many, failed to realize the close personal and social ties that were able to bridge it. Consequently they refused to acknowledge the claim of the *élite* to speak on behalf of the masses, or to make constructive use of them in a mediating role.[3]

[1] Cf. K. Mannheim's analysis of the function of *élites* in creating and assimilating culture. He points out that if the necessary 'minimum of exclusiveness is lost, then the deliberate formation of taste, of a guiding principle of style, becomes impossible'. At the same time, the *élites* should be 'reasonably accessible' and recruited from society in certain definite ways—in the Gold Coast, largely by education—if their culture is not to lose life and vigour through social in-breeding. *Man and Society* (London, 1940 edn.), pp. 86–88.

[2] S. F. Nadel, 'The Concept of Social Élites', in *International Social Science Bulletin* (Paris, 1956), vol. viii, no. 3.

[3] See Ch. II, pp. 87–91, above, Ch. V, pp. 213–14, and Ch. VI, *passim*, especially p. 228, below, for the role of educated advisers and the attitudes of administrators towards them in the nineteenth century.

The situation was, however, complicated by the existence of more than one *élite*, with potential and actual rivalries between them. K. A. Busia suggests that there are three main classes of *élite* in the Gold Coast: 'the traditional "royal" families, the European or alien rulers, and the educated Africans'.[1] It is possible to trace the social origins of nationalism to the fundamental conflict between the European *élite* and the educated African *élite*. As Balandier points out, 'The colonizing power has created a situation involving profound social changes, but the control which it exercises imposes an upper limit to these processes'.[2] As soon as Gold Coast Africans became sufficiently educated to hold European-type posts and to demand European status, they found increasing discrimination; and the resulting social frustration and resentment was channelled into a demand for political power, partly as a means of controlling the sources of status and influence.

During the twentieth century, however, a more significant conflict among Africans began to emerge, between the educated and the traditional *élites*. 'The Chiefs', as Busia puts it, 'secure as a standard-setting group in the traditional culture, wish also to exercise some degree of effective political authority, since this has been an aspect of their traditional role.'[3] He is writing of the period immediately preceding Independence, but his analysis is equally applicable to the attitudes of the paramount Chiefs—the 'Natural Rulers', as they somewhat nostalgically preferred to call themselves—during the 1920's. They were then asserting a claim to participation in the central Government, against opposition from the educated *élite*, who considered that their training for the problems of the modern world gave them a prescriptive right to leadership on the national scale.[4] This conflict was to remain unresolved for many years, with the scales becoming increasingly weighted against the Chiefs.

The changing social situation between 1850 and 1928 may be summed up in terms of the principles governing the selection of *élites*. Mannheim suggests that, historically, these have always been selected on the basis of blood, property, and achievement.[5] In the Gold Coast the traditional *élite* was based on blood or lineage. Western education then introduced the principle of achievement, and economic development attached a growing importance to wealth. But a barrier was imposed by the growing racial exclusiveness of the European *élite*—especially in the higher ranks of the civil service—and here the potential conflict provided strong motivation for nationalist agitation. The aspirations of the new *élite* towards political leadership were at first expressed in alliance with traditional rulers; but during the twentieth century

[1] Busia, 'The Present Situation and Aspirations of Élites in the Gold Coast', in *International Social Science Bulletin*, vol. viii, no. 3.

[2] Balandier, 'Social Changes and Social Problems in Negro Africa', in *Africa in the Modern World*, p. 63.　　　　　　　　　　　　　　　　　　　　　　　　[3] Busia, loc. cit.

[4] See Ch. X, pp. 389–96, and Ch. XII, pp. 491–7, below.

[5] *Man and Society*, p. 89.

they began to challenge the Chiefs directly, with a new claim to leadership on a national scale.

This *élite* covered a wide range of educational attainments, income levels, and occupational interests, from the junior clerk employed at an annual salary of £36 to the self-employed professional or business man earning over £1,000 a year.[1] The growing emphasis upon individual wealth and achievement gave some additional status to those at the top; but it would be rash to classify African society in terms of income received, since this often bore little relation to disposable income, which depended also on the financial help available from, or expected by, other relatives. The individual accumulation of capital, which had been virtually unknown under the traditional system, became possible to some extent, at first in trade; but towards the end of the nineteenth century the increase in the scale of expatriate enterprise eclipsed the efforts of the small African trader. Later, however, private practice in the professions (such as the law and medicine) enabled the fortunate few to invest their surplus income in house-renting, cocoa farming, or cocoa buying. By the 1920's it was noticeably the wealthier professional minority who took the lead in the National Congress movement.

The growth in numbers of the educated *élite*, taken as a whole, built up increasing political power behind nationalist demands. There was indeed a hierarchy of status within the *élite*; but this depended more on educational attainment than on income level as such; and the remarkable vertical mobility of individuals should prevent the assumption that there was any rigid stratification even among the educated. Participation in 'modernist-orientated'— i.e. in the Gold Coast context, nationalist—politics was effectively limited to those with some command of English. They alone were able to look beyond the tribe or State, to negotiate with the British governing *élite*, to use new concepts not readily assimilated into the vernacular, and to read the nationalist press. But an examination of the correspondence columns of these newspapers shows that an interest in politics and national affairs was not confined to the most highly educated; the illiterate majority, in so far as they became aware of any specific political grievance, increasingly gave what support they could.

It would be an over-simplification to regard the towns as the province of the new educated *élite*, and the rural areas of the traditional *élite*. In both there was conflict between the old and the new social order. Cocoa farming, in particular, brought modern social and economic change into the villages; and the position of the Chiefs in the towns raised some interesting problems of their relationship to the new political leaders. The cross-ties of kinship prevented any serious urban–rural dichotomy. Nevertheless, it was in the towns

---

[1] One might perhaps attempt to distinguish a semi-educated 'mid-*élite*' between the higher educated *élite* on the one hand, and the illiterate 'mass' on the other hand. Cf. H. D. Lasswell and A. Kaplan, *Power and Society* (London, 1952), pp. 201–3.

that the forces of social change were most uncomfortably at work; for this reason certain aspects of urban development will be briefly dealt with under a separate heading.

Some Social Problems of Urbanization

The rise of new towns around the early forts was one of the most obvious visible signs of European penetration. It was also the setting for the process of acculturation, for the earliest acceptance and diffusion of Western influences. As W. E. Moore has pointed out, writing of under-developed societies generally, 'Not only do the bearers of strange patterns first reach the cities, but the cities themselves act as internal distribution points and sources of change.'[1] Even under the traditional system, trading centres had attracted population from the surrounding villages; but European commerce and political influence combined to produce a different kind of urban community. The new coastal towns had about as much in common with the old-established market centres as a modern English conurbation with a medieval borough.

Cape Coast was for many years the chief British foothold, and during the nineteenth century its population grew with its administrative importance. Troops were sometimes billeted with the townsfolk; commercial activities increased under imperial protection; the more prosperous merchants built themselves European-style houses, and offered an increasingly wide range of goods and services. Similarly, the villages near Accra, originally 'a rude assemblage of fishermen's huts,' were said to have become transformed into 'places of constant resort', by the progressive development of their commercial resources, and the gradual addition of new houses, built for the influx of enterprising traders.[2]

But the methods of government—and particularly the sanitary arrangements—appropriate to villages soon proved inadequate for the expanding towns. An Army surgeon has left a vivid description of conditions in Cape Coast, written about 1850:

The part of the town occupied by the poorer classes consists of houses terribly huddled together, along the opposite faces of what is a deep valley, along which, in the rainy season, a considerable torrent runs, and where, during the dry, all kinds of filth the most abominable accumulate. From this ravine offshoots extend in various directions among the houses; myriads of frogs domesticate themselves . . . In the parts of the town where European merchants or wealthy natives reside the houses are of a superior kind, being composed of brick, flat-roofed, and well white-washed . . . The two principal streets are wide . . . like boulevards. On an eminence at one end

---

[1] W. E. Moore, *Industrialization and Labor* (New York, 1951), p. 181.
[2] W. F. Daniell, 'On the Ethnography of Akkrah and Adampé, Gold Coast, Western Africa', in *Journal of the Ethnological Society* (London, 1852), vol. iv.

of the principal street, directly facing the Castle, stands the Chapel of the Wesleyan Missionaries.[1]

Brodie Cruickshank, a contemporary, confirmed this picture; he described the African houses as 'huddled together in the most crowded manner, and without the slightest regard to light, or air, or the convenience of approach'.[2]

A few British administrators—notably Sir Benjamin Pine, who complained that the towns were 'at once dunghills and grave-yards'[3]—made repeated attempts to persuade the inhabitants to clean up and reorganize urban life.[4] But the main difficulty was the division of authority: the forts tended to overshadow and depress the power of the Chiefs, who yet retained sufficient authority to hamper direct control by the Government. There is no doubt that in theory there was what J. E. Casely Hayford called 'a system of municipal self-government', for sanitation, town planning, public works, and other communal necessities.[5] The towns were originally clearly divided into wards, or 'quarters', each with its own Asafo company, entitled to hold tribunals[6] and to be represented by its leader or Safuhene in the Chief's Council, sitting with the elders. To a description of the Council's functions, Cruickshank added his own estimate of their value:

Their duty, properly speaking, is to look after the police of the town, to suppress nuisances in the street, to clean the paths and roads in its neighbourhood, and to promulgate the edicts of the chief and his counsellors . . .

The institution of such a body of officials would be highly beneficial if they really acted up to their professed character; but whatever might have been the efficiency of their services on their first appointment, they are now utterly worthless.[7]

The Asafo companies had originally represented the main means of organized defence for the State in time of war; deprived of this function by the British *pax*, they seem to have taken more interest in corporate rivalries and matters of prestige than in the day-to-day business of town government. When traditional ceremonies aroused their martial spirit, they turned upon one another. After one of the worst Cape Coast riots, in 1859, the Chief Justice fined the companies mainly responsible, imprisoned the ringleaders, and made regulations for the display of company flags, which each had used to taunt and incite its rivals.[8] But this unsettled dispute dragged on for years,

---

[1] C. A. Gordon, *Life on the Gold Coast* (London, 1874), p. 4.

[2] Cruickshank, *Eighteen Years on the Gold Coast*, vol. i, p. 23.

[3] Dispatch No. 11 of 2 Feb. 1858, from B. Pine to Labouchere; CO/96/43.

[4] See Ch. IV, pp. 184–6, and Ch. V, p. 213, below.

[5] *Gold Coast Native Institutions*, pp. 109–11.

[6] For details of the Asafo tribunals, see Mensah Sarbah, *Fanti National Constitution*, pp. 31–32.

[7] Cruickshank, *Eighteen Years on the Gold Coast*, vol. i, pp. 249–50.

[8] Dispatch No. 24 of 13 Feb. 1860, from Bird to Newcastle; CO/96/47. See also *A Guide to Cape Coast Company Emblems, and Notes as to Customs, etc.* (Accra, 1909). Cf. the complaint of the Mayor of Cape Coast in 1859: 'The companies may be described as so many little republics, each independent of the rest, and having its own officers, laws, and customs . . . each has also a habit of exciting rival companies by singing insulting songs at the same time that the objectionable

and led to constant threats to municipal peace. The trouble was not peculiar to Cape Coast. Between 1863 and 1881, in four other coastal towns, thirteen different riots caused 160 deaths and were attributed mainly to company fights. The Government suppressed their worst excesses, but made little effort to divert their energies into constructive channels.

Meanwhile, the Chiefs had lost their initiative in municipal affairs, and any attempt to assert traditional authority tended to appear as a challenge to British rule;[2] while the various efforts of the educated *élite* to organize some new form of town government were at first stifled, and eventually completely ignored in legislation setting up local councils.[3] Mensah Sarbah had some justification for his allegation, in a petition of 1889, 'Today we are being ruled as if we had no indigenous institutions, no language, no national characteristics, no homes.'[4] Casely Hayford later complained, more reasonably, that 'The effect of intercourse with Europeans on the part of the people of the coast towns has been to disorganize their own former municipal arrangements, and to throw them back upon such haphazard provisions as the Government has felt inclined to make.' He vainly urged the authorities to restore 'the original municipal institutions of the people'.[5]

The drift to the towns continued. Some came in search of schooling for their children, others to find jobs for themselves, or to set up in trade. Differentiation of occupations proceeded fairly rapidly, although specialized skills were hard to acquire.[6] Anyone in paid employment might expect to be followed by other members of his extended family seeking work and support. Some may have been attracted by the prospect of escape from family obligations and other traditional social pressures, although this motive did not become important until later. The wealthy merchants built themselves fine family houses, which proved none too large for the demands of hospitality; and later, cocoa farmers followed their example. House-building increasingly became a popular form of what might be called 'conspicuous investment' for surplus capital. The growing differences in standards of living were illustrated by the contrast between the new 'storey houses' and the urban slums that sprawled around their feet.

Transport improvements and trade expansion during the twentieth century considerably increased the importance of the towns. Sekondi, as the first rail terminus, grew especially rapidly; later, the village of Takoradi mushroomed

flags are paraded.' Letter of 29 Nov. 1859, from R. Hutchison to Chief Justice; Mensah Sarbah, *Fanti Customary Laws*, pp. 11–13.

   [1] Dispatch No. 26 of 2 Feb. 1882, from Rowe to Kimberley; CO/96/137.
   [2] See Ch. V, below, for the conflict between King Aggery and the colonial authorities.
   [3] See Ch. XI, pp. 418–26, below.
   [4] Petition of 5 June 1889, to Secretary of State from principal inhabitants of Cape Coast, enclosed in Dispatch No. 180 of 18 June 1889, from Brandford Griffith to Knutsford; CO/96/202.
   [5] Casely Hayford, *Gold Coast Native Institutions*, pp. 111–13.
   [6] Occupational figures given in Ch. I, pp. 40–41 and 45, above, illustrate this tendency, although they are not comprehensive.

into importance with the new harbour of 1928. The further development of
railways attracted population to the villages *en route* and gave a particular
stimulus to Kumasi, Koforidua, and Accra.[1]

TABLE XVII. *Population of the Main Towns,*
1891–1931[2]

Census	Accra	Kumasi	Cape Coast	Sekondi	Tamale	Winneba	Koforidua
1891	16,267	3,000	11,614	1,276	n.a.	4,283	n.a.
1901	14,842	6,280	28,948	4,095	432	5,578	1,406
1911	19,582	18,853	11,269	9,122	2,138	5,842	3,891
1921	38,049	20,268	14,921	9,500	3,901	6,980	5,364
1931	60,726	35,829	17,685	16,953	12,941	10,926	10,529

Urbanization was also taking place on a smaller scale in many parts of the
country. By 1931, in addition to the seven towns with over 10,000 inhabitants,
there were nineteen with a population of 5,000–10,000 and 349 with 2,000–
5,000.[3] Many villages were expanding as a result of new wealth and new
activities; the pace of life quickened and the older generation, especially the
Chiefs, began to lament the loss of personal contacts on which old customs
were based. Nene Mate Kole said in 1912, 'I can recollect that in my own
boyhood, 50 years ago, my village was a very small place, but it has so increased in size and population that I am now unable to recognize all the young
men that I meet in the street.'[4]

The accelerated rate of urban growth during the twentieth century intensified some social problems, without necessarily raising any new ones. As the
towns sprawled outwards, there was more overcrowding, more dirt and
squalor, more disease—and more rootless young men in search of employment and security. The local Chiefs were powerless to control or improve the
lot of this great influx of population, most of whom owed them no allegiance.
The few municipal councils, on the other hand, which had been 'born in an
atmosphere of ill-will and sullen resentment', were unrelated to the traditional
authorities, while remaining ill-equipped and incompetent to deal with modern

[1] An interesting account of the growth of Accra is given by E. A. Boateng, 'A Geographical
Study of Human Settlement in the Eastern Province of the Gold Coast Colony West of the Volta
Delta'; unpublished B.Litt. thesis, 1954, University of Oxford.
[2] All these figures are taken from the contemporary Census Reports, except for Kumasi,
which appears for the first time in the 1911 Census, with comparative estimates for 1891 and 1901.
None of these figures, especially the earlier ones, should be taken as reliable. The revised estimates
published in later years serve only to increase such doubts. In 1911, for example, the previous
figures for Accra were revised, giving 1891: 19,999, and 1901: 17,892; the 1948 Census gave the
1931 population as 70,000. Presumably these were attempts to recast previous figures to allow
for new town boundaries.
[3] A. W. Cardinall, *The Gold Coast, 1931* (Accra, 1932), p. 158.
[4] Notes of evidence published with H. C. Belfield's *Report on the Legislation Governing the
Alienation of Native Lands in the Gold Coast Colony and Ashanti* (London, 1912), Cd. 6278.

needs. They also lacked the participation and even the confidence of the educated leaders of opinion; and their finances were insufficient to provide for even the basic physical needs of the towns, such as water supplies, drainage, or lighting.

A medical expert, appointed to inquire into an outbreak of bubonic plague in Accra in 1908, strongly criticized the Town Council as a sanitary failure. Thereafter, the central Government took some additional responsibility, for example, by directly appointing an Improvement Committee;[1] but although a piped water system had been under official consideration since 1894, it was not until 1910 that the first public drinking fountain was opened in Accra.[2] The following year the Town Council was once more blamed publicly for the filthy state of the town;[3] and in 1918 there were renewed press criticisms of the lack of drainage and sanitation.[4] A more promising start was made in Kumasi in 1925, when a Public Health Board was established, following a plague epidemic there, to regulate urban development.[5] This soon inaugurated a remarkable programme of town planning, on which nearly £1,000,000 was spent by the Board, by the Government, and by private property-owners, up to 1930.[6]

The shift of population towards the towns should not be allowed to obscure the importance of movements in the opposite direction, and the outward flow of new ideas and ways of life. As Balandier has pointed out, reciprocal relations between African towns and the surrounding villages are often extensive and influential. The urban population tends to be a mobile, impermanent, unsettled aggregate, made up largely of first-generation immigrants whose sojourn there may be only temporary.[7] This lack of permanence has often created serious labour problems, which add to the general restlessness and sense of insecurity; on the other hand, the possibility of returning home to the village offers to many an ultimate refuge that unemployed urban workers in Europe, for example, often lack. Kinship ties were still strong, and the new urban society was by no means 'detribalized'. The immigration of people of diverse origin did not mean that tribal differences ceased to matter. In Accra, for example, the Gãs still predominated, and in Cape Coast the Fantis; others, especially those from the Northern Territories, remained apart, often in their own quarter of the town, and did not even mix socially.

[1] Report by Professor W. J. Simpson on Sanitary Matters in Various West African Colonies and the Outbreak of Plague in the Gold Coast (London, 1909), Cd. 4718.
[2] See illuminated Address to Sir John Rodger, K.C.M.G., on laying Foundation Stone of a Drinking Fountain (Accra, 1910). By 1915 there were about sixty street fountains in Accra, at which the population queued throughout the day and most of the night.
[3] W. H. Grey, Legislative Council Minutes, 6 Nov. 1911.
[4] For example, The Gold Coast Independent, 20 July 1918.
[5] Kumasi Public Health Board Ordinance, 1925.
[6] Legislative Council Debates, 1930, p. 90.
[7] Balandier stated, as late as 1954, that more than two-thirds of the inhabitants of the larger towns of the Gold Coast had been there for less than five years. 'Urbanism in West and Central Africa', in Social Implications of Industrialization and Urbanization in Africa South of the Sahara (Paris, 1956), p. 499.

Nevertheless, one of the major difficulties confronting Africans coming to live in the towns was that of adjustment to an extended field of social relationships, where the 'stranger' or foreigner predominated. The breakdown of social restraints and moral values when members of different tribes—not to speak of races—come together has been more fully documented in recent years.[1] The 'demonstration effect' of close contact with higher standards of living, especially where the worker had no opportunity of emulation, was equally unsettling. Yet too much stress should not be placed upon the disintegrative, unsettling influences of the town. The urban immigrant was driven to seek new groups with which he could identify himself and which would meet the needs formerly supplied by his own kin. But it was precisely in the towns that he found such opportunities, and could begin to participate in a 'new, more interesting, and diversified civilization, with possibilities of greater liberty'.[2] The new associations that emerged are of considerable interest as positive expressions of this liberating aspect of urban life.

New Forms of Association

Educated Africans, in particular, felt the need for integration with those who shared their new interests and outlook, and their command of English helped to break down tribal barriers. During the latter half of the nineteenth century they seem to have attached great importance to building up all kinds of clubs and societies to foster social contacts and common interests.[3] At first these were nearly all modelled on European lines, with some attractive local variations. In 1859, for example, J. P. Brown with four of his young friends started a private literary club in Cape Coast, the Try Company, which remained active for two or three years,[4] and may have been responsible for the opening of the first Reading Room in 1860.[5] The Anomabu Temperance Society was founded in 1862 by R. J. Ghartey, who had recently visited England with F. C. Grant.[6] After a year's activity the members were able to report with pride the establishment of a temperance hotel, and a temperance goldsmith's shop, each with a light outside: 'the first lamp posts ever erected in the streets of any town in the Gold Coast'. It was claimed that 'Almost all classes have signed the pledge.'[7]

[1] For example, K. A. Busia, *Report on a Social Survey of Sekondi–Takoradi* (London, 1950).

[2] T. L. Hodgkin, *Nationalism in Colonial Africa* (London, 1956), p. 63.

[3] Perhaps the first example had been William de Graft's Society for Promoting Christian Knowledge, founded in 1831, which met regularly at Cape Coast to read and discuss the Bible; cf. Ch. II, p. 63 n., above. The early members included George Blankson, John Sam, Henry Brew, John Smith, John Aggery, and S. K. Mensah. A. E. Southon, *Gold Coast Methodism* (Cape Coast, 1934), pp. 27–28.

[4] Article commemorating J. P. Brown's 72nd birthday in *The Gold Coast Nation*, 8 Apr. 1915.

[5] J. B. Anaman, *The Gold Coast Guide* (London, 1902 edn.), p. 165.

[6] Letter of 23 Nov. 1862, from R. J. Ghartey to W. Pretty; Ghartey Papers, SC 7/2, G.N. Archives.

[7] *The African Times*, 23 Mar. 1863.

The Philanthropic Society of Cape Coast, formed in 1864 with the 'very laudable and desirable' object of raising public funds, met with less success. For this they blamed the Government and 'white men generally', who were said to have called their members half-educated and semi-civilized. Piqued by the alleged insult, they announced their intention of appearing on behalf of the Gold Coast Protectorate before the 1865 Select Committee in London; but they did not succeed in doing so.[1] For the next few years the energies of the educated handful were directed into political channels, especially while they were co-operating with the Chiefs in the Fanti Confederation. But after this had been broken up, there was a renewal of interest in more Europeanized forms of association. In 1874 the Rifle Club first met in Cape Coast, and an English merchant, G. H. T. Lyall, inaugurated the Masonic Club.[2] In 1877 the Good Templars were founded by the General Superintendent of the Wesleyan Mission and the Commanding Officer of the Castle garrison, with the help of J. P. Brown, who was made Lodge Deputy Grand Chief Templar.[3] In 1880 we meet the Oddfellows.[4] The next year a Literary Club was formed by a 'party of gentlemen', and a Mercantile Association presented a petition to the Governor.[5] At the end of 1882 yet another new organization was announced: the Grand Ancient Order of Foresters.[6]

But the seed fell at first on stony ground. 'I should like to know what the natives intend doing with the Reading Room and Literary Club', asked a writer in *The Gold Coast Times*. 'If they allow it to die out, like everything else, no more societies need be got up, at least on this side of 1900.' The editor tried to analyse the reasons for such failure, putting the main blame on the snobbishness of the organizers; they were accused of never using words of less than three syllables, looking down on others as inferior, and taking their main delight in wearing gold chains and green chokers for club meetings.[7]

A more fundamental reason for the difficulties experienced by these new forms of social grouping was suggested in a later article by W. E. G. Sekyi on 'Social Life in England and on the Gold Coast': 'The structure of the Akan family makes it impossible for groupings of members according to sex and age not to take place . . . Hence even within the family itself there is no room for the want of companionship of others which renders necessary in England the institutions known as clubs and "pubs" and social gatherings.'[8] This passage also suggests a certain rigidity in Akan social structure, and a failure to develop any sense of community extending beyond the family or at most the tribe. In any case, the fact that many kinship groups were no longer economically self-sufficient had already begun to impair their solidarity for

[1] Ibid. 23 Jan. 1865.   [2] *The Gold Coast Times*, 31 Aug. 1874.
[3] *The Gold Coast Nation*, 8 Apr. 1915.
[4] Report of 1st anniversary celebrations in *The Gold Coast Times*, 12 Nov. 1881.
[5] Ibid. 10 Sept. 1881, 21 Jan. and 29 Apr. 1882.
[6] Ibid. 23 Dec. 1882.
[7] Ibid. 16 Sept. 1882.   [8] *West Africa*, 1 Dec. 1917.

other social purposes.[1] Although so many of the new associations were over-ambitious, unstable, and short-lived—as, indeed, were many similar groups in the new towns of early-nineteenth-century England—this should not obscure their importance as modern means of expressing 'the African genius for sociability'.[2] They helped to make bearable the somewhat harsh, impersonal conditions of town life, and offered new, wider interests that to some extent replaced the warmth and colour of the extended family circle. The principles of continuity and loyalty, without the obvious bond of kinship, were naturally slower to develop. But these imported forms of association, however immature, might be regarded as helping to break down the social barriers to nationalism.

At first, the most successful were those in which a set European pattern was laid down in advance. The Good Templars, Freemasons, and Oddfellows, for example, were said to have defied all the predictions that they would fail.[3] Debating societies were also a popular method of spreading Western habits of thought. At a tea party in Saltpond in 1886, a debating club was proposed, on the ground that 'The Government neglect us intellectually, so we must educate ourselves'. But King Charles's head reared itself in unexpected places. The Cape Coast Debating Society was criticized for discussing whether the invention of gunpowder had been a blessing to mankind in general, and the legality or illegality of the execution of King Charles I, instead of more down-to-earth local matters. Even in Winneba, a lecture on 'The Ideal Standard of Education' was preceded by a debate on the topic 'that Celibacy was advantageous to mankind from an intellectual and religious point of view'.[4] Clearly such activities could only appeal to a limited and sophisticated circle.

Many groups were inspired by ideas of self-help and mutual improvement. In 1895, for example, a small study-circle of youths in Cape Coast was dignified by the title of the Star of Peace Society; this later became the Three Wise Men Society, sporting its own red, white, and black colours, with branches at Anomabu, Saltpond, and Mankessim.[5] Cape Coast also boasted a Young Ladies' Christian Association, and a City Club—whose secretary in 1897 was the young J. E. K. Aggrey—for 'social, physical and intellectual advancement'.[6] Similar developments had been taking place by fits and starts in Accra. In 1873 the Young Men's Free and Mutual Improvement Society had been born from the growing desire to gain additional knowledge; the Rev. W. Penrose gave help in ordering books, but when he returned to England

[1] Cf. K. Little, 'The Study of "Social Change" in British West Africa', in *Africa* (London, 1953), vol. xxiii, no. 4.

[2] Hodgkin, *Nationalism in Colonial Africa*, pt. ii, ch. 2, 'The New Associations'.

[3] *The Gold Coast Times*, 23 Dec. 1882. By the end of the century there were, for example, twenty-one Lodges and Juvenile Temples of the Independent Order of Good Templars. Anaman, *The Gold Coast Guide*, p. 137.

[4] *The Western Echo*, 11 Sept. and 7–13 Dec. 1886.

[5] *The Gold Coast Aborigines*, no. 35, 1899.

[6] *The Gold Coast Methodist Times*, Nov.–Dec. 1897.

the Society died. Later a Social Union was formed by Dr. B. W. Quartey Papafio; but this too was unable to survive the departure of the leading personality. In 1896 the Improvement Society was resurrected by the teachers of the Wesleyan Day School;[1] and the following year a Social and Literary Club was promoted.[2] The Rev. S. R. B. Solomon, who had helped to organize lectures, essay-writing, discussions, and debates in Accra, was now editor of *The Gold Coast Methodist Times*; and he was well placed to exhort young Africans to study all the books they could find concerning themselves, their motherland, and their laws: 'Again we say to all Young Men, Read, Read, Read.'[3]

Inevitably the new organizations developed a political slant. The Gold Coast Union Association, launched at Cape Coast in October 1881, with J. F. Amissah as President, was an early straw in the wind. Some Africans felt that there were more important things than imitating Europeans in clothes and ideas: 'Why, in a word, can we not imitate them in the one grand requisite—unity of purpose and of action?' The leaders hoped 'to unite all classes'; and by establishing branches in commercial centres, where most of the educated people were to be found,

to seek into the requirements of the country, to instil into us the absolute necessity for the development of the resources of our land, mineral, agricultural, or otherwise; in fact, to open our eyes to what is going on around us, and to teach us to give our aid towards advancing our country in the paths of civilization and enlightenment.[4]

But the Union Association soon followed its predecessors into oblivion. There was no difficulty in filling the platform for a public meeting and arousing enthusiasm for almost any issue of the moment; the problem was to maintain the initial impetus. At the end of the year an attempt was made to agitate more specifically for legal reforms; several European merchants were behind this move, and an ambitious organization was devised. There were to be branches at Accra, Cape Coast, and Lagos, subject to the control of a general council: 'we should have wheels within wheels, and gain enormous power thereby'. At a public meeting in Cape Coast, with G. T. H. Lyall in the chair, these paper plans received general approval;[5] but they were never carried out.

By 1885 the technique of organized protest was being studied. The English editor of *The Gold Coast News*, W. C. Niblett, urged the formation of an association of Africans, in order to bring public grievances more effectually to the notice of the Government. To this end, it must be non-sectarian, and 'composed of no more than a sufficient number of the representatives of all classes;

[1] *The Gold Coast Chronicle*, 9 July 1896.
[2] *The Gold Coast Methodist Times*, Nov.–Dec. 1897.
[3] Ibid. 31 July 1897.   [4] *The Gold Coast Times*, 8 and 22 Oct. 1881.
[5] Among those present at this meeting were F. C. Grant, J. Renner Maxwell, W. H. Selby, G. E. Eminsang, J. H. Brew, E. H. Richards, J. B. Elliott, D. W. Wylie, C. W. Burnett, Captain J. J. Pefingell, 'and upwards of twenty other gentlemen', including Chief Quassie Attah of Cape Coast. *The Gold Coast Times*, 10 and 24 Dec. 1881.

rich or poor, high or low, literate or illiterate, each could be represented'. The aim should be to have branches throughout the length and breadth of the country. The association might then be officially recognized by the Government, which would, it was optimistically suggested, pay close attention to its demands.[1] But it was not easy to organize a protest movement without a grievance. Even James Brew's much-publicized deputation scheme of 1885–7 failed to arouse the necessary enthusiasm to carry its promoters to England.[2]

The first African organization that was able to win and consolidate any lasting support was largely non-political, and grew out of the awakening of cultural consciousness among educated Fantis. In 1889 the *Mfantsi Amanbuhu Fékuw* (Fanti National Political Society) was formed in Cape Coast. As J. Mensah Sarbah put it, the founders, 'dissatisfied with the demoralising effects of certain European influences, determined to stop further encroachments into their nationality'.[3] As a practical step, they planned to collect, discuss, and compile a record of native sayings, customs, laws, and institutions.[4] It was at the suggestion of the *Fékuw* that Mensah Sarbah wrote a series of articles,[5] based on his study of Cape Coast court records, which was later elaborated into a full-scale work on *Fanti Customary Laws* (London, 1897). The deliberate revival of African culture—music, language, dress, and names—awakened a ready response in Cape Coast.[6]

The *Fékuw* struck deeper roots than its predecessors, and remained active for several years, until in 1887 it took on a new, political lease of life under a different name. Mensah Sarbah emphasized the essential continuity of policy: the *Fékuw*, 'now the Gold Coast Aborigines' Rights Protection Society', had always impressed upon people the necessity to reconsider the future of their native land.[7] This was only the most notable example of the tendency for existing groups to develop new functions and interests in response to a changing situation. From this time onwards, while many-sided social and cultural associations continued to proliferate, their members took an increasing interest in politics, and this often gave a new direction to their activities. Even those organizations apparently remote from political issues, such as friendly societies, old boys' associations, or football clubs, made an indirect contribution to the development of a national movement. As Hodgkin puts it, 'they have given an important minority valuable experience of modern forms of administration—the keeping of minutes and accounts, the handling of records and correspondence, the techniques of propaganda and diplomacy'. They have also provided 'the cells around which a nation-wide political organisation can be constructed'.[8]

[1] *The Gold Coast News*, 18 Apr. 1885.   [2] See Ch. XI, pp. 412–18, below.
[3] *Fanti National Constitution*, p. xvii.
[4] *The Gold Coast Aborigines*, 8 Feb. 1902.
[5] Johnson, *Towards Nationhood in West Africa*, p. 28 n.
[6] See Ch. XIII, pp. 517–20, below.   [7] *Fanti National Constitution*, pp. xvii–xviii.
[8] *Nationalism in Colonial Africa*, pt. ii, ch. 2.

Christianity and African Society

The Mission Churches could be regarded as just one more new form of social organization, on the lines of those already discussed. But the social changes brought about by Christianity go far deeper than this. R. S. Rattray emphasized in the 1920's 'the fact that to the African "religion" was co-extensive with every action and thought; that it is not possible to pick and choose from his culture and say, "I will retain this and this", if at the same time we destroy that which gave the whole its dynamic force'.[1] But by that time the new dynamic of Christianity had been at work for several centuries, inevitably challenging the old social order through its presentation of a new, positive way of life. The missionaries were also among the earliest bearers of alien culture, and resistance to the latter was sometimes expressed as hostility to the former.[2]

European influence in the Gold Coast can never in fact be entirely dissociated from the impact of Christianity, which has had a long and chequered history since 1471, when the first Portuguese Catholics to reach this part of the coast erected a wooden cross at Shama. Eleven years later, when a Portuguese fleet founded the settlement of A Mina, they 'assisted at the first mass that was celebrated in Guinea, and prayed for the conversion of the natives from idolatry'.[3] There is evidence that as trade developed at least some attempt was made to convert the local inhabitants,[4] not to mention Reindorf's allegation that the Portuguese 'catechised and baptized their slaves before shipping them off'.[5] Often the traders' frontier and the missionaries' frontier seem to have been interwined; for example, a mass baptism of the people of Efutu in 1503 is said to have owed something to a lucrative commercial offer made to the local Chief.[6]

It was not until later that missionary work was undertaken for its own sake, dissociated from commercial enterprise, and designed for the benefit of the inhabitants.[7] Various short-lived missionary efforts were launched over the

[1] *Ashanti Law and Constitution*, preface; part of this had been published previously in *Departmental Reports*, Special Commissioner for Anthropology, 1926–7. Cf. R. Firth's point that religious beliefs are 'not simply a set of intellectual ideas to be changed when a more logical set of ideas is presented. They are deeply infused with, indeed based upon, emotional attitudes of great strength and practical relevance.' *Elements of Social Organization* (London, 1951), ch. vii, 'Religion and Social Reality', p. 237.

[2] Cf. W. K. Hancock on the 'missionaries' frontier' in *Survey of British Commonwealth Affairs* (Oxford, 1940), vol. ii, pt. i, ch. i, sect. iii.

[3] R. H. Major, *The Discoveries of Prince Henry the Navigator, and their Results* (London, 2nd edn. 1877), p. 201.

[4] Duarte Pacheco Pereira, *Esmeraldo de Situ Orbis*, written c. 1505, and translated by G. H. T Kimble (London, 1937), pp. 120–1.

[5] C. C. Reindorf, *History of the Gold Coast and Asante* (Basel, 1895), p. 220.

[6] R. M. Wiltgen, *Gold Coast Mission History, 1471–1880* (Techny, 1956), pp. 12–13.

[7] There were chaplains appointed at various times for the coastal forts, but few of these ventured out to make conversions in the neighbourhood; see H. Debrunner, 'Notable Danish Chaplains on the Gold Coast', in *Transactions of the Gold Coast & Togoland Historical Society* (Achimota, 1956), vol. ii, pt. i.

years; for example, by Portuguese Augustinians in the sixteenth century,[1] French Capuchins in the seventeenth century,[2] and the Moravian Brethren in the eighteenth century.[3] From the start there were formidable obstacles, the most obvious being the sporadic hostility of the inhabitants and the devastating effects of local diseases upon Europeans. On this point a rare emotional touch even breaks into the Census report for 1891: 'The first Basel missionaries who came to the Colony [in 1828] all died to a man before they had time to organize their work, and from then till today the sacrifice of human lives among this and the other Missionary bodies in the Colony has been truly appalling.'[4] Almost as discouraging was the indifference and apathy encountered by the earliest English missionary to the Gold Coast, the Rev. Thomas Thompson, who was sent out by the S.P.G. from 1752 to 1756; when he attempted to extend his work beyond the official duties of a chaplain he found that 'Spiritual matters made no Impression on them. The Christian Religion they call *white Man's Fashion*, and *white Men*, they say, *know best*, but *black Man follow black Man's Fashion*: as much as to tell me, they would not be put out of their own Way.'[5] Thompson made very few converts, and baptized only a handful of adults. Two of the Cape Coast boys he sent to England for education died; but the third, Philip Quaque, became the first African to take orders in the Anglican Church,[6] and returned to the Gold Coast in 1766 to carry on the work for the next fifty years. He does not seem to have had much influence outside the castle walls of Cape Coast.[7]

The sacral aspect of chieftaincy has already been discussed; and it is hardly surprising that the traditional resistance to missionary penetration came largely from the 'Natural Rulers'. This appears to have been especially strong in Ashanti. The first Basel evangelist to visit Kumasi 'came back with the impression that we had to wait for better hints from the Lord'.[8] Despite elaborate

[1] *Informacão da Mina*, dated 29 Sept. 1572, at São Jorge Castle, quoted by Wiltgen, *Gold Coast Mission History*, p. 21.

[2] *Scritture di diversi paesi*, no. 83, Archives of the Sacred Congregation de Propaganda Fide, Rome; ibid. pp. 43–46.

[3] The Moravian Church sent out nine Brethren in all to the Gold Coast, from 1737 onwards, including Christian Protten, a Gã mulatto who had spent several years in Denmark. By 1770 all had died, some within a month of arrival, and the Mission station at Ningo was abandoned. See J. E. Hutton, *A History of Moravian Missions* (London, 1923), p. 156, and P. Steiner, *Ein Blatt aus der Geschichte der Brüdermission* (Basel, 1888).

[4] *Report on the Census of the Gold Coast Colony for the year 1891* (London, n.d.).

[5] *An Account of Two Missionary Voyages* (London, 1758); reprinted in facsimile with Introduction and Notes by the S.P.C.K. (London, 1937).

[6] In 1742 J. E. J. Capitein, a former slave from the Ivory Coast, had been ordained into the ministry of the Reformed Church of the Netherlands, and appointed chaplain at Elmina. See F. L. Bartels, 'Jacobus Eliza Johannes Capitein, 1717–1747', in *Transactions of the Historical Society of Ghana* (Legon, 1959), vol. iv, no. i.

[7] See Bartels, 'Philip Quaque, 1741–1816', in *Transactions of the Gold Coast & Togoland Historical Society* (Achimota, 1955), vol. i, pt. v. After Quaque's death, other Anglican chaplains were appointed to the forts; but the S.P.G. did not re-establish a Mission until 1904.

[8] Letter of 18 Dec. 1877, from the Rev. F. Ramseyer to Freeling, referring to the journey to Kumasi in 1839 by the Rev. A. Riis; CO/96/122.

and courteous exchanges between the Rev. T. B. Freeman and the Asantehene from 1839 onwards,[1] the Wesleyans had little success with the Mission station they established in 1843, and ten years later it was reported:

The state of the work of God in Asante is rather discouraging at present, from the circumstance of the people being afraid to expose themselves to the ire of the king, whose frown is indeed death for people becoming christians. Many of the Asantes are wishful to embrace christianity, but they are afraid to come forward . . . They always do whatever the king sanctions, whether good or bad, so that, the king himself being a pagan still, they all remain pagans still.[2]

The Mission house fell into disuse, and when the Wesleyans asked permission in 1876 to resume residence and start schools, they were told: 'We will accept the Mission, if you act as Mr. Freeman did to help the peace of the nation and the prosperity of trade, but you must understand . . . The Bible is not a book for us . . . We will never embrace your religion'.[3] This was not considered sufficiently encouraging; and a Colonial Office official commented: 'Apparently not much hope of the Christianization of Ashantee!'[4] A few years later, the Basel Mission was refused permission to settle in Ashanti, and although the Asantehene raised no objection to occasional visits, these were attempted 'all to no purpose; king and nation hardened their hearts'.[5] In 1882 the Catholics at Elmina sought permission to start work in Kumasi.[6] When Fr. A. Moreau asked for an assurance that the Protestants would not be granted anything refused to himself, the Asantehene diplomatically replied: 'I don't refuse you, and as for this minister, never fear; he won't get in.'[7]

The Wesleyans in fact returned in 1884, when the Rev. R. J. Hayfron was appointed to Kumasi. Some progress was made in outlying towns, such as Bekwai.[8] But a real opportunity for missionary work did not come until the exile of Prempeh in 1896, when the Governor personally invited the Basel Mission to Kumasi.[9] After three years' work, they had opened sixteen centres

[1] In 1841, for example, Freeman accompanied John Ossoo Ansah and William Inkwantabissa (two Ashanti princes who had been sent to England ten years previously) on their return to Kumasi, and presented the Asantehene with a wheeled carriage from the Wesleyan Missionary Society. T. B. Freeman, *Journal of Various Visits to the Kingdom of Ashanti, Aku and Dahomi, in Western Africa* (London, 2nd edn. 1844), pp. 123–37.

[2] Report of the Rev. T. Laing, quoted by Reindorf, *History*, pp. 242–3.

[3] Quoted by G. G. Findlay and W. W. Holdsworth, *The History of the Wesleyan Methodist Missionary Society* (London, 1922), vol. iv, p. 175.

[4] Minute of 8 June 1876, by A. W. L. Hemming; CO/96/118.

[5] D. Huppenbauer, *Von Kyebi nach Kumase* (Basel, 4th edn. 1905), pp. 52–60, and Scottish Mission, *The Basel Mission Centenary, 1828–1928* (Accra, 1928), ch. viii.

[6] The Catholics had been driven out of Elmina when the Dutch captured the fort in 1637. But when they returned in 1880, several traces of Christian worship and ritual were found to have survived, although their significance had been forgotten. Wiltgen, *Gold Coast Mission History*, ch. viii. The Catholics did not open a station in Kumasi until 1910.

[7] *Annales de la Propagation de la Foi* (Lyons, 1883), lv, quoted in translation by C. P. Groves, *The Planting of Christianity in Africa*, vol. iii (London, 1955), p. 189.

[8] Southon, *Gold Coast Methodism*, p. 115.

[9] Letter of 23 Jan. 1896, from Maxwell to Ramseyer; W. Schlatter, *Geschichte der Basler Mission, 1815–1915* (Basel, 1916), vol. iii, p. 121.

in Ashanti, with a total of 164 church members and 451 scholars; the Wesleyans then had 1,500 church attendants and 675 scholars (in Sunday and day
schools), in eight centres.[1] Then in 1900 came the Ashanti revolt, in the course
of which most of the churches were destroyed. A fresh start was made; but
for a long time the Christian religion was regarded by the Ashantis as an
alien influence.

Even farther south, where considerable progress had been made in education and evangelization during the nineteenth century, Christianity was still
generally regarded as 'White Man's Fashion'. This was partly an excuse to
avoid facing up to new and uncomfortable doctrines. But it was also perhaps
an inevitable reaction to the early missionaries' often unconscious assumption
that European civilization, as well as the Christian religion, was superior to
anything to be found in Africa. A few of them, ignorant of local customs,
condemned outright, in all its aspects, a culture that could sanction, for
example, human sacrifice. Similarly, it must have been difficult for many
Africans to distinguish between Christian doctrine and its European accretions and trimmings. So distinguished a Western writer as Dean Inge has
gone so far as to say:

As a great historical institution Christianity can be characterised only as the
religion of the white man . . . From the second century till the present day, Christianity has been the most European and the least Asiatic of religions. Its great expansion in modern times has been due to the unparalleled expansion of the white
race.[2]

Africans might therefore be forgiven if they sometimes imagined that the
insistence on 'decent' clothing, and the introduction of Christian instead of
'heathen' names, were as indispensable as the basic articles of faith. Dr.
E. W. Blyden was the first West African to attack the missionaries for the
spread of 'practices which, however useful they might be in Europe, become,
when introduced indiscriminately into Africa, artificial, ineffective and absurd'.[3] Later, many Gold Coast writers in turn were to protest that Christianity
had been 'presented Europeanised'.[4]

The Missions took some practical steps intended to dispel the idea that
Christianity was a white man's religion. The Rev. A. Riis, for example, took

[1] *Departmental Reports*, Ashanti, 1899.
[2] W. R. Inge, *Science, Religion and Reality* (London, 1925), p. 387.
[3] *Christianity, Islam and the Negro Race* (London, 1887), p. 75. E. W. Blyden was born in the
West Indian island of St. Thomas, a descendant of slaves imported by the Danes, mainly from
Christiansborg. He became a teacher at the College of Liberia, later Ambassador to the Court of
St. James, and in 1885 stood for the Presidency of Liberia. At one time he was a minister in the
Presbyterian Church of West Africa; in 1890–1 he visited Lagos, where he had a strong influence
on the foundation of the United Native African Church, and in 1901 he became Director of
Mohammedan Education in Sierra Leone. His censures against missionaries were not directed
particularly at the Gold Coast, but his views were influential among many educated West Africans.
See Ch. XIII, p. 538, below.
[4] Nana Annor Adjaye, *Nzima Land* (London, 1931), p. 160.

to heart a remark made by the Chief of Akropong: 'if you could show us some blackmen who could read the Whiteman's Book, then we would surely follow you'. Having secured the official support of the Mission in Basel, Riis himself sailed to Jamaica and in 1843 brought back twenty-four immigrants, including six couples with their children. The experiment was not an unqualified success. The West Indians had to cope with the problems of climate and language in the same way as Europeans, and some returned home when their five-year agreement expired. There were no large-scale conversions as a result of their example. Nevertheless, most of them remained as the nucleus of the resident Christian community at Akropong (in 1851, of a total of thirty-one, twenty-five were West Indians), and they intermarried with local families. The son of one of these marriages claimed that the immigrants had succeeded in proving to Africans 'that coloured people too could do without fetishes, live in monogamous Christian marriages, clothe themselves decently and work actively'.[1]

The Wesleyans were conscious of this problem, and it was undoubtedly fortunate that their first General Superintendent, the Rev. T. B. Freeman, was the son of an African; but his colour was so light that he was known as 'the great white prophet'.[2] The training of Africans as Wesleyan ministers began in 1841; and their missionaries were constantly directed to choose from among their converts men fitted for 'the trying and intricate work of native pastors'. According to the Rev. D. Kemp, one of their guiding motives was to demonstrate the Christian life as lived by Africans:

The life of the devoted white man is in danger of being misunderstood. By the native he is placed on a pedestal far above the poor black man. The native ascribes to superior nature and to propitious environment, that which ought to be ascribed to the transforming power of the Gospel of Christ. But the consistent life of the man of colour appeals to his fellow-countrymen. He is skin of their skin.[3]

The Basel Mission preferred to draw their converts into a new community life physically distinct from the old—to such an extent that J. B. Danquah later blamed them for creating a gulf between Christians and non-Christians. In Akim Abuakwa the Mission station itself was christened *Oburoni-kurom*, 'the white man's town'. A major source of friction was the idea that 'Christians were those who were free of the restraints and taboos of the heathen town, and, as they thought, of the authority and rule of princes of this earth'.[4]

---

[1] Unpublished MS. by N. T. Clerk, 'Centenary Report. The West Indians, 1843–1943'; cf. the account given by Schlatter, *Geschichte der Basler Mission*, vol. iii, esp. pp. 32–36.

[2] F. D. Walker, *Thomas Birch Freeman, the Son of an African* (Cape Coast, 1929).

[3] Wesleyan Methodist General Letter of 3 Nov. 1877, quoted by Kemp, *Nine Years*, pp. 144–5. See Ch. II, p. 64 n., above, for details of some of the early African ordinations.

[4] J. B. Danquah, *The Akim Abuakwa Handbook* (London, 1928), p. 90. In Akwapim there had even been an early suggestion that the Basel Mission should nominate a Native Christian Headman to sit in the local court at Akropong, 'in cases where Christians and Pagans are mutually interested'. Report by Freeman, dated 5 July 1867; CO/96/74.

There were, in fact, occasional outbreaks of violence between the sheep and the goats in Eastern Akim, especially during 1887. The traditional elders wrote to the Governor to say: 'Now we tell you plainly that we were here before [the Rev.] Mohr came, we do not want him or any of the Christians in this Eastern Akim.' At an official investigation it was found that 'the heathen complained of the conduct of the Christians who . . . refused to act in accordance with the native law and made themselves generally obnoxious', and that they attributed the death of their paramount Chief to Mohr, 'owing to an injudicious statement'.[1]

Similar, though less violent, conflicts arose in Ashanti once the Missions became established there. Some of the missionaries took special care to instruct their converts to obey the Chiefs.[2] But by 1905 it was reported that 'the Chiefs are afraid to encourage a movement that experience tells them will . . . undermine their power'. Sometimes the Government encouraged the Christians to form separate settlements in order to reduce the possibilities of discord. But friction continued. One grievance was the Christians' acceptance of slaves on equal terms with others in their new communities; another was the claim of converts to be freed from customary obligations of service to the Chief, where fetish practices were involved.[3]

A joint committee of officials and missionaries, set up in Kumasi in 1912, recommended that a distinction should be drawn between fetish and purely ceremonial services, so that Christians might be bound to perform the latter but not the former. It was also agreed that if a State oath were sworn against a Christian, he should be bound to accept it as a summons to attend court, but he should not be obliged to swear it back again.[4] The Ashanti Chiefs were not represented on this committee, all of whose members were Europeans.

---

[1] Letter of 16 Feb. 1887, from Chief Atcherey and others to Brandford Griffith, and Dispatch No. 396 of 31 Oct. 1887, from White to Holland; CO/96/184. The Mission version of the disturbances was that Nana Amoako Atta, who had been deported to Lagos in 1880, returned in 1884 determined to suppress Christianity; he 'destroyed the plantations of the Christians, robbed and illtreated them . . . death summoned him before a higher tribunal. On his coffin his adherents swore to finish his work.' A. Jehle, 'The Story of the Basel Mission Work in the Gold Coast', in *The Basel Mission Centenary.*

[2] For example, the Rev. F. Jost, who insisted on this, even if the Christians were treated unjustly. H. Huppenbauer, *Friedrich Jost, ein Berner Missionar in Asante* (Basel, 1943). The story is told of another missionary that when he reproved an Ashanti woman for disobeying the Chief, she complained, 'What is then the advantage of being a Christian?' L. Oehler, *Edmond Perregaux* (Basel, 1908), p. 73.

[3] *Departmental Reports*, Ashanti, 1905 and 1910.

[4] Ibid. 1912. The stool of each State, in both Ashanti and the Colony, had attached to it one or more oaths; these referred, usually indirectly, to some military defeat or other calamity—e.g. for Akim Abuakwa, *Wukuda ne Kwanyako* or Kwanyako Wednesday, the place and day of the paramount Chief's death from smallpox in 1811. The swearing of such an oath was strictly forbidden, and involved the payment of a heavy fine as well as a sacrifice to propitiate the ancestors (to which the Christians naturally objected). The State oath was often, however, 'used as a kind of challenge or wager by one of the parties in a dispute. The other party will either abandon his claim, if he is not prepared to back it up to the extent entailed, or will take up the oath in support of his own contention. In the latter case it will be necessary for the dispute to be submitted to the

Their conclusions could hardly be called an agreed solution, and in practice many local disputes were still left to be settled by the District Commissioners. Many years later Busia concluded, after a survey of the position in Ashanti, that 'the conflict between Christianity and the Chiefs is real, and has not been solved'.[1] It is not surprising, therefore, that some Africans, in both the Colony and Ashanti, attacked Christianity as being mainly disruptive and destructive of tneir social organization and of established authority.

Perhaps the biggest practical obstacle to the spread of Christianity was the fact that converts were expected to become monogamous. At first, there was less insistence on this; there is even an early record of a polygamist being knowingly baptized by the Basel Mission at Akropong.[2] But most of the missionaries soon came to the conclusion that polygamy was neither a social necessity nor a matter for the individual conscience. It was incompatible with the will of God. The Wesleyans decided in 1885 that no member of the Church should be allowed to marry a heathen man or woman—an ideal that has not always been attained in John Wesley's own country—and that no woman church member should be allowed to marry a man who already had a wife, 'both these being scriptural principles'. Further, 'no man having more than one wife should be admitted as a member of our Church, and . . . it should be left with the superintendent minister to decide whether, on an investigation of the case, the wives of polygamists should be received into Church fellowship.'[3]

In 1893 the Methodist Synod decided to insist on the Christian rite of marriage for all its members. 'In order to ease the situation', those who were already married according to native law were to be received for membership, but only 'on the distinct understanding that they cannot pass beyond the trial stage until they conform to the Christian rite'.[4] These rules were not always strictly interpreted in later years, as understanding of local conditions grew. The Presbyterians (who succeeded the Basel Mission after the First World War) agreed to recognize marriages already contracted by their members according to native customary law, and in 1927 an optional service of blessing was introduced; marriages of church members to heathens were regarded as 'not expedient', but were not banned.[5]

---

arbitrament of the Stool . . . in order that it may be resolved which of the parties has used the oath falsely.' The culprit would then have to pay the relevant penalty, as well as losing his case. C. W. Welman, *The Native States of the Gold Coast, I Peki* (London, 1925). A list of State oaths and a detailed description of their use is given in *The 'Sunlight' Reference Almanac* (Aburi, 1936), pp. 40–46. This unpretentious booklet contains a mine of information on Gold Coast tribes, customs, and institutions.

[1] Busia, *The Position of the Chief* (1951), p. 135.

[2] Personal communication from Dr. H. Debrunner.

[3] Kemp, *Nine Years*, ch. iv. Cf. the first authoritative Anglican pronouncement on this matter, when the Lambeth Conference ruled in 1888 that a polygamist might be admitted as a catechumen but not be baptized, while the baptism of the wives of polygamists was permissive. Groves, *The Planting of Christianity in Africa*, vol. ii (1954), p. 262 n.   [4] Kemp, *Nine Years*, ch. iv.

[5] *The Church in the State: the Reply of the Presbyterian Church of the Gold Coast to a Memorandum presented by the State Council of Akim Abuakwa* (Accra, 1942), pp. 15–19.

The existence since 1884 of three separate but—from different points of view —legal forms of marriage complicated social conventions,[1] and bedevilled the missionaries' own efforts to preach marriage as an indissoluble Christian bond. Social tensions were bound to arise from the persistence of customs which had been evolved to meet the conditions of a polygamous society, and which 'set standards sometimes prejudicial to the success of a monogamous marriage'.[2] But the Missions always refused to compromise on the basic question of polygamy.[3] Although they came to accept that the breaking up of polygamous marriages need not be considered an end in itself, none of them would—officially—accept a man with more than one wife as a full church member.

There was considerable pressure on the Churches to relax their views. The convert in Africa was being asked to make a much bigger sacrifice and 'change of life' than in many other countries; great strength of character and conviction was required to reject entirely so deeply rooted a social institution. Few Africans were ruthless enough to send away all but one of their existing wives to satisfy a little-understood principle. Some of the converts subsequently lapsed openly into polygamy; others followed the hypocritical example set by some white men. Non-Christians were probably made to feel vaguely guilty about the whole matter, while some Christians proceeded to try and justify polygamy with reference to the Old Testament.

In spite of the very real conflict between Christian beliefs and certain important aspects of African social organization, it is at least arguable that the missionaries were not the primary instigators of social change. It is noteworthy that when traditional authority was at its strongest—for example in Thompson's day, or during Ramseyer's detention in Ashanti—Christianity could hardly get a foothold. Once the country had been 'opened up' by the traders and administrators, and made receptive to Western influences, then the Missions became established. The development of competitive trade and of a money economy, the new roads that led out of the villages, the materialistic values of many Europeans,[4] even the introduction of English law, were far more decisive factors in the disintegration of a close-knit social system.

Government officials and traders knew and cared far less than most mission-

---

[1] Marriages could be contracted (1) according to native custom, (2) in a Christian Church, and/or (3) under the Marriage Ordinance of 1884. This was enacted after consultation with the main religious bodies; but in Dec. 1886 *The Gold Coast Methodist* called it a 'most impractical measure'.

[2] Busia, *Social Survey of Sekondi-Takoradi*, ch. iii, 'Married Life'.

[3] Occasional doubts were later expressed in Christian circles, e.g. by E. W. Smith: 'Most missionaries perhaps regard polygamy as a closed question. But a suggestion for reconsideration of this attitude ought not to be thrust aside lightly'. *The Christian Mission in Africa* (London, 1926), p. 278. The International Missionary Council Conference held at Le Zoute, Belgium, in 1926, of which his book is an account, reiterated the insistence of the Churches on monogamy.

[4] Cruickshank complained bitterly in 1853 of 'the very low standard of morality among the Europeans, the natural result of the demoralizing nature of the trade'. *Eighteen Years on the Gold Coast*, vol. i, p. 33.

aries about the structure and values of African society. As Governor Brandford Griffith wrote, somewhat complacently, in 1888: 'It cannot be considered probable that ... children educated in Christian schools will be
content when grown up to abide by or be contented with such justice as
conviction by Otootoo, a whistle which is supposed *ex mero motu* to discern
who are the guilty and who are the innocent.' He thought that although
native law should be preserved as far as possible, its extinction was only
a matter of time.[1] But it was the missionary who helped to mitigate the forces
of social change, through his intimate local contacts, and his assistance to
individuals facing the problems of transition. He was often the first to 'create
bridges of understanding between the people and himself', and to discover
and explore African culture.[2] The work of the Basel evangelists has been pre-
eminent in this field, for they took every opportunity to identify themselves
with the life of the country. Horton was impressed by the fact that some of
them married African wives, and that their numbers included shoemakers,
tailors, wheelwrights, carpenters, and coopers: 'they ... call themselves
Germano-Africans'.[3]

From 1828 onwards, numerous pamphlets and articles were produced by
Basel missionaries on Gold Coast life and customs.[4] The Rev. J. G. Christaller, introducing his collection of Twi proverbs, urged 'those Africans who
are enjoying the benefit of a Christian education' not to despise 'the sparks
of truth entrusted to and preserved by their own people'.[5] His *Dictionary* of
1881 constitutes an indirect mine of information about Twi society.[6] Another
full-scale work from Basel, on the Gã people, gives detailed descriptions of
their religious festivals and institutions.[7] But since this is woven round the
life-story of a fetish priest who became an evangelist, there is necessarily some
implied criticism. At least it seems clear that where African beliefs and
customs were rejected, the choice was usually made deliberately, and not out
of ignorance.[8]

Nevertheless, when educated Africans came to count the cost of social
change, it was often the missionaries who were blamed for the idea 'that

[1] Confidential Dispatch of 7 Apr. 1888, from Brandford Griffith to Knutsford; CO/96/191.

[2] Cf. G. W. Carpenter, 'The Role of Christianity and Islam in Contemporary Africa', in *Africa Today*, ed. by C. Grove Haines (Baltimore, 1955).

[3] Horton, *West African Countries and Peoples*, pp. 144–7.

[4] For example, Dieterle, 'Das Opfer der Neger auf der Goldküste' (1853), Mader, 'Priester und Propheten bei den Otschi-Negern' (1867), Breitenbach, 'Die Königs-Kostüme in Akropong' (1867), all in the magazine *Evangelische Heidenbote der Basler Mission*; also J. Bellon, *Kultus und Kultur der Tschi-Neger im Spiegel ihrer Sprichwörter* (Basel, 1907). For further examples, see A. W. Cardinall, *A Bibliography of the Gold Coast* (Accra, 1931), pp. 147–77.

[5] *Twi Mmebusem*, 'A Collection of Three Thousand and Six Hundred Tshi Proverbs' (Basel, 1879), p. xi.

[6] *A Dictionary of the Asante and Fante Language called Tshi* (Basel, 1881).

[7] H. Bohner, *Im Lande des Fetischs* (Basel, 1890), based on the life of Paul Mohenu.

[8] Cf. C. G. Baeta, 'The Challenge of African Culture to the Church and the Message of the Church to African Culture', in *Christianity and African Culture* (Accra, 1955).

everything African is necessarily evil, and must, therefore, be replaced with indecent haste'.[1] In particular, criticism fastened upon the incidental accompaniments of Church worship. As Casely Hayford asked:

Why, for example, should not the native convert sing his own native songs, and play his native airs in church? Why should he not attune his horns, his *adziwa*, his *gomey*, or for that matter, his *adankum*, to the praise of God, much as the Israelites of old praised Jehovah upon the cymbal and the harp? . . . Why, in the name of reason and common sense, should not the Native bear his own name and wear his own native garments? Why, indeed, except that the simple missionary has, from the beginning, ruled that all these things are against the letter, if not the spirit, of the Gospel? [2]

Sometimes the critics did not understand the reason behind these rules;[3] sometimes they were carried to excess, or continued after the original reason had disappeared. As Nana Annor Adjaye later remarked pointedly: 'There is a Church here which believes in the playing of drums to the glory of God. But they have selected European drums in preference to African drums. Is God a European?'[4] And he declared, 'I am a Christian myself, but I do not believe in a Christianity which spells denationalization.'[5]

A more fundamental criticism was sometimes made to the effect that the missionaries did not keep their eyes open, as St. Paul did in Athens, for the local altar 'to the unknown God', and that they failed to introduce Christianity in terms that would appeal to the already existing religious sense. Thompson had recorded in the 1750's, in his *Missionary Voyages*, 'I never spake with one of them, who did not confess Belief in a supreme Being.' The Akan name for this Being, *Nyankopon*, was taken over by the missionaries, some of whom made use of local proverbs to illustrate their message. But this was not felt to be enough. Casely Hayford claimed in 1903 that 'a different state of things would prevail if the missionary had first studied the Religious System of the Native'.[6] A generation later, J. W. de Graft Johnson wrote: 'In the natural religion of the African . . . was material that could be woven

---

[1] S. R. B. Attoh Ahuma, review of the Rev. M. Hayford's *West Africa and Christianity*, reprinted in app. to *Memoirs of West African Celebrities* (Liverpool, 1905). Cf. a Cape Coast writer who complained that as a child he had been led to believe that 'there was something peculiarly "devilish" about the celebrations of *Ahubaw* and that it would be awfully disgraceful and paganish for a Christian family to join in it.' *The Gold Coast Nation*, 13 Oct. 1917.

[2] *Gold Coast Native Institutions*, p. 105.

[3] At Odumase Krobo, for example, although African drums were used to call people to church services, the beating of gong-gong was forbidden, because it had to be accompanied by the swearing of a fetish oath. *The Church in the State: the Reply of the Presbyterian Church* (Accra, 1942), p. 20.

[4] Cf. the experience of the musician E. Amu, who introduced African music into church worship while a teacher at the Presbyterian Training College, Akropong; this, he claims, was considered by the church authorities 'improper and unedifying', and he was consequently expelled in 1933. Personal communication from E. Amu of Kumasi.

[5] Nana Annor Adjaye, *Nzima Land*, pp. 158 and 160.

[6] *Gold Coast Native Institutions*, p. 105.

into the very texture of Christianity.'¹ By this time some European observers
had become convinced of the need 'to naturalize Christianity in Africa', as
E. W. Smith put it. This meant 'not a paganization of Christianity for the
purpose of making it easier to Africans, but the Christianization of everything that is valuable in the African's past experience and registered in his
customs'.²

But this approach was not typical—or at least, not considered typical—of
the Missions. As Sir Gordon Guggisberg and the Rev. A. G. Fraser admitted,
'In our anxiety to Christianize, we have tended far too much to destroy, with
little thought of adaptation.'³ The reaction of many Africans was to extol the
virtues and past glories of their own religion, and this chimed in well with the
beginnings of cultural nationalism. Casely Hayford, for example, wrote with
considerable respect of 'that system of faith and worship known as Fetishism';
and he could see no reason for the 'uncultured Native . . . to forsake the gods
of his fathers'.⁴ Later, this theme was taken up and modified by Africans in
the Missions. As one teacher said in Kumasi in 1925: 'To the African the
whole universe breathes of God . . . the extent of his faith . . . is a locked-up
spiritual capital, which the Church has to learn to use.'⁵

The Churches and Nationalism

The training for leadership given to African ministers, and their growing
self-confidence in working alongside Europeans, may be regarded as a positive
stimulus to the development of the nationalist movement. A remarkably
prophetic account of this process was given by the Secretary of the C.M.S.
in London, as early as 1868. He suggested that racial consciousness would
'probably rise in intensity with the progress of the mission', and that 'as the
native race advances in intelligence, as their power of arguing strengthens, as
they excel in writing sensational statements, as they become our rivals in the
pulpit and on the platform, long-cherished but dormant prejudices, and even
passions, will occasionally burst forth'.⁶ Church organizations did not take
a definite part in nationalist agitation, but prominent members were often
outspoken on political issues. Most educated Africans were the product of
Mission schools, and accepted their religious teaching as a guide to the new,
Western ways of life, and a background to political thinking.

In the growth of self-governing institutions the Churches were usually
ahead of the Government, and they provided some African leaders with a
forum, and an unaccustomed freedom of expression, both in the pulpit and

---

¹ *Towards Nationhood*, p. 145.

² E. W. Smith, *The Golden Stool, Some Aspects of the Conflict of Cultures in Modern Africa*
(London, 1926), p. 260.

³ F. G. Guggisberg and A. G. Fraser, *The Future of the Negro* (London, 1929), ch. v.

⁴ *Gold Coast Native Institutions*, p. 101.

⁵ J. Mensah, *National Problems* (London, 1933), pp. 12–13.

⁶ W. Knight, *Memoir of . . . Rev. H. Venn* (London, 1880).

the press. The Wesleyans, for example, besides introducing a printing work-shop as part of their educational programme, were responsible for some of the earliest Gold Coast newspapers. *The Christian Messenger and Examiner* was produced in Cape Coast by the Rev. T. B. Freeman and the Rev. H. Wharton as early as 1859; this was succeeded by *The Christian Reporter*, which had an equally brief career. In 1885 two European missionaries, the Rev. W. T. Coppin and the Rev. W. M. Cannell, began to edit *The Gold Coast Methodist*, which was published quarterly for a year or so; the 'reasonable and just public demand' for African representation on the Legislative Council soon figured in its columns.[1] *The Gold Coast Methodist Times*, founded in 1894, appeared more frequently and had a much wider influence. It was originally intended to follow a strictly religious policy, 'entirely innocent of the odium of controversy and such like inventions of the Evil One';[2] but under the editorship of the Rev. S. R. B. Solomon the paper quickly became the outlet for major political grievances, and made a lasting reputation by its successful handling of the Lands Bill agitation. At the end of 1897 the Synod's misgivings about such emphasis on temporal affairs were redoubled by a libel case brought against the newspaper; Solomon then gave up the editorship, and soon afterwards publication ceased.[3]

The training of Africans, not only for church leadership but for democratic organization, was the basis of Wesleyan work in the Gold Coast, noted even in so neutral a document as a Census report: 'After the establishment of the native ministry in 1852, the Society spread very rapidly, especially among the Fantis on the Coast, its popularity being no doubt due, in some measure, to the democratic nature of its institutions and system of Church Government.'[4] According to J. W. de Graft Johnson, the Wesleyan Methodist Church was for years termed the 'National Church of the Gold Coast', and it consistently followed 'the policy to win Africa with the help of the Africans'.[5] In 1885, with only three Europeans, this Church had 15 African ministers, 43 cate-chists, 79 day-school teachers, and 259 local preachers.[6] By 1934, the cen-tenary year, there were 47 African ministers, 367 catechists, 479 day-school teachers, 1,500 local preachers, 2,500 class leaders, and 2,600 Sunday-school teachers.[7] This was a remarkably large group of articulate Africans, enjoying varying degrees of responsibility, and all conscious in some measure of belonging to a nation-wide—not to mention world-wide—organization. Un-doubtedly they played some part in stimulating the growth of national consciousness; and some of them found their way into politics, occasionally via separatist movements of protest against the parent Church.

---

[1] *The Gold Coast Methodist*, Dec. 1886.   [2] Vol. 1, no. 1, Mar. 1894.
[3] See Ch. IX, pp. 335–49, below.
[4] *Report on the Census of the Gold Coast Colony for the Year 1901* (London, 1902).
[5] J. W. de Graft Johnson, *Historical Geography of the Gold Coast* (London, 1929), ch. xxviii.
[6] *Census*, 1901.
[7] Southon, *Gold Coast Methodism*, pp. 126 and 135; he gives slightly different figures on p. 154.

In spite of the Methodists' insistence on African participation at all levels of leadership, there was at least one significant breakaway movement, under American Negro influence. The African Methodist Episcopal Zion Church of the Gold Coast was founded in 1898, mainly as a result of the initiative of Bishop B. J. Small from New York.[1] A few Wesleyan ministers as well as some critical members of their flock were attracted to join. The Rev. Fynn Egyir-Asaam was appointed Gold Coast representative;[2] and J. E. K. Aggrey, F. Arthur, and S. R. B. Attoh Ahuma went to the United States for further studies.[3]

The A.M.E. Zion Church appealed to awakening colour consciousness. The point was not so much that it was independent, as that it was wholly a black man's Church. At the inaugural meeting in Cape Coast in 1898, the Rev. T. B. Freeman jun. said that

this Church thus composed of Africans and entirely governed and worked by Africans was indeed 'bone of our bones and flesh of our flesh', which would naturally take a much greater interest in their missions in the Motherland than can be possible with Missionary Boards and Missionaries of an alien race who are *not above the colour question.*[4]

A few months later, at a similar function at Keta, details of the origin and aims of the new Church were publicized. *The Gold Coast Aborigines* reported:

It is, indeed, an entirely negro church; organized by negroes for negroes, manned, governed, controlled and supported by negro energy, intellect, liberality and contributions. In fact, it is the sentiment of the church, that however great may be the friendship, intellect or interest of any white man, in the well being, Christianization and enlightenment of the negro race be he European, American or Asiatic, he cannot successfully reach the emotional feelings of the masses of our people![5]

During the twentieth century a number of other separatist Churches, entirely West African in inspiration and membership, have arisen in the Gold Coast. A few early records survive, but the extent of the support for such sects can only be guessed at. Several of them were led by office-holders from the nonconformist Missions, inspired by a mixture of discontent, personal ambition, and spiritual conviction. The Church of God, for example, was

---

[1] *The Gold Coast Aborigines* gave an account, in its issue of 25 Feb. 1899, of the founding of the A.M.E. Zion Church in 1796 by coloured members of St. John's Street Methodist Episcopal Church in New York. Small was a West Indian, 'as black as ebony', who had first come to the Gold Coast as a sergeant in the West India Regiment, and later went to the United States to be ordained.   [2] *The Gold Coast Chronicle*, 15 Nov. 1898.

[3] Attoh Ahuma was the former Rev. Solomon who had edited *The Gold Coast Methodist Times*. Egyir-Asaam had formerly been W. F. Penny, and Arthur also changed his name, to F. A. Osam-Pinanko; after his return he became General Superintendent of the A.M.E. Zion Church. Aggrey, who had received his early education in the home of the Rev. D. Kemp, stayed in the United States for many years, until he returned to the Gold Coast permanently in 1924.

[4] *The Gold Coast Aborigines*, 26 Nov. 1898.

[5] Ibid. 25 Feb. 1899. For an account of the subsequent progress of this Church, see I. Sackey, 'A Brief History of the A.M.E. Zion Church, West Gold Coast District', in *The Ghana Bulletin of Theology* (Achimota, 1957), vol. i, no. 3.

launched in 1917 by the Rev. J. D. Taylor.[1] The Nigritian Church, which was
founded by the Rev. J. B. Anaman, made its appeal through the use of the
local language: 'Every part of the services in this Church is in Mfantsi . . .
pure and simple.'[2] The Musama Disco Cristo Church was founded by
'Prophet' Jehu Appiah, a former Methodist catechist, largely because he
wanted to give fuller scope to a desire for prayer-healing. In 1920 he formed
a small Faith Society, and in 1922, as the result of a vision, founded his own
Church, which is still in existence; it does not forbid polygamy.[3]

Most of these small Churches aimed at complete independence of European
authority and standards of conduct.[4] Sometimes this was due to irksome
discipline by the parent Church; the attraction was strongest for those who
had tried, and found themselves unable, to accept the full implications of
Mission Christianity. Doctrinal differences seldom went very deep; more
important was the desire for specifically African forms of worship. The
demand for prayer-healing, for example, derived from Akan religious tradition.[5] Some of the sects made use of traditional ceremonies, and encouraged
clapping and dancing by the congregation during services. But this was not
sufficient to hold a Church together; few of them developed branches, or
outlived their founders.[6] They hardly affected the position of the established
Churches, many of which had already made considerable adaptations over
the years in their forms of worship, thus reducing the field of conflict with
African tradition. According to the 1931 Census the membership of the principal Christian denominations was as follows:

Wesleyan Methodist	.	. 99,207	Ewe Presbyterian .	.	. 14,637
Roman Catholic .	.	. 85,087	Salvation Army	.	. 9,396
Presbyterian	.	. 50,167	A.M.E. Zion	.	. 5,478
Anglican	.	. 18,459	Seventh Day Adventist .	.	1,077

[1] *The Gold Coast Nation*, 30 June 1917.   [2] Ibid. 20 July 1918.

[3] Related to me by the present Prophet, who is the founder's son. Appiah produced a brief
Christ Mpiadua hu dom asornhu abakonsem (Koforidua, 1943) in Fante.

[4] The term 'Ethiopian' Churches is often used to indicate the desire for independence from
European control. Such movements were not so significant in the Gold Coast as in other parts of
Africa. The *locus classicus* on the subject of Ethiopianism and other separatist Churches is B. G. M.
Sundkler's *Bantu Prophets in South Africa* (London, 1948). G. Shepperson has discussed their
political influence: 'Ethiopianism and African Nationalism', in *Phylon* (Atlanta, 1953), vol. xiv,
no. 1. See also Hodgkin, *Nationalism in Colonial Africa*, ch. 3, 'Prophets and Priests'; and for
Central African contacts with Negro Churches in the United States at the turn of the century, see
G. Shepperson and T. Price, *Independent African* (Edinburgh, 1958), chs. iii and iv.

[5] Cf. Casely Hayford's account: 'The King, in the Native State System, is the Spiritual Head
of his people. But the actual working of the System is in the hands of the Priests, who combine with
their office the cure of disease.' *Gold Coast Native Institutions*, p. 106.

[6] In 1955 a survey of Accra recorded seventeen such independent Churches, with a total estimated membership of some 4,000. Nine of them had been founded later than 1944; only four had
managed to survive from the 1930's, and two since 1922; one claimed to have been founded in
1888. 'The Eternal Sacred Order of Cherubim and Seraphim' was said to have grown up independently of any other Christian Church; all the others had broken away from the established
Mission Churches, either in the Gold Coast or Nigeria. Ioné Acquah, *Accra Survey* (London,
1958), ch. viii.

The total membership, including smaller denominations not separately specified, was estimated at 283,911.[1]

In other parts of Africa, indigenous 'apocalyptic' or 'messianic' prophet-
led movements have sometimes whipped up fanatical anti-European feeling,
and encouraged extremist forms of nationalism.[2] But such tendencies have
been rare in the Gold Coast, and the two major examples were both channelled
into the work of the Methodist Church. In 1914 a Liberian evangelist, 'Prophet' Harris, reached Apollonia in his progress along the coast, and stayed
there for three months. Working with a Bible in one hand, and a staff to
which he fixed a small cross-piece in the other, Harris sternly denounced the
idolatry of the people, and called on them to burn their fetishes. Fifty-two
villages were reported to have done so, and eventually 8,000 converts were
clamouring for instruction. The Rev. E. Butler reported from Axim that 2,000
people were seeking admission into the Methodist Church, 'and many more
have given up their idol worship to serve the living God . . . the work is overwhelming for a single person to cope with'.[3] The Methodists, in fact, had not
enough staff to handle the situation, and later a reaction set in.[4]

In 1920 another mass movement was touched off in Ashanti by a local
Methodist preacher, Sampson Opon. He toured the country-side with the
Rev. W. G. Waterworth, arousing intense emotionalism, and in less than two
years 10,000 people had been baptized. The Basel Mission regarded Opon as
a fetish priest and would not let him preach in their Churches.[5] But the Methodists were less inclined to distrust an emotional revival, and were able to
make use of the movement as a basis for more enduring evangelical work. The
effects in Ashanti were so marked that the District Synod changed their plans;
so that in 1924 their Wesleyan Training College was opened in Kumasi instead
of in the Colony, with financial support from Fanti Methodists.[6]

[1] *The Gold Coast, 1931. Appendices containing Comparative Returns and General Statistics of
the 1931 Census* (Accra, 1932).
[2] J. S. Coleman has analysed the political significance of movements of this kind in 'Current
Political Movements in Africa', in *The Annals of the American Academy of Political and Social
Science* (Philadelphia, 1955), vol. 298.
[3] Quoted by Southon, *Gold Coast Methodism*, pp. 145–6.
[4] Contrast the development of this movement in the Ivory Coast, where Harris (who attacked
Roman Catholics as well as pagans) was banned by the French authorities in 1914; his disciples,
the 'Sons of God', later became strongly anti-European. For further details of one whom Smith
in *The Christian Mission in Africa* has called 'Africa's most successful evangelist', see Casely
Hayford, *William Waddy Harris: the Man and His Message* (1916), F. D. Walker, *The Story of
the Ivory Coast* (London, 1926), and W. J. Platt, *An African Prophet* (London, 1934).
[5] K. Schlosser, *Propheten in Afrika* (Braunschweig, 1949), pp. 272–8. Dr. H. Debrunner, who
has interviewed Opon, at his home near Dormaa, has pointed out to me that there was quite a
number of magical elements in his work, including 'a wonderful stone', in which he could 'read
the whole Bible from Genesis to Revelation thanks to the Holy Spirit, being by nature an illiterate'.
Debrunner also suggests that Opon's threats to bring down fire from Heaven frightened masses
into the Church, although there were many subsequent genuine conversions. For the standard
Methodist account, see Southon, *Gold Coast Methodism*, pp. 149–52.
[6] Ibid, p. 153.

In later years, a direct reaction against Christianity as the alleged tool of colonialism was to form one of the threads in the fabric of militant nationalism. The Missions were attacked for co-operating, or merely acquiescing, in European domination. In 1911 Casely Hayford gave an early hint of this theme, in an ironic fable depicting the partition of Africa:

One Nation said, 'How shall we do this thing, seeing that we are Christians?' Another said, 'Thou that doubtest, thou art merely slow of counsel. This thing is easily done. We shall go to the Ethiopians, and shall teach them our religion, and that will make them ours, body and soul—lands, goods, and all, for all time.' And the saying pleased them all.[1]

Such criticisms did not become widely current until a generation later, when the political atmosphere had become more bitter.[2] Then it was 'the apostates, the near-converts, and the many Africans exposed but unconverted to Christianity' who held the political platform.[3]

Yet the nationalist movement could hardly have got under way had it not been for the remarkable work of the Missions in the field of education. Christianity also made a far more direct contribution, though one less readily acknowledged; this was through the liberation of the individual. E. W. Smith has summed up very well the revolutionary impact of Christian teaching on African society, especially of the idea that every man is responsible to God for his own actions. The missionary, he points out, seeks individual conviction and conversion: 'For an African to respond means breaking in some degree from his group—an act which he has never before contemplated the possibility of doing.'[4] The preaching of the moral autonomy of the person, of his right—and duty—to act according to his Christian conscience, was one of the factors that led to the questioning of the authority of the Chief under the old order. It was only a matter of time before this in turn led to a questioning of European authority and of its moral basis.

*   *   *   *   *   *

In view of the many forces making for social change, it might seem surprising that so much of the customary way of life persisted into the twentieth-century Gold Coast. Yet the strong sense of family obligation, the pull of the home village, the influence of traditional religion, the tenacious attitude

---

[1] J. E. Casely Hayford, *Ethiopia Unbound* (London, 1911), p. 158.

[2] Italian aggression in Abyssinia, for example, was taken to prove 'to the African masses that Europe with all its civilisation is still enshrined in barbarism and . . . that Religion—especially Christianity—as it has been introduced by the whiteman to the blackman is a hideous mass deception'. *The Vox Populi*, 9 Nov. 1935. Soon afterwards, Wallace Johnson wrote an article on 'The Diplomacy of Christianity', in which he concluded: 'The 20th Century Christianity is no more for the Blackman.' Ibid. 29 Feb. 1936. For him, the attack on Christianity was a weapon in the war against colonialism; and for many, the dethronement of the European meant also the dethronement of his God.

[3] Coleman, *Nigeria*, p. 158.

[4] Smith, *The Golden Stool*, p. 256.

towards land—all these and many more remained as strong eddies and cross-currents in the rising tide of nationalism. In the story which follows, many of these themes will recur; perhaps the most significant is the role of the Chiefs. They appear initially as the natural representatives of the people in the Poll Tax Assembly of 1852; but soon they proceed to challenge British authority, either individually, as did King Aggery of Cape Coast, or collectively, as in the short-lived Fanti Confederation and the prolonged Ashanti resistance to British arms. The Chiefs next emerge in alliance with educated politicians in the A.R.P.S., only to resist the claim of the intelligentsia to leadership on a national scale in the National Congress of British West Africa; and finally we see them turning to the colonial Government for support in their defence of the traditional system.

The story of nationalist agitation is necessarily episodic, although organically connected; each protest grew out of the success—or, more often, the failure—of the last. The economic and social changes described above provide the backdrop for the political drama.

IV

TAXATION AND REPRESENTATION
1850–62

In January 1850 the British Forts and Settlements on the Gold Coast were separated from Sierra Leone and became a distinct dependency of the Crown, with their own Governor and Executive and Legislative Councils.[1] This step did not arouse any local protest, nor can it be said to mark directly the beginnings of a nationalist movement. Nevertheless, it was the necessary precondition for the emergence of such a movement, in that the Gold Coast thus became a separate constitutional entity.

Colonial nationalism is the product of what has been called 'the colonial situation'.[2] The impact of Western culture and commerce was not in itself enough to provoke an organized African reaction; the Gold Coast had already experienced nearly four centuries of European contacts, and a century of merchant government, without any serious protests or resistance movements, apart from a few isolated xenophobic risings.[3] The first brief period of direct Crown control, 1821–8, met with armed onslaught from Ashanti; but this was at least partly because the British became unwillingly involved in the Fanti–Ashanti quarrels, and there was no comparable pressure from within the area of British rule. In 1843 the Crown again resumed control; but the seat of government was still Freetown, and the local officials included several, notably George Maclean, whose power and influence had been exercised with a considerable degree of popular consent during the period of merchant government.[4]

But from 1850 onwards, the imported *élite* of colonial officials was increasingly in evidence, especially at Cape Coast, and the fact of British rule was brought home more directly to the people of the surrounding districts. In particular, certain administrative acts aroused specific protests, and encouraged a sense of resentment which was later to be channelled into the general political ferment of nationalism. The first major economic grievance arising directly out of the external pressure of alien rule was the poll tax episode.

[1] By Letters Patent of 24 Jan. 1850; reproduced in *Copies or Extracts of any Acts of Parliament, Orders in Council, Charters of Justice or Government, and Local Ordinances, defining the existing Civil and Judicial Constitutions of the British Settlements on the West Coast of Africa* (London, 1855), p. 383.

[2] Georges Balandier, 'La situation coloniale: approche théorique', in *Cahiers internationaux de sociologie* (Paris, 1951), vol. xi.

[3] For example, a massacre of the Augustinian monks at Efutu and Komenda in the sixteenth century. R. M. Wiltgen, *Gold Coast Mission History, 1471–1880* (Techny, 1956), p. 24.

[4] See Ch. V, pp. 193–4, below.

The Idea of Direct Taxation

The establishment of a more elaborate machinery of government impressed upon British officials the urgent need to increase revenue by some means or other. The annual parliamentary grant was only £4,000, and other sources of revenue were meagre,[1] while commitments continued to rise. The Secretary of State, Lord Grey, was anxious to employ more magistrates, and to extend the provision of roads, schools, hospitals, and dispensaries beyond the strict limits of the forts. He thought that such services should be provided out of local resources, rather than by an increase in the parliamentary grant; and of the two possible alternatives, customs duties or direct taxation, Grey strongly inclined to the latter.[2] He believed that in the enervating climate of the tropics it was necessary to create a 'motive for exertion', if the inhabitants were to attain any higher degree of civilization, and that this would be found in the pressure of a direct tax, which he had already introduced in Natal and other colonial territories.[3]

The local Government, on the other hand, would have preferred to increase customs duties; but so long as the British Settlements were interspersed with the Dutch and Danish along the coast, it was difficult to reach agreement over the enforcement of a uniform tariff. To raise the duties unilaterally might have resulted in a serious diversion of trade. In 1850, however, the Danish forts and trading posts at Christiansborg, Teshi, Ningo, Ada, and Keta, together with all their other territorial rights on the coast, were sold to the British for £10,000.[4] This appeared to be a favourable opportunity to

---

[1] The revenue for 1849 was as follows:

	£	s.	d.
Parliamentary grant	4,000	0	0
Customs duty of ½%	525	0	4
Lighthouse dues	35	0	0
Permits for landing goods and passports to canoemen .	19	7	0
Fines and summonses	976	3	10
Miscellaneous receipts	24	2	5
	£5,579	13	7

Dispatch No. 10 of 17 Jan. 1851, from Bannerman to Grey; CO/96/22.

[2] Earl Grey, *The Colonial Policy of Lord John Russell's Administration* (London, 1853), vol. ii, pp. 280–2.

[3] For example, a Road Ordinance in Ceylon, which required annually six days' labour, commutable by a small money payment, 'in fact . . . a direct tax'. The proceeds were to be spent by Provincial and District Committees. But Gold Coast reactions were not without precedent. In 1848 a rebellion in Ceylon was attributed to 'false reports' of the oppressive nature of the proposed taxes, spread by the Chiefs and priests, who 'felt that their influence over their countrymen was gradually fading away, from their being brought into contact with European civilization, and from the restrictions imposed by our laws'. Grey, *Colonial Policy*, vol. ii, pp. 171–80. No better illustration could be given of the conflict between traditional and external authority in a colonial situation.

[4] The ceremony of transfer of Christiansborg Castle took place on 6 Mar. 1870—107 years to the day before Ghana's Independence—and is described in detail by K. Larsen, *De Danske i Guinea* (Copenhagen, 1918), pp. 127–9. See also *Papers respecting the Cession to the British Crown*

negotiate an agreement with the Dutch, and the Governor, Sir William Winniett, discussed proposals for a higher customs duty with several of the merchants. James Bannerman (a mulatto) and Brodie Cruickshank (a Scotsman), the leading spokesmen of the trading community, stated that they did not anticipate any difficulty in raising a revenue of at least £10,000 for the first year, without risk to trade. They added, however, that it was essential to spend the proceeds on visible improvements, especially new schools and 'public works of general utility'; the proposed tax would never be popular if it were 'swallowed up in mere garrisoning of the forts and in the salaries of the officers of the Government'.[1]

But the authorities at Elmina were not prepared to collaborate; almost all the Dutchmen on the coast were merchants, more concerned with expanding trade than with increasing official revenue. In any case, they suspected that the proposed duties had been framed to fall most heavily on non-British imports. The Colonial Office knew that little help could be expected from the Ministry in Holland, which was dependent on the support of powerful mercantile interests in the legislature. So no immediate progress could be made in that direction.

The introduction of Crown Colony government had stimulated the merchants to take a keen interest in constitutional matters. They were anxious to secure adequate representation for themselves on the small Legislative Council, and to see the authority of the Government peacefully accepted by the surrounding Chiefs, so that the country might become sufficiently settled for the expansion of trade. During 1850, Bannerman and Cruickshank made some constructive proposals for an Assembly of Chiefs to be legally constituted for Protected Territories. This should meet twice a year at Cape Coast and, with the help of the Judicial Assessor, should frame laws 'generally binding upon the natives of the country', subject to the confirmation of the Governor. The members should receive a small annual stipend.[2]

This was in line with the policy Grey already had in mind. He had previously suggested such an Assembly, for the main purpose of raising a direct tax, and at the same time associating the Chiefs with the collection of the money and its expenditure on general welfare. Even though Winniett had pointed out the difficulty of securing the joint consent of numerous independent Chiefs, who were not directly under British rule,[3] Grey had not lost sight

of the Danish Possessions on the Coast of Africa (London, 1850–1). Probably the best account of the Danish establishments in the Gold Coast from *c.* 1650 to 1850 is G. Norregaard's 'De Danske Establissementer Paa Guineakysten', in *Vore Gamle Tropekolonier*, ed. by J. Brondsted (Copenhagen, 1953), pp. 431–615.

[1] Letter of 30 Apr. 1850, from Bannerman and Cruickshank to Winniett, enclosed in his Dispatch No. 37 of 20 May 1850, to Grey; CO/96/18.

[2] Letter of 22 Aug. 1850, from Bannerman and Cruickshank to Winniett, enclosed in his Dispatch No. 72 of 23 Aug. 1850, to Grey; CO/96/19.

[3] It had been estimated that there were twelve important Chiefs between Cape Coast Castle and the River Prah; although they were in the habit of assembling together on 'all matters of

of the possibility; and he now willingly gave his approval for the establishment of a yearly meeting of Chiefs, to make 'under proper superintendence,
and subject to the confirmation of the Governor, general Laws and Regulations for the arrangement of the Native Tribes'.[1] He also sanctioned annual
payments, or even regular salaries, to such Chiefs, in order to give them a
substantial interest in the maintenance of the Protectorate. To secure the
additional revenue which would be required, Grey emphasized the need for
a direct tax, suggesting that this might most easily be levied upon land,
possibly in the form of a tithe or some other fixed proportion of the produce.
If this were not sufficiently productive, then there might be a small graduated
levy, or 'perhaps a poll tax'.[2]

But Winniett died at the end of 1850 before this dispatch reached him; and
there was further delay, because Major S. J. Hill, the next Governor, did not
arrive until October 1851. Grey, when making this appointment, carefully
instructed Hill to secure the general consent of the Chiefs and people to some
form of direct taxation, using his discretion concerning the exact method to
be used.[3] During the interval, however, the influential Bannerman and Cruickshank, fearing the institution of a new tax, had changed their views concerning
an Assembly of Chiefs. They now advised that it would be unwise to call so
many rulers together, since each would bring 'a very large and imposing body
of followers fully armed', and such a gathering might show them 'their great
physical power as compared to ours'.[4] The Government might not even be
able to afford the large number of suitable presents that would be expected.
Hill was not unduly discouraged by such an opinion; if he could not bring
about the form of representation desired by Grey, at least he felt that a start
could be made on the taxation.[5]

The main problem was that the Legislative Council itself was not able to
authorize direct taxation, since as Grey pointed out, an Ordinance could
only apply 'within the very narrow limits by which the portion of territory
under British dominion is bounded'. The tax even in the towns surrounding
the forts could only be collected 'in virtue of treaty and usage', and so the
Governor was told to proceed with some caution.[6] Early in 1852 Hill visited
the eastern districts and took the opportunity while speaking to the Chiefs 'to

importance affecting the general welfare', they were otherwise independent of each other. Memorandum of 1 Aug. 1849, by W. Winniett; CO/96/19.

  [1] G. E. Metcalfe points out that Grey's readiness to establish an Assembly of Chiefs was due
to the fact that Britain 'had no intention of being saddled' with the direct government of the
Gold Coast. 'After Maclean', in *Transactions of the Gold Coast & Togoland Historical Society*
(Achimota, 1955), vol. i, pt. v.

  [2] Dispatch No. 55 of 18 Dec. 1850, from Grey to Winniett; CO/96/19.

  [3] Grey, *Colonial Policy*, vol. ii, p. 283.

  [4] As an imaginative official in London later put it: 'those who were responsible for the peace
of the Settlement shrank from encouraging the collection of tumultuous and combustible assemblies
for no very definite object'. Memorandum of 24 Mar. 1874, by E. Fairfield; CO/806/11.

  [5] Confidential Dispatch of 27 Oct. 1851, from Hill to Grey; CO/96/23.

  [6] Confidential Dispatch of 26 Jan. 1852, from Grey to Hill; ibid.

agitate the question of a small local taxation to be levied on all for their own benefit'. Their reactions encouraged him to press home his proposals in the western districts. He first suggested a house tax, but was soon convinced that 'the people generally would prefer a Poll Tax'. It was still not clear to Hill how such a tax should be imposed by a government 'possessing no territorial jurisdiction, and the natives not being British subjects'. An Ordinance of the Legislative Council being out of the question, he eventually came round to Grey's idea of a Legislative Assembly of Chiefs. He had no legal advice to draw upon, and so proceeded with some hesitation in this 'novel case'.[1]

It is interesting to note that, throughout the developments which followed, the Chiefs were the key figures. It was they whom the Government approached in the first instance, as the proper representatives of their people under British protection; it was they who first voiced the objections of the people both to the mismanagement of the tax and—later—to the principle of taxation; and it was they who finally led their people in armed revolt. The educated *élite*, although they were already beginning to inconvenience the Government, had not yet taken up a position either at the elbow of the Chiefs or in rivalry to them; nor was there any conception of a national leadership, transcending tribal loyalties. The poll tax episode might therefore be considered a 'traditional resistance movement' rather than a manifestation of modern nationalism.[2] Nevertheless, the Assembly of Chiefs was itself a supra-tribal structure, and it meant that a Westernized idea of representation was introduced *pari passu* with the alien concept of monetary taxation. The whole story of the poll tax points forward to the era of nationalist demands for self-government, rather than backward to the era of tribal resistance;[3] and theoretical distinctions cannot here be rigidly pressed.

The Legislative Assembly of 1852

Hill called together as many leading Chiefs as possible at Cape Coast Castle in April 1852, when several important resolutions were passed. The meeting, consisting of the Governor and his Council, together with the Chiefs and headmen of those 'countries' under British protection, constituted itself into 'a Legislative Assembly with full powers to enact such laws as it shall deem fit for the better government of those countries'. This Assembly was to be

[1] Dispatch No. 18 and Confidential Dispatch of 23 Apr. 1852, from Hill to Grey; CO/96/25.

[2] This distinction is made by J. S. Coleman, 'Nationalism in Tropical Africa', in *American Political Science Review* (New York, 1954), vol. xlviii, no. 2.

[3] Cf. E. Roux on the Natal poll tax rebellion of 1906, which he takes as the turning-point between the early period of tribal wars against white invaders, and the later struggle for national liberation and democratic rights. *Time Longer than Rope* (London, 1949), ch. ix. The parallel is not very close, however, since there was considerable violence and loss of life, costing the Natal Government nearly £1 million. For details see J. Stuart, *A History of the Zulu Rebellion, 1906* (London, 1913).

legally recognized by the British Government, and the Governor as President was to have power to assemble or adjourn it; all its enactments, once approved by the Governor, and given the Queen's consent, were to become immediately the law of the country, binding upon the whole population under British protection.

Further, it was agreed to be 'reasonable and necessary' that, in consideration of the advantages of protection, 'the Natives generally should contribute to the support of the Government', by means of such taxes as the majority of the Chiefs in council should decide. Stating that a poll tax would be 'the most productive, the least burthensome, and the most equitable' form of taxation under present conditions, the Chiefs and headmen, on behalf of themselves and their people, voluntarily agreed to the annual sum of 1s. per head for every man, woman, and child under British protection. The Chiefs also agreed, in return for annual stipends, to assist the official tax-gatherers both in taking a census of the population, and in collecting the money. An important clause added that the proceeds, after the payment of stipends and other expenses, should be

devoted to the public good, in the education of the people, in the general improvement and extension of the judicial system, in affording greater facilities of internal communication, increased medical aid, and in such other measures of improvement and utility as the state of the social progress may render necessary, and that the Chiefs be informed of the mode of its application, and entitled to offer suggestions on this point as they may consider necessary.

The resolutions were to be put into effect during the current year by a proclamation of the Governor, which should have 'in every respect the force of a law'. The seventy signatories were headed by George Fynn Aggery, Chief of Cape Coast;[1] and the Governor, in approving the resolutions, specifically recognized 'the legality of this self-constituted Assembly of the Chiefs.'[2]

Hill now congratulated himself on having brought the Chiefs into 'their proper position', in direct communication with the Government. This would enable him to secure their support in carrying out useful measures, and it would also curb the 'undue influence' of the educated inhabitants, whom he accused of opposing his efforts in an underhand manner; they had already started attacking the idea of a poll tax.[3]

[1] The others included King Eddoo of Fantee and King Enimilly of Wassaw, in addition to Chiefs and Cabboceers from the following towns and villages: Abbarsen and Eyen, Abrah, Adjumacoon, Agah, Aggonah, Annamaboe, Apollonia, Assam, Boosoomchie, Commendah, Daddeasa, Denkera, Dixcove, Donassie, Eccoonfee, Empohor, Emyenebrim, Eppinto, Essicoomah, Mansu, Mumford, Peppasal, Quarmin, Queen Ann's Point, Secondee, Sekkay, Takquah, Winnebah, Yancoomassie. The original spelling has been retained.

[2] Resolutions of 19 Apr. 1852 (proclaimed by Hill the next day), and covering Dispatch No. 32 of 29 May 1852, from Hill to Pakington; CO/96/25. The Poll Tax Ordinance was printed in full, with all the signatures, in Constitutions of the . . . West Coast of Africa (1855), and in Ordinances, &c. relating to Her Majesty's Forts and Settlements on the Gold Coast (London, 1860).

[3] Dispatch No. 18 of 23 Apr. 1852, from Hill to Grey; CO/96/25.

Although the Agreement referred to 'the whole of the population being under British protection', not even all the Fanti Chiefs were present when it was drawn up at Cape Coast. Hill soon summoned a similar meeting at Accra, which was attended by the Kings of James Town, Christiansborg, Akwapim, Akim Abuakwa, Akim Kotoku, and Krepi, and by Chiefs of towns from Labadi to Krobo and Ada. With the assistance of James Bannerman, the Civil Commandant, the Governor persuaded them, after some hesitation, to sign the Poll Tax Agreement, and agents were employed to start collecting the tax in four districts, Accra, Adangme, Akwapim, and Axim.[1] Hill seems to have visited Keta to assemble the Chiefs for a similar purpose,[2] although it was afterwards reported that the people of trans-Volta had 'positively refused to agree to the tax at all'.[3] Further signatures were added later in 1852, including some from Chiefs in the western districts who had not been present at the Cape Coast meeting. In addition, the Chief of Wassaw Amanfi placed himself and his people under British protection; he signed the Agreement, and promised to pay the poll tax for the current year, but he requested the assistance of one soldier and one scholar, 'as my people are the most unruly and ungovernable in the world'.[4]

Although Hill called three separate meetings of Chiefs, he seems to have thought in terms of only one Legislative Assembly. Its resolutions were not, however, confirmed in the character of Ordinances, since they were enacted for protected territory. All the same, the Governor thought that the Cape Coast Agreement would be a permanent part of the constitutional machinery of the Gold Coast; it was taken as having 'the force of law', and came to be known locally and historically as the Poll Tax Ordinance.[5]

Hill had drawn up preliminary estimates even before he met the Chiefs at Accra, calculating hopefully that a payment of 1s. per head for each man, woman, and child in an estimated population of 400,000 would yield a revenue of £20,000 per annum. He proposed to appoint a Collector-General, and to divide the Protectorate into twelve districts, each with a sub-collector— 'the best men I can procure'. Hill feared abuses if the Government delegated its authority to the Chiefs for the collection of the tax: 'Knowing that the Natives would be afraid to show any opposition, they would be induced to

[1] C. C. Reindorf, *History of the Gold Coast and Asante* (Basel, 1895), pp. 330–1.

[2] Dispatch No. 41 of 2 Aug. 1852, from Hill to Pakington; CO/96/25.

[3] Dispatch No. 28 of 31 Mar. 1858, from B. Pine to Stanley; CO/96/43.

[4] Letter of 10 Aug. 1852, from Quacoe Mensah to Hill, enclosed in his Dispatch No. 53 of 20 Oct. 1852, to Pakington; CO/96/25.

[5] It was printed as such in 1860, although it had not been passed by the Legislative Council. There was some confusion about its legal status, as illustrated by the evidence of Colonel H. St. G. Ord (who knew as much about it as anybody else) in 1865. When asked: 'In what sense is this agreement a legal ordinance?' he replied: 'It was so made, probably to give it additional validity . . . it was formally adopted as a legal ordinance of the settlements . . . It has certainly received the sanction of the Home Government. It is, however, doubtful whether, although called an ordinance, it did not pass the Legislative Council with the usual formalities.' *Report from the Select Committee on Africa (Western Coast)* (London, 1865), replies to questions 891–3.

increase the amount of the levy, thereby oppressing the people, and enriching themselves.' The salaries of the collectors, together with payments to the Chiefs, would bring the total expenses of collection to £5,000, i.e. 25 per cent., leaving an estimated net yield of £15,000.[1] The meetings of Chiefs, with all their followers, proved quite expensive; Hill spent over £500 on their subsistence, including a small donation to each, 'agreeably to the custom of the Country'.[2]

By October 1852 the gathering of the poll tax was proceeding with almost unnatural smoothness; collectors everywhere reported favourably on 'the cheerful disposition evinced by the masses of the people in the payment of this voluntary revenue'.[3] The Accra historian, the Rev. C. C. Reindorf, later wrote that the first collection was 'quietly and cheerfully given, yet some complained they had pawned their sons and daughters in paying it'.[4] In the Colonial Office it was noted with approval that this favourite scheme of Lord Grey's had at last been implemented, although he was no longer in office. Hill was congratulated on his zeal and ability in bringing about 'these important changes in our relations with the natives',[5] but was soon reminded not to create any supposition that the payment of the poll tax placed the people on the footing of 'British subjects inhabiting the dominions of the Crown'.[6] Grey himself wrote, with more enthusiasm than authenticity: 'I am persuaded I do not overrate the importance of the establishment of this rude Negro Parliament, when I say, that I believe it has converted a number of barbarous tribes, possessing nothing which deserves the name of a government, into a nation.' He looked forward to the time when the inhabitants should have grown into 'a nation capable of protecting themselves and of managing their own affairs' and the duty of governing and protecting them would no longer fall upon the British.[7]

There is no doubt that this new, exotic institution helped to hasten the day when the inhabitants were to think of themselves as a nation, and to demand the right to manage or mismanage their own affairs. But the progress in that direction was neither so direct nor so economical to the home Government as Grey had hoped, since the poll tax lamentably failed to produce either the revenue or the parliamentary experience required. The first difficulties, however, were simply practical problems of administration rather than objections of principle.

Problems of Collecting the Poll Tax

Payment of the tax continued to go well during the early months and Hill planned schools and other projects to be financed from the proceeds.[8] By May

[1] Dispatches Nos. 18 and 19 of 23 and 24 Apr. 1852, from Hill to Grey; CO/96/25.
[2] Dispatch No. 43 of 2 Aug. 1852, from Hill to Pakington; ibid.
[3] Dispatch No. 53 of 20 Oct. 1852, from Hill to Pakington; ibid.
[4] Reindorf, *History*, p. 331.
[5] Dispatch of 22 Dec. 1852, from Pakington to Hill; CO/96/25.
[6] Dispatch of 18 Mar. 1853, from Newcastle to Hill; CO/96/27.
[7] Grey, *Colonial Policy*, pp. 285-7.
[8] Dispatches Nos. 75 of 1 Dec. 1852, and 6 of 24 Jan. 1853, from Hill to Pakington; CO/96/25 and 27.

1853, however, he realized that much of the potential revenue would be lost owing to the inefficiency of several of the collectors.[1] Other difficulties were an unexpected drop in the exchange rate of cowries, which led to a loss of about £900,[2] and heavy transport expenses for this bulky currency.[3] Nevertheless, the proceeds for the period August 1852 to July 1853 amounted to £6,656, which left over £5,000 after deducting the expenses of collection. (See opposite page.) Although this might appear a promising start, the Government felt that much more could be collected.

Cruickshank had been made the first Collector-General; but he had not immediately taken up his appointment, owing to illness and private business, and on becoming Acting Governor in August 1853 he nominated another official to act for him on half-pay. Collection of the tax was hindered by the disturbed state of the country during an Ashanti invasion; but Cruickshank believed that the people still had no objections to the poll tax, and he gave them until the end of the year to complete the first payment.[4] In fact the Ashanti interruption came at a crucial period. Cruickshank appears to have mismanaged the tax, and failed to pay most of the Chiefs their promised salaries.[5] This was one of the main complaints made when he met the Chiefs of the eastern districts in January 1854, and announced that the second annual payment of the poll tax was now due. They refused to pay; and almost immediately trouble broke out in Accra. Hill hurried over from Cape Coast to investigate and found several thousand armed men, from all the coastal villages between Accra and the Volta, 'having Danish flags flying and menacing the Fort'.[6]

The Governor blamed this spirit of resistance on the tribes recently transferred from Danish protection, and attributed it entirely to the strict enforcement of the British rules concerning the sale or transfer of slaves.[7] But it is clear, especially from Reindorf's account, based on circumstantial detail from eye-witnesses, that the main grievance arising out of British rule was the collection of the poll tax. He describes how the sub-Chiefs and elders of Christiansborg led the protests against the tax at the beginning of 1854 by leaving the town and settling in Labadi. At a night meeting the leading men of Christiansborg, Labadi, Teshi, and other villages near Accra swore 'not to let the grandees go to the Fort nor pay any tax, even if the government should fight with them, and to make war with any party breaking this agreement.' According to Reindorf, this was why thousands of armed men soon assembled outside the castle, where they publicly confirmed their intention

[1] Dispatch No. 46 of 7 May 1853, from Hill to Newcastle; CO/96/27.

[2] Dispatch No. 36 of 31 May 1854, from Hill to Newcastle; CO/96/30.

[3] According to Dr. J. Africanus B. Horton, 2,000 cowries weighed 80–90 lb.: 'Lieutenant Forbes complains that to carry fifty dollars he had to employ five women.' *West African Countries and Peoples* (London, 1868), p. 267.

[4] Dispatch No. 88 of 1 Oct. 1853, from Cruickshank to Newcastle; CO/96/28.

[5] Dispatch No. 36 of 31 May 1854, from Hill to Newcastle; CO/96/30.

[6] Dispatch No. 6 of 29 Jan. 1854, from Hill to Newcastle; ibid.   [7] Ibid.

Poll Tax Income and Expenditure, 1852–3[1]

INCOME

Item	£	s.	d.	£	s.	d.
Western Wassaw				319	11	1
Eastern Wassaw (incl. Commenda, Dixcove, and Apollonia)				953	9	0
Cape Coast and villages	391	3	0			
Denkera	166	9	0			
Chifful	85	6	0			
				642	18	0
Anamaboe: Gold	819	11	10			
3,460 heads of cowries	475	15	0			
				1,295	6	10
Goomooh and Ahgoma: 5,312 heads and 33¾ strings of cowries				730	10	0
Accra, Croboe, and Aquapim: 10,862 heads of cowries	1,493	10	6			
Akim gold	1,204	0	0			
				2,697	10	6
Quitta: 118 heads and 37½ strings of cowries	16	6	6			
Gold	0	18	0			
				17	4	6
TOTAL				**£6,656**	**9**	**11**

EXPENDITURE

Item	£	s.	d.	£	s.	d.	£	s.	d.
Collection:									
Sub-Collectors: 6 at £100	600	0	0						
1 at £200 and 1 at £75	275	0	0						
				875	0	0			
Gold Takers				102	11	0			
Incidental Expenses: Windward	244	4	5½						
Winnebah	14	3	4						
Accra	171	13	10½						
				430	1	8			
							1,407	12	8
Stipends to Chiefs:									
from Accra to westward				800	0	0			
to eastward				371	15	0			
							1,171	15	0
Salaries:									
Governor (additional)	266	18	0	209	2	11			
Col. Secretary (additional)	106	5	0	373	3	0			
Clerk (additional)									
Collector General of P.T.	354	19	0	379	19	0			
Secretary	25	0	0						
Judicial:									
Asst. Judicial Assessor	233	6	8						
Civil Commandants: Winnebah	283	6	8						
Christiansborg	283	6	8						
Anamaboe	283	6	8						
Quitta	250	8	0						
Dixcove	114	8	7						
Mansue	150	0	0						
				1,597	15	3			
Collector of Customs				212	10	0			
							2,772	10	2
Schools: Apollonia &c.							45	17	0
Roads: Anamaboe road				112	10	9			
Yancoomassie road				81	8	8			
Roads: clearing				1	18	8			
Tools, materials &c.				274	4	2½			
							470	2	1⅛
Balance in hand							788	12	11⅛
TOTAL							**£6,656**	**9**	**11**

[1] This is a slightly rearranged form of the Statement of Poll Tax Income and Expenditure, 1852–3; CO/96/30.

N

not to pay the poll tax. Some wanted to go even further. Badu Asonko, for example, 'the powerful linguist of the infuriated people', urged the crowd not to 'serve the English Government' any longer; but through the influence of King Tackie he was forced to retract this suggestion.[1]

Hill tried unsuccessfully to restore order, using some of the missionaries and friendly inhabitants as mediators; but soon he was contemplating 'an appeal to force'.[2] Further large meetings of protest and minor disturbances took place early in 1854. Reindorf records that one of the songs sung by the people in Accra at this time was:

> Cannon they have loaded, but couldn't fire,
> Cannon they have loaded, but couldn't fire.
> White men dishonestly imposed poll-tax on the blacks.
> The poll-tax we will never pay, the grandees never deliver up,
> Go tell the white man to come out![3]

In fact, peace was restored without a shot being fired, and a fine of £250 was agreed upon; later the people at Ada—who had detained the Staff Assistant Surgeon as a hostage—were also fined.[4] But it would appear that, as Hill did not connect these disturbances directly with the poll tax, its payment was not made a condition of the settlement, so that the possibility of further trouble remained. According to Reindorf, the 'grandees' of Accra thought that the peace meant abolishing the poll tax.[5]

Meanwhile serious opposition to the tax had arisen in the western districts. At a meeting in Cape Coast, the neighbouring Chiefs belatedly received their stipends, and the statement of receipts and expenditure for 1852–3 was read out. From this it was clear that after paying the stipends, and the official salaries to be met in whole or in part from the funds, very little remained for the promised schemes of local improvement. The sum of £470 had been spent on roads and £45 on schools; but that was all. The Cape Coast spokesmen were particularly vocal in opposition; they protested against any magistrates or Chiefs receiving stipends from the funds, and after trying 'every dodge in vain to postpone the collection of the tax', they came out openly against it. They only agreed to pay under protest after Hill threatened to use force and 'punish according to the Law made by the Native Assembly of Chiefs'.[6]

The Colonial Office was not too happy about the reference to force in connexion with tax payments; and the Governor was told that any surplus receipts for 1854—over and above his estimate of £6,000—should be devoted not to augmenting salaries, but to schools, roads, and other public works which would encourage people to pay without coercion.[7] Hill had anticipated

---

[1] Reindorf, *History*, pp. 332–5.
[2] Dispatch No. 7 of 1 Feb. 1854, from Hill to Newcastle; CO/96/30.   [3] Reindorf, *History*, p. 334.
[4] Dispatches Nos. 10 and 11 of 7 and 17 Mar. 1854, from Hill to Newcastle; CO/96/30.
[5] Reindorf, *History*, p. 337.
[6] Dispatch No. 36 of 31 May 1854, from Hill to Newcastle; CO/96/30.
[7] Dispatch No. 113 of 3 Oct. 1854, from Sir G. Grey to Hill; CO/96/31

little difficulty in equalling the revenue of the previous year; but his calcula-
tions were seriously thrown out by subsequent events in the eastern districts.

The Christiansborg Rebellion, 1854

By now the natural reluctance to pay taxes as such was becoming equated
with a distaste for British authority; and a general emotional reaction began
to replace isolated, individual protests. Organized retaliation followed. As
soon as the alien economic pressure involved threats of coercion, it was
resisted by force.

Thus the sending of an Army officer to Accra, later in 1854, to collect the
tax touched off the most serious resistance yet encountered, which gathered
momentum as the official attitude stiffened. The Chiefs and elders assembled
together, including Akims, Akwapims, Krobos, and Accras, and 'made a
solemn compact never to pay the tax again'; they extorted 100 heads of
cowries from the James Town people, for having been the first to pay, 'and
intimidated them not to pay it again'.[1] When further attempts were made to
collect the poll tax, the people stoned the soldiers, and tried to cut off government supplies. Serious riots accompanied the crowded *Homowo* festival in
September; and as a result H.M.S. *Scourge* bombarded Labadi, Teshi, and
Christiansborg. The people in retaliation attacked the castle, led by hunters
with muskets.[2] This was the situation when Hill wrote to London from James
Fort, with some 4,000 rebels in arms between him and Christiansborg Castle.
He described the bombardment as a vindication of 'the insulted honour of the
British flag', blaming the Labadi fetish priests for instigating 'all the treason';
but he still did not give the Colonial Office any reason to connect the revolt
with the poll tax.[3]

After a second bombardment, during which some houses were burnt by
landing parties, many inhabitants fled inland.[4] Hill subsidized tribes in the
area to support the Government, and made a strong show of force with
regular troops.[5] In justification of his actions, he forwarded to London a
letter from some African merchants of James Town; they had begged him
to take severe measures to put down the rebellion 'among such a savage
and treacherous people', and in the interests of civilization 'to make them
feel the moral and physical superiority of the British Government'.[6]

---

[1] Letter of 21 Feb. 1855, from James Bannerman to Acting Colonial Secretary, enclosed in
Dispatch No. 37 of 16 May 1855, from Connor to Russell; CO/96/33.

[2] Reindorf, *History*, pp. 338–9.

[3] Dispatch No. 66 of 1 Oct. 1854, from Hill to Sir G. Grey; CO/96/31.

[4] 'Zimmermann and Steinhauser followed the scared people and settled with their seminarists
in the old rest houses at Abokobi under the most primitive conditions. From there they began to
carry the gospel to the great farming district around.' *The Basel Mission Centenary, 1828–1928*
(Accra, 1928), p. 10.

[5] Dispatch No. 76 of 8 Nov. 1854, from Hill to Sir G. Grey; CO/96/31.

[6] Letter of 1 Nov. 1854, from John Marman and other James Town merchants to Hill, enclosed
in his Dispatch No. 74 of the same date to Sir G. Grey; ibid.

The policy showed results; the insurgents submitted to the authority of the Government, and gave up six young hostages for their future good conduct. No fines were felt to be necessary, as so much property had been lost;[1] Hill was satisfied that he had laid the foundation for many years of peace. But he underestimated the length of Accra memories; and he was somewhat less than ingenuous in his final summing up of the causes of the rebellion as 'a resistance to any advancement of civilization together with a feeling of annoyance that they could not indulge in slave trading or any of their cruel and barbarous practices'.[2] Thus the Colonial Office was seriously misled, and officials were convinced that the Christiansborg rebellion was *falsely* reported to have had its origin from the levy of the Poll Tax'.[3]

Whatever view was taken of the causes of the rebellion, there could be no doubt about its effect on the collection of the tax. The Colonial Office insisted that the expenses of the outbreak must be met out of tax receipts, since the maintenance of peace and order was a necessary condition of that advance of civilization which the tax was designed to bring about.[4] When the accounts for 1854 were officially circulated, it appeared that only £3,625 had been collected, of which £840 had been set aside for the rebellion. Considerably less than that amount was spent on schools and roads, and all the rest went in salaries and expenses of collection.[5] This was not well received by the Chiefs and people. The King of James Town sent an abusive reply, signed by 'a set of bankrupt rebels who infest that District' (as they were officially described), and decorated with a vignette of 'a country war knife and across it the letter W written so as easily to be understood to mean "War" and the pages . . . joined with black Ribbon'.

The acting Governor now sent the 1854 financial statement to London, together with the first circumstantial account of some of the opposition and ill will aroused by the poll tax, and 'the difficulties, danger and labour' of collecting it. He admitted that from the time of its institution the collectors had had to be accompanied by one or two soldiers; but he still felt that its continuance was worth while, if only as a means of 'opening the country to civilization'.[6] The Colonial Office was no more favourably impressed by the latest poll tax accounts than the Chiefs had been. It was noted especially that the tax now yielded far less than had originally been expected, and that there were scarcely any items of expenditure for the public good, apart from the salaries paid to the Civil Commandants—'who may be partially useful to the

---

[1] 'Oh, that we were wiser in time, that we did not kick against the pricks!' exclaimed the Rev. Reindorf, lamenting these losses, in his *History*, p. 340.

[2] Dispatch No. 76 of 8 Nov. 1854, from Hill to Sir G. Grey; CO/96/31.

[3] Minute of 14 Feb. 1855, by G. Barrow; ibid.

[4] Minute of 19 Feb. 1855, by H. Merivale; ibid.

[5] Statement of Receipts and Expenditure of the Poll Tax Revenue in 1854; CO/96/33.

[6] This suggestion was lampooned in London as 'the Acting Governor's ingenious theory, that the visit of the tax gatherer in the bush itself advances civilization'. Minute of 28 July 1855, by Merivale; ibid.

natives as magistrates'—and to a Surgeon 'whose services they do not use'.[1]

Similar protests and problems continued during 1855;[2] these were especially marked in Accra, where the people were still nursing their grievances and the merchants counting their losses after the bombardment.[3] The Acting Governor decided that it would be 'pusillanimous, weak and unwise if not disloyal and unauthorized' to evade the responsibility of collecting the tax. Upon renewing the attempt, he encountered strong opposition from the merchants, who declared their 'large pecuniary interest in the tranquillity and peace of the country'; he found it 'peculiarly disgusting' that an Englishman, E. B. Cooper, took a leading part in this protest against a 1s. tax.[4] The merchants were also objecting to a recent increase in customs duties;[5] and in 1856 the Secretary of State decided to send out a special commissioner, Major H. St. G. Ord, to investigate the numerous complaints received from the Gold Coast, with particular reference to the poll tax.

Ord reported that the undoubted hostility to the poll tax was due more to irritation with government policy, and a feeling of general neglect, than to the tax itself. He criticized particularly the way the proceeds had been spent since the first year, but concluded that there was no form of tax that presented so many advantages and so few evils. If the details of its imposition were somewhat modified and the original intentions of its promoters strictly carried out, it could not fail to be of great benefit to the country, 'and ought to do more towards its gradual civilization than any other engine of which the Government could avail itself'.

At a conference with the Cape Coast Chiefs he promised that certain obvious defects in the collection of the tax would be remedied; but the people of Christiansborg and James Town could not be reconciled to payment on any terms. Ord suggested in his report, however, that since the people of the interior looked to the coastal Chiefs for leadership, a definite attempt should be made first to improve the coast towns out of the proceeds of the tax.[6]

---

[1] Dispatch No. 36 of 4 May 1855, from Connor to Secretary of State, and Minute of 28 July 1855, by Merivale; ibid.

[2] For example, Kate (the wealthy wife of the merchant Frank) Swanzy paid her tax only under protest, claiming that something ought to be done for the good of the country; and the Colonial Secretary replied gallantly that 'It is not His Excellency's habit to make promises, but as ladies like them, he authorises me to conclude with two', that the Government would make every effort to ensure faithful payment, and faithful expenditure, of the poll tax. Letters of Aug. 1855, enclosed in Dispatch No. 83 of 8 Sept. 1855, from Connor to Molesworth; CO/96/34.

[3] An interesting account of the situation at the time is given in the life story of a Basel Mission trader who arrived in Christiansborg at the end of 1854. *Gedenkfeier für H. L. Rottmann* (Basel, 1899).

[4] Protest of 8 Mar. 1855, and covering Dispatch No. 37 of 16 May 1855, from Connor to Russell; CO/96/33.

[5] See Ch. V, p. 197, below.

[6] Report of 16 May 1856, from Ord to Labouchere; CO/96/40.

Pine's Fresh Approach, 1857–8

It might perhaps be questioned whether the poll tax could not have been successfully managed if there had been more frequent and consistent consultation with the Chiefs or, better still, if they had had some voice in the expenditure of the proceeds. It was suggested by *The Accra Herald*,[1] towards the end of 1857, that all that was necessary was for the Government to supervise the collectors properly, and to see that provision was made for public health, road-building, and so on:

let the executive shew the people that it really takes an interest in their welfare, let all the clauses of the Proclamation be properly acted upon, and we venture to say there will not be too much grumbling about the Poll Tax which has been hitherto hateful because oppressively levied and iniquitously squandered.[2]

But once an emotional position is taken up, it may become a stock response that cannot easily be abandoned. Even the arrival of an enlightened Governor, who made every effort to introduce democratic control of expenditure and to give meaning to the principle of representation, could not rescue the scheme from decline.

When Sir Benjamin Pine came to the Gold Coast in 1857, he found the authority of the Government 'extremely limited' in the eastern districts, and practically non-existent in Accra, where most of the inhabitants had ceased even to appeal to British courts since the bombardment.[3] Their chief grievance was the poll tax, especially the manner in which it had been spent. On looking into this, Pine was appalled at the 'loose and unintelligible' state of the accounts, but managed to calculate that only about one-fifth of the amount collected in the eastern districts had been spent on the objects for which it was given. He also criticized the administration of the tax fund in one common treasury; separate accounts, if not two separate funds, should have been kept. The original Assemblies had thought that they were taxing themselves for purely local purposes, and the Accras, for example, 'never could have conceived that their money was to be applied in making roads and supplying medical aid for Fantees'.[4]

Pine's assessment of the situation was remarkably detached and fair. He thought the people would never have rebelled had they been ruled carefully

---

[1] This early newspaper had just been founded, in Sept. 1857, by Charles Bannerman, who produced manuscript copies at first. It became *The West African Herald* when its editor moved to Cape Coast and within two years he claimed, 'The subscribers now amount to three hundred and ten, of whom about two-thirds are natives.' Circular Letter of 11 July 1859, from Bannerman; 8071 Gold Coast, CO/96/46.

[2] 2 Nov. 1857.

[3] *The Accra Herald*, 5 Oct. 1857, called attention to 'unmistakable signs of the approach of disturbance and general disorder in the country. The influence of Government is daily declining ... we see the British authority hardly acknowledged in Axim, utterly cast off in Aquapim, Crobboe, Crepee and Awoonoh, and actually laughed at in places nearer to the seat of Government.'

[4] Dispatch No. 35 of 30 Apr. 1857, from B. Pine to Labouchere; CO/96/41.

and justly; but that now both the Government and the Chiefs had been brought into suspicion and disrepute. It would be difficult to remove the impression that the Government 'only condescends to consult them for the purpose of taking their money; and that, that obtained, it regards their humble counsel as useless'. The Chiefs had been used merely for collecting the taxes, without being given any sort of control over the expenditure, which had 'lowered them in the eyes of the people, and in some places almost destroyed their power'. Pine attributed these errors partly to ignorance on the part of the Government, and partly to the failure to live up to its own principle of taxation by means of representatives. He believed 'that that great principle founded in eternal justice is not above the understanding even of uncivilized men'.[1]

Pine immediately proceeded to take energetic remedial action. At a series of meetings in James Town, he frankly admitted previous irregularities in administration, promising to avoid them in future. He now proposed to appoint a committee of merchants and Chiefs to advise the Civil Commandant on the expenditure of the money, which need not be collected until after the harvest in October. The inhabitants were thus, to the admiration of the Colonial Office, persuaded to agree to pay the poll tax again.[2] He next met the people of Christiansborg and persuaded them to return and rebuild their town. Although advised not to mention the tax to them, Pine preferred frankness, even at the risk of downright opposition, to the possibilities of later misunderstanding. He told them openly that the poll tax would have to be paid once the town was rebuilt. This caused great commotion: 'the people told me that upon these terms they would not come back and rebuild their Town, but would remain for ever in the "Bush"; for that the Poll Tax had been the cause of the destruction of their Town and all their sorrow'.[3] He did not even attempt to win over the people of trans-Volta who had 'in effect ceased to acknowledge the Protectorate'.[4]

In September 1857 Pine issued a proclamation giving detailed rules for the collection of the poll tax in two separate funds; for the eastern districts it would be paid into a treasury at Accra, and for the western, at Cape Coast. Within these areas, the Governor could appoint District Councils to advise and assist him on the local expenditure of the tax receipts, after the expenses of collection and the Chiefs' stipends had been deducted. Pine felt that Grey's original suggestion for administering the tax through local representative institutions might have avoided much of the trouble. He now lost no time in establishing his District Councils—two in the west, at Cape Coast and Anomabu, and one in the east, at Accra—and he planned that they should

---

[1] Ibid.

[2] 'How ably Sir B. Pine can manage the Natives', minuted Barrow on 20 July 1857; ibid.

[3] Dispatches Nos. 40 and 47 of 14 May and 11 June 1857, from B. Pine to Labouchere; ibid.

[4] Dispatch No. 28 of 31 Mar. 1858, from B. Pine to Stanley; CO/96/43.

meet every two months, with power to make by-laws for suppressing nuisances.[1]

But the new machinery could not quickly wipe out old memories. The familiar complaint was made that no benefits had been seen from the tax so far,[2] and Pine even had to threaten to use force against the people of Labadi again. In March 1858 he summed up the general situation. A gradual improvement had taken place over the past year; but in spite of this, 'The Tax is very unpopular throughout the Country and the dislike of it increases as we go from the West to the East . . . It is now utterly detested.'[3] To revive the poll tax was proving far more difficult than its original imposition would have been for a man like Pine. His task was not made easier by the fact that Ord had agreed to the exemption of old and infirm persons as well as young children; this left wide and ill-defined powers in the hands of the collectors, and opened the way to further evasion and peculation.

Pine concentrated first on the improvement of the towns, as Ord had suggested, and gave them strong representation on his District Councils. But he soon found that the townspeople were spending the local improvement fund of the entire district upon themselves alone, 'at the expense of the bush people'. He complained that it was unfair to sacrifice the latter to the clamours of a few urban demagogues, and that in any case the poll tax revenue was insufficient even to develop the towns. So, rejecting this policy as utterly unsound, Pine decided that house rates should be levied instead of the poll tax in the towns, and that simple municipal corporations should be set up to regulate and administer them.[4]

The District Councils—or Assemblies, as he now decided to call them—were to remain as the tax authorities for the rural areas, but should give fuller expression to the wishes of the Chiefs. Pine preferred this scheme to Hill's original Legislative Assembly, which had never in fact consisted of all the Chiefs under British protection, and which he considered utterly impracticable.[5] He therefore enacted a District Assemblies Ordinance, which laid down their membership as consisting of the principal Chiefs in each district, with the Governor as President; members of the Executive Council might also attend meetings, which should take place at least once every year.[6]

At the same time, the Legislative Council approved an Ordinance to 'explain and amend' the original Poll Tax Ordinance, giving legal effect to Pine's reformed system of collection and expenditure. The tax was to be paid into

---

[1] Dispatch No. 79 of 4 Dec. 1857, from B. Pine to Labouchere; CO/96/41.

[2] The Chief of Eastern Akim complained: 'I have together with my people paid the tax three times, and we have not received a single piece of cloth or anything in return.' Report of 28 Dec. 1857, by the Rev. T. B. Freeman; CO/96/43.

[3] Dispatches Nos. 25 and 28 of 2 and 31 Mar. 1858, from B. Pine to Stanley; CO/96/43.

[4] Dispatch No. 44 of 7 May 1858, from B. Pine to Stanley; ibid.

[5] Dispatch No. 40 of 29 Apr. 1858, from B. Pine to Stanley; ibid.

[6] The District Assemblies Ordinance, 10 May 1858.

separate treasuries—at Accra and Cape Coast—and spent only in the district where it was raised. The net proceeds, after paying stipends and meeting the expenses of collection, were to be spent according to the following formula: 'Two-thirds on Medical Officers and Hospitals, on new Magistrates, and on Schools, and one-third on making Roads and Bridges, supplying tanks for water and the like matters.' Other provisions of this amending Ordinance were designed to check extortion and corruption, and especially to define clearly the exempted classes.[1]

The new system was completed by the establishment of municipal corporations, under yet a third Ordinance, enacted on the same day as the others.[2] In fact, this was Pine's most original contribution, arising directly out of his belief in the need for self-government: 'The best Government is that which teaches people to govern themselves, and certainly the object of this Government was not to clean out dirty towns, but to direct the people to that and other objects by controlling and modifying their own Government.' He decided to make use of the influential group of African merchants and traders in each of the main coastal towns, together with the few resident Europeans, to form 'a kind of Government, which should not directly supersede, but incorporate within itself the authority of the Chiefs'; they ought thus to be strengthened by the influence of the more intelligent inhabitants and of the Government itself. A related proposal for a house tax seemed innocuous enough, especially since it was to replace the detested poll tax, and was to be administered directly by the municipal corporation concerned. After discussions with the Chiefs and leading inhabitants of James Town, Accra, they were gradually persuaded to make a start.

Pine proposed a corporation of seven elected members, who should choose a Mayor from among themselves; a court was also to be established, with jurisdiction to impose fines of up to £50 in civil cases, and up to six months' imprisonment with hard labour in criminal cases. The Government decided to act quickly while the people were in the mood, and to confirm the proceedings afterwards by law. So the first municipal election ever held in the Gold Coast took place in Accra early in 1858.[3] The elected councillors,[4] with the King of James Town, celebrated the occasion by dining with the Governor; and then they commenced their duties with energy, passing several by-laws

[1] Dispatch No. 39 of 28 Apr. 1858, from B. Pine to Stanley; CO/96/43.

[2] The Municipal Corporations Ordinance, 10 May 1858. The inter-relationship was emphasized by providing that the Mayor and one member of each corporation should serve on their own District Assembly.

[3] Municipal government was thus already a *fait accompli* when Pine informed the Secretary of State of his new venture, commenting: 'Your Lordship will I think be surprised at receiving an Ordinance of this nature from this barbarous country.' Dispatch No. 44 of 7 May 1858, from B. Pine to Stanley; CO/96/43.

[4] These were: J. C. Hansen ('a very extensive and respectable coloured merchant'), W. Addy (a Chief), a West Indian commercial agent, 'three very well conducted black traders', and James Bannerman (the son of the late Commandant), who was then chosen as Mayor of James Town.

to suppress nuisances, and assessing the houses for rates on a sliding scale, ranging from 5s. to £3.[1]

Unfortunately for this experiment, Pine left the country almost at once. In July, however, a similar municipal corporation was set up in Cape Coast, with the encouragement of H. Bird, the Acting Governor.[2] The corporation quickly set about assessing houses into seven classes, to pay amounts varying from 1s. to £3, which were estimated to yield an annual revenue of £210. The Mayor and councillors were granted permission to wear insignia of office, partly to stimulate competition at the next election. Bird was impressed by their performance, and reported that 'there seems every likelihood of this novel and interesting experiment proving most beneficial'.[3]

It was one thing to assess the houses efficiently; but quite another to collect the money. When it came to paying up, a house rate did not seem so very different from the poll tax, after all. Difficulties seem to have arisen first in James Town, largely at the instigation of the Chiefs. In July 1859 they beat gong-gong at night, and ordered the people not to pay the municipal rate. There was sufficient noisy disturbance to bring the Acting Governor hurrying to Accra. The culprits appeared in court, to explain and eventually apologize; but they failed to lodge the required security for further good conduct, and so the King of James Town and his Chiefs were brought into Christiansborg Castle, there to remain until they could give satisfactory assurances.[4] Trouble soon followed in Cape Coast. The main issue there was the setting up of the new Mayor's court, which aroused the hostility of the King. Bird attributed this to the Mayor's dispensation of 'unpurchased, if not pure Justice', which cost no more than the official price of a summons, whereas in the traditional court heavy and often cruel exactions were made, mainly to support the King and his retinue.[5]

Pine's District Assemblies had never even been given a serious trial. In 1859 the Colonial Office decided to disallow the Ordinance on the grounds that 'the state of society on the Gold Coast is not yet ripe for an enactment of the kind'.[6] They relied mainly on the advice of E. B. Andrews, a Gold Coast official who was in London at the time, and who was soon to prove a most inefficient Governor. A fair example of his attitude was: 'our task will not be made easier by attempts to teach the people to govern themselves according to a more civilized state of society'.[7] On his arrival in 1860 it was easy to find excuses to criticize the municipal corporations, already faced with the prob-

[1] Dispatch No. 44 of 7 May 1858, from B. Pine to Stanley; CO/96/43.
[2] The seven municipal councillors elected were: F. C. Grant, J. Smith, J. Tandoe, H. Barnes, T. Hughes, J. R. Thompson, and R. Hutchison, who was then chosen as Mayor of Cape Coast.
[3] Dispatches Nos. 76 and 83 of 10 and 31 Aug. 1858, from Bird to Bulwer Lytton; CO/96/43.
[4] Dispatch No. 51 of 13 Aug. 1859, from Bird to Newcastle; CO/96/45.
[5] Dispatch No. 24 of 13 Feb. 1860, from Bird to Newcastle; CO/96/47.
[6] Dispatch No. 76 of 17 Sept. 1859, from Bulwer Lytton to Bird; CO/96/43.
[7] Memorandum of 23 July 1859, by E. B. Andrews; ibid.

lems of rate collection and squabbles over jurisdiction. Andrews had mis-
trusted Pine's policy from the start,[1] and soon complained of the scarcity of
people fitted to discharge the duties of councillors. The Mayor of Cape Coast
had died, and no one could be found to replace him, owing to ill will and
petty feuds, which Andrews attributed largely to the introduction of municipal
government. He claimed that not more than three or four interested gentlemen
could now be found to support the system, and forthwith secured the repeal
of 'an Ordinance so utterly unsuited to these Settlements'.[2]

Decline of the Poll Tax, 1859–62

Although the amended Poll Tax Ordinance was allowed to stand,[3] the time
was past for explanation and amendment, without a radical change in policy.
The diminishing receipts from the tax in subsequent years tell their own
story of the decline of the experiment:[4]

				£
1853	.	.	.	7,567
1854	.	.	.	3,625
1855	.	.		3,990
1856	.	.	.	3,353
1857	.	.	.	3,192
1858	.	.	.	2,921
1859	.	.	.	2,351
1860	.	.	.	1,725
1861	.	.	.	1,552

During 1858 the situation was exacerbated by a civil war in Krobo, where
the poll tax had never been paid willingly at the best of times, and where the
heavy-handed intervention of the Government only made matters worse. The
Chief of Yilo Krobo, 'who was known to be a palaverous man', refused to
acknowledge the authority of Odonkor Azu, the King of Manya Krobo, and
'collected a band of rioters against the payment of the poll tax'. The Rev.
T. B. Freeman, then Civil Commandant in Accra,[5] went to investigate the
disturbances, and a small force pursued the rebels up their sacred mountain;
but the soldiers were then set upon by all the Krobos, and there was an attempt
to destool Odonkor Azu for taking the side of the Government.[6]

---

[1] Dispatch No. 46 of 25 Apr. 1861, from Andrews to Newcastle; CO/96/52.

[2] Dispatch No. 6 of 8 Jan. 1861, from Andrews to Newcastle; CO/96/51.

[3] Its legal status was somewhat doubtful. The original Agreement was passed by Hill's Legislative Assembly, but not by the Legislative Council. Pine's amending Ordinance was passed by
the Legislative Council, but was not referred to an Assembly, as he considered the sanction of the
people was not required for a mere amendment. Dispatch No. 39 of 28 Apr. 1858, from B. Pine
to Stanley; CO/96/43.

[4] 1865 Report, app. i, p. 373. Hill's original figure of £6,656 was for the period Aug. 1852 to
July 1853. There are some other slight discrepancies between this table and the annual statements sent to the Colonial Office.

[5] Freeman had resigned as General Superintendent of the Wesleyan Mission in 1857, after
differences with the Missionary Committee in London.

[6] Enoch Azu, Adangbe (Adangme) History (Accra, 1929), pp. 57–60.

After the rebellion had been subdued, a punitive fine of £8,125 was imposed, to meet the cost of the expedition; but some injudicious arrangements for its collection by the merchants led to the palm oil hold-up of 1858–60.[1] This episode was accompanied by considerable resentment against both the merchants and the Government for what was considered an unjust penalty.[2] It added a flavour of moral indignation to the general dislike of the poll tax, and increased the difficulties of collection throughout the eastern districts. The situation there was not improved by the muddled state of the accounts under Freeman's supervision; he was later removed from the public service for financial irregularities in his poll tax records for 1859.[3]

During Andrews's period of office as Governor, 1860–2, attempts to collect the poll tax were even more ineffectual, largely because he himself thought the position was hopeless. There was some confusion between the poll tax and the new municipal rates; several villages on the outskirts of Cape Coast complained that they were being made to pay both.[4] But the fact that Andrews repealed the Municipal Corporations Ordinance merely encouraged the local Chiefs to hope that all forms of taxation could be removed. They 'resolved not to pay any more Poll Taxes, neither the assessment of our houses', and the Governor recommended the abolition of the tax.[5] The Secretary of State agreed that it had been a failure, but did not wish to appear to yield to the 'insolence' of the Chiefs of Cape Coast, and dismissed the idea of an increase in the parliamentary grant as out of the question.[6] In any case, the Colonial Office by now thoroughly distrusted Andrews's judgement, and were unwilling to make any important change on his advice;[7] he was simply told to limit expenditure to the revenue available.[8]

Meanwhile the payment of the poll tax gradually petered out, despite a brief revival under the governorship of Richard Pine in 1862. He persuaded the Chiefs of the Cape Coast District once more to agree to pay, provided the tax was spent on improvements under local control—even then, his 'strongest hope' was for a sum of only £400.[9] He felt that payment would be encouraged

[1] See Ch. I, p. 6, above.

[2] One of the Basel missionaries, the Rev. E. Schrenk, felt so strongly about the inequity of the fine that he printed a memorial and circulated it to all Members of Parliament while he was in England in 1864–5. S. Schrenk, *Elias Schrenk, ein Leben im Kampf um Gott* (Stuttgart, 1936), chs. 6 and 7. For some account of the situation among the palm oil farmers of Krobo at this time, see P. Steiner, *Saat und Ernte der Basier Mission auf der Goldküste* (Basel, 1895), pp. 37–42.

[3] Dispatches Nos. 86 of 31 Aug. 1860 and 96 of 9 Oct. 1861, with voluminous enclosures, from Andrews to Newcastle; CO/96/48 and 54.

[4] Cape Coast Municipality Minutes, 1 Sept. 1860, enclosed in Dispatch No. 2 of 2 Jan. 1861, from Andrews to Newcastle; CO/96/51.

[5] Petition of 3 Apr. 1861, from King, Chiefs, and other inhabitants of Cape Coast to Andrews, and his covering Dispatch No. 46 of 25 Apr. 1861, to Newcastle; CO/96/52.

[6] Minutes of 13 June 1861, by Barrow, and 26 June 1861, by Newcastle, and his Dispatch No. 102 of 16 July 1861, to Andrews; ibid.

[7] Minutes of 14 Apr. and 14 Oct. 1861, by T. F. Elliot; CO/96/51 and 55.

[8] Dispatch No. 102 of 16 July 1861, from Newcastle to Andrews; CO/96/52.

[9] Dispatch No. 111 of 29 Nov. 1862, from R. Pine to Newcastle; CO/96/58.

by an example of local initiative in Anomabu, where George Blankson had led a spirited voluntary movement to build a market, under the auspices of the local poll tax committee.[1] In 1864, after the shock of another Ashanti invasion, the Chiefs at Cape Coast again professed themselves willing to pay.[2] But this was only the last flicker of interest in a scheme which had once promised a real opportunity for experiments in local self-government. No serious attempt was made to collect the tax after 1862.

The Poll Tax in Retrospect

The most obvious defect in the poll tax scheme was the failure to eradicate the numerous abuses from the system of collection. Many of the publicans were also sinners. Andrews complained: 'it is a notorious fact that each Collector being a man of no pecuniary means when first appointed, acquires in four or five years that amount of property more or less which it is impossible to obtain by simply honest labour in his vocation'.[3] They did not always secure the assistance of the Chiefs, though this had been laid down in the Agreement. Poor communications added to the difficulties. Sir Benjamin Pine had at one stage suggested doing without the collectors altogether, and simply levying a lump sum on each Chief, leaving him to collect it as best he could. The Chiefs might still extort from their people under such an arrangement, but at least 'there would be only one class of extortioners', who would not be directly employed by the Government.[4]

But the system and its abuses remained. Receipts and accounts were not properly kept; and after several years' payment a regular system of auditing was still under discussion.[5] The Parliamentary Select Committee was told in 1865 that malversation had been the main reason for the failure of the poll tax; and that as a result, 'faith in the white man on the coast is very much shaken'.[6] These abuses might have been checked had there been one permanent Collector-General prepared to exert his authority; but in fact such a man proved difficult to find, and there was no continuity of administration. The first holder of this office, Cruickshank, occupied it only reluctantly, and one of his successors was suspended in 1856 after a petty squabble with the Acting Governor. An African merchant, Thomas Hughes, was then appointed provisionally, in spite of his earlier opposition to the tax, and official doubts about his morals.[7]

---

[1] This venture must be one of the earliest recorded examples of modern 'community development'. The Governor went to Anomabu to lay the foundation-stone, and decided to present the inhabitants with a public clock. Dispatch No. 113 of 12 Dec. 1862, from R. Pine to Newcastle; CO/96/58.   [2] See Ch. V, p. 200, below.

[3] Dispatch No. 46 of 25 Apr. 1861, from Andrews to Newcastle; CO/96/52.

[4] Dispatch No. 28 of 31 Mar. 1858, from B. Pine to Stanley; CO/96/43.

[5] Dispatch No. 60 of 13 June 1860, from Andrews to Newcastle; CO/96/47.

[6] *1865 Report*, evidence of Conran, reply to question 8,319.

[7] Confidential Dispatch of 20 Sept. 1856, from Connor to Labouchere; CO/96/38.

In view of all these practical difficulties, the amounts collected initially appear surprisingly large; the first sum of £7,567 represented the payments due from over 150,000 people. Any scheme for taxation was bound to be unpopular; but there seems to have been no objection to a poll tax *per se*. In fact, the Fanti Confederation later adopted the idea for its own purpose, and passed a 'law' in 1871 to raise its own revenue by means of a poll tax.[1] Again, among all the protests of 1853-62, there appears to be no evidence that the inhabitants could not afford to pay. Unfortunately, inefficient public relations, maladministration, and frequent changes of policy allowed the normal dislike of paying taxes to develop into a challenge to the authority of the Government.

It might even be argued that, had the original Agreement been carried out, the tax need never have been written off as a failure. Here there were two serious mistakes on the part of the Government. First, the original intentions concerning expenditure were not observed. The Chiefs were soon antagonized by the failure to pay them the stipends that had been promised; but later the stipends and expenses of collection swallowed up nearly the whole revenue, and the people became restless at the failure to provide the promised benefits. To ensure regular payment, it would have been essential to build some roads, schools, and hospitals, in both the eastern and western districts. It was comparatively easy to get people to pay 1s. in the first year, when such things were promised or expected; but not so easy after the fifth or sixth years, when there were still no visible results.

The fund was unwisely saddled with a disproportionately heavy burden of fixed charges. Several officials were paid entirely out of the proceeds, and others received additions to their salaries; the stipends of the Chiefs also had to be met. These amounts were calculated on the basis of totally unrealistic estimates. The proposed census of population was never carried out; but in any case expectations were never scaled down to realities. The system had the added disadvantage that practically everybody concerned with the collection of the poll tax was entitled to some share of the proceeds; however disinterested they might be, it was difficult for them to appear so. The Chiefs, in particular, were regarded as 'mere instruments of extortion'.[2]

Secondly, the principle of representation, which had been invoked when revenue was required, was dropped, for all practical purposes, once the tax began to be collected. The Legislative Assembly did not meet again after 1852; so it never had a chance of becoming the fully representative body of all the Chiefs of the Protectorate, referred to in the original Agreement. The discrepancy between theory and practice was particularly noticeable in the eastern districts. The Chiefs there were only consulted after the Cape Coast Agreement had been drawn up; and it was the inhabitants of Accra who

[1] See Ch. VI, p. 249, below.
[2] Dispatch No. 75 of 30 Apr. 1857, from B. Pine to Labouchere; CO/96/41.

were particularly unable to understand the point of the poll tax, even when it was driven home with cannon shot. Elsewhere, Sir Benjamin Pine found the people more amenable when they were fully consulted. His District Assemblies might have provided a workable alternative to the hypothetical central body; but the idea came too late to make much difference, and in any case it was turned down in London.

The abandonment of the poll tax, hastened by Andrews's distrust of the system, unfortunately created the enduring impression in the Gold Coast that direct taxation was an unjust imposition, to be resisted at all costs. It also encouraged the idea that the Government would yield to continued pressure. Officials, for their part, were reluctant for many years afterwards to consider schemes of direct taxation. It was not until 1877 that the suggestion was heard again; and the fear of potential opposition was such that no public proposal was made until 1898.[1]

But the idea of representation had taken root, and the abortive Legislative Assembly was not forgotten. It had been at least a potential unifying force, and became for later nationalist writers a powerful symbol of what might have been; it was assumed that Hill's intention to assemble all the Chiefs of the Protectorate had in fact been carried out. Fifty years afterwards Casely Hayford, referring to the 1852 Assembly, applied that stick to the backs of contemporary administrators: 'if any tax on the people be ever carried out, I conceive that it can only be effected in that manner, namely with the consent and the direct co-operation of the Chiefs themselves . . . Legislation, to be effectual, must be with the Chiefs in a representative legislative assembly.'[2]

Meanwhile, the unhappy experience of the poll tax had not made indirect taxes any easier to collect. After 1854 there was, in fact, almost a stock re-action against any government proposals to collect revenue, whatever their purpose or method. Repeated attempts were made to raise the level of customs duties, in order to fill the gap left by the poll tax. It was at this point that the interests of the European merchants were directly affected; they joined in the protests, helped to perpetuate the tradition of opposition, and strengthened it by new techniques of organization. The poll tax had marked the first clear division of interest between the Chiefs and people on the one hand, and the colonial Government on the other; and it set the pattern for a century of strenuous, if intermittent, political opposition to taxation in any shape or form.

---

[1] See Ch. VIII, pp. 307–12, below.
[2] J. E. Casely Hayford, *Gold Coast Native Institutions* (London, 1903), pp. 164–5.

V

KING AGGERY'S CHALLENGE
TO BRITISH JURISDICTION
1865–7

IT was not long after Governor Richard Pine's final failure to revive the poll tax that he found himself faced with a fresh challenge to British authority. This came from much nearer home, from King Aggery of Cape Coast, who was attempting to assert the right to dispense his own form of justice under the very walls of the castle, and even aspiring to achieve local self-government. The issue was considerably complicated by changing currents of opinion in England, especially when the advocates of retrenchment, allied with those of African advancement, succeeded in getting the aim of eventual self-government written into the Parliamentary *Report* of 1865; and Aggery was considerably encouraged in his intransigence by the outspoken, London-published newspaper, *The African Times*.[1]

But the question at stake locally was a simple one. Although the forts themselves were directly governed as a Colony, the British had acquired their rights of protection over the neighbouring territories only by the consent of the Chiefs. What was to happen if any Chief should repudiate the exercise of British jurisdiction? and further, how could the British govern the forts directly, and carry on their trade, without exercising something more than an indirect influence over the adjacent towns that they themselves were helping to create? The problem was particularly acute in Cape Coast, just because it was the headquarters of the Administration, although in strict legal theory the British had no more jurisdiction over that town than any other in the Protectorate.

The brief rise and fall of King Aggery is thus of greater significance than the mere events and personalities involved. Unlike Ja-Ja, King of Opobo in the Niger Delta, who was later to suffer a similar fate, Aggery was not a particularly dominant character, had no strong economic reasons for his stand against the British, and managed to put himself sufficiently in the wrong to justify deportation. Nevertheless, he was to become one of the earliest

---

[1] This was founded in 1861 as the journal of the African-Aid Society, and was published monthly just in time to catch the regular mail steamers to West Africa, where its influence was greater than a comparatively small circulation (about 350 in 1864) might suggest. The Secretary of the Society, F. Fitzgerald, was also the editor. When those whom he called 'The upholders of African abuses, mercantile and administrative', managed to get the Society closed down, he took over the newspaper himself as proprietor. *The African Times*, 23 June 1866. Fitzgerald remained editor until his death in 1884, at the age of 77.

national heroes of the Gold Coast, not so much to his contemporaries as to later generations. He was the first Chief in the Protectorate openly to express reasoned objections to British encroachment, the first actively to seek—or to be led by—the advice of educated confidants, and the first to send representatives to England to state his case. The outcome of this affair illustrates clearly how in the last resort it was impossible for British jurisdiction to coexist with the unfettered authority of the Chiefs; and it was only a matter of time before others besides Aggery were to learn this by experience. In order to unravel the origins of the dispute, however, it is necessary to start the story some years before Aggery's accession, and to indicate briefly the manner in which Britain had gradually acquired her jurisdiction on the coast.

The Growth of British Jurisdiction

The administration of British justice in the Gold Coast dates largely from the time of George Maclean. Up to 1821 the forts had been administered by the Company of Merchants Trading to Africa, and their officers on the coast had had no jurisdiction, either civil or criminal, nor any power of trial.[1] After the Crown took over from the Company, the Gold Coast Settlements were made subject to the laws and statutes of Sierra Leone,[2] and some magistrates were appointed. But this form of government did not last for long; trade declined, and the maintenance and defence of the forts against the Ashantis did not seem to be worth the cost, in lives and money. In 1828 the British Government withdrew from the forts, but was persuaded to retain them as nominal dependencies of Sierra Leone.[3] The responsibilities of the Crown were transferred to a Committee of Merchants in London, and the local administration was entrusted to a Council of Merchants at Cape Coast.

Several of the British traders on the coast were appointed Justices of the Peace, for the trial of petty cases arising within the walls of the forts; beyond this they had no authority or jurisdiction.[4] But after George Maclean became President of the Council in 1830, cases were increasingly brought to Cape Coast from the surrounding territories, and his judgements were generally accepted, although not strictly enforceable.[5] Dr. R. R. Madden, the investigating

---

[1] James Swanzy urged in 1816 that they should be given civil jurisdiction according to the English law. *Report from the Select Committee on Papers relating to the African Forts* (London, 1816), p. 41. For an account of the merchant administration, see E. C. Martin, *The British West African Settlements, 1750–1821* (London, 1927).

[2] Proclamation of 29 Mar. 1822, by Sir Charles Macarthy; J. J. Crooks, *Records relating to the Gold Coast Settlements from 1750 to 1874* (Dublin, 1923), pp. 138–41.

[3] As Brodie Cruickshank put it: 'A middle course was adopted, which relieved the government from the troublesome affairs of the Gold Coast, and, at the same time, gave its countenance and a slight pecuniary assistance [an annual grant of £4,000] to the merchants for their protection.' *Eighteen Years on the Gold Coast of Africa* (London, 1853), vol. i, p. 166.

[4] Letters of 30 Oct. and 14 Nov. 1828, from Hay (Colonial Office) to Barnes, Brown & Forster (of the London Committee of Merchants); CO/268/27.

[5] Ord later described this as 'a species of irregular authority, partly tolerated from a conviction of its usefulness, and partly compulsory, from the nature of our position'. *Copy of the Report of*

Commissioner sent out by the British Government in 1841, strongly criticized this system; although he admitted that the justice of Maclean's decisions was acknowledged by all parties, he felt that British law was not
sufficiently observed.[1] The 1842 Select Committee concluded that all jurisdiction outside the forts must be 'considered as optional and should be made
the subject of distinct agreement . . . with the Native Chiefs'.[2]

The Crown resumed control of the Settlements in 1843, and in the same
year the Foreign Jurisdiction Act was passed by Parliament 'to remove Doubts
as to the Exercise of Powers and Jurisdiction by Her Majesty within divers
Countries and Places out of Her Majesty's Dominions, and to render the same
more effectual'.[3] Maclean was then given the post of Judicial Assessor to the
Chiefs, with express instructions to maintain 'the exercise of that jurisdiction
which has been established . . . in the case of crimes and misdemeanours
committed among neighbouring tribes'.[4] The Judicial Assessor was to sit with
the Chiefs in important cases, but otherwise his duties were never clearly
defined.[5]

The next step was the so-called Bond of 1844, the first of a succession of
treaties under which certain Gold Coast Chiefs acknowledged the power and
jurisdiction of the Crown, and gave their formal consent to the trial of criminal cases 'before the Queen's judicial officers and the Chiefs of the district,
moulding the customs of the country to the general principles of British law'.[6]

---

*Colonel Ord, the Commissioner appointed to Inquire into the Condition of the British Settlements
on the West Coast of Africa* (London, 1865), p. 20. Contrast the view taken by King Aggery,
pp. 203–4, below. For an account of the establishment of British authority under Maclean, see
J. D. Fage, 'The Administration of George Maclean on the Gold Coast, 1830–44', in *Transactions of the Gold Coast & Togoland Historical Society* (Achimota, 1955), vol. i, pt. iv.

[1] 'I begged to be informed under what code, Russian or Turkish, justice was administered here,
and by what authority the [British] law had been set aside.' *Report from the Select Committee on
the West Coast of Africa* (London, 1842), pt. II, app. no. 3, p. 11.

[2] Ibid. pt. i, p. vi.

[3] Act 6 & 7 Vict., c. 94, of 24 Aug. 1843; reproduced in *Copies or Extracts of any Acts of
Parliament, Orders in Council, Charters of Justice or Government, and Local Ordinances, defining
the existing Civil and Judicial Constitutions of the British Settlements on the West Coast of Africa*
(London, 1855).

[4] Dispatch of 16 Dec. 1843, from Stanley to Hill; Crooks, *Records*, pp. 285–91.

[5] Early in the twentieth century, Gold Coast lawyers came to regard this period as a golden age
as far as relationships between Europeans and Africans were concerned; see J. Mensah Sarbah,
'Maclean and Gold Coast Judicial Assessors', in *Journal of the Royal African Society* (London,
1910), pp. 349–59.

[6] Declaration of 6 Mar. 1844, signed by eight Fanti Chiefs, including Joseph Aggery of Cape
Coast. This has been reproduced by several African writers, e.g. J. E. Casely Hayford, *Gold Coast
Native Institutions* (London, 1903), app. D5. Little publicity has been given to the subsequent
declarations by other Chiefs in identical terms, during 1844:

12 March	Braffo and Tuful Chiefs
18 March	Acoomfie and Bentil Chiefs
27 March	Adjumaccon Chiefs
12 April	Gomboah and Assambah Adjumaccon Chiefs
22 April	Esseecoomah Chiefs

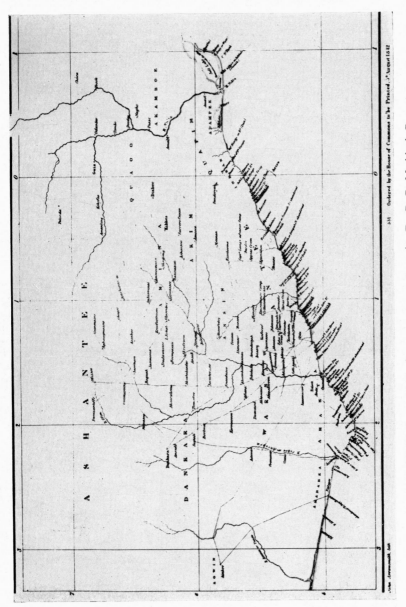

MAP 4. The Gold Coast, 1842—from a map accompanying Dr. R. R. Madden's Report.

331   Ordered by the House of Commons to be Printed, 1ˢᵗ August 1842

The document has since been described as of small intrinsic value, since at that time, 'whether by virtue of our protection or by consent or by usage or by usurpation, we had undoubtedly acquired the right of jurisdiction, civil and criminal'.[1] Nevertheless, it was of increasing psychological importance in determining local attitudes towards British protection.[2] As Dr. Africanus Horton wrote in 1868, 'the inhabitants submitted themselves to the British Government, not as subjects, but as independent nations, in alliance with, and protected by, the United Kingdom'.[3]

Soon after the Bond, the legal framework was completed by an Order in Council, which ordered judges, magistrates, assessors, and other officers, in the exercise of their jurisdiction outside the forts, to observe such local customs as were compatible with the law of England. In default of such customs, they were to 'proceed in all things as nearly as may be according to the said law of England'.[4] It has been pointed out that under the rule of the Chiefs there never evolved a unified system of customary law sufficiently comprehensive to be called a Common Law of the Gold Coast. There were so many independent States, with local differences and peculiarities, that this was almost impossible; and the fragmentation of the coast under different European powers further delayed the introduction of a unified legal system.[5] This may help to explain the rapidity with which British legal conventions came to be accepted, as British political influence increased during the second half of the nineteenth century.

When the Gold Coast was separated from Sierra Leone in 1850, no immediate change was made in the system whereby (in theory) the gravest offences were to be tried in Freetown.[6] In 1853, however, the Secretary of State was persuaded to agree to the establishment of a Supreme Court with jurisdiction inside the Forts and Settlements; an appeal lay to the Governor

8 May	Caboceer of Accra
29 May	Sarban and Odoomtoo Chiefs
22 July	Chiefs of Upper Wassaw
21 August	Caboceers of Dog Town, Big Town, and Darbanearty
2 December	Chiefs of Lower Wassaw

All are printed in *West African Treaties* (London, 1892), African (West) No. 411, pt. iii, Gold Coast, no. 4.

[1] W. Brandford Griffith, *A Note on the History of the British Courts in the Gold Coast Colony, with a Brief Account of the Changes in the Constitution of the Colony* (Accra, 1936).

[2] From 1949 onwards, the Bond was taken as the starting-point of '105 years of imperialist misrule'; and the date 6 Mar. acquired such emotive significance that it was chosen for the granting of Ghana's independence in 1957.

[3] J. A. B. Horton, *West African Countries and Peoples* (London, 1868), p. 243.

[4] Order in Council of 3 Sept. 1844, made under the authority of the Foreign Jurisdiction Act; Crooks, *Records*, p. 284.

[5] This point has been made by Sir Arku Korsah, for example, in his lecture on 'The Judicial System of the Gold Coast', Kumasi, Nov. 1948.

[6] Maclean had refused to observe this procedure, pointing out that he had no means of communication with Sierra Leone and no funds to meet the expenses. Letter of 30 Nov. 1836, from Maclean to the African Committee of Merchants in London; CO/267/136.

and Council of the Gold Coast.[1] The Judicial Assessor, J. C. Fitzpatrick, was then also appointed Chief Justice.[2] It was not clear to what extent English law should be held to prevail;[3] but Supreme Court trials were now conducted 'in the English manner', before a jury. As a result, the Chiefs' courts in the fort towns found their authority weakened by the increased powers and prestige of the new courts, especially in Cape Coast. An ex-Administrator later wrote of the British Government's 'solvent influence over native rule, which falls to pieces by mere proximity'.[4]

This process was clearly apparent in developments in Cape Coast during the next ten years. Both the traditional authorities of the town and the merchants—of all colours—were becoming restless and dissatisfied with the Government, and were challenging its jurisdiction in many minor judicial and economic matters. In 1853, mainly on the initiative of educated African merchants, a native court was set up for the whole town of Cape Coast, to replace the various Chiefs' courts held in private houses. J. R. Thompson, a schoolmaster, presided over the new court, at first with the sanction of the King; the Government did not interfere at this stage, apparently because no complaints were made.[5]

Later in the year there was an indirect challenge to the authority of the Government. Four African merchants—Henry Barnes, Joseph Smith, Thomas Hughes, and William de Graft—organized a 'most numerously signed' petition against Fitzpatrick in his capacity as Judicial Assessor. They alleged, among other complaints, that he had shown disrespect to the King, by bringing him to trial in a civil action. Brodie Cruickshank, then acting as Governor, was sympathetic,[6] and as a result the Judicial Assessor was virtually suspended from office. The Colonial Office disapproved of this action;[7] but the fact that, for private reasons, Fitzpatrick did not return to the Gold Coast was taken as a moral victory.

It was not long before the new native court attracted the attention, and the disapproval, of the Government. Early in 1854 some of the Cape Coast Chiefs agreed to destool Kofi Amissah, who had been King since 1851. He was held to be unfit for office and charged with attempting to blow himself up in his

---

[1] Supreme Court Ordinance of 26 Apr. 1853; *Constitutions of the ... West Coast of Africa* (1885).

[2] Fitzpatrick allowed his name (and salary) to be written into the Supreme Court Ordinance, which had to be amended by the Legislative Council in 1854 before a successor could be appointed.

[3] Memorandum of 9 May 1872, by D. Chalmers, concerning 'the law prevailing in Her Majesty's Forts and Settlements on the Gold Coast', enclosed in Dispatch No. 93 of 29 Oct. 1872, from Pope Hennessy to Kimberley; CO/96/94.

[4] C. S. Salmon, *The Crown Colonies of Great Britain* (London, 1886), pp. 90–91.

[5] Dispatch No. 94 of 18 Dec. 1854, from Connor to Sir G. Grey; CO/96/31.

[6] Dispatch No. 72 of 7 Sept. 1853, from Cruickshank to Newcastle; CO/96/28.

[7] The next year the Governor, commenting on objections to the poll tax, said: 'these oppositionists are the same clique to whose tumultuous clamour Mr. Cruickshank gave way and by an act of weakness led them to believe they could overrule the Government'. Dispatch No. 36 of 31 May 1854, from Hill to Newcastle; CO/96/30.

house with gunpowder. From that time, the townspeople considered the King deposed and 'politically dead', with no authority over Thompson's court. Amissah did not accept this, and took out a summons in the British court against Thompson, who was ordered to account for the money he had received by way of fines. Announcing this decision, the Chief Justice made it clear that the Government did not recognize either Amissah's deposition— 'a King could not be removed without the consent of the Governor'—or the imposition of fines and imprisonment by Thompson's court. Disturbances were feared as a result of this unpopular decision, especially as Thompson at first refused to obey the order. But the Chief Justice—who was now, to complicate matters, Acting Governor—took a firm stand, considering that if he gave in the people would become even more 'refractory and opposing to the Government'. His military preparations caused sufficient alarm for Thompson to appear in the British court, where he was fined.[1]

Amissah was left in an anomalous position; he was still recognized by the Government, which managed to forestall an attempt to enstool a new King. But in practice the main authority in Cape Coast was exercised by Thompson, who claimed that his office traditionally ranked second to the King, and that he was in effect 'Mayor of the Town'. Early in 1855 a memorial of protest from the townspeople to the Secretary of State stated that Thompson, as master-at-arms and town magistrate, had been appointed their leader, 'in charge of public affairs pro-tempore, until a new King be appointed by us'.[2]

The Secretary of State upheld the view that the King could not be deposed without the consent of the Governor;[3] but the Colonial Office was expecting further trouble in Cape Coast. The chief blame was laid upon certain 'half-caste and half educated' men, who were assuring the Africans 'that they are not "subjects" of Gt. Britain and therefore owe no obedience'.[4] Soon after Thompson's memorial, Smith and Barnes were suspended from office as Justices of the Peace, as a result of joining Hughes and de Graft in yet another complaint, this time against the Acting Chief Justice;[5] and further objections were made to the poll tax. To make matters worse there was an outcry against an Ordinance which raised the customs duty from $\frac{1}{2}$ to 3 per cent.[6]

---

[1] Dispatch No. 94 of 18 Dec. 1854, from Connor to Sir G. Grey; CO/96/31.

[2] Statement of 8 Dec. 1854, by J. R. Thompson, and Cape Coast Memorial of 5 Jan. 1855, enclosed in Dispatch No. 2 of 6 Jan. 1855, from Connor to Sir G. Grey; CO/96/33.

[3] Dispatch No. 9 of 3 Mar. 1855, from Russell to Connor; ibid.

[4] Minute of 19 Feb. 1855, by H. Merivale; ibid.

[5] *Executive Council Minutes*, 21 Feb. 1855.

[6] For example, enclosures in Dispatches Nos. 81 and 85 of 4 and 10 Sept. 1855, from Connor to Molesworth; CO/96/34. There was a long history of opposition even to the $\frac{1}{2}$ per cent. duty, which the merchants claimed had been continuously in force since 1829. In 1836 King Joseph Aggery and the people of Cape Coast petitioned the House of Commons, with the help of Sir Robert Peel, against this interference with free trade; see correspondence published by J. Mensah Sarbah, *Fanti National Constitution* (London, 1906), pp. 219–25. The following year Maclean was told by the Colonial Office that the duty was illegal, but in 1840 he was permitted to levy certain dues on trade at Cape Coast, Anomabu, and Accra. CO/268/34 and 36.

The Colonial Office was also anxious to placate the London and Liverpool merchants, whose lobbying was partly responsible for Major H. St. G. Ord's mission of investigation.[1] Soon after he arrived, in January 1856, a murderous riot took place in Cape Coast, which started as a demonstration against Kofi Amissah. Ord held a special inquiry, and in a Salomonic decision declared the King deposed, fined his opponents, and distributed the proceeds among those who had suffered in the disturbances.[2] His report revealed the interesting fact that the Chiefs from the interior relied almost implicitly upon those of Cape Coast for guidance in all their decisions; and although he suggested that this influence should be constructively used to further government measures, the Acting Governor refused to alter his policy of deliberately weakening any influence of the Cape Coast Chiefs which went 'beyond their own legitimate authority in their districts'. Ord considered that this had given great offence and needlessly irritated the Chiefs;[3] but his arguments went unheeded.

A further extension of British jurisdiction took place in 1856, when an Order in Council authorized the Supreme Court to hear cases arising in the Protected Territories, as well as inside the Settlements, 'without the co-operation of any native Chief or authority'. The influence of English law thus became more widespread, although the Court was adjured to pay equitable regard to local customs, where these were not repugnant to Christianity or to natural justice.[4] It had been originally intended that the Judicial Assessor's court should be held to assist the Chiefs, and that the functions of the Chief Justice should be exercised separately in the Supreme Court. But gradually the two courts drifted into one; and the regard paid to local customs became more and more perfunctory when professional lawyers were appointed to the dual office.

The years 1858–61 saw Sir Benjamin Pine's short-lived experiment in municipal government;[5] one of the difficulties that led to its failure in Cape Coast was the rivalry between the official Mayor's court (established under the Municipal Corporations Ordinance) and the King's court, originally set up under Thompson. Further memorials against the customs duty were sub-

---

[1] Ord was impressed by the need for co-operation with the Dutch over the enforcement of customs duties, and on his return from the Gold Coast he helped in the negotiations at The Hague which eventually led to the first definite proposals for an exchange of territory. See Ch. VI, p. 223, below. At the first meeting of the Legislative Council in 1850, F. Swanzy had proposed that 'a loan should be raised to buy out the Dutch because their dislike of duties was likely to prove a barrier to any advancement in the country, inasmuch as he regarded self-government as the most desirable thing for Africa'. *Legislative Council Minutes*, 4 Mar. 1850. No doubt he had self-government by the merchants in mind.

[2] Dispatch No. 16 of 2 Feb. 1856, from Connor to Labouchere; CO/96/38.

[3] Report of 16 May 1856, from Ord to Labouchere; CO/96/40.

[4] Order in Council of 4 Apr. 1856; *Ordinances, &c., relating to Her Majesty's Forts and Settlements on the Gold Coast* (London, 1860).

[5] Smith, Barnes, Hughes, and Thompson were all elected councillors for Cape Coast; see Ch. IV, p. 186 n., above.

mitted by both the merchants and the Chiefs, who were thus gradually gaining experience in the techniques of organized protest.[1]

Protection, Sovereignty, and Taxation, 1863–5

The increase in British powers and jurisdiction outside the forts might have been thought to carry with it some increased responsibility for the protection of these areas. This aspect received little consideration, however, during the years of comparative peace and prosperity; as Horton put it, 'There was a sort of happy lull in the political condition of the whole country', up to the end of 1862.[2]

But then a dispute arose over a demand from the Asantehene for the extradition of two Ashantis who had taken refuge in the Protectorate. The Governor, Richard Pine, was in a dilemma; he was anxious to preserve amicable relations with Ashanti, yet he felt it would be an injustice to hand the refugees over to certain execution: 'Their blood would be upon my head.'[3] He refused to surrender them, with the approval of the Secretary of State;[4] and as a direct result, the Ashantis invaded the Protectorate in 1863. The Fantis suffered heavy losses in this war, and their confidence in British protection was severely shaken. Pine wanted to strike a final blow at Ashanti power; he urged the home Government to supply sufficient soldiers to carry the British flag to Kumasi.[5] Early in 1864 there was an abortive expedition to the River Prah; but no contact was made with the Ashantis and many West Indian troops died of disease.

These misfortunes made a deep impression in Britain; severe criticisms were made in the House of Commons, and the Palmerston Government was urged to abandon such costly and troublesome Settlements. The Secretary of State agreed that 'it was not our duty to make expeditions into the interior', and protested that there was no desire for any extension of territory.[6] But *The Times* pressed him further: British commitments must be reduced—the Crown must have 'nothing whatever to do with such monstrosities as "protectorates" over savage tribes'.[7] On a motion of censure in the House of Commons about the responsibility for the 'so-called Ashantee war', there was an acrimonious debate, and the Government narrowly escaped defeat;[8] but it was Pine who became the scapegoat.[9] The Secretary of State knew that the Governor was not alone to blame; but he warned him that further retrenchment might be

---

[1] For example, the Cape Coast Memorial enclosed in Dispatch No. 81 of 8 Aug. 1860, from Andrews to Newcastle; CO/96/49.

[2] J. A. B. Horton, *Letters on the Political Condition of the Gold Coast* (London, 1870), p. 53.

[3] Dispatch No. 112 of 10 Dec. 1862, from R. Pine to Newcastle; CO/96/58.

[4] Dispatch of 4 Mar. 1863, from Newcastle to R. Pine; CO/96/60.

[5] Dispatch of 12 May 1863, from R. Pine to Newcastle; ibid.

[6] Cardwell, *Parliamentary Debates*, House of Commons, 20 May 1864.

[7] 21 May 1864.   [8] *Parliamentary Debates*, House of Commons, 17 June 1864.

[9] For example, 'Governor Pine was heedless of warnings and impervious to reproof. The delicate hints of the Colonial Office were lost on his fervid temperament.' *The Times*, 18 June 1864.

called for, and instructed him to 'take every possible means for bringing the Chiefs to an united and decided system of defence'. For this purpose they were to be given only advice, supplies, and such assistance as Pine could afford 'without exposing his officers and men to any protracted resistance in the interior'.[1]

In August 1864 Richard Pine called an important meeting of Chiefs from Cape Coast and the interior, together with merchants, members of the Legislative Council, and other prominent citizens. Cardwell's instructions were read and translated to them, with a general explanation of government policy, calling upon the people to pay their poll tax, develop their country in peacetime, and 'assist him (the Governor) in time of war', if they wished for the continuance of protection.[2] This did little to clarify an already confused situation. The Secretary of State, on the one hand, now feared that too much assistance had been promised, and Pine had to reassure him on this point.[3] The Fantis, on the other hand, feared that they were losing effective protection, and later claimed that Pine had said his instructions were 'not to interfere with any quarrels with the King of Ashantee, and that the Kings and Chiefs should be left to settle their own differences'.[4]

Meanwhile it had been decided in London that there should be a full-scale parliamentary inquiry into the state of the West African Settlements, and Ord was commissioned to visit them again and make an independent report. He was instructed to pay particular attention to the exercise of protection by the British, and their moral influence over neighbouring tribes; also to questions of treaty relationships and taxation.[5]

An awkward issue had arisen earlier in 1864, when Pine had passed an Ordinance requiring all traders in wines and spirits, wholesale or retail, to take out a £2 annual licence. This was to be enforced 'over the whole of the British possessions, and to a distance of two miles inland'.[6] It was designed more to limit the traffic than to increase revenue; but it was regarded locally as a form of taxation which the Government had no right to impose outside their narrow territorial limits. The Chiefs of Cape Coast made the significant claim—which owed much to Grey's approach to the poll tax—that the people ought not to be taxed without first being consulted, since they were not British subjects.[7] The Governor, however, claimed that he had consulted the Chiefs in advance, and had summoned a Council 'composed of men of

[1] Dispatch of 23 June 1864, from Cardwell to Hackett; CO/96/64.
[2] Report of meeting of 5 (and adjourned to 9) Aug. 1864, enclosed in Dispatch No. 75 of 12 Aug. 1864, from R. Pine to Cardwell; CO/96/65.
[3] Dispatch No. 108 of 10 Nov. 1864, from R. Pine to Cardwell; ibid.
[4] Quoted in preamble to the Fanti Confederation scheme of 1872; CO/96/94.
[5] Instructions of 25 Oct. 1864, from Cardwell to Ord; *Copy of the Report of Colonel Ord* (1865).
[6] *Report from the Select Committee on Africa* (*Western Coast*) (London, 1865), evidence of Ord, reply to question 932.
[7] Petition of 25 Oct. 1864, from Chiefs, Headmen and other inhabitants of Cape Coast to Governor; *The African Times*, 23 Dec. 1864.

influence in the country, and native merchants, who were required to consult with their constituents', as he put it, and to sound the Protectorate.[1] When the Chiefs complained that the Ordinance had taken them by surprise, they were told that the members of the Council had said that 'the people agreed to it'.[2]

Whatever the facts about the method of consultation, there was no doubt that Pine went beyond the letter of the law in imposing a tax without the explicit consent of the Chiefs in territory over which no sovereignty was claimed. The Ordinance was referred to the Secretary of State, who decided to disallow it. But owing to the unsettled state of the country after the Ashanti invasion, he delayed turning it down in order to avoid injuring the Governor's authority.[3] The exact nature and extent of British jurisdiction could hardly have been in a more confused and uncertain state, when a new and unpredictable character came upon the Cape Coast scene.

King Aggery and His Court[4]

In January 1865 the Chiefs of Cape Coast asked permission to elect a new King. The next month Richard Pine ratified their election of John Aggery, who was installed, 'for the first time in the annals of Cape Coast, without the usual semi-barbaric shouts, yells, clapping of hands and firing of muskets'.[5] Although government troops fired a salute of guns and composed a guard of honour, Aggery was not asked to swear allegiance to the Queen, an omission to which he himself attached considerable importance;[6] he said later that he took it as confirmation of his professed belief that the principal Kings were required to prepare themselves for self-government, 'so as to relieve the British Government of a task which they seemed so anxious to get rid of'.[7]

At first Pine welcomed Aggery to Government House as a Christian King,[8] and hoped he would prove a faithful ally; but only a few days later he noted 'symptoms of disaffection', arising out of a case in Aggery's court. A man was found guilty there of attempting to poison his neighbour, and was sentenced

---

[1] *1865 Report*, R. Pine, 7,843.   [2] Ibid. Martin, 8,429.   [3] Ibid. Ord, 8,511.

[4] The main Dispatches and documents covering this episode are contained in the Parliamentary Paper, *Deportation of King Aggery of Cape Coast* (London, 1867). For the purpose of the account that follows, reference has been made to the fuller documentation contained in the original Colonial Office records.

[5] Dispatch No. 29 of 8 Mar. 1865, from R. Pine to Cardwell; CO/96/67.

[6] The oath was 'somehow or another omitted in Aggery's case', according to Conran in his Dispatch No. 136 of 6 Nov. 1865, to Cardwell; CO/96/68. In view of the ritual nature of enstoolment and other local ceremonies, where words and gestures held great symbolic significance, Aggery's reaction is hardly surprising.

[7] Unsigned Petition from Aggery to Carnarvon, enclosed in his Dispatch No. 66 of 23 Jan. 1867, to Blackall; CO/96/74.

[8] *The African Times*, 23 Mar. 1865, contained an account of a speech by Aggery at the annual district meeting of the Wesleyan Chapel, a few hours after he had been 'crowned'. He recalled, in the presence of the Governor, how in his early evangelistic association with William de Graft (see Ch. III, p. 146 n., above) he had been taken before Maclean, on the complaint of the Chiefs, and later 'cast into prison' and publicly flogged for refusing to return to fetish-worship. Aggery was evidently a man prepared to defy authority when he thought fit.

to imprisonment. He escaped and appealed—although not a British subject—to the British court, where Joseph Martin (the King's magistrate who had sentenced him) was summoned for the technical 'assault', and fined £5. This was later paid by Aggery, but only under solemn protest, and the controversy over the powers of native courts was now renewed. Although Richard Pine had 'always approved of a country court of conciliation or of arbitration, with a right of appeal to the English court', he now declared that 'a British Governor could not permit irresponsible tribunals exercising the powers, at all events, of imprisonment'.[1]

In this view Pine was later supported by Ord, who stated in evidence before the 1865 Select Committee that the British did not recognize the right of the King of Cape Coast 'or any one's right to imprison throughout the length and breadth of the Protectorate'. He was closely questioned on this point:

That is assuming the sovereignty over the protected country to some extent?—Yes, with the assent of the natives.

It is at least a partnership in the sovereignty of the country with the chiefs?—To that extent.

Do you mean to say that the King of Cape Coast has assented?—I mean that the assent of all the natives has been obtained.

Or rather, should you not say implied?—Yes, implied; the right has been assumed, and never been contested. The King of Cape Coast is the first person who has ever, to my knowledge, doubted our right to protect the whole of the natives of Cape Coast from imprisonment at the hands of their masters.

... Within the Protectorate certain chiefs have exercised the power of imprisonment, have they not?—The chiefs exercise the power of adjudicating in criminal cases, according to the native law, at a distance from Cape Coast.

Do they exercise the power of imprisonment within the Protectorate?—They do, because we are not able to do it for them.

We go as far as we have the power of doing it; but where we cannot we do not?—Exactly.[2]

In practice, of course, it was only in Cape Coast, the headquarters of the British Administration, that the Governor could hope to enforce this pragmatic view; and here he encountered the resistance of Aggery, who feared the British might be intending to withdraw and was therefore anxious to restore 'the waning dignity of my court'.[3] Some conflict was inevitable, though the occasion for it was a trivial incident.

[1] *Executive Council Minutes*, 25 Mar. 1865. Also Dispatch No. 38 of 7 Apr. 1865, from R. Pine to Cardwell; CO/96/67.   [2] *1865 Report*, Ord, 8,477–80 and 8,482–4.

[3] Letter of 16 Mar. 1865, from Aggery to R. Pine, enclosed in his Dispatch No. 38 of 7 Apr. 1865, to Cardwell; CO/96/67. Cf. *The African Times*, editorial of 23 Aug. 1867, which argued that the Fanti Kings had gradually given up a portion of their power in return for substantial and effective protection; and that when it appeared that the protection was to be curtailed after 1864, it was 'not unnatural' for Aggery to consider he might re-establish an independent court, especially as this was his 'only regal source of revenue'. (The editor himself was not in favour of such courts, and criticized the system under which it was in the King's interest to pervert justice in order to increase his revenue.)

In March 1865 G. Blankson Wood, a clerk, was summoned before the same magistrate, Martin; because of his disrespectful language he was ordered to be imprisoned for contempt of the King's court. But he resisted arrest and escaped, no doubt with some violence on both sides. Blankson Wood was employed by W. C. Finlason, a coloured Jamaican advocate, who immediately complained to the Governor: 'My clerk does not acknowledge any authority, save that exercised by Her Majesty the Queen of England, and to that power he now appeals through me for redress.'[1]

Pine had evidently been awaiting such an opportunity: 'I have now been here nearly two years and a half, and I have watched these country courts very narrowly, and not until now could I ever prove a case where cruelty and injustice had been done.'[2] He at once requested an immediate and complete explanation from the King, alleging that the proceedings were 'unlawful, unconstitutional, unwarrantable', and that they had violated 'the compact, understanding, spirit, and usages existing' between the Government and the tribes under its protection.[3] But Aggery stood his ground, despite the warmth of the Governor's remarks. He claimed ignorance, if he had acted prejudicially to British jurisdiction, and complained that 'the compact, understanding, spirit, and usages spoken of, are left still so undefined and in the dark, that I am no wiser to-day than I was yesterday . . . I trust your Excellency is not unprepared to set bounds to my jurisdiction as King, and point out where I should go, where I should not go.'[4]

Pine replied that he would never recognize an irresponsible court not amenable to appeal to the British judiciary, that comparable decisions in the past had been invariably subject to reversal, and that Blankson Wood was a British subject. Consequently he demanded that all the proceedings and witnesses be transferred from Aggery's alleged court to one composed of the Judicial Assessor and the Governor himself; that all 'unlawful' proceedings be cancelled and annulled; and that Aggery should meet him to discuss the establishment of a King's court, 'upon such a basis as I can recognise'.[5]

Aggery immediately denied that his court was irresponsible, since an appeal lay to the 'King and Council'; and he then went on—in a remarkable statement—to question the whole basis and extent of British power and jurisdiction. He particularly criticized the methods of Maclean, who had, he alleged,

[1] Letter of 11 Mar. 1865, from Finlason to Acting Colonial Secretary; CO/96/67. In 1870 Finlason, when summoned before the King of Elmina, claimed that he was 'a white man . . . not a Fantee', and on this ground declared that he would 'obey no one but the Governor of Elmina'. Horton, *Letters*, no. viii, dated 12 Mar. 1870.

[2] *Executive Council Minutes*, 25 Mar. 1865.

[3] Letters of 11 and 12 Mar. 1865, from Aggery to R. Pine, enclosed in his Dispatch No. 38 of 7 Apr. 1865, to Cardwell; CO/96/67.

[4] Letter of 13 Mar. 1865, from Aggery to R. Pine; ibid.

[5] Letter of 14 Mar. 1865, from R. Pine to Aggery; ibid.

in a very peculiar, imperceptible, and unheard-of manner, wrested from the hands of our Kings, Chiefs, and head men, their power to govern their own subjects. The Governor, placing himself at the head of a handful of soldiers, had been known himself to travel to the remotest parts of the interior, for the purpose of compelling Kings, Chiefs, and head men (through fear of man or other feeling) to obey his Excellency's summons or to comply with his Excellency's decrees. A blow was thus firmly, slowly, and persistently struck . . . A white face, a red jacket was, in con‑ sequence, a terror on the Gold Coast . . . many a subject was encouraged and countenanced to throw off with impunity their very allegiance, an allegiance which could not well be disowned and ignored and denied without endangering the secu- rity of the King.

He recalled how in 1841 he had stood at the side of his father Joseph Aggery (who had soon afterwards signed the 1844 Bond) listening to the arguments of the Chiefs before Dr. Madden; they had maintained that the inhabitants of Cape Coast should not be considered subjects of the British sovereign. Madden had acknowledged in his report that they had 'a great deal of reason on their side'; and had found that the only territory belonging to the British consisted of the buildings within the walls of the castle, together with two small forts on the neighbouring heights. Aggery claimed that this view had recently been endorsed in Parliament; he now announced with a flourish that he would refer the matter to the British Government, and that pending an answer from London any further correspondence must be stopped.[1]

The Governor realized that times had changed. In Maclean's day the Blankson Wood affair could have been settled very simply, by sending a few troops; 'now I can do no such thing'.[2] But he told Aggery firmly that he was not prepared to accept such 'insolent and offensive communications', and even threatened to withdraw recognition from him as King of Cape Coast. This produced a reluctant letter of submission from Aggery; but he refused to commit himself when Pine insisted again that there must be a right of appeal from the King's court to British justice if the inhabitants were to continue to enjoy British protection. As if to emphasize the argument, Blank- son Wood was awarded damages and costs against Martin in the Judicial Assessor's court, despite the protests of Aggery and his supporters, who now referred for the first time to 'our deputation being despatched by us to England to have the case finally settled'.[3]

Pine was convinced that the King's pretensions and conduct were not approved by his councillors or by his subjects generally; and he therefore proposed 'to ascertain the views of the large majority'. He had already formed his own view, that one man should not be allowed to deprive the inhabitants of the Gold Coast generally of 'the boon of protection'.[4] He therefore hastened

---

[1] Letter of 16 Mar. 1865, from Aggery to R. Pine; CO/96/67. Also *1842 Report*, pt. ii, app. no. 3.
[2] *Executive Council Minutes*, 25 Mar. 1865.
[3] Dispatch No. 38 of 7 Apr. 1865, from R. Pine to Cardwell, and enclosures; CO/96/67.
[4] *Executive Council Minutes*, 25 Mar. 1865.

to call public meetings, at which 'all matters connected with the Protectorate, and the King of Cape Coast's attempt to sever it from British rule were discussed and explained'. The headmen and the captains of the Cape Coast companies refused to attend, but the people present were asked to declare whether they sided with Aggery against the British. A petition was then hurriedly prepared, signed by the King of Winneba and over 100 other 'inhabitants and natives of Cape Coast, Anamaboe, &c., &c.', and presented to the Governor. They expressed their desire for the continuance of English protection: 'To leave us now would be like the parent forsaking his offspring before being able to care for itself.' They dissociated themselves from Aggery, and claimed that he was not supported by 'the principal Kings and influential men of the Protectorate'. Pine left for England in April 1865, having obtained this useful document only one day beforehand.[1]

Shortly afterwards, Aggery sent messengers to the leading Chiefs of the Protectorate, in order—so it was later alleged—'to incite them to act in opposition to the British Government', and to spread rumours that Pine had announced, before leaving, that all native courts were to be abolished and slaves to be set free.[2] The Government countered this move by instructing all commandants of out-stations to inform the Chiefs of the error of these 'most wilful misstatements'.[3] In fact Aggery's messengers had been busy collecting contributions—or promises—towards the expense of a deputation to London; and soon Aggery's own commissioners, Joseph Martin and D. L. Carr, sailed from Cape Coast to appear before the House of Commons Select Committee then sitting.

The 1865 Select Committee

This Committee had been appointed to consider Colonel Ord's report, and to hear further evidence concerning the West African Settlements, largely as a result of the strong parliamentary criticisms of the previous year. Its chairman was C. B. Adderley, M.P., a noted free-trader and anti-expansionist, and several other members were strong advocates of retrenchment, while Lord Alfred Churchill represented the humanitarian and anti-slavery interests who for other reasons advocated the limitation of British authority. Some force was lent to the demand for complete withdrawal by the fact that the greatest volume of British trade was carried on in the Niger Delta, where there was no government agent or settlement, and where the merchants had long rejoiced in their freedom from 'extraneous interference'.[4] In the Gold Coast, by contrast, exports had been declining steadily under direct Crown control,

---

[1] Letter of 22 May 1865, from R. Pine to Cardwell, and enclosed Petition of 14 Apr. 1865; CO/96/67.

[2] Letter of 29 Apr. 1865, from Civil Commandant of Anomabu to Acting Colonial Secretary, enclosed in Dispatch No. 46 of 8 May 1865, from Jones to Cardwell; ibid.

[3] Circular Letter of 1 May 1865, from Acting Colonial Secretary; ibid.

[4] R. Jamieson, *An Appeal against the Proposed Niger Expedition* (London, 1841).

from £268,000 in 1850 to £166,000 in 1863, the year of the Ashanti invasion; during the same period the expense of maintaining the forts had risen from £5,000 to £12,000.[1] The fact that the Niger Delta was untroubled by the proximity of any such warlike power as Ashanti seems to have escaped the notice of many critics; but the Asantehene resented the attempts of the merchants to break his monopoly of the interior transit trade as much as the Government's repudiation of his title to the coastal forts.

The irony of the situation in 1865 has often been pointed out.[2] The 'little Englanders', together with the merchants who wanted a free hand in other parts of West Africa without government interference, gained the ear of Parliament and public opinion just at the time when the expansion of official British influence was required to maintain and protect commercial interests in the Gold Coast. The head of the Slave Trade Department in the Foreign Office—who pointed out before the Committee that, once a commercial establishment was set up, 'you cannot help interfering in the politics of the country'[3]—and the Gold Coast and Lagos administrators, who calmly disregarded its recommendations in continuing their expansionist policy during the 1860's and 1870's, were taking a more realistic view. Nevertheless, a combination of official parsimony, commercial pressure, and somewhat vague idealism succeeded in giving public expression in 1865 to the aim of self-government for West Africa. King Aggery stands alone as the only West African shrewd enough to make use of these cross-currents of opinion to further his own ambitions, and thus indirectly to encourage later leaders to aim at a more truly national form of self-government.

It was noticeable that the African witnesses before the Committee did not challenge British jurisdiction as such. The main point made by Martin was that neither King Aggery nor the Chiefs were respected by the European authorities. For example, they had not been consulted over the spirit-licence law; for this reason there was strong feeling against it, though it might otherwise have 'taken well with the people'. He was careful to urge that the white man should always remain as 'the chief justice before whom an appeal should be made'. Henry Barnes, who had been one of the organizers of the 1853 petition, commended imperial rule because 'when anybody has done anything wrong, they are fined and punished; that keeps the country in order; we are certainly very much obliged to the English'.[4]

The Committee was particularly anxious to discover from the various witnesses what they understood British protection to mean. Ord had reported

---

[1] *Gold Coast Colony Blue Book*, 1850 and 1863.

[2] See, for example, K. O. Dike's analysis from the standpoint of the Niger territories in *Trade and Politics in the Niger Delta, 1830–1885* (Oxford, 1956), ch. ix.

[3] *1865 Report*, W. H. Wylde, 2,715.

[4] Ibid. Martin, 8,365, and Barnes, 5,771. Besides Joseph Martin and Henry Barnes, the only other African to appear before the 1865 Committee was Joseph Smith, also a Cape Coast merchant, who was then living in England and was described as interpreter for Martin.

that the local Government was wrong in assuming that the people had been guaranteed complete protection against all their enemies: the only document implying this was the Poll Tax Ordinance, but the tax had never been paid in full and had now lapsed.[1] Ord thought it a distinct advantage that the exact position could not be too closely defined; if this were done, the people might be led away by 'mischievous advisers', whereas at present they were 'perfectly satisfied to accept the fiction that we rule'.[2] To some extent this view was confirmed by Martin's evidence, when he said of his fellow Africans: 'They understand the protectorate to be, that as the strong power has some influence over the weak, the former would not neglect the interests of the latter, especially if a good understanding exists between them.' He claimed that the Fantis had not the slightest fear of Ashanti; 'but since the British people have taken them up, nursed them, and are bringing them up, they would rather be with civilized men; and they like Europeans to be among them.'[3] The Committee was somewhat surprised to find the Colonial Secretary of the Gold Coast saying that the Protectorate amounted, in fact, to whatever any Governor chose to make it.[4] Such statements led them to conclude: 'The protectorate of tribes about our forts on the Gold Coast assumes an indefinite and unintelligible responsibility on our part, uncompensated by any adequate advantage to the tribes.'[5]

One of the potential advantages of protection, namely, assistance to the Chiefs in their administration of justice, was probed at some length by the Committee. But there was considerable criticism of the increased powers of the Judicial Assessor. A former Governor took the view that this official administered justice 'too much in the Queen's name and not in the name of the native authority'.[6] The current holder of the office admitted in evidence that he had never sat in conjunction with the Chiefs, and that he was unaware that this had ever been the intention.[7] The Colonial Secretary mentioned complaints from the Chiefs, especially in the interior, 'that we interfere much with them and their people, and that while we are unable to govern them we prevent them from governing themselves'.[8] Another 'very sore point' was the Judicial Assessor's habit of summoning an important Chief from the interior, and so lowering him in the eyes of his people.[9]

The 1865 Committee accepted the view of Aggery's commissioner that the judicial system led to needless technicalities and expense, especially through the employment of attorneys. The Committee also criticized the fact that the Judicial Assessor, instead of assisting the Chiefs in administering justice, had superseded their authority by decisions taken on his own authority alone. As a result, they recommended the virtual abolition of this office: 'The Chiefs

---

[1] *Copy of the Report of Colonel Ord* (1865).   [2] *1865 Report*, Ord, 8,629.
[3] Ibid. Martin, 8,453 and 8,457.   [4] Ibid. Ross, 8,142.
[5] Ibid. para. 43.   [6] Ibid. Sir Benjamin Pine, 2,997.
[7] Ibid. Hackett, 6,461–2.   [8] Ibid. Ross, 8,145.   [9] Ibid. Ord, 8,543.

should rather be left to exercise their own jurisdiction, with only an appeal, when necessary, to the English magistracy.'[1]

Nothing perceptible was done to translate this recommendation into action;[2] its publication, however, was clear proof in Cape Coast eyes of a radical change in British policy. How much more so was the famous Resolution No. 3 (out of seven presented to the House of Commons as summing up the gist of the Committee's *Report*). This ran as follows:

That all further extension of territory or assumption of Government, or new treaties offering any protection to native tribes, would be inexpedient; and that the object of our policy should be to encourage in the natives the exercise of those qualities which may render it possible for us more and more to transfer to them the administration of all the Governments, with a view to our ultimate withdrawal from all, except, probably, Sierra Leone.[3]

Resolution No. 4 added that this could not amount to an absolute prohibition of measures which, in peculiar cases, might be necessary for the more efficient and economical administration of the existing settlements. There were, in fact, serious differences of opinion within the Committee; but the full *Report* could have left no reader in doubt as to their general intentions, prompted mainly by the desire for retrenchment.[4] For example, it was said that a protectorate over the Gold Coast should only be retained while the Chiefs were as speedily as possible made to do without it: 'Nothing should be done to encourage them to lean on British help, or trust to British administration of their affairs, whether military or judicial.'[5]

West Africans were able to read these Resolutions for themselves in *The African Times*, which published them in full in July 1865, together with other extracts and considerable discussion of the *Report*. The editor expressed some disappointment; but Lord Alfred Churchill in reply claimed that they had enunciated 'an entirely new policy'. He urged West Africans to forgo all petty differences and to unite amongst themselves, so that the Government

---

[1] *1865 Report*, para. 55.

[2] The Judicial Assessor remained, but his status as Chief Justice was abolished, and in 1866 he became Chief Magistrate of a Court of Civil and Criminal Justice; see below, p. 215. As Judicial Assessor, he once again sat with the Chiefs; but now it was really he who tried the cases, with their advice, instead of vice versa. Nevertheless, the Chiefs did not formally surrender all their jurisdiction to him; and this argument was later used to great effect. See Ch. XII, below.

[3] The first draft of this Resolution was even stronger; the latter part of it ran: 'and that the object of our policy should be rather to transfer to the natives the administration of all the Governments, with a view to our ultimate withdrawal from all, except, probably, Sierra Leone.' The qualifying phrases were then added at the suggestion of Cardwell, the Secretary of State for the Colonies; and the fact was recorded in the *1865 Report*.

[4] The chairman later interpreted the Resolutions to mean 'that we should get out of the scrape in which we have involved ourselves, as speedily as we honourably can, leaving the tribes in a fair way of being able to hold their own and govern themselves'. C. B. Adderley, *A Review of 'The Colonial Policy of Lord John Russell's Administration', by Earl Grey, 1853; and of subsequent Colonial History* (London, 1869). He was Under-Secretary of State for the Colonies, 1866–8.

[5] *1865 Report*.

might better be able to carry it out.[1] This was the sincere belief of many humanitarians and reformers in Britain; and it was easily transformed into the—perhaps too facile—hopes of Aggery and others. Carr, on the voyage home from London, apparently assumed that as a preparation for the abandonment of the Gold Coast, measures were 'now being adopted for the teaching of Africans how to govern themselves eventually'.[2]

But the Colonial Office, having secured the toning down of the reference to withdrawal, was content to regard it largely as the expression of a pious hope for the future. As regards further extensions of territory, the Secretary of State seems to have given full weight to Resolution No. 3; and for the next few years at least, the policy of non-extension was strictly enforced from London, as far as possible. But the Gold Coast Government, in so far as it took any notice of the Resolutions at all, seems to have been more impressed by No. 4, with its loophole for extension of existing Settlements 'in peculiar cases'.[3]

First-hand news of the inquiry and *Report* reached the Gold Coast in August, when Colonel E. Conran returned as Administrator, and addressed a meeting of the Chiefs and people of Cape Coast. He emphasized how nearly it had been decided to give up the Gold Coast, and warned them that protection might yet be withdrawn; but since 'The Queen and noble England' had agreed to continue the relationship, 'with good advice and example', he urged them to show their gratitude by assisting in improving conditions in the town.[4] Yet when he wanted them to abolish markets on the Lord's Day, he found Thompson—who still styled himself Mayor of Cape Coast[5]—reluctant to co-operate. Eventually Aggery ordered the necessary gong-gong to be beaten, and Conran's first impressions were favourable, in spite of all he had heard against the King: 'I find him exceedingly well disposed towards upholding my authority.'[6]

British Authority in Cape Coast

One problem that the 1865 Committee left unsolved was the actual extent of the area claimed as British territory. Ord said in evidence that this had

---

[1] *The African Times*, 23 Aug. 1865.

[2] Letter of 31 Aug. 1865, from Carr to Fitzgerald; ibid. 23 Sept. 1865.

[3] See Ch. I, p. 12, above. Cf. Sir Charles Lucas's revealing comment on the Resolutions: 'Committees of the House of Commons cannot stop the working of natural causes. Neither peoples nor individuals ever stand still. They either go forward or they go back; and if a white race, not decaying in itself, keeps a hold among and is brought into daily contact with natives, it must, by a law of being which overrides all Parliamentary dicta, neither stand still nor go back, but extend its influence and widen its empire.' *Historical Geography of the British Colonies* (Oxford, 3rd edn. 1913), vol. iii, p. 130.

[4] Report of meeting of 24 Aug. 1865, enclosed in Dispatch No. 95 of 11 Sept. 1865, from Conran to Cardwell; CO/96/68.

[5] This in spite of R. Hutchison's brief period of office, 1858-60, as the first officially recognized Mayor. Cf. pp. 196-8, above.

[6] Dispatch No. 93 of 5 Sept. 1865, from Conran to Cardwell; CO/96/68.

never been distinctly defined, sometimes being spoken of as the ground on which the forts were situated, and at other times being said to extend to a cannon-shot from them.[1]

The issue had arisen in Cape Coast in 1863, when R. Pine removed all government civil staff from the dilapidated castle into nearby houses, and was surprised to find the Colonial Office expressing doubts whether the Supreme Court and the Legislative Council could legally function outside the forts.[2] Pine urged that the cannon-shot theory was generally accepted, and claimed that the inhabitants took an even more liberal view, 'considering our jurisdiction to extend over all land which has not been cleared, asking and receiving grants of it'.[3] But the Chief Justice was doubtful;[4] and so it was suggested in 1864 that a formal cession of the necessary land might be obtained from the Chiefs, and confirmed by proclamation. This proved difficult. The Chiefs were willing to state verbally that 'everyone knew the land to be the Queen's'; but, they protested, 'the signing of paper is what is doubtful to them'.[5] The Secretary of State then proposed an Order in Council and a proclamation to define British territory in Cape Coast as Fort William, Fort Victoria, the Castle, and all land within 500 yards of the main gate; but by this time Pine preferred to keep the existing ambiguity, 'which leaves us in the supposed possession of the contemplated five hundred yards and much more if it be required'.[6]

Ord had come to disagree with this by 1865, when he advised the Select Committee that British territory should be limited to the land on which the forts or buildings occupied by civil officers were situated.[7] Conran, too, wanted a precise definition; he was mainly concerned at the lack of any definite authority that he could exercise in the town of Cape Coast. He was particularly anxious to curb the violence of the annual 'Black Christmas' festival,[8] when the Asafo companies would meet together under their captains at some central spot for several days, each armed with distinguishing flags; as Conran described it, 'the state of intoxication from common American rum costing but 3*d.* or 4*d.* a pint is fearful to witness'. Hoping to prevent loss of life, which on some occasions had been serious, he made the Chiefs promise that this year no one should be hurt during the firing. But Conran soon felt that promises were not enough. When news came that four Africans had been killed and over sixty injured at Mumford, he issued a proclamation stating firmly that

[1] *1865 Report*, Ord, 8,629.

[2] Dispatch No. 106 of 3 Dec. 1863, from Newcastle to R. Pine; CO/96/62.

[3] Dispatch No. 23 of 12 Feb. 1864, from R. Pine to Newcastle; CO/96/64.

[4] His doubts were reinforced when Finlason, imprisoned in 1864 as an insolvent debtor, claimed that the proceedings were invalid because carried on outside the castle walls; ibid.

[5] Report of palaver at Government House, Cape Coast, 10 May 1864, enclosed in Dispatch No. 50 of 12 May 1864, from Hackett to Newcastle; ibid.

[6] Dispatch No. 86 of 9 Sept. 1864, from R. Pine to Cardwell; CO/96/65.

[7] *1865 Report*, Ord, 8,628.

[8] This was the 'yam custom', *Ahubaw*, referred to in Ch. III, pp. 132 n. and 160 n., above.

British law extended 'from each castle and fort to a distance of a cannon shot, or five miles'.[1] He hoped thereby to deter people from 'such dreadful practices', although he did not intend to interfere with the domestic slave question; and after three weeks he reported, 'not a single murmur from high or low have I heard against it, the better classes of Fantees everywhere rather approving of its purport and meaning'.[2]

The Secretary of State, noting that eight separate British forts were involved, was quick to disown Conran's proclamation and to instruct that it should be withdrawn. He approved of effects to prevent the loss of life due to barbarous customs; 'but the extension of British territory is a different matter, and cannot receive my sanction'.[3] Conran reported to London at the beginning of 1866 that he had recalled the proclamation;[4] but six years later the Fanti Confederation stated categorically that it had after all been allowed to stand, contrary to instructions.[5] Probably Conran had not been anxious to attract attention to his enforced *volte-face*; in any case his own attitude had far more influence locally than the remote, cautious voice of Whitehall.

Meanwhile, a serious riot had taken place in Cape Coast between the West Indian soldiers of the garrison and the townspeople. It had started one evening in September 1865, in the worst part of the town, after a day of excitement and drinking; two inhabitants were killed, and one soldier disappeared completely. Aggery saw his opportunity and immediately protested to Conran:

A frightful tragedy has been enacted in this town . . . The soldiers of the garrison have suddenly issued forth at night with some of their officers, and have treated this town as if they had taken it by assault in time of war . . . we have a right to expect that the Government will cause the most searching and complete judicial inquiry to be made . . . how it came to pass that the troops in garrison at Cape Coast were . . . rushing about the town in detached bodies, some with, some without officers, armed with muskets, bayonets, and clubs, forcibly entering the houses of sleeping persons, slaughtering the Queen's subjects, taking away property, beating peaceful citizens, dragging human beings about like dead cattle, and creating such terror and confusion as will never be forgotten here . . . it was not a riot on the part of the people; it was an attack on the town by the garrison.[6]

Cape Coast feelings were further inflamed by the ostentatious funeral of one of the victims. Aggery was officially reprimanded for parading the body round the town, and right up to the castle gate, instead of dutifully suppressing the general excitement. The inhabitants were accused of mocking Army funerals, and were asked to discontinue parades with music.[7] Charles Bannerman,

---

[1] Proclamation of 16 Sept. 1865; Crooks, *Records*, pp. 371–2.
[2] Dispatch No. 114 of 7 Oct. 1865, from Conran to Cardwell; CO/96/68.
[3] Dispatch No. 284 of 23 Nov. 1865, from Cardwell to Conran; ibid.
[4] Dispatch No. 5 of 2 Jan. 1866, from Conran to Cardwell; CO/96/70.
[5] Fanti Confederation scheme of 16 Apr. 1872; CO/96/94.
[6] Letter of 8 Sept. 1865, from Aggery to Conran, enclosed in his Dispatch No. 123 of 23 Oct. 1865, to Cardwell; CO/96/68.
[7] Letter of 11 Sept. 1865, from Acting Colonial Secretary to Aggery; ibid.

Aggery's 'professional adviser', denied these accusations on the King's behalf. He claimed that normal custom had been observed in parading the body of a scholar accompanied by 'a few young men with music'. This had never done any harm, nor been regarded as a mockery, 'any more than the fact of the natives crowding to chapel is a mockery of the religious rites of the Europeans'.[1]

A private soldier was soon afterwards tried, found guilty, and sentenced to death by the Acting Chief Justice for the murder of this man. Some officials criticized the conduct of the trial, and it was even alleged that the jury had been drunk. Although local feeling was running high, Conran commuted the sentence to hard labour for life, on the advice of the Executive Council, on the grounds that the soldiers had gone out in the execution of their duty, to suppress a riot.[2]

Influence of the Idea of Self-government

Aggery had now emerged as the spokesman not only of the Chiefs—in protest against British encroachment on their judicial preserves—but also of the townspeople, whose grievance against the very presence of the troops, the representatives of alien military power, had erupted into the recent riot. He had in fact already reached the point of no return, and was practically bound to continue to defy the British authorities, when his commissioners arrived home in September 1865.

Martin and Carr reported at some length to the Kings of Cape Coast, Abura, and Anomabu. Aggery complained to the Secretary of State that he had been unable to call a larger meeting to hear about this beneficial mission, because of what he still called the 'outrage', when the soldiers had made an 'attack upon the natives'.[3] Conran's explanation was, however, that the other Kings had not taken the slightest notice of such a presumptuous summons to Cape Coast. Again, when Aggery called upon them for their promised contribution towards the expenses of the commissioners, Conran alleged that these men had been despatched to London without the consent of the other Kings, who were now unwilling to pay; to make quite sure of this, he issued a circular telling them not to contribute.[4]

The ultimate clash was postponed by Conran's decision to 'wink at King Aggery's court'; for he admitted privately that there was some reason in the King's claim to be allowed the same privileges as his compeers further away in the Protectorate. He thought that Aggery on the whole dealt fairly with his

---

[1] Letter of 12 Sept. 1865, from Bannerman to Acting Colonial Secretary; CO/96/68.

[2] *Executive Council Minutes*, 16 Oct. 1865.

[3] Letter of 11 Oct. 1865, from Aggery to Secretary of State, enclosed in Dispatch No. 129 of 25 Oct. 1865, from Conran to Cardwell; CO/96/68.

[4] The commissioners claimed £400, most of which had been borrowed at a very high rate of interest. The debt continued to mount, and as a result Martin, Thompson, and one Catiline, who had stood security, were committed to prison in default of payment. CO/96/71 and 72.

own subjects in court, and was not in himself a bad man, although very ill advised by half-educated councillors, who were no better than Chartists. They had nothing to lose and everything to gain from political change, although 'they could not govern for a week in our absence'. Martin had even stated publicly that they would soon be allowed to govern the Protectorate them-selves 'according to Fantee laws with the advice and assistance of white men, who would have to live inside the Castle and Forts, as all outside belonged to them'.[1]

With the characteristic inability of the paternal administrator to believe that the masses and their educated advisers could have basically the same motivation, Conran assumed that it was possible to persuade the people not to heed such influences, and to accept gladly a form of government that was so patently designed for their own good. He was all the more surprised by the failure of the Cape Coast inhabitants to assist the Government, as they had promised, to clean up the town. Even such a trivial matter as the impounding of stray pigs showed how remote was the official viewpoint—unlike that of the educated African—from that of the people. Pigs had wandered loose in the streets from time immemorial; where human habitations left much to be desired, a pig-proof enclosure would have been hard to devise, and would have added nothing to the sanctity of an already well-respected form of property.

But the pigs got in the way of Conran's road improvements; so he simply proclaimed that any found loose in the streets of Cape Coast, Anomabu, or Accra would be impounded by the police, to put a stop to this ancient nuis-ance. The Secretary of State, although he approved of Conran's efforts to keep the towns in decent order, warned him once more against the public use of any expressions which bore the appearance of extending British juris-diction.[2] Even so, he could hardly have realized how this particular assump-tion of jurisdiction had brought the matter home to almost every family compound; if this was British protection, the people would rather have their pigs. Resentment over the proclamation persisted for some time, and nearly a year later Aggery and others were petitioning that 'the pig's law' should be revised and modified.[3]

During 1866 Conran became even more concerned at the increasing in-fluence of the 'so-called scholars (those natives who can read and write) and petty native lawyers who cling like leeches to the skirts of their more ignorant Kings and Chiefs'. He blamed Charles Bannerman particularly—'a native

---

[1] Dispatches Nos. 113 of 7 Oct. and 135 of 2 Nov. 1865, from Conran to Cardwell; CO/96/68.

[2] Public Notice of 1 Nov. 1865, and Dispatch No. 290 of 22 Nov. 1865, from Cardwell to Conran; ibid.

[3] They 'cheerfully' admitted, however, that Conran, in spite of crippled resources, had done more for the sanitary improvement of Cape Coast than any previous Governor during the past twenty years. Petition of Sept. 1866, forwarded by Blackall in his Dispatch No. 43 of 17 Oct. 1866, to Carnarvon; CO/96/72.

advocate possessing much talent, but totally devoid of principle'—for convincing Aggery and his councillors that the time had arrived when they themselves should govern the coast. Conran assured the Colonial Office that 'the merchants of all colours' strongly objected to this, fearing that without the protection of England they would be 'plunged back to the former condition of their ancestors'.[1] But he complained that the Blue Book containing the *Report* had misled 'many disaffected men and a few Chartists' into expecting a complete change in government policy.[2] The real danger, of course, lay in the fact that literal-minded Africans expected the British Government to mean what it said; whereas experienced administrators like Conran were able to read between the lines, and would have preferred to give the people their own interpretation direct, without the inconvenience of a published *Report*.

The 5th Resolution of the Select Committee, which had recommended the re-establishment of a central Government at Sierra Leone, with control over all the West African Settlements, was carried out early in 1866,[3] when Sir William Blackall took up office as Governor-in-Chief. During a visit to the Gold Coast, he received a letter from Aggery, 'respectfully' asking him to define the relationship 'between the King's court and the British magistrate's court; between the King and the Governor, and between the King and his brother Kings on the coast'. Aggery recapitulated many old grievances, and complained that the Government received customs and other revenues, while none went to him; he also announced his intention to form his own military corps, to be trained by British officers, for purposes of self-defence.[4] Conran took strong exception to this, and asked for Blackall's support 'in putting down this insolent, ignorant, and stubborn man'; the language was condemned as most seditious, showing a desire to overthrow the British Government and substitute his own. Aggery had just been convicted by the Supreme Court of cruelty, for chaining prisoners between logs, and would have been imprisoned had Conran himself not intervened, to avoid seeing the King so degraded.[5]

Blackall advised Conran to temporize, pending definite instructions from

---

[1] Dispatch No. 25 of 5 Feb. 1866, from Conran to Cardwell; CO/96/70.

[2] Dispatch No. 54 of 7 Apr. 1866, from Conran to Cardwell; CO/96/71. A superior official suggested that the 'untutored Natives' probably viewed the Blue Book as 'a kind of charm'. Minute of 18 May 1866, by T. F. Elliott; ibid.

[3] By Letters Patent of 19 Feb. 1866; *Ordinances of the Settlement of the Gold Coast; Royal Charters; Acts of Parliament; Orders in Council; Treaties of the Government of the Gold Coast with the Native Chiefs, &c. &c. &c.* (London, 1874).

[4] Letter of 13 Mar. 1866, from Aggery to Blackall, enclosed in his Dispatch No. 1 of 19 Apr. 1866, to Cardwell; CO/96/71. *The African Times*, 23 May 1868, claimed that Aggery's proposal to raise a military force was a direct result of the British injunction to the Chiefs in 1864 that they were to protect themselves in future.

[5] Dispatch No. 3 of 12 Apr. 1866, from Conran to Blackall; CO/96/71. Aggery considered 'unnecessary' even the reprimand for 'alleged cruelty in putting of his own people in irons for disobedient and refractory conduct'. Petition of Sept. 1866, forwarded by Blackall in his Dispatch No. 43 of 17 Oct. 1866, to Carnarvon; CO/96/72.

the Secretary of State. But in his own Dispatch to London he expressed certain grave doubts; he felt that if the present policy were pursued, 'we shall be in perpetual collision with the Chiefs, and incur incalculable expense'. He seriously questioned whether the occupation of Cape Coast was worth the annual cost. On the other hand, if the British were to stay, they could not allow Aggery to set up an armed force, probably consisting of 'the worst characters' and subject to no control.[1] The Secretary of State, who was anxious to avoid any sign of weakness following the 'misrepresentations' of the recent Parliamentary *Report*, strongly supported Conran: 'Aggery's proposal to establish a military force is mischievous, and his claim to revenue inadmissible, and his pretensions should be effectually discountenanced.' The King was to be told that in return for protection, he must pay deference to British authority.[2]

In November 1866 an Ordinance was enacted in Sierra Leone, abolishing the Gold Coast Supreme Court, and setting up in its place a Court of Civil and Criminal Justice under a Chief Magistrate (who continued to combine the office with that of Judicial Assessor). An Order in Council of 26 February 1867 established a West African Court of Appeal in Sierra Leone.[3] By removing the seat of judicial authority to Freetown, these enactments might have been thought to reduce the possibility of local conflict in Cape Coast. But they came too late to affect the tension between Aggery and British officials, which mounted to a crisis during the second half of 1866.

The King versus the Governor

At the end of July 1866 Thomas Hughes was chosen as 'Representative' of the King and people of Cape Coast, to assist Aggery 'as regards order, civilization, improvement, and welfare of the people'.[4] When Conran refused to recognize Hughes, or to correspond directly with him,[5] there were immediate protests, especially from the leaders of the seven companies of Cape Coast;[6] and Aggery suggested that the civil liberties of the people had been withheld in a manner unheard of in any civilized country, 'however despotic the sovereign may be'.[7] This bickering correspondence continued, and it became clear that the Government believed that Hughes was endeavouring to place himself on an equality with the Governor, the Queen's representative. It is doubtful whether this had been, in fact, the intention; but Conran attributed Aggery's move to either 'ignorance or impudence'.[8]

---

[1] Dispatch No. 1 of 19 Apr. 1866, from Blackall to Cardwell; CO/96/71.
[2] Dispatch No. 24 of 23 May 1866, from Cardwell to Blackall; ibid.
[3] *Ordinances of the Settlement of the Gold Coast . . . &c. &c. &c.* (1874).
[4] Letter of 30 July 1866, from Aggery to Conran, enclosed in Dispatch No. 43 of 17 Oct. 1866, from Blackall to Carnarvon; CO/96/72.
[5] Letter of 7 Aug. 1866, from Hamilton (Conran's private secretary) to Hughes; ibid.
[6] Letter of 8 Aug. 1866, from Chiefs Cudjoe Ayee and Cofie Attah, and others; ibid.
[7] Letter of 9 Aug. 1866, from Aggery to Hamilton; ibid.
[8] Letter of 8 Aug. 1866, from Hamilton to Aggery; ibid.

In September Aggery and his supporters formally protested against 'the undignified ill-treatment to which his Excellency [Conran] has at various times subjected the King of Cape Coast'. They objected particularly to the lowering of his dignity and authority by the recent court prosecution. The growing pressure of culture-conflict may be seen in their argument that the King was bound to observe local tradition in his own court, even if the punishments appeared harsh to others, for 'the people cherish their own customs, revere their own laws', while regarding European laws as 'an extraneous growth'. Other grievances were mentioned, including the treatment of Hughes; and then, with a prefatory assurance of 'love and respect', they launched a vigorous protest against the whole 'arbitrary' system of British rule. Its only object was alleged to be the 'abrogation of the real authority of the Chiefs and Headmen, the elimination of all moral influence and consequent disorganization of the Protectorate'.[1]

This petition was not considered on its merits. Forced to argue the case, colonial officials would probably have taken the view that such temporary conflicts of interest and authority were inevitable, but could be discounted when set against the benefits of a more enlightened form of government and code of morals, with the accompanying commercial advantages to both countries. The immediate reaction in Cape Coast Castle, however, was to discredit those behind the petition. Conran warned Blackall that the real sponsor was Hughes, who had recently been dismissed from his position as churchwarden for 'immoral' behaviour (unspecified). He called him 'a Fenian', and pointed out that of the hundreds of Chiefs in the Protectorate, not one seemed willing to sign his petition.[2] Blackall strongly supported Conran in refusing to recognize Hughes as the King's representative; and when forwarding the documents to the Secretary of State, he prophesied 'a return to the most barbarous and savage customs, were such men as have got up this petition entrusted with self-government'.[3]

Aggery by now stood alone, both in the intensity of his protest, and in the lengths to which he was prepared to go; furthermore, through his dependence on educated advisers, he had virtually isolated himself from his fellow Chiefs in the Protectorate. Nevertheless, discontent is infectious, and Conran probably had good reason for his inclination to blame Aggery's influence for any instances of 'insubordination' by neighbouring Chiefs, especially where the superiority of British courts was challenged. In October 1865 he had officially discouraged the use of force anywhere in the Gold Coast, 'so obedient are every King and Chief to this Government, except King Aggery'.[4] But now, only a year later, he took troops to Anomabu and handcuffed three Chiefs,

---

[1] Petition of Sept. 1866, from Aggery and 43 others, forwarded by Blackall in his Dispatch No. 43 of 17 Oct. 1866, to Carnarvon; CO/96/72.

[2] Dispatch No. 74 of 6 Sept. 1866, from Conran to Blackall; ibid.

[3] Dispatch No. 43 of 17 Oct. 1866, from Blackall to Carnarvon; ibid.

[4] Dispatch No. 128 of 24 Oct. 1865, from Conran to Cardwell; CO/96/68.

to ensure payment of a fine by their King, 'advice and kindness being totally lost upon such heartless men, resolute action being the only means of dealing with them, letting them see who is master'.[1] Back in Cape Coast, Conran proceeded to assert his judicial influence more energetically by releasing several of Aggery's prisoners, as a result of private petitions. The King was told that although there was no objection to his own court settling land disputes, petty debts, and minor offences, the sentences must not be of a cruel nature nor repugnant to British law; and even these cases must be regarded as subject to an appeal to Her Majesty's courts.[2]

Aggery at once held a large public meeting of his followers, and this evidently inspired him to send an even stronger letter than usual to Conran:

the time has now come for me to record a solemn protest against the perpetual annoyances and insults that you persistently and perseveringly continue to practise on me in my capacity as legally constituted King of Cape Coast. I presume your object is . . . to incite me and my people to enact more of those fearful things that took place in Jamaica that I have heard of . . . however much you may wish to have me and my people under martial law, you will never have that pleasure . . . the Earl of Carnarvon has laid it down in his speech on the 2nd August last, that we are all entitled to redress at his hands as the Colonial Minister.[3] To that quarter I shall appeal for the last time, and then if some tangible satisfaction is not accorded to me and those whose interest I am bound to protect, it will be time enough for me to adopt those measures which will ensure to me and my people something unlike the slavery that you are endeavouring to place us in.

He referred still more offensively to the Cape Coast riot, 'when my people were butchered by your soldiers, some by your own personal superintendence', and recurred to the familiar theme that 'the Government in England has expressed its desire that we, the Kings and Chiefs of the Gold Coast, are to prepare ourselves for self-government and no protection'.[4]

Aggery's Deposition

This 'very seditious communication' was the last straw for Conran, and he decided at once to imprison and depose the King. He took it to mean that Aggery, having now realized he could not succeed in achieving self-government, was threatening a repetition of the recent Jamaican rebellion; for this

[1] Dispatch No. 102 of 26 Nov. 1866, from Conran to Blackall; CO/96/72.

[2] Letter of 6 Dec. 1866, from Colonial Secretary to Aggery, enclosed in Dispatch No. 2 of 15 Jan. 1867, from Blackall to Carnarvon; CO/96/74.

[3] This passage reveals the direct influence of *The African Times*, which had recently added to its front page the following prominent motto: 'If any Colonist suffers from injustice, whatever may be his class, his condition, or his colour, he has a right to redress at the hands of the Colonial Minister in this country. Earl of Carnarvon, Secretary of State for the Colonies, 2 Aug. 1866.' The same newspaper had during the past year published reports and comments on 'The Sad News' of the Jamaican insurrection.

[4] Letter of 6 Dec. 1866, from Aggery to Conran, enclosed in his Dispatch No. 109 of 7 Dec. 1866, to Blackall; CO/96/72.

the King must answer at once, or there would be 'an end to our authority over the Gold Coast'.[1] Aggery was therefore summoned to attend personally at Government House. He refused to appear, and treated the Governor's messenger with disdain, declaring that 'he did not know who Colonel Conran was, but that he was the King of the people; he had no palaver with the Queen's representative, and that now he had no more letters to send or answer'.[2] Next day Conran took prisoner 'this arrogant man', and put him straight on the mail boat for Sierra Leone. He proclaimed Aggery no longer King of Cape Coast, and closed his court altogether.[3]

Conran explained his action thus to a meeting of merchants and towns-people:

From the moment King Aggery's Commissioners arrived from England, in September 1865, with the news of their being trained for self-government, I experienced from King Aggery much insubordinate and abusive language, indicating throughout his whole conduct the mad desire to govern, not only Cape Coast itself, but the whole Gold Coast, having lately adopted the title of King of Cape Coast and its dependencies . . . I received a production from him full of rebellious and insubordinate language, threatening me with the repetition of the late Jamaica scenes.

Conran emphasized that the British Government would be the judge of their fitness for self-government, and would never agree to hand over power to 'a few designing, needy, half-educated natives . . . at the expense of their more industrious neighbours'.[4]

When Blackall came to consider Aggery's case, he could not immediately decide what should be done. His legal adviser told him that the letter was seditious, but suggested that Aggery, if found guilty and simply imprisoned, might after his release return to Cape Coast and perhaps continue to 'incite, without detection, the populace to acts of insubordination and resistance to the authorities'. It might therefore be prudent to keep in exile 'so turbulent and mischievous a petty chief or king'. Blackall placed Aggery on parole for the time being, and referred the problem to the Secretary of State, adding his own opinion that Hughes was the real offender; Aggery appeared to know so little English that it was difficult to make him understand how insulting and threatening was the language of his seditious letter. This defect made him a most undesirable ruler, and a 'source of constant danger, as he is put forward by artful men whom we cannot reach so long as Aggery is the ostensibly responsible person'.[5] Blackall concluded that so long as Cape Coast remained

[1] Dispatch No. 109 of 7 Dec. 1866, from Conran to Blackall; CO/96/72.

[2] Undated statement by Hamilton, enclosed in Dispatch No. 62 of 24 Dec. 1866, from Blackall to Carnarvon; ibid.

[3] Proclamation of 10 Dec. 1866; Crooks, *Records*, pp. 378–9.

[4] Address of 10 Dec. 1866, by Conran, enclosed in his Dispatch No. 112 of 31 Dec. 1866, to Blackall; CO/96/74.

[5] This is the first mention of any deficiency in Aggery's knowledge of English, and it is likely that he had staged a politic withdrawal into semi-pidgin on his arrival at Freetown. Even if he

the headquarters of the Government, the division of authority between the Administrator and the King was bound to lead to constant conflict. There would, however, be no objection to recognizing a Headman, so long as it was clearly understood that he was directly under the orders of the Governor.[1]

The first news of Aggery's arrest and removal to Sierra Leone reached the Colonial Office in January 1867 from the British and Foreign Freedmen's Aid Society, quoting a correspondent in Cape Coast, 'in whose integrity and veracity the committee have the fullest confidence'.[2] His letter alleged that the whole Protectorate was losing faith in the British Government, in its intentions to implement the *1865 Report*, and particularly in its representative, Colonel Conran, who was punishing the King 'for giving him notice that he will complain to the Earl of Carnarvon'.[3] Aggery's promised appeal to the Secretary of State arrived in London by the same mail, recapitulating all his grievances against Conran, and asking for a new Governor: 'relieve us from military rule, and send us a civil gentleman of experience'.[4]

Lord Carnarvon, when he eventually came to review the case, found that there was no law authorizing deportation, and no precedent, except Ord's deposition of Amissah by local request:[5]

There is apparently no power to try Aggery at S. Leone. His deportation there is doubtful—& Col. Conran does not rest it on the ground of public safety. It is doubtful how he can be tried at the G. Coast—and the result of such a trial is doubtful. ... on the whole I think it will be simpler & better that Aggery's deposition sd be effected by the broad and undisguised exercise of the supreme Power wh created him 'King'.[6] The precedent quoted of Col. Ord's time is not applicable without a preliminary deposition of him by the other Chiefs. This it might be difficult & dangerous to attempt to obtain. His deposition sd therefore be at once pronounced in a formal manner and on the ground that it is required in the public interest.[7]

had been unable to discuss the purport of his letters in English, however, there was no need for Blackall to assume that he did not understand or approve them.

[1] Letter of 19 Dec. 1866, from Queen's Advocate to Blackall, and his covering Dispatch No. 62 of 24 Dec. 1866, to Carnarvon; CO/96/74.

[2] The letter was personally delivered in Downing Street by Lord Alfred Churchill. When asked to comment on it, Blackall complained that 'the facility which is given by certain societies and journalists, who assume to themselves a speciality of affection for the African race, of publishing garbled reports of supposed cruelties inflicted upon blacks, merely because they are blacks, is doing more to keep up ill-feeling, and to retard civilization, than any other means I am aware of'. Dispatch No. 5 of 13 Feb. 1867, from Blackall to Carnarvon; ibid.

[3] Letter of 8 Dec. 1866, from Cape Coast, quoted by the Freedmen's Aid Society in their letter to Carnarvon, delivered on 23 Jan. 1867; ibid.

[4] Aggery had not had time to sign this petition before his arrest, and it was forwarded direct to London by some of his sub-Chiefs. Dispatch No. 66 of 23 Jan. 1866, from Carnarvon to Blackall; ibid.

[5] For two precedents the Secretary of State might have quoted, see Ch. XII, p. 463 n., below.

[6] In the same way, the inhabitants of Cape Coast had argued in 1855, concerning Kofi Amissah: 'as we have the privilege of choosing our own King ... are we not competent to depose that King'. Memorial of 5 Jan. 1855, to the Secretary of State; CO/96/33. Now the Government was gradually assuming the prerogative as maker and unmaker of kings.

[7] Minute of 12 Feb. 1867, by Carnarvon; CO/96/72.

As for the future, the Secretary of State agreed that it would be better to avoid altogether the misleading title of King, which had only arisen out of the 'somewhat injudicious practice of white people in designating chiefs on the African coast'; henceforward the term 'Headman' would be far more appropriate. Aggery should be given an annual pension of £100 for life, subject to good behaviour; the Governor should decide if and when he could return as a private person, although it seemed safest for him to remain in Sierra Leone for one or two years, until recent events had been forgotten. The Secretary of State deplored the anomalous position of the British Government on the Gold Coast, which offered him no general principles on which to decide the question: 'I can only look to the history of the place.'[1] On this unsatisfactory note King Aggery's reign was closed.

1867–9—a Return to 'Docility'

Soon after the deportation of Aggery, Conran reported that peace and quiet had been restored throughout the district; Hughes, 'Aggery's Prime Minister', had hastened to Elmina, under Dutch protection, and Martin and Carr had 'run away from Cape Coast'.[2] Aggery himself, although bereft of his advisers, was still defiant. He wrote to the Secretary of State from Sierra Leone, justifying his fateful letter to Conran; and he now refused to sign a promise not to return to Cape Coast without the Governor's permission, since 'it would not be becoming in me as a King, to give my consent to the conditions therein contained'. Blackall asked him to reconsider this decision; but instead Aggery handed over the documents to F. A. Belgrave, a West Indian newspaper editor in Freetown, who published them immediately in *The African Interpreter and Advocate*. After this Blackall refused to see Aggery, cancelled his allowance, and took precautions to prevent his return to Cape Coast.[3]

In March 1867 H. T. Ussher, who was now acting as Administrator of the Gold Coast, issued a proclamation declaring that Aggery was for ever deprived of his stool, that the office and title of King no longer existed, and that the people should elect a Headman of Cape Coast, who must swear allegiance to the Queen and obey the orders of the Administrator. But the difficulty was to decide who were to be 'the proper representatives of public opinion'. He

---

[1] Dispatch No. 78 of 23 Feb. 1867, from Carnarvon to Blackall; CO/96/74. Mensah Sarbah took up this challenge in 1906, by giving an historical account of the rise of British jurisdiction in ch. iii of his *Fanti National Constitution*. He experienced difficulty in obtaining access to the relevant documents; but as one of the first generation of African lawyers his views had an important influence on public opinion. Looking back on these events in retrospect he admitted, for example, that Aggery's conduct had been 'tactless'; but while paying tribute to the work of Maclean he stressed the limited extent of the jurisdiction conferred on the British by the Bond of 1844.

[2] Dispatch No. 112 of 31 Dec. 1866, from Conran to Blackall; CO/96/72.

[3] Letter of 19 March 1867, from Aggery to Blackall, and his covering Dispatch No. 17 of same date to Carnarvon; CO/96/74.

summoned the senior Chiefs and captains of companies; but the latter, 'being under the influence of Mr. Hughes, and adherents of Aggery', refused to attend.[1] Eventually Quassie Attah was chosen, approved by Ussher, and sworn into office. Although Ussher thought that Hughes, Bannerman, and their friends were once more 'fomenting trouble and disturbances in the country', they called on Blackall during his visit to the Gold Coast to pay their respects and to assure him of their loyalty to the British Throne.[2]

Soon Ussher congratulated himself on the fact that Cape Coast was in perfect harmony and peace, chiefly due to the appointment of Quassie Attah: 'possessed of little or no influence, he is not regarded by any one as being in a position of importance; and though bearing the title of Headman, is a nonentity'.[3] In 1868, only a year after his appointment, the 'nonentity' was himself proclaimed an outlaw and deprived of his house and property for defying Ussher's instructions.[4] Nevertheless, the *Blue Book* for 1868 confidently reported: 'The people are docile, peaceable, and affectionate, and require only to be treated with kindness, gentleness, firmness, and strict impartiality, to make them willingly subservient to any orders or requirements that the Government may issue or demand of them.'[5]

During that year a large deputation from Cape Coast was received sympathetically when they asked for official help in securing the ex-King's release. The Acting Administrator invited the Chiefs and captains to dinner, and advised them to petition for the return of plain John Aggery.[6] Soon afterwards Sir Arthur Kennedy, in Freetown, recommended his repatriation, provided that he renounced 'all pretension to kingly power at Cape Coast'. Aggery was apparently now convinced that he had been the dupe of 'some semi-civilized mulatto adventurers . . . now thoroughly discredited, and no longer capable of doing any mischief'. Kennedy was anxious that the ex-King should not die in Sierra Leone, which would grieve the Fantis and probably affect adversely their relations with the British Government: 'My experience on this Coast has convinced me that these people may be conquered, and led by kindness, while harsh treatment, or coercion, are unavailing and expensive.'[7] The Secretary of State agreed.[8]

So John Aggery returned to Cape Coast in March 1869, and renounced his claim to be King;[9] he died later in the same year. But the idea of self-government—which he had used mainly to harass and provoke the Administration as far as he dared—lived on after him.

[1] Proclamation of 21 Mar. 1867, and covering Dispatch No. 21 of 25 Mar. 1867, from Ussher to Blackall; ibid.   [2] Dispatch No. 20 of 5 Apr. 1867, from Blackall to Carnarvon; ibid.
[3] Dispatch No. 99 of 5 Dec. 1867, from Ussher to Blackall; ibid.
[4] See Ch. VI, p. 228, below.   [5] *Gold Coast Colony Blue Book*, 1868.
[6] Dispatch No. 122 of 8 Oct. 1868, from Kennedy to Buckingham; CO/96/77.
[7] Dispatch No. 24 of 25 Jan. 1869, from Kennedy to Granville; CO/96/79.
[8] Dispatch No. 24 of 23 Feb. 1869, from Granville to Kennedy; ibid.
[9] In Apr. 1869 Quassie Attah was also pardoned. There was no Omanhene in Cape Coast until after his death in 1887, when Kojo Mbra was enstooled.

VI

THE FANTI[1] CONFEDERATION
1868–73

THE idea of self-government, originally based on the ambiguous Resolutions of the 1865 Select Committee, had gained currency during King Aggery's brief reign as a result of the tension between the colonial oligarchy and the traditional hierarchy in Cape Coast. So far there had been no conception of a 'national' unit of government—except for a vague and unsupported reference by Aggery to 'Cape Coast and its dependencies'.

During the next few years, however, the arbitrary and unimaginative implementation of certain imperial decisions was to spark off a much wider resentment against the attitude of the authorities. The immediate occasion was the exchange of certain Gold Coast forts between the British and the Dutch in 1868. This was partly designed to facilitate the British imposition of customs duties; but when the treaty came into force, the pattern of mercantile penetration and colonial influence which had grown up over the centuries was, for no good reason in African eyes, changed overnight almost beyond recognition.

The resulting disequilibrium and sense of insecurity might, one would think, have been foreseen. Less predictable, perhaps, was the intensity and character of the reaction. Temporarily thrown off balance, the Fantis were thrown together in unprecedented unity, the Chiefs of the interior soon coming to rely on one another rather than upon the inscrutable European. In an attempt to protect their mutual interests, they began to work out some united form of internal self-government. In fact, the contesseration of this mosaic of independent tribes was a considerable step forward in the direction towards which the poll tax Assembly had pointed. But the fact that it was taken on African initiative, and largely in secret, made it appear suspect in the eyes of officials, who were not reassured by the active campaigning of *The African Times* in London. The influence of the *1865 Report*, arousing mingled hopes and fears of British withdrawal, was still strong. But administrators continued to insist that Africans were deliberately misinterpreting this inconvenient document; and thus the Fanti Confederation was regarded as a sinister bid for power on the part of the same unscrupulous 'scholars' who had led King Aggery astray. The subsequent history of the movement is a sorry tale of misunderstanding and wasted opportunity.

[1] The original spelling was 'Fantee', as will be seen from most of the documents quoted. The organizers of the Confederation, however, adopted the spelling 'Fanti' in their constitution of 1871 and used it fairly consistently thereafter.

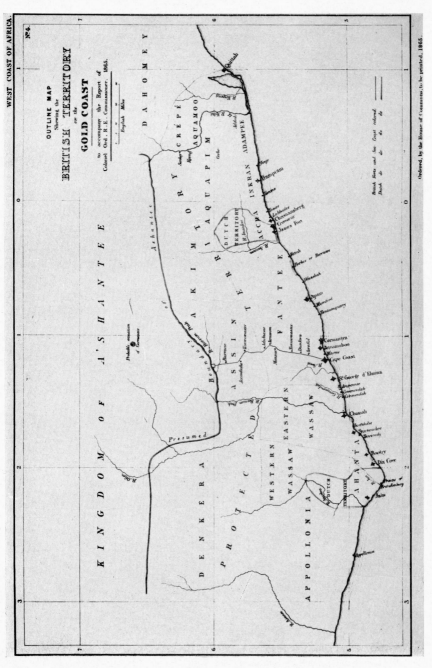

OUTLINE MAP
Shewing the
BRITISH TERRITORY
on the
GOLD COAST
to accompany the Report of
Colonel Ord. R.E. Commissioner.
1865.

English Miles

Ordered, by the House of Commons, to be printed, 1865.

British Forts and Sea Coast colored.
Dutch do do do

MAP 5A. The Gold Coast, 1865—a map accompanying Colonel H. St. G. Ord's Report.

The Exchange of Territory, 1868

Negotiations for an exchange of territory between the British and the Dutch—first seriously mooted in 1857—had been proceeding quietly, early in 1867. A Convention was signed in March, in London,[1] whose effect was to give each power a continuous coastline, administratively tidier and less expensive. This was inevitably coupled with the transfer of undefined rights of protection and influence over large areas.[2] The British then ascertained to their own satisfaction that the eastern tribes—with the exception of 'a few disaffected Accras'—would welcome the prospect of the cession of Dutch Accra;[3] but it seems to have been assumed that the transaction would have little or no direct effect upon the Africans involved. The Chiefs in the western part of the Protectorate were not even consulted before the exchange took place. H. T. Ussher, the Administrator, was more concerned with the need to assert 'unquestioned and undivided authority along the seaboard' than with the feelings of those to be transferred to the Dutch. In any case, he thought that an occasional present or complimentary message was generally sufficient to conciliate the Chiefs.[4]

At the end of the year Ussher issued a proclamation announcing that the transfer would be carried out on 1 January 1868, and giving details of the newly agreed boundary.[5] He also wrote friendly letters to the Chiefs of the Protectorate who were about to be transferred, informing them that, in order to facilitate trade and civilization, they would now be handed over to the Dutch Government; he hoped that their relations with the new Protecting Power would be as satisfactory as those hitherto maintained with Britain.[6] This was hardly a tactful approval to Chiefs who believed that the Queen of England had personally guaranteed them permanent protection in exchange for the rights they had voluntarily surrendered under the Bonds of 1844.

The King of Denkera was the first to take alarm. Fearing that his territory might be laid open to the Ashantis if it came under Dutch influence, he sent messengers to the leading Fanti Chiefs, asking them if they had had any say

---

[1] Convention of 5 Mar. ratified on 5 July 1867; E. Hertslet, *The Map of Africa by Treaty* (London, 1896), vol. iii, p. 977. The full text was reprinted by J. A. B. Horton, *Letters on the Political Condition of the Gold Coast since the Exchange of Territory between the English and Dutch Governments* (London, 1870), pp. iv–vi.

[2] The British gave up all their forts to the west of the Sweet River—Beyin, Dixcove, Sekondi, and Komenda—together with their protectorate over Denkera, Wassaw, and Apollonia; in exchange they received the Dutch possessions to the east of the Sweet River—Mori, Kormantin, Apam, and Dutch Accra. Maps 5A and 5B, facing pp. 222 and 256 show the boundaries before and after the exchange. A uniform customs tariff of 3 per cent. *ad valorem* was also laid down.

[3] Dispatch No. 42 of 6 July 1867, from Ussher to Administrator-in-Chief; CO/96/74.

[4] Dispatch No. 99 of 5 Dec. 1867, from Usher to Administrator-in-Chief; ibid.

[5] Only a few days' notice was given, according to Horton, *Letters*, no. i, dated 12 Aug. 1869. Ussher later admitted that the transfer was made public one month before the time fixed for carrying it into effect, and that this period was too short. Confidential Dispatch of 17 Oct. 1870, from Ussher to Kennedy; CO/96/85.   [6] Horton, *Letters*, no. i, dated 12 Aug. 1869.

in the matter. He also sent his family to Mankessim, for protection and further information. It was not long before a number of disturbed Chiefs arrived in the town with their elders and educated advisers; as a correspondent to *The African Times* of 23 April 1868 put it, 'up they all started for their ancient gathering place, Mankessim'.[1] By the time they were assembled, the exchange had come into effect, which meant that some of them were, strictly speaking, already under Dutch protection. They refused to accept this— especially as they had not previously been consulted—and were stimulated into proclaiming their solidarity.

Why did the Fanti Chiefs and their neighbours feel so strongly about the proposed transfer? One important reason was their fear of Ashanti, especially in view of recent alarums and excursions on the Prah frontier. They knew that the Dutch were favourably inclined towards the Ashantis, and feared that such 'protection' would not guarantee them against another invasion. The Denkeras and Wassaws, in particular, felt that they were in danger of being overrun. The second main objection was to the methods of Dutch administration; it was believed that they were hostile to many forms of social progress: 'No missionary is permitted to live amongst them, nor are there any schools worth noticing for the benefit of the rising generation.'[2] Thirdly, the presentation of this *fait accompli* confirmed the Fantis' growing suspicions that the British did not really respect their views and interests, nor even the sanctity of written agreements. Even those who were to remain under British protection had lost faith. Another newspaper correspondent underlined the Chiefs' deep distrust of the Cape Coast authorities: 'They believe that the Queen's Government at home means well to them, but that it is quite the other way with the men that they send out to govern the Coast.'[3] The whole transaction was a severe set-back to European prestige.

The Mankessim Council Goes to War

The Fantis now decided that independent, united action was necessary— a conviction that had been growing since the Ashanti war of 1863–4. The first step taken by those assembled at Mankessim in January 1868 was to form some sort of government, 'which would be to ourselves a head, having no King under the British'. After some initial bickering between those who

---

[1] Horton had written, just before this revival of the town's importance: 'Mankesin in former years was a famous Fetish town for all the Fantees, and exercised considerable control over the Government of the country; but, through the exertions of the Government, aided by the educated inhabitants, it has now no influence.' *West African Countries and Peoples* (London, 1868), p. 132. 'Mankesem' is shown on Map 2B on p. 29, above.   [2] Ibid. p. 256.

[3] *The African Times*, 23 July 1868. Cf. W. W. Claridge's comment on the transfer: 'with an utter disregard for the wishes of the people . . . and for the justice of their case, the Government calmly proceeded to carry out this change without so much as consulting those whose interests it so vitally affected, let alone attempting to gain their consent'. He also called it 'a monumental piece of folly and injustice'. *A History of the Gold Coast and Ashanti* (London, 1915), vol. i, pp. 560–2.

wanted a 'monarchial institution' and others 'for confederacy', it was decided that 'each state should give seven of its sensible and respectable men as national councillors, there, with the Kings and Chiefs, to form a Fantee Council'. Three leading Kings—Edoo of Mankessim, Otoo of Abura, and Ortabil of Gomuah—were accepted as joint 'Presidents of the Fantee Nation', and they proceeded to appoint Samuel Ferguson as Magistrate;[1] Joseph Dawson, according to his own account, was made Secretary.[2] The councillors were sworn to their duties, and all the Chiefs took an oath to work faithfully together; but no constitution was yet drawn up. As Dawson later wrote, 'still a proper form of the Confederation was to be prepared'.[3]

Ussher was already aware of the need for unification among the Fantis; he had suggested that periodical visits of district magistrates, dispensing impartial justice, would help to consolidate this collection of 'tribes' into a federation, or *Bund*, which would defy foreign invasion, and 'raise and elevate the people voluntarily composing it'.[4] But he was alarmed that the Chiefs themselves had taken the initiative, especially as it was rumoured that they were discussing a scheme of taxation with the help of some educated Cape Coast supporters of ex-King Aggery.

Yet it was to Aggery's former representative, Thomas Hughes, that Ussher turned, being now satisfied of his loyalty, in spite of former indiscretions. His mission was to find out the purpose of the meeting at Mankessim and 'to endeavour to counteract some mischief which I fear these people in their ignorance may be preparing'. Hughes was to warn the Chiefs still under British protection that 'any treasonable practices' against the supremacy of Her Majesty's Government would be punished as speedily as in the case of Aggery, and that if they did not at once leave Mankessim and go home they would be arrested on suspicion alone. Ussher also feared that armed resistance against the Dutch was being planned, and he therefore instructed Hughes to tell the deputations from the Wassaws, Denkeras, Komendas, and other tribes so recently transferred to Dutch protection that their presence now in British territory was highly suspicious and could no longer be sanctioned.[5]

The acquisition of forts by the British was going comparatively smoothly; but in the towns where the Dutch came to take over they found resentment, and at Komenda the inhabitants refused to lower the British flag. As Horton put it, 'This affront was not by any means savoury to the Dutch', who thereupon bombarded the town on 1 February 1868. This news, reaching

[1] Letter of 6 Feb. 1868, from Kings Edoo, Otoo, and Ortabil to Ferguson; Ghartey Papers No. 3, G.N. Archives.

[2] But there seems to have been some dispute over this. G. Amissah claimed to have been made President of the Council and Secretary to the Monarchs, and said that Dawson was only Clerk of the Court and Receiver-General. Letter of 17 Feb. 1868, from Amissah to Ghartey; Ghartey Papers No. 269, ibid.   [3] Letter from J. Dawson, *The African Times*, 24 Oct. 1870.

[4] Dispatch No. 99 of 5 Dec. 1867, from Ussher to Administrator-in-Chief; CO/96/74.

[5] Private and Confidential Instructions of 29 Jan. 1868, to Hughes from Ussher, enclosed in his Dispatch No. 17 of 6 Feb. 1868, to Blackall; CO/96/76.

Mankessim while Hughes was there, 'acted as an electric shock throughout the Protectorate . . . the whole of the Fantee race flew to arms', and the assembly of Chiefs turned itself into a 'council of war'.[1] They decided to enter the field on the side of the Komendas, and also to raise a poll tax in their aid. The general attitude was: 'The British Government has no right to transfer them like so many bullocks.'[2] When the Dutch counter-attacked, the King of Abura proclaimed the fight a righteous cause: 'We cannot understand that the people of Commendah, they being no slaves of either Government could be bartered off in this way, and when they refused to go under the Dutch Flag that their town to be bombarded and to be forced to leave their own home and soil.'[3]

It is clear that many tribal differences were submerged in this common attempt to drive out the Dutch. Ussher mentioned the Komendas, Denkeras, and Wassaws as being the most determined to resist Dutch rule; they were soon joined by the Apollonians,[4] who had initially accepted the transfer quietly. Many 'British Fantees' came to help; Horton listed the Kings of Assin, Fanti, Gomuah, Akenfee, Anomabu, and Winneba as having joined in the alliance with King Edoo of Mankessim. Sir Arthur Kennedy, Governor-in-Chief at Sierra Leone, commented: 'A strong National Sentiment has aroused the "Fantees".'[5]

The headquarters of the Dutch Government was now besieged by the Fantis, who welcomed the opportunity to try to settle the 'Elmina question'. For years there had been general coldness and occasional bitterness between the small tribe of Elminas, some 15,000 strong, and the 'Fantees proper', who surrounded them on all sides. Why was there this hostility? The Fantis and Elminas spoke almost the same language, and were virtually the same people, accustomed, in their own words, to 'marry the same wives and fish in the same waters'.[6] The explanation was to be found in the relationship between the Dutch Government and the Elminas with Ashanti; the Fantis feared and distrusted this because it gave their ancient enemies a pretext for entering their country and forcing their way to the coast at any time. The British, of course, had always helped to resist the establishment of this right of way through Fanti territory.[7]

[1] Horton, *Letters*, no. i, dated 12 Aug. 1869.   [2] Dawson, *The African Times*, 24 Oct. 1870.

[3] Letter of 2 Mar. 1868, from King of Abura on behalf of the Council at Mankessim to Ussher, enclosed in his Dispatch No. 21 of 6 Mar. 1868, to Kennedy; CO/96/76.

[4] Dispatch of 19 Mar. 1868, from Ussher to Kennedy; ibid.

[5] Dispatch of 30 Mar. 1868, from Kennedy to Buckingham; ibid.

[6] Dispatch No. 106 of 7 Nov. 1868, from Kennedy to Buckingham; CO/96/77. The 'deep-rooted enmity', as Brodie Cruickshank called it in 1853, dated back at least as far as the Ashanti invasion of 1807. It remained so acute that quite recently an Elmina man has been able to recall the difficulty of persuading a Fanti even 'to give a glass of water to a stranger known to hail from El Mina'. J. Sylvanus Wartemberg, *Sao Jorge D'El Mina* (Ilfracombe, n.d. [1950?]), p. 52. Cf. John, iv. 9.

[7] Memorandum by Kennedy, enclosed in his Confidential Dispatch of 7 Nov. 1868, to Buckingham; CO/96/77.

Ussher's Intervention

The Administrator was considerably perturbed by the outbreaks, although he was not displeased that the British flag was so strongly preferred to the Dutch.[1] He was particularly anxious to keep the peace throughout the Protectorate, no doubt remembering the unfortunate publicity that had surrounded the Ashanti invasion five years earlier. He feared, with some reason, that the Asantehene might now take the opportunity to intervene.[2] There was, too, some element of personal pique: the inhabitants should have taken his word as to what was best for their own interests. Nor did Ussher relish the increasing disobedience shown towards his administration. He was ready to check firmly any attempt at rebellion against Europeans, for if the natives got away with this show of force, there was no knowing what might happen next. This view was strongly supported in London: 'in the face of the symptoms which are reported of a general insubordination and disaffection towards Europeans amongst the natives of the Gold Coast, sound policy demands that they should gain no encouragement by inflicting unprovoked reverses on the White Race, whether Dutch or English'.[3]

In fact, the movement was specifically anti-Dutch; the tribal alignments were a faithful reflection of European interests and rivalries. Ussher's attitude was more calculated to inspire a general anti-European feeling than to reassure the remaining tribes of British protection. His diagnosis of the trouble was facile; the semi-educated African was now not only a scapegoat, but in danger of becoming a stereotype, as Ussher tried unsuccessfully to detach the Chiefs from such influences. Fortunately, the Fantis did not develop any general racial hostility, and both the Chiefs and their educated advisers remained surprisingly loyal to the British, though they now felt they had to rely mainly on their own resources.

Kennedy, from Sierra Leone, viewed the Fanti protest more sympathetically, and advised: 'Nothing short of dire necessity, or the prospect of dishonour, should, in my opinion, tempt us to use violence in coercing these people to adopt an alliance distasteful to them.'[4] Ussher, however, used all his influence to prevent the spread of resistance to Dutch authority. He issued a proclamation suspending indefinitely the sale of arms and ammunition, from the Sweet River to the Volta; he also warned the inhabitants of Cape Coast against 'meddling in these disturbances', and told them to preserve perfect neutrality.[5]

[1] 'The ceded tribes obstinately refuse to deliver up the British Flag, the symbol of their loyalty to us.' Dispatch No. 21 of 6 Mar. 1868, from Ussher to Kennedy; CO/96/76.

[2] The Fantis had recently captured several hundred Ashanti traders, some of whom had powder and lead concealed in gin bottles; the Government made haste to secure their release and a Fanti apology. Dispatch No. 17 of 6 Feb. 1868, from Ussher to Blackall; ibid.

[3] Minute of 3 June 1868, by T. F. Elliot; ibid.

[4] Dispatch of 30 Mar. 1868, from Kennedy to Buckingham; ibid.

[5] *Official Notice*, 26 Feb. 1868.

But while the siege of Elmina was quietly proceeding, some of the beleaguered townsmen counter-attacked an outlying Cape Coast village, and killed and captured several inhabitants. This was the signal for the men of Cape Coast, led by their Headman, Quassie Attah, to take up arms despite the strict instructions and threats they had received; Horton tells how they 'flew to arms and marched into the field, amidst the hurrahs of their women and children'.[1] Ussher described them as 'incited by their women, ever the instigators of mischief here', and ordered the deposition of Quassie Attah for this breach of his oath of allegiance.[2]

Ussher then sent the Rev. T. B. Freeman, W. E. Davidson, and W. Martin to the Fanti camp outside Elmina, to find out exactly what was going on, and to do everything possible to disperse this irregular army.[3] The Fantis were also to be told that even if they succeeded in driving out the Dutch, some other European nation would inevitably take over, and not Britain, who had already had 'so bad a return for her trouble and expense'.[4] Ussher advised the Fantis, instead of 'indulging in this suicidal and ruinous conflict', to draw up a memorial to London, which he would be prepared to forward.[5] While these negotiations were going on, a general engagement took place, and the Elminas and Dutch troops were driven back on all sides. But the besiegers were handicapped by inter-tribal jealousy and lack of co-ordination; and Freeman eventually persuaded the Fanti Chiefs that as they had avenged the insult to their honour, it would be best to place their dispute in the hands of the Administrator.

By now Ussher had decided that all the trouble had been due to the discreditable influence of 'discontented and unprincipled natives, principally mulattoes and semi-educated blacks (who appear to be an evil inseparable from all negro communities)'; they had been at work for the last three years, misrepresenting the resolutions of the 1865 Committee to the 'ignorant, impressionable and childlike Fantees', and attempting to set up King Aggery as an independent and irresponsible authority, under the walls of the British castle. He was convinced that 'unflagging secret agitation' by the very same people was responsible for the present disturbances. It was undoubtedly they who had urged the Chiefs to assemble a solemn council at Mankessim, ostensibly

---

[1] *Letters*, no. iii, dated 12 Oct. 1869.

[2] Dispatch No. 32 of 6 Apr. 1868, from Ussher to Kennedy; CO/96/76.

[3] The Governor-in-Chief later took the uncharitable view that 'Complications have been aggravated by the employment as Commissioners, by the Cape Coast Government, of such men as Thomas Hughes and Mr. Freeman; they are neither respectable, respected, nor honest. They derived a handsome livelihood from the disturbances which it has been their *interest* to foster and keep alive.' Confidential Dispatch of 7 Nov. 1868, from Kennedy to Buckingham; CO/96/77.

[4] But Ussher told Kennedy privately that he thought the only solution would be to purchase the Dutch settlements. The irony of the situation is emphasized by the Administrator's suggestion, two years earlier, that an exchange of territory with the Dutch would help to 'steer clear of troubles and broils'. Dispatch No. 25 of 5 Feb. 1866, from Conran to Cardwell; CO/96/70.

[5] Letter of 11 Apr. 1868, to Freeman, Davidson, and Martin from Ussher, enclosed in his Dispatch No. 52 of 18 May 1868, to Kennedy; CO/96/76.

to collect money and combine against a non-existent Ashanti threat, but in reality to plan armed opposition to the treaty of interchange. Rumour had it that a large quantity of gold had been collected, and that Ashanti messengers had been told there was 'no Governor now, and Fantees ruled the coast'. Ussher therefore decided that it was necessary to make some salutary examples, in order to 'crush out the spirit of disaffection so glaringly evident in the whole conduct of the people of Cape Coast'.[1]

The Fanti leaders now formally requested Ussher to arrange a truce, so that they could meet and negotiate with the Elminas.[2] They were not all ready to make peace;[3] but heavy rain eventually discouraged even those from Cape Coast who wanted to continue fighting, and the Fanti battle camp was broken in June. Ussher at once sent a small commission to Elmina, consisting of W. H. Simpson (the Collector of Customs), Dawson (representing the Fanti Chiefs), and Freeman, to negotiate peace terms with the Dutch and the local inhabitants. His plan was to get them to suspend their alliance with Ashanti for six months, and a treaty was drafted on these lines. But the Fanti Chiefs and their educated advisers remaining at Mankessim refused to sign. They considered this far too short a period for any security, and maintained that neither Freeman nor Dawson had been authorized to consent to a peace which allowed the Elminas to remain neutral in the event of another Ashanti war. They were therefore unwilling to abandon entirely the blockade of Elmina, which continued intermittently for some months.

Ussher was furious at what he took to be a fresh defiance of British influence and of his personal authority; he considered the Fanti objections 'frivolous and unworthy of notice'. He therefore sent an ultimatum to Mankessim, demanding entire compliance with his draft treaty as the only possible reply.[4] Twelve days later, just before going on leave, he tartly informed the Chiefs that thanks to their conduct he could no longer have any relations with them: 'In case of a war with Ashantee as you will have provoked it, you will bear the brunt thereof without help from this Government.'[5]

The Aim of Self-government

One result of this letter was to arouse the educated few to a keener political consciousness. By this time, some of them were ready to look beyond the

---

[1] Dispatches Nos. 32 of 6 Apr. and 52 of 18 May 1868, from Ussher to Kennedy; ibid.

[2] Letter of 1 June 1868, from Fanti Kings and Chiefs to Ussher; Cape Coast Historical Society Papers, SC 3/5, G.N. Archives.

[3] For example, when G. Amissah presided over a meeting held at Mankessim on 11 June 1868, to discuss Ussher's reply, they could not agree whether to hand over four Elmina hostages as a token of good faith before the negotiations. Cape Coast Historical Society Papers, SC 3/8, ibid.

[4] Letter of 6 July 1868, to Kings Otoo, Ortabil, and Edoo ('Presidents of the Fantee and other allied tribes at Mankessim') from Ussher, enclosed in his Dispatch No. 85 of 17 July 1868, to Kennedy; CO/96/76.

[5] Letter of 18 July 1868, to 'Presidents and other Chiefs of Fantee at Mankessim' from Ussher, enclosed in his Dispatch No. 93 of 7 Aug. 1868, to Kennedy; CO/96/77.

horizons of the village or tribe towards a possible wider unity; but thanks to the attitude of the Administration, they were becoming increasingly dissatisfied with the political direction of the British, and their influence upon the Chiefs was exerted accordingly. The need to help the Chiefs to draw up 'some measures for our self-government and our self-defence' was being strongly canvassed during 1868, and a general invitation was issued from Mankessim to all 'Friends and Countrymen' to assemble for discussion.[1] Later, another notice was circulated to the inhabitants of Cape Coast, especially those who were educated, inviting them to a meeting at Mankessim on 1 October.[2]

The most influential voice at this time was that of Dr. J. Africanus B. Horton, whose political ideas were being discussed among his friends in Cape Coast and Accra. A native of Sierra Leone, Horton had been stationed in the Gold Coast for some years as Staff Assistant Surgeon to the Army, and had written two works of some medical interest.[3] He had just published *West African Countries and Peoples* (London, 1868), which set out to discuss 'the Requirements necessary for establishing that Self-Government recommended by the Committee of the House of Commons, 1865'. This was the first exposition of the aim of self-government to be written by a West African. Horton's theme was 'that great principle of establishing independent African nationalities', which he attributed to the 1865 Resolutions. Considering how this might be applied in practice, he suggested that the British Gold Coast should be divided into two parts, a Kingdom of Fanti and a Republic of Accra, the latter extending from Winneba to the River Volta, and including Eastern Akim, Adangme, Akwapim, Krobo, Akwamu, Krepi, and Avatime. Each of these should remain under the auspices of the British Government, with a British consul always ready to advise them in political matters and guarantee them against foreign invasion.

It is interesting to note that Horton was thinking in terms of two independent regions, and virtually ignored the possibility of a central government for both as the road to autonomy. In fact, tribal loyalties were still so strong that it was a significant extension of the word 'nationality' to use it to cover groups of several tribes. Horton's originality lay in his insistence on the need for a strong, compact form of internal government for each region, if necessary at the expense of parochial pride. He ridiculed the proliferation of kings in

[1] 'Address of a Native of the Gold Coast to His Fellow-Countrymen', later published in *The African Times*, 23 Sept. 1868.

[2] Circular of 15 Sept. 1868, by Ferguson; ibid. 23 Nov. 1868.

[3] *The Medical Topography of the West Coast of Africa, with Sketches of its Botany* (London, 1859); and *Physical and Medical Climate and Meteorology of the West Coast of Africa* (London, 1867). This included 'valuable hints to Europeans for the preservation of health in the Tropics'; e.g. 'Persons accustomed to licentious indulgences are to be avoided, especially on first arrival', and 'The companionship of persons of irritable and violent temper should, as much as possible, be avoided, as in the tropics such habits are peculiarly catching, and have an injurious effect on the health.' Details of this enterprising doctor's later career have already been referred to in Ch. I, pp. 22 and 27, above.

every small *croom* or hamlet along the coast; 'any man who can plant a village, make a stool, and sit himself on it' might call himself a King. Their title should be changed; and at one point in the book he even put forward the idea that, as they died, each stool should be done away with. But quite apart from this rather naïve suggestion, his proposals involved a radical change in the system of government.

Taking first the Fantis, Horton pointed out that in their present disunited state, if a war should break out with Ashanti, they had no superior authority to look to, except the Governor, who was no longer allowed to support them in the interior. The only way to achieve unity was to choose a strong leader to be crowned 'King of Fantee' with the consent of all the Kings and Chiefs. He considered such an appointment all the more urgent, after the deposition of Aggery. Horton did not appear to mind greatly whether this supra-tribal King should be chosen by universal suffrage, or appointed by the Governor; but he must in any event be a man of great sagacity and education, who had served the British Government well, besides being 'versed in native diplomacy, and well known and respected by the various Kings'. Horton suggested that the Hon. George Blankson might meet such exacting requirements. But events were to prove him over-optimistic in imagining the Kings capable of accepting the leadership of an educated commoner. Their inability to agree even on a leader chosen from among themselves remained one fatal flaw in the whole Fanti Confederation movement.

The immediate object of this proposed appointment was strategic. Lacking a leader, the Fantis lacked discipline and organization to fight their own battles; with one, they could concentrate a large force at short notice at any given point of attack from their powerful neighbours. But the long-term aim was to pave the way for self-government. Horton feared that the premature withdrawal of the British would lead to 'intestine warfare . . . fearful and barbaric massacre and bloodshed'; and so their help must be sought in bringing about the radical reforms needed, before it was too late. The King of Fanti must therefore be 'crowned, assisted, acknowledged and supported by the British authority, both on the Coast and in Downing-street'. The Governor should refer to him domestic matters concerning the other Kings, advise him, and enforce his decisions. Other detailed suggestions were made, a mixture of the ideal and the practical. The King should be assisted by a number of councillors, some educated, and some traditional office-holders; these should swear allegiance to the British Government, 'until such time as the country is considered fit for delivery over to self-government'. Each State was to be made to contribute towards the expenses of government, and a volunteer force was to be raised.

Horton felt, however, that there were better possibilities in the eastern districts than in the western for 'a good, useful native self-government', because the people there were more united, with Accra as a natural headquarters; and because the Ashantis, their only enemies, were unlikely to try to overrun that part of the country. The main aim of the proposed Republic of Accra would be to regulate the internal government of the country by an alliance of the Kings and Chiefs under the supervision of the Governor, who should nominate an educated African as President. The Government should vote a yearly grant out of revenue, which might be increased by customs duties at the eastern and western boundaries of the Republic. Under such a system, Horton was confident, the Republic of Accra could be made one of the richest provinces in West Africa; its resources were vast and extensive, and required only to be developed.[1]

Although the educated group in Accra was only too ready to try out these proposals in practice, it was among the Fantis that Horton's ideas had the greatest influence on subsequent developments. This was because the external pressures of the Anglo-Dutch exchange and the threat from Ashanti were already driving them into some form of alliance.

Simpson's Attempts at Conciliation, 1868-9

Meanwhile the Governor-in-Chief was not altogether happy about the deadlock between the Fantis and the Cape Coast authorities. He believed that 'a little better judgement and patience' at the beginning of the disturbances would have saved a great deal of trouble, and maintained friendly relations with the Fantis.[2] In August 1868 Simpson became Acting Administrator and tried, in his own words, 'by temperate language and a conciliatory manner' to gain the confidence of all parties. He hoped to make the Chiefs conscious of their isolation and weakness, and thus to deter them from their 'suicidal' hostility to the Dutch and the Elminas. Then they might see that it was in their own interest to submit to the paramount influence of the British. Thus there was an ulterior motive behind his cordial reception of the Cape Coast deputation seeking the return of Aggery,[3] and he also courteously sent word of developments concerning Ashanti to the Chiefs at Mankessim.[4] They, however, were quietly sending out their circulars, including at least one version designed for Accra, in an attempt to achieve some sort of united front.[5]

Kennedy now took a personal hand. He visited the Gold Coast and at the beginning of November had a lengthy conference with the Chiefs of Cape Coast and neighbourhood, 'representing the Fante Nation'. He was greatly

[1] Horton, *West African Countries and Peoples*, ch. x, 'Self-Government of the Gold Coast—Kingdom of Fantee', and ch. xi, 'Republic of Accra'.

[2] Dispatch No. 73 of 13 Aug. 1868, from Kennedy to Buckingham; CO/96/77.

[3] See Ch. V, p. 221, above.

[4] Dispatch No. 122 of 8 Oct. 1868, from Simpson to Kennedy; CO/96/77.

[5] For example, 'Circular to all the Educated Chiefs, and Head Men of James Town, Christiansborg and Ussher Town' proposing a meeting to discuss general matters concerning the coast, referred to by G. F. Cleland in his Letter of 3 Oct. 1868, to S. Ferguson; Ghartey Papers No. 361, G.N. Archives.

impressed with their general bearing, intelligence, and 'comparative civilization', and described their proposals as just and reasonable.[1] He also listened
sympathetically to their complaint that the mode of procedure in the law
courts was 'dilatory, complicated, unreasonably expensive and unsatisfactory'.[2] But the meeting was mainly concerned with military matters. The
Fantis still wanted the Elminas to break completely with Ashanti and to join
them in an offensive and defensive alliance. They argued that 'they would
never consent to remain between two fires as at present, with Ashantee their
old, barbarous, and treacherous enemy in their front,—and the Elminas in
their rear'.

Kennedy agreed that the Fanti terms were an essential condition for peace
and prosperity in the area. He proceeded to Elmina, still subject to an effective
blockade by land, and advised the King and Chiefs there to enter into an
alliance with the tribes comprising the Fanti Confederation; but they would
not concede anything beyond the promise of neutrality. This would, as
Kennedy pointed out, enable them to sell ammunition to both the Fantis and
the Ashantis in the event of war. He believed that they were encouraged in
their attitude by the Dutch, who feared interference with the so-called 'emi-
gration' of West Coast soldiers to Java. Kennedy himself was convinced that
these Africans were being purchased by the Dutch Government from Ashanti,
and that this was why the Netherlands kept up an otherwise unprofitable
establishment at Elmina.[3] In the event, he advised the Colonial Office that the
Fantis should not be coerced against their traditions and interests and that
there was only one solution: the retirement of the Dutch and the acquisition
of Elmina by Britain.[4] But the Secretary of State, echoing the inhibitions of
the *1865 Report*, refused to entertain any idea of extended occupation on the
coast.[5]

Simpson continued to try and regain personal control and influence over
the Chiefs of the Protectorate and to revive their confidence in the Government. As soon as he had succeeded in obtaining a general cessation of hostilities, he invited them to meet him at Cape Coast and indicated his intention
of openly recognizing and supporting 'the council of the Kings assembled
at Mankessim'. Simpson was anxious that the authority and influence of
the Administration should be substituted for the 'interested services and

---

[1] Dispatch No. 106 of 7 Nov. 1868, from Kennedy to Buckingham; CO/96/77.

[2] Letter of 20 Dec. 1869, from Kennedy to Ussher, enclosed in his Confidential Letter of
4 May 1872, to Pope Hennessy; CO/96/94.

[3] Confidential Dispatch of 7 Nov. 1868, from Kennedy to Buckingham; CO/96/77.

[4] Dispatch No. 1 of 11 Jan. 1869, from Kennedy to Granville; CO/96/79. Horton gives details
of a memorial of the Fanti Kings and Chiefs drawn up by W. Cleaver, the European agent of
Swanzy's, in Nov. 1868, urging 'that negotiations be at once opened for the purchase of the
Dutch settlements'. *Letters*, no. vi, dated 12 Jan. 1870. Their aim was to influence Kennedy while
he was visiting the Gold Coast, but the memorial was not received by him until the following
year. CO/96/80.

[5] Dispatch No. 18 of 9 Feb. 1869, from Granville to Kennedy; CO/96/79.

pernicious interference of the "scholars" or semi-educated natives hitherto in uncontrolled ascendancy'. He suggested that some simple scheme might be devised, without usurping the prerogatives of the Crown, to create a Union for self-defence of all the different nations within the Protectorate. This might be the first step, under the guidance of the British Government, for testing their fitness for anything approaching self-government. On his reading of 'the temper of these people and times', as well as of British policy, Simpson concluded that 'an attempt at political advancement must and will be made', and, more important, that it should be officially anticipated and controlled.[1]

The Chiefs and their advisers hesitated to commit themselves again to allegiance and obedience; they remembered Ussher's previous conduct, and feared that he might soon return. Only a few of them came from Mankessim to Cape Coast in January 1869; but Simpson was anxious to meet the full Council, as he felt that 'the spirit of disaffection' was still spreading from Mankessim, and so far he had only been able to counter it indirectly.[2] Eventually, by 'a certain amount of diplomatising', he secured—and accepted— an invitation to go to Mankessim, where a few months earlier 'it would have been deemed sacrilege if not dangerous or impossible to have placed a foot'.[3] In the Colonial Office, however, it was thought 'rather strange' that Simpson should go there at all, to hold a conference with a British-protected tribe who had placed themselves in a hostile position towards a British ally.[4]

The Secretary of State had already made it clear—contrary to the advice of Kennedy—that the desire of the Fantis for an alliance with the Elminas against the Ashantis was considered unreasonable.[5] But Simpson could not bring himself to 'avow broadly and directly' to the Chiefs something so opposed to what he had previously led them to expect, fearing to arouse suspicions of his own honesty.[6] In any case, he believed that it was only the Elmina question that was keeping the Chiefs together and giving them cohesion; without that the Mankessim Council would die a natural death. He therefore gave most weight to Kennedy's instructions to encourage the spirit

[1] Dispatch No. 131 of 5 Dec. 1868, from Simpson to Kennedy; CO/96/77.

[2] Simpson had written to the King of Wassaw, for example, warning him not to allow his power to be challenged by 'the persons styling themselves Councillors of Mankessim . . . should any attempt be made to tax your people, you will do well to arrest them immediately, and report to me'. Letter of 15 Feb. 1869, to King Ennimil, enclosed in Dispatch No. 38 of 9 Apr. 1869, from Simpson to Kennedy; CO/96/79.

[3] Dispatches Nos. 38 of 9 Apr., 41 of 19 Apr., and 43 of 5 May 1869, from Simpson to Kennedy; CO/96/79 and 80.   [4] Minute of 21 May 1869; CO/96/79.

[5] Confidential Dispatch of 22 Jan. 1869, from Granville to Kennedy, and his covering Confidential Dispatch of 27 Feb. 1869, to Simpson; ibid.

[6] Dispatch No. 103 of 23 Aug. 1869, from Simpson to Kennedy; CO/96/81. Simpson was unaware that the recall of his commission had been under consideration in London for his 'hazardous' encouragement of the Fantis against the Ashantis, although he was still regarded as an 'efficient and zealous public servant'. Dispatch No. 43 of 17 May 1869, from Granville to Kennedy; CO/96/77.

of unanimity and self-reliance among the Chiefs; and although he did not actually promise them any material aid, which had been strictly forbidden, he proceeded by 'humouring those who believe that the regeneration and independence of their country is at hand'. Simpson's conduct appears all the more contradictory in view of his own lack of faith in the prospects of self-government. He privately deplored the absence of honest and capable leaders, and the fact that the Chiefs derived their power from slavery; he believed that, if the British withdrew, sacrifices would recommence in Cape Coast within a week, 'and the Country return to a state of utter barbarism and ruin'. Therefore the Government must take the lead in directing 'native national affairs'.[1] But he took care not to reveal these doubts to the Fantis.

Simpson arrived at Mankessim in April 1869, not knowing what to expect. He found that the Council consisted of the Kings themselves, or their sworn delegates, and that all the important Fanti States were represented, except Assin, whose leaders were guarding the Ashanti frontier; there were also a few representatives from Accra. The Acting Administrator first gained their confidence by sympathetically reviewing recent events; in particular, he agreed that the hand-over to the Dutch in the west without consultation had been a mistake, that the attack on Komenda had been countenanced by the British Governor, and that with regard to Elmina 'the Fantees were right and the Government wrong'. He thought they were justified in taking the House of Commons debate in 1864 as a serious warning,[2] and he approved their efforts to promote Fanti unity.

Simpson then reminded them that a council of war for a definite purpose was simple enough, but a council to regulate the internal affairs of a country in time of peace was another and more difficult matter. He asked for full details of the origins and functions of the Mankessim Council, and said that he would then be prepared to give a 'qualified assent'. If they wanted official recognition, the articles of union would have to be approved by the Governor-in-Chief and sanctioned by the Secretary of State. Simpson offered personally to prepare such a constitution, with the assistance of any competent person they wished to nominate, to help achieve 'the unity of the Fantee nation and its progress towards self-government'. This elicited the significant statement from the Fanti Kings that they were 'now ready to disclose everything and do nothing without consultation and concurrence of Acting Administrator'. They also put forward a number of grievances against the Government, shrewdly insisting that everything must be in writing, so that 'when another Governor came he might see the Policy pursued by Acting Administrator and stick to the same'.

The Kings announced that they had appointed R. J. Ghartey as Chief

---

[1] Dispatches Nos. 30 of 7 Apr. 1869, from Kennedy to Simpson, and 43 of 5 May 1869, from Simpson to Kennedy; CO/96/79 and 80.

[2] See Ch. V, p. 199, above.

Magistrate of the Fanti National Supreme Court,[1] and George Blankson jun. as their Agent;[2] and that these two would act for them in assisting Simpson, who approved their choice. He himself politely declined the appointment of 'Field Marshal Commanding in Chief of the Fantee Forces', but said he was ready to lead them against their enemies should they be invaded. He called attention to the disgraceful state of the roads, and promised that the Government would contribute a small sum if the Kings would take on the responsibility for their upkeep; but taxes on transit trade must cease. British courts must be obeyed; and the Judicial Assessor might come to Mankessim two or three times a year to assist them in settling their palavers. The Kings agreed to all this, and said they would consult Simpson concerning better tax schemes. During the proceedings, which continued for several days, the question of self-government was amicably discussed, with verbal concessions on both sides. Simpson declared that the British did not desire to rule them if they showed themselves capable—but this must first be proved; and the Kings assured him that 'they had never wished to govern themselves except from being told they had been cast off'.

Simpson believed that as a result of this meeting he had succeeded in re-establishing the influence of the Government over the whole of the western districts, wiping out old grievances, and securing 'reconciliation and union under the British Flag, which in their hearts the natives love so well'.[3] Kennedy, on the whole, was also pleased, hoping that this personal contact with the Chiefs would obviate misunderstandings and neutralize the influence of bad advisers.[4] But Colonel Nagtglas, the new Commissioner of the Netherlands Settlements, protested angrily against Simpson's alleged warlike pronouncements 'that the British policy towards the Fantees was wrong, that Elmina *must* go and that he had the entire *concurrence* of Earl Granville in all he was doing'.[5] So Simpson was told from Freetown to disavow promptly the language and sentiments complained of.[6] He later defended himself on the grounds that his rapidly delivered speech had been inadequately reported;[7] but it was felt in the Colonial Office that such indiscreet language had been regrettable at an otherwise sensibly conducted meeting. In any case it was seriously questioned whether Simpson ought to have recognized the Council

[1] Ghartey carefully preserved his sealed letter of appointment, dated 5 Dec. 1868; Ghartey Papers No. 9, G.N. Archives.

[2] Dawson commented, in a letter to Ghartey dated 15 May 1869, 'I am glad you have got Mr. G. Blankson. I believe the young man is a true patriot.' Ibid. No. 82.

[3] 'Notes of the Proceedings at the Meeting of Fantee Kings with His Excellency the Acting Administrator William Henry Simpson at Mankessim, April 22–28, 1869', and his covering Dispatch No. 43 of 5 May 1869, to Kennedy; CO/96/80.

[4] Dispatch No. 46 of 26 May 1869, from Kennedy to Simpson; ibid.

[5] Letter of 20 May 1869, from Nagtglas to Kennedy, enclosed in his Confidential Dispatch of 1 June 1869, to Granville; ibid.

[6] Dispatch of 31 May 1869, from Kennedy to Simpson; ibid.

[7] Dispatch No. 103 of 23 Aug. 1869, from Simpson to Kennedy; CO/96/81.

at Mankessim, which was to all intents and purposes 'a *Council of War* . . . against a British Ally'. The view in London was that he was pursuing right objects by rash and unjustifiable means.[1]

At Mankessim discussions continued, and an attempt was made to place the organization on a more permanent footing; and it was at this juncture that the title Confederation (or Confederacy) seems first to have been used, especially by some who were anxious to draw in more educated men 'for the great business'.[2] The Fanti Kings, however, were anxious to find a single President from amongst themselves, but they were unable to agree. King Edoo of Mankessim considered he should have the title; but this antagonized King Otoo of Abura, 'who from time immemorial has been regarded as the leader of the Fantee nation', and a 'slight coldness between the two potentates' resulted.[3] It was Ghartey, therefore, who became the first President, at a time when the Fantis were becoming more and more resentful of Dutch rule.[4]

Increasing Tension[5]

The Acting Administrator while at Mankessim had done his best to influence the Confederation to keep the peace; but soon several incidents occurred which further inflamed feeling against the Dutch, and made his task more difficult. For example, when the Dutch destroyed several towns in Apollonia in May 1869, this created the greatest indignation. The Fantis were also suspicious of the Elminas, and accused them of instigating the Ashanti army to advance to the borders of Wassaw. But Simpson refused military aid and managed to persuede the Fanti leaders to 'postpone' any reprisals.[6]

Potentially a more serious affair was the kidnapping of four Dutch sailors by the villagers of Komenda. Simpson, however, called together some of the neighbouring Fanti Chiefs, and they promised to arrange for the release of the prisoners in exchange for four of their own messengers who were detained in Elmina. This episode prompted Ghartey to take official action as 'President

[1] Minutes of 21 and 24 June 1869; CO/96/80.

[2] Letter of May 1869, from J. Halford to Ghartey; Ghartey Papers No. 80, G.N. Archives.

[3] Horton, *Letters*, no. ii, dated 12 Sept. 1869.

[4] The British authorities did not take Ghartey very seriously. 'He proposed himself as the first President of the Fantee Confederacy, and caused some merriment by ordering a gold laced suit of uniform from England in anticipation of his office.' Dispatch No. 125 of 16 Dec. 1871, from Kennedy to Kimberley; CO/96/89.

[5] The main Dispatches and documents concerning the subsequent history of the Fanti Confederation were published in the Parliamentary Paper, *Copies or Extracts of all Correspondence between the Colonial Office and the Administrator of Cape Coast and with Mr. Pope Hennessy as Administrator in Chief, relative to the Fanti Confederation: And, of the Instructions given to Colonel Harley, the present Administrator at Cape Coast, with reference to the said Fanti Confederation and its Constitution* (London, 1873). For the purpose of the account that follows, reference has been made to the fuller documentation available in the Public Records Office, London, and the Ghana National Archives, Accra.

[6] Dispatch No. 50 of 5 June 1869, from Simpson to Kennedy; CO/96/80.

of the Fantee Confederation', using the title for the first time. Blankson wrote on his behalf, instructing the Chief of Komenda to hand over the Dutch prisoners to the messengers of 'the Confederate Government'.[1] But the Komendas did not obey these orders and procrastinated by arguing about ransom. The Confederation, in fact, was not very effective in this matter; only after considerable delay were the Dutch sailors released.[2]

Soon afterwards, fighting broke out in Dixcove between pro-Dutch and pro-English factions, and the town was bombarded from the Dutch fort, which did not help matters. Simpson reported 'the grossest mis-management' on the part of the Commandant, and warned that the Fantis were now determined to drive the Dutch from the coast by force of arms.[3] They were already collecting a poll tax to support their plans[4]—though there is no record of the amounts so raised—and they were encouraged by a report that the Elminas might agree to make an alliance with them.[5] Simpson did his best to ease the tension by helping to arrange a meeting in July 1869, between the Dutch authorities, accompanied by representatives of Elmina, and some influential Fantis, including Ghartey. Nagtglas now agreed that the Elminas might, if they desired, join the Fantis in alliance. But this concession had come too late to provide any good result and was probably interpreted by the Fantis as 'an indication of weakness'.[6]

The Fanti Confederation met in August to discuss disturbing reports of Ashanti advances.[7] The border tribes were now sending complaints to Mankessim concerning the failure of the Fantis to honour their promises and begging them to send practical aid instead of 'plausible words';[8] so the Chiefs decided to plan their own defensive action. Simpson was informed;[9] but he immediately accused them of taking the matter into their own hands without obtaining the prior approval of the British Government, and warned them that any action would be entirely on their own responsibility, nor could they expect to receive assistance. Their part of the Protectorate had not yet been

[1] Letter of 28 May 1869, from Blankson to Chief of Komenda, enclosed in Dispatch No. 70 of 20 June 1869, from Simpson to Kennedy; CO/96/80.

[2] Dispatch No. 77 of 24 June 1869, from Simpson to Kennedy; ibid. Also Horton, *Letters*, no. vii, dated 12 Feb. 1870.

[3] Dispatch No. 83 of 8 July 1869, from Simpson to Kennedy; CO/96/80.

[4] Ghartey Papers No. 89, G.N. Archives.

[5] Charles Bartels said at this time that he had told the Elminas not to expect the white man to remain for ever, for 'the people are getting enlightened and civilized, and soon will cry out, to govern themselves like Liberia.' Letter of 13 July 1869, to Ghartey; Ghartey Papers No. 93, ibid.

[6] Dispatch No. 75 of 27 July 1869, from Kennedy to Granville; CO/96/80.

[7] Replies to invitations to meeting at Mankessim, 25 Aug. 1869, preserved among the Ghartey Papers; e.g. Nos. 98 and 177, G.N. Archives.

[8] For example, undated Letter from King of Wassaw to Fanti Kings, and Letter of 17 Aug. 1889, from 'Deputies to the ceded tribes to the Dutch' to King Edoo; ibid. Nos. 183 and 367.

[9] Ghartey evidently did not tell Simpson of their plan also to take offensive action against Elmina; but this came to nothing, owing to ineffective leadership, according to a letter published in *The African Times*, 23 Nov. 1869.

attacked by the Ashantis, and Simpson did not think that it was likely to be.[1]

This unexpectedly discouraging reply was probably due to the fact that Simpson was still smarting under a recent Colonial Office reprimand for having too directly implicated the British Government when the Ashantis had been threatening the eastern districts. The combined effects of the Ashanti advances, Horton's publications, official vacillation, and the example of the Fantis led to somewhat similar developments in Accra during 1869. These merit brief examination, although Horton's Republic of Accra never came near to realization.

When the Ashantis, in alliance with the Akwamus, had been actively engaged against the Krepis early in 1869, Simpson had come hurrying over to Accra to rally the Chiefs in their own defence. He gave money to some of them to prepare an expedition, wrote a threatening letter to the Asantehene saying that the British fully intended to protect the former Dutch tribes to the east of the Volta, and even went up to Akwamu hoping to win over that State. His militant zeal was unabated after being held prisoner by the Akwamus for a few days;[2] but there soon came a crushing reminder from London that the British Government could not be held responsible for the defence of the tribes, and did not regard their wars as its own.[3]

Meanwhile, the educated community in Accra were becoming increasingly anxious about the absence of any united system of defence against Ashanti. A few of them attended the discussions at Mankessim during April and May, and were hoping against hope that their own traditional leaders would give a similar lead. Horrified to discover that the Chiefs had done nothing with Simpson's money except to share it, and unaware of the official side-stepping in London, they decided to take matters into their own hands and to form an alliance which they hoped might be the germ of the republican form of government advocated by Horton.[4]

William Lutterodt, 'the acknowledged head of the educated natives of Accra', took the initiative in August 1869 by calling a meeting in his house of all the educated inhabitants, numbering about sixty, at which the Kings of James Town, 'Dutch Accra', and Christiansborg were invited to outline their plans for defence. Dissatisfied with what they heard, several of them met again to elect a Managing Committee of six—Lutterodt as President, with James Bannerman, L. Hesse, G. F. Cleland, W. Addo, and J. E. Richter—to act in conjunction with the Kings and to draw up rules for their joint guidance.

[1] Letter of 8 Sept. 1869, to Ghartey from Simpson, enclosed in his Dispatch No. 118 of 3 Oct. 1869, to Administrator-in-Chief; CO/96/81.

[2] Letter of 8 Mar. 1869, to King of Ashanti from Simpson, enclosed in his Dispatch No. 26 of 22 Mar. 1869, to Kennedy; CO/96/79.

[3] Dispatch No. 43 of 17 May 1869, from Granville to Kennedy; ibid.

[4] Letter of 21 Sept. 1869, from James Bannerman to Horton, quoted in his *Letters*, no. iii, dated 12 Oct. 1869.

According to Bannerman, the Kings 'at once joyfully consented' to the proposal that they should renounce their initiative in matters affecting peace and order, and act only after consultation with the educated Africans. The day after the Committee had been appointed, they informed the Government, and proposed immediately to raise a force to meet the marauding bands who had crossed the Volta, claiming that they alone had power to act, but modestly applying for 'some slight assistance in the way of ammunition and money'.[1] Simpson replied in only lukewarm terms, doubting their estimate of their own ability and of the incompetence of the Chiefs, and querying the necessity for their appeal to arms.[2] But in London it was felt that even this had gone rather too far.[3]

Bannerman's optimism was undaunted, and he wrote to Horton: 'I doubt not that, with God's help, we shall soon learn practically the art of self-government.'[4] The educated group managed themselves to raise several hundred pounds; and in October Simpson found 'a national war' in progress, with all the eastern tribes in arms to drive the Ashantis out of Krepi.[5] He still felt they deserved some assistance; but the return of Ussher the following month put paid to any such hopes.

The Accra Committee would have liked to establish some permanent link with the Fanti Confederation, and towards the end of the year the two were reported to be 'in daily communication'.[6] But there was no continuing organization in Accra to compare with that of the Fantis; the educated leaders were able to stir up enthusiasm to fight against Ashanti, but there were no really powerful Chiefs to support them. Their attempt to supersede the traditional rulers seems to have been premature; at all events, nothing was heard of the 'Managing Committee of Educated Natives' in Accra after the end of 1869. By contrast, the persistent influence of the Fanti Confederation was acknowledged by implication in the severe report made on them by Ussher soon after his return:

This small knot of men, consisting of three or four Chiefs, with a semi-educated black at their head, as president, is quite powerless for good in the country. But although their orders are ridiculed by the other Chiefs, their constables beaten, and their attempts at collecting revenue met with defiance, they are still supported and approved by Fantee opinion in any acts which they may attempt hostile to Ashantee or Elmina.

[1] Letter of 14 Aug. 1869, from 'some educated natives of Accra' to Acting Civil Commandant, Accra, enclosed in Dispatch No. 108 of 3 Sept. 1869, from Simpson to Administrator-in-Chief; CO/96/81.
[2] Letter of 21 Aug. 1869, from Simpson to Civil Commandant, Accra; ibid.
[3] Minute of 9 Oct. 1869; ibid.
[4] Letter of 21 Sept. 1869, from James Bannerman to Horton; Letters, no. iii, dated 12 Oct. 1869.
[5] Letter of 13 Sept. 1869, from 'Members of the Managing Committee of Educated Natives of Accra' to Civil Commandant, and covering Dispatch No. 117 of 3 Oct. 1869, from Simpson to Administrator-in-Chief; CO/96/81.
[6] The African Times, 24 Jan. 1870.

To add insult to injury they were, he alleged, trying to impress the Ashantis with the idea that Ghartey was the 'Governor of the Gold Coast'.[1]

After the invaders had returned to Ashanti, the Administrator continued Simpson's negotiations with the Asantehene for the exchange of prisoners and the release of the European missionaries who had recently been captured in Anum.[2] The Fanti Chiefs seemed prepared to co-operate with Ussher and, in obedience to his orders, started to collect all the captured Ashantis in the Protectorate with the aim of an interchange on the banks of the Prah. But Ussher suspected Ghartey of carrying on separate negotiations with Kumasi, in spite of his denials,[3] and made him publicly acknowledge before the Ashanti messengers that the Fantis at Mankessim had no power 'to usurp Her Majesty's Prerogative' in this matter. To make this quite clear, Ussher wrote to inform the Asantehene that any communications he might receive direct from the Fanti Chiefs would have no weight whatever.[4]

A new and serious complication now arose. A small band of Ashantis, initially estimated at 200, led by the warlike Chief Adjiempon, was on the way to Elmina, committing atrocities in the Dutch coastal districts.[5] Ussher issued a proclamation warning Fantis against going into Elmina, and refused to issue arms or ammunition except in the case of an actual attack by Ashanti; but he feared that it would be difficult to keep the peace much longer.[6] Kennedy blamed the Dutch severely for having encouraged and let loose an uncontrolled horde of 'blood thirsty barbarians' upon a comparatively civilized community, 'whose original and only offence, was their refusal to accept and live under the Dutch flag, without their wishes or interests having been ever consulted'.[7] He visited the Gold Coast again, and after complaining to Nagtglas came to the conclusion that the Dutch Government, 'having vindicated the national honour by burning some villages, and killing some natives', would be glad to relinquish their Gold Coast possessions on any terms that might be offered.[8]

Ussher was also concerned to prevent the Fantis from provoking the

---

[1] Dispatch No. 142 of 2 Dec. 1869, from Ussher to Administrator-in-Chief; CO/96/81.

[2] See Ch. VII, p. 269, below.

[3] Ussher's suspicions were later confirmed by a published account of the delivery of a message from the Asantehene to the Fanti Confederation at Mankessim on 7 Dec. 1869. *The African Times*, 23 Feb. 1870.

[4] Letter of 10 Dec. 1869, to King of Ashanti from Ussher, and his covering Dispatch No. 145 of 17 Dec. 1869, to Kennedy; CO/96/84.

[5] For details of the dramatic career of Adjiempon, see Horton, *Letters*, no. viii, dated 12 Mar. 1870.

[6] Dispatches Nos. 20 of 15 Jan. and 30 of 26 Jan. 1870, from Ussher to Kennedy; CO/96/84.

[7] Confidential Dispatch of 8 Feb. 1870, from Kennedy to Granville; ibid.

[8] Dispatch No. 32 of 23 Mar. 1870, from Kennedy to Granville; ibid. Meanwhile the British Minister at The Hague had reported that the Dutch Government 'would be too glad to get rid of them if they could, but they are afraid to broach the matter to the King of the Netherlands, who is very sensitive about losing territory'. Confidential Dispatch No. 90 of 29 Sept 1869, from Harris to Clarendon; CO/96/82.

Ashantis. He complained early in 1870 of frequent and unnecessary outrages by the Assins on inoffensive Ashanti traders and messengers; and he asked the Fanti Confederation to settle this affair, although he had no confidence in their ability to do so.[1] Later, when an embassy arrived from Kumasi to negotiate the exchange of prisoners, Ussher was pessimistic about the chances of the Fantis making peace after the recent unprovoked attacks by the Ashantis in the Volta area, and their aid to the Elminas in the west. He realized, however, that any peace concluded without Fanti consent would be futile, and was particularly apprehensive of the possible obstinacy and jealousy of 'the small group of disaffected and silly persons styling themselves the "Fantee Confederation"'.[2] The King of Anomabu was still in the field with some of his troops; but when Ussher ordered him to leave Dutch territory, in order to avoid prejudicing the Ashanti negotiations, he obeyed at once. This left Ghartey as 'the only "Power" making actual war against the Dutch natives'. Ussher had by now discounted the Fanti Confederation as an active force. He himself hoped to introduce a town council for Cape Coast, which he believed would 'be more calculated to infuse a spirit of self-reliance, as a commencement of real self-government, than any hare-brained schemes of crafty and illiterate adventurers and drunken and barbarous "Bush Chiefs"'.[3]

Nothing came of Ussher's plans for local government; but he continued to refer scathingly to the bad management of the Fanti Confederation and their lack of ability even to establish unity or to carry out a single plan, except the attack on Elmina, which he attributed simply to 'a rush of popular passion and excitement'. Ussher considered that it had 'fallen to pieces of itself' without any opposition from the local Government.[4] But in fact he had, as he later admitted, taken fairly positive steps, out of loyalty to the Dutch as a friendly Power, to encourage this 'falling to pieces'; while behaving courteously to the leaders, he had succeeded in detaching the Chiefs one by one. Unable to see any good resulting from the activities of the Confederation, he 'ended by ignoring it, and allowed it to lapse of itself'.[5]

An example of Ussher's treatment of the leaders was his reception of their 'national seal'. This had been carefully made in England, and depicted an elephant standing against an oil-palm tree, encircled by the words 'The Government of the Fantee Confederacy, Mankessim'.[6] Ghartey was so proud of this that he sent it to Ussher to prove that union between the Fanti Chiefs was now an established fact; but the Administrator took great exception to the

[1] Dispatch No. 10 of 2 Jan. 1870, from Ussher to Kennedy; CO/96/84.

[2] Dispatch No. 96 of 11 July 1870, from Ussher to Kennedy; CO/96/85.

[3] Dispatches Nos. 135 of 19 Sept. and 143 of 11 Oct. 1870, from Ussher to Kennedy; ibid.

[4] Dispatch No. 148 of 13 Oct. 1870, from Ussher to Kennedy; ibid.

[5] Confidential Letter of 4 May 1872, from Ussher to Pope Hennessy, enclosed in his Dispatch No. 93 of 29 Oct. 1872, to Kimberley; CO/96/94.

[6] A newspaper correspondent even expressed the hope that soon 'another seal may have the words, "The Government of the Fantee and Accra Confederacy"'. The African Times, 24 Jan. 1870.

use of the word 'Government', summoned the President and alleged that this was treasonable. Ghartey wrote to apologize, with assurances of 'our attachment to the British Crown';[1] but the seal had to be sent back to England to have the word 'Council' substituted for 'Government'.[2]

During the latter part of 1870 government officials were preoccupied with the proposed final transfer of Dutch interests and property in the Gold Coast. No secret was made of these negotiations, on Ussher's advice, after his experience of 1868;[3] and it was hoped that the Elminas would gradually become accustomed to the idea if they had sufficient warning. A recent declaration of theirs was not very encouraging: 'On no account will we become English . . . We have suffered so much from the exchange of territory that we are tired and exhausted. Surely a man can be sold only once!'[4] The Convention was eventually signed in Holland in February 1871,[5] although it was not ratified until a year later.[6] It was therefore common knowledge that Britain was preparing to increase, rather than to withdraw from, her existing commitments in West Africa. But F. Fitzgerald, the editor of *The African Times*, saw the proposed transfer as an essential preliminary to handing over the Gold Coast to a united native government.[7] His newspaper still took the line that British withdrawal was only a matter of time.

The Influence of Africanus Horton

Meanwhile some hard thinking was going on among the educated handful. Horton was still very interested in the Confederation movement, through which, as he claimed in *Letters* published in 1870, 'the whole of the Fantee race, numbering some 400,000 souls, can now, for the first time, boast of a national assembly'. He called this 'the commencement of an independent self-government or confederation of all the provinces in the former Protectorate'; and blamed its 'present drooping state' upon the lack of official recognition, claiming that the Administrator 'circumvents the officers of the Confederation with petty annoyances, and humiliates its President . . . before the eyes of the nation'. Horton suggested that the Confederation required to be bound by a constitution and a code of law, in order to guide them 'in the mystic labyrinth of constitutional self-government'.

Horton urged that the relative position and jurisdiction of the British

---

[1] Letter of 14 Jan. 1870, from Ghartey to Ussher; Ghartey Papers No. 33, G.N. Archives.

[2] F. Fitzgerald criticized Ussher's handling of this episode in an editorial headed 'The Dog in the Manger'. *The African Times*, 23 Mar. 1870.

[3] Confidential Dispatch of 17 Oct. 1870, from Ussher to Kennedy; CO/96/85.

[4] Statement by Kings and Chiefs at Elmina on 19 Dec. 1870, quoted by Sir W. Lawson, M.P., who commented that such sentiments only showed 'how ignorant they were of civilised life'. *Parliamentary Debates*, House of Commons, 4 May 1874.

[5] For text, see J. J. Crooks, *Records relating to the Gold Coast Settlements from 1750 to 1874* (Dublin, 1923), pp. 393–6.   [6] See p. 256, below.

[7] Letter of 19 Apr. 1870, from Fitzgerald to Granville; CO/96/86.

authority and the Fanti Confederation must be strictly defined, and possible sources of revenue considered. For a start, the Administrator of the Gold Coast should be *ex officio* the 'Protector of the Fantee Confederation'. There should then be elected a President, two Ministers—one for internal and external affairs, and the other for industry and education—and a Chief Justice. A Confederate Diet should be established at Mankessim, with two divisions: 'the Royal', for all the Kings, with the principal Chiefs; and 'the Representative Assembly', to which each Province should send a certain number of members, elected by the votes of all the citizens. The President of the Confederation should be *ex officio* a member of the Legislative Council, to attend only when subjects relating to the interests of the Confederation were to be discussed.[1]

It was Dawson who acted as the most enthusiastic publicist for Horton's ideas. In August 1870 he sent an interesting letter to *The African Times*, addressed to 'the educated class of Fantees, through your kind and valuable paper'.[2] The history of the Mankessim Council was traced and then a possible form of constitution propounded, which closely followed the lines laid down by Horton. The Confederation was to be under the protection of the British Government in a carefully defined relationship. Dawson used Horton's word 'Diet' for the Parliament of the Confederation, which was to consist of two Houses: one for the Kings, and one, which he called 'the Commons', for members selected by each State. He added his own suggestion for a 'permanent Federative Diet' consisting of 'plenipotentiaries of all the States', who would be the executive ministers of the Confederation, entrusted with the management of its current affairs. They were to elect a President from among the Kings; but Dawson, evidently anxious to avoid further discord, suggested that the Kings should be 'taken in turns'. He also put forward detailed financial regulations, including provision for the plenipotentiaries to submit to the Diet all accounts of revenue and expenditure. Dawson ended with an appeal to educated Fantis 'to root out the love of prejudice and the desire to rise on the ruin of their neighbours, so as to make way for this Confederacy'.

The African Times commented editorially in the same issue that the Government 'ought to endeavour tenderly to guide this effort at federation in the right way'. Fitzgerald reminded his readers that ever since 1865 he had been contending that the Chiefs 'should be called to Council in assembly at regular periods', by which means they might learn to rule in association with the British Administrator and his officials, and become 'acquainted with the fundamental principles of civilised government'.[3]

---

[1] Horton, *Letters*, nos. ii, dated 12 Sept. 1869, and ix, dated 2 May 1870.

[2] Dawson had to write to London to reach a Gold Coast audience, since at that time there was no local newspaper apart from *The West African Herald*, then being published somewhat infrequently, in Freetown.

[3] Letter of 21 Aug. 1870, from Dawson, and editorial comment; *The African Times*, 24 Oct. 1870.

These publications aroused considerable interest; and by the beginning of 1871 Ussher was once more apprehensive that the Government was 'gravely menaced by the proceedings of the small knot of persons desirous of re-establishing the old and mischievous scheme of a "Bush" Fantee Government or Confederacy'. He appears to have been convinced—probably by the publication of the *Letters*—that Horton was the principal schemer; and he accumulated further incriminating evidence, to the effect that Horton had been acting as agent for *The African Times*, that he was not a native of the Gold Coast, and that he had been known to criticize the Dutch transfer 'in native society at Accra'. Ussher therefore warned the Army Staff Surgeon of the doctor's 'derogatory' conduct, expressed his intention of cancelling Horton's commission of the peace, and urged the Governor-in-Chief to have him removed to another Settlement.[1]

But Kennedy was not impressed. He did not believe in the 'grave menace', and took Horton's part, advising London that he had never heard a word against him either privately or professionally: 'Dr. Horton is undoubtedly "a Negro" as stated by the Administrator, but I cannot see that it disqualifies him from holding an opinion (which I have never seen improperly or violently stated in his writings) on the present or future of his native land.'[2] The Colonial Office dismissed the matter as 'another hasty indiscretion' of Ussher's, and saw nothing to justify Horton's removal; even if he had been acting for the Press, this could have been sufficiently dealt with by a caution.[3] It was fortunate for Horton, in fact, that his *Letters* had been sent to London and read on the files, even before publication, as they were formally addressed to the Secretaries of State for War and the Colonies. One official commented: 'Dr. Horton's letters have been very intelligent and temperate, and I was not prepared to hear that he was a negro.'[4]

Most of the Fanti tribes laid down their arms in response to a proclamation issued by Ussher at the end of 1870; but he complained that 'the silly representative of the Fantee Confederacy, Mr. Ghartey', was still fighting against the so-called Dutch tribes on the coast near Shama and Sekondi, outside British jurisdiction.[5] Ussher's critical reports were not taken very seriously in London, where he had the reputation of being rather an alarmist.

[1] Letter of 16 Jan. 1871, to Dr. Mosse from Ussher, and his covering Confidential Dispatch of 16 Jan. 1871, to Kennedy; CO/96/87.

[2] Confidential Dispatch of 25 Jan. 1871, from Kennedy to Kimberley; ibid. Horton's latest book had been dedicated to Kennedy and contained several compliments to him as 'the right man in the right place', to whom the people of the Gold Coast must look 'as the steersman at the helm of the Fantee national vessel'. *Letters*, no. ix, dated 2 May 1870.

[3] One official suggested that 'Mr. Ussher must have read the Doctor's letters, & found something in the description of "what is requisite in the character of an administrator of the Gold Coast" which he fancied was aimed at himself. His action appears to me arbitrary & injudicious.' Minute of 2 Mar. 1871; the Secretary of State noted, 'I agree'. CO/96/87.

[4] Minute of 28 Feb. 1871; ibid.

[5] Dispatch No. 14 of 26 Jan. 1871, from Ussher to Kennedy; ibid.

In April 1871 he was reassured by his success in getting the Chiefs and their representatives to meet the Governor-in-Chief, and to discuss the Ashanti question, without referring to the Fanti Confederation or applying for assistance to them.[1] By July, when Ussher went on leave, his suspicions had been allayed, and he reported that the Gold Coast was 'in perfect peace'.[2]

The Constitution of the Fanti Confederation, 1871

The development of the Confederation falls reasonably clearly into two phases. The first, precipitated by the high-handed attitude of the European Powers, had been marked by actual fighting against the Dutch, which was broken off only by the stern discouragement of Ussher, in spite of the brief interlude of friendly advances from Simpson. The *raison d'être* of the military alliance was removed by the negotiations for the final purchase of all Dutch territory; but the habit of consultation and co-operation among the Fanti Chiefs and their educated advisers continued, and the Confederation, although temporarily subdued, had not been dissolved or dispersed in any meaningful sense. While Ussher was away, the organization shook off its 'apathetic slumber', and entered upon a second phase of more peaceful and constructive planning. In view of what followed, it is important to insist upon the essential continuity of development from one stage to the other.

In October 1871 a meeting of all the Chiefs of the Fanti Confederation and their advisers was convened at Mankessim. *The African Times* in London hinted that important new developments were to be expected; and, in fact, Dawson had already written to Fitzgerald, who now publicly called upon the Confederation to fulfil the growing hopes of Gold Coast advancement. He also renewed his criticism of the Government for not recognizing the 'mighty germ of power for good' in the organization: 'This . . . was the true "dog in the manger" spirit; they could not eat the hay of power throughout the interior countries themselves, and they could not bear that the kings, chiefs, and educated natives should eat it.'[3] C. S. Salmon, the Acting Administrator, was already suspicious of the activities of the Mankessim group, especially of Ghartey, who was accused of having always acted in opposition to the policy and wishes of the Government.[4]

The educated leaders, aware of the official attitude, decided, unlike *The African Times*, that caution was necessary. The following pencilled memorandum, later found among their papers, indicated their new plan of campaign:

[1] Confidential Letter of 4 May 1872, from Ussher to Pope Hennessy; CO/96/94. See also *The West African Herald*, 31 Mar. 1871.

[2] Dispatch No. 82 of 15 July 1871, from Ussher to Administrator-in-Chief; CO/96/88.

[3] *The African Times*, 23 Nov. 1871. Also issue of 23 Jan. 1872, for reference to Dawson's Letter of 5 July 1871.

[4] Dispatches Nos. 140 of 7 Dec. 1871, from Salmon to Kennedy, and 125 of 16 Dec. 1871, from Kennedy to Kimberley; CO/96/89.

Ghartey's issuing circulars creates distrust, first with Govt. & with natives. Confederation to be commenced by Kings—Confedertn. to be confined as clearly as possible to Chiefs in interior leaving sea coast for present. Ground work of Constitution to be first formed—then others can join—by these means collision with Govt. will be avoided—& when things are properly worked others will join. Kings & Chiefs should avoid communicating with people at C.C. Confederation should be confined as closely as can be to the Chiefs in the interior for the present because the B. Govt. exercises supreme authority on the sea coast. The educated people may be sent for—& any interference of the people with Coast towns may bring the Confedrn. into collision with the Govt. Confederation for express purpose of improving the interior & developing resources of country.[1]

Although this document was subsequently taken by officials as confirmation of their worst suspicions, it is difficult to find any fault with it on constitutional grounds. There is no challenge to the direct colonial rule exercised by the British on the coast, and no apparent subversive intentions concerning the Protectorate. The main inference to be drawn from it is that any overt collaboration between the Chiefs and their educated subjects was being driven underground by official disapproval; and this might indeed have led to serious trouble.

But the main business of the latest Mankessim meeting was to draw up a constitution for the Fanti Confederation.[2] This was signed by thirty-one Kings and Chiefs (or their representatives) on 18 November 1871, and its main features were as follows:

1. An *Executive Council* was to consist of five elected officials, 'the Ministry' (viz. a Vice-President, Secretary, Under-Secretary, Treasurer, and Assistant Treasurer), who must be 'men of education and position', plus such others as might be thereafter appointed. Their main duties would be to prepare legislation and see that it was administered, 'to examine carefully the financial condition of the Confederation', to hear certain appeal cases and disputes, and to determine enstoolments according to a majority vote of the people.

2. A *Representative Assembly* was to be responsible for legislation. Each of the Kings and principal Chiefs was to nominate two representatives: one to be an educated man, the other a Chief or headman. The Vice-President would preside.

3. A *National Assembly*, composed of all the Kings and principal Chiefs, was to meet annually in October. The Kings attending would elect a King-President for each year; and the National Assembly would hear the business done during the year by the Representative Assembly, discuss the forthcoming programme, and elect members of the Ministry to hold office for three years.

[1] Enclosure A in Confidential Dispatch of 3 Jan. 1872, from Salmon to Kennedy; CO/96/92.
[2] Enclosure A in Dispatch No. 128 of 16 Dec. 1871, from Kennedy to Kimberley; CO/96/89. It was later printed for Parliament under the title, 'Constitution of the New Fantee Confederacy' —see *Correspondence . . . relative to the Fanti Confederation* (London, 1873), pp. 3–8—and again reproduced in that form by J. E. Casely Hayford, *Gold Coast Native Institutions* (London, 1903), pp. 327–40, and by J. Mensah Sarbah, *Fanti National Constitution* (London, 1906), pp. 199–209. But the title did not form part of the original document, and must have been added for the printers in London by those who thought it was a 'new' venture; see pp. 253 and 255–6, below.

4. The *King-President*—a kind of constitutional monarch—was to act on the advice of his Ministry, and to sanction all laws passed by the Representative Assembly.

5. *Administration*. The members of the Representative Assembly were to be responsible in their own areas for the implementation of legislation. Provincial Assessors were to be appointed in each district; their duties were to include the holding of courts.

6. *Finance*. Arrangements were to include a Board of Officers (viz. a Vice-President, Secretary, Treasurer, and one King) to check the cash in hand each quarter. Surplus cash was to be placed in a special chest, for which three officials would each hold a separate key.

7. *Oaths of Allegiance* to the King-President were to be taken by all Kings and Chiefs, their captains and headmen, and 'the educated persons who express a wish to join the Confederation', as well as the office bearers.

8. *Relations with the British Government*. Summonses from the British authorities were to be carried into effect without delay. If appeals were made to British courts, then the minutes of the proceedings were to be forwarded, and assistance was to be given by the officers of the Confederation.

The constitution also contained a statement of aims which included the promotion of friendly intercourse between the Fanti Chiefs, a union for offensive and defensive purposes, and 'the improvement of the country at large', including the building of roads and schools, as well as the development of agriculture, industry, and mineral resources.

Although the constitution reveals the direct influence of Horton's book, as interpreted by Dawson and others, it is of considerable significance as the first written scheme to emerge from this joint venture of the Chiefs and the educated *élite*. It differs in one important respect from previous suggestions: instead of keeping the Houses for Chiefs and for commoners rigidly apart they were now to sit together in the main legislative body, the Representative Assembly. This would seem to indicate that their co-operation and mutual trust were greater than had originally seemed possible, and certainly closer than the Government would have liked. The constitution did not, however, propose any direct link with the Legislative Council, as Horton had done, presumably because of the great care taken not to tread on any official toes. Finally, a constructive programme was offered, which, however vague and lacking in practical 'know-how', could have tapped a considerable fund of local initiative and enthusiasm.

After the constitution had been signed and sealed, the Chiefs proceeded to hold the first meeting of the National Assembly, and to elect the officers of the Confederation. But no agreement could be reached on who should be President. The two rival Kings, Edoo of Mankessim and Otoo of Abura, were therefore appointed 'to perform jointly the duties of the office of the King-President of the Fanti Confederation, pending the election of the said King-President'. The other officers were:

Vice-President:	W. E. Davidson
Secretary:	J. F. Amissah
Under-Secretary:	J. H. Brew
Treasurer:	F. C. Grant
Assistant Treasurer:	J. M. Abadoo

In addition, R. J. Ghartey, G. Amissah, S. Ferguson, G. Blankson jun., J. M. Insaidoo, and J. D. Hayford were appointed to the Fanti Executive Council.[1] Fitzgerald of *The African Times* was appointed agent in England, to 'further the interests of the Confederation'. He promptly published the constitution and other documents in full, and greeted the episode, optimistically if a little prematurely, as 'the birth of a NATION'.[2]

After the elections the Fanti National Assembly took decisions on organization and policy. It was agreed that, by the end of the year, the Kings and Chiefs should forward the names of their representatives for the legislature; until then the executive should be empowered to appoint officers in the field 'for the purpose of carrying on the Government'. A 'law' was passed providing for the collection of a poll tax, and for import and export duties.[3]

Rejection by Salmon

The National Assembly also approved a letter to be sent to the Governor-in-Chief, informing him of these developments, and enclosing a copy of the new constitution and other relevant documents for the information of the Secretary of State. They assured Kennedy that their sole object was to improve the condition of their peoples, and 'not to interfere with but to aid our benefactors on the Sea Coast'; and they asked for his assistance.[4] On 30 November 1871 Davidson and Brew called upon the Acting Administrator, who seems to have lost both his head and his temper. Salmon at first refused to receive and forward the documents, and said they must be withdrawn within 48 hours; later the same evening he had Davidson and Amissah arrested. Warrants were then issued for the arrest of the other members of the executive of the Confederation; and Ferguson, Insaidoo, Hayford, Abadoo, and G. Blankson jun. were quickly apprehended. The eight prisoners were released on bail, but were warned not to leave Cape Coast.[5]

It is clear that Salmon was furious at being presented with a *fait accompli*.

[1] Ghartey was now publicly thanked for his past services, presumably to prevent hard feelings. But he had signed the constitution as 'President', evidently considering himself still in office until the elections had been held. This would seem to support the view that the 'new' Confederation was merely a more systematic development of that of 1869, which Salmon was later to deny.

[2] *The African Times*, 23 Jan. 1872.

[3] Resolutions passed at first meeting of the National Assembly of the Fanti Confederation, 18 Nov. 1871, enclosed in Dispatch No. 128 of 16 Dec. 1871, from Kennedy to Kimberley; CO/96/89.

[4] Letter of 24 Nov. 1871, from Kings-President of the Fanti Confederation and others to Kennedy; ibid.

[5] Dispatch No. 134 of 4 Dec. 1871, from Salmon to Kennedy; ibid. The episode was colourfully described in *The African Times*, 23 Jan. 1872, under the heading, 'Real African Martyrs'.

The Confederation documents were handed over 'for information', without any request for his sanction to their proceedings. When he came to question individually those he had arrested, the office-holders told him that their intention had been to seek the sanction of the Government. But Salmon claimed that this was exactly what had not been done;[1] he should have been informed of the nature of the latest meeting at Mankessim, and invited to send a representative if he so desired. In this there was a certain amount of personal pique; 'I consider that I have not been treated with the proper respect due to the Queen's representative', he later told the Fanti Chiefs.[2]

Salmon was also shocked to find that some of the most prominent Africans, whose confidence he thought he had won, had been involved in the proceedings behind his back; especially F. C. Grant—a prosperous merchant and a member of the Legislative Council—whose name appeared as Treasurer. One of his first steps was to demand a written disavowal from Grant, who, fearing governmental anger, improbably denied all knowledge of the affair.[3] But the sense of personal insult persisted, as shown in Salmon's private letters to Kennedy.[4]

In spite of this, the harshness of Salmon's action seems difficult to explain. He appears to have deduced that since they had succeeded in keeping him in the dark, this must be a dangerous conspiracy, threatening British control; it therefore had to be destroyed for good, or the country would become 'altogether unmanageable'.[5] He assumed that because the proceedings at Mankessim were unauthorized, they were also illegal,[6] and with enviable certitude stated: 'The law of the matter is clear. The authority of the Protecting Power respecting life and death, the levying of taxes and the making of treaties with foreign powers, and the supremacy of its Courts is well established by custom and precedent, and could not be departed from without dire confusion resulting.'[7]

---

[1] Dispatch No. 148 of 10 Dec. 1871, from Salmon to Kennedy; CO/96/89.

[2] Letter of 20 Dec. 1871, to Kings and Chiefs from Salmon, enclosed in his Dispatch No. 24 of 16 Feb. 1872, to Administrator-in-Chief; CO/96/92.

[3] Grant claimed that he did not even know his name had been mentioned as Treasurer, and added: 'I would not encourage any acts having a tendency to lessen British rule and influence in the Country.' Letter of 1 Dec. 1871, to Salmon, enclosed in Dispatch No. 128 of 16 Dec. 1871, from Kennedy to Kimberley; CO/96/89. But Grant had already written to Amissah on 21 Nov. 1871: 'I . . . can see no reason why I should refuse their offer of acting as treasurer to the Confederation', and added: 'The grand principle is, Help yourself . . . The Government will make a colony of the coast if we do not stir ourselves to self-government.' The African Times, 23 Mar. 1872.

[4] For example, 'Grant behaved bad in keeping me in the dark, also Blankson.' Private Letters of 4 Dec. 1871, from Salmon to Kennedy; CO/96/89. George Blankson sen. was, like Grant, a member of the Legislative Council.

[5] Dispatch No. 134 and Private Letter of 4 Dec. 1871, from Salmon to Kennedy; ibid.

[6] The Parliamentary Under-Secretary of State pertinently commented: 'If we approve of the Administrator's conduct, it appears to me that we shall be saying in effect that we will allow no attempt at the development of the principles of self-government in the Protectorate unless & until we initiate it ourselves.' Minute of 9 Jan. 1872, by E. H. Knatchbull-Hugessen; ibid.

[7] Dispatch No. 148 of 10 Dec. 1871, from Salmon to Kennedy; ibid. Two weeks later, however,

The Confederation had not challenged British authority on any of these matters, except perhaps in drawing up an agreement binding the Wassaw Chiefs to put an end to human sacrifices,[1] and in their tax proposals. In fact, they had been levying various dues on trade for some time, and had been anxious to substitute a permanent poll tax, following the war-time precedent of 1869.[2] But Salmon seems to have assumed that these were now intended to be levied throughout the Protectorate, and that they would supplant government taxes, since 'people would not stand a double taxation'. He argued that the export duty would be pernicious, even if levied only at the ports; but that if exacted from the producers on the way to the coast it would be disastrous.[3] He was later assured by persons whom he considered responsible that the proposed taxes would soon have led to civil war, requiring British intervention.[4] Salmon complained that the Government had for a long time been attempting to achieve the stated objects of the Confederation, while the originators had, 'more than all else, hindered us, by keeping up a state of feud, and destroying unity and confidence'.[5]

But in the heat of the moment Salmon had not thought out all the detailed arguments for action; he simply arrested all those he could lay hands on because he was afraid of their going to Mankessim and setting the Government at defiance. A few days afterwards he reported that the Confederation had received its *coup de grâce*, and things were settling down quietly again: the episode had caused no ill-feeling whatever in the country, and the hand of the Government would be strengthened thereby.[6]

The Governor-in-Chief was easily convinced that the main motive was pecuniary speculation, by means of the levy, on the part of individuals without any education, means, or character. But he took a more detached view of the whole matter from Sierra Leone, saying that he had long known of the contemplated movement, which was 'too absurd and impracticable to be seriously considered'. He did not believe it was supported by the Fanti Chiefs, and attributed the constitution to Fitzgerald and Rainy of *The African Times*,[7]

Salmon reported 'the Judge is here now, he is very cautious, he thought the arrest of parties a false move'. Private Letter of 24 Dec. 1871, to Kennedy; CO/96/92.

[1] This agreement was executed by Dawson in the name of the Fanti Confederation on 19 Nov. 1871, and published in *The African Times*, 23 Jan. 1872; but it is not clear whether the Government yet knew of this.

[2] On 5 Feb. 1870 Ghartey wrote as 'Representative of the Council of Fantee Confederation' to Ussher, saying that the people objected to their tollage on palm-oil and would prefer to pay the poll tax which he said had been recommended by Simpson at the Mankessim meeting. As recently as Aug. 1871 salt was being collected as a form of taxation, one-third being retained by the local Chief and two-thirds by the Confederation. Ghartey Papers Nos. 34 and 145, G.N. Archives.

[3] Confidential Letter of 23 Dec. 1871, from Salmon to Kennedy; CO/96/92.

[4] Confidential Dispatch of 20 Jan. 1872, from Salmon to Administrator-in-Chief; ibid.

[5] Dispatch No. 134 of 4 Dec. 1871, from Salmon to Kennedy; CO/96/89.

[6] Private Letter of 10 Dec. 1871, from Salmon to Kennedy; CO/96/92.

[7] W. Rainy, a West Indian barrister, was reported in 1865 to have 'attained the highest eminence as an advocate in the Supreme Court of Sierra Leone'. He was associated with several

'whose powers of mischief are happily decreasing as the violence of their language and recklessness of assertion increase'. Nevertheless, Kennedy supported Salmon for his firmness and moderation in promptly taking the only possible course, where there was no precedent to guide him.[1]

Kennedy believed that if the purport of the constitution were explained to the signatories they would at once repudiate it. This had also occurred to Salmon; and he sent a letter to the leading Chiefs, asking them whether they approved the proceedings, which, he claimed, if fully carried out would cause disunion in the country and sever its connexion with England. Only one answer was possible: 'favourable' replies were received from the Kings of Ekkoonfie, Essie Coomah, Gomuah, Western Gomuah, and the Chief of Tantum.[2] The King of Edjumakoo claimed that he had been represented at Mankessim by a messenger who was forced by Ghartey to hold a pen putting the King's name to a letter, 'which he knows not content neither myself. . . I shall not, therefore, be able to approve of the proceedings.'[3] But a Gold Coast correspondent to *The African Times*[4] warned readers against attaching too much weight to these disclaimers; if a man of Grant's education, position, and influence could be frightened into a denial, although he had committed himself in writing, what could be expected from 'poor, ignorant, semi-savage kings'?

Salmon also succeeded in stopping the tax imposed by the King of Mankessim on produce passing through his territory, which had nearly brought the Cape Coast interior trade to a standstill.[5] But his main efforts were directed towards finding incriminating material to discredit those responsible for the constitution, whom he considered 'a parcel of half-educated schemers'. Apart from the influence of Fitzgerald, who was in direct correspondence with Mankessim, he thought the constitution had been drafted by James Brew, 'a penniless lawyer, with an *awful* private character (a half caste)';[6] Horton's assistance was suspected, but difficult to prove.[7] Salmon's researches resulted in a sketch of the Chiefs and office-holders so full of scandal that the Secretary of State later commented: 'If the Administrator's account is correct the Chiefs of the "Confederacy" are a set of drunken scoundrels.'[8]

Freetown newspapers, and founded *The West African Liberator*; but after three years of struggle he published a 'Farewell Address' to the paper's subscribers and left for London in 1871, where he collaborated with Fitzgerald and harried the Colonial Office about Sierra Leone affairs. *The African Times*, 23 Dec. 1865, and 22 July 1871.

[1] Dispatch No. 128 of 16 Dec. 1871, from Kennedy to Kimberley; CO/96/92.

[2] Letter of 20 Dec. 1871, from Salmon to Fanti Kings and Chiefs, with their replies, and covering Dispatch No. 24 of 16 Feb. 1872, from Salmon to Administrator-in-Chief; ibid.

[3] Letter of 29 Dec. 1871, from King of Edjumakoo to Salmon, enclosed in his Confidential Dispatch of 20 Jan. 1872, to Administrator-in-Chief; ibid.   [4] 21 Feb. 1872.

[5] Dispatch No. 153 of 25 Dec. 1871, from Salmon to Kennedy; CO/96/92.

[6] Salmon really let himself go in describing Brew: 'a native practitioner in the Courts here, rather a sharp fellow, his private character is infamous, he had even to leave here once for some time on account of having had a child by his own sister'.

[7] Private Letters of 4 and 24 Dec. 1871, from Salmon to Kennedy; CO/96/89 and 92.

[8] Minute of 29 Jan. 1872, by Kimberley; CO/96/92.

Salmon attempted to make a distinction between what he called the first Confederation, and the recent 'audacious assumption'. When Simpson had visited Mankessim, all the Fanti Kings and Chiefs had been there and even some representatives from Accra; now there were only Mankessim and Abura. He enclosed a map to show the farthest limits of the support they could claim; this consisted of a small circle drawn around Mankessim, with the note: 'all except within the circle marked have declared against the Confederacy'.[1] But this, as had already been pointed out in *The African Times*, did not prove that the other Chiefs had not been involved in the drafting of the constitution; and the argument was hardly relevant to the relationship between the earlier and later forms of the Confederation. The Governor-in-Chief at this stage took Salmon's representations on trust, dismissing the scheme as a failure and its leaders as worthless, 'for the most part bankrupt and characterless mulattoes'. He reported to London: 'I cannot learn that there is a single English speaking native or person of whole character connected with this foolish project; the promoters ... having failed in all honest business have now as a last and desperate resource adopted Patriotism.'[2]

Meanwhile there was considerable concern in the Colonial Office, where lengthy minutes were being written on the episode. It was felt that Salmon had made a grave mistake in his arrests and was unlikely to secure a conviction for conspiracy: that the articles of the constitution were probably not intended to conflict with British jurisdiction: and that the sponsors would have been ready enough to submit their scheme to the Administrator for modification if he had exercised a little more judgement.[3] If the movement was 'too absurd and impracticable to be seriously considered', as Kennedy said, it was surely not worth while to make so many political martyrs, each of whom would be bound to claim compensation. The *1865 Report* was recalled: if the Fantis were now honestly seeking to develop those qualities which would fit them for self-government, 'with what face can we arbitrarily oppose them?' It was suggested that Salmon should have received and forwarded the Mankessim documents, though he could still have deferred recognition of the constitution until he had received advice from London.[4]

The Secretary of State agreed that Salmon had made a great blunder, but suggested that his action should be disavowed 'in as gentle a manner as is consistent with disavowal'.[5] As a result, instructions were sent that if the court proceedings had not yet taken place they should be stayed, and the parties freed from bail. But this was accompanied by a reprimand so mild as

---

[1] Private Letter of 24 Dec. 1871, from Salmon to Kennedy; ibid.

[2] Confidential Dispatch of 2 Jan. and Dispatch No. 14 of 9 Jan. 1872, from Kennedy to Kimberley; ibid. Cf. Dr. Johnson: 'Patriotism is the last refuge of a scoundrel.' And note the official correlation between 'English speaking' and 'of whole character'.

[3] Minute of 6 Jan. 1872, by H. T. Holland; CO/96/89.

[4] Minute of 9 Jan. 1872, by Knatchbull-Hugessen; ibid.

[5] Minute of 11 Jan. 1872, by Kimberley; ibid.

almost to amount to an endorsement of Salmon's attitude; Kimberley simply regretted the arrests and stated that the Administrator should have confined himself to issuing a proclamation warning British subjects against taking office under the Confederation.[1]

Salmon, as yet unaware of Colonial Office reactions, had decided to look for further incriminating evidence. A search was made under warrant for 'Mankessim papers' in Cape Coast, in the course of which three more Fantis were arrested for alleged obstruction of the police; this time bail was refused.[2] Few documents were found, but Salmon was confirmed in his belief in the rightness of his own action. Although the 'educated gentlemen' who planned the scheme were aiming to rule only in the Protectorate 'for the present', he was sure that they intended to supplant British rule as quickly as possible in the coast towns as well as in the interior.[3] The worst feature was the way in which all the power was to be taken from the Chiefs and placed in the hands of the 'Ministry', composed of young men of doubtful respectability and scanty means.[4]

Salmon's Dispatches took on a more conciliatory tone after he had received the 'gentle disavowal' from the Colonial Office. He released the Confederation leaders from bail, and claimed that he had not after all intended to prosecute them, as their absence from Mankessim had had the desired effect. But even during this period, further appeals for Fanti support had been sent out;[5] although they were couched in respectful language, Salmon was still nervous that such statements might cause further mischief.[6] The Secretary of State's suggestion no doubt made him feel on safe ground in issuing a proclamation in February 1872, 'to warn all loyal subjects against taking office under the said Constitution'. This announced that almost all the Kings and Chiefs had repudiated the constitution, and added the more doubtful statement: 'the Queen's Government has likewise disapproved thereof deeming the so-called Constitution to be subversive of those relations which have for a long time past subsisted between Great Britain and this Country, and certainly leading to the discontinuance thereof.'[7] Kimberley was glad to learn that so many had disavowed the Confederation, which he now felt could not have been countenanced by the British, although he noted that the words 'deeming . . . continuance thereof' went somewhat beyond the terms of his previous Dispatch.[8]

Meanwhile Fitzgerald was bombarding the Colonial Office with protests,

[1] Dispatch No. 147 of 16 Jan. 1872, from Kimberley to Kennedy; CO/96/89.

[2] Dispatch No. 93 of 29 Oct. 1872, from Pope Hennessy to Kimberley; CO/96/94.

[3] Confidential Dispatch of 3 Jan. 1872, from Salmon to Kennedy, and enclosures; CO/96/92.

[4] Confidential Dispatch of 20 Jan. 1872, from Salmon to Administrator-in-Chief; ibid.

[5] For example, Circular of Jan. 1872, from Kings Edoo, Otoo, and others at Mankessim 'To the Educated Gentlemen of Fanti'. The African Times, 23 Feb. 1872.

[6] Dispatches Nos. 23 and 24 of 16 Feb. 1872, from Salmon to Administrator-in-Chief; CO/96/92.   [7] Proclamation of 12 Feb. 1872; ibid.

[8] Minute of 19 Apr. 1872, by Kimberley; CO/96/93.

in his capacity as London agent of the Confederation.[1] For example, he complained that the arrests and imprisonments were 'a wanton and brutal outrage', at least by proxy, against all the Fanti Kings, Chiefs, and people; and he asked for their immediate release. Again, he argued that it had been necessary to promulgate and act upon the constitution before submitting it to the Government, in order that there might be a real organization to deal with.[2] He even claimed that the proposed transfer of Dutch territory had been made possible entirely by the Confederation; the Colonial Office justifiably called this 'a sheer piece of presumption'.[3] Fitzgerald's *pièce de résistance* was a 23-page letter, in February 1872, which was officially filed under the heading 'Past, Present & Future of the West African Settlements'. This largely took the form of a defence of the rights of 'The Educated Native Mercantile Communities'; but he also criticized past civil servants as inferior and disreputable, and urged that a higher class of European influence and example was needed, because: 'Nations are forming; and proper and adequate impulse and direction ought to be given by the Supreme power.' In particular, the union of all the Fantis in the Confederation should be promoted, not discouraged, as he had been urging ever since the British Government had renounced 'the efficient Protectorate', as he put it, in 1865. He hoped that educated Africans, with the Chiefs forming the Fanti Confederation, would be granted 'an independent voice and co-operating action in the Government of the British West African Settlements'.[4]

Salmon, when asked to comment on these letters, was not to be outdone—his reply ran to 35 pages. He took the occasion to deny again that there was any connexion between the old and the new Confederation. He had already reported: 'The promoters of the new scheme seeing their difficulties, are now endeavouring to confound the new with the previous Confederacy'.[5] Salmon now sought to prove that the original Confederation had been a spontaneous movement of the Chiefs, for the sole purpose of carrying on hostilities against the Dutch and their allies, and against Adjiempon;[6] that the movement had requested but never been given British support; and that the projected annexation of Dutch territory, together with the Ashanti peace negotiations, had caused it to die out altogether.

---

[1] *The Gold Coast Times*, 28 Mar. 1874, hailed Fitzgerald 'as the good Samaritan of our people. ... There certainly had been before ... such men as Wilberforce, Buxton and others ... But ... there was no regular, honest, thorough exponent of official African abuses—no genuine representative of our neglected interests, in the favoured land of the "superior order of white skinned beings".'

[2] Letters of 2 and 20 Jan. 1872, from Fitzgerald to Kimberley; CO/96/95.

[3] Letter of 3 Feb. 1872, from Fitzgerald to Kimberley, and minute thereon; ibid.

[4] Letter of 2 Mar. 1872, from Fitzgerald to Kimberley; ibid.

[5] Confidential Dispatch of 3 Jan. 1872, from Salmon to Kennedy; CO/96/92.

[6] Yet in Dec. 1868 (long before Adjiempon was heard of) Simpson had complained of 'the "scholars" or semi-educated natives hitherto in uncontrolled ascendancy' over the Council; see p. 234, above.

The 'new Confederacy' on the other hand, according to Salmon, was organized entirely by the individuals he had arrested, materially aided by Fitzgerald. The Chiefs were outside the movement—or so they had protested to him—while the great majority of the inhabitants had had 'no hand whatever' in drawing up the constitution.[1] Salmon was no doubt correct in challenging Fitzgerald's assertion that the documents represented the views and desires of the entire Fanti people, and in emphasizing their preference for old traditions. But it is difficult to see how he expected the majority to have had a hand in the drafting; nor did he show how the Confederation conflicted with tradition. His only purpose seems to have been to dismiss the latest developments as an isolated criminal conspiracy.

The Fanti Confederation Scheme, 1872

The Confederation, however, survived even Salmon's public arrests and private calumny. A change of officials early in 1872, both at Freetown and Accra, relieved the tension and induced what might almost be called an Indian summer. The Fanti spokesmen received such reasonable treatment from J. Pope Hennessy, the new Administrator-in-Chief, that they were soon encouraged to put up a reasoned scheme for a limited form of internal self-government, subject to British approval and support.

Ussher, on resuming the government, issued a new proclamation in March 1872, threatening to prosecute anyone 'committing any overt acts on the part of the said Confederation, especially the levying of taxes, assumption of judicial power, and molestation of peaceful inhabitants'. He sent copies of this to all the Chiefs, asking them to spare no endeavours to make such arrests.[2] But Pope Hennessy quickly told Ussher to suspend the proclamation until he himself had an opportunity of looking into the whole question on the spot.[3] In London it was regarded as milder in tone than Salmon's proclamation but not altogether wise.[4] Meanwhile Adjiempon, who had been the main obstacle to a settlement with the Dutch, had at last been removed from Elmina. The treaty of cession had been ratified in February 1872, but Pope Hennessy had been instructed that he was not to take over finally from the Dutch unless he was personally satisfied that it was the general wish of the people concerned.[5] He therefore travelled to the Gold Coast and effected the transfer in April in an atmosphere of apparent calm.[6] Soon afterwards, however, a riot

---

[1] Dispatch No. 24 of 16 Feb. 1872, from Salmon to Administrator-in-Chief; CO/96/92.

[2] Proclamation of 9 Mar. 1872, and Confidential Circular, enclosed in Dispatch No. 31 of 9 Mar. 1872, from Ussher to Pope Hennessy; ibid.

[3] Dispatch No. 44 of 18 Mar. 1872, from Pope Hennessy to Ussher; ibid.

[4] Minute of 8 Apr. 1872; ibid.

[5] For the Elmina deputation of protest to the Netherlands early in 1872, see Ch. XI, p. 411, below. In Mar. 1873 the King refused to take the British oath of allegiance, and was imprisoned in Cape Coast Castle. CO/96/97. He was then deported to Sierra Leone for twenty-one years.

[6] Ussher's map, reproduced on the opposite page, shows the extent of territory which

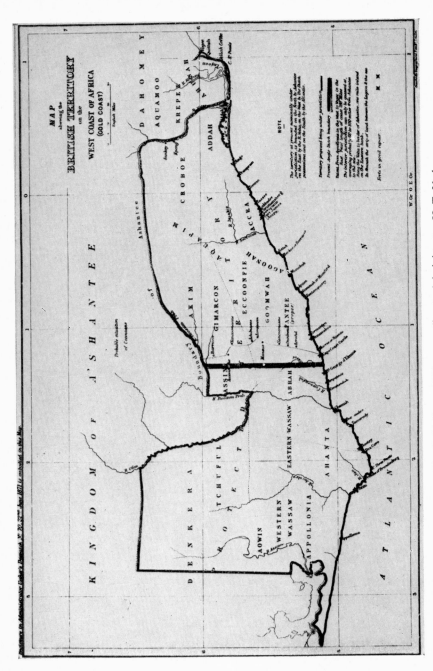

MAP 5B. The Gold Coast, 1871—according to Administrator H. T. Ussher.

took place in Elmina, and a Dutch officer was killed. Ussher was censured for inaction;[1] and the following month he left the country, his health broken.[2]

Pope Hennessy had been annoyed on arrival in Cape Coast to find the latest proclamation still in force, due to an 'oversight', as Ussher had explained. The Fanti Confederation leaders took advantage of the public reversal of policy to lobby Pope Hennessy. He gave verbal approval to some of their plans, and promised to consider their full programme favourably if they sent it to him for transmission to London. A few days later he received a detailed scheme, under which the Fanti Confederation was to carry on a government in the interior, with the 'recognition, countenance and support, and hearty co-operation of Her Majesty's Government'.

Three main matters were dealt with in the scheme. First, there were to be two distinct judicial systems, the authority and jurisdiction of the Confederation and of the local Government being clearly defined. The balance of power was tilted slightly in favour of the British courts, which were to have the right to hear appeals from those of the Confederation; there was also to be mutual provision for the extradition of criminals. Secondly, the Vice-President of the Confederation and 'four other gentlemen, natives or residents of the Gold Coast', were to be added to the Legislative Council, as elected and not nominated members; both eastern and western districts were to be represented.

Thirdly, came a set of financial proposals, based on an ambitious estimate of annual expenditure, which read as follows:

Pay of Principal Officers[3] . .	£2,000
Stipends to Kings and Chiefs[4] .	1,600
Police	1,440
Interior	3,000
Roads	4,000
Education	4,000
Medical	2,000
Rents and Buildings . . .	1,000
Miscellaneous	1,000
	£20,040

was now united under British jurisdiction. In June 1871 he commented: 'I have no one here sufficiently skilful to produce a complete and correct chart; so that I have been forced to rely upon my personal knowledge of the positions of the various countries, aided by a chart of the coast line published by the Admiralty.' *Correspondence relative to the Cession by the Netherlands Government to the British Government of the Dutch Settlements on the West Coast of Africa* (London, 1872).

[1] Minute of 11 June 1872; CO/96/93.

[2] The Colonial Office commented, 'When patched up a little he should be very competent to administer a minor Government elsewhere.' Minute of 24 June 1872; ibid. Ussher returned to the Gold Coast as Governor in 1879.

[3] Detailed estimates showed: King-President £200 per annum; Vice-President £350, Secretary £250, Under-Secretary £200, Treasurer £200, Assistant Treasurer £150, Foreign Secretary and Legal Adviser £250, Minister of the Interior £200, Minister of Justice £200.

[4] This allowed for sixteen Kings at £50 per annum, and thirty-two Chiefs at £25.

The Chiefs' stipends were to be paid in lieu of their court fees and fines, now to be diverted to the Confederation, which would dispense justice 'far more impartially, expeditiously, and at less cost'. The Confederation expected to raise in this way half the required sum, and proposed that the Gold Coast Government should find the remaining £10,000. This optimistic suggestion was felt to be justified since the British would be relieved of the trouble of controlling the interior of the Protectorate, and of the expense of establishing schools, hospitals, roads, canals, and so on. If such a grant were not forthcoming, then the Confederation itself would have to levy taxes or duties. The only alternative course would be for the Queen's Government 'to take over the whole country, and govern it as vigorously and on the same system and principles as it does Her other Colonies, but not permit us to be governed and ruled in the shameful and neglectful way in which we have been for years past, and give free scope for our legitimate aspirations'.[1]

Pope Hennessy was prepared to think out the whole position afresh, but his first step was to consult Gold Coast officials. Ussher was thus given the opportunity, just before he left the country, to fire a parting shot at the Confederation, its leaders, and the hidden hand behind it—'the scheme itself has been made up by other than they'—and to declare that the latest proposals were too complicated to succeed. Ussher was in favour of a Native Council of Chiefs; but it should be designed to place them, and not the 'scholars', in direct communication with the Government.[2] At this time the whole problem of the relationship between the British and the traditional authorities was also under serious consideration. D. Chalmers, the Chief Magistrate and Judicial Assessor, prepared three separate memoranda on British jurisdiction and the current state of the law, exposing existing defects, and suggesting reforms;[3] he also made new proposals for the judicial system, designed to associate the Chiefs more closely with the Government than hitherto.[4]

Meanwhile the Confederation leaders moved cautiously. In July 1872 a meeting was held at Mankessim which registered further important decisions, carefully noted as 'subject to the approval by the British Government of the Constitution, &c., of the Fanti Confederation'. At last, one King-President was chosen—Edoo of Mankessim—and Otoo of Abura was consoled with the post of 'General Field Marshal of the Fantee Nation'. The Chiefs who had repudiated the Confederation as a result of Salmon's threats were now

---

[1] 'Scheme to be submitted to His Excellency Governor J. Pope Hennessy and to the Home Government for their approval as regards the Fanti Confederation', signed by J. H. Brew and dated 16 Apr. 1872, and covering Dispatch No. 93 of 29 Oct. 1872, from Pope Hennessy to Kimberley; CO/96/94.

[2] Confidential Letter of 4 May 1872, from Ussher to Pope Hennessy; ibid.

[3] Memoranda (1) on 'the power of the Administrator and Legislative Council to legislate for the "Protected Territories"', dated 16 Apr. 1872, (2) concerning 'the Jurisdiction of Commandants and Magistrates', and (3) on 'the law prevailing in Her Majesty's Forts and Settlements on the Gold Coast', both dated 9 May 1872; ibid.

[4] See Ch. XII, p. 459, below.

persuaded to take the oath of allegiance. They were said to be all anxiously awaiting the British Government's decision.[1]

But Pope Hennessy took several months to consider their scheme and to discuss its implications. He gave due weight to the views of the Confederation, though he did not come to the conclusion they had hoped for. In October 1872, when he eventually forwarded all the documents to London, he took the trouble to repudiate the accumulation of scandal about the Fanti leaders as largely inaccurate; and he reported that every educated inhabitant at Cape Coast sympathized with the Confederation, including Grant, 'a native gentleman, who is certainly not the inferior of any European on the Gold Coast in character, ability or mercantile position'. If Ussher's judgement on their moral conduct and character were sound, it would be 'a painful commentary on the so-called Christianizing and civilizing effect of the Gold Coast Administration'.

Pope Hennessy accepted the view that the judicial authority of the Chiefs had been usurped and nothing tangible put in its place: hence the frequent stoppage of roads, and 'the natural uprising of a spirit such as that of the Fanti Confederation'. But he also pointed out that the British administrators had lacked the first element of government—power—and that lately the Chiefs in the interior had been able to laugh at their threats. While, therefore, agreeing with the leaders of the Confederation that an important change in the system was required, he recommended their second alternative, a firm extension of Crown Colony government, in preference to their scheme for 'a native Government, with certain financial and judicial powers'. At the same time Pope Hennessy was willing to appoint another African to the Legislative Council; he also suggested that municipal institutions should be established in the main coastal towns, and that Chiefs in the interior should exercise a certain amount of judicial power in conjunction with district magistrates.[2] To the Fanti Confederation, therefore, credit is due for having stimulated indirectly several legislative, municipal, and judicial reforms which were to be gradually implemented over a long period of years.

But their ambitious scheme was viewed with disapproval when it reached the Colonial Office. It was felt that the whole episode proved that the educated natives 'have been, are, and are likely to be the source of much trouble to the administration of affairs upon the West African coast'.[3] The Secretary of State therefore pronounced a decision destined to be far-reaching in its effects on British policy: 'I would have nothing to do with the "educated natives" as a body.[4] I would treat with the hereditary Chiefs only, and endeavour as far

---

[1] Report of meeting at Mankessim, 30 July 1872; *The African Times*, 23 Oct. 1872.

[2] Dispatch No. 93 of 29 Oct. 1872, from Pope Hennessy to Kimberley; CO/96/94.

[3] Minute of 18 Feb. 1873, by Knatchbull-Hugessen; CO/96/104.

[4] Kimberley was advised to go as far as 'preventing their association with the Kings and Chiefs, and entirely opposing and discouraging their attempt at any co-ordinate jurisdiction with the latter'. Ibid. But this did not become an explicit policy.

as possible to govern through them.' The question of ultimate self-government was also considered and quietly relegated to some distant date, in spite of the 'unfortunate influence' of the undue publicity given to the *1865 Report*. Kimberley admitted that at some future time the inhabitants might have improved so much as to be fit to govern themselves; but for a long time to come such an experiment would destroy all hopes of opening the interior to commerce, a result which 'would commend itself neither to philanthropists nor to traders'. For all practical purposes, therefore, he dismissed the question of retiring from the coast.

In this frame of mind it was not difficult for Kimberley to reject entirely the Fanti Confederation scheme. But he was also unable to accept the alternative recommended both by Pope Hennessy and by his own London advisers: namely, the extension of authority over the whole territory as a Crown Colony. He was able to offer some cogent reasons for doing nothing. The cost, in both lives and money, of defending the territory, especially against Ashanti, would be unthinkable; and the existence of domestic slavery, so interwoven with the whole life of the people that it could not easily be interfered with, would be contrary to British law. These he considered two fatal obstacles to the plan.[1]

But the Secretary of State was willing to agree that the powers and obligations of Britain, as Protecting Power, needed to be more carefully defined and established. A Dispatch was therefore drafted in March 1873, suggesting that this was to be done by agreement with the Chiefs, presumably replacing and expanding the Bonds of 1844. The Fanti Confederation in its existing form could not be recognized as an intermediary between the Chiefs and the Government; but the Chiefs were to be encouraged to form their own confederation for the purpose of defence along their internal frontier. The slave trade was not to be permitted; they were not to conduct relations with a foreign State (African or European) without the sanction of Britain; nor were they to levy transit dues on goods, Britain retaining the sole right to control customs duties. The limits of British sovereignty should be narrow; but the Government should have the right to enforce court decisions and maintain peace and order throughout the Protectorate. In return for these undertakings, stipends might be paid to the Chiefs; and the Governor was to be asked to consider any possible system of taxation instead of court fees to support their dignity. Various suggestions were also made, concerning the development of vernacular education, for example, and the employment of educated Africans in subordinate appointments.[2]

Kimberley was not anxious to introduce changes too hastily, nor to bind himself to any particular detail; there was no hurry to carry through the whole programme at once. The draft Dispatch would probably have been

---

[1] Minute of 22 Feb. 1873, by Kimberley; CO/96/104.
[2] Draft Dispatch of Mar. 1873, from Kimberley to Keate; ibid.

modified; but, as matters turned out, it was never sent. Reports of an Ashanti invasion relieved the Secretary of State from the burden of decision. In the event he merely informed the Governor-in-Chief that the moment was inopportune for discussing and settling questions affecting the permanent organization of the Government and its relations with the 'Native tribes'. He promised to deal with the matter further 'when a more favourable juncture of affairs presents itself'.[1] That juncture never came, for when the Ashantis had been dealt with his party was out of office, and his successor rejected the course of negotiating with the Chiefs.[2]

Unfortunately for the Fantis, their scheme had merely served to remind the London authorities of the insecure and doubtful nature of the Queen's jurisdiction in the Protectorate; and this, combined with the shock and expense of the latest Ashanti war, impelled a somewhat reluctant Colonial Office to establish British authority more decisively than hitherto. It was ironical that the Fantis, by appealing once again to the ideas of the *1865 Report*, should have prompted the British finally and publicly to turn their backs on that policy altogether. Their scheme had yet another unwelcome result, in that the stereotype of the designing, troublesome, educated African became firmly fixed in the official mind, adversely affecting policy for a considerable number of years.[3]

The Fantis Once More Disunited

During the many months of inaction that followed the submission of the 1872 scheme, the Confederation had been 'left to shift for itself', and its organization had virtually withered away. The King of Mankessim, however, wrote as 'Head of the Fanti Confederation' to ask for government assistance early in 1873, when news came of the Ashanti invasion.[4] He cannot have had much hope of success. R. W. Harley, the new Administrator, followed precedent in branding the letter as one dictated by certain individuals who wished to make capital out of the crisis, although he replied in a friendly manner.[5] Harley's personal prejudices were revealed when he received a further petition, this time from the Fanti Chiefs,[6] asking for 'pecuniary assistance, say, a loan of £7,200' to maintain their troops in camp. He reported that

---

[1] Dispatch No. 258 of 10 Mar. 1873, from Kimberley to Keate; ibid. This undertaking has recently been interpreted as 'a promise of Gold Coast self-government'. J. B. Danquah, 'The Historical Significance of the Bond of 1844', in *Transactions of the Historical Society of Ghana* (Achimota, 1957), vol. iii, pt. i.

[2] See Ch. VIII, pp. 302–3, below.   [3] Cf. Ch. II, pp. 87–92, above.

[4] Letter of 1 Feb. 1873, from King of Mankessim to Harley, enclosed in his Dispatch No. 26 of 4 Feb. 1873, to Pope Hennessy; CO/96/96. Sir Garnet Wolseley wrote later in the year, 'we left them almost entirely to themselves at the beginning of this contest'. Dispatch No. 301 of 4 Nov. 1873, to Kimberley; CO/96/103.

[5] Dispatch No. 27 of 11 Feb. 1873, from Harley to Pope Hennessy; CO/96/96.

[6] Petition of 16 May 1873, from Fanti Kings and Chiefs to Harley, enclosed in his Dispatch No. 101 of 24 May 1873, to Kimberley; CO/96/99.

this request had been inspired by 'men of no social status or means whatever', whom he had so far managed to ignore, by refusing to communicate with the Chiefs except personally or through a government officer.[1]

The Fanti Confederation was dead. An ironic legacy of its passing was the difficulty experienced by the civil and military authorities during the Ashanti campaign of 1873–4 in bringing about any united Fanti action under one leader.[2] For example, in June 1873, after a heavy defeat from the Ashantis, a meeting of Fanti Chiefs was held at Cape Coast, and Harley admonished them on the need for unity. Chief Green, 'the orator of the Fantees', then told him all he could have wished to hear: 'They [the Kings and Chiefs] do not feel able to take the management of affairs. It would be impossible for them to do so; nor could they elect one to be their Chief King, that power must come from the Governor, and if any one has said that they wished to govern themselves it was untrue.' Although Harley urged them to appoint a King themselves—offering to give him the necessary power for a temporary period—they insisted 'that that appointment should come from your Excellency'.[3]

Harley considered this public declaration a complete answer to the designs and intrigues of those who had endeavoured to organize 'the so-called "Fantee Confederation"'.[4] All it proved was, however, that the Administration had succeeded by alternate threats and neglect in reducing the Chiefs to a state of complete subservience to the Protecting Power. Browbeaten out of their plans for co-operation, and robbed of the will for united action, they were left in a helpless state of confusion, which turned out to be highly inconvenient for the British in the face of an Ashanti invasion. It is arguable that had the Fanti initiative been encouraged and turned to constructive purposes from the outset, they could have put up a resistance against the Ashantis at least as determined as their stand against the Dutch and Elminas, incidentally saving the Government considerable expense. But the opportunity had been lost, and never presented itself in that form again.

Certainly the movement for self-government was never again so closely associated with the Chiefs. The seeds of distrust between the traditional and the educated leaders had been carefully sown, and germinated much bitterness. But the Confederation was not easily forgotten; in fact, in later years its scale and importance tended to be exaggerated by Africans. There is no reason to suppose that *The African Times* was justified in describing it as 'the birth of a NATION'; nor even that the promoters were entirely disinterested. Its

[1] Dispatch No. 101 of 24 May 1873, from Harley to Kimberley; CO/96/99. In the Colonial Office it was noted that £7,200 was 'curiously enough' the amount claimed by 'Messrs. Brew & Co.' as the expenses of organization already incurred by the Fanti Confederation; ibid.

[2] Brew complained that it was the Government who had disunited them, and prevented them from collecting funds for joint action. Letter of 28 Feb. to *The African Times*, 29 Mar. 1873. Carnarvon soon afterwards admitted: 'We taught them to lean so much on us that they lost all dependence on themselves.' *Parliamentary Debates*, House of Lords, 12 May 1873.

[3] Report of meeting at Cape Coast, 6 June 1873; *The West African Herald*, 28 June 1873.

[4] Dispatch No. 136 of 30 June 1873, from Harley to Kimberley; CO/96/100.

importance lies in the aim rather than the performance; for towards the end of the century constant references by the leaders of the Aborigines' Rights Protection Society were to elevate it into a symbol of the wider national unity yet to be achieved.

Meanwhile, the ever-present threat from Ashanti was to draw the British Government, despite official reluctance to extend financial and territorial commitments, into closer and closer relationship with the fortunes of the Fantis. Withdrawal from the coast from 1873 onwards would have looked too much like retreat before the Ashantis to be either politically feasible for the British, or remotely attractive to the Fantis. A state of uneasy hostility for the next twenty-five years was to culminate in the destruction of Ashanti military power and its replacement by the pattern of British authority.

VII

ALARUMS AND EXCURSIONS IN ASHANTI
1873–97

ASHANTI has inevitably been impinging more and more upon the Gold Coast scene, as the story of nineteenth-century political movements unfolds. During that century, however, the story of Ashanti was not a part of the history of Gold Coast nationalism; rather, it appeared as a potential threat from outside, driving the Fantis and other tribes to commit themselves further to British protection. Nevertheless, Ashanti could be said to be the nearest approximation to a modern nation that was reached independently of European influence. The idea of 'Ashanti' owed nothing either to any reaction against alien forms of government or to the European example of national sovereignty. When Ashanti's conflict with her neighbours brought her up against the force of British arms, and when her desire for a monopoly of the interior trade was challenged by the penetration of European merchants,[1] a pre-existing national unit was reinforced by a twofold urge to preserve her independence.

In a sense, therefore, Ashanti's intermittent warfare against British-sponsored forces might be classed as a 'primary resistance movement', to use the terminology of J. S. Coleman. Yet it was not simply a question of 'resistance to the initial British penetration and occupation'; the objective of the Ashantis was nearer to 'the self-government and independence of ... a nation-state existing on a basis of equality in an international state system', which Coleman isolates as the distinguishing feature of modern nationalism.[2] In fact, such analytical distinctions cannot be pressed too far. It is useful to discern the operation of these two elements in Ashanti nationalism; but it is more fruitful first to study its development in the historical context, in order to understand fully the role of Ashanti in later nationalist movements. The origins of this influential nation-state must therefore be briefly outlined, as the key to its military and psychological significance.

---

[1] T. E. Bowdich, *Mission from Cape Coast Castle to Ashantee* (London, 1819), p. 337, reported that the Ashantis prevented 'all intercourse but their own with the waterside nations'. Nearly fifty years later, according to the Rev. E. Schrenk, it was still 'not the custom' of traders to visit the Ashantis, who preferred to come down to the coast themselves to trade. *Report from the Select Committee on Africa (Western Coast)* (London, 1865), reply to question 3,268.

[2] J. S. Coleman, *Nigeria: Background to Nationalism* (Los Angeles, 1958), pp. 169–70. See, for example, Prempeh's dignified claim to remain 'independent as of old', p. 281, below. The fact that Ashanti was not a sufficiently large unit to stand alone in the modern world does not affect the argument.

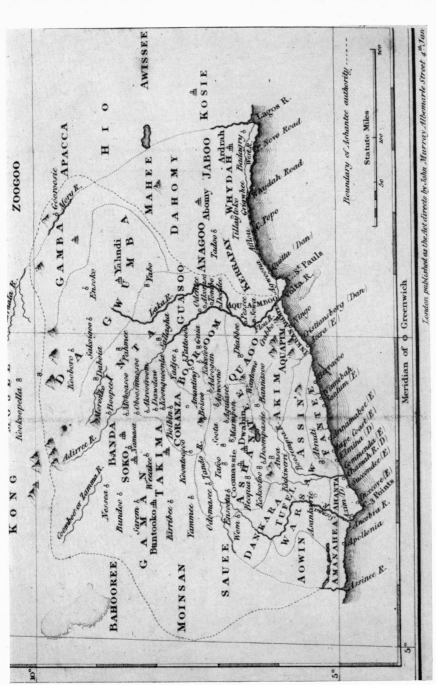

MAP 6. The extent of Ashanti authority—from a map published by T. E. Bowdich in his *Mission from Cape Coast Castle to Ashantee* (London, 1819).

The Nature of the Ashanti Union

The Ashanti Union was originally formed out of a loose association of tribes, the Amansie, who in the seventeenth century owed allegiance to Denkera. They freed themselves at the turn of the century, and developed their own military and political organization, under the leadership of Osei Tutu and the inspiration of his priest, Okomfo Anokye.

The Golden Stool, traditionally celebrated as having been brought down from heaven by Anokye,[1] was established as the symbol of Ashanti nationhood;[2] as R. S. Rattray says somewhat cynically of Anokye, 'with a true insight into the psychology of the people with whom he had to deal, he realised that the only way to unite independent and mutually jealous factions was by playing upon their superstitious beliefs'.[3] Thus religious sanctions were added to military force as a means of holding the Chiefs together. Kumasi became the centre of the kingdom, and its supremacy was emphasized by the destruction of the old Amansie stools and their replacement by new stools presented by Osei Tutu to the Chiefs who swore allegiance to him. He was no longer paramount Chief of a tribal State, but Asantehene, the head of the Ashanti nation.

Osei Tutu's successors continued to consolidate this position until, by the end of the eighteenth century, the supremacy of Ashanti extended over a wide area, and included a large number of States in a loose confederacy, linked by their common allegiance to the Asantehene, and by their common language, religion, and customs.[4] T. E. Bowdich, who visited Kumasi in 1817, described how 'every subject state was placed under the immediate care of some Ashantee chief, generally resident in the capital, who seldom visited it but to receive the tribute from the native ruler, for whose conduct he was in a reasonable degree responsible'.[5] The Chiefs thus subordinated, however, preserved their independence in matters affecting their own States; they were in any case cut off from one another by the absence of effective communications and by the relative economic autarchy of each small community. Heads of clans, villages,

---

[1] For the traditional account of this miracle, see R. S. Rattray, *Ashanti* (Oxford, 1923), ch. xxiii, 'The Golden Stool'.

[2] K. A. Busia describes the Golden Stool as 'the sacred shrine which symbolizes the unity of the Ashanti'. *The Position of the Chief in the Modern Political System of Ashanti* (Oxford, 1951), p. 96. The whole of his ch. v, 'The Ashanti Union', gives a useful background to the above section.

[3] *Ashanti Law and Constitution* (Oxford, 1929), p. 73; see also ch. xxiv for a biography of Anokye.

[4] The six leading States of Ashanti were Kumasi, Juaben, Kokofu, Nsuta, Bekwai (all belonging to the Oyoko clan), and Mampong, according to Busia, *The Position of the Chief*, p. 85. In addition, Essumeja, Kumawu, Adansi, Offinsu, Ejisu, and Agona should be included in the inner circle of the Union. But W. W. Claridge also lists the following States as owing allegiance to the Asantehene at the beginning of the nineteenth century: Nkoranza, Banda, Gyaman, and Techiman (Brong tribes); Wassaw, Sefwi, Denkera, Tufel, Aowin, Assin, Akim, Akwapim, Kwahu, and Akwamu. *A History of the Gold Coast and Ashanti* (London, 1915), vol. i, p. 228. Also under the dominion of Ashanti were Salaga and Yendi, which lay farther north, on the main trade routes to the Fulani emirates across the River Niger. I. Wilks, *The Northern Factor in Ashanti History* (Legon, 1961), p. 24.   [5] *Mission to Ashantee*, pt. ii, ch. ii, 'History'.

and households had important responsibilities in their own sphere, and in many respects the system of government might be said to have lacked cohesion.

On the other hand, unity of action was the ideal for purposes of warfare. K. A. Busia has suggested that the main achievement of the Kings of Kumasi was the building up of this loose political system into a strong military power.[1] Within his own kingdom the power of the Asantehene was paramount, reinforced by the ever-present menace of the state executioners. But if he wanted to go to war, the active participation of the leading Chiefs of other States was essential, in order to raise troops, for there was no standing army. On matters of war and foreign policy, decisions were taken by what Bowdich called 'the Privy Council, or Aristocracy, which checks the King'; this was originally made up of all the 'peers and associates' of Osei Tutu, but by 1817 was reduced in number to four. Bowdich noted that on subjects of war or tribute they could even veto the King's decision; and that this system was believed to make the nation more formidable to its enemies, 'who feel they cannot provoke with impunity where there are so many guardians of the military glory'.[2]

Interesting confirmation of the accuracy of Bowdich's record, and of the continuity of Ashanti tradition, is given by the account of the Rev. F. Ramseyer and J. Kühne, written over fifty years later:

the reins of the Ashantee government are not exclusively in the hands of the king, nor does he possess unlimited power, but shares it with a council which includes, besides his majesty, his mother, the three first chiefs of the kingdom [Juaben, Bekwai and Mampong], and a few nobles of Kumasi . . . This council is called 'Asante Kotoko', or the Ashantee porcupine, which means that like the animal of that name, nobody dare touch them . . . It is the Kotoko council which rules the entire kingdom, and deals with the people, who must obey, whatever their own wishes or inclinations may be, in the most despotic way . . . In important matters all the other chiefs of the kingdom are called together to discuss the case, but they are sure to vote in accordance with the view of the council, for who would dare to oppose the Kotoko?[3]

This account may tend to overstress the powers of the Council, since the writers were in Kumasi during a particularly warlike reign. Busia's recent description of the four main functions of the Council may serve to correct the balance:

It met to discuss war; this was its primary function. Later, the periodic *Odwera* ceremonies were instituted, when the chiefs met to participate in those rites which rekindled their sentiments of solidarity and nationhood. Thirdly, it met as a national tribunal before which even the Asantehene himself could be tried. And, finally, it met for the enstoolment or destoolment of an Asantehene.[4]

[1] *The Position of the Chief*, p. 89.
[2] *Mission to Ashantee*, pt. ii, ch. iii, 'Constitution and Laws'.
[3] F. Ramseyer and J. Kühne, *Four Years in Ashantee* (London, 1875), app. iii, 'The Government of Ashantee'.   [4] *The Position of the Chief*, p. 101.

The decisions of the Council did not always go unchallenged. As Rattray has pointed out, the great Chiefs remained jealous of their privileges and powers, and were ever ready to take up arms if the central authority acted in too despotic a manner.[1] On the other hand, all valued the military security provided by the Confederacy, and if one State attempted secession others would rally to the support of the Asantehene. In the last resort, the strength of the Union depended upon success in war. Local jealousies were naturally subdued in any national emergency; both to the south and to the north were potentially hostile States, whose very existence 'gave unity and solidarity to the segmentary organisation of Ashanti'.[2]

Paradoxically enough, it was this very hostility between Ashanti and the southern tribes that eventually led to both being brought directly under a British Governor. During the eighteenth century the Ashantis made little effort to approach the coast. But after that, starting with their crushing punitive expedition against the Fantis in 1807,[3] they came into increasing conflict with the coastal tribes, and hence with the British.

British–Ashanti Relations before 1873

Ashanti remained virtually unknown territory to Europeans long after the traders had settled on the coast. But as a result of the Ashanti invasion of 1807 it was thought wise to establish diplomatic relations, and there followed a period of power politics, when the Asantehene was treated with the ceremony due to a foreign sovereign, in marked contrast to later British attitudes. In any case, successive invasions had led to fears for the safety of the forts themselves, and respect for Ashanti military power was no mere polite fiction.

It was probably about 1810 that the Asantehene made the first move in the diplomatic game, and asked the Governor of Cape Coast Castle to send an officer to reside in his capital. The evidence for this is somewhat indirect,[4] and little is known of the motives prompting such a request; but it is certain that the Asantehene would not have intended to suggest anything in the nature of a colonial relationship. The first British officers visited Kumasi in 1817, when Bowdich concluded a treaty guaranteeing perpetual peace and harmony between the Kings of Ashanti and Juaben on the one hand, and the British on

---

[1] Rattray, *Ashanti Law and Constitution*, p. 105.

[2] Busia, *The Position of the Chief*, pp. 90–91.

[3] Ellis, followed by Claridge and Ward, wrongly dates this invasion as 1806. The mistake derives from the contemporary record by H. Meredith, *An Account of the Gold Coast of Africa* (London, 1812), which gives two incompatible dates. Claridge appears to have noticed the discrepancy, but to have settled it by silently altering the date of one of the letters he quotes from Meredith. For fuller details of contemporary documents, establishing the date beyond doubt as 1807, see E. C. Martin, *The British West African Settlements, 1750–1821* (London, 1927), ch. x.

[4] James Swanzy suggested before the 1816 Parliamentary Committee that this message had not been made known to the British Government. The Governor's reply was, however, approved by the London Committee of Merchants. *Report from the Select Committee on Papers relating to the African Forts* (London, 1816), pp. 37 and 116.

the other, together with 'all nations of Africa residing under the protection of the Company's Forts and Settlements on the Gold Coast'.[1] W. Hutchison, another member of the mission, was left in Kumasi to act as Resident,[2] while an Ashanti captain was sent in return to Cape Coast.

After Hutchison had been recalled to the coast, J. Dupuis was sent out from London as Consul, and in 1820 he made another treaty (revoking the previous one), under which the Asantehene took an oath of allegiance to the Crown and promised to support British interests with his armies; but at the same time 'the Fantee territories' were recognized as Ashanti dominions, and the natives of Cape Coast town as subjects of the Asantehene.[3] The Governor and Council of Merchants were so annoyed that they refused to receive Dupuis on his return to Cape Coast, or to allow the Ashanti messengers to travel to England. The treaty was never ratified in London, and no successor to Dupuis was appointed when he left the coast the same year.[4]

For the rest of the nineteenth century, relationships with Ashanti remained largely military in character,[5] and British policy was mainly directed towards protecting their own traders—and, incidentally, the Fantis—from what might otherwise have been an irresistible Ashanti drive towards the sea. The Ashantis were officially regarded, by successive merchant and colonial governments, as wealthy but disturbing neighbours, whose power continually offered a potential threat to British trade and influence. Their defeat at the battle of Dodowa in 1826 discouraged further forays towards the coast for the time being; and under Maclean's treaty of 1831, the Asantehene renounced 'all right or title to any tribute or homage from the Kings of Denkera, Assin, and others formerly his subjects'.[6] In spite of several subsequent quarrels over fugitives, and a warlike Ashanti expedition to Assin in 1853, the British

[1] The first recorded mention of 'protection' for the Fantis was thus prompted by the threat from Ashanti. On this occasion the King of Juaben seems to have been accorded equal status with the Asantehene, and Bowdich took care to secure the assent of both. But in 1820 the Asantehene remarked indignantly, 'Is there any other King besides me?' J. Dupuis, *Journal of a Residence in Ashantee* (London, 1824), p. 138.

[2] Hutchison kept a diary from Sept. 1817 to Jan. 1818, which was reproduced in Bowdich, *Mission to Ashantee*, ch. xii.

[3] See Dupuis, *Journal*, app. iii, for the text of the treaty, and a markedly partisan account of these negotiations. Claridge, *History*, vol. i, chs. xvi–xviii, has made a gallant attempt to sift and assess the conflicting evidence concerning the treaties and the Asantehene's claim to ownership of the land on which the most important coastal forts stood.

[4] W. Hutton, author of *A Voyage to Africa* (London, 1821), who had accompanied Dupuis to Kumasi, was appointed by him Acting Consul; but despairing of recognition by the Council of Merchants, and growing tired of looking after two leopards consigned to the King of England by the Asantehene, he also left the coast.

[5] There were, however, several attempts to establish a Christian Mission in Ashanti. See especially *Evangelisches Missions-Magazin* (Basel, 1840), pp. 174–238, for an account of the visit of the Rev. A. Riis to Ashanti; also T. B. Freeman, *Journal of Various Visits to the Kingdom of Ashanti, Aku, and Dahomi in Western Africa* (London, 2nd edn. 1844), for a first-hand contemporary description of Kumasi; and cf. Ch. III, pp. 152–4, above.

[6] J. J. Crooks, *Records relating to the Gold Coast Settlements from 1750 to 1874* (Dublin, 1923), pp. 262–4.

managed to avoid further direct conflict for many years; meanwhile the Ashantis continued to trade direct with the coastal forts, and also maintained their friendly relations with the Dutch at Elmina.

But the inconclusive war of 1863–4 aroused Fanti fears of the ability and willingness of the British to protect them; and these were not dispelled by the exchange of territory in 1868, which prompted them to form the Fanti Confederation. The Ashantis for their part welcomed the fact that, as a result of the exchange, Dutch protection—and hence their own influence—might be extended to Denkera. But they were alarmed by the Fanti attack on Elmina, which was regarded as a direct threat to Ashanti interests.

Kwaku Dua, 'the most peaceful and wise ruler of the kingdom of Ashantee', died in 1867, and was succeeded by his nephew, Kofi Kakari, 'a fiery young man of thirty-five',[1] who paid little heed to the moderating influence of Prince Ansah.[2] During 1869 an Ashanti force under Adu Boffo was sent to raid the eastern districts towards the Volta; this provoked stern resistance from the Krepis, and a threatening letter from W. R. Simpson, the British Acting Administrator.[3] Although the Secretary of State refused to countenance direct intervention, the Asantehene was not to know this, and an unofficial military expedition from Accra lent substance to Simpson's threats. The invaders returned to Kumasi, taking with them the Basel missionaries Ramseyer and Kühne, who had been captured at Anum, and a young French trader, J. Bonnat, from Ho.[4] Later in the year Adjiempon commenced his bloody expedition towards Elmina, which was intended to protect Ashanti interests there at all costs.[5]

The Dutch were now anxious to leave the coast altogether, and Kakari protested vigorously when he heard of the proposed treaty whereby the British would purchase all their possessions, including Elmina. There was considerable delay in ratifying the Convention, which was initially signed at

[1] J. A. B. Horton, *Letters on the Political Condition of the Gold Coast* (London, 1870), pp. 82–84.

[2] Prince John Ossoo Ansah, the son of a former Asantehene, was one of the two young men who had been handed over under the treaty of 1831 for education in England. He returned to Kumasi in 1841 with the Rev. T. B. Freeman, but later married a Fanti and settled at Cape Coast with an annual allowance from the Government, visiting Ashanti occasionally. The Rev. F. Ramseyer and J. Kühne spoke highly of his help and kindness during their captivity in Kumasi, and of his attempts to pacify Kofi Kakari. *Four Years in Ashantee*, pp. 74–76 and 113. Prince Ansah was afterwards suspected, by the Government and by the Fantis, of intriguing with factions in Ashanti, and in 1873 he nearly lost his life when several members of his household were beheaded by an angry Cape Coast mob. He was sent to Sierra Leone for his own safety (see p. 271 n., below); but later he returned to Cape Coast and again fell under suspicion as 'a mischievous intriguer'. The Governor and Council recommended in 1884 that he should be deported to St. Helena, but he died in November of that year.

[3] Letter of 8 Mar. 1869, to King of Ashanti from Simpson, enclosed in his Dispatch No. 26 of 22 Mar. 1869, to Kennedy; CO/96/79.

[4] See Ramseyer and Kühne, *Four Years in Ashantee*, and J. Gros, *Voyages, aventures et captivité de J. Bonnat chez les Achantis* (Paris, 1884).

[5] Cf. Ch. VI, above, which briefly recounts these events and the subsequent negotiations from the point of view of the coastal peoples, especially the Fantis.

The Hague in February 1871. At first the British were afraid of provoking an Ashanti war by taking over Elmina in defiance of Kakari, especially while Adjiempon was still in the neighbourhood; but their suspicions were lulled by the Dutch Governor's exposition of his Government's claim to sovereignty over Elmina, and by his willing co-operation in arresting Adjiempon, who was eventually sent away to Half Assini as a prior condition of the transfer.[1]

The Dutch possessions were then formally handed over in April 1872, and the British authorities flattered themselves that all had gone smoothly, apart from a short-lived riot in Elmina. At the end of the year it even seemed that the Basel missionaries were about to be released. But these negotiations fell through, apparently because the Ashantis feared that the ransom would not be paid; and after Adjiempon had been allowed to return to Kumasi, their attitude stiffened.[2] It became clear that they were resolved not to accept the loss of Elmina, and at the beginning of 1873 a large Ashanti force invaded the Protectorate under the command of Amankwatia, the Bantamahene.[3] Later, the Asantehene himself took the field.

The War of 1873–4

Of all the Ashanti wars, this was the first to be inspired largely by anti-European sentiment, and it therefore deserves somewhat fuller treatment. The invasion of 1863 had been a direct reprisal for the British refusal to surrender two Ashanti refugees; and that of 1869 had been designed to warn the Fantis 'hands off Elmina'. But now, with the final departure of the Dutch, it became clear that the strengthened British position was a direct threat to Ashanti interests, and a determination to drive the strangers out was added to their long-standing ambition to subjugate the Fantis. The scale of the operation was commensurate with this wider aim.

The Ashanti invasion swept forward successfully to the outskirts of Cape Coast, where thousands of Fanti refugees huddled miserably for several months. In Elmina the intrigues of the pro-Ashanti faction led to a British bombardment of the town; and to the west, several of the former Dutch tribes joined forces with the Ashantis, notably at Sekondi, Shama, Axim, and Dixcove.[4] However anxious the British might have been to withdraw voluntarily from the coast in 1865, they were not now prepared to be driven out by

---

[1] The Dutch also obtained a letter from the Asantehene purporting to renounce his claim to Elmina. This has been dismissed (e.g. by Claridge, *History*, vol. ii, pp. 610–11) as probably a forgery drawn up by the African messenger, H. Plange; but D. S. Coombs has recently argued convincingly that it was genuinely authorized by Kakari, in a deliberate attempt to conceal his warlike intentions until he was ready to fight. 'The Place of the "Certificate of Apologie" in Ghanaian History', in *Transactions of the Historical Society of Ghana* (Achimota, 1958), vol. iii, pt. 3. See also *Correspondence relative to the Cession by the Netherlands Government to the British Government of the Dutch Settlements on the West Coast of Africa* (London, 1872), C. 670.

[2] Ramseyer and Kühne, *Four Years in Ashantee*, and Gros, *Voyages . . . de J. Bonnat*.

[3] See *Despatches respecting the Transfer of the Dutch Possessions . . . Negotiations for the Release of German Missionaries . . . and the Ashantee Invasion* (London, 1873).

[4] The early stages of the campaign are fully described by Claridge, *History*, vol. ii, chs. i and ii.

the Ashantis. The Administrator-in-Chief, R. W. Harley, was relieved of his post, and General Sir Garnet Wolseley was appointed as civil administrator and military commander with full power to free the Gold Coast from the Ashanti 'menace'.[1]

On his arrival from England in October 1873, Wolseley found more than 20,000 Ashantis occupying threatening positions within an easy march of Elmina and Cape Coast.[2] The Fantis believed the forts were about to be attacked at any moment, and public confidence in the British was at a very low ebb.[3] Within a fortnight Wolseley had made a successful raid on the main Ashanti camps, which helped to precipitate their return to Kumasi. At this stage he could do little more than harass their rear, and was unable to rally the Fantis in pursuit. Little information was then available about conditions in Ashanti,[4] and the military precedents were not encouraging; only two British Governors had previously crossed the River Prah, and of these one (Sir Charles Macarthy, in 1824) had lost his head.[5] But the landing of over 2,000 British troops in December made possible Wolseley's hard-fought march to Kumasi early in 1874, supported by Captain J. H. Glover, R.N., who took the eastern route with a force of West African soldiers. Wolseley found Kumasi itself undefended, in the absence of the Asantehene, and he stayed there only two days;[6] but the occupation and destruction of the town was officially regarded as a decisive victory.[7]

[1] For Wolseley's Instructions from the War Office and the Colonial Office, see Crooks, *Records*, pp. 460–8.

[2] The Ashantis called this the *Fanti'sa*, or sometimes the *Toto* war, an indirect reference to the sound of the English cannon at the forts. Rattray, *Ashanti Law and Constitution*, pp. 134 and 175.

[3] Dispatch of 15 Dec. 1873, from Wolseley to Secretary of State for War; Crooks, *Records*, p. 486.

[4] The sketchy knowledge of the country in 1873 is illustrated by a *Map of Ashantee and Gold Coast* (War Office, London, 1873). H. Brackenbury and G. L. Huyshe compiled *Fanti and Ashanti* (London, 1873), and extracts from R. J. Ghartey's *Guide for Strangers Travelling to Kumasi* (Cape Coast, 1864) were republished in London in 1873, as aids to the British expedition. Nothing new was added by J. Dalrymple Hay, *Ashanti and the Gold Coast and What we Know of it* (London, 1874). *The Times* of 29 July 1873 published an account of the kingdom of Ashanti and of the outbreak of the war, by 'Prince Ossoo Ansall, uncle to the Ashantee King, and at present detained in a kind of honourable captivity at Freetown, Sierra Leone.'

[5] Macarthy crossed in pursuit of the Ashantis, although he did not actually enter their territory. H. I. Ricketts, *Narrative of the Ashantee War* (London, 1833). The first Governor actually to visit Kumasi was Sir William Winniett in 1848; Crooks, *Records*, p. 315.

[6] Although Wolseley had undertaken to get the British troops out of the country before the rains, the abruptness of the withdrawal caused some criticism. Winwood Reade claimed that Wolseley's initial failure to organize a proper system of carriers had vitiated the whole expedition, and made him 'run into Coomassie and out again like a ferret in a rabbit-hole'. *The Story of the Ashantee Campaign* (London, 1874), p. 393. Sir W. Lawson, M.P., said the campaign reminded him of the old rhyme,

> 'The King of France with twenty thousand men
> Marched up a hill and then marched down again.'

Parliamentary Debates, House of Commons, 4 May 1874.

[7] See H. Brackenbury, *The Ashantee War* (London, 1874), 2 vols., prepared from official documents by Wolseley's Assistant Military Secretary.

The extent to which the British Government was prepared to man and finance this expedition indicates their realization that not only military honour but the very survival of imperial and commercial interests on the coast was at stake. Yet at this stage they thought it sufficient to confine the Ashantis within their own boundaries and prevent any further warlike excursions. There was no suggestion of destroying or supplanting the military power of Ashanti; and with the *1865 Report* still fresh in memory it was hardly to be expected that anyone should have foreseen the shift in British policy in favour of colonial expansion which, towards the end of the century, was to force a final trial of strength with Ashanti.

Wolseley himself predicted as a result of his expedition such a diminution in the prestige and military power of the Asantehene as might result in the complete break-up of the kingdom. But he did not consider that this would be any great gain, because there was no power among 'the feeble races of this coast' to replace that of Ashanti.[1] It was perhaps for this reason that in his capacity as civilian negotiator he refrained from pressing home his military advantage; the treaty handed to the Asantehene's messengers at Fomena, after the withdrawal from Ashanti, did not contain any severely punitive clauses, apart from the very heavy indemnity of 50,000 oz. of gold (over 1,000 oz. of which were paid on the spot). Its main concern was to repudiate the Asantehene's claim to supremacy over Elmina and any other British possessions on the coast; and to guarantee the freedom of inland trade routes. By its other provisions, Adansi was added to the list of tribes no longer owing allegiance to Ashanti, but was not offered any protection;[2] 'perpetual peace' was agreed between England and Ashanti, without any guarantee to maintain it; and the Asantehene promised his 'best endeavours', for what they were worth, to check the practice of human sacrifice. Perhaps more obviously than most, this treaty helped to sow the seeds of the next war.[3]

There were still some influential people in Britain who would have liked to see a complete withdrawal from the coast, after this decisive—but costly— show of force. H. Brackenbury, for example, the official historian of the war, argued that there was no moral obligation to protect the Fantis, since they had ceased to pay the poll tax; that it was impossible to get 'a first-class man to rule in such an accursed country',[4] and that there was no advantage in

---

[1] Dispatch No. 31 of 7 Feb. 1874, from Wolseley to Kimberley; CO/96/111.

[2] According to Wolseley, the King of Adansi told him that he intended to leave Ashanti and bring his people under British protection. Dispatch of 13 Feb. 1874, from Wolseley to Secretary of State for War; Crooks, *Records*, pp. 513–14. Prempeh, however, later complained that the Adansis had been told by Wolseley that they *must* leave Ashanti and come into the Protectorate. Letter of 20 Jan. 1891, to Knutsford; *Further Correspondence relating to Affairs in Ashanti* (London, 1896), C. 7917.

[3] For the text of the Treaty of Fomena, dated 13 Feb. 1874, see Crooks, *Records*, pp. 521–4. This was ratified in Cape Coast the following month by envoys from Ashanti.

[4] Three senior officers in turn refused to accept office as Governor in succession to Wolseley; Lieutenant-Colonel J. Maxwell was then appointed, but he died at sea a month later. Dispatch of

retaining settlements that were not even self-supporting.[1] On the other hand, the idea of obligation towards the Fantis was not so easily dismissed, especially since they were urging the British to avoid the dishonour of withdrawal from the coast. *The Gold Coast Times*, arguing that such a possibility was beyond contemplation, rejoiced at the recent victory, and hoped to see it consolidated, remarking: 'England has, under Providence, justly punished an aggressive, savage, and bloodthirsty nation.' Doubting whether the Ashantis would keep the terms of the Treaty of Fomena, this newspaper urged that a clear policy should be laid down, so that the Protectorate would be in a position to defend itself in any future war.[2]

In London the Ashanti campaign had forced a general realization of the extent to which Britain was committed on the coast. As *The Times*[3] put it, 'The King of Ashanti has bound us to the Gold Coast by the ties of honour and reputation.'[4] Defence against Ashanti had been recognized as inevitable, however costly, if trade was to be carried on. The issue was never really in doubt, in spite of some beautifully turned periods at the Colonial Office: 'Complete annexation or total abandonment are I fear the only sound alternatives. The former is too ghastly a scheme to contemplate, the latter too charming to be capable of execution.'[5] Lord Carnarvon, the Secretary of State for the Colonies in the new Conservative Government, commented: 'A very evil choice to have to make.'[6]

The issue was debated in the House of Commons, where there was a strong minority opinion in favour of withdrawal. Some critics were uneasy about the whole purpose of the campaign: 'The most extraordinary way of carrying on trade was to commence business by killing one's customers.' The destruction of Kumasi was condemned as an act of vandalism, and the treaty as not worth the paper on which it was written. But there had been a general reversal of opinion since 1865; and even one former member of the Select Committee now stood out against abandoning the coastal tribes, hoping that there would be no attempt to 'extemporise a negro Government and a negro Parliament'. A member of the previous Government defended its policy towards the Fanti Confederation, and claimed that the Ashanti campaign had been fought 'to vindicate the honour of our flag . . . in the interests of future peace, civilization and progress'. He hoped that the British would now stay on the coast, but would limit and define their territory and obligations.[7]

27 Feb. 1874, from Wolseley to Kimberley; *Further Correspondence respecting the Ashantee Invasion No. 8* (London, 1874).   [1] Brackenbury, *The Ashantee War*, vol. ii, pp. 345–8.
    [2] *The Gold Coast Times*, 11 and 29 Apr. 1874.   [3] 28 Apr. 1874.
    [4] Even before Wolseley arrived in the Gold Coast, *The African Times*, 29 Aug. 1873, had claimed that his appointment meant the abandonment of 'the do-nothing or surrender policy which was so disgraceful to Great Britain'.
    [5] Minute of 20 Apr. 1874, by J. Lowther (Parliamentary Under-Secretary); CO/96/114.
    [6] Minute of 21 Apr. 1874, by Carnarvon; ibid.
    [7] *Parliamentary Debates*, House of Commons, 4 May 1874; the quotations are from Sir W. Lawson, A. Mills, and E. H. Knatchbull-Hugessen, in that order.

This was exactly what Disraeli's Government, elected while Wolseley was on the road to Kumasi, hoped to do, although the detailed lines of policy were far from clear. The Prime Minister promised an early statement; and, as almost always, a middle course was found. Letters Patent and an Order in Council were issued in London on 24 July 1874, transforming the Gold Coast Settlements into the Gold Coast Colony. This (with Lagos) was to have its own administration, once more separate from Sierra Leone. The British intention to remain on the coast was thus reaffirmed; and the position in the adjacent Protected Territories was made clearer a few days later, when an Order in Council of 6 August empowered the Legislative Council of the Colony to legislate also for them.

The new policy retained the advantage that no one knew exactly how far these territories extended, nor what degree of protection was offered to them.[1] In particular, the Colonial Office was exceedingly anxious not to become further involved in Ashanti affairs, largely owing to British scruples over the continuing practices of slavery and human sacrifice. After a British officer had assisted the Juabens to declare their independence in July 1874,[2] the Ashantis were left severely alone. The British were not sorry to see the break-up and weakening of the Ashanti kingdom, but no further action was sanctioned for some years, either to encourage or prevent it.

The Weakening of the Confederacy, 1874-88

The disintegration of Ashanti seemed imminent immediately after the war. The shock of military defeat had acted as a stimulus to the separatist tendencies within a union that was by nature multipartite. The revolt of the Juabens encouraged Nsuta and other neighbouring tribes to declare their independence. The strongest group to reject the supremacy of Kumasi was made up of the Brongs;[3] on the more distant borders of the kingdom, Salaga and Yendi took the opportunity to break off their more tenuous relationship. Discontent was also spreading nearer home, especially among the Kokofus and Bekwais, who were opposed to the Asantehene mainly on personal grounds.

Later in 1874 Mensa Bonsu succeeded his elder brother Kakari—who had been destooled for robbing and desecrating the royal tombs—and set about reasserting the central power of Ashanti. The Juabens were quickly reconquered, the Gold Coast Government this time refusing to intervene when asked to do so;[4] and the other nearby tribes, including the Nsutas, Bekwais,

[1] See Ch. VIII, p. 313, below.

[2] Details of their struggle for independence are given in the Juaben tribal history recorded by Rattray, *Ashanti Law and Constitution*, pp. 175-6.

[3] See 'Concise History of Abruno Rebellion against Ashanti', by C. V. E. Graves; *Further Correspondence regarding Affairs of the Gold Coast* (London, 1882), C. 3386.

[4] A. B. Ellis blamed the Government for its failure to restrain the Juabens from provoking the Ashantis. *A History of the Gold Coast of West Africa* (London, 1893), p. 356. After they had been conquered, Dr. V. S. Gouldsbury, sent up to investigate, unsuccessfully advocated the British

and Kokofus, returned to their old allegiance. Some of the defeated Kings and Chiefs, with numbers of their people, took refuge in the Protected Territories,[1] and there was constant intrigue and skirmishing along the borders.

The Gold Coast Times was soon calling for further positive intervention in Ashanti. Since the war had destroyed the monarchy and disintegrated the component tribes of Ashanti, Britain herself should take the power to 're-construct and rebuild that which is now broken down'.[2] By 1877 many Fantis had convinced themselves: 'Never was a greater mistake made than when Sir Garnet Wolseley left the Ashanti Kingdom to itself, satisfied with his paper treaty and his few ounces of Gold Dust.'[3] British administrators on the coast came increasingly to endorse this view, feeling that a lasting peace could be ensured only by extending their influence farther inland. Many of the European and African merchants were also looking hopefully towards the wealth of the interior; meanwhile, the dissident Ashanti tribes had been encouraged by the terms of the Treaty of Fomena to expect British protection and assistance. But soon a direct threat to Adansi revealed only too clearly both the inability of the British to enforce the treaty, and the determination of the Colonial Office not to become involved in any further inter-tribal disputes, let alone extensions of territory.

The Gold Coast Government protested to Mensa Bonsu in 1879 against his interference in Adansi, calling upon him to fulfil his treaty obligations, and sent an army officer there to 'request' any Ashantis to leave.[4] But the Lieutenant-Governor, C. Lees, was immediately reminded by the Secretary of State that Adansi was not within the Protectorate,[5] and that he should not have acted without previous consultation in a matter of external policy, especially since he was not in a position to enforce his demands.[6] In spite of this, Lees's successor proposed to send a strong warning to the Asantehene against interference with Adansi or any British-protected country;[7] and he in his turn was reminded that Adansi was not under protection.[8] In any case, there was no intention in London of enforcing the Treaty of Fomena by active intervention, so long as the Ashantis did not enter the Protectorate. Instead, the Permanent Under-Secretary of State recommended a Downing Street

occupation of Juaben, to avoid the recovery of Ashanti prestige. His report of this journey into the interior, 1875–6, is printed in African No. 95.

[1] For example, the Juaben migration to Koforidua; cf. Ch. I, p. 18, above. The British adhered rigidly to their policy of non-intervention; later Asafu-Adjaye, the ex-King of Juaben, was exiled to Lagos, and King Tackie of Accra was sent to Elmina, for conspiring together against the Ashantis. CO/96/126 and 132.

[2] *The Gold Coast Times*, 17 Aug. 1875.

[3] Ibid. 5 Dec. 1877.

[4] Dispatch of 25 Feb. 1879, from Lees to Hicks Beach; *Affairs of the Gold Coast and Threatened Ashanti Invasion* (London, 1881), C. 3064.

[5] Cf. p. 272, above.

[6] Dispatch of 25 Apr. 1879, from Hicks Beach to Lees; C. 3064.

[7] Dispatch No. 346 of 30 Dec. 1880, from Brandford Griffith to Kimberley; CO/96/132.

[8] Dispatch of 4 Feb. 1881, from Kimberley to Brandford Griffith; C. 3064.

pipe-dream: 'a strong and solemn warning which does not actually commit us to anything'.[1]

The local Government's policy during the first part of 1881 was dominated by the fear that the Ashantis intended at any moment to force another war upon the Colony.[2] The history of the resulting negotiations and misunderstandings has been fully covered by Ellis and Claridge;[3] but the episode of the Golden Axe, which was originally regarded by the British as a threat of war, but finally handed over by the Ashantis with great ceremony as a token of good faith to the Queen,[4] produced some increase of respect for the Ashantis as a nation and for their customary emblems.

After this the Secretary of State, Lord Kimberley, had time to consider the need for a recommencement of the trade with Ashanti, which had decreased considerably; he attributed this partly to the decline in the Asantehene's political influence and the scorn of his former allies. He did not wish to restore the former supremacy of the Ashantis, but he thought that they might be brought into cordial relations with the British, and induced to give up 'their revolting practice of human sacrifice'.[5] In particular, he felt that the unpaid balance of the indemnity imposed by Wolseley in 1874 was too severe a burden, and 'a source of humiliation to them in the estimation of their neighbours'. Kimberley therefore suggested that it might be waived, as a preliminary step towards the extension of commerce.[6] No definite decision was taken on this; but positive efforts were now made to increase trade with the surrounding tribes.

The Ashanti embassy that brought the Golden Axe to Accra had requested that a European officer should accompany them on their return to Kumasi.[7] Here was a useful opportunity for making contacts that might result in increased trade; so Captain R. La T. Lonsdale was sent back with them, and also journeyed north of Kumasi, returning through Krepi to Accra early in 1882. The Government was particularly anxious to break the Ashanti monopoly over the northern transit trade, and Lonsdale's mission succeeded in opening up again some of the trade routes to the east. He found that the Gonjas, the Krachis, and the Brong tribes generally—with the important exception of Nkoranza—had sworn an oath by the Krachi fetish, Dente, and

---

[1] Minute of 2 Feb. 1881, by R. G. W. Herbert; CO/96/132.

[2] Dispatch of 24 Jan. 1881, from Brandford Griffith to Kimberley; C. 3064.

[3] Ellis, *History*, ch. xxviii, and Claridge, *History*, vol. ii, ch. xi.

[4] Dispatch of 30 May 1881, from Rowe to Kimberley; C. 3064. Rowe commented: 'I believe I cannot exaggerate the value of the presence of this axe as a public proclamation on the part of the Ashanti King of his submission to the authority of Her most gracious Majesty.' But Claridge thought, more simply, that the Ashantis gave it up because they had lost all faith in its power. *History*, vol. ii, p. 243.

[5] Cf. *The Gold Coast Times*, 1 Oct. 1881, for a sensational editorial on 'Human Sacrifices in Coomassie'.

[6] Dispatch No. 447 of 18 Oct. 1881, from Kimberley to Rowe; CO/96/136.

[7] Dispatch of 9 July 1881, from Rowe to Kimberley; C. 3064.

entered into a defensive alliance to protect themselves against any Ashanti attack.[1] Almost immediately, Lonsdale was sent up-country again, this time to settle Mensa Bonsu's latest dispute with Gyaman.[2] Mindful of the western trade routes, he returned via Sefwi and Denkera to Cape Coast, and found that the main problem was to prevent the irresponsible molesting of traders, even where the Chiefs professed co-operation.[3]

The encouragement of commerce did not involve any political concessions towards Ashanti. Kimberley agreed with his advisers that 'till they have changed their nature it is better for us that they should be "down" and not "up" '. The revival of Ashanti power would be sure to bring serious trouble to the British, and so it was better to encourage the independence of the border countries, and to cultivate good relations with them.[4] The policy towards Ashanti might be described as political attrition, combined with economic competition. At the same time, the bitterness among the Fantis was beginning to die down. *The Gold Coast Times* suggested that a Consul should be sent to Kumasi;[5] and followed this up with a serialized article on the 'Future of the Gold Coast', which went so far as to say: 'The Kingdom of Ashantee can be fairly and without dispute called a Gold Coast country, for putting aside the little peculiarities observable in the inhabitants of its nations they speak a common language and they both come from one and the same stock or progenitor.'[6] Such sentiments, however, were as yet far from general acceptance.

Lonsdale was profoundly impressed by the internal dissension that was tearing the Ashanti kingdom apart, and reported that the people were praying for direct intervention by the British Government, to shield them from the injustice and cruelty of Mensa Bonsu. He suggested that European officers should be stationed as consuls at various points in the interior. But Kimberley firmly rejected what he called 'the usual recommendation, white men to take care of the black men and all will be well. All over the world . . . this is the panacea.'[7] He remained adamant, in spite of strong representations from London and Manchester merchants.[8] In 1883, when Mensa Bonsu had been forced to flee from Kumasi,[9] the Governor refused an invitation to settle the dispute over the succession to the Golden Stool. The British authorities were,

[1] Report of 18 Mar. 1882, by Lonsdale on his Mission to Kumasi, Salaga and Yendi; C. 3386.
[2] Instructions of 24 Mar. 1882, from Rowe to Lonsdale; ibid.
[3] Short Report of 2 Aug. 1882, by Lonsdale, on his Mission to Ashanti and Gyaman; also his Full Report, enclosed in his Letter of 14 Apr. 1883, to Derby. *Further Correspondence regarding Affairs of the Gold Coast* (London, 1883), C. 3687.
[4] Minutes of 6 June 1882, by E. Ashley (Parliamentary Under-Secretary), and of 7 June and 28 July 1882, by Kimberley; CO/96/139.
[5] The same editorial was almost equally concerned that Cape Coast should have another letter-box. *The Gold Coast Times*, 25 Feb. 1882.
[6] Ibid. 20 May 1882.
[7] Minute of 4 Dec. 1882, by Kimberley; CO/96/143.
[8] *The Times*, 13 Dec. 1883; also correspondence in CO/96/152.
[9] Précis of Report of 20 Aug. 1883, by Captain K. Barrow on his Mission to Kumasi; *Further Correspondence regarding the Affairs of the Gold Coast* (London, 1884), C. 4052.

however, reluctantly becoming a party to Ashanti's internal quarrels. Their disinclination to intervene in any decisive manner simply had the effect of prolonging a period of unrest, without convincing anybody that Ashanti was being left to its own affairs.[1]

There followed several years of confusion, intensified by the death of the next Asantehene shortly after his enstoolment, and later of his chosen successor, and by the unexplained failure of the Government to respond to another Ashanti request for a European 'peacemaker'.[2] By 1886 the Chiefs were sharply divided into two factions, each supporting rival candidates for the Golden Stool;[3] one was Agyeman Prempeh, then in his early teens, and the other was Yaw Achiriboanda, a cousin of Mensa Bonsu.[4] Excessive delay and indecision in Accra had no doubt contributed to the critical situation in Ashanti. *The Gold Coast Methodist* complained with some justification of the policy towards Ashanti and the other tribes: 'What a halting, helpless one it is.'[5] Soon afterwards, the Manchester Chamber of Commerce, prompted by a memorial from Gold Coast merchants, strongly attacked the failure of the Government to maintain its authority and to check the depredations of the border tribes, especially the Adansis.[6]

In 1887 Lonsdale was sent up to Ashanti again, this time accompanied by E. A. Barnett. Their instructions were to make peace between the Bekwais and the Kokofus, and to assist in establishing a strong central government in Kumasi. Lonsdale was unable to stay long enough to ensure a permanent settlement, but the Chiefs begged Barnett to remain until they could rally sufficient support for Prempeh.[7] Strictly speaking, he could not be made Asantehene without the formal participation of the Kings of Mampong and Kokofu; but their representatives gave assurances of support, and in March 1888 Prempeh was chosen as King-elect, with the consent of the linguists, under the title of Kwaku Dua III. Barnett was present at this preliminary ceremony, when Prempeh was given the care of the 'royal stool', and referred to him thereafter as King of Ashanti;[8] but in fact his position was not yet secure. The Kokofus, who soon rebelled, had to be driven across the Prah;

[1] Cf. Minute of 6 Oct. 1883, by R. H. Meade: 'let them fight it out and if the Ashantee Kingdom breaks up, all the better for its neighbours. We don't want a strong united Ashantee.' CO/96/151.

[2] Interviews with Ashanti Messengers in Accra on 16 Oct. and 21 Nov. 1884; Palaver Book, 1877–87, G.N. Archives.

[3] C. W. Badger's Report of 20 Oct. 1886; *Further Correspondence respecting the Affairs of the Gold Coast* (London, 1888), C. 5357.

[4] Rattray says that Prempeh was backed by most of the Chiefs of Kumasi and the Kings of Bekwai and Juaben, and Achiriboanda by the Kings of Kokofu, Mampong, and Nsuta. *Ashanti Law and Constitution*, p. 177.

[5] *The Gold Coast Methodist*, Dec. 1886.

[6] Petition of 8 Feb. 1887, to Secretary of State from Manchester Chamber of Commerce; C. 5357.

[7] Dispatch of 13 Apr. 1888, from Brandford Griffith to Knutsford, and enclosures; *Further Correspondence respecting the Affairs of the Gold Coast* (London 1888), C. 5615.

[8] Letters of 29 Mar. and 9 May 1888, from Barnett to Brandford Griffith; ibid.

the King of Mampong fled to Attabubu, and Achiriboanda went down to the coast, where he continued to hope and intrigue for the Golden Stool.

Renewed British Interest in Ashanti, 1888–94

The Colonial Office, which was watching Ashanti almost as anxiously as the Home Office watched Ireland, was hoping for a period of peace and quiet under this new ruler. Barnett, while in Kumasi, had added his voice to the chorus urging the Government to appoint an officer to remain there; and the refrain was taken up once more by the merchants of Cape Coast. The Governor, W. Brandford Griffith, had no objection in principle, although he was anxious not to risk the life of a European during the rainy season; but in London it was felt that there were strong objections to the appointment of a Resident, especially the estimated annual cost of £7,000. Further, it was argued that the ultimate result would be the inclusion of Ashanti in the Protectorate;[1] and no one was yet prepared to answer to Parliament for that.

During this period local officials were usually several steps ahead of Colonial Office opinion, revealing clearly how, in the absence of definite guidance from London, policy could virtually be made by the man on the spot. Brandford Griffith had already pointed out the danger to British interests from French colonial ambitions, which were being revived by exploration in the hinterland of the Gold Coast.[2] Fearing that they might penetrate to Ashanti and prevail upon the people to come under French protection, he had urged in 1886 that the territory should instead be quickly brought under British jurisdiction.[3] The following year the Governor sent further warnings, against German expansion. At first these were not taken very seriously in London;[4] and the Secretary of State even minuted, 'If Ashanti is to be annexed to any European power let it be by the Germans.'[5] But the next few years of competitive penetration in the interior, combined with diplomatic haggling in Europe, convinced the Colonial Office that some action must be taken, at least to the north of Ashanti.

[1] For example, Minutes of 24 and 26 May 1888 by A. W. L. Hemming; CO/96/191.

[2] Captain L. G. Binger had been entrusted by the French Government in 1886 with a mission of reconnaissance along the bend of the Niger. He started from the interior, in order to avoid arousing British suspicions, and by 1889 had covered a vast area between Bamako, Kong, and Wagadugu, treading on British heels at Salaga and Kintampo, and getting into Bontuku just before them with a treaty of protection for Gyaman. See Binger, *Du Niger au Golfe de Guinée par le pays de Kong et le Mossi, 1887–89* (Paris, 1892), 2 vols. The British mission to Bontuku in 1888 is described by R. A. Freeman, *Travels and Life in Ashanti and Jaman* (London, 1898), ch. vii.

[3] Dispatch No. 51 of 5 Feb. 1886, from Brandford Griffith to Stanley; CO/96/172. Also Confidential Dispatch of 22 Apr. 1886, from Brandford Griffith to Granville; CO/96/173.

[4] A young official at the Colonial Office, Sidney Webb, wrote: 'I should pause before going further *north*. It would no doubt be inconvenient to have the Germans behind our backs at the Gold Coast, but . . . The Gold Coast Colony has cost England some 6 lives this year alone. Is it worth extending?' Minute of 22 Aug. 1887; CO/96/188.

[5] Minute of 21 Sept. 1887, by H. T. Holland (later Lord Knutsford); ibid.

The Anglo-French Agreement of 1889, defining the western boundary of the Gold Coast for only 20 miles inland, after which it could be prolonged up to the ninth parallel according to treaties made with the local Chiefs, encouraged the spirit of competition for treaties and trade.[1] Similarly, the Anglo-German Treaty of 1890, by establishing a Neutral Zone to the north-east of Ashanti within which both nations bound themselves not to acquire protectorates,[2] served only to sharpen colonial rivalries in the surrounding territory.[3] Thus, when the King of Attabubu requested British protection, the Secretary of State was content to follow the advice of the Governor, then on leave in London,[4] and a treaty of friendship and protection was executed by George Ferguson, the pioneer African surveyor, in 1890.[5]

But London's new-found tolerance towards extensions of the Protectorate was not yet applied to Ashanti itself. When Brandford Griffith was advised to send another fact-finding mission to Kumasi,[6] he bettered his instructions by dispatching one of his officers in March 1891, with a draft treaty of protection and a letter to Prempeh strongly recommending its acceptance. He neglected even to inform the Colonial Office until two months later.[7] This was not well received, and on his return to London he was reprimanded for having broached so important a matter without previous authority from the Secretary of State, especially since he could have telegraphed for permission.[8] But, as it happened, influential Ashantis had ceased to look to the British for assistance; most of the internal wars had been settled, and the people were hoping for a restoration of their former power under their new King. So Prempeh refused the Governor's offer firmly, but with some courtesy:

---

[1] E. Hertslet, *The Map of Africa by Treaty* (London, 3rd edn. 1909), vol. iii, p. 730.

[2] Ibid. p. 893.

[3] The treaty also defined the southern Gold Coast–Togoland boundary in general terms, but its interpretation in detail aroused much local resentment. At Peki, for example, the King of Krepi told the Anglo-German Boundary Commission: 'I myself gave myself and people to the Governor it is not the Governor that asked me ... If the Queen says she does not like me I take my freedom. ... I gave it to you whole, now you want to divide my land ... If the English want to "dash" any of my people to their friends they must first come to me and we will talk.' His right-wing commander, the Fia of Awudome, declared defiantly: 'they say these sticks are our boundary ... kindly go and take away those sticks'. Report of meeting at Peki, 17–18 Apr. 1892, enclosed in Confidential Dispatch of 10 May 1892, from Brandford Griffith to Knutsford; CO/96/223. Sticks or no sticks, the European-made boundary remained.

[4] Dispatch No. 23 of 14 Jan. 1890, from Hodgson to Knutsford, and Colonial Office minutes thereon; CO/96/208.

[5] G. E. Ferguson, *Report on Mission to Atabubu* (London, 1891). The map opposite, reproduced from *The Times*, 24 Feb. 1898, shows both the Neutral Zone and most of the European treaties of the 1890's.

[6] Dispatch of 15 Oct. 1890, from Knutsford to Brandford Griffith; C. 7917.

[7] Dispatch of 19 May 1891, from Brandford Griffith to Knutsford, and enclosures; ibid.

[8] Letter of 3 Sept. 1891, from Colonial Office to Brandford Griffith; ibid. It was now quicker to send a message from Accra to London than to Kumasi, since the opening of a direct telegraphic link between Accra and Liverpool in 1886. CO/96/175. For some years previously, urgent messages had been sent by mail steamer from Accra via Madeira to Lisbon, and thence by telegraph to England. CO/96/107.

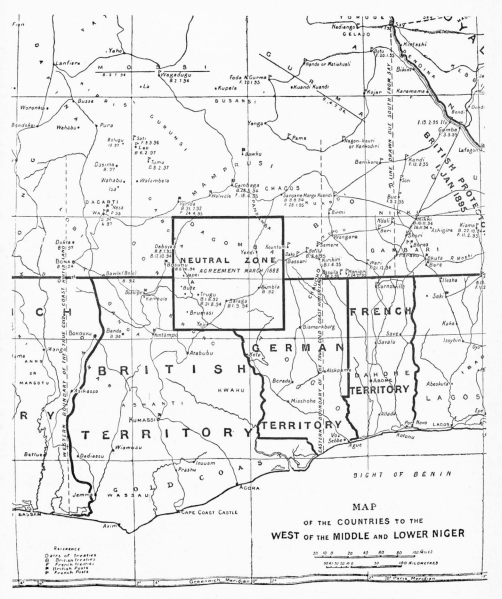

MAP 7. European territories and treaties—from a map published in *The Times*,
24 February 1898.

'I am happy to say we have arrived at this conclusion, that my Kingdom of Ashanti . . . must remain independent as of old, at the same time to be friendly with all white men. . . . Believe me, Governor, that I am happy to inform you, that the cause of Ashanti is progressing'.[1]

Five years of precious independence were all that remained to Prempeh. Brandford Griffith, somewhat chastened and overworked, now preferred merely to watch the disintegration of the kingdom, and 'gather the fruit when it is ripe'.[2] But the Colonial Office, while still refusing to entertain the idea of British responsibility for Ashanti, continued the policy of expansion farther north that made its eventual inclusion within the British sphere virtually inevitable. During 1892, for example, Ferguson concluded a series of treaties with several important northern tribes, including Dagomba, binding them not to accept the protection of any other Power without the consent of the British.[3]

In 1893, when the Ashantis appeared to be on the point of attacking Attabubu, a strong warning was sent to Kumasi, and a force of Hausas, under Sir Francis Scott, to Attabubu itself.[4] Although they had strict instructions to avoid an engagement, the opportunity was taken to conclude treaties of 'friendship and freedom of trade' with several neighbouring tribes who wished to assert their independence of Ashanti, including Nkoranza;[5] and although these did not grant the full protection the Chiefs had asked for, such subtle distinctions were not generally appreciated.[6]

F. M. Hodgson, the Acting Governor, had now made up his mind that Ashanti must ultimately be annexed. He advocated a settled policy to this end, which would avoid the expense of constant skirmishes, and make possible an increase in trade sufficient to justify an annual expenditure even of several thousand pounds. Hodgson claimed that the most powerful tribes would welcome annexation, although he was not certain whether the Hausa constabulary could cope with the Ashanti army. But he was able to quote the opinion of Ramseyer, now at Abetifi, that Kumasi could be brought under the British flag without a single shot being fired.[7]

Scott, on his way north, had found the Juabens and Agogos, as well as the Nkoranzas, asking for protection; and he urged that an ultimatum should

[1] Letter of 7 May 1891, from King of Ashanti to Brandford Griffith, enclosed in his Dispatch of 3 June 1891, to Knutsford; C. 7917.

[2] Dispatch of 13 Dec. 1892, from Brandford Griffith to Ripon; ibid.

[3] *Collection of Treaties with Native Chiefs, &c., in West Africa* (London, 1914), African (West) No. 1010, pt. iii, nos. 1–5.

[4] Dispatch of 29 Sept. 1893, from Hodgson to Ripon, and enclosures; C. 7917.

[5] African (West) No. 1010, pt. iii, nos. 6–12.

[6] As Scott commented, Africans would find it difficult to understand 'how anyone who has received a flag and "made paper" with "the white man" can be otherwise than under his protection'. Letter of 7 Feb. 1894, to Colonial Secretary, enclosed in Dispatch of 21 Feb. 1894, from Hodgson to Ripon; C. 7917.

[7] Confidential Dispatch of 13 Nov. 1893, from Hodgson to Ripon, and enclosed Letter of 31 Oct. 1893, from Ramseyer to Acting Governor; CO/96/238.

be sent to Prempeh to bring Ashanti under British protection, which he thought could be done without bloodshed. The Acting Governor welcomed this support for a 'forward policy' towards Ashanti; unlike Scott and Ramseyer, he expected some resistance, but this should not be very serious, since the Ashantis were poorly armed and without money. Nevertheless, he was not prepared to issue an ultimatum unless he could count on British troops to back it up if necessary.[1] His views found some support in the Colonial Office:

> As regards Ashanti the present moment seems more favourable than we may get again. The King is cowed & the bulk of his people wish for protection, so the time is ripe for a bold stroke such as tells with savages. The Colony is rich & can afford the outlay (say £10,000) which will be necessary for a few years.[2]

But Lord Ripon, then Secretary of State, was not prepared for such drastic action: 'I do not desire to annex Ashanti in name or in fact and thereby greatly to increase the responsibilities of the Gold Coast Government.'[3] Hodgson must have regarded this as merely postponing the inevitable; but he was not given sanction to proceed with his forward policy, and Scott was ordered to return to Accra, which he did with considerable regret.[4]

Hodgson was asked instead to consider the possibility of a *via media*, by which the object desired might be attained without the use of force; the King and his principal Chiefs might be paid stipends, in return for accepting a British Resident at Kumasi and promising not to make war on the Nkoranzas, Attabubus, and other neighbouring tribes.[5] The only flaw in this scheme was the failure to consider what would happen should the King refuse. Even though in the event he evaded a direct answer, local officials were ready to take this as an excuse to follow up the offer with threats of force. The Secretary of State clearly intended his proposal to mean no more than it said; but once committed to this apparent compromise, the gradual abandonment of the ideal of non-intervention was almost inevitable.

Meanwhile the British were rapidly becoming more deeply involved in the race against France and Germany for treaties with the northern tribes. Ferguson, who had travelled with the Attabubu expedition, continued his journey northwards during 1894 to complete a belt of treaties all round the west and north of the Neutral Zone, bringing such important tribes as the Dagartis, Mamprussis, and Mossis under some obligation to the British.[6] Later in the year he moved into the Neutral Zone itself for a series of treaties designed to improve Britain's bargaining position with Germany.[7] 1894 was also marked

---

[1] Confidential Dispatch of 18 Nov. 1893, from Hodgson to Ripon, and enclosed Letter of 8 Nov. 1893, from Scott to Colonial Secretary; CO/96/238.

[2] Minute of 21 Dec. 1893, by J. Bramston; ibid.

[3] Minute of 15 Jan. 1894, by Ripon; ibid.

[4] Letter of 5 Mar. 1894, from Scott to Hodgson, enclosed in Dispatch of 22 Mar. 1894, from Brandford Griffith to Ripon; C. 7917.

[5] Confidential Dispatch of 30 Jan. 1894, from Ripon to Hodgson; ibid.

[6] African (West) No. 1010, pt. iii, nos. 13-17.   [7] Ibid. nos. 18-24.

by a German expedition into the hinterland of Togo,[1] and the following year saw further penetration into the Kong region by the French, who had already declared a Protectorate over Dahomey.[2] While the Great Powers of Europe were thus elbowing for position on the African map, it was hardly to be expected that Ashanti would be left to its own devices. Yet even now the Colonial Office was hoping to evade the responsibility of a direct challenge to Prempeh, and to get by with its *via media*.

It was in March 1894 that Hendrick Vroom, an African Commissioner, was sent to Kumasi, armed with a draft agreement and a letter from the Acting Governor to Prempeh asking him to accept a British officer stationed at Kumasi 'as the Agent of this Government, and as your friend and adviser'.[3] Vroom was authorized to pledge the Government to pay stipends up to a total of £2,000 a year, including a suggested £600 to the King of Ashanti, and lesser sums to the Kings of Mampong, Kokofu, Bekwai, and Juaben, and to the Queen Mother, Yaa Kyia.[4]

It was difficult to get any answer to Hodgson's request, since Prempeh was observing the funeral custom for his sister. After a few weeks' stay the most Vroom could obtain was a letter from Prempeh deferring a formal reply until his 'District Kings, Chiefs and principal men' arrived in Kumasi, when they could discuss 'the subject of the British Government, which is not a small case'.[5] Vroom suspected that an embassy to Christiansborg was being planned, in order to win better terms from the Government. There was now strong support for Prempeh to be placed on the Golden Stool, in order to reunite the Confederacy and to negotiate more effectively with the Governor; and the Chiefs were extremely anxious to get Vroom out of the way before this took place.[6] He did not stay long in Kumasi.

In June 1894 Prempeh was formally enstooled as Asantehene, this time with full ceremony, in the presence of two new Kings of Mampong and Kokofu, who had been appointed to replace the exiles. Prempeh wrote to inform the Governor that he had 'entered at the Royal Palace', and also that his 'grandson' John Ansah would come shortly, with six others, to give the

[1] See *Further Correspondence respecting the Missions of Mr. G. E. Ferguson and the Extent of the Sphere of British Influence in the Hinterland of the Gold Coast Colony* (London, 1895), African (West) No. 479.

[2] See J. Scott Keltie, *The Partition of Africa* (London, 1895 edn.), ch. xvi, 'The Struggle for the Niger', and R. L. Buell, *The Native Problem in Africa* (New York, 1928), vol. i, ch. 55, 'The French Occupation of West Africa'.

[3] Confidential Dispatch of 26 Feb. 1894, from Hodgson to Ripon, and enclosures; CO/96/243.

[4] Letter of 23 Feb. 1894, from Hodgson to Vroom; ibid. The letter to the King made no mention of the stipends, on Vroom's advice, to avoid giving Prempeh the impression 'that he and his country were being bought by British gold'; but it did contain an indirect reference to the possibility of Achiriboanda's succession to the Golden Stool, which probably had the reverse effect from that intended.

[5] Letter of 7 Apr. 1894, from King Kwaku Dua III to Acting Governor, enclosed in Confidential Dispatch of 7 May 1894, from Brandford Griffith to Ripon; CO/96/245.

[6] Report of 24 Apr. 1894, by Vroom; ibid.

Governor the final decision concerning the recent important proposal.[1] This letter was brought by Prempeh's sword-bearer and court crier, but Brandford Griffith would not receive the messengers personally, 'as their rank was not such as to make them worthy of having an interview with me',[2] and he later informed Prempeh that he still awaited a reply.[3]

When reports of the enstoolment ceremonies reached the coast, they were accompanied by numerous atrocity stories. *The Gold Coast Methodist Times* of 31 August reported 'A dreadful slaughter of human victims', and claimed that 400 had been killed. *The Gold Coast People* of 24 September wrote: 'We have no wish to pollute our pages with a description of the revolting, cruel and savage iniquities committed in open day in the streets of the Ashanti capital.' There seems to be no doubt that some sacrifices took place, though fewer than these reports suggested. Brandford Griffith refused to recognize the enstoolment; he alleged that it was a sham ceremony, performed by selected puppets. Until now the British authorities seem to have assumed that Prempeh was already King of Ashanti; but Brandford Griffith took this opportunity to refuse even titular recognition and began to address him merely as 'King of Kumasi'.[4] This left open the possibility of supporting Achiriboanda, but did nothing to improve the chances of friendly relations with Ashanti.[5]

In September 1894 Brandford Griffith urgently recommended that a strong mission should be sent to Kumasi if there should be any further delay in replying to the British proposal.[6] The Secretary of State reiterated that 'it is *not* the policy of HM's Govt. to annex Ashantee, and that it would be very unacceptable to us to advance in that direction'.[7] But the Governor believed that non-intervention had proved 'neither humane nor politic', and that a firm policy was essential. He suggested that the Ashantis had been united in arms only by the threat of common foes, who were now under British protection;

---

[1] John Ansah, the eldest son of Prince Ansah, was the grandson of a former Asantehene, and thus a grandson of the 'stool', although he was in fact older than Prempeh himself. During 1889 he had endeavoured to get himself appointed as Prempeh's ambassador to the Governor, but Brandford Griffith refused to recognize him (Memorandum of interview between Ansah, Governor and Colonial Secretary, dated 13 June 1889; C. 7917). He later returned to Kumasi, and was now said to be acting as Prempeh's 'Prime Minister'. Claridge makes him the scapegoat in the course of his apologia for Prempeh: 'Ansa's connection with him in all probability did more than anything else to bring Prempeh into a discredit that was largely undeserved.' *History*, vol. ii, p. 380.

[2] Confidential Dispatch of 26 July 1894, from Brandford Griffith to Ripon, and enclosed Letter of 28 June 1894, from Kwaku Dua III to Governor; CO/96/247.

[3] Letter of 3 Aug. 1894, from Governor to 'King of Kumasi', enclosed in Confidential Dispatch of 10 Aug. 1894, from Brandford Griffith to Ripon; ibid.

[4] Letter of 1 July 1895, from Brandford Griffith to Colonial Office; CO/96/268.

[5] The draft agreement offered to Prempeh a few months earlier had been made out as between the Queen and the 'King of Ashanti'. Claridge suggests that this invalidated the Government's 'ridiculous' refusal to recognize Prempeh as King of Ashanti. *History*, vol. ii, pp. 390–1.

[6] Confidential Dispatch of 28 Sept. 1894, from Brandford Griffith to Ripon; CO/96/247.

[7] Note of 23 Oct. 1894, by Ripon, on his conversation with Hodgson (Colonial Secretary), then in London; CO/96/248.

and that the policy of the past twenty years—whereby the British had 'striven loyally and earnestly to prop up Ashanti', and to make it 'at unity with itself, and self-reliant'—had now been proved a failure.

It might be argued that the trouble was not, as Brandford Griffith thought, a policy that had been tried and found unavailing, but the lack of any clear British policy at all. Nevertheless, whatever the cause, Ashanti was no longer a compact State; in the words of Brandford Griffith, it was 'nothing but a few tribes with difficulty held together by the power and the recollection of the former influence of Kumasi, each tribe biding its time to become independent'. To attempt seriously to restore the former balance of power would, according to the Governor, endanger security and trade. He therefore recommended that Ashanti should be included in the Protectorate, either by annexing its several sections one by one, or preferably by asserting British power over the whole country at once.[1]

The local newspapers were continuing to build up feeling against the Ashantis. In Accra *The Gold Coast Chronicle* called for direct action:

we must go straight to Kumasi and occupy or annex it, declaring Ashantee a British protectorate . . . if there are 800 Hausas in this Colony, send them all to Ashantee with the Union Jack, and let the whole of that country be declared once and for all a British protectorate in spite of all opposition . . . It is a reproach moreover to the civilization of this country, that any savage King should be suffered by the British Government to do what King Prempeh is daily doing.[2]

At the end of 1894 a deputation from the Cape Coast Chamber of Commerce asked that Ashanti should be brought within the sphere of British influence and a permanent Resident appointed.[3] They were not satisfied with the Governor's reply; but most of them had direct business or personal links with Manchester, and the petition was forwarded to the Chamber of Commerce there.[4] In England, increasing pressure had recently been brought to bear on the Secretary of State, from the Chambers of Commerce of Liverpool, London, and Glasgow, to bring Ashanti under British protection.[5]

The Ashanti Embassy to London, 1894–5

The obvious reluctance in Kumasi to accept the proposal for a British Resident was mainly prompted by the well-founded fear that such a step would soon be followed by the conversion of Ashanti into a Protectorate, with all that that implied in the way of abolishing slavery and other customs.[6] It was

---

[1] Memorandum of 24 Oct. 1894, by Brandford Griffith, enclosed in his Confidential Dispatch of 31 Oct. 1894, to Ripon; ibid.   [2] *The Gold Coast Chronicle*, 30 Nov. 1894.

[3] Petition and Notes of Interview on 4 Dec. 1894, enclosed in Confidential Dispatch of 2 July 1895, from Maxwell to Secretary of State; CO/96/259.

[4] Letter of 15 Feb. 1895, from Secretary, Manchester Chamber of Commerce, to Colonial Office; CO/96/269.   [5] C. 7917.

[6] Article in *The Graphic*, 4 May 1895 (soon after the embassy had arrived in London), quoted by Maxwell in his Confidential Dispatch of 13 June 1895, to Ripon; CO/96/258.

felt that a direct threat to the independence of the country was involved, and that a mere message of refusal to the Governor would not suffice to avert this.[1] The Ashanti leaders were more aware than the Secretary of State of the realities of the situation, perhaps because they were more sharply conscious of the attitudes of the men on the spot. In particular, Brandford Griffith's professions of friendship were distrusted, while he was 'at the very time seeking to detach from the King certain of his feudatories'.[2] Prempeh had therefore decided—or been persuaded—that a deputation to England was necessary. John Ansah was confident of success; he must have taken an interest in the Cape Coast deputation scheme of 1885-7,[3] and he was in touch with James Brew, its main sponsor, who was now in London.

It was in October 1894 that reports of Prempeh's new plan first reached the coast. The Governor now understood earlier rumours he had heard of a 10s. tax being levied on every person in Ashanti;[4] evidently sufficient had been collected to defray the expenses of messengers to England, for they were on their way from Kumasi to see him first.[5] Meanwhile, in Axim, Albert Ansah[6] (the brother of John) informed the Government that an embassy—which he himself was to join—was on its way from Kumasi 'direct to Her Britannic Majesty', and asked that the special envoys might be officially received before their embarkation, in accordance with the wishes of 'His Majesty the King'.[7]

The prospect was not welcomed in the Colonial Office. It was hoped that the Ashantis could be prevented from coming to London, where they might be used by political opponents to harass the Government; there was even a danger that they might go on to Paris and stir up 'the most anti-English views'. The embassy was dismissed as a scheme of the Ansahs to enhance their own importance, and get a holiday at the expense of the Ashanti government; it was regarded as irrelevant to the negotiations with Kumasi.[8] So Brandford Griffith was instructed by telegram to tell the 'King of Kumasi' that he should reply through the Governor to the original message brought by Vroom; and that his envoys could under no circumstances be received by the

---

[1] It has been argued that Prempeh's failure to accept the British proposals was due to his inability to commit Ashanti as a whole, since so many States had seceded from the Union. But no such argument was put forward by Ashanti spokesmen at the time, and all the contemporary evidence supports the view that the embassy was a last desperate attempt by the King to retain control of an independent Ashanti.

[2] Circular Letter of 5 Sept. 1895, from J. Ossoo Ansah, to enlist support in England; CO/96/267.

[3] See Ch. XI, pp. 410–18, below.

[4] Confidential Dispatch of 10 Aug. 1894, from Brandford Griffith to Ripon; CO/96/247.

[5] Confidential Dispatches of 24 and 31 Oct. 1894, from Brandford Griffith to Ripon; CO/96/248.

[6] Albert, the second son of Prince Ansah, was born in Cape Coast, and became a government clerk. In 1884 he was dismissed for 'insolence, irregularity and disobedience of orders'; he was reinstated, but resigned in protest against being put on a lower grade. Since then he had been trading at Cape Coast and Axim.

[7] Letter of 7 Nov. 1894, from A. A. Ossoo Ansah to District Commissioner, Axim, enclosed in Confidential Dispatch of 15 Nov. 1894, from Brandford Griffith to Ripon; CO/96/249.

[8] Minute of 27 Nov. 1894, by Hemming; ibid.

Queen, coming as they did 'from a ruler who is accused on apparently good grounds of allowing human sacrifices'.[1]

On their arrival at Cape Coast in December 1894, the Ashanti envoys had several interviews with the Governor. Brandford Griffith read aloud 'a message from the Queen' (his Colonial Office telegram) after a band had played a few bars of the National Anthem; he also did his best to discredit both the Ansah brothers, especially John, whom he accused of having 'got at the young King' to put him in a false position, and of working under the influence of 'an unprincipled native in England'.[2] (This was James Brew.) The other envoys came in for their share of abuse, which caused some mild surprise in Whitehall; as one official commented: 'The Governor's tongue wagged a little too much I think.'[3]

After this, the Ashanti envoys informed the Governor in writing that they still intended to carry out their mission, even if they were denied the liberty and courtesy normally accorded to British subjects.[4] They had already sent a telegram to a M.P. in London, asking him to communicate with the Foreign Office in order to obtain the Queen's permission for them to proceed to England.[5] This was designed partly to bear out their claim to be an independent nation, partly as a means of by-passing the usual channels. But the reply came from the Colonial Office, confirming the decision that they could not be received;[6] and the Governor was instructed to forbid them to sail.[7] Brandford Griffith must have been only too pleased to transmit this message immediately to the Ashantis:[8] but they asked with some reason and even more dignity whether Her Majesty's Government had ever exercised the right of excluding visitors from any part of the world; as an embassy, they had no alternative but to obey the commands of their King.[9]

The Governor sent Captain D. Stewart and Vroom to explain to Prempeh why his messengers had been stopped.[10] But after a fortnight in Kumasi they

[1] Telegram of 30 Nov. 1894, from Ripon to Brandford Griffith; ibid.

[2] Notes of Interviews on 12, 13, and 15 Dec. 1894, enclosed in Confidential Dispatches of 14 and 26 Dec. 1894, and 21 Jan. 1895, from Brandford Griffith to Ripon; CO/96/249 and 254.

[3] Minute of 22 Feb. 1895, by E. Wingfield; CO/96/254.

[4] Letter of 15 Dec. 1894, from Special Messengers to Brandford Griffith, enclosed in his Confidential Dispatch of 26 Dec. 1894, to Ripon; CO/96/249.

[5] Telegram of 13 Dec. 1894, to H. Labouchere, M.P.; CO/96/253.

[6] 'The King of Ashantee is now only the Head of a tribe, and does not hold a position which would entitle him to send "ambassadors" to the Queen of England; neither are they the class of person whom the Queen could be asked to receive.' Letter of 15 Dec. 1894, from Colonial Office to Labouchere; ibid.

[7] Telegrams of 20 Dec. 1894, from Colonial Office to Brandford Griffith; CO/96/249.

[8] Letter of 20 Dec. 1894 from Governor to 'Mr. John Osso Ansah, Chief Buatin, Kwaku Freku, Mr. A. A. Ansah and others composing the party of Special Messengers from the King of Kumasi', enclosed in Confidential Dispatch of 26 Dec. 1894, from Brandford Griffith to Ripon; ibid.

[9] Letter of 29 Dec. 1894, from Messengers from Kumasi to Brandford Griffith, enclosed in his Confidential Dispatch of 31 Dec. 1894, to Ripon; ibid.

[10] Confidential Dispatch of 26 Dec. 1894, from Brandford Griffith to Ripon; ibid.

could still get no reply to the proposal for a British Resident, and blatant cynicism prevailed on the coast: 'As the Ethiopian cannot change his skin, so also the Ashanti cannot change the natural bent of his mind in the direction of deceit, hypocrisy, mendacity, treachery, and unreliableness.'[1] Stewart and Vroom returned from Kumasi early in 1895 with complaints about their treatment by Prempeh, who had insisted that his envoys must give to the Queen alone the answer to the original letter brought by Vroom ten months previously.[2] In Cape Coast they were again warned that they would not be received by the Queen;[3] but John Ansah assured the Governor that nothing would deter them from going to England. He also said they would return unopened any further messages, unless properly addressed to the Ashanti embassy.[4]

This was too much for the already irate Governor. Brandford Griffith immediately urged the Secretary of State to deal a crushing blow to Ashanti, which would bring it under complete control.[5] There was some exasperation in London at the continued defiance from 'this petty King, who is no doubt egged on by the "educated natives", who have always been at the bottom of every intrigue & disturbance'.[6] But the suggestion of military action was not welcomed, especially as the Colonial Office did not now completely trust Brandford Griffith's advice. In any case, it was too late for an expedition before the next rainy season. The matter was discussed by the British Cabinet, and it was decided that Sir William Maxwell, who was shortly to replace Brandford Griffith, should examine and report on the whole situation afresh.[7] His first task would be to secure, if possible, a peaceful settlement. Failing this, Maxwell was authorized to approach Prempeh again, calling on him to fulfil his treaty obligations, and demanding a reply within a fixed time-limit. If this were not complied with, a military expedition would have to be sent. It was emphasized that no such ultimatum should be sent without direct authority from the Secretary of State, and that no preparations must be made for an expedition without his knowledge and approval.[8] But it is clear that the British had now reached the point of no return, and were at last beginning to face up to the consequences of their actions—and periods of inaction—over the past twenty years.

In London, James Brew inquired on behalf of the 'Princes at the head of

[1] Confidential Dispatch of 25 Jan. 1895 from Brandford Griffith to Ripon; CO/96/254.

[2] Report of 5 Feb. 1895, by Vroom and Stewart, and covering Confidential Dispatch of 6 Feb. 1895, from Brandford Griffith to Ripon; CO/96/255.

[3] Letter of 6 Feb. 1895, from Governor's Private Secretary to 'Mr. John Ossoo Ansah and the other persons sent by the King of Kumasi as Special Messengers to Cape Coast', enclosed in Confidential Dispatch of 13 Feb. 1895, from Brandford Griffith to Ripon; ibid.

[4] Letter of 11 Feb. 1895, from 'J. O. Ansah of Ashanti, Head of Embassy, for self & other Members of the Ashanti Embassy' to Governor; ibid.

[5] Telegram of 12 Feb. 1895, from Brandford Griffith to Ripon; ibid.

[6] Minute of 13 Feb. 1895, by Hemming; ibid.

[7] Minutes of 1 and 9 Mar. 1895, by Ripon; ibid.

[8] Confidential Dispatch of 15 Mar. 1895, from Ripon to Maxwell; ibid.

the Ashanti Embassy now at Cape Coast (to whom I am related)' whether
they were to be restrained by force by the Gold Coast Government from proceeding to England, and whether they would be received—either officially or
unofficially—if they did arrive.[1] In reply, he was merely referred to a parliamentary statement explaining why they would not be received.[2] Brandford
Griffith was instructed not to interfere with the envoys, legally or otherwise,
if only through fear of reciprocal action against British messengers sent to
Ashanti,[3] although it was suggested in the Colonial Office that the Ansahs
would be better locked up.[4]

The Ashanti embassy which eventually set sail from Cape Coast in April
1895 is of some significance as the first deputation to take to London a grievance which could in any sense be called national.[5] It consisted of the following
members: John Ansah, Albert Ansah, Kwamin Boatin (a Chief), Kwaku
Foku (a linguist), and four other court officials: Inkrumah, Bonnar, Dabban,
and Tufuor.[6] They left a week before Maxwell arrived, which he considered
a deliberate act of disrespect. Although the Colonial Office had repudiated
them in advance, Brew was not deterred. He wrote (on printed 'Ashanti
Embassy' notepaper) to inform two Secretaries of State—for the Colonies
and Foreign Affairs—of the arrival of the eight members of the embassy, and
inquired what day and hour 'after Wednesday next' would be convenient for
a formal call.[7] The Colonial Office merely repeated that the Ashantis would
neither be recognized nor received, and that they should deal direct with the
new Governor in the Gold Coast.[8]

Brew thereupon produced voluminous documentary evidence to establish
the status of Prempeh as King of Ashanti and of the mission as an embassy,
and also to deny the charges of human sacrifices.[9] On these points the Colonial
Office preferred to accept a detailed analysis by the late Governor.[10] The
Ashanti embassy remained in England for over six months, but to no political
purpose. A change of Government brought no concessions to their demands,
and the doors of the Colonial Office remained closed to them.[11]

---

[1] Letter of 9 Feb. 1895, from Brew to Ripon; CO/96/267.

[2] S. Buxton, Parliamentary Under-Secretary of State, *Parliamentary Debates*, House of Commons, 14 Feb. 1895.

[3] Minute of 25 Mar. 1895, by Meade, and Telegram of 26 Mar. 1895, from Colonial Office
to Brandford Griffith; CO/96/255.   [4] Minute of 17 Mar. 1895, by Hemming; ibid.

[5] For an earlier but abortive deputation project, see Ch. XI, pp. 410–18, below. Cf. also King
Aggery's commissioners, who spoke mainly for Cape Coast, Ch. V, pp. 204–9 and 212, above.

[6] The spelling of these names varies considerably, even in Government Dispatches; Foku (or
Fokoo), for example, was sometimes called Freku.

[7] Letters of 6 May 1895, from Brew to Secretaries of State for the Colonies and Foreign Affairs;
CO/96/267.   [8] Letter of 9 May 1895, from Colonial Office to Brew; ibid.

[9] Letter of 22 May 1895, from Brew to Secretary of State for Foreign Affairs, with numerous
enclosures; ibid.

[10] Letter of 1 July 1895, from Brandford Griffith (at 'The Chestnuts', Ealing) to Colonial
Office; CO/96/268.

[11] It is interesting to contrast the treatment of the Ansahs with that of the Bechuanaland Chiefs

The British Ultimatum, 1895

Meanwhile, in the Gold Coast, Maxwell was studying the situation and formulating a new policy towards Ashanti. He expected the deputation to return disappointed by their failure in England, and proposed to tell them firmly that the proper place for the discussion of the future of Ashanti was Kumasi itself, and that he would be willing to go there to treat with the King in person on being invited to do so. Matters for negotiation should, Maxwell suggested, include the acceptance by all Ashanti tribes of British protection with guarantees for the freedom of trade between the coast and the interior, the safety of missionaries, and the abolition of human sacrifices. If such an approach were refused, then an ultimatum threatening military action would have to be sent to Prempeh. Simultaneously with this, separate messages could be sent to the other Ashanti Kings, and also to the scattered remnants of the refugee tribes, offering them formal admission within the Protectorate. Though the 'quarrel' of the Colonial Government was with Kumasi only, tribes which did not actively help must be directed to 'hold aloof or take the consequences'.[1]

This new approach merits careful examination, since it was the first official reference to any quarrel with Prempeh or any need for help from the other tribes. Until then, the only question at issue had been the peaceful proposal to station a British Resident at Kumasi as the Asantehene's 'friend and adviser', and the failure of Prempeh to reply to the Governor, though irritating, could hardly be called a quarrel; while no serious attempt had ever been made to enforce the Treaty of Fomena. Hodgson's 'forward policy' had been designed to crush the desire of the Ashantis for independence; this had not found sanction in London, and it was only seven months since Brandford Griffith had been sharply reminded that Ashanti was not to be annexed. But now Maxwell was proposing to exercise to the full the limited discretion that had been offered to him on his appointment.

As it happened, it was a new Secretary of State, Joseph Chamberlain, who took the decision on Maxwell's proposals. He replied by cable in September 1895 that Prempeh must be told to carry out the 1874 obligations, including the payment of the indemnity, to refrain from making attacks upon his neighbours, and to accept a British Resident at Kumasi, who would exercise control in these matters but would not otherwise interfere with the administration or institutions of the country. Protection was now to be extended to the tribes of Mo and Nkoranza, and others who had asked for it; and the Governor was instructed to meet Prempeh personally, either at Kumasi or on the road to Prasu. This was to be no empty threat; the Colonial Office was now

who came to England in the same year to press for the continuance of British protection, and who were probably the earliest deputation of Africans to be received in London, according to Lord Hailey. *An African Survey* (Oxford, 2nd edn. 1945), pp. 162 and 506.
[1] Confidential Dispatch of 13 June 1895, from Maxwell to Secretary of State; CO/96/258.

prepared to back Maxwell's policy to the extent of authorizing a military expedition.[1]

This telegram from Chamberlain at last filled the twenty-year policy vacuum with a surprisingly emphatic ultimatum. No doubt the Colonial Office had listened more readily to the recommendations of Maxwell than to those of the elderly, irascible Brandford Griffith. But at last it had been officially recognized that British inaction might stimulate rival European Powers to encroach across their agreed borders. There had been reports during 1894 of increasing purchases of arms and gunpowder by the Ashantis, and the Colonial Office hoped that the French and German Governments might jointly agree to prohibit—at least temporarily—this traffic.[2] The British Chambers of Commerce had continued during 1895 to urge the need for effective action in Ashanti, in order to increase the trade and revenue of the Protectorate.[3] Their arguments were not likely to be lost on Chamberlain. The new approach was summed up by *The Times* when it complained that the Ashantis had 'long formed a solid block of savagery' between the British coast and the Muslim interior, thus preventing a considerable amount of trade, and that the French were now opening up markets in the interior, which might well be lost to Britain.[4]

In 1896 Chamberlain indignantly denied that the new policy towards Ashanti had any reference to what the French were doing. He claimed that it was designed solely to put a stop to the 'intolerable nuisance' of the government of Ashanti, which since 1874 had obstructed the interests of civilization, of trade, and of the people themselves.[5] But several years later he admitted that when the Unionist Government came into office they were anxious about the advance of other nations: 'The danger was serious that in a very short time we should find all our colonies on this coast enclosed and depreciated, just as Gambia had been many years ago.'[6] This was the background to the firmness now adopted towards the Ashanti embassy, and towards Prempeh himself.[7]

As a result, Stewart and Vroom were sent to Kumasi again, in September 1895, with an ultimatum to Prempeh, requiring of him either a written reply or a personal interview with the Governor at Prasu before the end of October. They were empowered to make a separate treaty of protection with any Ashanti Chief who might ask for one, and especially to offer such a treaty to Bekwai; the Adansis were to be invited to return to their own lands.[8] The two

---

[1] Telegram of 6 Sept. 1895, from Chamberlain to Maxwell; ibid.

[2] Reports and Minutes in CO/96/248.

[3] *Further Correspondence relative to Affairs in Ashanti* (London, 1896), C. 7918.

[4] *The Times*, 21 Jan. 1896.

[5] *Parliamentary Debates*, House of Commons, 12 Mar. 1896.

[6] Ibid. 18 Mar. 1901.

[7] The Ashantis, however, attributed very different motives to the British; see Ch. II, p. 75, above.

[8] Letter of 23 Sept. 1895, from Governor to 'King of Kumasi', and Instructions to Stewart

officers were given a good reception in Kumasi, but no direct reply; and they refused to delay their return when asked to do so. They found a general distaste for the idea of the Asantehene leaving his own country, and reported that there was no chance of his meeting the Governor outside Kumasi.[1] On their return journey Stewart and Vroom concluded a treaty of friendship and protection with the Adansis at Prasu;[2] but the King of Bekwai refused to follow suit, fearing Prempeh's reactions unless he could give the excuse that he had been coerced.

Failure of the Embassy

In London the Ashantis were running into difficulties. The novelty of their arrival had worn off, and despite the help of some English friends they had still not been received at the Colonial Office, let alone by the Queen. They heard a rumour that the Governor was planning an expedition to Kumasi;[3] most of them could not speak English, and they began to quarrel among themselves. To make matters worse, they were running out of money. In September Tufuor and Dabban left for the Gold Coast,[4] and the Ansahs tried one last gamble, in conjunction with a British business man. They decided to form a British company to acquire 'all rights now possessed by the King of Ashanti in the dominions over which he rules'. The six Ashantis remaining in London then signed a concession whereby the proposed chartered company should appoint resident agents in Ashanti, build railways and factories, publish newspapers, issue coinage, grant licences for trading, mining, and other purposes, and develop the country generally, 'the King to receive an annual grant from the Company of one-fourth of the nett profits'.[5]

Chamberlain declined to recognize this 'alleged concession' for the development and administration of Ashanti,[6] 'arrangements which the King of Kumasi has no right or authority to make'.[7] In any case, it was too late. Since the Governor had received no reply within the time-limit, Chamberlain had decided that the proposed expedition must go forward, and that it might even

and Vroom, enclosed in Secret Dispatch of 26 Sept. 1895, from Maxwell to Chamberlain; CO/96/260.

[1] Report of 26 Oct. 1895, by Vroom and Stewart, enclosed in Confidential Dispatch of 28 Oct. 1895, from Maxwell to Chamberlain; CO/96/261.

[2] Treaty of 18 Oct. 1895; African No. 1010, pt. iii, no. 25.

[3] Letter of 5 Sept. 1895, from J. Ossoo Ansah to Colonial Office; CO/96/267.

[4] The Governor reported that they had returned for further funds to bring their colleagues home, but 'leaving the Ansahs altogether'; according to D. M. Abaddo, a Cape Coast trader just returned from England, 'the real Ashanti members of the mission' thought that the Ansahs and Brew had been 'squandering the money supplied to them on their own amusements'. Confidential Dispatch of 28 Oct. 1895, from Maxwell to Chamberlain; CO/96/261.

[5] Concession to G. Reckless, dated 21 Oct. 1895; C. 7918.

[6] Since Ashanti was still nominally independent, Chamberlain had no *locus standi* in the matter, either to grant or deny recognition; but no one queried this anticipation of British supremacy, which was clearly only a matter of time.

[7] Letter of 11 Nov. 1895, from Colonial Office to Harris; C. 7918.

be necessary to remove Prempeh from 'the position he now occupies'.[1] A sword-bearer and court crier eventually arrived in Accra from Kumasi, only to say that the Asantehene had already sent messengers to the Queen of England.[2] They brought no reply in writing; so this was regarded as a rejection of the ultimatum. Preparations for an expedition under the command of Sir Francis Scott were well under way in the Gold Coast towards the end of 1895, and Maxwell was expecting formidable resistance.[3] He summoned the Chiefs of the Protectorate in order to explain what was expected of them during the forthcoming expedition.[4]

It was at this juncture, just when Prempeh was putting his last hopes in them, that the embassy in London became really alarmed by an intimation from the Colonial Office that the expedition would proceed unless the King accepted the original terms of the ultimatum. This was the first time they had seen details of the British demands, and they hastily decided to accept, hoping thus to forestall a military disaster. They enlisted the help of a London barrister, T. Sutherst, and offered through him to execute a treaty of submission, sending copies of certain documents in support of their claim to act on behalf of the Asantehene.[5] Sutherst maintained that the Government could 'at once obtain all that can justly be demanded, without either firing a shot, sacrificing a life, or spending a pound'. He was quickly told that the expedition would not be delayed, and that if his clients had any real desire to avert the consequences, they should advise the King by telegram to accede to the demands made on him, and return to their country immediately to settle the matter at Kumasi.[6]

The Ashantis then sent a formal acceptance of the British terms, still hoping against hope for official recognition:

Acting on behalf of Kwaku Dua III, King of Ashantee, and as his envoys with full powers contained in the documents of which you have seen a copy, we have the honour to acknowledge the receipt of the Queen's ultimatum to our King, and we now, on his behalf and on behalf of the Chiefs and people of Ashanti, tender submission thereto.[7]

They telegraphed J. G. Halm, their Fanti agent at Cape Coast, the same day: 'We have accepted Resident. Hope to conclude treaty to-morrow. Inform King quickly. Ashanti Envoys.'[8] Sutherst tried to salvage something from the

---

[1] Letter of 9 Nov. 1895, from Colonial Office to War Office; CO/96/262.

[2] Telegram of 12 Nov. 1895, from Maxwell to Chamberlain; ibid.

[3] Secret Dispatch of 14 Nov. 1895, from Maxwell to Chamberlain; ibid.

[4] Confidential Dispatch of 18 Nov. 1895, from Maxwell to Chamberlain; ibid.

[5] The main document appointed John Ansah as Ambassador Extraordinary and Minister Plenipotentiary, and purported to have been signed with Prempeh's mark at Kumasi on 8 Sept. 1894. Enclosure in Letter of 16 Nov. 1895, from Sutherst to Chamberlain; CO/96/269.

[6] Letters of 14 and 15 Nov. 1895, from Colonial Office to Sutherst, and of 15 Nov. 1895, from Sutherst to Chamberlain; ibid.

[7] Letter of 16 Nov. 1895, from six Ashanti Envoys to Chamberlain, forwarded by Sutherst; ibid.

[8] Confidential Dispatch of 23 Nov. 1895, from Maxwell to Chamberlain; CO/96/262.

wreck of his clients' hopes, and begged the Secretary of State to meet one 'if not all' of them.[1]

But the Colonial Office was determined to win all the advantage it could from the situation. There were serious doubts of the ability of the embassy to pledge Prempeh or his people. In any case, why had they not notified their acceptance earlier? Now the only thing for them to do was to return to Kumasi, in company with the British officers who were to install the Resident. The military expedition would in the meantime proceed, and would not be stopped except by the complete submission of the King in person.[2] Sutherst attempted to explain the delay: the Ashanti envoys had been trying to see the Colonial Office since May, and when Prempeh received the ultimatum, he had naturally referred the Governor to his embassy in London. They had received no copy of the ultimatum until after the date of expiry, and had then accepted it within 24 hours.[3] But the Colonial Office would not budge; and, deciding it was too late to stand any longer on their rights, John Ansah announced that they were returning at once to Ashanti.[4]

Four more of the envoys, though not yet the Ansahs, arrived back in December, and the Governor immediately interviewed them. They claimed that the major grievances they had hoped to discuss in London were, first, the indirect threat to Prempeh of deposition and supersession by Achiriboanda, and secondly, the policy whereby States formerly subject to Ashanti were being taken under British protection.[5] They now attempted to impute all their difficulties and grievances to Brandford Griffith, whom they blamed for the fact that they were not received in England: 'we could see nobody . . . We cannot read, we cannot write. It is Governor Griffith who has wronged us; the present Governor has not done us anything wrong.' They even claimed that if they had known that Maxwell was on his way to the Gold Coast they would have waited to deliver their message to him.[6]

But Maxwell was not to be mollified. Despite Stewart and Vroom's warning, he insisted that Prempeh should come to Prasu to meet him, and should pay all the expenses of the expedition. In addition, he demanded hostages for the fulfilment of the treaty conditions, recognition of the independence of all tribes seeking British protection, and the grant of land for a fort in any place that the Government required.[7] The Ashanti envoys then left for Kumasi with the Governor's message.

When the Ansahs reached the Gold Coast, Maxwell was amazed at their

[1] Letter of 16 Nov. 1895, from Sutherst to Chamberlain; CO/96/269.
[2] Letters of 18 and 19 Nov. 1895, from Colonial Office to Sutherst; ibid.
[3] Letter of 22 Nov. 1895, from Sutherst to Chamberlain; ibid.
[4] Letter of 26 Nov. 1895, from John Ansah (on crested notepaper with a lion on a stool beneath the words 'Asante Kortorkor') to Colonial Office; CO/96/267.
[5] Confidential Dispatch of 23 Dec. 1895, from Maxwell to Chamberlain; CO/96/263.
[6] Notes of interview on 17 Dec. 1895, enclosed in Dispatch No. 493 of 18 Dec. 1895, from Maxwell to Chamberlain; ibid.
[7] Confidential Dispatch of 23 Dec. 1895, from Maxwell to Chamberlain; ibid.

naïve belief that they could have secured the suspension of all government action by simply remaining in England. He cross-examined them minutely on their credentials, and under pressure they admitted that the main document had been prepared in Cape Coast, and that the mark of Prempeh had actually been made by John Ansah with the help of Foku; the seal had been manufactured in London, and the impressions added after their arrival.[1] This 'forgery' effectively undermined in official eyes the Ansahs' claim to act on behalf of the Asantehene and his Chiefs.[2] The Colonial Office commented: 'This exposé is a fine climax to the farce of "The Ashanti Ambassadors".'[3] It was conveniently forgotten that the last message received from Prempeh in Kumasi had referred the Governor to his ambassadors in England; he evidently retained his trust in them, even when they were not present to influence him.

The Deposition of Prempeh, 1896

The stage was now set for a demonstration of British supremacy; how conclusive this was to be, probably no one could then have foretold, even Maxwell himself. The Fantis welcomed the expedition, and *The Gold Coast Chronicle* was in fighting mood:

We have reason to believe that the King of Ashantee means nothing but mischief. He may pretend to be a friend; he may do a great deal to induce us to believe that he does not wish to fight . . . We must go straight to Kumasi this time. The King must be deposed and sent about his business. Atchereboandah must be put upon the throne. A District Commissioner with a strong force of Haussas must be left in Kumasi . . . When we have once annexed Ashantee, the moral, intellectual and social elevation of the people in the interior of our part of the dark continent, will be thoroughly effected . . . With Ashantee once conquered, we shall have the foundation for a West African Empire (12 December 1895).

As soon as Prempeh heard that the expeditionary force had crossed the Prah, he sent down two young boys—said to be his own sons—as hostages, in a vain attempt to stay the British. But Scott had been instructed that, once across the river, the troops must reach Kumasi without any further halt for negotiation.[4] A week later they were met just outside Kumasi by Foku and Boatin, with an offer from Prempeh to pay the indemnity and 'come under

[1] Notes of interview with Ansahs on 27 Dec. 1895, and covering Confidential Dispatch of 28 Dec. 1895, from Maxwell to Chamberlain; ibid.

[2] There was now no difficulty in incriminating the Ansahs further by means of gossip from the other members of the embassy, which was duly passed on to London: 'Foku said that in their hotel . . . the Ansahs represented them as mere followers; and that whilst the Ansahs were drinking the best wines, they had to content themselves with beer or whisky. The Ansahs spent the money they took freely, about £400 was paid to Mr. Brew, being a private debt due to him by Ansah. They say they were kept in the dark as to what was going on with regard to their mission.' Secret Memorandum by Vroom, enclosed in Confidential Dispatch of 23 Dec. 1895, from Maxwell to Chamberlain; ibid.   [3] Minute of 28 Dec. 1895, by Bramston; ibid.

[4] Instructions of 22 Nov. 1895, from War Office; C. 7918.

the white men's government'. The only reply was that Prempeh would be required to submit personally to the Governor in Kumasi, though he would not be deposed if he made full submission and paid the cost of the expedition.[1]

The troops under Scott entered Kumasi on 17 January 1896. They met no opposition; and it has been argued that the Kumasis and their allies miscalculated the intentions of the British, deliberately deciding not to oppose them in the hope that they would quickly return to the coast after a display of force.[2] The Governor reached Kumasi the next day, and soon called a public meeting, at which Prempeh was told to make submission before all his people; he was also asked to produce immediately 50,000 oz. of gold (about £175,000) to help pay for the expedition.[3] Prempeh, to quote Maxwell's account, 'duly made submission in the Ashanti fashion, by grasping my feet in the attitude of a suppliant', asking at the same time that his country might be placed under British protection.[4] But the 680 oz. of gold which he said was all he could pay was not regarded as a serious offer.

To the horror of the assembled Ashantis, Maxwell then took the Asantehene prisoner, together with his mother, father, brother, two other close relatives, two linguists, the Chiefs of Bantama and Asafu, and the Kings of Mampong, Offinsu, and Ejisu. The Ansah brothers, too, who had reached Kumasi just before the expedition, were detained in custody and sent down to the coast to stand trial for forgery.[5] The mausoleum at Bantama was destroyed, and the sacred trees blown up. Valuable gold ornaments were sent to England, and the remaining contents of the Asantehene's palace were sold by auction ('to check looting' by the carriers).[6] The main body of troops was quickly ordered back to Cape Coast, escorting the political prisoners, who were then sent by sea to Elmina Castle.

The Government had stated previously that if Prempeh acceded to the terms stated he would not be deposed. His removal on what seemed a technical pretext concerning the amount of compensation, after his formal act of submission, was for many years regarded by the Ashantis as deliberate British perfidy.[7] Claridge has argued that the demand for compensation was

[1] Confidential Dispatch of 13 Jan. 1896, from Maxwell to Chamberlain; CO/96/270. R. S. S. Baden-Powell commented: 'Alas! this looks like a peaceful end to all our work', in his vivid diary of the march to Kumasi. *The Downfall of Prempeh* (London, 1896), p. 107.

[2] Letter of 29 Jan. 1901, from Hodgson to Colonial Office; CO/96/391.

[3] Maxwell had telegraphed to London to discover the approximate cost of the expedition, and the Colonial Office was surprised to find that this came to over £200,000, more than four times the original estimate. CO/96/270.

[4] For an eye-witness account, see G. S. Musgrave, *To Kumasi with Scott* (London, 1896).

[5] Notes of palaver at Kumasi, 20 Jan. 1896, and covering Confidential Dispatch of same date, from Maxwell to Chamberlain; CO/96/270.

[6] Despatch No. 13 of 24 Jan. 1896, from Maxwell to Chamberlain; ibid.

[7] It may be worth noting that the French had similarly deposed and exiled King Behanzin after their hard-fought conquest of Dahomey in 1893. H. H. Johnston, *A History of the Colonization of Africa by Alien Races* (Cambridge, 2nd edn. 1913), p. 206. The Ashanti expedition, however, had met with no armed resistance, and the Asantehene offered voluntary submission.

fixed at an exorbitant level, beyond the means of the kingdom, that the cost of the recent embassy had been met only by the imposition of a special tax, which had taken some time to collect, that the trade of the country had been at a standstill for years owing to civil wars, and that the defection of large numbers of his people had still further impoverished Prempeh.[1]

It seems unlikely, however, that Maxwell deliberately made a demand that he knew could not be met. More likely, he was ill-advised; Vroom told him that Prempeh and his family could easily have produced £20,000, and therefore the offer of just over £2,000 appeared a deliberate slight. Further, the Governor wanted a decisive moral victory, realizing that he could not gain a physical one, for the absence of armed resistance had made it impossible to strike a crippling blow and thus lower the prestige of Kumasi.[2] But the means he chose were not perhaps the best calculated for the purpose, and the episode did not escape comment from nationalist leaders farther south. J. E. Casely Hayford later strongly criticized the Government for having 'saddled the sins of omission of *all* Ashanti upon Prempeh, whose claim to the sovereignty of *all* Ashanti they had previously denied'. That might be British justice, he commented wryly; but it certainly did not appeal to the sense of justice of 'the untutored Ashanti'.[3]

The Aftermath

The future system of government for Ashanti was not easy to determine. Maxwell from the start disclaimed any intention of annexing the country or including it within the Gold Coast Protectorate. He proposed to consult as many Ashanti Chiefs as possible, before making any recommendations for a permanent settlement.[4] But this had been made infinitely more difficult by the removal and imprisonment of the Asantehene. Before returning to Cape Coast, the Governor met the remaining Chiefs in Kumasi, and found that what they wanted was a provisional Ashanti Government with full control, in the name of the Golden Stool, over all subordinate Kings, Chiefs, and tribes. Maxwell would not hear of this, and nominated a local committee of three Kumasi Chiefs, Opoku Mensah, Kwaku Nechi, and Kwami Efilfa, 'simply to conduct local affairs according to native custom'.[5] He also appointed Captain D. Stewart as Resident.[6]

Outside Kumasi, the policy was to make separate treaties of protection with all the Ashanti States. The first had been made with Adansi, even before the expedition took place. After crossing the Prah, Scott had taken Bekwai

---

[1] Claridge, *History*, vol. ii, pp. 420–2.

[2] Confidential Dispatch of 28 Jan. 1896, from Maxwell to Chamberlain; CO/96/270.

[3] *Gold Coast Native Institutions* (London, 1903), p. 265.

[4] Confidential Dispatch of 28 Jan. 1896, from Maxwell to Chamberlain; CO/96/270.

[5] Confidential Dispatch of 20 Feb. 1896, from Maxwell to Chamberlain; ibid. The spelling of the names differs in Maxwell's version.

[6] Confidential Dispatch of 29 Jan. 1896, from Maxwell to Chamberlain; ibid.

and Abodoom under British protection; while Ferguson had been sent to Kumasi via Nkoranza, where he signed a treaty of protection. Now the refugee Kings of Mampong and Kokofu were able to return from British territory, whither they had fled in 1888, and to sign treaties with the Governor, along with other important Chiefs. A flying column was also sent north-westwards, and several further treaties were made during the next few months.[1]

The Governor left detailed instructions for the Resident. He was to treat the separate tribes as absolutely independent of any authority in Kumasi; any claim to act as the agent of Prempeh or the 'palace party' was to be summarily repressed. Apart from this complete disruption of the remnants of the Union, there was to be as little interference as possible, and the Ashantis were to be 'encouraged to manage their own affairs'; they could even hold their own courts of justice—with the important reservation that they were not to inflict the death penalty. The Resident was to exercise all ordinary civil and criminal jurisdiction, being guided by 'the general principles of English Law and of Equity and good conscience'; human sacrifice and slave-trading were to be dealt with severely. One of his most important duties was the encouragement of trade, and the clearing of a road to the north. No concessions of land were to be granted without the sanction of the Governor, but a quarter of Kumasi could be assigned for foreign traders, and sites allocated for Mission schools.[2] Work was also started later in the year on the construction of a fort in Kumasi.[3]

Maxwell had been relieved to discover that the Ansahs were now widely discredited in Ashanti. Asafu Buakyi had said in Kumasi, pointing to John Ansah: 'Why should we suffer and he be left alone?'[4] On reaching Elmina, Prempeh denied having given the Ansahs any authority to go to England: 'I myself proposed that we send a messenger accepting the English Flag; but the Ansahs instanced a case of the people of Dahomey who sent home Ambassadors to England and are now free.'[5] Even after allowing for the somewhat garbled facts, too much reliance should not be placed on this claim, since Prempeh, anxious to return to Kumasi, clearly had an ulterior motive for disclaiming the Ansahs. The brothers were committed for trial on charges of forgery, conspiracy, misappropriation, larceny, and receiving stolen property;[6] but they were discharged for lack of evidence. They were ordered not to re-enter Ashanti;[7] and soon afterwards they returned to London.

[1] See African (West) No. 1010, pt. iii, nos. 26–40.
[2] Instructions of 10 Feb. 1896, from Governor to Resident, Kumasi, enclosed in Confidential Dispatch of 22 Feb. 1896, from Maxwell to Chamberlain; CO/96/270.
[3] Report of 20 Oct. 1896, by Pigott, enclosed in Confidential Dispatch of 19 Nov. 1896, from Maxwell to Chamberlain; CO/96/279.
[4] Notes of palaver at Kumasi, 20 Jan. 1896; CO/96/270.
[5] Account of examination of Prempeh at Elmina Castle, 5 Feb. 1896, enclosed in Confidential Dispatch of 26 Nov. 1896, from Maxwell to Chamberlain; CO/96/279.
[6] *The Times*, 11 Mar. 1896.
[7] Dispatch No. 232 of 10 June 1896, from Hodgson to Chamberlain; CO/96/274.

It was more difficult to decide what should be done with the prisoners from Kumasi. A petition was drawn up in July 1896, by two African lawyers at Cape Coast, on the instructions of Boatin and Foku, in which Prempeh begged for the release of himself and his compatriots, so that they could return to Kumasi and collect the indemnity.[1] But Maxwell felt that he could not place the smallest reliance on this professed intention to pay.[2] The Secretary of State also agreed that, so long as Prempeh and his party were within reach, it would be difficult to convince people in Ashanti that they could safely 'fall in with the new order of things', and obey the British Resident.[3] Ironically enough, Prempeh's repeated requests for recognition of the independence of his kingdom were at last being given due weight, in that his continued presence within reach of Ashanti was recognized as a threat to British domination. On 1 January 1897 the whole Ashanti contingent of forty-four persons (including wives, children, and attendants) was sent to Sierra Leone.[4]

But even this was not sufficient to destroy Ashanti hopes. They were becoming united in resentment more firmly than the British could divide them by treaties. Vroom, on a visit to Ashanti in June 1897, received several requests for the return of Prempeh, and for the restoration of the sovereignty of Kumasi over certain towns and villages. Maxwell was annoyed to hear that the three Chiefs of the Native Committee were interfering in political matters;[5] he visited Kumasi himself in August, and found persistent rumours that Prempeh was going to be released. He also found the Chiefs determined to cling to the great oath of Ashanti, although he had publicly declared: 'There is no King and there is consequently no great oath.'[6] Maxwell then recommended that Prempeh and the other Ashanti prisoners should be removed to the distant Seychelles,[7] to make it quite clear that there was no hope of their return.

Between 1883 and 1895 the waning military power of the Ashanti Confederacy, together with the increasing internal dissension under a young and inexperienced ruler, had been leading almost inevitably to its downfall. The dispatch of ambassadors to London, seeking a British guarantee of Ashanti

---

[1] Petition of July 1896, to Secretary of State from Prempeh, drawn up by C. Sapara Williams and Rotinu Aladé, and enclosed in Confidential Dispatch of 26 Aug. 1896, from Hodgson to Chamberlain; CO/96/276.

[2] Confidential Dispatch of 26 Nov. 1896, from Maxwell to Chamberlain; CO/96/279.

[3] Confidential Dispatch of 26 Oct. 1896, from Chamberlain to Maxwell; CO/96/276.

[4] CO/96/288 and 289. Boatin and Foku had been accused by the Cape Coast Chamber of Commerce of interfering with Ashanti traders, and were deported with the other prisoners.

[5] Report of 19 June 1897, by Vroom and covering Confidential Dispatch of 14 July 1897, from Maxwell to Chamberlain; CO/96/295.

[6] Maxwell suggested an alternative: 'Cannot you use the Fanti oath "by Sir Charles McCarthy's red coat"?' Opoku Mensah: 'That is a good oath, but we cannot do without the great oath.' Memorandum of interview between Governor and Ashanti Chiefs on 16 Aug. 1897, enclosed in Confidential Dispatch of 4 Sept. 1897, from Maxwell to Chamberlain; CO/96/298.

[7] Ibid. Confidential Dispatch.

independence, had been a counsel of despair to a nation that had previously maintained its independence by force of arms. The failure of the embassy marked the end of an epoch; but the manner in which British supremacy was asserted in Ashanti, by the unexpected arrest and deportation of Prempeh, ensured the persistence of a strong, and often embittered, national sentiment.

Maxwell died on the voyage home at the end of 1897, leaving a legacy of growing unrest in Ashanti. But Hodgson, who was promoted to succeed him, remained for some time blissfully unaware of the gathering storm. He was far more concerned by the agitation over the 1897 Lands Bill, by the mining boom, and by the technical problems of British jurisdiction in the Protected Territories, which together succeeded in diverting official attention from Ashanti during the next few crucial years.

VIII

THE PATTERN OF BRITISH AUTHORITY
1874–1902

THE last quarter of the nineteenth century had seen the extension of British influence and interests far beyond the limits of the old coastal settlements. During the complicated negotiations which culminated in the 1896 invasion of Ashanti, the British authorities had been taking part in an often undignified scramble for treaties and territory, mainly farther to the north, in competition with both the French and the Germans. In 1874 'the Gold Coast' had consisted of several scattered Forts and Settlements along the coast, with a largely undefined sphere of influence stretching towards Ashanti. By 1900 a boundary had been drawn around approximately 78,000 square miles of territory stretching from a 334-mile coastline back to the 11° N. parallel. Yet the legal status of this expanding territory was far from clear; and, indeed, the British hold over Ashanti was far from secure, although the Government were the last to realize this.

The new boundary of the Gold Coast and its hinterland enclosed a disparate assortment of cultural and linguistic groups. Some of these had little in common save propinquity and colour. They varied in social organization, political structure, occupations, living standards, religion, and outlook; they often had far more in common with their neighbours on the other side of the 'international' line. There are few countries in the world where political boundaries coincide exactly with ethnologic or linguistic frontiers; in the Gold Coast there was never even a chance of this. All types of communities were included, from the (formerly) highly organized political kingdom of Ashanti to the scattered, independent compounds of the Fra-Fras: from the small forest villages, relatively isolated from the forces of change, to the growing towns with their emergent, vocal groups of teachers, traders, and clerks. Nevertheless, there were important forces making for unity. Sir Ernest Barker's 'formula' for the making of a nation begins: 'Take first a territory: add some form of organisation (or State) to hold its inhabitants together.'[1] It therefore becomes important to understand how, while the territorial unit was taking shape, the pattern of British authority came to be established; for this in turn provided the background against which nationalist protests—military, emotional, economic, or constitutional—can be seen as an emergent or a latent challenge to alien rule.

[1] *National Character and the Factors in its Formation* (London, 1927), p. 15.

British Jurisdiction Redefined

The four years commencing with 1874 marked a crucial change in Britain's relations with the Gold Coast. By Letters Patent issued on 24 July 1874, the Gold Coast Forts and Settlements (with Lagos) were separated from the government of Sierra Leone, and were 'erected into' a Colony. This step marked the final rejection of the policy of gradual withdrawal recommended by the 1865 Select Committee; and the Colonial Office dilemma—complete annexation versus total abandonment—was for the time being resolved.[1]

It was not so easy to cut through the legal tangle concerning the extent of British jurisdiction. The Chief Magistrate had already urged the need to put beyond question the power to enforce customs duties and to legislate generally for the Protected Territories.[2] He had also pointed out that the legal jurisdiction of commandants and magistrates was inadequate for the functions they habitually exercised.[3] In 1874 Lord Derby could say: 'I greatly doubt whether any man in or out of the Colonial Office exactly knows or could define the limits of our authority and of our responsibility in regard to the tribes included within the protected territory.'[4]

The Colonial Office, however, now set about the problem in earnest. On 6 August 1874 an Order in Council for the first time authorized the Legislative Council of the Gold Coast to legislate for the Protected Territories. The scope of any Ordinances was limited to the exercise of 'such powers and jurisdiction as Her Majesty may, at any time before or after the passing of this Order in Council, have acquired' in the territories adjacent to the Colony. It was then felt to be necessary to define the nature and extent of the 'peculiar jurisdiction' exercised by the British in the Protected Territories, for certain rights were held to have been acquired, by usage and by the sufferance and tacit assent of the inhabitants, over and above those specifically granted by the Bonds of 1844.

At one time officials in London had favoured the course of negotiating a fresh agreement with the Chiefs.[5] But after the Ashanti war was over, the new Secretary of State, Lord Carnarvon, was not anxious to follow the precedent

[1] Cf. Ch. VII, p. 273, above. The Administration was soon afterwards advised to move its headquarters from Cape Coast to Accra, mainly on the grounds of a healthier climate; and this was done in 1877. See J. M. Akita, 'The Transfer of the Seat of Government from Cape Coast to Accra', in *Gold Coast Teachers' Journal*, Mar. 1956.

[2] Memorandum of 16 Apr. 1872, by D. Chalmers, on the power of the Administrator and Legislative Council to legislate for the Protected Territories, enclosed in Dispatch No. 93 of 29 Oct. 1872, from Pope Hennessy to Kimberley; CO/96/94. The Smuggling Ordinance of 1867 and the Spirit Licence Ordinance of 1869 had been applied to the coastline beyond the forts 'without demur', although no authority could be traced for this. W. Brandford Griffith, *A Note on the History of the British Courts in the Gold Coast Colony, with a Brief Account of the Changes in the Constitution of the Colony* (Accra, 1936).

[3] Memorandum of 9 May 1872, by D. Chalmers, on the jurisdiction of commandants and magistrates; CO/96/94.

[4] Quoted by Sir W. Lawson, *Parliamentary Debates*, House of Commons, 4 May 1874.

[5] Cf. Ch. VI, pp. 260–1, above.

of 1844, since 'It is not for Her Majesty to take as a grant what is already claimed and held as a right'. Further, it would be embarrassing, to say the least, if any considerable body of Chiefs refused their consent; and the Government might even unwittingly neglect to invite some who would afterwards claim that they should have been consulted.[1]

Carnarvon therefore decided to proceed by way of a proclamation of authority, which was accordingly drafted, for the guidance of the legislature, and of the Chiefs under British protection. The Queen's powers and jurisdiction were now declared to include the preservation of peace; the administration of both civil and criminal justice; the establishment and regulation of courts of justice (including native courts); the enactment of laws, 'framed with due regard to native law and customs where they are not repugnant to justice, equity and good conscience'; the hearing of appeals from native tribunals; the apprehension and trial of criminals in any part of the Protectorate; the abolition of human sacrifice, panyarring, judicial torture, and slave trading; measures concerning domestic slavery and pawning; the protection and encouragement of trade, by means of roads, bridges, telegraphs, and other public works; the settlement of Chiefs' disputes; the promotion of public health and education; the establishment of municipalities; and the raising of revenue.[2]

The proclamation was also intended to define the extent of the Protectorate. The Prah and the Volta were suggested as the natural boundaries, but the draft was sent to the Governor, Captain G. C. Strahan, with a blank space for him to insert a list of the relevant territories. He was also asked to exercise the most delicate tact and judgement to avoid alienating the feelings of the inhabitants, and was warned that too hasty an assumption of authority might create discontent.[3]

Strahan was more concerned with exercising power than with defining it. He eventually reported to London that as the Queen's authority was still being extended, exact territorial limits could not yet be given.[4] But first he took into his own hands the powers proposed in the proclamation. He summoned the leading Chiefs of both the western and eastern districts in turn, and informed them that it was the Queen's desire to do away with the slave traffic, in return for the protection they had had against the Ashantis. Strahan reported that they had agreed; the question of slavery being 'thus settled',[5] he proceeded to pass two Ordinances in December 1874, not only to abolish slave dealing but also to emancipate existing slaves throughout the Protectorate.[6] This came as a severe shock, and several petitions and

---

[1] Secret Dispatch of 20 Aug. 1874, from Carnarvon to Strahan; CO/96/113.

[2] This important draft proclamation was first publicized by J. Mensah Sarbah, *Fanti Customary Laws* (London, 2nd edn. 1904), pp. 293–5.   [3] CO/96/113.

[4] Dispatch of 27 Mar. 1875, from Strahan to Carnarvon; CO/96/115.

[5] Dispatch of 7 Nov. 1874, from Strahan to Carnarvon; CO/96/112.

[6] The Gold Coast Slave Dealing Abolition and Emancipation Ordinances, Nos. 1 and 2 of 1874.

memorials were received—including one from the Chiefs of the Cape Coast area, who had been misled, according to Strahan, by 'characterless' advisers with a smattering of education.[1]

In London the Governor's action was considered somewhat precipitate, although it was felt that now there could be no looking back.[2] Since the local Government had already been able to carry through 'a measure so vitally affecting the interests of the whole protectorate', the proposed proclamation was no longer considered necessary to authorize the lesser measures of administrative and legal reform originally suggested. It was therefore officially 'reserved', although the details became known, having been published for Parliament in draft.[3] From 1874 onwards the Crown was held to be fully and legally entitled to exercise all the rights and jurisdiction it had hitherto assumed in the Gold Coast, as if the proclamation had in fact been published locally.

Strahan then decided to change the title of Civil Commandant to District Commissioner, in preparation for the exercise of fuller judicial powers.[4] In 1876 the Supreme Court Ordinance and the associated Criminal Procedure Ordinance were enacted to apply both to the Colony and to the Protected Territories. Both the Court of Civil and Criminal Justice and the Judicial Assessor's Court were abolished, and replaced by the Supreme Court. The office of Judicial Assessor now finally disappeared; his appellate jurisdiction over native courts was vested in the Chief Justice. District Commissioners' courts were set up in place of the old magistrates' courts, their sentences being subject to review by the Chief Justice, with a right of appeal to the Supreme Court. In 1877 provision was made for appeal thence to the Privy Council in London, instead of to Sierra Leone.[5]

The main effect of these changes was to widen the sphere of influence of English law. The Supreme Court Ordinance provided for the application of the Common Law, doctrines of equity, and Statutes of general application, as they existed in England in 1874, except where specifically modified by local Ordinances.[6] English rules of evidence and methods of procedure were followed. The Chief Justice was empowered to admit barristers, solicitors, or other 'fit and proper persons' to appear in the Supreme Court. This gave

---

[1] To eradicate such influences the Governor even suggested that the Chiefs should not make use of written petitions at all, but should meet him personally or send their 'trusted swordbearers'. Dispatch No. 2 of 3 Jan. 1875, from Strahan to Carnarvon; CO/96/115. For details of the protests, see *Correspondence relating to the Queen's Jurisdiction on the Gold Coast and the Abolition of Slavery within the Protectorate* (London, 1875), and *Further Correspondence relating to the Abolition of Slavery on the Gold Coast* (London, 1875). Some were printed in *The African Times*, 1 Apr. 1875, including 'the humble petition of the ladies of the Gold Coast Protectorate'.

[2] Minute of 6 Feb. 1875, by A. W. L. Hemming; CO/96/115.

[3] Minute of 9 May 1875, by E. Fairfield; ibid.

[4] Dispatch of 24 June 1875, from Strahan to Carnarvon; ibid.

[5] Order in Council of 23 Oct. 1877, revoking that of 1867.

[6] Section 14 of the Supreme Court Ordinance, 1876.

scope for some of the unqualified attorneys to continue to practise; but they were soon to be replaced by the first generation of professional African lawyers.[1] The fact that these were all trained in England, and grounded in the principles of English law, only hastened the process of assimilation.

It has been argued that the 1876 Ordinance gave preference to native law, by providing that it should be observed in all cases between Africans, and in most cases between Africans and Europeans, unless excluded by a contract.[2] Lord Hailey points out that the Gold Coast was one of the few colonies where such trials in British courts led to 'the growth of a case law based on native law'.[3] But generally speaking, customary law proved too uncertain and localized in its application to be of much importance outside the Chiefs' courts; and it was never likely to provide a legal framework for the new political structure that was rapidly developing.

The jurisdiction of the Chiefs' courts was in theory not affected by the Supreme Court Ordinance;[4] but inevitably they became somewhat eclipsed by the paraphernalia of modern justice, especially in the coastal towns where District Commissioners were stationed.[5] Mensah Sarbah claimed that such an appointment weakened the Chief's influence and quickly undermined his jurisdiction; and that this was mainly because 'In the African mind, leadership carries with it the administration of justice.'[6] Now it was the District Commissioner who had to combine the exercise of executive and judicial functions, rather in the manner of an important Chief. In the early days young and inexperienced men, often Constabulary Officers, were appointed;[7] later, legal qualifications became obligatory.[8] They may sometimes have been tempted to abuse their powers, and their methods may have appeared rough and ready in the eyes of African lawyers with a professional axe to grind.[9] But for the

---

[1] Cf. Ch. II, pp. 68–70 and 96 n., above.

[2] Section 19 of the Supreme Court Ordinance, 1876. See H. W. Hayes Redwar, *Comments on some Ordinances of the Gold Coast Colony* (London, 1909), p. 8.

[3] *An African Survey* (Oxford, 2nd edn. 1945), p. 275. Some of the British merchants were uneasy at this tendency, and organized a public meeting in Cape Coast 'to agitate for the abolition of the existing laws of the Gold Coast Colony, which are often unjust, and the enactment of measures assimilating the laws of the Colony to those of England'. *The Gold Coast Times*, 10 Dec. 1881. Cf. Ch. III, p. 149, above.

[4] According to the 1887 Full Court judgement in Oppon v. Ackinnie. Sarbah, *Fanti Customary Laws*, p. 232.

[5] According to the *Gold Coast Colony Blue Book*, 1878, there were District Commissioners at Cape Coast, Accra, Elmina, Saltpond, Winneba, Ada, Keta, Sekondi, Dixcove, and Axim.

[6] J. Mensah Sarbah, *Fanti National Constitution* (London, 1906), pp. 128 and 134.

[7] Dispatch No. 310 of 4 June 1884, from Young to Derby; CO/96/158.

[8] Brandford Griffith was the first Governor to insist on this; in 1889 it was claimed that the policy had already raised the level of district reports. CO/96/203. Cf. Ch. II, p. 99, above.

[9] Cf. W. E. G. Sekyi, speaking later of 'the development of strange courts with strange procedure, presided over by non-professional political officers'. Lecture, 'Political Development in the Gold Coast since 1900', Achimota, 1952.

The Accra Divisional Court once had to award damages against the District Commissioner of Keta, who had arrested and detained a man without charge and then reprimanded him in court for saluting the Queen's representative in a manner which was considered not respectful, 'though

most part, the District Commissioners built up a reputation for the impartial administration of justice.

The Chiefs in the interior were not greatly affected by these changes. The foundations of British authority were, however, completed by the Native Jurisdiction Ordinance of 1878, as re-enacted and applied in 1883. This purported to regulate the powers and jurisdiction of Chiefs' tribunals, but in practice it served also to confirm and extend the jurisdiction of the Government *vis-à-vis* the Chiefs.[1]

Taxation, Sovereignty, and Protection, 1874–1901

These legal and constitutional developments did not impinge very closely upon the ordinary inhabitants of the Gold Coast, except in so far as the abolition of slavery and other measures could be enforced by the handful of District Commissioners and their courts. In practice, the main impact of British authority was felt, as it had always been, through the imposition of taxes; and this, from the days of the poll tax onwards, had been strongly resisted, even though a general direct tax was not again publicly proposed until nearly the end of the century. Indirect taxation, unlike direct, did not involve any pressure towards wage employment, with its consequent changes in status and increasing economic insecurity. It was opposed primarily by the merchants and traders, whose grievances were personal rather than in any sense national; nevertheless, it was recognized as an alien form of economic coercion resulting from the new political order, and it increasingly became one of the main points at issue between the people and the Government.

In 1874 an increase in the customs duty on spirits had led to a remarkably united protest from the 'Kings, Chiefs, headmen, native merchants, European and American merchants, native petty traders and retail dealers in spirits, and others of Accra and the Eastern Districts'.[2] Even though the general public might not realize the effect of the duty on prices, the traders whose income would be affected had been able to rally the support of the Chiefs, who were concerned about the cost of their customary fines and presents. The main result of this petition was to convince the Colonial Office of the need to establish beyond doubt the right of the Queen through her officers to collect customs and other revenue,[3] and thus to influence the preparation of the constitutional instruments of 1874.

The Letters Patent of that year left no doubt that taxes could be levied upon the Colony. The accompanying draft proclamation, which was neither pro-

whether the disrespect consisted in the mere touching of his hat, instead of raising it, or touching it with a hand in which he carried a stick, or in "the expression of his countenance", is not clear'. Tamaklo *v.* Mitchell, 22 Jan. 1892; Hayes Redwar, *Comments*, app. iv.

[1] For an account of the Chiefs' jurisdiction and their relationships with the Government from 1878 onwards, see Ch. XII, below.

[2] Petition of 8 May 1873, to Kimberley; CO/96/99.

[3] Secret Dispatch of 20 Aug. 1874, from Carnarvon to Strahan; CO/96/113.

mulgated nor withdrawn, authorized the Legislative Council to raise revenue in the Protected Territories 'by licences and customs, and by such direct imposts as the native Chiefs and rulers, or a major part of them, may agree to'. Legal qualms concerning customs duties were thus removed; and it now appeared that direct taxes could be imposed in the Colony by consent of the Legislative Council, and in the Protectorate by consent of the Chiefs as well. But the formal assumption of sovereignty was not marked, as in most other British territories in Africa, by the imposition of a direct tax. The unhappy experience of the poll tax may have discouraged a fresh attempt; this simply added to the eventual difficulties of imposing direct taxation. As Lugard later pointed out, 'If delayed, its imposition is certain to be resented, and to lead to trouble'.[1]

Customs duties continued to be levied after 1874, although their collection was hampered by the growing tension between the Government and the mercantile community, who considered that British rule should offer special protection and encouragement to traders.[2] In 1877 a new Customs Tariff Ordinance authorized an *ad valorem* duty of 4 per cent. on almost all imports, and the Cape Coast merchants were up in arms at once. They lobbied the Governor, S. Freeling, in vain for any concession,[3] but he was so impressed by the difficulties of imposing indirect taxation successfully that he advocated a house tax as a means of raising revenue in the thirteen main coastal towns. Since these contained over 5,000 houses, he estimated that a tax of 10s. per annum—to be collected quarterly—might raise £2,500. There might be some awkwardness and excitement at first, but even if the tax were too unpopular to raise much revenue, it might still be used for another purpose. It could be implemented only when and where the Governor's orders were disobeyed concerning the cleanliness of a town; and then the mere threat of its operation might be sufficient to ensure improvements being carried out.[4]

The scheme had a mainly cautious reception in London: 'If the natives are dissatisfied at the imposition of customs duties, how great will be their objection to any system of direct taxation.'[5] The Secretary of State suggested that if anybody was to be taxed, the people of the Protectorate should also make a direct contribution, especially towards the cost of the constabulary; could there perhaps be a general poll tax, or a fixed contribution from each district to be collected by the Chiefs?[6] There followed one of the frequent delays during an interregnum between Governors, when policy could only be mulled over in the Colonial Office. The unhappy poll tax experience of 1852–61 was analysed, and it was argued that direct taxation might be safely and profitably

[1] F. D. Lugard, *The Dual Mandate in British Tropical Africa* (London, 1922), p. 234.
[2] For example, Andrew Swanzy, *Trade on the Gold Coast* (London, 1874).
[3] Jan. 1877; CO/96/120.
[4] Dispatch No. 117 of 3 May 1877, from Freeling to Carnarvon; CO/96/121.
[5] Minute of 2 Jan. 1878, by R. H. Meade; CO/96/122.
[6] Dispatch No. 4 of 8 Feb. 1878, from Carnarvon to Freeling; ibid.

reimposed, now that there were better means of checking abuses, and a greater degree of jurisdiction and authority over the Chiefs.[1] The question was next referred to H. T. Ussher, who returned to the Gold Coast as Governor in 1879. He criticized the scheme strongly, mainly on the grounds that there was not enough order and obedience throughout the Protectorate.[2] These arguments were not found very convincing by permanent officials in London, who had been urging the need for additional funds for education:[3] but eventually a new Secretary of State was persuaded to drop the idea of direct taxation.[4] Lord Kimberley was the more open to persuasion because the revenue in 1880 was flourishing.

The Government therefore continued to rely mainly on customs duties— which a London official had commended because their 'insidious operation' made them easy to levy upon a population 'too ignorant to understand the objects of taxation and too indifferent to its results'.[5] But this was certainly not true of the merchants, especially their principals in England, who intermittently prodded the Colonial Office with criticisms. For example, in 1883 a deputation from London and Manchester complained to the Secretary of State that the increased revenue from the 4 per cent. duty had not led to any improvements in roads, sanitation, or town conditions.[6] In 1887 the Manchester merchants returned to the attack. In addition to their complaints about the British failure to deal with Ashanti and prevent border incidents, they alleged that the import duties were helping to maintain an unnecessary and expensive staff of officials on the coast, while scarcely anything was being done for the development of trade or for the general good; ten years earlier, by contrast, a much smaller customs revenue had sufficed to maintain an administration 'quite as efficient and less grievous to the people'. They claimed that official apathy and inactivity had brought about a serious decline in trade, and quoted detailed supporting figures.[7]

The persistence of the merchants was rewarded, and in 1888 the 4 per cent.

---

[1] Memorandum of 27 Dec. 1878, by Hemming; CO/96/125.

[2] Dispatch No. 151 of 11 May 1880, from Ussher to Kimberley; CO/96/131.

[3] Minute of 9 Mar. 1880, by Hemming; CO/96/130.

[4] Minute of 27 June 1880, by Kimberley; CO/96/131.

[5] Minute of 16 June 1877; CO/96/121.

[6] *The Times*, 13 Dec. 1883, and CO/96/152. Comment in the Colonial Office lent some weight to their arguments: 'The Establishment is larger now than it has ever been, & costs, with travelling, about £100,000 out of a total expenditure of £140,000. We are doing absolutely nothing for the people out of the money we extract from them, except what benefit this large staff may be supposed to give, & a mere trifle on education. Public Works have been restricted to ordinary repairs for several years.' Minute of 25 Oct. 1883, by S. Webb; CO/96/151. See also Ch. I, p. 9, above.

[7] For example, the annual value of cotton goods exported to West Africa (£'000):

1867	.	. 300	1885	.	. 388
1877	.	. 350	1886	.	. 318
1884	.	. 591			

Petition of 8 Feb. 1887, to Secretary of State from Manchester Chamber of Commerce; *Further Correspondence respecting the Affairs of the Gold Coast* (London, 1888), C. 5357.

ad valorem tariff was abolished, although some specific duties remained. As a result government revenue, which had already been falling short of expenditure, fell further still.[1] Optimists in the Colonial Office took the opportunity a year later to suggest a return to direct taxation, only to meet local arguments that this would be both impolitic and inexpedient. The Governor, Sir William Brandford Griffith, had just encountered vehement protests against his proposal for municipal rates, when Cape Coast petitioners had maintained that they had a right to enjoy representative institutions without direct taxation.[2] The Governor felt that any wider scheme would equally be opposed by the educated inhabitants, who would rouse the interior districts, and spread all sorts of untrue reports; force would be needed to put down opposition and collect the tax, and this would greatly diminish the influence of the Government. His references to possible disturbances and bloodshed—followed by the inevitable questions in Parliament—were sufficient to dissuade the Colonial Office from any such course.[3] Every year's delay was another nail in the coffin of direct taxation.

The alternative put forward by the Governor—a 10 per cent. *ad valorem* duty on certain specified goods—was accepted, and came into operation on 1 January 1890. In the first year this yielded £22,791, which was sufficient to eliminate the government deficit. But it was the last straw for the merchants, who had been increasingly restless under Brandford Griffith's administration.[4] Swanzy's now decided to support any steps necessary to secure the abolition of the duty;[5] and in 1892 their acting chief agent, W. Waters, prepared a memorial to the Secretary of State, signed by over 500 Africans and Europeans, mainly connected with trade. It was undoubtedly the most impressive and best-organized protest yet seen in the Gold Coast, having been signed in Accra, Axim, Dixcove, Sekondi, Shama, Elmina, Cape Coast, Saltpord, Apam, Winneba, Pram Pram, Ada, Keta, Akuse, and Kpong.

The main complaint was against the 10 per cent. duty. It was alleged that the vacillating customs policy of the Government had been highly detrimental to the trade of the Colony, and in particular that the proceeds had not been spent upon the objects mentioned in the preamble to the Ordinance; these included the development of roads, telegraphs, education, and the judicial

---

[1] According to the *Gold Coast Colony Blue Books* the figures were as follows (£'000):

Year	Revenue	Expenditure	Year	Revenue	Expenditure
1885	194	153	1888	98	133
1886	123	202	1889	111	125
1887	123	139			

[2] See Ch. XI. p. 421, below.   [3] Minute of 3 Nov. 1889, by Hemming; CO/96/204.

[4] One disgruntled European barrister complained that 'English merchants cannot afford to offend the Governor'. E. Eiloart, *The Land of Death*, 'A Pamphlet addressed to the Members of both Houses of Parliament' (London, 1887).

[5] Letter of 10 Jan. 1894, from F. and A. Swanzy to Ripon; CO/96/253.

system. The signatories claimed that they were not opposed to an *ad valorem* duty as such—although it should not exceed 5 per cent.—provided the money in hand was spent at once on sanitation and economic development. They contradicted in detail a recently published report from the Governor, which had claimed that town improvements had been carried out to the utmost possible extent.[1] This was refuted by a 'statement of existing latrines' and scavengers; and his remark that 'Every town on the seaboard is now admirably lighted' was flatly denied. A strong request was also made for adequate unofficial representation on the Legislative Council; and for an Imperial officer to visit the Colony forthwith, to inquire into its needs.

Brandford Griffith took these allegations very seriously, as a personal challenge, which indeed they were. After a delay of nearly eight months— during which he had taken care to secure the Secretary of State's agreement to the continuance of the duty[2]—the Governor forwarded the memorial to London, together with a 30,000-word reply, itemizing the progress of the Colony during his term of office, with voluminous supporting documents.[3] A useful argument was the fact that imports had risen considerably in 1890 and 1891, in spite of the higher duty. Even more damaging was his description of how the memorial had been organized, with many people signing loose sheets of paper, 'against the 10% duty', in ignorance of the detailed complaints.[4]

In the Colonial Office the memorial at first sight appeared a formidable indictment of Brandford Griffith's administration, but on further examination most of it was dismissed as exaggerated, inaccurate, and groundless.[5] His

---

[1] Dispatch of 10 Nov. 1890, from Brandford Griffith to Knutsford, published in *Colonial Reports, Miscellaneous No. 1. Gold Coast* (London, 1891).

[2] Confidential Dispatch of 28 Feb. 1893, from Brandford Griffith to Ripon, and his reply of 16 June 1893; CO/96/231.

[3] Dispatch No. 171 of 12 June 1893, from Brandford Griffith to Ripon, and enclosures, including Memorial of 31 Oct. 1892; CO/96/234. This was published as *Dispatch from Governor Sir W. Brandford Griffith, K.C.M.G., forwarding a Memorial from Merchants, Agents, and Traders of the Gold Coast Colony, with his Observations and the Secretary of State's Reply* (London, 1893), C. 7225.

[4] The Governor attempted to minimize the effect of the numerous signatures by tabulating them as follows:

29 Europeans (merchants, agents, sub-agents, and 'nondescripts')
19 Native merchants and agents
42 Native traders
100 Clerks and subordinate employees
86 Petty native traders, 'mostly hucksters'
8   Clerks to petty traders
58 Non-commercial persons (including 'shoemakers, drunkards, bankrupts, convicts, photographers' etc.)
47 Unknown
119 Crosses unwitnessed

518

[5] Minute of 19 Sept. 1893, by Hemming; CO/96/234.

recent Dispatches had left London in no doubt about the strained relations existing between the Government and the merchants, especially Swanzy's, who were held to be mainly responsible for the agitation. The Secretary of State had little choice but to support the Governor, with some reservations concerning roads.[1] Some of his advisers thought, however, that it was time for Brandford Griffith to retire.[2]

Proposals for a general direct tax were revived by the next Governor, in 1897. Municipal house rates were already due to be levied in Accra, under the Town Councils Ordinance, although strenuous opposition had delayed their introduction. Even against this unpromising background, Sir William Maxwell felt that there was an urgent need for additional revenue, to meet the expenses of the recent Ashanti war and to finance a harbour and railways. He believed that a false impression had been created by the procedure over the unsuccessful poll tax, and that consent was not a prerequisite for taxation; it would be a fatal error to consult the Chiefs in advance. Maxwell preferred a hut tax, since it was easier to count houses than heads, and proposed a flat rate of 5s. per annum. He did not anticipate any more serious resistance than a few local riots, which could be dealt with by the police; as a last resort, the Ashantis might even be used for coercion.[3]

But Maxwell died before he could implement his policy. Early in 1898 the Chief Justice strongly advised that the draft House Tax Bill should be postponed. The Chiefs and people generally had already had their hostility aroused by the Compulsory Labour Ordinance and the Lands Bill; he feared that their reactions would be: 'the Government seize our persons to make us carriers, they are trying to take our land, and now they want to take our money.' F. M. Hodgson, the new Governor, considered that direct taxation was only suitable for small-scale, local expenditure, directly benefiting the people who paid. Furthermore, the collection of municipal rates had proved so difficult in Accra that he was unwilling to enforce any wider scheme of taxation; this would only stir up the country and interfere with trade, for the sake of a possible £70,000.[4]

The contemporary hut tax experiment in Sierra Leone was not auspicious. Serious riots had already taken place there, and in England some influential criticisms were now heard. Mary Kingsley alleged in *The Spectator* of 19 March that a tax on individual possessions was abhorrent to African law, which held that if a man paid a regular fee for anything, it was not his own. This tax, she argued, implied to the African that his hut had been confiscated by the Government, hence the 'recurring rows'.[5] When Chamberlain met the

---

[1] Dispatch No. 309 of 17 Oct. 1893, from Ripon to Acting Governor; ibid.

[2] See Ch. XI, p. 428 n., below.

[3] Confidential Dispatch of 8 Jan. 1897, from Maxwell to Chamberlain; CO/96/288.

[4] Letter of 24 Feb. 1898, from Brandford Griffith C.J. to Hodgson, and his covering Confidential Dispatch of 18 Apr. 1898, to Chamberlain; CO/96/314.

[5] A year later she wrote to Major M. Nathan alleging that this 'confiscation' of property was

A.R.P.S. Lands Bill deputation in August 1898,[1] he took the opportunity to ask them whether they would prefer a hut or a poll tax, since one or the other was essential: 'no taxation means no improvement'. The deputation declined to give an immediate answer to this unexpected proposition.[2] After a peremptory telegram from Cape Coast, 'House Tax Instruct Solicitors Urgent Insist 1844 Bond',[3] they rejected both forms of direct taxation, on the grounds that either would lead to rebellion. To show willing, however, they suggested that the tax on alcohol might safely be increased.[4]

The Gold Coast press, in support of the delegation, refused to entertain the idea of direct taxes.[5] This issue could evoke a wider national sentiment than could customs duties, especially since the traditional rulers were already exercised over the land question. When the Chiefs of the Western Province discussed the proposal in 1899, they advanced the argument that the Government had no right to impose any form of direct tax, because they themselves had not been conquered and were not subject to the paramount authority of the British.[6] Constitutionally, they were quite correct, since the 1874 Proclamation had authorized taxation in the Protectorate only with the consent of the Chiefs. But a London official now argued that the Government had virtually acquired rights of conquest over the protected peoples, since 'they would have been destroyed by the Ashantis if we hadn't come to their rescue in 1873-4'.[7] Hodgson took a more practical view, and warned that dire results might be expected from a tax which would probably have to be collected at the point of a bayonet.[8] Little could be done against the wishes of the Governor, Chiefs, and people, so no more was heard of a general house tax.[9]

The Chiefs, for their part, realized that their united voice had been heard to some effect on two important matters; but this did not strengthen their position in constitutional relations with Britain. Local Ordinances might sometimes be withdrawn or disallowed as a result of such protests, while the Chiefs themselves attached most weight to negotiated treaties by which they could be voluntarily bound. Royal Orders in Council, on the other hand, neither required consent nor admitted appeal. In cold fact, despite the success

---

a breach of faith. Letter of 8 Mar. 1899, in S. Gwynn, *The Life of Mary Kingsley* (London, 1932), pp. 217-19.   [1] See Ch. IX, pp. 353-4, below.

[2] *Report of the Proceedings of the Deputation from the Kings and Chiefs of the Western Province of the Gold Coast* (London, 1898).

[3] Letter of 18 Aug. 1898, from Ashurst, Morris, Crisp & Co. to Colonial Office; CO/96/333.

[4] Letter of 23 Aug. 1898, from A.R.P.S. Deputation to Chamberlain; CO/96/332.

[5] For example, *The Gold Coast Aborigines*, editorial of 26 Nov. 1898, headed 'Hut or Poll Tax, Which? None!'

[6] Letter of 26 May 1899, from Kings and Chiefs of the Western Province to Chamberlain; CO/96/352.   [7] Minute of 17 July 1899, by R. W. A.; ibid.

[8] Confidential Dispatch of 20 Dec. 1899, from Hodgson to Chamberlain; CO/96/346.

[9] The experiment, if tried, would probably have been no more successful than it was in Uganda, where the hut tax levied under the 1900 Agreement with Buganda was alleged to encourage overcrowding and immorality; it was supplemented from 1905, and entirely superseded in 1909, by a poll tax. K. Ingham, *The Making of Modern Uganda* (London, 1958), p. 115.

of their 1898 deputation, the Chiefs were unable to exert any influence upon the constitutional status of the country, which had been determined in 1874, and was to be redefined in 1901, without any reference to their attitude or wishes.

The repeated failure to introduce direct taxation was only one of the difficulties in the way of establishing British sovereignty in practice after 1874. Other, more technical, problems continued to arise concerning the meaning and extent of British jurisdiction. In particular it proved almost impossible to define satisfactorily the terms 'Colony' and 'Protected Territories'.

Between 1874 and 1895 Britain, it has been aptly said, 'gradually glided into' her jurisdiction on the Gold Coast.[1] The fact that the Legislative Council was empowered to make laws for both the Colony and the Protectorate encouraged officials to neglect the legal distinction between them,[2] although it was carefully observed in Ordinances enacted during this period. Geographically, it was almost impossible to say where the Colony ended and the Protectorate began, The Letters Patent of 1874 and 1886 were not much help; the Gold Coast Colony was there defined as 'all places, settlements and territories belonging to Us on the Gold Coast in Western Africa' between 5° W. and 2° E. No one was prepared to state exactly which were the territories belonging to the Crown. As the Chief Justice admitted in 1900:

When natives desired to embarrass the Government they would endeavour to draw a distinction between the powers of the Governor in the Colony and his powers in the Protected Territories,[3] and would ask for the treaties under which we exercised jurisdiction, and the general absence of such treaties bred disaffection of a sort.[4]

The Rev. S. R. B. Attoh Ahuma, a leader of the newly founded Aborigines' Rights Protection Society, put his finger on the disputed point when he asked in a newspaper article in 1897, 'Colony or Protectorate—Which?' He claimed that the term 'Colony' should be reserved for the original settlements of European merchants, and that therefore the only British possessions on the Gold Coast were the actual forts. The A.R.P.S. 'must begin by claiming the rightful name of "Protectorate" for this country, and all other things will follow in time as a matter of course'.[5] There were few other Africans alive to the legal

---

[1] Brandford Griffith C.J., 28 Oct. 1908, Rex v. Kojo Ayensu; quoted in Hayes Redwar, *Comments*, pp. 241–4.

[2] The Chief Justice later complained that 'It used to take officials quite a long time to appreciate the distinction between Colony and Protected Territories.' Memorandum of 22 Mar. 1900, by Brandford Griffith C.J.; CO/96/371. A senior London official wrote in 1887, with unintentional amphibology, 'the greater portion of the Gold Coast Colony still remains a Protectorate'. Letter from R. H. Meade to A. McArthy, M.P., quoted by J. E. Casely Hayford, *Gold Coast Native Institutions* (London, 1903), p. 149.

[3] He had already explained that in the past when such questions arose, the practice had been 'not to settle them and in that way to avoid hard and fast solutions'. Memorandum of 9 Aug. 1899, by Brandford Griffith C.J.; CO/96/342.

[4] Memorandum of 22 Mar. 1900, by Brandford Griffith C.J., on the status of the Protected Territories; CO/96/378.

[5] *The Gold Coast Methodist Times*, 30 Apr. 1897, 'Thoughts on the Present Discontent'.

technicalities of the position; and in any case the matter was discussed mainly in confidential Dispatches and private minutes.[1]

On the strictest interpretation, excluding what had been acquired from the Dutch, the actual area of the Gold Coast Colony in 1886 would have been less than one square mile. But at that time the Colonial Office was averse to laying down an accurate line of demarcation between Colony and Protectorate.[2] In 1895, after several years of doubts and queries, the local Government grasped the nettle—too boldly, as it turned out—and attempted to abolish altogether the distinction between Colony and Protected Territories by means of a Statute Law Revision Ordinance. Four years later, when the legal position of Ashanti was also under review, Brandford Griffith developed at some length the theory that this Ordinance had made possible automatic expansion of the Colony. During the last ten years, he said, the Colony had extended itself from the coast foreshore to the banks of the Prah.[3] The Secretary of State, realizing that this was contrary to the view of his own advisers, sought the opinion of the Law Officers. They rejected firmly any such notion, on the grounds that the Queen alone had power to enlarge her jurisdiction—by her own Order in Council, not by a Gold Coast Ordinance.[4]

This authoritative opinion posed some legal conundrums for the Secretary of State. It was now necessary to redefine the Colony in unambiguous language, and to limit the term to territory that had been formally annexed. Joseph Chamberlain did not then consider that either the Protected Territories or Ashanti should be annexed, preferring to keep them separate from the Colony proper.[5] But the Chief Justice argued strongly that it would be difficult, if not impossible, to go back from what had been done in 1895 and to draw a dividing line between Colony and Protectorate. If the Ordinance was *ultra vires*, then other steps must be taken to proclaim all the country south of Ashanti to be a Colony.[6] The Governor later assured the Colonial Office that no difficulty was likely to arise concerning slavery, since it had practically been abolished; the inhabitants were 'ready for annexation', and would give no trouble 'if the state of affairs which they regarded as already existing *de facto* were established *de jure*'.[7]

Chamberlain eventually yielded to pressure from Gold Coast officials, and

---

[1] Brandford Griffith (previously C.J.) admitted in 1936 that the constitutional changes through which the Colony had passed were still 'a sealed book even to most lawyers', owing to the difficulty of obtaining information. *A Note on the History of the British Courts in the Gold Coast Colony.*

[2] The Colonial Office suggested to the War Office that a reference to the Gold Coast in a confidential précis should merely say: 'Some portion of these possessions is British Territory but the greater part is a British Protectorate.' Cf. Minute of 11 Oct. 1887, by Hemming: 'This commits us to nothing and is I think quite sufficient. It is accurate and yet vague.' CO/96/188.

[3] Memorandum of 9 Aug. 1899, by Brandford Griffith C.J., on whether Ashanti should be regarded as part of the Colony; CO/96/342.

[4] Letter of 21 Oct. 1899, from Law Officers' Department to Chamberlain; CO/96/347.

[5] Confidential Dispatch of 19 Feb. 1900, from Chamberlain to Hodgson; CO/96/349.

[6] Memorandum of 22 Mar. 1900, by Brandford Griffith C.J.; CO/96/371.

[7] Minute of 2 Oct. 1900, by R. W. A.; ibid.

early in 1901 he decided to annex the Protected Territories (as they had existed on 29 December 1887); this would make the whole area a Colony, whose inhabitants would be British subjects, bound by the British anti-slavery laws.[1] Meanwhile, a major rising in Ashanti had considerably modified the plans that had been made for the exercise of British jurisdiction there. To the developments in Ashanti between 1896 and 1901 we must now turn.

The Last Struggle for Power in Ashanti

After the Ashanti campaign of 1896 the Government was urged to take positive steps to establish law, order, and security there.[2] Hodgson later came to regret that a comprehensive scheme of administration had not been worked out immediately, and European officers stationed among the Ashanti tribes.[3] But the necessary staff was not available, and for several years the Government was preoccupied with the agitation in the Colony over the Lands Bill, and with developments in the Northern Territories; so valuable time was lost in Ashanti.

Meanwhile, Prempeh from Sierra Leone,[4] and the Ansahs from London,[5] continued vainly to press for his release. Resentment and discontent were growing among the Ashanti Chiefs and people. The Basel missionaries were well aware of this, and the Rev. F. Ramseyer several times warned the Government of an impending revolt. During 1899 the Resident, Captain D. Stewart, passed on reports of a rising; but the reinforcements ordered from Lagos were soon cancelled.[6] When more convincing rumours of serious unrest reached Kumasi, the Chiefs were made to swear oaths of loyalty to the British.[7]

The Governor, after discussions with various commercial firms in England, was anxious to formulate a more complete system of government for Ashanti, as much 'in the interests of trade and mining capitalists', as from political considerations. He was convinced of the need to be in closer touch with the various tribes without disturbing the local administration of the Chiefs.[8] In particular, Hodgson hoped to encourage the idea that they were under the same obligations of service to the Government as they had been to their Asantehene; he felt that to make separate treaties had unduly raised the status of individual Chiefs, and weakened the power of any central authority.[9]

---

[1] Confidential Dispatch of 5 Feb. 1901, from Chamberlain to Nathan; ibid.

[2] For example, 'Policy and Wealth in Ashanti', by Sir George Baden-Powell, M.P., in R. S. S. Baden-Powell, *The Downfall of Prempeh* (London, 1896).

[3] Confidential Dispatch of 24 July 1900, from Hodgson to Chamberlain; CO/96/361.

[4] Petitions of 5 May 1898, and 27 Oct. 1899, to Secretary of State from Prempeh; CO/96/316 and 345.

[5] Feb. 1898; CO/96/333.

[6] Confidential Dispatches of 20 and 27 Mar. 1899, from Low to Chamberlain; CO/96/338.

[7] See F. Fuller, *A Vanished Dynasty; Ashanti* (London, 1921), p. 186. Hodgson later complained, in his Confidential Dispatch of 7 Apr. 1900, to Chamberlain, that none of these rumours had been reported to him at the time. CO/96/359. In fact, all except the last were on record on his files.

[8] Letter of 29 Jan. 1901, from Hodgson to Colonial Office; CO/96/392.

[9] Confidential Dispatch of 23 Oct. 1899, from Hodgson to Chamberlain; CO/96/345.

A clear definition of the legal position of Ashanti could no longer be delayed. The question came to a head in 1899 when an Accra barrister, A. B. Quartey-Papafio, asked whether Kumasi fell within the jurisdiction of the Supreme Court.[1] The previous Governor had advised against allowing this.[2] Ashanti had not been formally annexed, and in London was regarded as a foreign country;[3] although the 1896 Ashanti treaties were regarded locally as having incorporated these countries into the Colony, the Colonial Office realized that they had only been brought into the Protectorate.[4] Now the Chief Justice produced a long memorandum on his theory of 'automatic expansion' of the Colony by the provisions of the 1895 Statute Law Revision Ordinance; and he suggested that the Government should unhesitatingly claim that Ashanti was part of the Colony.[5] Hodgson fully supported this; it was more than ever desirable that the Supreme Court should exercise jurisdiction over Ashanti, especially since 'capitalists are turning their attention to the gold reefs'.[6]

At this point, however, the Secretary of State had no intention of annexing Ashanti, and even went so far as to tell Hodgson that 'any right of conquest which might have been claimed has been waived by the conclusion of treaties with the various Kings and Chiefs'. Ashanti, therefore, should become a Protectorate. But he did not agree that it should be on the same footing as the Protected Territories to the south; the Resident in Kumasi should be entrusted with judicial as well as executive functions, and the Governor of the Gold Coast should have power to legislate by proclamation for Ashanti. An Imperial Order in Council would be prepared, vesting in the Governor all powers and jurisdiction over Ashanti. Approval was given for a direct tax of 4s. per head, to be collected by the Ashanti Chiefs, who should be entitled to 10 per cent. of the proceeds. This was not to be called a 'tax' or 'tribute', but 'interest' on the war debt from the expeditions of 1874 and 1895–6.[7] The Governor received this important Dispatch only two days before he was due to leave for Kumasi. There was not time to reply to Chamberlain; so he left

---

[1] The Acting Resident in Ashanti had sent a case to Accra for trial, and the Supreme Court decided that it had the necessary jurisdiction; the European manager of the Ashanti Goldfields Corporation and two of his African staff were then tried on charges of torturing (causing 'dangerous harm' to) certain individuals, to obtain evidence concerning a robbery at Obuasi. Confidential Dispatch of 24 Feb. 1900, from Hodgson to Chamberlain; CO/96/357.

[2] Confidential Dispatch of 28 Jan. 1896, from Maxwell to Chamberlain; CO/96/270.

[3] For example, 'We do not hold Ashanti either by conquest or cession—both terms imply annexation and we are there only in exercise of H.M.'s jurisdiction in a foreign country.' Minute of 14 Dec. 1896, by J. Bramston; CO/96/277.

[4] Minute of 26 Oct. 1896, by R. L. Antrobus; CO/96/275.

[5] Memorandum of 9 Aug. 1899, by Brandford Griffith C.J.; CO/96/342.

[6] Confidential Dispatch of 21 Aug. 1899, from Hodgson to Chamberlain; ibid. Cf. Ch. I, pp. 22–24, above. Under the regulations of 7 Aug. 1899, a certain amount of official supervision was required over the acquisition of concessions in Ashanti; but the Governor wanted fuller powers than this.

[7] Confidential Dispatch of 19 Feb. 1900, from Chamberlain to Hodgson; CO/96/343.

the whole matter for detailed consideration by the Chief Justice, while including the interest payment in the agenda for his own discussions with the Chiefs of Ashanti.

Thus it was against a background of political unrest and legal uncertainty that Hodgson, accompanied by his wife, and a small escort of about thirty Hausas, left Accra in March 1900, cheerfully confident that 'whatever may be the opinion of the Government the Ashantis without exception regard themselves as a conquered people'.[1] A French historian later made some shrewd comments on the characteristic British illusion that, once a Protectorate had been declared over a country, complete submission would automatically follow. The local authorities were taken by surprise in Ashanti in 1900—as in Sierra Leone in 1898—owing to their inability to understand that alien rule might be unpopular: 'On ne comprit pas comment les indigènes pouvaient avoir eu même l'idée de se révolter.'[2]

The true situation in Ashanti was very different from what Hodgson supposed. The removal of Prempeh had been a deep and galling wound; the young men were bitter and resentful that they had not been able to prove their strength in 1896. Rumours were circulating that the British had suffered severe losses in South Africa, and that no white soldiers were available for Ashanti, so that there was every chance of beating any African troops sent against them. It was also whispered that the Government intended to bring back Achiriboanda as Asantehene, and to remove some of the remaining powerful Chiefs.[3] On the Governor's entry into Kumasi, one Chief was heard to remark that if he had not brought them a good message, they intended to fight. Unfortunately, the Acting Resident did not take this seriously, and failed to report it to the Governor until later.[4]

One major object that Hodgson hoped to achieve while in Ashanti was to gain possession of the Golden Stool. Ever since the removal of Prempeh the Government had feared that an attempt might be made to enstool another Asantehene, so long as the Stool remained in secret Ashanti hands. The Resident in Kumasi had been instructed from the start to try to ascertain its hiding-place, by offering a reward or by taking advantage of local dissensions. If found, the Golden Stool was to be sent to Cape Coast for safe custody.[5] A small expedition under the command of the Governor's private secretary, Captain C. H. Armitage, had recently been dispatched on a wild-goose chase to look for it, on information from an Ashanti youth, who had then panicked

---

[1] Confidential Dispatch of 23 Oct. 1899, from Hodgson to Chamberlain; CO/96/345.

[2] E. Baillaud, *La Politique indigène de l'Angleterre en Afrique Occidentale* (Paris, 1912), pp. 530–6.

[3] Confidential Report of 14 Jan. 1901, by Resident, Kumasi, enclosed in Secret Dispatch of 29 Jan. 1901, from Nathan to Chamberlain; CO/96/377.

[4] Letter of 27 Mar. 1900, from King of Juaben to Acting Resident, enclosed in Confidential Dispatch of 16 Apr. 1900, from Hodgson to Chamberlain; CO/96/359.

[5] Instructions of 22 Feb. 1896, to Resident, enclosed in Confidential Dispatch of 22 Feb. 1896, from Maxwell to Chamberlain; CO/96/270.

and run away. Hodgson still had hopes of the capture of this 'very valuable asset' for the Government, and regretted that its delivery had not been insisted upon in 1896.[1]

The Governor was surprised to find that the majority of the inhabitants of Kumasi were still living away from the deserted town, and had not accepted the new régime;[2] the garrison was insufficient and the Ashantis were not 'over-awed', as they ought to be.[3] He evidently decided that this was the occasion for a display of firmness—although unsupported by the necessary troops—and at a public meeting in Kumasi he announced that annual payments would be levied on each tribe; the separate amounts required to be collected by the Chiefs were read out, making a total of £15,000. The Governor now proceeded to drop one of the great bricks in African history:

> Let me tell you once and for all that Prempeh will never again rule over this country of Ashanti . . . The paramount authority of Ashanti is now the great Queen of England whose representative I am at this moment . . . Under the Governor the Resident at Kumasi exercises the powers of King paramount . . . Where is the golden stool? Why am I not sitting on the golden stool at this moment? I am the representative of the paramount power; why have you relegated me to this chair?[4]

Ignorant of the profound impression these remarks had created, and of the Chiefs' immediate plans for war, sealed by a secret fetish oath, Hodgson proceeded privately to ask two members of the Kumasi Native Committee to produce the Golden Stool. When they told him they did not know where it was, the Governor said he did and would get it.[5] A small force of Hausas and hammock-men was immediately dispatched, again under Armitage, to locate the Stool near Bali, north of Kumasi. The search was unsuccessful; then the party was attacked by the Offinsus as well as the Kumasis, and had to fight its way back to the town.[6]

This disturbing incident—the first clash between Ashantis and government troops since 1874—stiffened the Governor's resolve to stay and settle the matter permanently, 'in the interests of trade and of the gold mining concessions'.[7] The Acting Resident, still confident that the trouble was not

---

[1] Letter of 22 Feb. 1900, from Armitage to Hodgson, and his covering Confidential Dispatch of 7 Apr. 1900, to Chamberlain; CO/96/359.

[2] Letter of 29 Jan. 1901, from Hodgson to Under-Secretary of State; CO/96/391.

[3] Confidential Dispatch of 7 Apr. 1900, from Hodgson to Chamberlain; CO/96/359.

[4] Notes of palaver at Kumasi, 28 Mar. 1900; ibid.

[5] Confidential Dispatch of 19 Mar. 1901, from Nathan to Chamberlain; CO/96/378.

[6] As the Ashantis closed in, their war song was heard:

'The Governor came up to Kumasi on a peace palaver.
He demanded money from us and sent white men to bring him the Golden Stool.
Instead of money the Governor shall have the white men's heads sent to him to Kumasi.
The Golden Stool shall be well washed in the white men's blood.'

C. H. Armitage and H. F. Montanaro, *The Ashanti Campaign of 1900* (London, 1901), p. 10.

[7] Confidential Dispatch of 11 Apr. 1900, from Hodgson to Chamberlain; CO/96/359.

serious, departed for the coast on leave; and when military reinforcements arrived Hodgson sent them out to burn some nearby villages, apparently by way of a demonstration. The resistance forces then closed in on Kumasi; the Basel Mission was attacked, and the missionaries took refuge in the Fort.[1] By the end of April it was in a state of siege, with several hundred occupants, and several thousand refugees around the walls.

It is notable how quickly, in spite of the large number of separate treaties that had been made by the British, the Ashantis reunited in opposition to them. The following tribes joined the rising: Kumasi,[2] Ejisu, Offinsu, Atchima, Ahafo, Kokofu (though not all), Bechem, Nkwanta, and Adansi (later).[3] The military organization was largely in the hands of Kofi Kofia; but the main leadership and inspiration came from Yaa Asantewa, the Queen Mother of Ejisu, whose grandson had been deposed and exiled with Prempeh.

The tribes that stood out, though of some importance, were fewer in number. The Chiefs of Mampong, Nsuta, Juaben, and Agona were taken into the Fort, and their people took no organized part in the rising.[4] Some of the outlying tribes, including Bompata, Kumawu, and Attabubu on the north-east, British Gyaman on the north-west, and—eventually—Nkoranza, refused to take up arms against the British.[5] The Bekwais were expected to take the opposite side from the Adansis, whose lands they had occupied since 1886, and had recently leased profitably to the Ashanti Goldfields Corporation. The Governor upheld their claim, and relied on them to safeguard the property of the mines at Obuasi.[6] But the King of Bekwai wavered, and was only restrained from joining the rising by the presence of an advance column of the West African Frontier Force at Essumeja.

The Governor's attempts to negotiate with the rebel Chiefs—or freedom fighters, as they might nowadays have been called—during a brief truce proved unsuccessful; but their peace terms, which he dismissed as absurd, are of some interest:

1. Prempeh to be given back, and to regulate and collect any annual payments to be made,
2. Permission to buy and sell slaves as in the old time,
3. To be freed from demands for carriers,

[1] For the indomitable Ramseyer's own account of his second period of detention in Kumasi with his wife, see F. Ramseyer and P. Steiner, *Dark and Stormy Days at Kumassi, 1900* (London 1901).

[2] Kwame Afilfa and Kwaku Nenchi, of the Kumasi Native Committee, took an active part; but the senior member, Opoku Mensa, warned the Government of this, and he remained in the Fort, where he later died of pneumonia.

[3] Confidential Report of 14 Jan. 1901, by Resident; CO/96/377.

[4] Many years later the Juabens told R. S. Rattray: 'A people cannot fight when their master is not there to advise them.' *Ashanti Law and Constitution* (Oxford, 1929), p. 178.

[5] Confidential Dispatch of 19 Mar. 1901, from Nathan to Chamberlain; CO/96/378.

[6] Lady Hodgson, *The Siege of Kumassi* (London, 1901), pp. 39–40 and 111. At the time of the rising, there were about sixty Europeans at Obuasi. H. C. J. Biss, *The Relief of Kumasi* (London, 1901), p. 69.

4. To be freed from the obligation of building houses and supplying thatch,

5. All huxters and traders to be sent away.[1]

Armitage later gave a slightly different list, which included specific demands for the departure of all white men and the destruction of the Fort. Whichever version may have been the original, the basic theme was the desire of the Ashantis to be free from European interference.

The arrival of a small relief column from the north after a strenuous march was regarded by the Ashantis as a breach of the armistice, and the blockade was renewed.[2] The story of the three months' siege, the escape of the Governor's party by night, and the relief expedition from the coast under Colonel J. Willcocks, is too well known from several eye-witness accounts to bear repetition here. The Fort was not relieved until July 1900, and the expedition did not finally dispose of the guerrilla fighters and leaders until November, when Yaa Asantewa was captured. Public opinion in Britain was moved and alarmed; but in answer to repeated questions in the House of Commons, the Secretary of State was unable to say what were the causes of the rebellion, and especially unwilling to attribute it to the 'trivial incident' of the Golden Stool.[3] He discussed the matter in London with Stewart, who was about to return to Ashanti to resume his post as Resident, and impressed upon him the importance of obtaining possession of this emblem of Ashanti sovereignty.[4]

Chamberlain's private comment on this episode was 'I must get the Governor transferred as soon as possible as I do not think he has been wise.'[5] Hodgson left for England shortly after his escape from the siege, and his successor, Sir Matthew Nathan, was unable to visit Ashanti until March 1901. Several urgent matters then remained to be settled, including the fate of the leaders of the rising. The new Governor did not accept the suggestion that half a dozen of them should be hanged in front of the Residency 'to mark the occasion': this would, said the old King of Bekwai, have an excellent effect.[6] Instead, forty-six political prisoners were sent down to the coast,[7] and in May, Yaa Asantewa and fourteen other Ashantis sailed for the Seychelles,[8] to join Prempeh and his party, who had been sent there soon after the relief of Kumasi the previous year. The deposed Chiefs were replaced by safe nominees;[9] and an amnesty was proclaimed in April 1901, to all others who had

---

[1] Confidential Dispatch of 16 Apr. 1900, from Hodgson to Chamberlain; CO/96/359.

[2] Armitage and Montanaro, *The Ashanti Campaign*, p. 65 and ch. vii.

[3] *Parliamentary Debates*, House of Commons, 13 Dec. 1900; also CO/96/366.

[4] Confidential Dispatch of 21 Aug. 1900, from Chamberlain to Hodgson; CO/96/362.

[5] Letter of 6 Aug. 1900, to Mrs. Chamberlain, quoted by J. L. Garvin, *The Life of Joseph Chamberlain*, vol. iii (London, 1934), p. 588.

[6] Confidential Dispatch of 25 Mar. 1901, from Nathan to Chamberlain; CO/96/378.

[7] The prisoners were hooted at on leaving Kumasi, not apparently because they had made the attempt to free Ashanti from British rule, but because they had failed. Confidential Dispatch of 27 May 1901, from Nathan to Chamberlain; CO/96/380.

[8] *Departmental Reports*, Ashanti, 1901.

[9] Telegram of 8 Mar. 1901, from Nathan to Chamberlain; CO/96/378.

taken up arms. Nathan also took the opportunity while in Kumasi to announce the amount of indemnity tax to be paid by each tribe. But he offered a little balm in Gilead: he would not interfere with Ashanti religion—so long as it prompted no inhuman or immoral acts—and he did not want the Golden Stool.[1]

That the demand for the Golden Stool was only one of several factors leading to the rising, is certain; that it was the main precipitant is equally certain. Writing many years later from memory, a British officer recalled that Yaa Asantewa was heard to say during the Governor's speech: 'Good, he is calling the Ashantis to arms for me! He could not do it better than he has done it in demanding the Golden Stool.'[2] It is the more difficult to understand Hodgson's blunder since the psychological importance of the Golden Stool was well understood by at least some of his subordinates.[3] There were other factors. Stewart reported that the leaders of the rising listed their reasons for it in the following order: '1st. Search for the Golden Stool, 2nd Demanding payment of the tribute tax, 3rd Removal of Prempeh, 4th Taking away stools from Big Chiefs.' He himself thought that trouble would have been inevitable at some time, even if it had not happened when it did.[4]

It is clear that at the time of Hodgson's visit to Kumasi a very slight mishandling of the Ashantis would have been sufficient to produce armed resistance. Nathan attributed the rebellion basically to a profound dislike on the part of the Chiefs and other leaders to alien rule. The British, he said, had deprived the Ashantis of the power of making war, of keeping their people in order by barbarous punishments, and of recruiting slave labour. In return they had been given protection from external aggression, peace within their own boundaries, law enforced by civilized methods, and opportunities of making money by labour. But the Ashantis had formerly been able to protect themselves from aggression, and peace within the country had no attraction to those who derived their title to respect, their power, and their wealth from feats of war; while personal labour of any kind was 'beneath their dignity'. Nathan's careful analysis throws light on the attitude of the British officials as well as on the Ashantis themselves:

A complicated system of administration, hallowed by antiquity and historic precedents, which our ignorance and policy have alike tended to break down, and a

---

[1] Confidential Dispatch of 25 Mar. 1901, from Nathan to Chamberlain; ibid.
[2] W. M. Hall, *The Great Drama of Kumasi* (London, 1939), p. 280.
[3] For example, Letter of 30 Sept. 1900, from F. H. Kelly to Colonial Office; CO/96/372. The point was perhaps exaggerated in later years, and Rattray's statement (apparently based on the account of only one informant) that not even the Asantehene ever sat on the Golden Stool has been taken too literally by some; e.g. E. W. Smith, *The Golden Stool* (London, 1926), p. 7. By contrast, nineteenth-century accounts make no mention of any such rigid taboo. Dr. R. A. Freeman, normally a careful observer and reporter, wrote of the Golden Stool: 'On this the King takes his seat on his formal appointment to his royal office, and it is said he occupies it thereafter once in every year'. *Travels and Life in Ashanti and Jaman* (London, 1898), pp. 100–1.
[4] Confidential Report of 14 Jan. 1901, by Resident; CO/96/377.

deep rooted superstition which we are unable to understand and from which our presence in the country has detached a proportion of the people, further help to make our rule distasteful to the Ashanti.[1]

The revolt was the last, unsuccessful attempt of the Ashantis to assert by force the right of their traditional State to survive as a national unit in the modern world. Their impetus was exhausted in this final struggle with the British; and although they could never be said to have acquiesced voluntarily in alien rule, yet during the first part of the twentieth century Ashanti, unlike the Colony, was notable for the absence of any resistance to specific administrative actions and decisions. It took many years for the old Ashanti nationalism to be revived and subsumed in a new, wider Gold Coast nationalism. Ironically enough, the framework for this later development was now about to be laid down, by Orders in Council designed to settle once and for all the vexed question of British sovereignty.

The Annexation and Protection Orders in Council, 1901–2

Almost immediately after Hodgson had reached the safety of the coast he proposed that all the land of Ashanti, with certain exceptions, should become Crown property.[2] Fortunately for all concerned, Nathan rejected the idea, as he did a suggestion that the lands of the rebel tribes should be confiscated and transferred to the 'loyal' tribes.[3] The Governor's policy was not entirely disinterested, since he realized that to allow the Chiefs to retain their lands and rents would be to give them a vested interest in keeping their country quiet, and would be almost a guarantee of their co-operation, especially in providing labour for the mines.[4]

The main reason for Nathan's visit to Kumasi in 1901 was to formulate his own views and advise the Secretary of State on the definition of British jurisdiction in Ashanti. After the rising, Chamberlain no longer considered that it would be sufficient to declare a Protectorate over Ashanti. Having already decided to annex the Protected Territories to the south, he was the more ready to listen to the continued requests for annexation made by the British Chambers of Commerce; and he believed that since Ashanti had been conquered, the people would be ready to acquiesce in a new form of government. Conscious of the large gold-mining operations already in progress,[5]

[1] Confidential Dispatch of 19 Mar. 1901, from Nathan to Chamberlain; CO/96/378.
[2] Confidential Dispatch of 24 July 1900, from Hodgson to Chamberlain; CO/96/361.
[3] The only confiscations were two Adansi villages, which were given to the Bekwai stool, and Agogo, which was put under Bompata. *Departmental Reports*, Ashanti, 1901. In 1905 the lands of Kumasi were declared to belong to the Crown; seven years later the Chief Commissioner suggested that this should be extended to all land in Ashanti, but his advice was not accepted. *West African Lands Committee: Minutes of Evidence, &c.* (London, 1916); evidence of Sir Francis Fuller in reply to questions 4,648 and 4,653–4.
[4] Confidential Dispatch of 20 Mar. 1901, from Nathan to Chamberlain; CO/96/378.
[5] The Ashanti gold rush recommenced almost as soon as the troops had cleared the country; in one year alone, 124 permits for prospecting were issued. *Departmental Reports*, Ashanti, 1901.

which might be expected to increase when the railway reached Kumasi, Chamberlain suggested that Ashanti should be annexed to the Colony, provided that this could be done without injustice to those tribes who had supported the British, and without risk of difficulty over the abolition of slavery.[1]

Nathan agreed with the Secretary of State that Ashanti should be annexed by the Crown, so that the people would become British subjects. He proposed, however, that it should not form part and parcel of the Gold Coast Colony, but should be administered separately.[2] He was supported by the Chief Justice, Brandford Griffith, who now argued that it would be undesirable to deal with Ashanti affairs from headquarters in the Colony;[3] the railway would only encourage Chiefs and others to come down to Accra, 'Kumasi would cease to be the focus that it ought to be for Ashanti affairs, and the centre of gravity of Ashanti would be shifted from Kumasi to the Coast'. An elastic system of government was needed, in order to allow British administrators to interfere far more than would have been thought necessary before the rising.[4]

The Colonial Office accepted this view; and Ashanti was separately annexed by an Imperial Order in Council of 26 September 1901, which specifically declared that it had been 'conquered by His Majesty's forces'.[5] The Governor of the Gold Coast was given full powers and jurisdiction to provide for peace, order, and good government; in particular he, and not the Legislative Council, was empowered to legislate for Ashanti. He was enjoined to respect native laws, except where they were incompatible with the powers and jurisdiction of the Crown, or clearly injurious to the welfare of the inhabitants.[6]

The future status of the peoples to the north was easier to decide. Rights of protection had been acquired by direct treaty negotiations, with the voluntary consent of the Chiefs. Resistance to European influence had been isolated and infrequent, and mainly inspired by the arbitrary imposition of boundaries with little reference to African interests or wishes.[7] By 1899 the

[1] Confidential Dispatch of 5 Feb. 1901, from Chamberlain to Nathan; CO/96/371.

[2] Confidential Dispatch of 28 May 1901, from Nathan to Chamberlain; CO/96/380.

[3] Brandford Griffith C.J. admitted that this reversed his view of 1899 that Ashanti *should* be treated as part of the Colony.

[4] Memorandum of 23 Apr. 1901, by Brandford Griffith C.J.; CO/96/380.

[5] The Ashantis in later years have strongly denied this assertion; e.g. Cobina Kessie's rider, 'purely of academic interest', to the Coussey Report. He claims that the separate treaties concluded with the Ashanti States in 1896 made them allies of Britain, and that as far as the Gold Coast Government was concerned Ashanti as a unit ceased to exist. The Asantewa War of 1900 could not therefore be a war against—or a defeat of—Ashanti. The text of the Report, however, says that the question will remain 'one of the moot points of . . . history'. *Report to His Excellency the Governor by the Committee on Constitutional Reform* (London, 1949), Colonial No. 248, para. 17.

[6] This Order in Council retains traces of a previous draft under which Ashanti was to become a Protectorate. The term 'treaty' is initially defined, but being irrelevant to annexation by 'conquest' it is nowhere subsequently mentioned.

[7] The King of Yendi refused to sign a treaty in 1894, since he feared the eventual partition of his territory: 'Did you ever see two men riding one donkey?' he asked. It was not surprising

international rivalries were virtually over; agreement had been reached with both the French and the Germans, and the newly christened Northern Territories of the Gold Coast, though not united amongst themselves, were at least readily amenable to British influence. The Chief Justice at that time assumed that the Government had undertaken the protection of 'the rest of the back territories up to the French boundary'.[1] Hodgson hoped that eventually the whole area would become part of the Colony, although the north might have to be administered as a Protectorate until communications could be improved and civilizing influences had made their mark.[2] But after the Law Officers had considered the Colony-Protectorate problem, it became clear that a new Order in Council would be required to legalize even this limited form of jurisdiction in the north.

By 1900 Chamberlain had come to the conclusion that the Northern Territories needed a semi-military administration.[3] At that stage he envisaged three separate divisions of the Gold Coast Protectorate. During the subsequent year the Chief Justice, as we have seen, persuaded Chamberlain to annex the Protected Territories, and circumstances forced him to annex Ashanti; but the proposals for the north survived more or less intact. So a Protectorate was declared over the Northern Territories of the Gold Coast by another Order in Council,[4] of the same date as the Ashanti Order. Apart from the major difference—protection instead of annexation—its terms were very similar; the powers and jurisdiction of the Crown were again vested in the Governor, who alone had power to legislate for the Northern Territories.

The annexation of the Protected Territories was implemented by the Gold Coast Order in Council, also passed on 26 September 1901;[5] these now became part of, and subject to the laws of, the Colony. A fourth Order in Council was necessary to sweep away the uncertainty over the 'automatic application' of earlier laws; this revoked the 1887 Order in Council, and validated all Ordinances or reputed Ordinances enacted since then by the Legislative Council.[6]

that when his kingdom was in fact divided between the British and the Germans in 1899, some of the Dagomba Chiefs resisted by force; but the area was soon pacified. *Further Correspondence respecting the Mission of Mr. G. E. Ferguson and the Extent of the Sphere of British Influence in the Hinterland of the Gold Coast Colony* (London, 1895), African (West) No. 479; also 1953 Acc. No. 1288, G.N. Archives.

[1] Memorandum of 9 Aug. 1899, by Brandford Griffith C.J.; CO/96/342.

[2] Confidential Dispatch of 21 Aug. 1899, from Hodgson to Chamberlain; ibid.

[3] Confidential Dispatch of 19 Feb. 1900, from Chamberlain to Hodgson; CO/96/349.

[4] Passed under the authority of the Foreign Jurisdiction Act of 1890, which had superseded that of 1843.

[5] Sometimes called the Boundary, Annexation and Ordinance Extension Order in Council. This, together with the Ashanti and Northern Territories Orders in Council of the same date, was reprinted in Mensah Sarbah's *Fanti National Constitution*, pp. 170–82.

[6] The Revocation and Validation Order in Council of 23 Oct. 1901. After the prolonged Colony-Protectorate controversy, Brandford Griffith C.J. had the last word. He argued that the Ordinances thus validated included the 1895 and 1898 Revision Ordinances, and therefore that the

All these Orders in Council came into force together, on 1 January 1902. From that date 'the Gold Coast' consisted of three separate but related territories: the Colony, Ashanti, and the Northern Territories. For the two latter, the new system of government was set forth in Administration Ordinances, the major provisions of each being almost identical.[1] In each area the powers of the Governor were to be exercised by a Chief Commissioner, whose Court should have the same powers and jurisdiction as a Divisional Court in the Colony; at first, he did not even need to consult the Governor before carrying out a death sentence. No criminal appeal was allowed; but appeals to the Supreme Court of the Colony were possible in civil cases involving £100 or more, by leave of the Governor.[2] Local branches of the Chief Commissioner's Court were to be presided over by District Commissioners, on similar lines to those in the Colony.[3] From 1902 onwards, although the Governor of the Gold Coast remained the Governor of all three territories, and they were all covered by the budget of the Colony, their legislative and judicial systems were quite distinct.[4] Up to 1934 all Ordinances had to be enacted separately for each of the three territories; and from 1906 to 1933 barristers and solicitors were specifically excluded from courts in Ashanti and the north.

The new Orders in Council gave the Governor full power to raise revenue in all the territories under his jurisdiction. They were still not accompanied by the introduction of a direct tax. A half-hearted attempt to collect some payment on account of the Ashanti war debt had already been made, but was well on the way to being dropped. Nathan believed that it would only serve to increase discontent among those who did not want the benefits of civilization. It would be impolitic to remit the tax in response to threats, for this would amount to an admission of weakness;[5] but he agreed to abolish it within two years at most, to end the disputes, quarrels, and extortion that had already arisen, and hoped soon to substitute indirect taxation.[6] A mutiny in the West African Regiment at Kumasi further complicated the situation and weakened the Government position in Ashanti.[7] The collection of the

effective date of annexation of the greater part of the Protectorate was 1895. See his judgement of 9 Dec. 1907, *in re* Mutchi *v.* Annan, Inketsia, and Kudo. *Report of the Gold Coast Local Committee of the Society of Comparative Legislation* (Accra) for the quarter ending 30 Sept. 1907.

[1] For Ashanti alone it was provided that 'It shall not be lawful for any headchief to exercise any powers as headchief until he shall have been recognised as such by the Governor'; the Government was also empowered to requisition land there for public purposes.

[2] The full jurisdiction of the Supreme Court was not extended to Ashanti and the Northern Territories until the Courts Ordinance of 1935.

[3] Ashanti Administration Ordinance, No. 1 of 1902, and Northern Territories Administration Ordinance, No. 1 of 1902; *Government Gazette*, 1 Jan. 1902.

[4] Brandford Griffith C.J., *A Note on the History of the British Courts in the Gold Coast Colony.*

[5] Confidential Dispatch of 23 Apr. 1901, from Nathan to Chamberlain; CO/96/379.

[6] Confidential Letter of 2 Aug. 1901, from Stewart to Nathan, enclosed in his Confidential Dispatch of 17 Aug. 1901, to Chamberlain; CO/96/382.

[7] The troops' grievances over pay and conditions of service were not dealt with; so they marched

indemnity tax was left to the Resident's discretion; it was reduced by half in 1902 and abolished in 1903.[1]

Experience in the Northern Territories was very similar. It had been agreed in 1898 that there should be some sort of annual tax, and Lieutenant-Colonel H. P. Northcott, the first Commissioner and Commandant, was anxious that it should be collected as soon as possible, 'before the pernicious doctrines of individual irresponsibility filter through from the Coast natives'.[2] He believed strongly that the essence of easy rule over the inhabitants of West Africa was the existence of some convincing proof of paramountcy.[3] While visiting the districts, he explained the advantages of British rule, at the same time emphasizing the necessity for taxation.[4] Apparently there was no public dissent, and Northcott proceeded to draw up a realistic schedule of the limited amounts that he thought might be expected from each district for a start, making a total of £875.[5]

But the so-called 'maintenance tax' was never seriously pressed. The next Commissioner persuaded the Governor that it would create increasing disaffection, and that the trouble of collection was not worth while.[6] Only small sums had been raised, and even these had given the Chiefs useful opportunities for extortion. An inquiry into customary taxation showed that only the Dagombas were used to paying an annual tribute to their King; the Mamprussis were merely required to provide free agricultural labour, while a regular, recurring imposition was completely foreign to the Dagartis, Gurunshis, and Fra-Fras, who lacked any central form of government. The tax was therefore dropped altogether at the end of 1901, in the hope of securing more free labour instead.[7]

Thus at the beginning of the twentieth century the whole tenor of official opinion was against direct taxation for the Gold Coast. The difficulties were undoubtedly great, and the need did not appear very urgent. In 1900 over £280,000 was collected in import duties, and the following year over £350,000 —considerably more than half the total expenditure.[8] The day of reckoning

back to Cape Coast, and threatened the Bank of British West Africa, where they thought their money was. Confidential Dispatch of 5 May 1901, from Nathan to Chamberlain; CO/96/379.

[1] *Departmental Reports*, Ashanti, 1902 and 1903.

[2] Letter of 10 Aug. 1898, from Northcott to Colonial Secretary, enclosed in Confidential Dispatch of 14 Feb. 1899, from Low to Chamberlain; CO/96/337.

[3] Report of 9 July 1899, by Northcott, quoted in Confidential Dispatch of 22 Aug. 1901, from Nathan to Chamberlain; CO/96/382.

[4] The main source of revenue was caravan dues; in addition, there were local taxes (e.g. on butchers for the slaughter of animals) and some fines. The total collected in the north in 1899 was £2,913; but expenditure was running at a much higher rate.

[5] Letter of 5 Mar. 1899, from Northcott to Colonial Secretary; 1953 Acc. No. 1288, G.N. Archives.

[6] Confidential Dispatch of 14 July 1900, from Hodgson to Chamberlain; CO/96/360. Also Report of 21 Feb. 1900, concerning disaffection in the Bole Sub-district; 1953 Acc. No. 1288, G.N. Archives.

[7] Undated Letter from Morris to Nathan, enclosed in his Confidential Dispatch of 8 Nov. 1901, to Chamberlain; CO/96/383.   [8] *Gold Coast Colony Blue Book*, 1900 and 1901.

was therefore postponed. As in 1874 with the Colony and Protected Territories, so now in 1902 with Ashanti and the Northern Territories, the Government failed to observe Lugard's principle that 'The inauguration of British rule is the moment at which to lay the foundations' of a tax system, not merely with a view to subsequent increases in expenditure, but in order to establish the principle of personal contribution to the State.[1] The Gold Coast remained without direct taxation for many more years.[2]

The 1901 Orders in Council, supplemented by the Administration Ordinances of 1902, at last provided a complete definition of the meaning and extent of British jurisdiction. Their full significance was not immediately apparent to African politicians. One reason was, no doubt, the legal confusion surrounding the whole situation, and the fact that the Government had been acting as if the country had long previously been annexed. No special publicity was given to the Orders in Council at the time, in marked contrast to the detailed negotiations with Chiefs in East Africa which led up to the 1900 Buganda Agreement. The absence of any national protest in the Gold Coast, however, has been attributed to the fact that the annexation was carried out only a few years after the people had been reassured that the Government would not lay claim to their land.[3]

The subsequent nationalist contention has been that, whatever the legal niceties, the fundamental relationship between Britain and the Gold Coast should be traced back to the Bond of 1844 as 'one of friendship between a weaker and a stronger people'.[4] Indeed, for many years the zealous leaders of the A.R.P.S. were doggedly insisting, in spite of the *fait accompli* of the Orders in Council, that 'countries like the Gold Coast are not Colonies at all, but Protectorates'.[5] But the pattern of British authority was now plain for all to see, whether they chose to accept it or to challenge it. The Gold Coast had acquired a constitutional as well as a territorial identity.

The manner in which this authority was exercised appeared both administratively simple and politically expedient in its tendency to emphasize regional divisions. Ashantis and northerners, as they became politically conscious, had every reason to consider themselves to some extent separate from the Gold Coast Colony—attached to it and yet not of it. Although the Ashanti Union had been constitutionally decapitated, the people continued to preserve what they could of their traditional organization, and did not think of themselves as being incorporated in any larger unit. This tendency was sedulously

---

[1] Lugard, *The Dual Mandate*, p. 234.

[2] Income tax proposals, although more equitable as well as more efficient than a regressive poll tax, had to struggle during 1931–4 against serious opposition, which was the indirect legacy of the past. It was not until 1943 that an Ordinance was finally pushed through the Legislative Council, assisted by the exigencies of war and the hope of fuller representation under a new constitution.

[3] M. A. Ribeiro, 'Political History of the Gold Coast', in *Quo Vadimus or Gold Coast Future* (Achimota, 1940).

[4] *Report . . . on Constitutional Reform* (1949), para 7.

[5] W. E. G. Sekyi, *West Africa*, 23 July 1932.

encouraged by the Chief Commissioner. For example, when the Ashanti Chiefs were first told of the annexation in 1901, they expressed some misgivings concerning the introduction of what they called Coast Law; but they were officially reassured that 'things would go on much the same as before'.[1] The Ashantis did not, however, readily accept the idea of defeat; and Nathan suggested that the numerous endeavours made to get the Government to search again for the Golden Stool were instigated by the war leaders, who wanted an excuse to appeal to the young men to take up arms.[2] His refusal to take any action helped to prevent fresh trouble arising.

During the 1920's and 30's there was to develop an uneasy, though fruitful alliance between Gold Coast and Ashanti nationalism. In the Northern Territories, on the other hand, with their dispersed social organization and subsistence economy, even the idea of regional unity was slow to develop, and the people remained in political isolation from the rest of the country for many years. This sprang partly from the deliberate policy of the Administration, partly from the comparative poverty of the area and the consequent slowness of social and economic development.

Ultimately, a wider sense of national unity was bound to come, if only in that very tenuous form 'imposed by all imperial powers upon colonial peoples under their control; namely, an awareness of being under a common alien master to whom all grievances could be ascribed.'[3] Meanwhile, the mere existence of British rule meant, for example, that British ideas of law and justice were applied throughout the separate judicial systems. Administrative officers, and to some extent their African subordinates, were interchangeable between any of the three territories, and policy trends were similar, in spite of marked differences in regional emphasis. Officials were neither so physically remote from one another, nor so emotionally partisan where their own regions were concerned, as seems to have been the case in Nigeria.[4]

Almost everywhere in the Gold Coast, Africans who worked with Europeans had to learn the English language; and this gradually became a means of inter-communication between people of such diverse language groups as Ewes, Gãs, Dagombas, and Akans, at the same time tending to cut them off from French and German speakers across the border.[5] Within the boundary lines, the old, tribal units of society began to melt and diffuse, and the crosscurrents of new ideas and information began to flow across a wider area. More important still, the development of communications, resulting in a new economic interdependence, began to link the various regions more firmly than any tripartite scheme of administration could divide them. As Attoh Ahuma

---

[1] *Departmental Reports*, Ashanti, 1901.

[2] Secret Dispatch of 3 May 1902, from Nathan to Chamberlain; CO/96/396.

[3] J. S. Coleman, *Togoland* (New York, 1956), *International Conciliation*, No. 509, p. 6.

[4] Cf. J. S. Coleman, *Nigeria: Background to Nationalism* (Los Angeles, 1958), pp. 46–47.

[5] See Ch. XIII, pp. 507–17, below.

put it: 'We are being welded together under one umbrageous Flag . . . The Gold Coast under the *aegis* of the Union Jack is the unanswerable argument to all who may incontinently withhold from us the common rights, privileges, and status of nationality.'[1]

[1] S. R. B. Attoh Ahuma, *The Gold Coast Nation and National Consciousness* (Liverpool, 1911).

IX

THE A.R.P.S. AND THE LANDS
1889–1900

THE creation of the Aborigines' Rights Protection Society in 1897 was perhaps the first organized protest on anything approaching a national scale in the Gold Coast—i.e. in the former 'Colony and Protectorate'. Although the A.R.P.S. centred primarily in Cape Coast and the Western Province, it was not, as some government officials liked to believe, a mushroom growth fostered by mercenary land speculators, but had its roots in the past. The long, though chequered history of attempts to form associations among educated Africans, the growing tradition of protest against government actions, the conscious revival of respect for national traditions, especially since the foundation of the *Mfantsi Amanbuhu Fékuw* in 1889, and a deep-rooted reverence for land as the foundation of community life, all played a part in the emergence of this new organization.[1]

The evolution of the *Fékuw* into the A.R.P.S. probably owed more than its name to the example of the Aborigines' Protection Society in London. This was already well known for its tireless campaigning on humanitarian and political issues affecting Africans, and was showing an increasing interest in the Gold Coast.[2] In 1891 H. R. Fox Bourne, the Secretary of the Society, planned to visit West Africa. He informed the Colonial Office, where A. W. L. Hemming immediately scented danger: 'it would be wise policy to suggest that he should be made much of, & entertained & not allowed to fall into the hands of the opponents of the Govt.'[3] But Fox Bourne had other ideas. He wrote to *The Gold Coast Chronicle* suggesting that 'patriotic residents' in the principal towns should form local committees in order to supply useful information to his Society. He hoped that this might help to secure a just, generous, and humane government policy, with peace throughout the Protectorate.[4]

This letter was given considerable publicity in the Gold Coast, and Hemming was stung into more than his usual asperity: 'Mr. Fox Bourne ought to be ashamed of . . . inviting complaints & accusations against the Colonial authorities from ignorant and mendacious people like the natives of

---

[1] For urban associations during the nineteenth century, see Ch. III, pp. 146–50, above.

[2] So many letters were sent from the A.P.S. to the Colonial Office during 1890–1 that officials wondered who were the 'busybodies' in the Gold Coast 'inciting' them to protest. Minute of 22 Apr. 1891, by A. W. L. Hemming; CO/96/220.

[3] Minute of 14 Sept. 1891, by Hemming; ibid.

[4] Letter of 13 Nov. 1891, from Fox Bourne; *The Gold Coast Chronicle*, 21 and 28 Dec. 1891.

W. Africa.'[1] But *The Gold Coast Chronicle* declared that Europe might well be proud of Fox Bourne and his Society; the proposed visit was used as a text to preach the gospel of political unity and the need for a petition to present grievances to the Governor. The difficulty was to get people to act together; but this was not for want of press persuasion. The campaign continued from week to week: 'we can not be transported and persecuted or imprisoned by the local Government for simply holding a few meetings, with respect to our grievances, and making some arrangements in reference to a reception for the Secretary of such an important association as the Aborigines' Protection Society.'[2] The projected visit never took place; but as a result of these plans, united action was now almost a catchword. Journalists in Accra welcomed *The Gold Coast People*, which first appeared in 1891, as 'an excellent mouthpiece' for the people of Cape Coast and the west, and suggested that later there could be a meeting of delegates: 'We are all one, and natives of the same colony.'[3] The only thing that was lacking was a nation-wide grievance.

In 1894 the first Lands Bill provided a ready-made issue for agitation. It tended to divert attention, however, from the aims of the *Fékuw*; it was not until 1897 that political and social aspirations were fused, and the A.R.P.S. was formed to defend both land rights and the social structure based upon them. The new legislation was not, however, primarily intended as the insidious attack upon native institutions that its opponents made it out to be; nor was it an unpremeditated move on the part of the Government. Some account of their underlying motives is necessary at this stage in order to bring the ensuing conflict into sharper focus.

The Background to Land Legislation

With the rise of the gold-mining industry after 1874,[4] and the increasing number of concessions that were being granted, land disputes were bound to arise. The Government had already found it by no means easy to establish a title to land for public buildings. In 1876, partly to facilitate the acquisition of land for the new seat of administration in Accra, a Public Lands Ordinance was enacted.[5] Even then, difficulties arose. In 1887 King Tackie complained that a wall he was building had been broken down: 'Since the English Government took possession Sir they have not asked us for land. But we only see them building.'[6] He was shown a plan of the boundaries of government land; but further misunderstandings arose, especially over areas occupied by the Government before 1876. It was therefore suggested that a retrospective

---

[1] Minute of 7 Feb. 1892, by Hemming; CO/96/219.
[2] *The Gold Coast Chronicle*, 21 and 28 Dec. 1891.
[3] Ibid. 4 Jan. 1892.   [4] See Ch. I, pp. 15–16 and 21–25, above.
[5] *The African Times*, 1 Apr. 1875, carried away by enthusiasm at Strahan's abolition of slavery, suggested that he should proceed to lay the foundations of a civilized State by declaring 'the whole land of the country . . . to be vested in, and held from the Crown'.
[6] Report of meeting between Administrator, King Tackie, and others, in May 1887; CO/96/181.

Ordinance was needed, declaring the title of the Government to all lands taken for public purposes before the passing of the Public Lands Ordinance.[1] But the Secretary of State refused to sanction further legislation, unless there was a chance of the Crown's title being seriously challenged, which he thought unlikely.[2]

In 1889, however, as a result of a mining land dispute, the Governor, Sir William Brandford Griffith, proposed a sovereign remedy: namely, that the whole country should be taken over as Crown land, and administered to greater advantage than the inhabitants could do it for themselves. Individual rights could be preserved for the lifetime of the holders, and the revenues from the sale or lease of lands could be devoted to the exclusive benefit of the district.[3] The Colonial Office realized that this plan had the merit of simplicity, and might get rid of the many troublesome questions of jurisdiction in a country 'practically ruled as if it were British territory, tho' nominally it is not so'.[4] On the other hand, it was feared that to turn the whole country into Crown land would be something of a social revolution, and might raise a ferment without much corresponding advantage.[5] The cautious admission was placed on record that there were 'many reasons in favour' of making the whole of the Colony and Protectorate British territory and, therefore, Crown land; and the Governor was asked for more detailed proposals.[6]

In 1891 the Chief Justice, J. T. Hutchinson, carefully considered the policy of taking over all 'waste lands' as Crown property. He pointed out that all the land in the Colony and the Protectorate, whether occupied or not, had according to native law an owner. A large part of the litigation in the courts concerned land, and such cases were argued with great pertinacity. There might, however, be two possible gains from expropriation: an increase of revenue from sales and leases of the land, and a benefit to the community from the creation of indisputable titles derived from the Crown. But these would be of doubtful value, and more than offset by the disadvantages: the importance of Chiefs and heads of families would be reduced, and a sense of injustice and consequent hostility to the Government would be created in the minds of the people. Another problem would be the payment of compensation to the owners, even though the land was lying waste. Hutchinson therefore rejected the proposal, so far as *all* waste lands were concerned; but he suggested that the Crown might simply take possession of minerals, and of unused and unoccupied forest lands. Minerals, he argued, had not been a source of revenue. except to a few owners, and were not likely to have any sentimental value, Therefore no hardship and no consequent public hostility should arise if these

[1] Minute of 24 July 1887, by Hemming; CO/96/181.
[2] Dispatch of 12 Aug. 1887, from Holland to White; ibid.
[3] Confidential Dispatch of 25 June 1889, from Brandford Griffith to Knutsford; CO/96/202.
[4] Cf. Ch. VIII, pp. 313–15, above.
[5] Minutes of 11 and 25 Nov. 1889, by Hemming and R. H. Meade; CO/96/202.
[6] Letter of 4 Dec. 1889, from Colonial Office to Brandford Griffith; African No. 513.

were appropriated by the Crown for the general benefit, provided that mines already worked and concessions previously made were not interfered with.[1]

Brandford Griffith was not convinced by Hutchinson's arguments that legislation should be limited to minerals and forests. He felt he needed further advice, especially over the tricky question of compensation, and consulted his son, recently transferred to Jamaica, who now produced some cogent arguments to support the case his father wanted to make. He agreed that all the land undoubtedly belonged to some person or group. It would be almost impossible to value each claim; but compensation would not be necessary if existing rights were preserved when the Crown took over the land. This would not be confiscation: 'The Crown does not take the land for itself. It would not really be taking the land from the natives of the Gold Coast Colony. It would simply aim at holding the land for them as a trustee ... This I submit disposes of the moral questions which to my mind at first seemed serious'.[2] The younger Brandford Griffith admitted that it would hardly be politically possible to expropriate all the land at once. But he suggested an ingenious scheme to achieve this object in time, without injustice, by means of a graduated land tax. Where the tax remained unpaid for, say, ten years the land should be liable for forfeiture. Owners would thus be compelled to formulate definite, fixed claims; at the same time, no one need lose any existing rights. By this means, however, the Crown could get possession of all unoccupied land, which would be a form of payment in return for protection; and the system should only be applied to the coast, at first.[3]

This drastic scheme, after being pigeon-holed in Accra for some time, was eventually rejected as impracticable for a country which had never been surveyed and lacked fences and boundary marks.[4] Meanwhile the Government was becoming increasingly concerned about the uncontrolled acquisition of land from Chiefs by speculators. In August 1891 a circular letter was sent to District Commissioners enclosing a form of monitory notice to Chiefs;[5] but the traffic in concessions continued unchecked. In 1893 a government official told Liverpool business men that it would be difficult to find a square mile of land from Apollonia to Shama which had not been conceded, at least once, to some speculator.[6] The Governor thought that the rapid expansion of the timber trade, too, would make legislation necessary 'at no distant date' in order to ensure fair play to the landowners, and to prevent the

[1] Letter of 7 Apr. 1891, from Hutchinson to Brandford Griffith, enclosed in his Confidential Dispatch of 29 Aug. 1894, to Ripon; CO/96/247.

[2] Unfortunately the 'natives' were never able to follow this line of reasoning and the moral issue to them remained 'serious'.

[3] Memorandum of 21 Jan. 1892, by W. Brandford Griffith jun. (in Jamaica); CO/96/247.

[4] Letter of 26 July 1894, from Hutchinson to Brandford Griffith; ibid.

[5] Circular of 24 Aug. 1891, from Acting Governor to District Commissioners; CO/96/218.

[6] H. J. Bell, *The History, Trade, Resources, and Present Condition of the Gold Coast Settlement* (Liverpool, 1893).

loss of valuable resources.[1] The Secretary of State was disturbed by further reports of reckless felling of timber in the Axim district;[2] and he was surprised to receive an application to construct a railway from Elmina to Cape Coast and thence to the River Prah, from a British entrepreneur who stated that he had already negotiated all the necessary concessions from the Chiefs. In 1894 Brandford Griffith was pointedly asked what had happened to the proposals for land legislation, which had been under consideration for so long.[3]

The Crown Lands Bill of 1894

As a result of this long-distance prodding, legislation was drafted by the Chief Justice in 1894 'to vest Waste Lands, Forest Lands and Minerals in the Queen'. The main object was to control further exploitation of timber resources and minerals, existing grants and concessions being safeguarded; the Crown would also acquire all waste lands, this term being given the same interpretation as unoccupied lands in the earlier Public Lands Ordinance. Hutchinson now felt that this could be done without hardship or injustice to anyone.[4] Members of the family or tribe could continue to occupy and use the land; but Chiefs would be deprived of the right to make grants to 'strangers', particularly Europeans, on the slender grounds that these were 'probably illegal according to native law and custom.'[5] Under his Bill, all such concessions of waste lands, minerals, and forests would be made by the Crown alone. An end would thus be put to the system whereby rival Chiefs could concede mining or timber rights over vast and ill-defined tracts of country, with little likelihood of a safe title, and with no obligation to work them efficiently, or even to work them at all. In future, the area of each concession would be defined, and the grantee would be required to work it within a reasonable time and in a proper manner; he on his part would be able to bargain with the Government for the improvement of transport facilities, and, most important of all, he would get an indefeasible title.[6]

When the Governor forwarded the proposed Bill to London, the Colonial Office agreed that it was most desirable that the Government should be able to prevent the lands of the Colony 'falling into the hands of concession mongers for a bottle of rum or a case of gin'.[7] So the draft was approved, subject to minor amendment.[8] Apparently no official in the Gold Coast foresaw serious political difficulties. Brandford Griffith reported in September

[1] Dispatch No. 85 of 21 Mar. 1893, from Brandford Griffith to Ripon, commenting on enclosed Reports by District Commissioners for the quarter ending 31 Dec. 1892; CO/96/232.
[2] Confidential Dispatch of 2 Jan. 1894, from Ripon to Brandford Griffith, CO/96/242.
[3] Confidential Dispatch of 1 May 1894, from Ripon to Brandford Griffith; CO/96/253.
[4] Letter of 26 July 1894, from Hutchinson to Brandford Griffith; CO/96/247.
[5] Cf. Ch. I, pp. 16–21, above.
[6] Confidential Letter of 2 Aug. 1894, from Hutchinson to Brandford Griffith; CO/96/247.
[7] Minute of 27 Sept. 1894, by Hemming; ibid.
[8] Confidential Dispatch of 10 Oct. 1894, from Ripon to Brandford Griffith; ibid.

1894, when outlining financial progress, 'The people of the Colony appear to be quiet, contented and peaceful.'[1] But the peace was not destined to last for long. Seldom can a measure so far-reaching in its impact on society have been introduced with so little understanding of its implications.

The Crown Lands Bill was given its first reading in November 1894, on the same inauspicious day as the final passage of the Town Councils Ordinance, against strong opposition in the Legislative Council.[2] The new Bill was not published until the end of January;[3] but agitation had already commenced, led by M. Burtt, Swanzy's main European agent. A meeting in Accra protested against both measures, and a deputation was appointed, which met the Governor early in 1895 'to petition for the repeal of the one, and the withdrawal of the other'.[4]

The newspapers were not slow to take up the lands issue. *The Gold Coast Methodist Times*, edited by the Rev. S. R. B. Solomon, 'that able young man . . . then in the active ministry of the Wesleyan body',[5] announced from Cape Coast that it could no longer restrict itself to religious matters, since there had arisen from all quarters a 'fiery indignation likely to devour the Colony, on account of the Bill intituled Crown Land Ordinance'.[6] In Accra, *The Gold Coast Chronicle*[7] claimed that if this ever came into force, in its present form, 'the natives of the Gold Coast will not consent for 24 hours to remain at home! They will leave the Colony.' The heart of the controversial matter was contained in the widely quoted clause vesting all waste and forest land in the Queen 'for the use of the Government of the Colony'. Since the Government was not felt to be identified with the people, the object of the Bill was commonly interpreted as being 'to take away from the people all their lands'. The very obscurity of the legal phraseology was suspect: 'The authorities appear to be desirous of concealing their real motives.' Later issues of these newspapers were full of reports of meetings, plans, and petitions, as well as editorials, articles, and letters about the proposed legislation.

Early in February 1895 a meeting was held in the market-place at Elmina,[8] and messengers were sent to the Governor in Accra with a written protest, respectfully declining to consent to the Crown Lands Bill.[9] The King of Abura came to Cape Coast to ask the District Commissioner about the rumours he

[1] Confidential Dispatch of 6 Sept. 1894, from Brandford Griffith to Ripon; CO/96/248.

[2] *Legislative Council Minutes*, 14 Nov. 1894. See Ch. XI, p. 423, below.

[3] *Government Gazette*, 31 Jan. 1895.

[4] Report of meeting at Swanzy's factory, 22 Jan. 1895, and covering Dispatch No. 39 of 30 Jan. 1895, from Brandford Griffith to Ripon; CO/96/254. Also Report of meeting between Governor and Accra deputation, 2 Feb. 1895, and covering Letter of 3 July 1895, from Brandford Griffith to Meade; CO/96/268.

[5] J. E. Casely Hayford, *Gold Coast Native Institutions* (London, 1903), p. 178.

[6] Vol. 1, no. 12, Feb. 1895.   [7] 25 Mar. 1895.

[8] Report by District Commissioner, Elmina, for quarter ending 31 Mar. 1895, enclosed in Dispatch No. 265 of 20 June 1895, from Maxwell to Ripon; CO/96/258.

[9] Petition of 12 Feb. 1895, to Governor from inhabitants of Elmina; G.N. Archives.

had heard, and then sent for his Chiefs, headmen, and councillors. They appealed to history in their petition against the Bill: 'Sir Chas. Macarthy lost his life for the tribes of the Gold Coast, the great Maclean dwelt long with our ancestors; but these men never made such a proposition.'[1] Several other protests were forthcoming. The Chief and headmen of Himan complained that they were to be ousted, with their families and their people, from the land of their ancestors; they prayed that the proposed Ordinance might be 'abandoned, dropped and thrown overboard'.[2] King Inkwanta Bissa sent his head linguist and two court criers to inform the Government that his people disliked the 'Waste Lands Ordinance' and did not desire it to be passed.[3]

But it appears from the records that Brandford Griffith did not keep the Colonial Office fully informed of these reactions. He apparently discounted most of the petitions, merely because they used similar language, and seemed to reveal a good deal of misunderstanding. The only one that he forwarded was an elaborate, printed document addressed to the Secretary of State by the Chiefs, merchants, and residents of Accra. This affirmed that all the people of the Gold Coast were, 'as one man', opposed to the Crown Lands Bill ever becoming law. The people under British protection had been repeatedly told by former Governors that the Queen did not claim a right to any lands whatever outside the walls of the forts. Now, however, with a stroke of his pen, this Governor was depriving them of 'their lands, their gold mines, their gum trees, their rubber trees, their kola trees, and everything of theirs that is worth having and which descended to them from their remote ancestors'. The petitioners argued that the Public Lands Ordinance of 1876, which was still in force and 'in daily application', was quite sufficient to enable the Government to acquire whatever land was really required for bona fide public purposes. Their major objection to the Bill was that there was no such thing as 'waste land', since it was all owned by Kings, Chiefs, or private individuals.[4] So much for Hutchinson's painstaking analysis and imagined safeguards.

Meanwhile, the Attorney-General and the Colonial Secretary, who had been away while the Bill was being drafted, had returned and recorded their own criticisms. The former suggested that the proposed control of concessions might frighten off the speculative capitalist, who was the chief hope for the future of the Colony.[5] The Colonial Secretary, on the other hand, expressed his private dissatisfaction with the Bill's wholesale annulment of all existing ownership of vast tracts of land and forest, which had already caused extreme

---

[1] Petition of 23 Feb. 1895, to Governor from King, Chiefs, headmen, and councillors of Abura, enclosed in Dispatch No. 196 of 11 May 1895, from Maxwell to Ripon; CO/96/257.

[2] Petition of 29 Mar. 1895, to Governor and Legislative Council from Chief and Headmen of Himan; ibid.

[3] Minute of 1 Apr. 1895; G.N. Archives.

[4] Petition of 30 Mar. 1895, to Secretary of State from Kings of Accra and Christiansborg, Chief Ababio of James Town, and 52 merchants and residents, enclosed in Dispatch No. 140 of 6 Apr. 1895, from Brandford Griffith to Ripon; CO/96/256.

[5] Minute of 27 Feb. 1895, by E. B. Hindle; M.P. No. 5644/94, G.N. Archives.

dissatisfaction. What the Government needed was simply the right to watch the interests of both the inhabitants and the capitalists; this might have avoided 'the universal irritation which has not yet found its full vent'.[1] Brandford Griffith left the Gold Coast in April 1895, and was succeeded by Sir William Maxwell. The full weight of the opposition was first realized in London when the new Governor began to send copies of the petitions which had already accumulated, as well as those he received himself.

The inhabitants of Cape Coast, for example, now addressed the Secretary of State, referring in detail to the Bond of 1844 and the 1874 Proclamation defining British jurisdiction, neither of which had stated that the soil of the Gold Coast was the property of the Queen. In the past, no encouragement had been given for development; now, when private enterprise had proved the value of their lands, an Ordinance was to deprive them of their property and hand it over to the Government, in the appointment of whose members 'no native of the Gold Coast has a voice and over whose policy and conduct the people of this country have no control whatever'.[2] Numerous Chiefs from districts farther to the west came to Elmina and, on behalf of the territory 'formerly under the kind protection of His Majesty the King of Holland', they reminded the Secretary of State that at the 1872 transfer they had been assured that their rights would not be interfered with.[3] Yet another petition came from the Chiefs and headmen of the Anomabu area;[4] and there was considerable agitation at Tarkwa.[5] The Accra merchants also returned to the attack, and in May a deputation of Europeans and Africans from the Chamber of Commerce, led by Burtt, urged Maxwell that the Crown Lands Bill should be considerably amended.[6]

Before any of these protests had reached London, James Brew, who was already corresponding with the Colonial Office concerning the Ashanti embassy,[7] had delivered his own lengthy attack upon the Bill. He argued that long before the advent of the European every inch of land had been owned by some Chief, individual, family, or community: and that these rights had been recognized implicitly by the Ordinance of 1876 and whenever the Colonial Government had paid money for lands purchased. The Gold Coast

---

[1] Minute of 27 Mar. 1895, by F. M. Hodgson; ibid.

[2] Petition of 9 Apr. 1895, to Secretary of State from King, Chiefs, natives, and 'other inhabitants' (a few European merchants and agents) of Cape Coast, enclosed in Dispatch No. 196 of 11 May 1895, from Maxwell to Ripon; CO/96/257.

[3] Memorial of 29 Apr. 1895, to Secretary of State from Kings, Chiefs, and headmen of Elmina, Shama, Sekondi, Adjuah, Axim, Apollonia, and including Eastern and Western Wassaw; ibid.

[4] Petition of 9 May 1895, to Secretary of State from King, Chiefs, and headmen of Anomabu, Ayan, Egimaku and Kwaman, enclosed in Dispatch No. 219 of 28 May 1895, from Maxwell to Ripon; ibid.

[5] Report by District Commissioner, Tarkwa, for quarter ending 30 June 1895, quoted in Dispatch No. 390 of 28 Sept. 1895, from Maxwell to Chamberlain; CO/96/260.

[6] Report of meeting between Governor and Chamber of Commerce deputation, 16 May 1895, enclosed in Dispatch No. 211 of 23 May 1895, from Maxwell to Ripon; CO/96/257.

[7] See Ch. VII, pp. 286-9, above.

Protectorate was on a different footing from any other British dependency: 'Its position is unique. It has not been acquired either by conquest, cession, or treaty.' Although the Government exercised certain powers and jurisdiction, it possessed no inherent legal right to deprive the inhabitants of their lands.[1] The phrase 'conquest, cession, or treaty' was to appear like a refrain in protests for many years afterwards.

In May 1895 the Governor made a lengthy analysis of Brew's arguments, which were already familiar to him from the numerous local petitions he had read:

The African view of the position is, apparently, that, within the Protectorate, the Colonial Government may collect a revenue on imports (paid in the first instance by merchants on the Coast, and therefore not understood by the African consumer to really fall on him), provide the machinery of administration, make roads and maintain order. But anything like direct taxation is resented, and sovereign rights are claimed over land, the rights of Her Majesty being denied in respect of any land not purchased from a King, Chief, community or individual.

He found it intolerable that the protected Chiefs and tribes should receive everything and yield nothing. In the Malay Peninsula, as soon as Protectorates had been established, all concessions had had to be countersigned by the British authorities before they could be recognized. Maxwell believed that this should have been done in the Gold Coast as soon as concessions had begun to cause embarrassment, around 1890. The difficulty had been enhanced by delay, by the quasi-recognition of existing concessions, and by the courts' practice of admitting native law as governing the situation. But the Governor felt, all the same, that the Crown Lands Bill was open to certain objections and might have to be withdrawn in favour of stronger legislation.[2]

Brandford Griffith, from his retirement, urged that the thing to do was to take a firm line at the start:

Africans are rather peculiar to deal with . . . If they detect anything like hesitation or indifference in transacting with them, they will give a great deal of trouble. If, on the contrary, they consider that the Government is determined . . . they will acquiesce in its decision almost without a murmur. Let them at once understand that Her Majesty's Government wills that the Crown Lands Bill—possibly with some amendments—shall become law, then, I think, no further opposition of any consequence will be made to it.[3]

This look-your-adversary-straight-in-the-eye philosophy might have been appropriate for shooting big game in the bush; but the elephant of African public opinion had been aroused, and was not so easily to be deterred.

[1] Letter of 22 Mar. 1895, from Brew to Ripon; CO/96/267.
[2] Dispatch No. 187 of 9 May 1895, from Maxwell to Ripon; CO/96/257.
[3] Letter of 8 July 1895, from Brandford Griffith to Colonial Office; CO/96/268.

Joseph Chamberlain, the new Secretary of State, thought the Chiefs were misinterpreting the Crown Lands Bill, possibly owing to faulty translation. He agreed in principle that some legislation was needed to prevent indiscriminate felling of timber, and to prevent improvident dealings in land and minerals; but he was not yet ready to take a final decision.[1] Maxwell was increasingly anxious to place land tenure on a more satisfactory legal footing, especially after touring the mining and timber districts. Natural products must at least be made liable to a royalty, and this would make clearer the duty of the Government to improve communications.[2] He had already instituted a local inquiry into customs relating to land tenure, in order to strengthen the hand of the Government; but its report was inconclusive.[3] In any case, so many alterations to the original Crown Lands Bill had been officially proposed that Maxwell decided in October 1895 to drop it altogether, having begun to discuss the draft of an entirely new Bill.[4] He was convinced of the urgency of the situation, especially after reading the published claim of one company to mineral and timber rights over an area of 7,000 square miles; this had apparently been conceded by the Chiefs of Beyin for only £90, not all of which had been paid.[5] But there was further delay, mainly because of the military expedition to Kumasi early in 1896.

The final drafting of the Bill was assisted by Maxwell's presence in London later in the year. Complaints of the proposed legislation and prophecies of impending trouble reached England and inspired one sympathetic editor to comment: 'The native's untutored mind does not grasp the idea that the colour of his skin justifies the confiscation of his property.'[6] The Governor returned to find a general spirit of opposition, which officials complained had been 'fostered and fed on every conceivable opportunity by African lawyers'.[7] *The Gold Coast Methodist Times* picturesquely renewed its attack upon the original Bill, fearing that this was to be reintroduced: 'That the Crown Lands Ordinance is pregnant with fell and butcherly stratagems goes without saying.' Worst of all, by an 'erroneous, mutinous and unnatural hypothesis', land of economic importance was being 'diplomatically enveloped' in the term 'waste', so that it could be wrested from its owners—a procedure stigmatized as 'civilised Robbery or British Brigandism'.[8]

---

[1] Dispatches Nos. 304 and 313 of 10 and 13 Sept. 1895, from Chamberlain to Maxwell; CO/96/257 and 268.

[2] Dispatch No. 389 of 28 Sept. 1895, from Maxwell to Chamberlain; CO/96/260.

[3] *Report upon the Customs relating to the Tenure of Land on the Gold Coast* (London, 1895).

[4] Dispatch No. 412 of 12 Oct. 1895, from Maxwell to Chamberlain; CO/96/261.

[5] Dispatch No. 150 of 17 Apr. 1896, from Maxwell to Chamberlain; CO/96/272.

[6] *Truth*, 22 Oct. 1896.

[7] Report by District Commissioner, Cape Coast, for quarter ending 30 Sept. 1896, enclosed in Dispatch No. 18 of 14 Jan. 1897, from Maxwell to Chamberlain; CO/96/288.

[8] *The Gold Coast Methodist Times*, vol. 1, no. 27, Nov. 1896.

The 1897 Bill and the Formation of the A.R.P.S.

The new Lands Bill was formally introduced into the Legislative Council on 10 March 1897. This was framed to give the Crown rights of administration but not of ownership, for it was announced that the intention of vesting waste and forest lands in the Queen had been abandoned. The Government held that what might properly be called 'public land' must be administered 'for the general advantage'. Chiefs would still be allowed all reasonable authority, but the paramount Protecting Power would ensure that private rights were not improvidently created over so-called public land.

African rights of ownership would no longer be automatically recognized. Occupiers of land would not be disturbed; but they would be entitled only to a 'settler's right', a permanent heritable right of occupancy, which could be transformed into an absolute right, on application to the Governor, by the grant of a land certificate. The Government could also declare that any piece of land had no owner, and then authorize its occupation. This provision was based on the same assumption as the previous Bill, that there was some unoccupied land which had no owner. Furthermore, land held under a land certificate could devolve and be transmitted only according to English law. Africans could make grants and concessions to other Africans, but not to Europeans except by express permission of the Governor. In practice, most concessions would be granted directly by the Government, using its powers of administration. This was clearly designed to ensure that concessionaires would get a firm title, and would not be subject to varying local uncertainties. But it was bound to appear as a threat to native law and custom, especially as a new Concessions Board, independent of the courts, was to be set up to investigate all such cases.[1]

The first reactions to the Bill were concerned mainly with the wide powers to be assumed by the Government, and little attention was paid to the fine distinction between ownership and administration. *The Gold Coast Methodist Times* printed some stirring headlines, and offered Biblical texts for the campaign:

> Your Land, Strangers devour it in your presence. Isaiah i. 7.
> Other men have Our Lands. Nehemiah v. 5.[2]

The Gold Coast Chronicle began to serialize the Governor's message and the text of the Bill, together with critical editorial comment:

> Historically, from Cruickshank to Lucas,[3] this country has never been conquered or ceded to Her Majesty's Government, and as recently as 1887, if we are not mistaken as to the time, Sir Henry Holland, Her Majesty's principal Secretary of State

---

[1] *Government Gazette* (*Extraordinary*), 10 Mar. 1897.

[2] Vol. 1, no. 34, Mar. 1897.

[3] B. Cruickshank, *Eighteen Years on the Gold Coast of Africa* (London, 1853), and C. P. Lucas, *Historical Geography of the British Colonies*, vol. iii (Oxford, 1894).

for the Colonies, admitted, in correspondence with Mr. Sarbah . . . that Her Majesty did not lay claim to the soil of this Colony which belonged to the people of the Gold Coast (29 March, 1897).

The next four issues all dealt, at great length, with the Bill. The rallying cry was: 'We confidently call upon the people of this country, from North to South, from East to West, to give to this measure their most unremitting opposition.'[1]

On the day the Bill was laid before the Legislative Council, J. H. Cheetham, one of the two African members, sent his own annotated copy to J. W. de Graft Johnson in Cape Coast.[2] The tinder was dry; this spark was all that was needed. de Graft Johnson immediately consulted his friends, and 'provoked an agitation', as his son later wrote.[3] A meeting was held with J. Mensah Sarbah, Chief J. D. Abraham, and 'Father' J. P. Brown, at the latter's house, to organize a movement of protest against Maxwell's Lands Bill.[4] A Committee was chosen: J. W. Sey was made President and Brown Vice-President, with two other Vice-Presidents, a Treasurer, a Secretary, and a *Kyiami* to speak for them at meetings with Chiefs, who would each have their own 'linguist'. It soon became clear that the issue was beyond the scope of the *Mfantsi Amanbuhu Fékuw*, and after two or three meetings they adopted a new name, the Gold Coast Aborigines' Rights Protection Society.

Parallel developments were taking place at Axim, thanks to the Rev. Solomon, who was then Superintendent of the local Wesleyan circuit. As soon as he received a copy of the *Gazette* with the text of the Bill, he called together the literate inhabitants to discuss it, and a committee was formed for the purpose of 'educating' the Chiefs of Axim and Apollonia. Under their auspices, a meeting was held in April; a unanimous resolution of protest was passed, and telegrams were sent to Elmina, Cape Coast, and Accra through the Chiefs: 'We strongly protest against the Land Ordinance, 1897. What do you say? Reply paid.' To ensure unity of action, the Axim Committee voluntarily affiliated itself to the body which had been simultaneously established in Cape Coast as the A.R.P.S.[5]

The Society's first public statement was issued towards the end of April 1897:

The Gold Coast Aborigines' Rights Protection Society

Whereas in former times, all measures intended by the Government for the whole Protectorate were brought before a meeting of the various Kings and Chiefs of the

---

[1] *The Gold Coast Chronicle*, 27 May 1897.   [2] K. Taylor, *Our Political Destiny* (Winneba, 1941).

[3] J. W. de Graft Johnson, *Towards Nationhood in West Africa* (London, 1929), p. 155. Earlier in this book the son is at pains to stress that the agitation over land was not the *fons et origo* of the A.R.P.S. But his story makes it clear that the 'pernicious legislation' was the main reason why the *Mfantsi Amanbuhu Fékuw* 'blossomed into' the Society; and in quoting the 1907 constitution, he comments that its major function, 'to watch the acts of the Government', arose from persistent attempts to alienate the lands of the people. Ibid. pp. 28–32.

[4] M. J. Sampson, *Gold Coast Men of Affairs* (London, 1937), p. 98.

[5] *The Gold Coast Leader*, 28 Jan. 1922; obituary notice of Attoh Ahuma.

Protectorate convened for the purpose, and who in turn communicated them to the people of their respective districts by gong-gong And Whereas this time-honoured and effective custom has for some time been set aside and superseded by the Gazette And Whereas a very large majority of the population of the Gold Coast Protectorate are still unable to read And Whereas even the greater part of those able to read cannot well comprehend the meaning of the Bills passed from time to time by the Government, the above Society of which natives and residents alike can be members,[1] has been formed to discuss the various Bills intended to be passed by the Government from time to time, with a view to fully understand the meaning purport object and effect thereof that every person may have the opportunity of understanding the same.[2]

Since it was the educated, politically-conscious group who took the initiative in forming the Society, they evidently felt some justification was needed for this intervention in what had been regarded, especially by the Government, as the affairs of the Chiefs. Their main motive, of course, was not so much to explain gazetted Bills to ignorant or illiterate Chiefs, as to put themselves in a position to protest effectively against the Lands Bill and any other measures they disliked, backed by as many Chiefs as possible, since they knew that the Government habitually discounted protests from 'scholars' alone.

The Gold Coast Methodist Times under Solomon—who later changed his name on nationalist principle to Attoh Ahuma—played an important part in rallying support for the new Society and against the Bill. The crusade was featured in every issue for many months, either in passing or, more often, as a major item. This was popular, if not strictly orthodox in the eyes of the Methodist Synod:

The paper was the property of that body, and Attoh Ahuma was but their servant. But the intrepid editor did not think it right to confine the columns of the paper to church news and religious controversy . . .

The Gold Coast Methodist at once took up the gauntlet [the Lands Bill], and fought like a veritable Achilles; and right loyally was it supported by the best intellect of the land.[3] It fought and won.[4]

The campaign was conducted in a legitimate manner, as the authorities admitted.[5] *The Gold Coast Methodist Times* reminded the newly formed A.R.P.S.:

[1] Presumably this was meant to include Europeans, if they wished to join; the 1907 constitution of the Society seems to have excluded them, but in later years 'foreigners' were specifically invited to join. See Ch. X, pp. 361–2 and 373, below.

[2] This was published in all the local newspapers, e.g. *The Gold Coast Express*, 22 Apr. 1897, and *The Gold Coast Independent*, 1 May 1897.

[3] It is interesting to note that the young J. E. K. Aggrey, just before he left for the United States, helped the Rev. J. B. Anaman to write articles against the Lands Bill for this newspaper, and on one occasion in July 1898 walked 36 miles to send off an important telegram for the A.R.P.S. See E. W. Smith, *Aggrey of Africa* (London, 1929), p. 52.

[4] Casely Hayford, *Gold Coast Native Institutions*, pp. 178–9.

[5] For example, Report by District Commissioner, Cape Coast, for quarter ending 31 Mar. 1897, enclosed in Dispatch No. 330 of 23 July 1897, from Maxwell to Chamberlain; CO/96/297.

'To achieve the highest good—the *summum bonum*—in the Gold Coast, we must agitate, but agitate constitutionally.'[1]

It was some months before the A.R.P.S. leaders in Cape Coast were able to get all the neighbouring Chiefs together in conference. At first, individual contacts and isolated protests were made in many centres, until the resistance to the Lands Bill began to gather momentum.

Mounting Opposition

Towards the end of April 1897 Maxwell undertook a tour of the western districts, and encountered several public demonstrations against the Bill. At Cape Coast, for example,

A red banner, supported by two poles, one on either side, bore the simple but effective words: 'We protest against the land Bill'. It is carried by two illiterate women in native costume. They are followed by a long procession of other illiterate women, also in native costume. They are chanting a monotonous dirge, the refrain of which is somewhat in these words: 'Arise my soul and Praise the Lord'.[2]

The Governor, it was said, had to go about under armed escort there; and at Axim popular feeling was 'manifested, if anything, in a more intensified, perhaps ruder form'.[3]

Maxwell ascribed most of the opposition to African land speculators, who disliked the idea of the Governor's sanction being required to render a grant or concession valid.[4] There was something in this allegation. For example, Sey, the President of the A.R.P.S., and Brew, one of the most outspoken critics of the Bill, had both been concerned in the Gold Coast Native Concession Purchasing Co. Ltd. of 1882, and no doubt their business colleagues were equally active in protest. Brown, an A.R.P.S. Vice-President, was one of several Africans who had helped to negotiate a lucrative Adansi concession which later became the property of the Ashanti Goldfields Corporation.[5] There is no reason to suppose, however, that the African brokers stood to gain as much from such transactions as the European concessionaires, or that they were incapable of making protests on behalf of the general interest as well as their own; while the Chiefs, if consulted, might even have preferred to have their land dealings negotiated by educated fellow countrymen rather than by a remote, alien Government.

Maxwell's accusations of wilful misrepresentation by interested parties aroused much resentment, especially when he singled out the educated

[1] 30 Apr. 1897.

[2] This was the account given by *The Gold Coast Methodist Times*, 15 June 1897, 'Letters to Flavia'. The Governor, however, simply dismissed the Cape Coast demonstration as 'a noisy crowd of women and boys' who had displayed a banner bearing words of protest, and suggested that they had been employed by men who were 'too prudent to risk anything' themselves. Confidential Dispatch of 1 July 1897, from Maxwell to Chamberlain; CO/96/295.

[3] *The Gold Coast Methodist Times*, 12 May 1897.

[4] Dispatch No. 169 of 4 May 1897, from Maxwell to Chamberlain; CO/96/292.

[5] See Ch. I, pp. 23–24, above.

leaders for blame. *The Gold Coast Methodist Times* on 15 June alleged that during his tour the Governor was 'continually spicing his most pungent remarks with the mysterious but ominous refrain—"Scholars like these";— "Men like J. P. Brown" ' and denouncing them by name, 'as if veritable firebrands in the popular movement against the intolerable Land Bill'. Brown, in particular, was held up by the writer as a shining example to the public. He was the son of a Wesleyan minister, a cultured member of the aristocracy, not convicted of any crime, a preacher and General Superintendent of Wesleyan schools, a landowner, a Christian Socialist, and a Vice-President of the A.R.P.S.: 'Surely a gentleman so stuffed with such honourable virtues cannot be the butt of public execration! . . . Men like J. P. Brown? Would to God we had more of them!' Rather, the Government was blamed for resenting and fearing constructive criticism.

Anxiety in the Colonial Office was aroused particularly by protests received direct from commercial interests in England.[1] During the first week in May alone, protests against the Lands Bill were sent by the Wassaw Mining Co. Ltd., the Tarquah and Abosso Gold Mining Co. Ltd., a group of merchants including Swanzy and Cleaver, and, more disquieting still, by the Chambers of Commerce of London, Liverpool, and Manchester. James Brew, of course, was still corresponding vigorously; and Fox Bourne wrote on behalf of those Africans who had appealed to the Aborigines' Protection Society.[2] Even *The Financial Post*[3] reported in London that a vast amount of opposition and feeling had been evoked against the new Lands Bill.

In the Gold Coast protests were multiplying. The following were among those organized in May 1897:[4]

Letter of 6 May to Governor from King of Elmina.

Telegrams of 17 May to Queen, Prince of Wales,[5] and Secretary of State from Axim.

Petition of 18 May to Governor and Legislative Council from Chiefs and people of Axim and Apollonia (with 150 signatures).

Petition of 18 May to Secretary of State from Chiefs and people of Axim and Apollonia (with over 180 signatures: 'Writer and witnesses to Marks: Sam. Rich. Wood').

Petition of 25 May to Governor and Legislative Council from Head Chief and leading men of Cape Coast.

Petition of 25 May to Governor and Legislative Council from King of Abura and other inhabitants (witnessed, and probably drafted, by T. F. E. Jones), stating that

---

[1] Correspondence in CO/96/306 and 309.

[2] Letters of 8 June and 4 July 1897, from Fox Bourne to Chamberlain; CO/96/306 and 266.

[3] 24 May 1897.

[4] Enclosures in Dispatches Nos. 235 of 10 June and 306 of 15 July 1897, from Maxwell to Chamberlain; CO/96/294 and 295.

[5] The Prince of Wales was unable to make 'head or tail' of this Telegram, and his Secretary asked the Colonial Office, 'Would you kindly cause an answer of some sort to be sent to it.' Letter of 20 May 1897, from Marlborough House to Colonial Office; CO/96/306.

they had 'secured the services of as competent a person as could be got to explain to them in their mother tongue the meaning of the said Bill'.

Petition of 27 May to Governor and Legislative Council from King of Anomabu and other inhabitants.

At the end of that month the Legislative Council met, with the second reading of the Lands Bill on the agenda. Cheetham presented the petitions from Abura, Cape Coast, and Anomabu, asking that counsel should be heard on their behalf.[1] As a result, Mensah Sarbah and P. Awoonor Renner were allowed to appear at the bar of the Council.

Mensah Sarbah cited the 1895 report on land tenure in support of his fundamental contention that every piece of land in the Gold Coast had an owner, whether or not it was described as 'waste'. Family land remained the property of the family, whether cultivated or not; only on the failure of successors, he pointed out, did it fall back into the common land of the village, subject to the control of the Chief and elders. The main objection to the Bill, from Chiefs and people alike, was the fundamental alteration of their natural right of absolute ownership into that of mere holders and settlers. There was now to be no distinction between individual, family, and communal rights; and the Bill would destroy the control exercised by headmen over villages and families. 'Not only are the bonds of society to be snapped but family ties are to be broken and family relationships destroyed.'

Furthermore, the fact that a settler's right would be forfeited by three years' non-user of his own property was unnecessary hardship, especially for artisans, clerks, or traders, who after that length of absence from their village would lose their title and interest in the family land. Other, minor objections were that the definition of 'Natives' in the Bill by excluding mulattoes directly destroyed their right as members of the community; and that under the Bill shifting cultivation conferred no title to land. Mensah Sarbah brought into the open the suspicion underlying the whole case for the opposition:

I am specially instructed to say that this Land Bill is an elaborate and expanded form of the Crow Land Bill of 1894. That Bill refers only to what is termed waste and forest land whereas this Bill refers to the whole land of this Country, depriving the aborigines of their right in the soil of their native land.[2]

The progress of the hearing was reported soon afterwards to a big meeting in Wesley Square, Cape Coast, attended by the Kings of Abura and Denkera; the delegates who had accompanied counsel to Accra gave an account of their mission and the reaction of the Legislative Council.[3] Mensah Sarbah

---

[1] *Legislative Council Minutes*, 27 May 1897.

[2] The quotations in these paragraphs have been taken from Mensah Sarbah's own notes for his speech, published in *The Gold Coast Methodist Times*, 30 June 1897; he disputed the official shorthand report.

[3] Ibid. 15 June 1897, for report of Cape Coast public meeting, 12 June 1897.

made a great reputation for himself over this issue, especially as he refused
the offered retainer of 400 guineas.[1] In a letter to the A.R.P.S. he explained
that he had initially been reluctant to go to Accra, because he was not sure to
what extent his countrymen were in earnest in their opposition; 'When, however, I was fully convinced in my own mind that they were never so united nor
so determined in all parts of the country, I left home to do their bidding.'
And he urged that no effort should be spared to provide every Gold Coast
African with 'a correct and true knowledge of the constitutional history of
his dear native land'.[2]

Maxwell was not likely to be swayed by the legal arguments he had heard.
But he was sufficiently impressed by the volume of the opposition to adjourn
the second reading, and to inform the Secretary of State that he did not feel
justified in proceeding further without express instructions.[3] The Colonial
Office was already giving serious consideration to the objections received
from the commercial world. A Dispatch had been drafted, warning the Governor that the alarm and uncertainty amongst capitalists in Britain might discourage enterprise in the Gold Coast. At the same time, African criticisms of
the alleged confiscation of their rights were seriously considered and various
alternatives to the principle of Crown disposal of lands were discussed. It was
also suggested that the proposed levy on concessions granted under the Bill
should not be so great as to make it appear that the object of the Government
was to seize the full value of the land; the charge could be reduced to an
annual rent of 1s. for four or five acres. Even for sixty years ago, this sounds
unduly generous; but it was pointed out that many of the mining companies
were unable to make a net profit, and that only one had been able to pay even
a single dividend.[4]

It was, therefore, unlikely that the Bill would be allowed to go through as it
stood; but on receipt of Maxwell's urgent message, Chamberlain instructed
him by telegram to proceed with the Bill until the committee stage was completed, and then to refer it with all the associated protests to London.[5] This
course succeeded only in giving people in the Gold Coast the impression that
the Bill was to be forced through at all costs, and thus in stimulating even
more desperate opposition. In fact the Secretary of State, by postponing full
consideration of the matter to the latest possible time, made the eventual
reversal of policy (after the arrival of a deputation in London) appear more
dramatic than it actually was.

The Legislative Council soon reassembled to conclude the second reading;

---

[1] Forty years later J. B. Danquah wrote: 'Nothing nobler was ever uttered from the heart of
a patriot.' Introduction to Sampson's *Gold Coast Men of Affairs* (1937).

[2] *The Gold Coast Methodist Times*, 30 June 1897; Letter of the same date from Mensah
Sarbah to J. P. Brown.

[3] Telegram and Dispatch No. 235 of 10 June 1897, from Maxwell to Chamberlain; CO/96/294.

[4] Draft Dispatch of June 1897, from Chamberlain to Maxwell; CO/96/306.

[5] Telegram of 14 June 1897, from Chamberlain to Maxwell; CO/96/294.

C. J. Bannerman and Awoonor Renner were given permission to appear on behalf of petitioners from Axim and Winneba.[1] Some amendments were made in committee, but in spite of these Cheetham and J. Vanderpuiye, the two African members, recorded their dissent at every opportunity.[2] Maxwell forwarded the amended Bill and the full proceedings to London, and in his comments attempted to meet the lawyers on their own ground. He quoted references to 'public lands' from Mensah Sarbah's *Fanti Customary Laws* which, he claimed, contradicted what had been said in the Legislative Council. The Governor remarked reassuringly that opposition to the Lands Bill had been much exaggerated; once more he attributed the campaign entirely to African middlemen who had been negotiating concessions for English speculators, especially in Cape Coast, Elmina, and Axim. He called attention to the 'remarkable fact that where the native land-broker does not exist, there is no remonstrance on the part of the Chiefs . . . no agitation, no protest and no petitioning'.[3] But the Colonial Office was not fully convinced. The Bill in its amended form was considered a great improvement, but still open to substantially the same objections as had been successfully urged against its predecessor.[4]

There seems to have been a consistent tendency on the part of the local Administration to play down, or at least to underestimate, the strength of feeling on this matter. The District Commissioners' reports for this period were concerned mainly with details of the celebrations of the Queen's Jubilee, and the land question was hardly mentioned. Even in Axim the agitation was reported to be subsiding, although the few European merchants were said to be against the Bill as much as the Africans.[5] Nevertheless, further protests continued to accumulate, including:[6]

Telegram of 25 July to Secretary of State from King and Chiefs of Abura, confirming the objections made in London by Brew.

Petition of 26 July to Secretary of State from King and Chiefs of Eastern Wassaw, claiming: 'That the provisions of this Bill have terrified us greatly for that by the passing of a law we and the people whom we represent should lose all our rights as natives of the soil where our lot did cast us.'

Petition of 31 July to Secretary of State from Kings and Chiefs of Ahanta, Dixcove, and Bushua.

The Gold Coast Methodist Times continued the campaign, and defied rumours of a press censorship: 'Thank God, we are not in Russia . . . if the

---

[1] *Legislative Council Minutes*, 29 June 1897. Also Petition of 23 June 1897, to Governor and Legislative Council from Head Chief of Gomua and Chiefs of Egimaku and Winneba, enclosed in Dispatch No. 306 of 15 July 1897, from Maxwell to Chamberlain; CO/96/295.

[2] *Legislative Council Minutes*, 5 to 10 July 1897.

[3] Confidential Dispatch of 1 July and No. 306 of 15 July 1897, from Maxwell to Chamberlain; CO/96/295.   [4] Minute of 25 Aug. 1897, by T. Mercer; ibid.

[5] Reports by District Commissioners for quarter ending 30 June 1897, enclosed in Dispatch No. 369 of 3 Sept. 1897, from Deputy for Governor to Chamberlain; CO/96/298.

[6] CO/96/306 and G.N. Archives.

Legislature so far forgets itself as to descend against public rights conceded to us by the Constitution of England, we will resist unto blood.'[1] But the opposition was sometimes expressed in a lighter vein:

BAND OF HOPE ENTERTAINMENT Axim . . . In *The Land Bill 1897* the scene commenced with an assembly of the Legislative Council when Mr. S. R. Wood as 'Governor' spoke at length upon the object and scope of the Bill . . . Native women hearing of this at the market place rush in furiously to interview the Governor at his residence where they are driven away by an armed force. The Chiefs next arrive and they are similarly treated . . . The Queen (Mrs. H. B. Plange) dressed in all her Royal paraphernalia announces her readiness to hear official matters, whereupon the Secretary of State for the Colonies (Mr. H. B. Plange) seeks audience for a Deputation.[2]

The amended version of the Bill was published in August 1897, together with the Governor's reply to counsel.[3] This did nothing to allay the general fear and suspicion. A strong emotional appeal was provided by the publication of a letter from King Ghartey, written on his death-bed to a Vice-President of the A.R.P.S.:

Now in the big struggle before us *re* the Land Bill &c. the history past, present and future call with one loud voice for Loyalty, Unity of purpose, and perseverance in actions . . . Hopefully therefore I fall in this Battle field with many wounds fresh and old and deep scars of the defunct Fanti Confederation[4] . . . Be constitutional. God bless you, our Country and the Queen.[5]

The Chiefs had no thought of unconstitutional action; but they were fully convinced of the importance of the Bill, and urgent consultations were going on in many parts of the country.[6]

Towards the end of 1897 *The Gold Coast Methodist Times* declared: 'While we have breath and while the Governor is bent on forcing this measure on us we must not tire in our efforts to destroy the pernicious Bill.'[7] By now the newspaper was evidently being severely criticized in some quarters. The editor was unrepentant:

We have been indoctrinated as to how a religious paper should be conducted . . . we do not intend to wrap up our religion for Sunday use only: we shall continue to go on, so long as we are permitted to be organically connected with this periodical. Our silence in matters political, so far as they traverse the fundamental principles of the Christian faith, will only synchronise with our absence from the editorial chair which position of course we occupy by sufferance.[8]

---

[1] *The Gold Coast Methodist Times*, 31 July 1897.   [2] Ibid. 16 Aug. 1897.

[3] *Government Gazette* (*Extraordinary*), 13 Aug. 1897.

[4] In 1872, shortly after the collapse of the Confederation, its first President, R. J. Ghartey, had been installed as King Ghartey IV of Winneba.

[5] Letter of 28 July 1897, from Ghartey to Brown; *The Gold Coast Methodist Times*, 15 Sept. 1897.

[6] For example, Report by District Commissioner, Tarkwa, for quarter ending 31 Dec. 1897, enclosed in Dispatch No. 190 of 7 May 1898, from Hodgson to Chamberlain; CO/96/315.

[7] 15 Oct. 1897.   [8] 15 Nov. 1897.

An enforced absence from the editorial chair very soon followed. According to J. E. Casely Hayford, the Wesleyan Synod 'suddenly awakened to a sense of an alleged incongruity in the discussion of political issues in a spiritual organ, and with the awakening Attoh Ahuma gave up the editorship, and the paper died'.[1]

The A.R.P.S. had already felt the need for their own newspaper; and it seems clear that the fee refused by Mensah Sarbah was now used to help finance *The Gold Coast Aborigines*, which first appeared on New Year's Day, 1898, with the motto ' For the safety of the public, and the welfare of the Race'. An appreciative note of thanks to *The Gold Coast Methodist Times*, for going out of its religious way to play such a noble part in the struggle, showed that the new weekly paper intended to take on the *Times*'s political mantle.[2] Several of the full- and part-time staff moved over, including Attoh Ahuma himself, and the Rev. F. Egyir-Asaam, who was the first editor of the *Aborigines*.

Maxwell did not live to see this journalistic metamorphosis. He had been in poor health for some time; and when at last he went on leave, in December 1897, he died at sea. The local obituaries were bitter. One, for example, contrasted his ability, energy, and advanced views with 'the grasping tyrannical landgrabbing and rotten Policy marked out for him', which he was alleged to have implemented with a cold and unsympathetic spirit, 'contempt for natives characterising most of his measures'.[3] The Fanti Kings, meeting at Cape Coast, took the opportunity to send the Queen the compliments of the season, and to ask for a new Governor who would be sympathetic and study their interests. Queen Victoria thought this 'quaint'; not so London officials, who realized only too well that this was an oblique reference to the Lands Bill.[4]

The Deputation to England, 1898

In the Gold Coast it appeared that the agitation was quietening down. In fact, the A.R.P.S. had decided to *reculer pour mieux sauter*. Attempts were being made to improve their methods of consultation; *The Gold Coast Aborigines* suggested that the Chiefs should be regularly represented at monthly or quarterly meetings, instead of sending their linguists only now and again. Furthermore, owing to the size of the Protectorate, there should be properly organized branches in all the principal coastal towns, and at other centres where there were important Chiefs. So far, only Axim and Elmina had branches,

---

[1] Casely Hayford, *Gold Coast Native Institutions*, p. 179.   [2] 1 Jan. 1898.
[3] *The Gold Coast Chronicle*, 3 Jan. 1898. By contrast, the same newspaper had recently published an editorial on 'The Late Sir William Brandford-Griffith, K.C.M.G.', saying that 'in all parts of the Colony the memory of the late Governor will be long remembered and cherished'. Ibid. 20 Sept. 1897. This was mainly because he, and not Maxwell, was credited with the withdrawal of the 1894 Bill.
[4] Telegram of 31 Dec. 1897, from Fanti Kings to Queen Victoria, and Colonial Office Minute thereon; CO/96/306.

but others should be formed without delay, so that the Government might recognize in some practical form 'this SOCIETY which is in reality the mouthpiece of the nation'.[1]

The leaders in Cape Coast had already decided to take legal advice in London, and were busy collecting historical ammunition. Casely Hayford was asked by the executive committee of the A.R.P.S. to prepare a brief against the Bill; and he later used his detailed researches for this purpose as the basis of a pioneer study of native institutions.[2] The Society was already contemplating the idea of a deputation, but did not court publicity, since this had been of little help to the abortive deputation scheme of 1885-7.[3] The first the Colonial Office heard officially was in March 1898, when a London firm of solicitors informed the Secretary of State that they had received instructions from the Kings and Chiefs of the Western Province to bring before him in Parliament their objections to the Lands Bill.[4]

The Colonial Office were none too pleased to hear this, nine months after the debate in the Legislative Council. Maxwell's death had delayed a final decision; but it now seemed essential to settle the land question as soon as possible, so the solicitors were informed that any representations must be received within a month, otherwise no promise could be made to wait for them.[5] But exactly one month later the solicitors reported that a deputation of Kings and Chiefs was already on its way; they therefore requested a further extension of the time-limit.[6] Presented with what appeared to be a *fait accompli*, it was difficult for the Colonial Office to turn down this request, especially in the absence of any clear indication from the new Governor, F. M. Hodgson, who was evidently unaware of any serious plans for a deputation.

About this time Hodgson was suggesting that as the Chiefs seemed more or less resigned to the inevitable, it would be best to amend the Bill and get it through quickly, 'before the feeling begins to work off'. His proposed amendments, after discussion with the Chief Justice, included the appointment of judges to the Concessions Court, thus bringing it under the control of the Supreme Court, which went some way towards meeting the local objections.[7] The Colonial Office, somewhat baffled, decided to await the arrival of the Western Province representatives, although the delay was considered

---

[1] *The Gold Coast Aborigines*, 8 Jan. 1898.

[2] Casely Hayford, *Gold Coast Native Institutions*; for the genesis of the book, see his 'Preliminary', pp. xi–xiii. Upwards of thirty *Blue Books*, Parliamentary Reports, &c., were sent to the London solicitors to help them prepare their case. CO/96/333.

[3] Letter of 17 Mar. 1898, from Ashurst, Morris, Crisp & Co. to Chamberlain; ibid.

[4] See Ch. XI, pp. 429–31, below.

[5] Minute of 21 Mar. 1898, by Mercer; CO/96/333.

[6] Letter of 21 Apr. 1898, from Ashurst, Morris, Crisp & Co. to Chamberlain; ibid.

[7] Dispatch No. 147 of 9 Apr. 1898, from Hodgson to Chamberlain; CO/96/314. For an account of the part played by the Chief Justice, Sir William Brandford Griffith, see his reminiscences, *The Far Horizon* (Ilfracombe, 1951).

PLATE 4

The 1897 London Deputation of the Aborigines' Rights Protection Society

b. J. W. Sey (President)

a. George Hughes, E. F. Hunt, T. F. E. Jones

'unfortunate, as it seems as though we were encouraging the agitation and the sending of the deputation'.[1]

But the appointed members had not yet left the Gold Coast; they were still worrying about the prospects of being received, and anxious to know if their credentials were acceptable. The recent experience of the Ashanti embassy was not very encouraging. They now cabled to inquire whether a deputation leaving early in June would be heard;[2] but Chamberlain was surprised to learn that they were not already on the way, and said that he could not wait so long.[3] So a final cable from the London solicitors advised the Society that if the deputation did not leave before June it would not be received.[4] This was sufficient encouragement for the A.R.P.S. leaders to make up their minds; in any case they feared that if there was further delay Hodgson would try to push the Bill through.[5] On 24 May 1898 three prosperous Cape Coast merchants—J. W. Sey (President), T. F. E. Jones, and George Hughes—sailed for London.

There was a curious ambivalence of view as to whether they really constituted a deputation or not. *The Gold Coast Aborigines*, a few days after they had left the Gold Coast, seemed to consider them merely as harbingers: they were being sent to ascertain on the spot, with the assistance of the most eminent counsel of the English Bar, the best way to secure a patient and impartial hearing for the public objections to the Lands Bill. Under Maxwell there had been something approaching unity—'we were getting to be a cohesive mass'—and now, it appeared, the time was 'nearly ripe for something to be done . . . we repeat that if the necessity arises to England a deputation must go'.[6] The writer may simply have been anxious to leave a loophole for retreat. In fact the delegates took with them a number of State swords (more than they could comfortably carry between them) as their authority from the Chiefs,[7] remembering the ridicule occasioned by the Ansahs' forged credentials.

So much stress was laid on the fact that the deputation genuinely represented the 'Natural Rulers' that the A.R.P.S. was not mentioned either in the petitions drawn up in London, or in the official report of their interview with the Secretary of State. This led the Government to argue later that the deputation was sponsored directly by the Chiefs, and not by the A.R.P.S. at all.[8] It

---

[1] Minute of 22 Apr. 1898, by Mercer; CO/96/333.
[2] Letter of 28 Apr. 1898, from Ashurst, Morris, Crisp & Co. to Chamberlain; ibid.
[3] Letter of 5 May 1898, from Colonial Office to Ashurst, Morris, Crisp & Co.; ibid.
[4] Letter of 24 May 1898, from Brown to Colonial Secretary, Accra; G.N. Archives.
[5] *The Gold Coast Aborigines*, 14 May 1898.   [6] Ibid. 28 May 1898.
[7] It was later suggested to the Colonial Office that as the swords were rather cumbersome, it might be sufficient for the members to bring one each. CO/96/333. When the deputation was introduced to Chamberlain, their solicitor said: 'Sir, the kings and chiefs of the Gold Coast exhibit to you their swords as evidence that the deputation really represents the kings and chiefs. These swords have never been out of their country before.' *Report of the Proceedings of the Deputation from the Kings and Chiefs of the Western Province of the Gold Coast* (London, 1898).
[8] For example, in Notes on the 1926 A.R.P.S. Petition by H. S. Newlands; S.N.A. Acc. No. 1503, G.N. Archives.

is therefore useful to examine in some detail the contemporary evidence on this point.

On the day the deputation sailed, J. P. Brown informed the Government that 'the Gold Coast Aborigines' Rights Protection Society, at the request of the Kings and Chiefs of the Western Province of the Gold Coast Protectorate', had instructed a London firm of solicitors to present their case before the British Government, to be followed by a deputation.[1] The Governor telegraphed to warn the Colonial Office that a delegation from the 'A.P.S.' was on its way;[2] and, while noting that the Society was not altogether a representative institution, he did not try to stand in their way. 'I see no good objection to delegates being admitted to an interview if you are good enough to grant one.'[3] The Colonial Office then asked the solicitors for further information about the members of the deputation; some private doubts were expressed as to whether they should be received, especially if they represented the 'A.P.S.' rather than the Chiefs.[4] Probably the A.R.P.S. was conscious of this danger, and therefore deliberately played down its role. Yet the deputation consisted of the President and two leading members of this new organization; and there can be no doubt that it was the Society which had managed to canalize the opposition of the leading Chiefs of the Western Province, and to get them to agree to the idea of a direct approach to London, though it was careful always to act in their name.

The Colonial Office was now considering Hodgson's suggested amendments, especially concerning the constitution of the Concessions Court. In June he forwarded yet another petition, from influential Chiefs in the Cape Coast area, noting that they did not object to the establishment of such a court, provided they had a voice in its constitution.[5] There seemed to be an agreed basis for action in this limited field. It was felt in London that such a step might be 'sufficient for all present requirements', though it would fall far short of Maxwell's original proposals.[6]

With this in view, and remembering that the Governor had raised no serious objections, Chamberlain agreed to see the deputation; but first he asked for a written statement of their views and proposed amendments.[7] Their 'Petition Against the Lands Bill of 1897'[8] was quietly and reasonably

---

[1] Letter of 24 May 1898, from Brown to Colonial Secretary; G.N. Archives.

[2] Hodgson may have imagined that this was a Gold Coast branch of the Aborigines' Protection Society in London.

[3] Telegram of 28 May 1898, from Hodgson to Chamberlain; CO/96/316.

[4] Minute of 31 May 1898, by E. Wingfield; ibid.

[5] Petition of Apr. 1898, to Governor from Kings of Anomabu, Abura, and Inkusukum, and Chiefs of Cape Coast and Elmina, enclosed in Confidential Dispatch of 3 June 1898, from Hodgson to Chamberlain; ibid.

[6] Minute of 6 July 1898, by W. A. M.; ibid.

[7] Minute of 7 July 1898, by Chamberlain; ibid.

[8] The original version of this Petition, dated 27 May 1898, had been drawn up by the solicitors, who took the advice of counsel, including H. Asquith, Q.C. When Sey, Jones, and Hughes arrived in London, they made minor amendments and then signed the final, undated version, adding the

framed to suggest careful amendment, limitation, and revision, rather than the complete abandonment which was their tacit hope. No stops were left unpulled: 'Some Chiefs may have made improvident bargains. This, however, can hardly justify taking from your Petitioners the power to make any bargains whatever.' They attached a complete new version of the Bill, incorporating all their amendments, and also a 'Petition for the Alteration in the Constitution of the Government', which Chamberlain refused even to discuss.[1] The deputation asked for an audience at Buckingham Palace;[2] but noting loftily that 'These people are too small to see the Queen',[3] Chamberlain granted them an interview at the Colonial Office on 5 August 1898.

On this historic occasion, Sey, Jones, and Hughes were accompanied by their legal advisers, including an English barrister, C. Grant, who acted as their main spokesman. His speech presented a more succinct statement of their case than their own final petition, and is therefore worth quoting *in extenso*:

> The main objection to the Lands Bill was that it proceeded on an assumption which the natives deny, and which they were not allowed to argue before the Governor . . . that what is called in the Bill the 'unoccupied land' in the Colony does not belong to anyone . . . Either they belong to a family or a chief or to a king. But the whole of the land is so allotted . . . and no one, whether he comes from another family or tribe, or whether he is a foreigner, can occupy any of that land without the permission of the stool . . .
>
> The second was an objection as to procedure . . . The Lands Bill proposed that persons appointed by the Governor, who were to be called 'Commissioners', were to have the whole power of dealing with every concession . . . without any definite course of procedure laid down . . . they asked that it should be judicial and not administrative.
>
> The third objection, 'also a very important one', concerned the proposal 'that everyone who obtains land by land certificate should take it subject to English law, instead of subject to native law. Now that would amount to a revolution in the land system in the Colony. At the present time the land descends through the women to the children.'

Several other provisions of the Bill required amendment. The public purposes for which unoccupied land could be taken were defined too broadly, and should be limited to a specific list; the Chiefs would then be willing to give up their land for recognized public purposes. They felt that a notice in the *Gazette* would not be sufficient warning to those affected by concessions procedure; there should also be a notice personally delivered to the Chiefs concerned by a qualified interpreter.

names of fourteen Kings and over seventy Chiefs. *Report of the Proceedings of the Deputation* (1898).
  [1] See Ch. XI, pp. 429–31, below.
  [2] Letter of 27 July 1898, from Ashurst, Morris, Crisp & Co. to Chamberlain; CO/96/333.
  [3] Minute of 31 July 1898, by Chamberlain; ibid.

After a short discussion, the deputation was gratified to hear Chamberlain say:

'I think I can give you the assurance which you wish . . . I am willing that in all cases where the natives are concerned the native law shall remain and prevail . . . with regard to the devolution of land. And I am also willing that the Court which is to decide upon these questions should be a judicial Court.'

Mr. Corrie Grant: 'Those are the two main questions that we have been anxious about'.[1]

The deputation left England convinced that they had achieved a great victory. As we have seen, theirs were not the only objections that weighed with Chamberlain, who also had commercial interests very much in mind. Although no hint of weakening had been apparent in the Gold Coast, there had been heart searching in the Colonial Office for a long time over this Bill. The death of its main author perhaps removed the major objection to its withdrawal, which could now be effected without too much loss of face. It is arguable that had Maxwell lived, he might have persuaded the Secretary of State not to see the deputation, and to retain the Bill, perhaps in a modified form.

Nevertheless, other interpretations have been offered. George Padmore argues that Chamberlain acted as he did partly because he was already under attack for his alleged complicity in the Jameson Raid, and mainly because he realized that West Africa was not suitable for permanent white settlement: 'The mosquitoes saved the West Africans, not the eloquence of the intellectuals.'[2] Martin Wight is equally disparaging, from the opposite point of view; he comments that the success of this deputation established a lasting tradition in the Gold Coast of opposing government measures, 'as much for the sake of opposition as because of their intrinsic demerits'.[3]

Whatever the reasons for the withdrawal of the Bill, there is no doubt that the A.R.P.S. had a strong case and, making the most of it by constitutional means, succeeded in precipitating a favourable decision. To speak of opposition for its own sake is to misunderstand the nature of nationalist protests; whatever the merits of each individual case, there is felt to be an overriding national cause sanctifying all kinds of opposition to the Government. The prestige gained by this A.R.P.S. deputation gave a considerable aura of respectability to the movement, and won them publicity on almost a national scale. They were given a tremendous welcome on their return in October 1898.[4] A large number of Chiefs assembled in Cape Coast to receive their report, and to arrange for the payment of their expenses. It was then unanimously resolved that the A.R.P.S. should not be dissolved, 'but be firmly and permanently established for the protection and good government of the

[1] *Report of the Proceedings of the Deputation* (1898).
[2] G. Padmore, *The Gold Coast Revolution* (London, 1953), p. 38.
[3] M. Wight, *The Gold Coast Legislative Council* (London, 1947), p. 25.
[4] *The Gold Coast Aborigines*, Nov. and Dec. 1898.

Rulers and people of the Gold Coast'.[1] A Declaration was signed by all the Chiefs present, empowering the President and executive committee to act on their behalf.

Hodgson, who was on a tour of the western districts, reported that he had been interviewed by the principal residents of Cape Coast together with the assembled Chiefs, and that he had been presented with an address from the Society.[2] This was the first time that the Governor had met the A.R.P.S., and de Graft Johnson later interpreted the occasion as meaning that it was 'recognized' by the Government. He claimed that Hodgson, meeting the Society in session, had commended the Chiefs and officers for founding it, congratulated them on what had been accomplished, 'and added that the Government looked to them for ready assistance and cordial co-operation at all times in the difficult task of beneficial government'.[3] There is no doubt that this was the impression current at the time. It was afterwards disputed by the Government, but not until 1906,[4] and by then it was too late to prove anything, since no shorthand notes had been taken at the meeting (the Governor's clerk had been asked to interpret instead). The unofficial version persisted.[5]

The 1898 deputation brought the Society to the high-water mark of its success. Referring to those early days, de Graft Johnson wrote:

Composed of practically all the principal Chiefs of the country,[6] with the few amongst the most enlightened and influential of their educated brothers elected by themselves into office, the assemblage of the Society was truly imposing, grand and impressive. It was the Confederation all over again. It was called to power not by the accident of birth but by the free choice of the nation and it embraced all that the people possessed of political wisdom and practical statesmanship. It was the noblest embodiment of the nation; in consistency and political sagacity, in unanimity and patriotism, it represented the best thought of the Gold Coast peoples.[7]

The Concessions Ordinance, 1900

In spite of the failure of the Lands Bill, the Government was still anxious to find some means whereby unscrupulous prospectors and concession-

[1] Preamble to the A.R.P.S. *Bye-laws, Rules and Regulations* (Cape Coast, 1907).
[2] Dispatch No. 525 of 24 Dec. 1898, from Hodgson to Chamberlain; CO/96/324.
[3] de Graft Johnson, *Towards Nationhood*, p. 31.
[4] Letter of 4 May 1906, from Colonial Secretary to President of A.R.P.S.; G.N. Archives.
[5] Subsequent A.R.P.S. petitions habitually quoted Hodgson as saying that he 'looked to the Society for ready assistance and co-operation at all times in the difficult task of beneficial government, and that for these reasons the Government wishes the Society a career of usefulness and great prosperity'. E.g. *Gold Coast Aborigines' Rights Protection Society, 1934 Petition* (London, 1934).
[6] The preamble to the A.R.P.S. *Bye-laws, Rules and Regulations* (1907) claimed that the following twenty-six Head Chiefs had supported the Society at its foundation: Apollonia, Axim, Dixcove, Ahanta, Shama, Komenda, Elmina, Cape Coast, Denkera, Western Wassaw, Eastern Wassaw, Abura, Kwaman, Anomabu, Nkusukum, Aguna, Egimaku, Mankessim, Ekumfi, Gomua, Assin Apimenim, Assin Atanesu, Tafur, Ayan, Esikum, and Winneba. But the Society had little support in the Eastern Province, and no contacts with Ashanti or the Northern Territories.
[7] de Graft Johnson, loc. cit.

mongering Chiefs could be protected from one another, and the development of mining and commerce could be assisted. Hodgson was in London during the first half of 1899, and the Colonial Office took advantage of his presence to discuss the framing of new legislation to cover the limited field of agreement concerning concessions. Conversations were held with representatives of the British Chambers of Commerce, and other interested parties, including the London solicitors, who were still representing the Gold Coast petitioners.

In the event, a Concessions Bill was drafted, which was virtually an amended version of Part III of the original Lands Bill, all reference to public lands being omitted; in particular, there was to be no interference with the right of African owners to make grants, provided they could establish their title. A special judicial tribunal of the Supreme Court was to be set up to investigate all concessions; its approval would be necessary before any concession could be declared valid. Mining concessions were to be limited to five square miles, and others to twenty; a definite period was also to be fixed for the duration of concessions and options, thus preventing land from being tied up too long in the hands of those unable to work it. The main purpose was to obtain security of title for concession-holders, and to protect landowners from fraud.

On his return from leave in July 1899, Hodgson was given a uniquely demonstrative reception with speeches, processions, triumphal arches, flags, and flowers.[1] At Accra the whole town was *en fête*; a special committee had been formed to organize the festivities, and the President and members of the newly established Town Council congratulated the Governor on his recent knighthood. Hodgson commented, somewhat naïvely, that never before had he seen such a large and enthusiastic assembly, nor, so far as he knew, had any Governor received a public welcome on such a scale.[2] Fortunately he did not see the rather spiteful Colonial Office minute on this: 'I am afraid that this popularity is to some extent due to Sir F. Hodgson's being a weak rather than a strong Governor.'[3] More likely, however, he was being fêted because the Lands Bill was dead. Word of the new Concessions Bill had already reached the Gold Coast, and it was realized that African views had been considered sympathetically.

The latest proposals, when published, were of course studied critically, even suspiciously, by *The Gold Coast Aborigines*: 'the voice is the voice of the *Concession Bill* but the hands are the hands of the Lands Bill, and Time alone will reveal this fact to us, and then—it will be too late'.[4] For the debate in the Legislative Council in February 1900, the Governor appointed four extra-ordinary members.[5] One of these was Mensah Sarbah, to put the views of the A.R.P.S., although curiously enough he was said not to be a member. At

[1] *The Gold Coast Free Press*, 1–14 Aug. 1899.

[2] Letter of 12 July 1899, from Accra Town Council to Hodgson, and his covering Dispatch No. 268 of 14 July 1899, to Chamberlain; CO/96/341.

[3] Minute of 11 Aug. 1899, by R. W. A.; ibid.

[4] 16–23 Dec. 1899.   [5] *Legislative Council Minutes*, 26 Feb. 1900.

Hodgson's suggestion he agreed to second the Bill, in order to show that the Chiefs were grateful for this new approach.[1]

The vote was unanimous; a few amendments were made at the committee stage, although Mensah Sarbah did not secure all that the A.R.P.S. would have liked, and soon afterwards the Concessions Ordinance reached the statute book. The Society sent delegates from its Cape Coast and Axim sections to listen to the proceedings.[2] Afterwards a writer in *The Gold Coast Aborigines* expressed the viewpoint of the minority who were irrevocably opposed to any form of land legislation: 'The Bill as it was, at its second reading, was nothing else but the despicable Lands Bill clothed in fine, smooth words... it was in some respects even worse.'[3] But this was only minor carping, and the Society was well content to rest on the laurels of its victory in 1898.

[1] Dispatch No. 95 of 5 Mar. 1900, from Hodgson to Chamberlain; CO/96/358.
[2] Letters of 8, 16, and 31 Mar. 1900, from Sey to Ashurst, Morris, Crisp & Co.; CO/96/371.
[3] *The Gold Coast Aborigines*, 17 Mar. 1900.

X

THE A.R.P.S. AND THE NATIONAL CONGRESS
1901–30

DURING the twentieth century the Aborigines' Rights Protection Society retained the same guiding principles as had sustained it during the Lands Bill agitation, and continued to apply these to the changing political situation. For example, the leaders took for granted that the Society would continue to act as the main medium of communication between the Government and the people, and hardly seemed to notice that both the form of government and the peoples under its rule had changed beyond recognition during the few years 1897–1902.

The A.R.P.S. appeared to believe that the political leadership of this wider national unit would automatically remain in the hands of a small circle in Cape Coast, and that the Government was bound to respect the united opposition of the Fanti Chiefs, with their educated advisers and spokesmen. They also continued to oppose all legislation affecting lands and forests, often assuming wrongly that the economic interests of the Chiefs were identical with those of the country as a whole. Consequently, the Society failed to adapt its structure and tactics to the changed circumstances of the twentieth century; and its leaders hardly realized that power was slipping away from them, in favour of those who were more concerned with a fundamental change in the colonial relationship than with the preservation of traditional rights.

Readjustments within the A.R.P.S.

After the noteworthy success of the 1898 deputation against the Lands Bill, disagreements over policy, as well as the lack of a strong central organization, began to be felt within the A.R.P.S. The Society really consisted of little more than the parent body at Cape Coast, with a vigorous scion at Axim, often acting independently; in August 1899 *The Gold Coast Aborigines* published an editorial under the title 'Wanted: Organization for the Gold Coast Aborigines' Rights Protection Society', stressing the need for a permanent Secretary. This newspaper was having its own difficulties. Early in 1901 the printer was changed twice, and soon there was trouble between the editorial staff and the executive of the Society, who requested the return of their property;[1] the paper then temporarily ceased publication.

Any real or imagined threat to native land rights was guaranteed to bring the Society sharply to the defensive. In 1901 the Government took powers to

---

[1] *The Gold Coast Aborigines*, 13 May 1901.

acquire any land within the area of a town under the Public Lands Ordinance, 1876, as though it were required for the service of the Colony. Land so acquired in the new township of Sekondi was then advertised for public auction.[1] This took the A.R.P.S. by surprise; and the Axim leaders sent a long and respectful petition to the Governor, claiming that this action denied 'the rights of the people to their ancestral lands', as reaffirmed by Chamberlain in 1898. If the main object was to promote town development, they suggested, then the landowners could be directed to build substantial houses, or else to lease their land to those who could; but the Government was not entitled to dispose profitably of lands acquired at a nominal sum for the public interest. They asked, therefore, for the repeal of the 1901 Towns (Amendment) Ordinance, in the name of 'the Aborigines of the country, whom we have the honour of representing'.[2]

Sir Matthew Nathan, the new Governor, was not going to allow anything to be taken for granted; he wanted to know when the A.R.P.S. was formed, who were its members, the dates on which they joined, and the authority under which they claimed to represent the aborigines of the country. The Axim branch replied that the previous Governor had 'over and over again' granted interviews to members of the executive committee of the Society, at which important issues affecting the welfare of the country were discussed. They complained that there was, under the present system of government, no other means for the people to express their sentiments and opinions. But their petition was returned, and they were told that it should be laid on the table of the Legislative Council by a member, according to the standing rules.[3] After two months of official punctilio they were back where they were.

But Nathan appears afterwards to have recognized the Society, at least by consulting it on more than one occasion when considering Bills,[4] and in 1903 by asking for details of the traditional titles of Chiefs.[5] The Commissioner for the Central Province later admitted that the A.R.P.S. had rendered some assistance to the Government, mainly he thought in the interests of the trade of Cape Coast; questions of native custom, in disputes between Chiefs and others, had also been referred to them.[6] In 1902 *The Gold Coast Aborigines* resumed publication, and announced an attempt to resuscitate the *Mfantsi*

[1] *Government Gazette*, 27 July 1901.

[2] Petition of 23 Sept. 1901, to Governor and Legislative Council from Axim branch of A.R.P.S., signed by S. Sacoom (President) and A. Bissoe (Secretary). J. E. Casely Hayford, *Gold Coast Native Institutions* (London, 1903), app. E. 1.

[3] Letters of 9 Oct. and 15 Nov. 1901, from Governor's Private Secretary to Sacoom, and Letter of 24 Oct. 1901, from Sacoom and Bissoe to Nathan; ibid.

[4] According to Dispatch No. 398 of 12 June 1912, from Thorburn to Harcourt; S.N.A. No. 1503, G.N. Archives.

[5] *Government Gazette*, 30 Jan. 1904.

[6] Letter of 20 Mar. 1912, from Provincial Commissioner, Cape Coast, to Colonial Secretary; S.N.A. No. 25/1922, G.N. Archives. A list of minor collaborations between the Society and the Government during 1901–4 was proudly set out in *Gold Coast Aborigines' Rights Protection Society, 1934 Petition* (London, 1934).

Amanbuhu Fékuw: 'We want Educated Fantis not europeanised natives. We simply want our education to enable us to develop and to improve our native ideas, customs, manners and institutions.'[1] In the same year J. W. Sey died, and J. P. Brown was elected President of the Society, an office which he held for the next five years. In spite of some official criticism, relations with the Government were maintained, until the establishment of town councils brought about an open rupture.

The 1894 Town Councils Ordinance was applied in 1904 to Sekondi, and there was immediate opposition, especially to the idea of municipal rates. Although the protests were not organized by the A.R.P.S. as a body, they emanated largely from Cape Coast.[2] The Chiefs there, for example, petitioned the Governor to amend the Ordinance on lines not too far removed from their own traditions, and repeated earlier requests for a direct government grant to finance the councils.[3] The Press joined issue in a lively campaign, whose theme was 'boycott'. At the Sekondi elections in March 1905 four Europeans were returned unopposed. The opposition grew more intense when it appeared that the Ordinance would next come into force in Cape Coast.[4] *The Gold Coast Aborigines*[5] had much to say on the subject; so strong were local feelings that troops were transferred from Kumasi 'because a row was expected'.[6] The Omanhene continued to bombard the Government with formal protests, fully supported by the A.R.P.S., who were now on their home ground.

Contributions were collected from the Chiefs of the Central and Western Provinces, and in 1906 the Rev. K. Egyir-Asaam was dispatched to England.[7] He carried a petition to the King signed by over seventy Chiefs, including those from Axim, Elmina, Wassaw, and Abura, as well as by many other inhabitants. This recalled a promise by Chamberlain to the 1898 deputation that he would not impose legislation against the will of the people, declared that the whole of the Colony was opposed to municipal house rates, and demanded the repeal of the Town Councils Ordinance.[8] J. Mensah Sarbah records that the thirty-one Members of Parliament who sympathized with this protest 'added more to the prestige of the British nation in West Africa, than a score of punitive expeditions could possibly do'.[9] Egyir-Asaam was granted an interview with the Secretary of State, Lord Elgin; but secured

---

[1] *The Gold Coast Aborigines*, 8 Feb. 1902.

[2] For details of the Ordinance and the underlying motives of the opposition, see Ch. XI, pp. 422–6, below. An interesting account of the Cape Coast objections is given by E. Baillaud, *La Politique indigène de l'Angleterre en Afrique Occidentale* (Paris, 1912).

[3] Petition of 1 Nov. 1904, to Governor from Cape Coast Chiefs; G.N. Archives.

[4] *Departmental Reports*, Native Affairs, 1904 and 1905.   [5] June 1905.

[6] Captain A. W. Norris, 'Three Tours on the West Coast of Africa', *The Gold Coast Review* (Accra, 1928), vol. ii, no. ii: 'There were one or two very funny things said in the local native paper about us coming down ... But one soon learns not to take any notice of the babblings of the native press.'   [7] Rodger, *Legislative Council Minutes*, 7 Nov. 1906.

[8] *West Africa*, 2 Feb. 1906.   [9] *Fanti National Constitution* (London, 1906), preface.

nothing more than a courteous letter agreeing that the representative element on the councils might be enlarged when they had gained sufficient experience. The Colonial Office was not prepared to concede any immediate change in their composition, especially as public money was involved.[1] Meanwhile, in the absence of Cape Coast candidates for election, the Acting Governor optimistically nominated four councillors: Mensah Sarbah, J. P. Brown, Chief J. Sackey, and W. J. Hooper. But they never took their seats.[2]

Relations with the Government were further upset by a most unfortunate incident at the end of 1906. Sir John Rodger visited Cape Coast to open an agricultural show, also hoping to allay suspicion and smooth the passage for the new town council. But many rowdy protests were made. As the Governor and his wife prepared to leave by the next steamboat for Accra, the market women discovered their movements and gathered at the landing stage, many clothed in sackcloth and ashes; some threatened, others shouted, hooted, and rushed, and Lady Rodger was alarmed. It was widely believed that the Governor never forgave the inhabitants; certainly he did not revisit the town before he left the Gold Coast in 1910, and it seems that Cape Coast—and the Society—remained under an official cloud for several years.[3]

In 1907 the constitution, aims, and objects of the A.R.P.S. were 'revised carefully, and diligently construed'.[4] This was not so much a revision, however, as the first formal constitution to be drawn up. Only a very brief statement of the Society's aims had previously been issued, in 1897. It had now been proved in practice that when the Chiefs could act together, their united voices carried some weight. But the problem was to create some form of permanent association that would neither limit their traditional authority within their own States, nor set any one of them in a higher position than the others. This was eventually solved by the expedient of formally delegating power to non-Chiefs, i.e. to the educated officers of the Society's executive, who would thus be empowered to act on behalf of the Chiefs in summoning them together and in carrying out any joint decisions. Each paramount Chief thus remained wholly independent of the others, while the President of the Society had the unique honour of being in a position to invite any or all of the Chiefs to a conference, to discuss common problems or united action.

---

[1] Letter of 19 June 1906, from Colonial Office to Asaam; quoted by W. S. Kwesi-Johnston, in a lecture to the Youth Conference, Accra, 27 Jan. 1943.

[2] Elections fell due every two years, but none was contested before 1914, and then only fifty-three votes were cast. In Sekondi only two of the first five elections were contested; in 1914 no election was arranged at all, 'through an oversight'; in 1916 three votes were cast and in 1918 seven. 'Report by the Town Councils Committee on the Constitution and Working of the Existing Town Councils in the Colony', *Sessional Paper No. XVII of 1922–23*, app. no. iii.

[3] J. W. de Graft Johnson alleged that 'by the merest accident of the headquarters of the Society being at Cape Coast, the organisation fell into disfavour with the Governor and his successors unto this day'. *Towards Nationhood in West Africa* (London, 1928), pp. 66–67.

[4] K. Taylor, *Our Political Destiny* (Winneba, 1941), a pamphlet written to commemorate the 43rd anniversary of the A.R.P.S.

This, however, was a very different thing from the effective union towards which the Fanti Confederation Chiefs had striven, or the sense of a common cause, outweighing local jealousies, which alone could have allowed the Chiefs to retain active leadership in the new, wider, national framework.

The general aims of the Society, now stated fully for the first time, were not only to protect the rights and interests of the Aborigines of the Gold Coast, but to 'promote and effect unity of purpose and action', and to be the medium of communication and 'right understanding' between the Government and the people. Special stress was laid upon the need for constitutional methods of action and upon the importance of continued loyalty to the British Crown; but the members must be educated to a 'proper and correct understanding' of the 400-year-old relationship between Britain and the Gold Coast. To this end, the Society would provide facilities for the Chiefs and people to study legislative measures and 'watch the acts of the Government'; but its zeal was clearly of a conservative rather than a reforming character.

The constitution of the A.R.P.S. laid down rules for membership (open to any native of the Gold Coast), entrance fees (6*d.* and 1*s.*) and subscriptions (6*d.* per month, or £10 annually for Chiefs), for procedure at meetings, and for the general structure of the organization, which could include sub-committees on such matters as commerce, sanitation, the Press, and education. The management of the Society was still to rest in the hands of the officers at the Cape Coast headquarters of the parent Society: the President, three Vice-Presidents, a Recording Secretary, a Corresponding Secretary, a Treasurer, and a *Kyiami*.[1] The Society was thus drawn up constitutionally for the next affray with the Government. Proposals for forest reserves soon brought them back to the land question.

Forest Legislation, 1907–11

The forests were an old problem. The 1883 Native Jurisdiction Ordinance had empowered Chiefs to make local by-laws for forest preservation; but in fact none were made. In 1899 the Governor was planning legislation for the conservation of forests and the regulation of the timber trade.[2] This would have introduced licences for cutting timber and collecting rubber and kola-nuts, and a programme of reafforestation.[3] But the whole question was shelved, for fear of political repercussions so soon after the Lands Bill agitation; it was felt that expert study and advice were first necessary.

---

[1] A.R.P.S., *Bye-laws, Rules and Regulations* (Cape Coast, 1907). The constitution was signed by J. P. Brown (President), J. E. Casely Hayford (Delegate, Tarkwa and Dunkwa Sections), S. Sacoom (President, Axim Section), and by thirty-seven Chiefs. It was dated 9 Apr. 1907, and was witnessed by T. F. E. Jones (a Vice-President) and J. A. Mills (Secretary); afterwards other signatures were added.

[2] Dispatch No. 561 of 18 Dec. 1899, from Hodgson to Chamberlain; CO/96/346.

[3] Dispatch No. 108 of 12 Mar. 1900, from Hodgson to Chamberlain; CO/96/358.

In 1907 the Timber Protection Ordinance prohibited the cutting of immature trees; and the next year the Conservator of Forests in Southern Nigeria was invited to advise on more radical measures. He found two main problems; the 'wasteful system' of African farming, and the over-exploitation of the forests for timber, fuel, and other produce; the former was by far the greater danger, and would, he was convinced, eventually result in the virtual extermination of the forests.[1] The main solution he proposed was to establish forest reserves in important strategic situations, such as hill-tops and watersheds; and on his recommendation a Forestry Department was created in 1909. Legislation was soon drafted to provide for the establishment of forest reserves which could be set up by the Governor over any 'Waste lands, i.e. lands unoccupied and uncultivated'. Titles to ownership would not necessarily be affected, but might lapse if not claimed within a given time-limit. The very phraseology sounded echoes of the original Crown Lands Bill of 1894, and the reaction that might have been expected was not long delayed.

As soon as the Forestry Bill was introduced into the Legislative Council in October 1910, representations were made against it by the unofficial members, and the Government undertook to amplify the attached statement of objects and reasons, prior to its publication.[2] The Acting President of the A.R.P.S. wrote rather belatedly in January 1911, having only just seen the Bill, to ask for a postponement of the second reading, so that the Society might have time to study it and register their objections.[3] But the Bill was already dead, for certain defects of procedure had become apparent, and it was now felt that Southern Nigerian precedent had been followed too closely.[4] Slightly different legislation was therefore drafted, while the Gold Coast Conservator of Forests continued to press for early action.[5]

The ripples of the old Bill continued to spread outwards, stirred up again by a petition from the Gã Mantse;[6] and in May, when a new Forest Bill came before the Legislative Council,[7] the Chiefs of the Central and Western Provinces were in conference with the A.R.P.S. at Cape Coast discussing the earlier version. Many present were suspicious simply because there was no explanatory preamble to the Bill, and they felt that it violated the pledge given in 1898 by Chamberlain, 'the Magna Charta of the people of the Gold Coast'. They sent a formal petition—preceded by a telegram to London— against the version which they thought was still before the Legislative Council,

[1] H. N. Thompson, *Gold Coast. Report on Forests* (London, 1910), Cd. 4993.

[2] *Legislative Council Minutes*, 28 Oct. 1910, and *Government Gazette*, 16 Nov. 1910.

[3] Letter of 3 Jan. 1911, from Jones to Colonial Secretary; Forestry Department Records, Accra (hereinafter referred to as F.D. Records).

[4] Thorburn, *Legislative Council Minutes*, 13 Sept. 1911.

[5] Letter of 13 Dec. 1910, from Conservator of Forests to Colonial Secretary; F.D. Records.

[6] Petition of 24 Mar. 1911, to Governor from Gã Mantse, Mantsemei, and people of Eastern Province; ibid.   [7] *Legislative Council Minutes*, 13 May 1911.

claiming that the principle involved was the same as that of the Lands Bill, unnecessarily infringing private property rights.[1]

The Conservator of Forests eventually went to Cape Coast to explain the provisions of the latest Bill to the Chiefs. But they had already gone home; and the A.R.P.S. officers failed to meet him at the appointed time, so that he merely handed over a copy of his address[2]—a very brief document, which left them little the wiser. The Society then arranged another full-scale conference of Chiefs and their supporters in August, at which the Acting Provincial Commissioner tried to persuade them that the Forest Bill was intended for their good.[3] In spite of this, they sent the customary telegram of protest to the Secretary of State,[4] followed up by yet a further petition to the Governor.[5]

The suspicions planted during 1894–7 were proving difficult to uproot; J. E. Casely Hayford's pamphlet, *Gold Coast Land Tenure and the Forest Bill*,[6] published after the latest conference, indicates how African minds turned automatically to the land question. He argued that the 1911 Bill was in some respects more drastic than that of 1910; and that it sought to make the Public Lands Ordinance almost of general application, by giving the Government the 'remarkable and dangerous power' of compulsorily acquiring any land for forest reserves, subject to certain provisions. The people, the owners of the land, were, he complained, with a stroke of the pen to be reduced to 'mere squatters, depending, in effect, upon the foreign capitalist for a daily wage as hewers of wood and drawers of water'. Such emotional appeals struck right home.

When the Legislative Council met in September 1911, T. Hutton Mills presented the latest A.R.P.S. petition, together with one from the Gã Chiefs and people,[7] against the proposed forest legislation. Permission was given for counsel to appear in support of these petitions, and the following extracts from their speeches reveal the main African fears and criticisms:

J. E. Casely Hayford

To draw one or two obvious comparisons between the Land Bill of 1897 and the Forest Bill, 1911, it is clear that the administration of Public Lands by the Government is the same thing as the 'management' by the Government of reserved lands . . . both words are practically synonymous . . . whether you call land 'waste land', 'unoccupied land', 'forest land' or 'bush land', the result is the same to the persons claiming proprietary rights to such land.[8]

[1] Telegram of 15 May 1911, and Petition of 23 May 1911, to Secretary of State from Kings and Chiefs of Central and Western Provinces 'in Conference assembled'; F.D. Records.
[2] Letter of 28 July 1911, from Conservator of Forests to Colonial Secretary; ibid.
[3] Casely Hayford, *Legislative Council Minutes*, 13 Sept. 1911.
[4] Telegram of 10 Aug. 1911, to Secretary of State from 'Amanhin, Ahinfu people, Central and Western Provinces, in Conference'; F.D. Records.
[5] Petition of 23 Aug. 1911, to Governor and Legislative Council from A.R.P.S.; ibid.
[6] London, 1911.
[7] Petition of 11 Sept. 1911, to Governor and Legislative Council from Gã Mantse, Mantsemei, and people of Eastern Province; F.D. Records.
[8] The Conservator of Forests commented: 'if this misconception is genuine it is incomprehensible'. Letter of 14 Sept. 1911, to Colonial Secretary; ibid.

... it is inconceivable in the native mind that any jurisdiction can exist without land, or without the right and power of active management of such land. Take away the control of the lands by the Amanhin and Ahinfu and you have practically destroyed the whole fabric of native institutions.

C. J. Bannerman
... to the idea of the Native such a Bill is wholly unnecessary. If it is for their good, my clients say they do not want it, and if it is for the benefit of any other person or persons they object to it.

E. J. P. Brown
The soil of this country has never been acquired by Conquest, Cession or Purchase; and since 1898 the land question of this country was a settled one and not open to argument.

The Governor at once stated that he would consider amending the Bill,[1] in order to make its purpose still clearer and dispel the misconceptions which had arisen; and so the next stage was deferred.[2]

In November the amended Forest Bill came up for its second reading; it was now emphasized that there would be no change in ownership when forest reserves were established. An owner could continue to do as he pleased with his own part of the reserve, but if he failed to manage it properly the Government would take it on lease, to be supervised by the Forestry Department. The Governor hoped that this would allay unfounded suspicions; and Hutton Mills was so reassured by this that he was now willing to second the Bill. He felt that the amendments had wholly removed those aspects 'which might have frightened people'. Nene Mate Kole raised no objection; and the forest proposals were passed, to the relief of the Governor, who remarked that such a controversial Bill had seldom had such a smooth passage. He hoped it was now clear that the Government had no intention whatever of confiscating land.[3]

But the enactment of this Ordinance marked the beginning of a fresh political storm. Before the end of the month the A.R.P.S. produced a memorial to the King, and announced their intention of sending a deputation to England. They maintained that the Ordinance had made no 'tangible alteration' in the principles which they had already complained of before the bar of the Legislative Council. Although the Government had abandoned the right of compulsory acquisition, the power to take up leasehold grants would 'in effect be the same' as the official acquisition of lands. They therefore viewed with grave apprehension the return to a land policy 'long proved to be inapplicable and untenable'.[4]

---

[1] The Conservator foresaw such drastic amendments that he offered to draft a new Bill, omitting the creation of government reserves, and compelling the Chiefs to manage their native reserves on sound principles under the direction of the Forestry Department; ibid. This might have afforded a workable compromise, but his offer was not taken up.

[2] *Legislative Council Minutes*, 13 Sept. 1911.   [3] Ibid. 6 and 9 Nov. 1911.

[4] Memorial of 30 Nov. 1911, to King George V from A.R.P.S., and covering Letter from Attoh Ahuma to Colonial Secretary; F.D. Records.

This came as a sharp surprise, so soon after the acquiescence within the Legislative Council. The main reason was the lack of political representation; there had been no opportunity to register a formal protest at the time of the debate, for printed copies of the latest draft were not available until a month later. But in any case the A.R.P.S., once having taken up an issue that affected land, was not likely to let it rest, whatever amendments the Government might have made.

The Head Chiefs of Accra and Christiansborg were officially persuaded to admit that they had signed the A.R.P.S. memorial under the impression that it referred to the unamended version of the Forest Bill. But they refused to withdraw their protest, even after studying the final Ordinance.[1] It was discovered, however, that only one of the thirteen Head Chiefs who had signed the document had any land likely to be affected. So the Governor, apparently not admitting the possibility of a disinterested protest, advised the Secretary of State that it was not a true exposition of the view of the signatories but had been 'engineered by certain interested persons who are collecting money . . . to secure a free trip to England and a little transient notoriety'.[2] In January 1912 Casely Hayford arrived in London to make advance arrangements for the full A.R.P.S. deputation, and especially to brief their solicitors.

Death of an Ordinance, 1912–16

Meanwhile, the Secretary of State had decided to take advantage of the opposition to the Forest Ordinance to study the whole land problem. So he appointed a Special Commissioner, H. C. Belfield, to inquire into the general conditions governing the alienation of land in the Gold Coast, with special reference to concessions since 1901; the A.R.P.S. were to be given an opportunity to state their case.[3] Casely Hayford, on hearing this, returned at once to the Gold Coast to assist the Society.

Belfield spent nearly three months taking evidence in Accra, Cape Coast, Sekondi, and Kumasi; his report was published in July 1912. He had been careful to include sufficient references to African land-ownership to satisfy even the most sensitive members of the A.R.P.S.:

It must . . . be taken as established that all land belongs to the people which has not been acquired by other parties by specific process, such as cession, purchase, exchange, or inheritance: consequently such general appropriation by the Crown as was contemplated by the Land Bill of 1897 is, in my view, out of the question.

On no account must the fact be lost sight of that the land is the property of the people, that a concession is a contract . . . to which the Government is no party; that intervention must therefore be limited to supervision and guidance only.

---

[1] Memoranda of 4 and 8 Jan. 1912, by Acting Colonial Secretary; F.D. Records.
[2] Dispatch No. 12 of 8 Jan. 1912, from Thorburn to Harcourt; G.N. Archives.
[3] Dispatch No. 37 of 13 Jan. 1912, from Harcourt to Thorburn; ibid.

With regard to concessions, Belfield found that far too many had been granted on terms unfavourable to the inhabitants, mainly because the Chiefs had little idea of area measurements and were usually unaware of the extent of the land they signed away.[1] But the total area granted since the Concessions Ordinance of 1900 was not as excessive as reports had suggested, as the following annual figures show:

Colony		Ashanti	
Year	Square miles	Year	Square miles
1901 .	3·529	(1897 .	100—Ashanti Gold-
1902 .	15·133		fields Corp.)
1903 .	90·965		
1904 .	131·609		
1905 .	109·673		
1906 .	40·695	1906 .	76·367
1907 .	35·390	1907 .	147·190
1908 .	59·041	1908 .	69·970
1909 .	145·920		
1910 .	45·366		
1911 .	201·756	1911 .	15
879·077		408·527	
out of approx. 24,300 square miles		out of approx. 24,800 square miles	

In addition, many more concessions were 'under notice', i.e. not yet issued with certificates of validity. Probably the vast majority of these had lapsed, but there was no method of telling, since they continued to remain on the court records.

Belfield heard nothing to bear out the stories that Chiefs were knowingly granting the same pieces of land twice over; nor had they infringed local custom in the distribution of the proceeds. But he made the more important point that these customs were not always a satisfactory guide under modern conditions. Certain defects were also apparent in the existing Concessions Ordinance and, disregarding the earlier struggle for judicial control, Belfield suggested that this should now be transferred to the executive. A Commissioner of Lands should be appointed; but all local negotiations in the first instance should take place through District and Provincial Commissioners. He also recommended that the maximum area for each mining concession should be reduced from five square miles to one, and that operations should be required to commence within two years.

Belfield gave full consideration to the view of the A.R.P.S., although he had been told in advance that the educated leaders in Cape Coast really dictated

[1] Chief Esselkojo of Appintoe said in evidence: 'The land is usually described in square miles. I do not know what a square mile is. Sometimes I have given more land than I intended, and if I had known the true extent I would have given less.' *Report on the Legislation Governing the Alienation of Native Lands in the Gold Coast Colony and Ashanti; with some Observations on the 'Forest Ordinance', 1911* (London, 1912), Cd. 6278, by H. C. Belfield, p. 76.

the policy of the Society, and that the Chiefs had little or no voice. He strongly rejected such a view, maintaining that the inception of the Society had clearly been due to the expressed wish of the Chiefs themselves, and that they took as active a part in its proceedings as any of the educated members. In general, he found that the people in Ashanti did not feel so strongly about land. The Government had been in a position, when Ashanti was annexed, to proclaim the land Crown property; but since any claim to ownership had then been waived, it could not now be asserted. He found the relations between government officers and Chiefs closer and more harmonious in Ashanti than in the Colony, and he attributed this to the natural deference shown to 'the representatives of the conquering nation'.

Special attention was paid to the pending Forest Ordinance. Belfield analysed the opposition in some detail, but it was only at Cape Coast that he heard objections urged. Elsewhere it did not seem to be regarded as a matter of importance, and he assumed that there was no general desire throughout the Colony for its withdrawal. He reported that no one who complained against the Ordinance could be induced to show the smallest interest in the preservation of forests or to admit, even when the system was explained, that the country would be any better for its introduction. He summed up their attitude as 'obstructive to improvement and apathetic of consequences'.[1] In spite of this, Belfield made certain suggestions which yielded some ground to the A.R.P.S. For example, under no circumstances should more than a certain proportion of stool land be appropriated for forest reserves, since if the whole were so used, the tribe would probably break up and disperse. The Government should also dispel local fears by stating clearly that it did not intend to vest interests in such reserved areas to third parties.[2]

The *Belfield Report* as a whole, therefore, while giving some official blessing to the traditional A.R.P.S. arguments against Crown expropriation or management of land, and to the Society's claim to represent the Chiefs, exposed their isolation from general opinion in the Colony, and scarcely affected the immediate issue of the Forest Ordinance.

Meanwhile the A.R.P.S. had not given up the idea of a full-scale deputation. In April 1912 their solicitors had informed the Colonial Office that their clients were anxious to come to London, and to appear again before Belfield in case any further questions arose which might affect them.[3] One of the main reasons for their anxiety was that money had already been collected for the

---

[1] This is not the main impression gained from reading the minutes of evidence appended to the *Belfield Report*. Several of the witnesses, notably those from the A.R.P.S., suggested—or welcomed suggestions made to them for—improvements in the Ordinance. Casely Hayford had previously urged that well-trained forest instructors should advise the Chiefs, in their own language, how to cultivate their lands better, and encourage them to pass by-laws—as they were entitled to do under the Native Jurisdiction Ordinance—for the conservation of forests. *Legislative Council Minutes*, 13 Sept. 1911.   [2] *Belfield Report*.

[3] Letter of 10 Apr. 1912, from A.R.P.S. Solicitors to Under-Secretary of State, enclosed in Confidential Dispatch of 16 Apr. 1912, from Harcourt to Thorburn; F.D. Records.

specific purpose of a deputation. The Chiefs had paid up handsomely, no doubt with gratifying memories of the 1898 success; Lower and Upper Wassaw and Aowin had each contributed £300, and £150 each came from Gomoa, Elmina, Eguafo, Anomabu, Nkusukum, Abura, and Ekumfi. As a result of these special contributions, there was a sum of over £3,000 in the bank; about £400 had already been spent, partly on Casely Hayford's brief visit to London, and partly on the revival of the Society's newspaper.[1]

The Secretary of State at once inquired about the status and motives of the proposed deputation, only to be told that the four members had already left. In a series of official thumb-nail sketches, J. E. Casely Hayford and E. J. P. Brown were described as barristers-at-law—the former having had a wide experience of concession cases—T. F. E. Jones as a 'well-connected native', and Dr. B. W. Quartey-Papafio as a retired medical officer. Nothing could be found to damn them in advance: 'These gentlemen are probably interested in concessions but I can obtain no proof thereof.'[2] But the Governor had no reservations in his condemnation of the A.R.P.S., which he alleged existed primarily to oppose all government measures, 'frequently stirring up prejudice by an absolutely distorted interpretation of the Government's intentions'.[3]

When the A.R.P.S. deputation arrived in London, the Colonial Office was being lobbied by an influential group who wanted to protect West African land against concession-hunters, and who were pressing for the appointment of a committee of inquiry into the whole question of land transfers, with special reference to the Northern Nigerian system of complete control and disposition by the Governor. In a letter to *The Times* they had urged the need for immediate action in the Gold Coast, owing, on the one hand, to the rush for mining and agricultural concessions and, on the other, to the widespread destruction of valuable timbered areas: 'it is inconceivable that the native peoples, did they fully appreciate the matter, would be consenting parties to a system destructive of their own most vital interests'.[4]

When the deputation was received by the Secretary of State on 28 June 1912[5], they were simply informed that the West African Lands Committee had been appointed, with Sir Kenelm Digby as Chairman; other members included E. D. Morel and an ex-Governor, Sir Frederic Hodgson. They took the opportunity to appear before the Committee, and to submit various documents;[6]

---

[1] Letter of 20 Mar. 1912, from Provincial Commissioner, Cape Coast, to Colonial Secretary; S.N.A. No. 25/1922, G.N. Archives.

[2] Telegram of 9 June 1912, from Thorburn to Harcourt; F.D. Records.

[3] Dispatch No. 398 of 12 June 1912, from Thorburn to Harcourt; ibid.

[4] Letter from E. D. Morel, Noel Buxton, Ramsay MacDonald, Philip Morell, Sir Albert Spicer, and Josiah C. Wedgwood; *The Times*, 6 June 1912.

[5] They were introduced by T. Healey, K.C., M.P., and were supported by the Rev. W. R. Griffin (Chairman of the Wesleyan Mission), the Rev. Dr. M. Hayford (of the Baptist Mission), and J. M. A. Oppon, of the Gold Coast.

[6] See *West African Lands Committee: Minutes of Evidence, &c.*, and *West African Lands Committee Correspondence* (London, 1916), African (West) Nos. 1047 and 1048.

Casely Hayford spoke strongly against the Forest Ordinance, but his views were not treated very seriously by some members, who were no doubt annoyed when those whom they wished to benefit presumed to argue with them.[1]

The future of the Ordinance was still uncertain when the A.R.P.S. delegates returned to the Gold Coast, more in sorrow than in anger.[2] Local administrators were pressing for it to be implemented as soon as possible, since 'Injury that is irreparable within any reasonable period is being done yearly to the Gold Coast Forests.'[3] But the Secretary of State took the view that, as the whole subject of land tenure was under such detailed consideration, the Chiefs should simply be told to stop felling trees indiscriminately.[4] The Committee continued to sit in London for several years, and the A.R.P.S. rejoiced to see the hated Ordinance being gradually buried under the weight of these deliberations. Eventually a draft report was produced—but not published—in 1916, recommending legislation to prohibit all individual ownership and sale of land, and to limit very severely the Chiefs' powers to grant leases.[5] The new Governor of the Gold Coast, Sir Hugh Clifford, flatly rejected these proposals, declaring that such legislation would be a severe blow at native rights; and in any case the 1911 Forest Ordinance had already gone by default.

Thus although the A.R.P.S. had really lost the battle in London, it was won for them in Accra. Numerous commentators have deplored this on economic grounds. As R. L. Buell put it: 'The same considerations which led the government to hold up the Public Crown Land Act of 1897 [sic] and the Forestry Law of 1911, again kept it from saving the natives from themselves.'[6] Such a judgement seems to ignore political and social realities. Nevertheless, it is true that the opposition which had prevented interference with African land rights continued to inhibit the development of any constructive policy for conserving the forests or regulating dealings in land.[7] It was not until 1927 that the Government managed to get a long-overdue

---

[1] For example, 'But how can you, who have not a forestry knowledge, or how can anybody without scientific knowledge, take up a position of that sort?' *W.A.L.C. Evidence*, question 881.

[2] A Nigerian deputation was also sent to London in 1913 to protest against an apparent threat to African land-ownership in Southern Nigeria; but they were even less effective, due largely to financial difficulties and internal dissension. See J. S. Coleman, *Nigeria: Background to Nationalism* (Los Angeles, 1958), pp. 180–1.

[3] Dispatch No. 741 of 21 Oct. 1912, from Bryan to Harcourt; G.N. Archives.

[4] Dispatch No. 747 of 30 Nov. 1912, from Harcourt to Bryan; ibid.

[5] *West African Lands Committee Draft Report* (London, 1916), African (West) No. 1046.

[6] *The Native Problem in Africa* (New York, 1928), vol. i, pp. 823–4.

[7] Cf. W. K. Hancock's treatment of 'the paradox . . . that a government which wished to dispossess a Native people could hardly do better than proclaim the principle of absolute ownership by the Native communities'. *Survey of British Commonwealth Affairs* (London, 1940), vol. ii, pt. ii, p. 182. The problems raised by the West African Lands Committee are not intended to be fully dealt with here. In addition to the works cited, C. K. Meek, *Land Law and Custom in the Colonies* (London, 1946), ch. xiv, and F. D. Lugard, *The Dual Mandate in British Tropical Africa* (London, 1922), chs. xiv–xvi, are indispensable for reference.

Forests Ordinance enacted, winning the co-operation of the Chiefs through their Provincial Councils.

The A.R.P.S. in Decline

The A.R.P.S. had by no means returned to favour in official eyes. In 1912 a Provincial Commissioner, attempting to analyse the extent to which it represented educated opinion, remarked shrewdly that 'An organisation of this nature composed of and guided by educated natives naturally creates a public opinion, which probably without it would not make itself heard to any degree.' The Society was chiefly conspicuous in opposition to the Government, and because self-interest was their principal argument, they were 'bound to appeal to and receive the support of the general community whether educated or not'. He mentioned the Head Chiefs of Anomabu, Abura, and Nkusukum as educated, intelligent, and influential members of the Society, but remarked on its lack of support in the Eastern Province, and concluded: 'There is no united national sentiment amongst the various tribes in the Colony, and the Society cannot therefore claim to be a national organisation. Its interests are principally those of Cape Coast and the District'.[1]

This was the considered official view of the Society. The leaders were well aware of government suspicions of anything emanating from Cape Coast; they therefore took it very kindly when Clifford attended an A.R.P.S. banquet there in 1913. This was the first visit of a Governor to the town for seven years, and his friendly gesture reminded Casely Hayford of the days of the Judicial Assessors—'There was a time when the officers of the Government mixed freely with the people'—which had been followed by a period of isolation, distrust, segregation, and suspicion, now 'blotted out' by the Governor's action.[2] The officers of the A.R.P.S. could not resist the temptation to hand Clifford a memorandum of mainly local grievances. But this still placed the land question first and foremost: 'There is no matter which is nearer the hearts of the people of this country.'[3]

Speaking at the banquet, the Rev. S. R. B. Attoh Ahuma, now Secretary, took care to deny accusations that the Society existed for the sole purpose of opposing all legislative measures, that its members were influenced by 'a morbid love of cheap notoriety', or that it was 'engineered by a band of

[1] Letter of 20 Mar. 1912, from Provincial Commissioner, Cape Coast, to Colonial Secretary; S.N.A. No. 25/1922, G.N. Archives.

[2] Casely Hayford was proposing the toast of 'Our Distinguished Guest'; *The Truth about the West African Land Question* (London, 1913), app. B. 3. Three years earlier Mensah Sarbah had quoted the last of the Judicial Assessors as saying: 'one who treats these Natives with consideration and, as far as possible, with respect for the beliefs, law, and customs which are theirs . . . soon finds that he gains an influence among them which nothing else will bring him. Instead of starting a steam-engine and smashing the cart, get into the cart and ride with the Native driver.' J. Marshall, quoted by J. Mensah Sarbah, 'Maclean and Gold Coast Judicial Assessors', in *Journal of the African Society* (London, 1910), pp. 355–6.

[3] Memorandum of 16 May 1913, from A.R.P.S. to Clifford; Casely Hayford, *The . . . Land Question*, app. B. 2.

educated men'. He stressed their positive aims, especially the preservation of native traditions and the development of unity among the Chiefs; and he maintained that the Society was an essential aid to the Administration, so long as officials were unfamiliar with the 'idiosyncrasies, customs, laws, habits and modes of thought peculiar to the natives', and ignorant of what it meant to 'think black', as Mary Kingsley had put it. The Society had always stood for 'combination of the scattered interests and the unity of our natural Rulers'. Finally, he expressed the hope that the Governor would be sufficiently impressed by the capabilities of the A.R.P.S. to make it 'the authorised channel for the practical realisation of that frank co-operation which he seeks'.[1]

This hope was not to be realized. J. W. de Graft Johnson later complained that the atmosphere created by the banquet was transient, and that during Clifford's administration the gap between the Society and the Government tended increasingly to widen.[2] This was perhaps inevitable, since the new Governor was mainly preoccupied with the social and economic developments arising from the expansion of the cocoa industry, and with the need to make corresponding adjustments in the machinery of government, rather than with assisting the Chiefs to preserve their rights and privileges unimpaired under modern conditions, or giving free rein to the electoral ambitions of the educated *élite*. Possibly in self-defence, the A.R.P.S. leaders about this time began to acquire their habit of nostalgia, which was to prove a handicap to effective action in the years to come. On 20 August 1914, for example, *The Gold Coast Nation* published an editorial on the '17th Anniversary of a Great Political Success', and looked comfortingly back to the time when 'as soon as our lands were touched . . . the whole nation for the first time tasted of the sweetness of Unity'.

The Society seemed somewhat ineffective to most educated Africans outside Cape Coast. The Axim branch had ceased to function some years previously[3] (although S. R. Wood still remained the nominal Secretary), that in Sekondi had only a theoretical existence, and in Accra jealousy of the Cape Coast officers had for many years prevented the formation of a section. In 1911 a European business man in Accra had suggested the creation of a Gold Coast Auxiliary of the Anti-Slavery and Aborigines' Protection Society of London, and several Africans welcomed this move, until they realized that the Auxiliary would not deal with political matters, and withdrew their support. The Gold Coast Native Institutions Conservation Society was then formed in Accra, and was said to co-operate with the A.R.P.S. at Cape Coast.[4]

---

[1] *The . . . Land Question*, app. B. 3.

[2] *Towards Nationhood* (1928), p. 67.

[3] Letter of 20 Mar. 1912, from Provincial Commissioner, Cape Coast, to Colonial Secretary; S.N.A. No. 25/1922, G.N. Archives.

[4] *W.A.L.C. Evidence*; Dr. B. W. Quartey-Papafio, replies to questions 839–44, and Governor J. J. Thorburn, 1,588–9.

Eventually, towards the end of 1912, an Accra section of the Society was set up, with C. J. Bannerman as President;[1] but this never flourished and had little contact with Cape Coast.[2]

The Society in fact only existed in Cape Coast, where it was firmly in the hands of the same rather elderly officers, with their backward-looking tendency to rest on the laurels of the successful Lands deputation.[3] In August 1914 a so-called 'minor conference' elected T. F. E. Jones as President, together with several new officers; but all were Cape Coast men, steeped in the old tradition.[4] To some extent these leaders realized that they were not universally appreciated. Their own newspaper stated: 'The notion seems prevalent that the Society is limited as to its membership and its operations are restricted to the efforts of a few individuals who hold the monopoly of service to the country'. And it then went on to invite 'all the natives of the country, Ashanti and the Northern Territories' to join, with a special appeal to the young, to all foreigners, and to the Churches of every denomination.[5]

But the response was not encouraging. The Cape Coast organization did not regard itself as one of a possibly increasing number of branches, but as the 'parent Society', with whom naturally and constitutionally rested the initiative.[6] Although the general executive committee theoretically included the Presidents of all local sections, in practice the Cape Coast leaders took decisions in the name of the A.R.P.S. as a whole. They seem to have failed to realize that unless the Accra, Sekondi, Axim, and other sections were represented on the main executive, the Society would not retain a national significance. While the A.R.P.S. was in this parlous condition, two controversial Bills relating to palm produce were brought forward by the Government; the opposition that the Society could rally had only a fraction of its former weight. The Palm Oil and Palm Kernels Ordinances were far more damaging to the economic interests of the country than anything in either the

---

[1] S.N.A. 445, Case 4/1913, G.N. Archives.

[2] J. P. Brown subsequently complained that the Accra section of the A.R.P.S. had been 'a little lukewarm and backward in its working', and that although T. Hutton Mills was supposed to be a member, he did not consult the parent Society. *The Gold Coast Nation*, 8 Apr. 1915.

[3] As J. B. Danquah later put it: 'the Aborigines' Society had nearly spent itself in the effort of "protecting" an empty sanctuary or guard-room of "rights" which were not there to protect'. Introduction to M. J. Sampson, *Gold Coast Men of Affairs* (London, 1937).

[4] The full list was:

President . . .	T. F. E. Jones	Linguists . .	C. J. Bartels and J. A. Wilson
Senior Vice-President.	J. E. Biney	Secretary . .	W. S. Johnston
Vice-President .	W. Coleman	Press Manager .	Rev. F. A. Pinanko
V.-P. and Treasurer .	J. D. Abraham	Editor of *The Nation*	C. E. Graves
Financial Secretary .	G. Amissah		

The Gold Coast Nation, 6–13 Aug. 1914.

[5] Ibid. 3 Sept. 1914.

[6] Contrast this unworkable concept with Casely Hayford's technique (p. 399, below) whereby the National Congress was to meet in each of the four colonies, so that organizationally it should be as West African as possible.

well-intentioned lands or forests legislation; but they were defeated by economic circumstances, not by the A.R.P.S., nor even by more influential critics in England.[1]

In fact, the Society had lost, and was never to recapture, the political initiative in the Gold Coast. Their main trouble arose not so much from lack of government recognition—which has never proved a serious handicap to nationalist leaders—nor from any lack of interest in constitutional development, the main internal political issue during these years, but largely from their inability to adapt the leisurely, parochial techniques of nineteenth-century Cape Coast politics to the more militant outlook and wider horizons of the twentieth century.

The Idea of West African Unity

Although there was genuine respect for the achievements of the A.R.P.S., and their 1898 success remained an important historical landmark for all future leaders, more modern forms of nationalist association were bound to arise. These derived some impetus from the ideas of self-determination that gained international currency towards the end of the First World War, and from a growing racial consciousness. More important, the emergence of a national movement no longer depended upon the voluntary consent of a handful of independent rulers, but was being accelerated by increasing political and economic interdependence; while the new political leaders were drawn largely from the educated younger generation. To some extent, therefore, conflict with the Chiefs was inevitable, especially where the politicians had no traditional standing. This first came to a head in the post-war period; but the struggle was neither so serious nor so prolonged in later years, largely because political aspirations were temporarily directed beyond the boundaries of the Gold Coast to the ideal of a united West Africa.

The concept of a West African nationality preceded the ideal of Gold Coast nationhood as an active political force. This can be partially explained by the obvious disparity between the three regional units so recently grouped together under the Gold Coast Government. More important was the fact that educated West Africans from the various British territories had more in common with one another than with the illiterate peasants of their own countries. Education was apt to breach tribal barriers; but it was also likely to establish a community of interest, stretching beyond the new and artificial colonial boundaries, between Africans in neighbouring territories. Another important aspect was the growing 'African' consciousness of the 1920's, which began to encourage the expression of national sentiment in terms of race and colour.

'British West Africa' was itself an artificial concept: but *rapport* with

---

[1] See Ch. I, pp. 46–47 and 53–55, above.

neighbouring French West Africans, though it might even then have been politically and psychologically feasible, was practically ruled out by the barriers of language, education, and different political systems. These were the very factors which facilitated contact between the politically conscious minorities in Nigeria, the Gold Coast, and Sierra Leone. Other predisposing factors were the relative ease of east–west coastal communications, compared to the difficulties of travelling inland, the established habit of crossing colonial boundaries in search of education or employment, and the intermarriage of several educated families in the various British territories.

J. E. Casely Hayford, for example, who supplied the inspiration for a united West African movement, was the first to see that a sense of unity could be most readily awakened by an appeal to race or colour, and fostered by the growing consciousness of political disabilities under colonial rule, regardless of territorial divisions.[1] Thus he wrote in 1913:

> One touch of nature has made all West Africa kin. The common danger to our ancestral lands has made us one—one in danger, one in safety. United we stand divided we fall . . .
>
> United West Africa . . . shall take her true part among the nations of the earth.[2]

This was the dream behind the formation of the National Congress of British West Africa. Although there was never any question of mass support, for in fact it was little broader-based politically than the A.R.P.S., yet it was more of a 'national movement' than the Society had ever been, in that its political horizons were wider and that it was working towards a fundamental change in the colonial relationship.

A conference of leading men from the four British West African colonies was probably first suggested during 1914.[3] Casely Hayford talked the plan over with Dr. R. A. Savage of Nigeria, who was then editing *The Gold Coast Leader*, and they asked F. W. Dove, a barrister friend in Freetown, to discuss the matter with influential people there, including the editor of *The Sierra Leone Weekly News*. But they thought it unwise to press the idea of such a conference before the war ended.[4] It might have been expected that any fresh initiative would be taken through the A.R.P.S. In fact, Casely Hayford fell out with the Society as soon as he suggested united West African action. Why was this? And why did he find it necessary to form a completely new organization?

[1] Like his two elder brothers, Casely Hayford had received some of his education in Freetown; and his second wife was the sister of the Sierra Leonean judge, Frans Smith.

[2] Casely Hayford, *The . . . Land Question*, pp. 99 and 112.

[3] Early the next year the idea was already being criticized, e.g. in *The Gold Coast Nation*, 11 Feb. 1915: 'I fail to see the utility of politicians of the different West African Colonies meeting together to discuss questions which . . . do not affect the same common ground as regards interests, conditions, and systems of administration . . . At present it seems to me a remote possibility.'

[4] It would appear that these contacts arose from an earlier project for 'associated press action in the British West African Colonies', suggested by J. P. Herbert Brown, the proprietor of *The Gold Coast Leader*. Personal communication from W. S. Kwesi Johnston of Cape Coast. Casely Hayford later took over the editorship of *The Leader*, after Savage had returned to Nigeria.

The answer lay partly in the structure of the A.R.P.S. itself, and partly in personal rivalries.

Casely Hayford's first brush with the A.R.P.S. hierarchy came as soon as the war started. With the help of Savage he initiated the Sekondi Gold Coast Imperial War Fund, which had an immediate success. The Governor set the seal on its respectability by agreeing to act as patron and making a personal donation. By December 1914 over £3,700 had been forwarded to London. But the leaders of the Society in Cape Coast were outraged because the idea had not been referred to them first—more especially as they had taken the lead in 1900 by contributing £100 to the South African War Relief Fund.[1]

Determined not to be outdone this time, the A.R.P.S. launched their own fund, 'to demonstrate in a practical form their gratitude and loyalty to His Majesty's Government'; they appealed especially to the Natural Rulers not to be persuaded into subscribing to any scheme other than the one organized by the Society, 'through whom they have always expressed their national will and desire'. Theirs was to be a fund for the aboriginal inhabitants only; Casely Hayford was attacked for collaborating too much with Europeans, and for claiming to have promoted the scheme from an imperial point of view (although that word itself had not yet become a term of political abuse). They argued that charity began at home, 'and before you can effectively think imperially you need to be conscious of nationhood as an essential component of imperialism'.[2]

This sounded effective enough. But nothing could have been further from the minds of the A.R.P.S. than a conscious drive towards nationhood, although it might have provided them with a useful counter to Casely Hayford's wider ambitions. The collection of money was organized on the same lines as that for the Forest Bill deputation, certain sums being apportioned to each Chief. Despite strenuous efforts at Cape Coast, only £600 had been collected in this fashion by March 1915. But where Casely Hayford had succeeded, the Society was determined to do likewise. Three months later £1,500 had been raised for an aeroplane to be called after the Society; and after a further two years that sum had been doubled.[3] (It is worthy of note that during the war eleven aeroplanes all told were presented to the British Government by the people of the Gold Coast.[4])

It was against this background of jealousy and recrimination that Casely Hayford was formulating his own plans for a conference. Meanwhile, the idea of West African unity was gaining ground. The inclusion of a representative from India at the Imperial War Conference prompted queries from Gold Coast newspapers, 'Why not West Africa as well?'[5] *The Gold Coast*

---

[1] Dispatch No. 16 of 8 Jan. 1900, from Hodgson to Chamberlain; CO/96/358.
[2] *The Gold Coast Nation*, 19 Nov. 1914.
[3] Ibid. 12 Aug. 1915, and 28 July 1917.
[4] Clifford, *Legislative Council Debates*, 28 Oct. 1918.
[5] This suggestion was not without influential official support. In 1922 Sir Frederick Lugard,

Leader in 1917 recalled the separate deputations sent to London from the Gold Coast and Nigeria some five years earlier, which might have made common cause. Now, it claimed, West Africa could be as easily represented as India or any of the Dominions.[1] *West Africa* publicly doubted the possibility, owing to the number of races, and the difficulty of choosing any one man to represent the whole 'country'.[2] But these doubts culminated in a challenge from the London editor 'to prove us mistaken, by letting the British public see and know that West Africa has public men' who would command the support of the great bulk of the people.[3] Such articles were closely followed by Gold Coast leaders—and leader-writers.

Nana Ofori Atta, the powerful paramount Chief of Akim Abuakwa, was thinking along similar lines. In 1917 he suggested to T. Hutton Mills the desirability of initiating some movement to voice the needs and grievances of West Africa. To this end he proposed that major conferences should be held at various centres, and that their conclusions should be embodied in a memorandum by a central committee. Hutton Mills was asked to confer privately with the leading members of the Accra community; but he had his own doubts concerning the feasibility of 'this colossal racial movement', and felt that the A.R.P.S. executive was a suitable body to formulate a plan of procedure. Nana Ofori Atta agreed about the difficulty, but suggested that the first task was to organize firm support in the Gold Coast, after which means could be devised to get into touch with people elsewhere, by 'the instrumentality of "pen" '[4].

Casely Hayford was still hoping to carry the A.R.P.S. with him. In May 1918, when the Society met in conference at Cape Coast, he and E. J. P. Brown were asked to prepare a petition for elective representation, and their draft was approved; but serious disagreement arose over the procedure to be followed. Casely Hayford wanted all the British West African colonies to be associated with it, arguing that to make common cause would carry greater weight; in 1898, and again in 1912, they had 'gone singly and failed'.[5] He took the opportunity to press hard for a Pan-West-African Conference. But the A.R.P.S. cherished the memory of their 1898 success concerning the lands, and their reception by the Secretary of State in 1912; the Cape Coast leaders were by no means convinced that the advantages to be gained from a hypothetical West African movement would outweigh the loss of their historical prestige and personal influence. In the year of the Society's 21st anniversary, they wanted to continue to make political representations in their own time

a former Governor-General of Nigeria, asked 'whether the time has not yet come when the Crown colonies and protectorates may justly demand some representation on Imperial Conferences'. *The Dual Mandate*, p. 191.

[1] Quoted in *West Africa*, 29 Sept. 1917.
[2] Ibid. 2 June 1917.   [3] Ibid. 29 Sept. 1917.
[4] *The Gold Coast Independent*, 30 Apr. 1921.
[5] Casely Hayford, *Legislative Council Debates*, 25 Apr. 1921.

and way. As a result, the petition remained on the shelf, no doubt in a place of honour.

The Gold Coast Nation,[1] referring to criticisms that the A.R.P.S. had been 'conspicuously reticent' concerning the latest proposals for a wider political movement, agreed that there was a need throughout British West Africa for major reforms in 'this hoary system of Crown Colony Government', especially the grant of the franchise. But the Society was not necessarily willing to participate in joint political action unless its own leadership was recognized. It claimed to have surmounted 'insuperable' problems of domestic bickering and jealousy, and to be 'a living aboriginal organisation to be reckoned with'. In any case it would have been difficult to persuade an association acting in the name of the Gold Coast Colony Chiefs, many jealous of their own local dignity, to accept the unknown implications of a still wider association. No decision was reached at the time, but it was clear that the Cape Coast leaders were not pleased with the steps Casely Hayford had already taken on his own initiative.

Meanwhile the new movement was gaining support outside Cape Coast, irrespective of the attitude of the A.R.P.S. One Accra newspaper considered that such a grand scheme should appeal to every patriot; Cape Coast and Sekondi each had a conference committee already, and the sooner Accra had one at work the better.[2] Another editor looked to India (via London) for encouraging political comparisons: 'As it is rightly put forward by the Editor of "West Africa" we natives in West Africa have no religious difference or that amount of illiteracy which make for disintegration as in India. Here we are all Negroes and our united front is more easily realised than that of the Indians.'[3] In September 1918 the A.R.P.S. met again at Cape Coast, mainly to consider, at considerable length, the suggestions for West African collaboration. Eventually it was resolved that the Chiefs could not take part in the proposed conference,[4] and that each of the four colonies should present a separate petition for constitutional reform, through its own Governor. Immediately after this decision, E. J. P. Brown was ridiculed and criticized in Casely Hayford's mouthpiece, *The Gold Coast Leader*, and the two became open enemies.[5]

Casely Hayford and his friends now went ahead with their own plans to organize a West African Conference. An Eastern Province section of the movement was formed, with Hutton Mills as President, and one for the Western Province, led inevitably by Casely Hayford. They abandoned the idea of

---

[1] 24–31 Aug. 1918. [2] *The Voice of the People*, 31 Aug. 1918.

[3] *The Gold Coast Independent*, 17 Aug. 1918.

[4] E. J. P. Brown, *Legislative Council Debates*, 30 Dec. 1920.

[5] There were some personal as well as political reasons for this enmity. Both men came from Abura State, but Brown apparently resented the fact that Casely Hayford ranked above him by birth in the traditional hierarchy. Personal communication from Dr. J. W. de Graft Johnson of Cape Coast.

working through the A.R.P.S., though they would still have welcomed its support. The Society never forgave them for acting in this fashion. Nana Ofori Atta, however, was still a powerful potential ally for the new movement. He was not a member of the A.R.P.S., and was thus unaffected by their jealousy and distrust of the projected Conference. Towards the end of 1918 he discussed the idea further with the promoters in Accra, and still favoured the principle of West African collaboration. But they did not consult him about their next move.

In February 1919 Dr. F. V. Nanka-Bruce wrote, on behalf of the 'Gold Coast Section of the Projected West African Conference', to ask when the Governor could receive a deputation;[1] and he enclosed a set of resolutions to be cabled not only to the Secretary of State, but through him to the Prime Minister, to President Wilson, and to each of the Allied Powers, in order that 'the voice of West Africa' might be heard at the Peace Conference. The resolutions included protests against the handing back of any African colonies to Germany, and against the return of a German government to any part of Africa. There were also requests for an effective voice for West Africans in their internal affairs, with the grant of free institutions and the franchise: for freedom from all exploitation and interference with the rights of natives to their ancestral lands: and for the abolition of the liquor traffic throughout West Africa.

Clifford asked for further information. How had the Gold Coast section been formed? What was the nature of its mandate to speak in the collective name of the Chiefs and tribal communities of the country? And how could the resolutions be forwarded in advance, if the Conference was only projected?[2] They replied that it was not necessary to have the mandate of all the Chiefs, since the educated classes were a substantial, influential, and integral part of the people of the Gold Coast.[3] The Governor met a deputation led by Hutton Mills, and the Secretary of State was informed of the resolutions received from 'a body of influential, educated natives'.[4]

Nana Ofori Atta only heard by chance afterwards about this exchange with the Governor. He sharply reminded Casely Hayford and Hutton Mills that all the Chiefs should be informed in advance if they were expected to participate in a national movement. But, according to him, they replied that it was high time that the educated natives established their position as the natural leaders of their country, and that they must be heard by the Government. Such sentiments, he later declared, 'at once cut away from them the Chiefs

---

[1] Letters of 14 and 17 Feb. 1919, from 'Secretary, Eastern Province Section of The Projected West African Conference' to Governor's Private Secretary; 'Correspondence relating to the National Congress of British West Africa', *Sessional Paper No. VII of 1919–20.*

[2] Letter of 17 Feb. 1919, from Governor's Private Secretary to Nanka-Bruce; ibid.

[3] Letter of 24 Feb. 1919, from Nanka-Bruce and Woolhouse Bannerman (Joint Secretaries) to Governor's Private Secretary; ibid.

[4] Telegram and Dispatch No. 189 of 7 Mar. 1919, from Clifford to Milner; ibid.

and the uneducated people in this Country'.[1] This was a serious tactical error, and as a result Nana Ofori Atta became an increasingly influential enemy of the Conference scheme. Casely Hayford ascribed his attitude to wounded pride; but it was the untraditional method of procedure, and its implications for chieftaincy, to which Nana Ofori Atta really took exception. At the end of 1919 he wrote to several of the Eastern Province Chiefs, criticizing not the objects of the movement but the way in which it had been brought into being. This had violated constitutional principles: 'unless the national authorities of the country are given their due place, I consider any such movement as a farce'.[2] Nana Ofori Atta later described the reaction of his own Chiefs and councillors when he received a letter about the Conference from Nanka-Bruce: 'One of the very first questions that was put to me . . . was "Who is Nanka-Bruce? Is it the name of the Gã Mantse?"'[3]

In May 1919 a final attempt was made to get the backing of the A.R.P.S. and the western Chiefs, who were again in conference at Cape Coast; but they simply reiterated their refusal to associate themselves with the other colonies of West Africa to bring about the reforms desired. They also demanded that Casely Hayford should 'satisfy' both E. J. P. Brown and the executive of the Society with substantial gifts of cash and drinks, in order to settle the strained relations between them. Casely Hayford was particularly taken to task for having written to Sierra Leone and Lagos before consulting the executive committee. *The Gold Coast Nation* later added fuel to the fire by reporting verbatim some of the plain speaking of the Chiefs: 'You must know you are *not* the King of the Gold Coast, and that if even you were, you would have your big men to consult with first.' The writer commented loftily that men with education could be very useful to their country in political movements; but this should not encourage them 'to create a following and *condemn the authority of their Natural Rulers* and thus sow seeds of the spirit at the present moment upsetting Europe, namely, Bolshevism'.[4] It was repeatedly emphasized that the Chiefs were the recognized political representatives through whom the British Government administered the affairs of the country.[5]

Meanwhile the West African Conference organizers were set on their course, and found useful support from *The Voice of the People*, which declared, 'We shall have the Conference, come what may', admitting that this would be easier if petty quarrels could be forgotten. It was false to suggest that the Chiefs and headmen were against the plan, for those who had had the objects of the new movement 'properly explained to them' had fallen in readily with the views of the educated classes, and in any case it was 'rather late in the day to be saying that a Conference is not necessary'.[6]

[1] Nana Ofori Atta, *Legislative Council Debates*, 27 Apr. 1921.
[2] Circular Letter of 31 Dec. 1919, from Nana Ofori Atta; *The Gold Coast Independent*, 26 Mar. and 23 Apr. 1921.   [3] Nana Ofori Atta, *Legislative Council Debates*, 30 Dec. 1920.
[4] *The Gold Coast Nation*, 16 Aug. 1919.
[5] Ibid. 20–27 Dec. 1919.   [6] *The Voice of the People*, 2 Dec. 1919.

The 1920 Conference and Deputation

In March 1920 six representatives from Nigeria, three from Sierra Leone, and one from the Gambia, with a Gold Coast contingent of over forty, assembled in Accra for the first West African Conference. In view of the allegations that were soon to be made concerning the unrepresentative nature of this movement, it is useful to examine the initial support from the Gold Coast. There were seventeen lawyers, in addition to a sprinkling of Chiefs, clergy, journalists, doctors, merchants, and 'independent gentlemen'—all from the Colony. Casely Hayford was at pains to analyse in public detail the extent of his support.[1] He went on to claim, significantly, that this was a movement of the intelligentsia—the educated classes of British West Africa. It would never be possible 'to dissociate the educated African from his un-educated brother (Cheers)'; but as advances were made in education, naturally he would become the leader of his people. This was a clear break with the past; previous organizations had always relied on support from the most influential Chiefs, or used them as intermediaries. Hutton Mills then developed a novel claim to leadership: since each delegate belonged to a 'Distinctive African Family', with rights of property, they were the natural leaders of the people, and had in themselves the right to appeal to His Majesty's Government for 'such constitutional reforms as in their judgement are necessary'.[2]

The Government initially welcomed the Conference as an opportunity 'to find out what was really wanted'; and Guggisberg said that he would personally have attended every meeting, if he had not been away from Accra on tour.[3] His deputy attended the opening and thought that the speeches were characterized by extreme moderation of tone. He had reservations about the representation from other colonies; but as far as the Gold Coast delegates were concerned, he had no doubt that they represented 'a fairly large body of the educated Coast natives'.[4]

Although a few interested unofficial Europeans were also present, there was no attempt to encourage them to collaborate. *The Gold Coast Leader* later asked for their sympathy, but not their participation, and denied that there was any exclusiveness in trying to secure a voice in legislation for 'ourselves'

[1] Casely Hayford named the leading figures present from each part of the Colony, as follows. *Accra*: the Gã Mantse, and the officers of the local section of the A.R.P.S., including C. J. Bannerman, T. Hutton Mills, and the James Town Mantse. *Axim*: S. R. Wood (who brought a resolution from the Chiefs and people of Apollonia in which they declared themselves 'fully convinced that the time is ripe for a United West Africa'), a representative of the Chief of Atuabo, and W. G. Essien. *Cape Coast*: H. Van Hien, Prince Atta Amonu, W. Ward Brew, and W. E. G. Sekyi. *Western and Central Provinces*: a few Chiefs from Lower Wassaw, Shama, Saltpond, and Winneba, although not present, were represented on local Conference committees. *The Gold Coast Leader*, 30 Oct. 1920, claimed that many other Chiefs favoured the new movement, but were deterred from open support because of the attitude of the current office-holders of the A.R.P.S. at Cape Coast.   [2] *Sessional Paper No. VII of 1919–20.*

[3] Guggisberg, *Legislative Council Debates*, 27 Apr. 1921.

[4] Dispatch No. 289 of 9 Apr. 1920, from Harper to Milner; *Sessional Paper No. VII of 1919–20.*

in 'our own country'.[1] But the following year Casely Hayford appeared more sensitive to criticism on this count, and protested that they had been appealing for the representation of the whole community, European as well as African. He thought that those who provided the capital of the country should 'have their place in any scheme of electoral representation'.[2]

A great deal of preparatory work had been done before the Conference met. On the first day the members proceeded to appoint officers, and these included the following Gold Coast figures:[3]

President	T. Hutton Mills
Vice-President . . .	J. E. Casely Hayford
Joint Secretaries[4] . .	Dr. F. V. Nanka-Bruce
	L. E. V. M'Carthy (from Sierra Leone)
Joint Treasurers . . .	A. B. Quartey-Papafio
	H. Van Hien

Five additional Vice-Presidents were appointed, giving some voice to the other West African colonies. The main aims of the movement were publicly summarized by Casely Hayford. These included 'the better and more effective representation of our people', a clear distinction between the functions of the executive and the judiciary, 'equal opportunities for all without consideration of creed or colour', and, of course, control of the land: 'we . . . like to feel that, on one spot of the earth at least, the black man can claim the land as his own absolutely'. Such matters required publicity,

to let the Government know plainly and fully what is passing in the mind of the African. We do not believe in subterranean grumblings. We believe in open explanation of our wants, because our experience teaches us that when these wants are fairly placed before the executive, generally they are attended to, if not today, the next day or the day after. We desire further, as the intelligentsia of British West Africa, to promote unity among our people.[5]

The session lasted for over two weeks, and eleven major subjects were discussed, each introduced by a different speaker, as follows:

From the Gold Coast:

J. E. Casely Hayford	Legislative (including municipal) reforms and granting of the franchise
W. E. G. Sekyi	Education, with particular reference to a West African university
A. Sawyerr	Judicial reforms

---

[1] *The Gold Coast Leader*, 30 Oct. 1920.

[2] Casely Hayford, *Legislative Council Debates*, 25 Apr. 1921.

[3] *West Africa*, 3 Apr. 1920, commented: 'It is the beginning of a new era . . . The first West African Conference has commenced well. The two greatest Africans in the Gold Coast are to lead it.'

[4] Soon after the Conference, S. R. Wood of Axim took over the office of Secretary.

[5] *Sessional Paper No. VII of 1919–20*.

Dr. F. V. Nanka-Bruce	West African press union
H. Van Hien	The inauguration of the Congress of Africans of British West Africa
Prince Atta Amonu	Representation of West African views

Sierra Leone:

F. V. Dove	Alien problems
L. E. V. M'Carthy	Commercial enterprise
Dr. H. C. Bankole-Bright	Sanitary and medical reforms

Nigeria:

Patriarch J. G. Campbell	The policy of the Government in relation to the land question

Gambia:

E. F. Small	The right of the people to self-determination

At the close the Conference resolved itself into a permanent National Congress of British West Africa,[1] to be composed of the several committees already established; its headquarters would be in Sekondi—the home of Casely Hayford at that time—and the next session would be held in Sierra Leone. The number of resolutions passed reached the remarkable total of eighty-three. First, and foremost, these put forward requests for constitutional reforms, both in central and local government. It was resolved that half the members of the Legislative Council should be elected, and half nominated. The Executive Council should remain as it was; but a new House of Assembly, with special financial powers, should be created. This should consist of all the members of the Legislative Council, together with six other elected representatives; there would thus be an elected majority for controlling finance. The methods of election were left somewhat vague; they were to be held through 'such local groups as may be found most convenient and expedient'. But where indigenous institutions did not provide a ready means of ascertaining the will of the people, property or educational qualifications would be necessary. For municipal affairs, corporations with full powers of local self-government were to be established in each principal town.

The following extracts give the gist of the many other resolutions:[2]

University education: 'the time has come to found a British West African University on such lines as would preserve in the student a sense of African Nationality'.

The Syrian question: the Colonial Office should be asked to consider whether the Syrians were 'undesirables and a menace to the good Government of the land' and consequently should be repatriated from the West African colonies.

[1] The resolutions embodying this decision were originally headed 'The Inauguration of the Congress of Africans of British West Africa'; but later the term 'Africans' seems to have been quietly dropped.

[2] It seems probable that many of these resolutions had been drafted in advance by the Gold Coast organizers; but they were carefully discussed during the Conference. For the full text, see *Resolutions of the Conference of Africans of British West Africa* (London, 1920).

Economic development: 'the natural resources of the British West African Dependencies are not for the exploitation of Concessionaires under State control.
. . . the time has come for . . . the formation of a Corporation, to be known as
the British West African Co-operative Association . . . to found Banks, promote
shipping facilities, establish Co-operative Stores, and produce buying centres, in
such wise as to inspire and maintain a British West African National Economical
development.'

Judicial reforms: 'the time has come to open definitely to African practitioners of
experience all Judicial appointments . . . experienced Judges outside the British
West African Judiciary might be appointed to form an Appellate Court for British
West Africa.'

The Press: a committee of experienced journalists should be appointed to
investigate the best means of promoting greater co-operation in the British West
African Press; the Congress should publish its own quarterly magazine.[1]

Medical reforms: 'this Conference views with marked disfavour the Trades Union
spirit of the West African Medical Staffs, which attempts to exclude qualified
African citizens of British West Africa from entering the Medical Service in their
country.' In future more attention should be paid by the sanitary authorities to the
improvement of the general conditions of the community than to the 'fanciful
theory' of European segregation in cantonments.[2]

Land: 'the principle of Trusteeship with respect to the lands of the people of
British West Africa by Government has been overdone . . . the average British
West African is quite capable of controlling and looking after his own interests in
the land.'

Self-determination: 'the Conference views with alarm the right assumed by the
European powers to exchanging or partitioning Countries between them, without
reference to, or regard for, the wishes of the people, and records the opinion that
such a course is tantamount to a species of slavery.' They condemned specifically
the partitioning of Togoland and the handing over of the Cameroons.

President Wilson's doctrine of self-determination, as J. B. Danquah has
recalled, was being 'pronounced from high places and from low in the chancelleries of the world powers'.[3] It raised immediate echoes in West Africa,
and was quickly adopted and adapted by the Conference organizers. Casely
Hayford wrote just after the war: 'To-day entire West Africa has clasped
hands over . . . a common constitutional demand . . . She is asking for

---

[1] But the projected *British African National Review*, which was to have been edited by Casely
Hayford, never appeared.

[2] In 1912 a conference of Principal Medical Officers of all the British West African colonies
had laid down certain rules to safeguard the health of Euopeans, including absolute segregation
in new towns and quarters, and the gradual evacuation of 'residential premises' in existing 'native
areas'. But these were never enforced in the Gold Coast, since Clifford considered they could
'work untold mischief' in breaking the close associations of missionaries and merchants with the
people, and also because he considered that the health of Europeans was not the first priority for
the Government. *Legislative Council Debates*, 28 Oct. 1918.

[3] J. B. Danquah's Introduction to Sampson's *Gold Coast Men of Affairs*, p. 27.

self-determination'.[1] Danquah has emphasized that the Conference did not make any 'fatuous demand' for the Gold Coast to be declared an independent nation.[2] The 1920 resolutions placed on record their 'unfeigned loyalty and devotion' to the King-Emperor, and promised to preserve 'strictly and inviolate' the connexion of the West African dependencies with the British Empire. The main point of this, however, was 'to preserve unreservedly all and every right of free citizenship of the Empire and the fundamental principle that taxation goes with effective representation'.[3]

The aim of self-determination no doubt seemed vague and idealistic from the more sophisticated London viewpoint of *West Africa*, which later[4] commented that the inaugural Conference had taken place under conditions unfavourable to reasoned consideration, and that the whole political atmosphere had been unreal, 'thanks to the injurious influence of that misleading phrase, "self-determination".'[5] But Casely Hayford and his friends saw in it a new hope for West Africa, as well as a suitable and most specific title for a group of their resolutions.[6]

The local Government was still mildly sympathetic. The Secretary of State was informed that the main objects of the Conference were a reform of the Legislative Councils on some electoral basis, and the throwing open of higher administrative posts to natives.[7] When Guggisberg saw the full text of the resolutions he did not consider them very revolutionary, and afterwards declared that there was scarcely one concerning which he had not previously invited the co-operation of the African members of the Legislative Council and other leading citizens.[8] The Bishop of Accra, for his part, declared the movement deserving of the greatest respect, and its resolutions wise and prudent.[9] *West Africa* described the Congress as 'evidently modelled to some extent upon the lines of the National Congress in India'.[10] But the Government was not prepared for the speedy—and in official eyes unconstitutional—action which followed.

The technique of the deputation was by now an established West African convention. This was the immediate resort of the Congress; the inaugural Conference resolved that representatives from each colony should be sent to London to take legal advice on the best method to secure the franchise and

---

[1] J. E. Casely Hayford, *United West Africa* (London, 1919), pp. 43–44.
[2] Danquah, loc. cit.   [3] *Sessional Paper No. VII of 1919–20.*
[4] 31 Mar. 1923.
[5] One writer had even complained: 'It will raise hopes which can never be realised . . . What a calamity that the phrase was ever uttered!' R. Lansing, *The Peace Negotiations: A Personal Narrative* (London, 1921).
[6] The A.R.P.S., if they were concerned with the principle at all, applied it to themselves rather than to the Ewes, in 'praying for the annexation of Togoland to the Gold Coast'. *The Gold Coast Nation*, 28 June 1919.
[7] Dispatch No. 289 of 9 Apr. 1920, from Harper to Milner; *Sessional Paper No. VII of 1919–20.*
[8] *Legislative Council Debates*, 27 Apr. 1921.
[9] Letter of 20 Sept. 1920, from the Rt. Rev. M. S. O'Rorke (in England) to Wood; *The Gold Coast Independent*, 18–25 Dec. 1920.   [10] 25 Sept. 1920.

the other reforms advocated, and that no time should be lost in preparing their case.[1] A special fund was immediately opened for the expenses; in addition, it was decided to launch an appeal for a Congress inaugural fund of £100,000. This proved to be a wildly optimistic figure, although Hutton Mills gave a 1,000 guineas.

The deputation did not wait for all the necessary funds to be subscribed. The leaders managed to assemble a small group who were able to contribute to the cost of their passage and residence, or who wished to visit London for personal reasons.[2] The representation fell below their initial hopes, especially from Nigeria;[3] but by September 1920 the following West Africans were in London:

Nigeria: Chief Oluwa of Lagos, J. Egerton Shyngle.
Gold Coast: T. Hutton Mills, H. Van Hien, J. E. Casely Hayford.
Sierra Leone: Dr. H. C. Bankole-Bright, F. W. Dove.
Gambia: E. F. Small, H. N. Jones.

Bankole-Bright was appointed Secretary; and only at this stage did they inform Guggisberg of their intention to approach the Secretary of State direct. Printed copies of the Conference resolutions were sent to the Gold Coast, to enable the Governor to consider the proposed memorial fairly and impartially.[4]

The members of the deputation took what opportunity they could to canvass their case in London. They seemed to attach considerable importance to a meeting with the League of Nations Union, under the chairmanship of Professor Gilbert Murray; possibly they were under a misapprehension as to the relationship of the L.N.U. to the League itself. Casely Hayford took great care to establish their credentials and explain their resolutions. Hutton Mills appealed to that section of the Covenant according to which members of the League of Nations undertook to secure just treatment of the native inhabitants of territories under their control. The officers of the L.N.U. questioned

[1] *Sessional Paper No. VII of 1919–20.*

[2] It would appear that several of the members of the deputation had heavy commitments in the cocoa market and were anxious to get to London as soon as possible owing to the onset of the slump of 1920–1. This would account for the haste with which they left. Personal communication from W. S. Kwesi Johnston of Cape Coast. Their 'rush' tactics were criticized by *West Africa*, 11 Dec. 1920. It is interesting to notice that Dr. F. V. Nanka-Bruce, another leading Congress figure in Accra, described himself at this time as 'a planter and shipper of cocoa'. Nanka-Bruce *v.* The Commonwealth Trust Limited, in *Judgments of the Judicial Committee of the Privy Council on Appeal from the Gold Coast Colony, 1874–June, 1928* (Accra, 1929), pp. 85 ff.

[3] Protests were made by some Nigerians who objected not to the Congress aims and objects—which had their 'hearty and unalloyed support and sympathy'—but to the methods adopted to represent Nigeria; e.g. Letter of 5 Sept. 1920, from Dr. Obassa to Hutton Mills. 'Further Correspondence relating to the National Congress of British West Africa . . .', *Sessional Paper No. X of 1920–21.*

[4] Letter of 21 Sept. 1920, from Bankole-Bright to Colonial Secretary, Gold Coast; *Sessional Paper No. VII of 1919–20.*

the deputation closely, but that was all.[1] During their stay in London, contacts were also made with the *Bureau International pour la Défense des Indigènes*, the Welfare Committee for Africans in Europe, West African students, and various interested Members of Parliament.

The deputation soon got down to their main business, by addressing a petition to the King, asking primarily for constitutional and electoral reforms, in addition to the other matters mentioned in their resolutions. This was accompanied by a voluminous memorandum in sixty-three parts; other supporting documents included not only the Conference resolutions but all the inaugural speeches.[2] Many trivial details were interwoven with important demands and the discussion of fundamental principles. The petitioners even reproduced the formal acknowledgements returned by the West African Governors to the Conference greetings, thus naïvely—or perhaps disingenuously—suggesting that they had received official recognition.[3] But they did not send copies of these documents to the Gold Coast Government until nearly a fortnight later.

Guggisberg was annoyed by the repeated failure to keep him informed in advance. In particular, he felt that it was most unreasonable to put to him 'certain extraordinarily important points' referring to three other colonies with which he had nothing to do. He claimed that he was unable to take any official notice of the resolutions, although had they come 'in the orthodox manner' from the citizens of the Gold Coast, he would have given them every consideration in his power.[4] It seems unfortunate for the deputation that they should have fallen foul of a progressive and sympathetic Governor on this technical point. There was no particular reason why their political ambitions should have fitted into pre-existing administrative compartments; in fact, they must have realized that no individual Governor could deal fully with their memorial, so London would have appeared to be its logical first destination,[5] and the requirements of courtesy to be met by their letter to Accra. But they failed to appreciate the difficulties that would be caused by offended official susceptibilities.

The petition claimed that the Congress represented 'the intelligentsia and the advanced thought' of British West Africa and that it stood for the funda-

---

[1] *Report of the Proceedings of a Meeting held in London between the League of Nations Union and the Delegates of the National Congress of British West Africa* (London, 1920).

[2] Petition of 19 Oct. 1920, to King George V from National Congress of British West Africa; *Sessional Paper No. VII of 1919-20*.

[3] This was criticized in *West Africa*, 12 Feb. 1921. Clifford, in Nigeria, later maintained that his personally friendly reply had been completely misinterpreted.

[4] Guggisberg, *Legislative Council Debates*, 27 Apr. 1921.

[5] Casely Hayford offered a defence on these lines: 'If you ask for a modification on some such basis as Sir Hugh Clifford's enlarged Council, that certainly is a scheme that may be considered locally, but when you are asking for a majority and also asking for a voice in the executive, that is a proposition beyond this Government.' Ibid. His reference to 'asking for a voice in the executive' seems a curious slip.

mental principles 'that have always actuated communities that have arrived at the stage of national consciousness'. Furthermore, it also claimed to represent the bulk of the indigenous inhabitants, 'as sons of the soil', with the inherent right to submit complaints and propose reforms. In answer to the expected argument that they were not united and that there were too many factions and feuds for election purposes, the petition recalled that unfriendly Chiefs had often met on common ground for united action in the past.

The Colonial Office took a long time to consider this extensive material, mainly because they had to refer back to the four Governors for their detailed comments. *West Africa*, which had already given the visitors a sympathetic welcome,[1] now found time for further reflections, which were not quite so encouraging. The deputation could only be of importance if it had behind it 'the nation in West Africa—or rather, the several powerful and numerous smaller nations'. But there were a number of doubts on this point. In particular, no pronouncement in favour of the Congress had come from the Chiefs, 'the people's natural organs of expression'. Their only public statement appeared to have been made at a gathering of some Gold Coast Chiefs, who had come to the conclusion that at present they did not associate themselves with the Congress.[2]

West Africa appears to have misunderstood one of the objects of the Congress leaders, and to have misrepresented their claims by stating that they had come to London to seek self-government.[3] It is probably true that Casely Hayford's personal dreams went beyond the immediate aims of the deputation. At the inaugural Conference he had said of Crown Colony government: 'It is my sincere hope that in the enlightened year 1920, it will be found possible to do away with this archaic system.'[4] But no such demand appeared in their resolutions, or their petition; and unfortunately they gave little or no further public explanation of their case. It would seem that in private conversation someone had unwittingly given the impression that their proposals for a new House of Assembly, with powers of financial review, meant full self-government. But later they informed Reuters that the Congress had never, directly or indirectly, asked for complete self-government; on the contrary, they did not even seek to disturb the existing Executive Councils.[5]

Probably their disclaimer was a matter of immediate tactics rather than long-term ambitions; but in any case the *canard* took a long time to die. Two years later *The Gold Coast Independent*[6] still thought it necessary to deny that elective representation meant 'self-government, in which ministers carry portfolios and control the administration through a Cabinet and Prime Minister!' The idea was dismissed as remote, 'the vague fancy of an alarmist or a scarecrow'. This passage was set in somewhat bewildering juxtaposition to their

[1] *West Africa*, 25 Sept. 1920.   [2] Ibid. 11 Dec. 1920.
[3] Ibid. 6 Nov. and 11 Dec. 1920.   [4] *Sessional Paper No. VII of 1919–20*.
[5] *West Africa*, 22 Jan. and 5 Feb. 1921.   [6] 3 Feb. 1923.

newly stated ideal of British West Africa as a partner in the British Commonwealth of Nations, free to enjoy the liberties and privileges of the self-governing Dominions.[1] But they were now careful to point out that 'as *trustee nation*
to guide and direct the destinies of Africans of British West Africa there is
none to equal the British Government'.

Nana Ofori Atta versus the National Congress

As soon as the Congress deputation had left for London, Nana Ofori Atta
had decided to rally the Chiefs in opposition. In the Eastern Province he
wrote confidentially to several Chiefs, suggesting that the educated men were
usurping their rights, and that they should protect themselves. He received
several assurances of support, although his correspondents appeared to know
little about the Congress.[2] To reach the Central and Western Provinces, he
simply sent a letter to the A.R.P.S. at Cape Coast. J. E. Biney, the President,
replied emphatically that the executive, holding full authority from the
Natural Rulers, were in complete agreement that 'an exposure of the fraud
should no longer be delayed'.[3] Nana Ofori Atta was sufficiently encouraged
to launch a devastating attack on the claims of the Congress leaders in the
Legislative Council in December 1920.

This speech is worthy of detailed study as a frank exposition of the fears
and suspicions of the Chiefs. Nana Ofori Atta claimed to speak on their
behalf, as natural and legitimate custodians of the institutions and customs of
the country. They were determined to see that their own system of government should not be superseded by any other, nor disturbed in any way or
form. Furthermore, they would actively resist any attempt to usurp their
exclusive 'rights, privileges and prerogatives' in matters affecting the interests
of the country and its relationship with the British Government. He declared:

I stand here to ask who these individuals are who say that they represent the Gold
Coast . . . ?
. . . the Colony is not of one entire Native State, and it is not ruled by one Native
Potentate.

[1] Casely Hayford later stated explicitly that the aim of British West Africa was eventually to
achieve Dominion status, though this would 'necessarily take time'. Presidential address to second
session of Congress at Freetown, Jan. 1923; M. J. Sampson (ed.), *West African Leadership*
(Ilfracombe, 1950), ch. iii.

[2] Some of the replies were later published in *The Gold Coast Independent*, 23 Apr. 1921. For
example: 'As matter of fact, I have not as yet read any of the papers as regards the movement
now known as the National Congress of British West Africa, and I am therefore in agreement
with you in anything . . . in your experienced sense of duty for the uplift of our country I endorse the same' (M. A. Awah II, Manche of Shai). 'Matters occurring in this country are
terrible. I am surprised that an individual youngman should have the courage to write that he
represented Akuapemman' (F. W. K. Akuffo, Omahene of Akwapim).
    Nano Ofori Atta's original letter, which must have been strongly worded, was not published,
although one Chief referred to the 'Confidential Letter No. 1244 69/20 of the 20 Sept. 1920,
asking my consent and support in your fight'.

[3] Nana Ofori Atta, *Legislative Council Debates*, 25 Apr. 1921.

On the contrary it consists of a great number of States, each with its Paramount Chief, Chiefs and Councillors and other Officers in a State of its own, absolutely independent of any other State in the Colony[1]. . .

. . . can any of them say whether they hold any authority from the Division, of which I am the elected head and the elected representative, to carry on as they have done? . . . In other words the Chiefs are a flock of sheep which can be dragged wherever these highly educated people take them . . .

Whatever may be the height of the intelligence and the sagacity in politics of the Hon. Mr. T. Hutton Mills or of the Hon. Mr. Casely Hayford, or of any other member of the Congress, they have no influence or power over my Division . . . it is the same with every other State in the Colony.

So long as a paramount Chief remained in his position, said this forceful spokesman, it must be assumed that his Chiefs and people were satisfied with him; consequently there was no excuse for any one to 'jump over his head' to discuss with outside people matters of political importance affecting his territory. They refused to relinquish their stewardship in any way, and therefore very bitterly resented the attitude taken by the Gold Coast leaders of the Congress. They claimed to be the natural, rightful, and legitimate successors of those Chiefs who had, both by written documents and by mutual consent, 'so magnificently connected this country with His Majesty's Government'; and they questioned whether the individuals composing the Congress had the legal right, without the necessary authority from these native rulers, to go before the King to demand the reconstitution of the Government. The Chiefs were not prepared to 'submerge' rights acquired by their ancestors to please any other colony not so favourably situated.

Never, Nana Ofori Atta affirmed, had so base an attempt been made to denationalize the Gold Coast, and never had a handful of people so wilfully and deliberately resolved to break to pieces so solid a structure, 'erected on a most concrete and substantial foundation', as their system of government. Even more disturbing was the fact that other people were following the example of the Congress in various parts of the country: 'The fact is that the movement sets out a dangerous precedent . . . If this is the sort of benefit to be derived by the country from our sons and relatives who are educated, then, I am afraid, the position of the Gold Coast is in great danger.' He described an incident in his own State, as an example and a warning. A Union of the

---

[1] Almost simultaneously Clifford was ridiculing in the Legislative Council of Nigeria 'the suggestion that there is, or can be in the visible future such a thing as a "West African Nation" ', or even such a thing as a Nigerian nation: 'at all events until the arrival of the Millennium'. *Governor's Address to the Nigerian Legislative Council*, 29 Dec. 1920. Similarly he had earlier spoken of the Gold Coast Colony (leaving Ashanti and the north out of account) as 'a collection of little States, each of which is self-contained and entirely independent of its neighbours, to which a measure of unity is imparted by their common allegiance to His Majesty the King'. Clifford, *Legislative Council Debates*, 28 Oct. 1918.

It is interesting that it was now the Gold Coast Chiefs, rather than the Administration, who openly attacked the concept of national unity, and denied the existence of a nation.

very small number of literate people in Akim Abuakwa had been formed, and had sent him a somewhat threatening letter, demanding that the Chiefs should support the Congress, and suggesting that the State councillors were obstructive owing to lack of education.[1] He had promptly sent for the local President, and persuaded the Scholars' Union leaders to withdraw the resolutions they had passed; his Chiefs then charged them with exceeding the rights and powers of the Union. Nana Ofori Atta went on to underline the moral of his tale. If the Chiefs of Akim Abuakwa had not held 'dear to their very hearts' the fundamental principles of their tribal constitution, this small band of people would have assumed the right to dictate to the Chiefs, simply because they were educated.[2]

Nana Ofori Atta was supported in the Legislative Council by the other three nominated Africans present. Nana Amonoo V urged that the powers of the Chiefs should be increased, and Dr. B. W. Quartey-Papafio saw no reason why the National Congress should ignore them. E. J. P. Brown was even more vigorous in his protestations: 'Whatever may be our political ideals we must learn to respect and obey our Natural Rulers.' At present, the educated section of the community was only a drop in the bucket, and they had thousands and thousands of 'unlettered people' to consider, as well as those on the coast.[3]

The full text of Nana Ofori Atta's onslaught was not published immediately in the Gold Coast, so its impact there was delayed. But Guggisberg cabled a summary to London, and this was probably the decisive factor influencing the Secretary of State. *The Gold Coast Independent* later[4] alleged that the Governor's action was timed to cause the maximum embarrassment, just when the delegation was on the edge of success, so that the very next day the tables were turned. Clifford, in Nigeria, also discredited the Congress, calling them a 'self-appointed congregation of educated African gentlemen',[5] and his opinion was bound to carry considerable weight, reinforced by his Gold Coast experience.

Early in 1921, nearly three months after the petition had been presented, the Secretary of State, Lord Milner, made it clear that he would have nothing to do with the National Congress of British West Africa. He had now been convinced that it was in no way representative of the native communities, that its claim to speak on their behalf was repudiated by the most influential voices expressing public opinion, including practically all the Chiefs in the Gold Coast, and that the scheme put forward would be 'inimical to the best

---

[1] This letter, signed by R. K. Ofosu, 'Speaker and Acting Secretary' of the Union, had just been published in *The Gold Coast Independent*, 18–25 Dec. 1920. Nana Ofori Atta later alleged that the Union had been 'got at' by Congress members. *Legislative Council Debates*, 27 Apr. 1921.
[2] Ibid. 30 Dec. 1920.
[3] Nana Amonoo V, Quartey-Papafio, and E. J. P. Brown, ibid.
[4] 23 Apr. 1921.
[5] Reported in *The Gold Coast Independent*, 29 Jan. 1921.

interests of the community'.[1] The demands for elective representation, unofficial majorities, and legal reforms were bluntly turned down, and an interview was refused.

The delegates were not so easily silenced. In a lengthy 44-point reply, they repeated their request for an interview, and re-emphasized their claims to be fully representative.[2] But the damage was done, mainly by the speech of Nana Ofori Atta. *West Africa* had published the official summary, at Guggisberg's request,[3] and the editor commented, 'The present London delegation may for practical purposes be written off.'[4] Although the Congress leaders were bitterly disappointed, they had no thought of using radically different methods in the future. Bankole-Bright publicly denounced an anonymous caller who had told him, 'You can never succeed until you allow us Bolsheviks to do the work for you'. He himself declared, 'If we have to fight year after year, we shall fight constitutionally.'[5]

Back in the Gold Coast, the newspapers were almost entirely pro-Congress, and a counter-attack was already being launched. J. T. Arkong, who edited *The Gold Coast Independent* for Nanka-Bruce, and T. Laing of *The Eastern Star & Akwapim Chronicle*, who had both attended the inaugural conference, probably had the greatest influence at this time. Backing them up was *The Voice of the People*, which had been the first in Accra to support the plans of Casely Hayford, and of course *The Gold Coast Leader*, of which he was now editor. In the other camp, the A.R.P.S. newspaper, *The Gold Coast Nation*, was in financial difficulties.

The Gold Coast Independent led the field, vigorously rebutting Clifford's references to the absence of unity and uniformity among the people of West Africa, 'which he says is not a "Nation" but fails to tell us what it is'. This newspaper cited the Indian National Congress, which had been established in a country with 220 vernacular dialects, whose people showed great diversity of race, religious belief, degree of civilization, and political and social institutions. The West African Congress leaders had been called Europeanized and detribalized;[6] but this article, referring to the Roman occupation of Britain and Norman-French cultural influences, claimed that a similar process of absorption must take place in West Africa before 'civilisation of the

---

[1] Letter of 26 Jan. 1921, from Colonial Office to Bankole-Bright; *Sessional Paper No. X of 1920–21*.

[2] Letter of 28 Jan. 1921, from Casely Hayford and Bankole-Bright to Milner; ibid.

[3] Guggisberg explained, 'That request would never have been made had the delegates confined themselves to approaching the Secretary of State but they went in for influencing public opinion in England.' *Legislative Council Debates*, 27 Apr. 1921.

[4] *West Africa*, 12 Feb. 1921. Casely Hayford criticized this weekly journal to the African Progress Union in London: 'I will tell you what must be written off, and that is this unwholesome influence. We feel that an attitude has been taken up which is not impartial.' Ibid. 26 Feb. 1921.

[5] Speech by Bankole-Bright to the African Progress Union dinner; ibid.

[6] Cf. 'Now, Sir, what has brought about all this? It is education. Education typical of foreign designs.' Nana Ofori Atta, *Legislative Council Debates*, 30 Dec. 1920.

masses' was possible. At the same time, the British were accused of deliberately neglecting the education of Chiefs, in unfavourable contrast with the French process of civilization: an educated African brought up in the Christian religion should not be forced to submit to 'the unenlightened decisions of an uneducated and illiterate fetish ruler'.[1]

As soon as Casely Hayford returned from London he wrote to a number of Chiefs, and received enough favourable replies to show that Nana Ofori Atta had given only one side of the picture—or at least, that some of the Chiefs were coming round towards the Congress movement. He received letters of support from all three Provinces of the Colony. The Omanhene of New Juaben stated that Nana Ofori Atta had had no authority from him, 'either by writing by parole or by inference to make those heinous statements against the National Congress'; the Konor of Manya Krobo said he had never discussed the objects and aims of the Congress with Nana Ofori Atta; the Omanhene of Akim-Kotoku disclaimed any knowledge of what had been said in the Legislative Council, and declared himself in sympathy with the Congress; while the Omanhene of Western Nzima emphatically repudiated 'his utterly false position' as not representing their sentiments and wishes. The views of Nana Ofori Atta were also denounced in telegrams of protest sent to the Secretary of State from both the Axim and Sekondi sections of the A.R.P.S.,[2] and from a group at Cape Coast.[3]

Casely Hayford next tried to persuade the A.R.P.S. executive to call a conference in April 1921, so that he could rally additional support for the Congress before addressing the Legislative Council. Needless to say, the office-holders at Cape Coast were in no hurry to put themselves out, and only a few Chiefs attended; so the full conference was postponed till July. His hand was strengthened, however, by an editorial in *The Gold Coast Independent*,[4] which maintained that Nana Ofori Atta's previous diatribes had been disowned by many Chiefs, and by the A.R.P.S., except E. J. P. Brown and a few 'insignificant followers'.

Armed with the letters and telegrams he had received, and fortified by the rising feeling against Nana Ofori Atta, Casely Hayford proceeded to make a vigorous personal attack in the Legislative Council at its April meeting. He assailed Nana Ofori Atta's position there, as a Chief nominated by the Government, who had no right to present even the views of his own people. Still more objectionable was the claim to speak for the Chiefs of the country; Casely Hayford quoted his own evidence to the contrary. Had Nana Ofori Atta, he asked, ventured to appear before a public meeting with his brother Chiefs to criticize the Congress? 'He knew very well that he was not supported

---

[1] *The Gold Coast Independent*, 29 Jan. 1921.

[2] *West Africa*, 30 Apr. 1921.

[3] Telegram to Secretary of State from Sekyi, Secretary of Congress Committee, 'on behalf of a meeting of Chiefs and inhabitants of Cape Coast'; quoted by Casely Hayford, *Legislative Council Debates*, 25 Apr. 1921.   [4] 23 Apr. 1921.

by the people.' Casely Hayford went on to defend the right of the educated to an independent voice in the legislature:

After all who buys the motor cars, the patent boots, the high collars, the fine shirts, who builds the fine houses? It is the educated class. We contribute largely to the taxation, and I am asking very respectfully, if we do this, have we not the right to ask that we may have a voice in the disbursement of the money that is derived from taxation?

The claim of the educated leaders, 'as sons of the soil', to represent both the intelligentsia and the bulk of the inhabitants was repeated, and Casely Hayford refuted emphatically the idea that when a man was educated and had adopted European ways he lost his identity with his people.

With some vehemence he attacked the 'very dangerous principle' implied in Nana Ofori Atta's speech 'that no body of men within his district can say or express an opinion upon a question common to the whole of the Gold Coast without his consent'. Casely Hayford countered this by suggesting that whereas private individuals had the right to express their opinions in matters of common interest to the country, the Chief, as a Chief, had not that right. The Chief did not represent himself; he was not an autocrat in his State but responsible to his community, and not even allowed to express an opinion except through his linguist. Casely Hayford wound up with increasing bitterness, alleging that Nana Ofori Atta had rendered himself liable to impeachment under customary law, for making unauthorized statements and communicating in his capacity as Chief with 'the head of a Government outside our own' upon national matters. 'I regret I cannot impeach you before this Council', he declaimed, 'But I impeach you before the bar of your own conscience, and in the silence of the night, in your beds, you and your supporters will acknowledge to yourselves that you have proved traitors to the cause of British West Africa.'[1]

Nana Ofori Atta was now on the defensive, and answered in detail most of the sallies made in the debate, without yielding an inch on the main question of 'this bosh that an ordinary native simply because he is educated becomes the natural leader of the State to which he belongs. It is a wrong doctrine; a very wrong one indeed.' He challenged the claim of the educated few to special representation, arguing that illiterates were just as much entitled to such rights, and that the educated man's conspicuous consumption—as it would be called today—was made possible by the work of the cocoa farmer. As a paramount Chief, Nana Ofori Atta emphasized that he spoke not for himself, but for his people, with whom he had discussed in advance the matters raised at the previous Legislative Council meeting. In order to comply fully with native custom, he always took a linguist and an elder with him to the Council. This time, he was able to point out, he was accompanied by a literate councillor,

[1] Casely Hayford, *Legislative Council Debates*, 25 Apr. 1921.

the Vice-President of the Akim Abuakwa Scholars' Union—which had pre-sumably been brought back under the paramount umbrella. For Nana Ofori Atta was determined that in his State there should be no separation between the literate and illiterate communities, and that 'our good and worthy institu-tions should suffer no undue or radical change'.[1]

The Governor in his reply welcomed the claim of the educated African to take a part in government, but made it clear that this had to be fitted into the traditional framework. It was not, he thought, a fair thing for 'the people of the stools' to be approached by a political party on big public questions in any other way than through the Chiefs and their councillors. Any attempt to get at the people behind the backs of traditional authority would be bound to evoke 'enormous opposition from those who support the maintenance of national institutions'. Guggisberg attributed the Congress members' complete failure to co-operate with the Government to the inherent weakness of trying to represent all four colonies at once. More serious, in his view, was the bitterness expressed in the newspapers, which had been growing since the formation of the Congress, and especially since Nana Ofori Atta's December speech in the Legislative Council. Such attitudes were, the Governor felt, 'widening day by day and month by month the gap between the black man and the white man; they were increasing and creating this racial feeling'. The main difference of opinion in the Legislative Council had been on a technical point, although a very important one: was the Congress representative or not? He emphasized his own major criticisms: that the dispatch of the delegation to England had been unduly hasty, and that the Government, in spite of its desire to help the people of the country, had been ignored.[2]

When Nana Ofori Atta left the Legislative Council after this debate, he was loudly hooted by the crowd outside. This was unusual enough for the Govern-ment to announce publicly that he had been fully justified in raising such an important constitutional issue; and that the regrettable demonstration had been a grave breach of courtesy and respect towards an important visiting Chief.[3] With a little official prompting, Nana Ofori Atta complained to the Gã Mantse about his treatment, and after the latter had sent an evasive reply, the Secretary for Native Affairs took a hand, reproving him for his 'weakness and want of frankness'.[4] It is clear that there was a close relationship between Nana Ofori Atta and the Government at this time.

What were the fundamental issues at stake in all this? It was certainly not a contest between obscurantism and enlightenment. Nana Ofori Atta was an exceptionally intelligent and forceful personality, more receptive than many

[1] Nana Ofori Atta, ibid. 27 Apr. 1921.   [2] Guggisberg, ibid.
[3] *The Gold Coast Independent*, 21 May 1921; Letter of 11 May 1921, from Colonial Secretary.
[4] 'I interpret his action as that of a weak character, afraid of putting himself in the wrong with the Congress people, of whom there are of course many in his Division. I . . . will note the incident in the Gã Mantse's record.' Minute of 27 May 1921, by C. W. Welman; S.N.A. 1/1921, G.N. Archives.

of his fellow Chiefs to new ideas, and anxious to encourage social progress. But this, he felt, must be within the limits of the traditional framework. He was not willing that the Chiefs should relinquish their claim to leadership, even if it meant sacrificing a wider national unity to the cumbersome local machinery of numerous independent States. At this point he was confronted by a newly articulate group, with no traditional standing, asserting their right to national political leadership simply because they were educated. They claimed to be better qualified than, but yet not isolated from, the mass of the people; and the fact that they also earned sizeable incomes from commerce and the professions was put forward as an economic argument for representation at the national level.

The inherited privileges of chieftaincy were thus challenged by the acquired privileges of education and private property. The appeal to immemorial custom was matched by an appeal to individual rights, as the justification for political representation. The Congress leaders went so far as to challenge the position of the Chiefs in the Legislative Council, while the latter appeared to deny the right of individual expression except through inflexible customary channels. Both sides could deploy powerful arguments; neither could claim conclusively to be the sole spokesmen of the illiterates; and neither could fully understand the other's point of view.

This deep cleavage of interest and sentiment is still an unsettled issue in West Africa. The role of the Chiefs *vis-à-vis* the Congress was not forgotten, and Casely Hayford's charge of treachery to the national cause was later to be revived in different circumstances. The immediate result of this episode was an attempt by the Government to associate the Chiefs more directly with the legislative process at the national level, a step which to some extent widened the gap between the Chiefs and their educated subjects.[1] But the problem did not become acute during the 1920's, and even after these acrimonious debates some degree of reconciliation was still possible. Meanwhile the Congress leaders found some satisfaction in routing the remnant of the old guard of the A.R.P.S., which they had already condemned as 'defunct' and 'unrepresentative',[2] thus emerging unchallenged as the spokesmen of educated opinion.

The Capture of the A.R.P.S., 1921–2

When a reasonably well-attended conference of the A.R.P.S. was at last held at Cape Coast in July 1921, it was the Congress leaders who won the support of the majority of Chiefs present.[3] The members of the executive were found 'guilty' of secretly corresponding with Nana Ofori Atta, and of

[1] For Guggisberg's Provincial Councils scheme, see Ch. XI, pp. 440–2, below.
[2] *The Gold Coast Leader*, 26 Feb. 1921.
[3] Nana Ofori Atta was not a member of the A.R.P.S., which had virtually no organized support in the Eastern Province, but he was represented at this conference by J. B. Danquah, his young half-brother.

allowing the President to pledge the support of the Society without consulting any of the Natural Rulers, even those living close at hand. Fines were
imposed, and the officers were instructed to cable the Secretary of State confirming what the Congress leaders had said and done in London. Not surprisingly, they could not bring themselves to do this, and asked the Omanhene
of Cape Coast to send the cable,[1] making the excuse that they did not know
the contents of the Congress petition.

There was very little difference between the two opposing factions within
the A.R.P.S. concerning the general reforms required, especially the demand
for an elected Legislative Council. Apart from the clash of personalities, the
main issue was the relative status of the Chiefs and the educated class; and
this left unsettled the important point as to who should constitute the electorate. There was also the subsidiary question of tactics: the majority considered that their aims could best be obtained by uniting with the three
neighbouring colonies, while the minority thought that the dissimilarity of
customs was too great to allow united action to succeed.

The executive of the A.R.P.S. had already prepared their own scheme for
elective representation, which had been issued in the name of 'the Aboriginal
unofficial members' of the Legislative Council while Casely Hayford and his
colleagues were in London. They had proposed that the A.R.P.S. itself should
become an electoral body, to return twelve unofficial representatives and three
members of the Executive Council.[2] Casely Hayford was determined to discredit this move. He had attacked it in his Legislative Council speech, claiming
that the A.R.P.S. leaders were seeking the self-same thing as the Congress
had done when they combined with Sierra Leone, the Gambia, and Nigeria,
the only difference being that the electors would be the A.R.P.S. and the
Chiefs, instead of the masses. 'Why? Because my friend there [E. J. P. Brown]
knows that if today he were to solicit the vote of the populace he would not
get a single vote.'[3]

Casely Hayford now repeated these charges at the A.R.P.S. conference,
and as a result the executive was put on oath not to send any constitutional
proposals to the Government without further consultation. A few of the
Chiefs left the meeting in protest; but Casely Hayford had clearly won the
second round, and the officers had virtually, though not formally, been suspended.[4] Great bitterness resulted. As the aged J. P. Brown, now editor of
The Gold Coast Nation, complained: 'we parted not as friends, and the Congress people set about writing all sorts of nonsense in the papers against the
other party'.[5]

Early in 1922 the Governor announced that he had received a scheme for

[1] Published in *West Africa*, 9 July 1921.   [2] For details, see Ch. XI, p. 437, below.
[3] Casely Hayford, *Legislative Council Debates*, 25 Apr. 1921.
[4] Letter of 22 Aug. 1921, from Acting Provincial Commissioner to Acting Colonial Secretary;
S.N.A. 1/1921, G.N. Archives.
[5] Letter of 9 Aug. 1922, to Colonial Secretary; S.N.A. 23/1922, G.N. Archives.

elective representation from the A.R.P.S. This was the last straw for the Congress leaders, who now decided to try and remove the A.R.P.S. officers. The Omanhene of Cape Coast was persuaded to call an emergency conference of the Society in April; but the members of the executive did not attend because they considered it unconstitutional, nor were there enough Chiefs present to settle matters finally. It was, however, resolved to ask the Governor to defer consideration of the surreptitiously forwarded scheme until the Society as a whole had met to consider it.

A larger conference was held during June and July 1922. Again the A.R.P.S. officers declined to attend, since they argued that it had not been called by the President, as provided in their Declaration. In their absence they were then removed from office. Minor disturbances followed in Cape Coast; stones were thrown, and Nana Ababio (one of the few supporters of the old executive) was hit on the head. At this stage the Acting Provincial Commissioner strongly advised J. E. Biney (ex-President), W. S. Johnston (ex-Secretary), and the other former members of the executive to attend. They eventually did so, and reluctantly handed over the Society's press and documents.[1] For contravening the sworn instructions of the previous conference, they were 'fined' drinks totalling £45.12s., and a bullock. The new officers of the Society were all younger men, supporters of the Congress movement. H. Van Hien was appointed President; J. E. Casely Hayford, J. W. de Graft Johnson, and W. Ward Brew were made Vice-Presidents; and K. Sakyiama became the new Secretary. The conference then proceeded to a solemn ratification of the Society's aims and constitution.[2]

The Government soon came to dislike the new leaders of the A.R.P.S. still more than the old. In retrospect, the Secretary for Native Affairs even felt that the latter had been comparatively reasonable, and that the nine or ten years up to 1922 had been marked by a distinct growth of understanding and confidence between the people and the Administration, and by a genuine readiness on the part of the Society to assist the Government by explaining its proposals to the Chiefs and people, thus 'predisposing them to acceptance'. E. J. P. Brown and the Chiefs of Abura, Anomabu, and Nkusukum had been particularly helpful in their refusal to associate the Society with the irregular procedure and 'blatant methods' of the Congress. The transfer of power was described as the revenge of Casely Hayford and his associates against Brown and the moderate Chiefs, especially Nana Ofori Atta, and they were accused

[1] Great significance was attached to the Declaration, which was supposed to be always in the custody of the President. About this time it had been 'mislaid in the house' of the Secretary, and later found with a leaf missing, on which had been some of the original 1898 signatures and seals. J. P. Brown was at great pains to justify this lapse, in a letter to the Colonial Secretary of 9 Aug. 1922, which throws a pathetic sidelight on the transfer of power. S.N.A. 23/1922, G.N. Archives.

[2] The 1907 version was republished in identical form, except that the first paragraph now read as follows (the words in italics having been added): 'To protect the Aborigines of the Gold Coast *in the free enjoyment of their ancestral lands and ancient institutions* at all times by constitutional means and methods.' A.R.P.S., *Bye-laws, Rules and Regulations* (Cape Coast, 1922).

of stirring up 'the perverse and wrongheaded elements for which Cape Coast has always been unamiably notorious ... with every circumstance of misrepresentation, vilification, insult and even personal assault'.[1]

Yet if the A.R.P.S. was to face up to political realities in the twentieth century, some radical change in its outlook was essential, whether by fair means or foul. The main result of the change of leadership was, first, that the Society now came out openly in favour of the interests of the educated class; in fact, the old executive had represented similar influences behind the scenes, but had tended to use the Chiefs more as a stalking-horse for their real aims. Secondly, the way was open for the Congress to become an influential national force, now that the opposition from within the A.R.P.S. had been removed, or at least silenced. Strange as it may seem, the very reverse happened, and the influence of the Congress gradually became weaker throughout the 1920's. This may be explained largely by the lack of any effective local organization. A detailed programme of reform was thought out and impressively argued at successive sessions; but in the absence of any concerted effort to get this carried out in each colony, the movement took on the character of an intermittent pressure group rather than a political organization.

The Last Travels of the Congress

The Congress really came to life only when in joint session, and had little separate existence in each colony. Casely Hayford had been so preoccupied with his personal struggle for leadership in the Gold Coast that he had hardly paid any attention to branch activities and organization there, let alone in the other three territories. There was little support in Nigeria, only a handful of enthusiasts in Sierra Leone, and hardly any scope for politics at all in the Gambia.

Nevertheless, the aim was to meet in each capital in turn, and subsequent sessions were held at Freetown in 1923, at Bathurst at the turn of the year 1925–6, and eventually at Lagos four years later. On each occasion the same pattern was followed, platform addresses being followed by discussion of a long list of resolutions. As the years passed, the opening speeches claimed more achievements to the credit of the Congress and the resolutions grew slightly less in number. But the main subjects of interest remained constant: constitutional and judicial reform, education, the press, Africanization of the civil service, and—increasingly during the 1920's—'the growing consciousness of our race the world over', and 'its growing articulateness'.[2]

The Freetown session was not very well attended; the twenty-five delegates included only four from the Gold Coast and none from Nigeria.[3] But it was

[1] Memorandum of 17 July 1924, by C. W. Welman; S.N.A. No. 1503, G.N. Archives.
[2] Presidential address by Casely Hayford, Freetown, Jan. 1923; Sampson, *West African Leadership*, ch. iii.
[3] *The Gold Coast Independent*, 3 Feb. 1923.

notable for the production of a formal constitution for the National Congress of British West Africa—consisting of fifty-four items[1]—and for the election of Casely Hayford as President, an office which he held until his death in 1930. As before, telegrams of greetings were dispatched to the King and the West African Governors. This time Clifford was determined that no one should be able to misunderstand his reply. While finding himself unable to regard 'this self-appointed Congress' as in any sense representative of African interests or public opinion in Nigeria, His Excellency looked forward to reading the report of their deliberations, 'which cannot fail to be of interest as an example of the opinions held on a variety of public questions by a number of educated African gentlemen'. The Congress decided not to let the implications of this message go unchallenged, and repeated once more that they represented not only the intelligentsia, but also the bulk of the inhabitants.[2] Special attention was paid to educational problems at this session, and the thoughtful nature of their approach is illustrated by the following statements:

We do not subscribe to the view that a peculiar kind of education is desirable for the African *per se*. We believe in the African being trained by the African with an African outlook, which is a very different thing. Experience has taught that it is oftener than not the half-educated African who is de-Africanised rather than the thoroughly educated African.

For these reasons, Casely Hayford urged upon the attention of the colonial Governments the early foundation of a British West African university.[3]

Back in Accra, Casely Hayford held a 'mass meeting' at the Native Club, and gave a glowing account of the Freetown session, which was interpreted into Gã.[4] But a mass meeting in those days was no doubt considerably smaller than it would be today; and Casely Hayford has recently been criticized, probably with some justice, for limiting his appeal to middle-class intellectuals. The Congress, from this somewhat doctrinaire viewpoint, was bound to fail 'without the active support of the plebeian masses, especially the peasantry, who form the bulk of the population'.[5]

Certainly the Congress leaders showed little awareness of the needs and problems of the rural areas. A plan was announced to sell thousands of badges: 'only 2/6 to help your country's cause, to make you free citizens of the Empire'. Soon the mantle of bourgeois respectability began to settle rather too heavily round their shoulders. A ladies' section was founded in

---

[1] *The Gold Coast Leader*, 28 Nov. 1925, and 2 Jan. 1926.
[2] *West Africa*, 31 Mar. 1923.   [3] Sampson, *West African Leadership*, ch. iii.
[4] The interpreter was John Buckman. *The Gold Coast Independent*, 24 Mar. 1923. Cf. his pamphlet appealing for support for the educated political leaders 'fighting our battles for us unaided'. *The Future of the African of the Gold Coast* (London, 1922).
[5] George Padmore writes of Casely Hayford: 'educated under Nonconformist middle-class influences, he reflected all the virtues and political limitations of mid-Victorian liberalism . . . unlike men of the type of Gandhi and Nehru and Kwame Nkrumah'. *The Gold Coast Revolution* (London, 1953), p. 52.

Accra, which discussed the desirability of forming a similar association amongst illiterate women,[1] but there is no record of any action being taken on these lines. By 1924 Congress had become almost an institution. The 28th of March—the last full day of the inaugural conference—was set aside as Congress Day, when social-political meetings were held, and celebrations of some kind were arranged in many Eastern Province towns. Money was still being collected towards the outstanding expenses of the London deputation; and the local newspapers at this time had little news other than the commemoration of Congress Day.[2]

It seemed, however, that the Congress had begun to look backwards rather than forwards. With the passage of time the leaders could afford to assess more charitably the bitter attacks that had marked their early days, which were now felt to have brought home to the people, even in the most remote parts, the objects for which they stood.[3] *The Gold Coast Independent* reported a grand reception given by Congress ladies in honour of the Rev. A. G. Fraser and his Achimota staff, the Director of Education, and Woolhouse Bannerman: 'Practically everybody who mattered was present', including the Governor.[4] The movement was almost in danger of being killed with kindness. In 1925 Hutton Mills, as President of the Gold Coast Section, welcomed the Prince of Wales during his visit to Accra; an address of welcome was presented, to which the Prince briefly replied.[5] But some government officials regarded the Congress leaders as anything but innocuous, and resented their control over the A.R.P.S., which now seemed to have 'reverted from calculated policy to the original attitude of suspicion and opposition... It is in fact ... merely a political engine in the hands of Mr. Casely Hayford and his supporters'.[6]

Difficulties of organization in the Gambia caused the third session to be postponed several times during 1925, especially while Casely Hayford and his colleagues were anxiously awaiting the outcome of Gold Coast constitutional discussions; and it was not until December that the full session eventually opened in Bathurst.[7] Once again Nigeria was unrepresented. This time the

---

[1] *The Gold Coast Independent*, 28 Apr. 1923.
[2] For example, ibid. 29 Mar. 1924.
[3] Ibid. 5 Apr. 1924.   [4] Ibid. 22 Nov. 1924.
[5] Guggisberg also arranged for the Prince of Wales to meet members of the Gold Coast Bar, and the A.R.P.S., and to reply to their addresses of welcome; see *Visit of His Royal Highness The Prince of Wales to the Gold Coast Colony* (Accra, 1925). The A.R.P.S. and Congress were now closely interlocked, as shown by the signatures to their addresses:

Congress: T. Hutton Mills (President); J. E. Casely Hayford (Vice-President); H. Van Hien (President, Central Province); F. V. Nanka-Bruce (Secretary, Eastern Province).

A.R.P.S.: H. Van Hien (President); J. W. de Graft-Johnson (Vice-President); Gã Mantse (President, Accra Section); F. V. Nanka-Bruce (Vice-President, Accra Section).

[6] Memorandum of 17 July 1924, by Welman; S.N.A. No. 1503, G.N. Archives.
[7] Presidential address by Casely Hayford, Bathurst, Dec. 1925; Sampson, *West African Leadership*, ch. iv.

D d

delegates devoted much attention to a constitutional memorandum, which was later incorporated in the A.R.P.S. petition of 1926 against the new Gold Coast constitution.[1] Casely Hayford and S. R. Wood were re-elected as President and Secretary, and J. Glover-Addo and J. Kitson-Mills as joint Financial Secretaries. All of them being from the Gold Coast, it was clear that this was still the fountain-head of the Congress, which had only rudimentary support elsewhere.

West Africa continued to take a polite interest in the movement—including the time-honoured comparison with the Indian National Congress—and published a full report of the Bathurst session. The editor suggested that the Congress had made a positive contribution towards broadening the constitutions, especially by hastening the enlargement of the Legislative Councils and the introduction of the elective principle. Such an organization could act as a useful check on 'the great power and the sheltering from public opinion which mark almost every Crown Colony Government'. Indeed, the more competent the Governor, the less likely would he be to resent this.[2]

Eventually the fourth session was held at Lagos, with the support of the Nigerian Democratic Party, from December 1929 to January 1930, thus completing the tour of the four capitals, and—it was hoped—strengthening the limited support from Nigeria. Casely Hayford's review of ten years' progress now claimed credit for the Congress in the extension of the franchise in Nigeria, Sierra Leone, and the Gold Coast; in the foundation of Achimota as 'a direct response' to their resolution demanding a university that would preserve in the students a sense of African nationality; and in the establishment of a West African Appeal Court.[3] For the future, he felt that elective representation did not yet go far enough, and that the principle of an official majority could not remain undisturbed if British West Africa were to have an effective voice in her own affairs. He referred specifically to the proposed constitutional changes in Ceylon as a useful precedent.[4]

Casely Hayford no longer underestimated the difficulties. He stressed the need for Africans to accept the responsibility of initiating policy, and carrying it out effectively. While retaining his faith in the liberating power of education, he was conscious of lack of unity as the major obstacle to be overcome: 'the African God is weary of your wranglings, weary of your vain disputations, weary of your everlasting quarrels which are a drag upon progress and which keep from you, as a people, the good that is intended for you'.[5] These were

---

[1] See Ch. XI, p. 449, below.   [2] *West Africa*, 6 Mar. 1926.

[3] Cf. Martin Wight's verdict on the Congress, twenty years later: 'It had had no direct effect, but it crystallized demands which received partial fulfilment in the Constitution of 1925, and in the foundation of Achimota College.' *The Gold Coast Legislative Council* (London, 1947), p. 27.

[4] The Donoughmore Report (implemented in the Ceylon constitution of 1931) had proposed to 'transfer to the elected representatives of the people complete control over the internal affairs of the Island'. *Ceylon: Report of the Special Commission on the Constitution* (London, 1929).

[5] Presidential address by Casely Hayford, Lagos, Dec. 1929; Sampson, *West African Leadership*, ch. v.

virtually the last rites of the National Congress. Casely Hayford, who had founded it, and had ever since been its main energizer, died in 1930. Although a fifth session in Accra was later suggested,[1] this never materialized, and the movement ceased to have any influence in the Gold Coast, whence it had always drawn its main vitality. In any case, the growing divergences in the direction and pace of political development in each territory were making it increasingly difficult to present unified demands for reform, so that the leading African politicians had become more and more preoccupied with their own local problems, at the expense of the Congress as a whole.[2] The attempt at West African unity had certainly been premature, though in some ways it had been more far-sighted than the Governors who condemned such an approach as unconstitutional.

The restless, controversial post-war decade thus closed with nationalist activity almost at a standstill, or at least quiescent. The A.R.P.S. was virtually moribund, while the National Congress was unable to survive the death of its founder and moving spirit. As far as the Gold Coast was concerned, perhaps the economic prosperity and social progress achieved under Guggisberg's administration temporarily removed many of the usual nationalist grievances, which were to be revived in the 1930's, in the harsh aftermath of the world slump.

More important was the fact that the Governor, in introducing the 1925 constitution, had offered a challenge to nationalist leaders to make the new Legislative Council work, before they could reasonably present any fresh constitutional demands. For many years Gold Coast politicians had been seeking elective representation at the centre, and although the latest reforms were not entirely what they had hoped for, sufficient ground had been gained to make necessary a period of consolidation. Several of the provisions of Guggisberg's constitution were fiercely attacked; nevertheless, the Legislative Council had now come to be generally accepted as a forum for the expression of national opinion, and as a possible basis for responsible African government. From this time onwards, Europeanized political institutions gradually superseded traditional forms of government in spite of official attempts to bolster up the latter. The next chapter traces the development of the Legislative Council from its first establishment in 1850, and the successive demands for fuller representation and the introduction of the franchise, which did not come near being satisfied until 1925.

[1] *The Times of West Africa*, 27 Oct. 1932.
[2] For the special reasons that led to the waning of enthusiasm for the Congress in Nigeria, see Coleman, *Nigeria*, pp. 191–5.

XI

THE CONSTRUCTION OF THE
LEGISLATIVE COUNCIL
1850–1928

FOR a full understanding of the rise of Gold Coast nationalism, it is necessary to study not only specific protests and movements, but also the development of political institutions within the national framework. Central to this process is the Legislative Council. Although at first of little practical importance, it was always in theory a check upon the absolute power of the Governor—and also perhaps a symbolic reflection of the British parliamentary conscience. For, as has been pointed out, there is an inherent anomaly in the situation where a democratic assembly exercises sovereign power over a population other than that which it represents. J. E. Powell suggests, for example, that the dilemma can only be resolved if the ruling assembly creates in the dependent territory 'representative institutions in its own image'.[1] It was perhaps under some such compulsion that the first step taken by the British Government, when the Gold Coast became a separate dependency of the Crown in 1850, with its own Governor responsible to London, was to establish a Legislative Council.

From the outset there seem to have been two separate aspects of the Council's functions; from one point of view, it was advisory, from the other, representative. The former was the usual interpretation of Governors on the spot, though the latter seems to have been nearer to the mind of Lord Grey when he established the Council: 'It was my object . . . without relinquishing the power possessed by the Crown, gradually to bring these legislative bodies more under the influence of the opinion of the intelligent and educated inhabitants of these Colonies.'[2] It must be granted that for the first seventy-five years of its existence the Legislative Council was representative only in a very limited sense, since all its members were appointed by the Governor. Nevertheless, the attempt was consistently made—with varying degrees of success according to the Governor concerned—to nominate unofficial members who would fairly represent moderate local opinion. Africans in the Gold Coast never had to fight for the principle of unofficial representation—only once, after a lapse of some years, for its restoration.

The main constitutional bone of contention was the principle of elective

---

[1] 'The Empire of England', in *Tradition and Change* (London, 1954).
[2] Earl Grey, *The Colonial Policy of Lord John Russell's Administration* (London, 1853), vol. i, p. 30.

representation. This was sometimes demanded as the privilege of a special group—for example by the merchants in 1850, by the Chiefs in 1898, or by the A.R.P.S. in 1918—but it was consistently regarded as a popular right which must eventually replace the system of nomination. A limited electoral scheme was at last written into the 1926 constitution, but this was strongly criticized by educated Africans as inadequate and ill-advised; and it did not disturb the official majority on the Council, which was to remain intact for nearly another generation.

Thus throughout the period under review the Legislative Council hardly even approximated to an image of the Mother of Parliaments. The mid-nineteenth-century West African Settlements had not been expected to follow the path of the British-settled colonies in their advance to responsible government on the lines of the 1840 Durham Report.[1] Nevertheless, West African forms of government owed much to the belief that the essential rights of the British constitution both could and should be exported for the benefit of those capable of exercising them. Sierra Leone, even under merchant government in the 1790's, had elected its own legislative body,[2] and as Martin Wight points out, this was the first instance in modern history of a self-governing colonial community of non-European population.[3] Although the principle of election was not retained by the Crown when it took over the West African colonies, the Legislative Council remained as a potential stepping-stone to fuller representation. It is therefore profitable to study the way in which nationalist demands, themselves conditioned by the very existence of such a Council, succeeded in modifying, hastening, or directing its evolution.

The First Unofficial Members, 1850–63

In 1850 the European merchants, who had until recently been accustomed to managing the affairs of the coastal forts, tried to persuade the Colonial Office to let them have a majority voice on the new Legislative Council. But Grey considered that their interests were not identical with those of the inhabitants, and his London advisers argued that to give the merchants any authority to interfere with the government of the protected districts would be 'both anomalous in principle and mischievous in effect'.[4] So the first Legislative Council of the Gold Coast followed the normal Crown Colony pattern, with an official majority. Two merchants—Brodie Cruickshank, and James Bannerman, a prosperous African—were nominated to sit with three full-time unofficials.[5]

---

[1] By contrast to the nominated Legislative Councils in Africa, New South Wales in 1842, only two years after transportation had ended, was given a Council with a two-thirds elected majority.

[2] 'The British constitution, as far as it is applicable to the circumstances of the place, is of course transferred thither.' Report of the Directors of the Sierra Leone Company (London, 1794), p. 4.

[3] The Development of the Legislative Council, 1606–1945 (London, 1946), p. 43.

[4] Minute of 14 Nov. 1850, by H. Merivale; CO/96/19.

[5] Many of the merchants undertook government duties at various times, so that the distinction

During these early years, the Executive Council had virtually the same membership as the Legislative Council. Their composition was not rigidly fixed. Various merchants were occasionally summoned to attend, especially in the absence of the regular members: for example, F. Swanzy and W. M. Hutton in 1851, and C. Clouston in 1852–3. At this stage the choice depended largely on who was available, regardless of colour. The mercantile members repeatedly but unsuccessfully urged that they should be elected rather than nominated.[1]

In an attempt to meet the merchants' objections, Grey insisted that draft legislation should be gazetted well in advance of its introduction, so that they might have an opportunity to express their views outside the Legislative Council.[2] He favoured the idea of a Chamber of Commerce, which was founded in 1851, and which sometimes organized deputations of protest;[3] but the merchants remained critical of the new constitution. According to G. E. Metcalfe, their co-operation could not always be relied on: 'their opposition was some times open and often suspected; ... their alienation, such as it was, weakened government seriously'.[4] As a result, the European merchants and the small but growing numbers of educated Africans sometimes found themselves united in opposition to the Government. (This spasmodic but crucial alliance was to achieve its most spectacular expression in 1892 against Brandford Griffith.)

Cruickshank died in 1854. Bannerman attended meetings very infrequently, since he had to travel from Accra to Cape Coast; he retired from public life, in poor health, in 1857. As a result, Sir Benjamin Pine found, on his arrival in that year, that the Legislative Council consisted only of four officials; the Governor, the Chief Justice, the Colonial Secretary, and the Officer Commanding the Gold Coast Corps.

Pine considered this extremely unsatisfactory. Major H. St. G. Ord had already recommended strongly that the Legislative Council should contain some merchants;[5] and the Governor now suggested that six further members should be appointed, to serve for three years. In addition to the Civil Commandants of Accra and Anomabu, he named four merchants, from Accra and Cape Coast. He was not convinced of the need to preserve a strict official

between them and the permanent officials was not always very clear. Bannerman, for example, was Civil Commandant of Accra from 1850 to 1857, and even acted as Lieutenant-Governor from Dec. 1850 to Sept. 1851. A few of his letters have survived from this period, among the Bannerman Papers, SC. 2/4 to 19, G.N. Archives.

[1] For example, Letter of 22 Aug. 1850, from Bannerman and Cruickshank to Winniett, enclosed in his Dispatch No. 22 of 23 Aug. 1850, to Grey; CO/96/19. Also proposal by F. Swanzy 'for the Establishment of an Elective Council' in *Legislative Council Minutes*, 1 Apr. 1851.

[2] Minute of 16 Nov. 1850, by Grey, and his Dispatch No. 55 of 18 Dec. 1850, to Winniett; CO/96/19.

[3] Dispatch No. 43 of 6 May 1851, from Bannerman to Grey; CO/96/22.

[4] 'After Maclean', in *Transactions of the Gold Coast & Togoland Historical Society* (Achimota, 1955), vol. i, pt. v.

[5] Report of 16 May 1856, from Ord to Labouchere; CO/96/40.

majority, so long as the Governor had an exclusive right to introduce legislation, and a veto.[1] In practice, the unofficial attendance would have varied according to whether the Council met in Cape Coast or Accra, and the officials would have been unlikely to be outvoted; nevertheless, Pine's proposal was too radical for the Colonial Office, which refused to alter the proportions laid down seven years earlier.

Between 1857 and 1861 unofficial representation on the Legislative and Executive Councils remained largely on an *ad hoc* basis. In 1861 the Governor complained of the difficulty of finding merchants to attend, and proposed the appointment of three 'native gentlemen'.[2] The Colonial Office agreed to two of the names he put forward: George Blankson of Anomabu,[3] and Robert Hutchison of Cape Coast. When Hutchison died in 1863,[4] the Colonial Office accepted two further Cape Coast names: F. C. Grant and A. B. McIntyre, a European agent.[5] It was also agreed that two others should be invited to attend when the Council was held in Accra; the Civil Commandant and N. Irvine, the leading merchant there.[6]

Demands for Representation, 1864–82

In 1864 there was some criticism of the lack of consultation over the unpopular spirit licence law.[7] Arising out of this, Joseph Martin, King Aggery's commissioner, complained in London to the 1865 Parliamentary Committee: 'we have no suffrage in this place to elect a member of the Council to protect the interests of the country'. Lord Alfred Churchill then cross-questioned Martin on this new application of British ideas to the Gold Coast:

Do the natives express any wish to enjoy the suffrage?—
I believe, if it is not asking too much, that they are entitled to the suffrage.[8]
Do you think that, if they had the suffrage, they would fall in with the ordinances of the Governor more readily than they do now?—
They would readily comply with them.[9]

Such views, though heard with respect, were not due to be accepted for another sixty years.

[1] Dispatch No. 50 of 12 June 1857, from B. Pine to Labouchere; CO/96/41.
[2] Dispatch No. 7 of 9 Jan. 1861, from Andrews to Newcastle; CO/96/51.
[3] See J. M. Akita, 'Biographical Sketch of George Blankson of Anomabu', in *Transactions of the Gold Coast & Togoland Historical Society* (Achimota, 1955), vol. i, pt. v.
[4] Richard Pine then described Hutchison as 'highly educated, exceedingly intelligent . . . [and] a firm supporter of my Government'. Dispatch No. 62 of 14 July 1863, from Governor to Newcastle; CO/96/61.
[5] Three years later a correspondent from Cape Coast complained, referring to McIntyre and others, 'Forster and Smith's people still *rule* in the Legislative Council'. *The African Times*, 23 May 1866.
[6] Dispatch No. 39 of 11 May 1863, from R. Pine to Newcastle; CO/96/60.
[7] See Ch. V, pp. 200–1 and 206, above.
[8] Lord Alfred Churchill's own recollection of this answer was that Martin had said that the natives 'were afraid to ask' for the suffrage. *The African Times*, 23 Aug. 1865.
[9] *1865 Report*, questions 8,430–1, and replies.

The main constitutional outcome of this parliamentary inquiry was that from 1866 to 1874 the Gold Coast was again administered from Sierra Leone, as part of the West African Settlements. The Administrator was made responsible to the Governor-in-Chief at Freetown, who soon queried the number and the method of appointment of the unofficial members.[1] When the Administrator formally requested authority for Blankson, Grant, McIntyre, and Irvine to renew their membership of the Legislative and Executive Councils, he was reminded that the latter had now been abolished, and that the members of the former should be as few as possible.[2] The legislature was therefore reduced in importance, and comprised, during most of this period, only the Administrator, the Collector of Customs, the Chief Magistrate, and, less frequently, Blankson; in addition, Grant was invited to attend in 1869 and 1871.

The Fanti Confederation scheme of 1872 proposed the election of four 'gentlemen, natives or residents of the Gold Coast', in addition to the nominated members;[3] and the Secretary of State was horrified at the idea of a majority of independent members. But the liberal Administrator-in-Chief, J. Pope Hennessy, thought it fair that another African should be appointed to the Legislative Council, and recommended Grant, as 'the leading native merchant of Cape Coast, a gentleman who seems to have the confidence of the educated natives, as well as of the Chiefs'.[4] The following year, before any decision on this had been taken, the Fanti Chiefs secured Blankson's arrest on charges of complicity with the King of Ashanti.[5] The Administrator took the opportunity to recommend the appointment of two mercantile members: Grant, and Swanzy's main European agent, W. Cleaver, also of Cape Coast. The Colonial Office saw no objection, since the Government would still have a majority in the Council.[6] But these appointments did not satisfy the Chiefs and merchants of Accra. At a protest meeting, Edmund Bannerman was appointed spokesman to press their claim for two local members. It was argued that this had been granted previously, when both the Civil Commandant and Irvine had been in the Council: but that now the new unofficials were ignorant of the needs of the eastern districts.[7]

[1] Dispatch No. 38 of 30 July 1866, from Blackall to Conran; CO/96/71.

[2] Dispatch No. 46 of 22 Aug. 1866, from Blackall to Conran; CO/96/72.

[3] Cf. J. A. B. Horton's earlier suggestion in his *Letters on the Political Condition of the Gold Coast* (London, 1870), p. 167, that the President of the Confederation should be *ex officio* a member of the Legislative Council.

[4] Confidential Letter of 4 May 1872, from Ussher to Pope Hennessy, and his covering Dispatch No. 93 of 29 Oct. 1872, to Kimberley; also Kimberley's marginal comments. CO/96/94.

[5] Blankson denied the charges—on which no evidence was offered—and later published *A Vindication of the Hon. Geo. Blankson* (Cape Coast, 1874). This included a letter from the Chief Magistrate, who, while not expressing an opinion on the facts of the case, agreed that he had been 'most basely and cruelly used'.

[6] Minute of 21 May 1873; CO/96/98.

[7] Report of meeting at Accra, 13 Aug. 1873, enclosed in Dispatch No. 214 of 30 Aug. 1873, from Harley to Governor-in-Chief; CO/96/101.

In 1874 the Gold Coast reverted to a separate government. The Governor and Executive Council were restored, and Lagos (with its own Administrator)[1] was now attached to the Gold Coast. The importance of the Legislative Council was also considerably increased, at least in theory, by the new powers to legislate for the Protected Territories as well as for the Colony. Its legislative authority was thus co-extensive with the exercise of British jurisdiction, ill-defined as that might be.

The number of officials on the Legislative Council was now increased.[2] But the Governor did not feel the need for outside advice, and he chose to govern without any unofficial members at all. For the next twelve years none was appointed, and all his successors during this period were opposed to the idea.[3] This practice was reinforced by a decision of the Secretary of State in 1877 'that it was not desirable to admit any unofficial members into the Legislative Council'.[4] One theory was that the Chief Justice was to a certain extent independent of the Government and thus able to represent the people and safeguard their interests.[5] But by 1878 some merchants in Cape Coast were beginning to lose patience, and made a strong plea for representation in the Council again: 'We have hitherto kept silence upon this matter thinking that a change would shortly come.' The Government, however, was satisfied with the existing system whereby merchants were invited to express their opinions verbally on proposed Ordinances, which were available for inspection at Cape Coast, Elmina, and Accra.[6]

The merchants' appeal was supported in the editorials and correspondence columns of *The Gold Coast Times*.[7] This Cape Coast newspaper, founded in 1874 by James Brew,[8] commenced weekly publication in 1881, and intensified the campaign for constitutional reform: 'Were a Roumanian sent to govern

[1] This post was abolished in 1883, and Lagos was administered from the Gold Coast until 1886, when it became a separate Colony.

[2] During 1879–80 one of these, S. Bannerman, then Acting Collector of Customs, was an African.

[3] According to Brandford Griffith's Confidential Dispatch of 6 Mar. 1893, to Ripon; CO/96/232.

[4] Minute of 16 Feb. 1878, by A. W. L. Hemming (referring to a decision by Carnarvon); CO/96/123.

[5] The Chief Justice, Sir William Brandford Griffith, endorsed this view in 1899, pointing out that the Government thus had 'an independent critic with a bias towards itself'. But this degree of independence was never likely to satisfy African critics; nor did it appeal to the Colonial Office, which thought that the Chief Justice should be expected to give general support to the Government, and that if he could not conscientiously do so, he should abstain from voting. Confidential Dispatch of 30 June 1899, from Chamberlain to Hodgson; CO/96/338. This did not prevent Brandford Griffith from strenuously opposing the 1910 Bill amending the Native Jurisdiction Ordinance; see Ch. XII, pp. 468–9, below. After he retired in 1911, no further Chief Justice was appointed to the Legislative Council.

[6] Letter of 16 Jan. 1878, from F. C. Grant, John Sarbah, and other merchants to Freeling, and his covering Dispatch No. 14 of 21 Jan. 1878, to Carnarvon; CO/96/123.

[7] For example, 25 Jan. 1878.

[8] Although *The Gold Coast Times* subsequently underwent reorganization and changes of printers, publishers and editors, Brew continued to be intimately associated with its policy.

Venezuela would he be capable of doing so without the assistance of some of its inhabitants? If our rulers cannot know our needs without their first being brought to their notice, then we ought to have natives in the Council who know and could represent them.'[1] As yet, there was no explicit demand for the franchise. But a scheme for representative government in Cyprus did not escape editorial comment. After several years as a Colony, the Gold Coast, it was observed, had not heard of 'the elaboration of any scheme for the righteous government of its people'.[2]

The Deputation Scheme, 1882–7

Eventually an important suggestion was published, almost casually, in August 1882:

> Never was there a better opportunity for patriots to wake up than now . . . A few hundred pounds would easily convey a party of natives to England and when there how excellent the chance for them to drop a word for the country . . . We would suggest a subscription, for a deputation to be sent to England with the view of asking for this 'desideratum',—popular representation.[3]

The idea of a deputation did not awaken any immediate response. But *The Gold Coast Times* during succeeding months continued to air local grievances, with an eye on influential opinion elsewhere. Brew's main demand was for a considerable number of non-official members of the Legislative Council. In order that they should not be the 'mere tools' of a Governor, they must be elected by the people. But he disclaimed any idea of universal adult or even household suffrage. There should be a property qualification, to include 'all respectable persons', in small constituencies; admitting that this would be class legislation, he pointed out that it would be a larger class than that which now monopolized power.[4]

The attention of the British press and Parliament was optimistically called to the general state of the Colony, as it appeared to Brew: 'its resources are entirely underdeveloped, its sanitation neglected, its police inefficient, its prisons mismanaged, its taxation improperly levied and its whole civilization backward'.[5] For this sorry state of affairs the Governor was held responsible; and a direct appeal to the British Government did not seem unreasonable. The origin of this idea might perhaps be traced as follows, although such thoughts were not overtly expressed: European monarchs had been held up to Africans as infallibly just and righteous; their representatives in Africa were demonstrably not so. Surely a visit to Europe and a personal explanation would lead to things being put right. Even Paul had appealed to Rome.

There was a more recent precedent, in the deputations sent to the Netherlands from Elmina. After the Fanti attack on the town in mid-1868, the

---

[1] *The Gold Coast Times*, 3 Sept. 1881   [2] Ibid. 10 June 1882.   [3] Ibid. 26 Aug. 1882.
[4] Ibid. 20 Jan. 1883.   [5] Ibid. 10 Feb. 1883, and repeated in several subsequent issues.

inhabitants had commissioned two men—a Dutch officer and George Emin-sang, an African merchant—to go to The Hague to request support. It was believed locally that they had succeeded in securing the recall of an ineffective Governor.[1] In 1870 the people of Elmina, perturbed by reports that they were to be handed over to the British, were encouraged by this experience to propose another deputation. The Governor was first approached with a demand for the facts; finding that the transfer was not yet settled, they publicly suggested:

we may perhaps succeed in putting a stopper on those proceedings. Let Governor Nagtglas select one man, and we another, to proceed to Holland and tell the head man there our opinions on this subject.

The Governor (smiling): Good. I agree to that, provided you will pay the expenses.

Dontah (indignantly): Pay! Of course we'll pay! I'll pay![2]

The Convention transferring Dutch territory to the British was signed in February 1871, not long after this meeting; but it was not ratified for some time, and the inhabitants of Elmina still felt it worth while to draw up a petition of protest, asking indignantly how the Netherlands would like to 'turn English', and submit to foreign authority.[3] D. M. Graves, an educated African trader, was deputed to carry this petition to the States General at The Hague. His arrival there early in 1872 was well timed to encourage the Dutch opposition to the transfer;[4] during a three-day debate in the legislature, he was seated in a conspicuous place in the gallery.[5] But the Convention won a majority vote, ratifications were exchanged, and the actual transfer took place in April 1872. Nevertheless, Graves was granted an audience by the King and Queen;[6] and, according to a later tradition, the Dutch Colonial Minister commended the intelligence and good humour of the delegate, and the cultural development of his people.[7] A standard of courteous and favourable reception had apparently been set; and these Elmina deputations may have encouraged Brew in his plans.

The idea of by-passing the local Government was further reinforced by the example of some European merchants from Cape Coast, led by G. T. H.

[1] Horton, Letters, no. vii, dated 12 Feb. 1870.

[2] Report of meeting at Elmina, 19 Dec. 1870, by C. Bartels; Correspondence relative to the Cession by the Netherlands Government to the British Government of the Dutch Settlements on the West Coast of Africa (London, 1872), C. 670, p. 16.

[3] Petition of 10 Dec. 1871, to States General of the Netherlands from inhabitants of Elmina; CO/96/95.

[4] The Dutch Governor, Nagtglas, was then living in Rotterdam, and was privately instructed by his Government to intercept Graves and try to 'neutralize his action'. Confidential Dispatch of 5 Jan. 1872, from Harris to Granville; FO/37/500. The British Ambassador later invited Graves to a friendly discussion at which Pope Hennessy (shortly to leave for West Africa as Administrator-in-Chief) was also present.

[5] Confidential Dispatch of 18 Jan. 1872, from Harris to Granville; ibid.

[6] The King remained silent on the subject of the mission, and Graves 'could get nothing beyond kind words and gracious smiles'. The Times, 6 Feb. 1872.

[7] J. S. Wartemberg, Sao Jorge D'El Mina (Ilfracombe, n.d.? 1950), p. 37.

Lyall and W. H. Selby[1], who arranged a public meeting in London in 1883 to air their grievances against the Gold Coast Government. They managed to organize a deputation of London and Manchester merchants, who, with the assistance of several Members of Parliament, obtained an interview with the Secretary of State and presented a memorial. Their requests were courteously dealt with, including one for adequate unofficial representation; Lord Derby remarked that he did not know that there had been any desire for it, or that there were competent persons available, but he promised to consider their views.[2] *The Gold Coast Times* displayed much interest in this move, suggesting that 'monster meetings' should be held at Axim, Accra, and Cape Coast, to pass resolutions of support.[3] Lyall received a great welcome on his return to Cape Coast,[4] especially as this coincided with a change of Governor. The episode encouraged those who were dissatisfied with long-distance petitions as the standard method of approaching those in authority. As *The Gold Coast News* remarked, 'Petitions here and there from no recognised political organisation can, and will, not answer any salutary purpose', owing to the official belief that their contents represented the views of only a small clique, and not of the community as a whole.[5]

In November 1885 Brew founded another newspaper, *The Western Echo*.[6] Profiting from his previous experience, he made a great effort to cater for the whole Colony, not just for Cape Coast. In the first issue Brew announced his immediate aim, the one thing needful to save the country from ruin, namely the immediate and prompt dispatch of a deputation to England. Petitions and conventional memorials 'can, and will, not do any good'. If the inhabitants wanted to be treated with serious attention, their representatives would simply have to appear at the Colonial Office.[7] There followed a systematic campaign to reach public opinion in London, over the head of the Governor. Several copies of each issue of the newspaper were sent to the Colonial Office, and others so favoured included the leading members of the Liberal and Conservative Parties, peers as well as commoners: 'nor do we forget the twelve leading papers in Great Britain and Ireland'.[8]

[1] They had collaborated with Brew and Grant in forming a semi-political association in 1881; see Ch. III, p. 149, above.

[2] *The Times*, 13 Dec. 1883; also correspondence in CO/96/152.

[3] *The Gold Coast Times*, 11 Jan. 1884.   [4] Ibid. 10 May 1884.

[5] *The Gold Coast News*, 11 Apr. 1885. This newspaper, launched and edited by an English barrister, W. C. Niblett, had a briefer career than most, issuing the following valediction after only a few months' publication: 'The reading community apparently care very little whether there is such a thing as a journal in their midst; this apathy is really unpardonable . . . We bid you farewell; and pray that Providence may shower His blessings on your country.' Ibid. 29 Aug. 1885.

[6] According to J. E. Casely Hayford, Brew's nephew, he 'developed . . . into the most brilliant journalist the Gold Coast has ever known . . . With all his ability, I never knew a humbler man . . . Never did he pass an article to the head printer without first reading it aloud to us, and inviting our free criticism. The "Owl" column of *The Western Echo* is spoken of to this day.' *Gold Coast Native Institutions* (London, 1903), p. 176.

[7] *The Western Echo*, 18 Nov. 1885.   [8] Ibid. 31 May 1886.

The Governor, Sir William Brandford Griffith, soon began to complain of alleged libellous and seditious remarks in *The Western Echo*; but he did not think it advisable to take any action, lest this should increase the sales and popularity of the new Cape Coast newspaper.[1] He heard rumours of a petition to be sent to the Secretary of State, concerning the state of the roads and the interior generally, and the conduct of the constabulary. On investigation, this proved to be an incomplete report of the deputation scheme.[2] The Governor was particularly annoyed at such attempts to unsettle the minds of the Chiefs, and he warned the Colonial Office of Brew's plan to collect money to send himself and a friend to London.[3]

The main aim of the proposed deputation was to secure some form of representative government or, as Brew preferred to call it, self-government. He had no doubts about the justice of the cause; the British Government could never have intended 'that a body of officials, 4 or 5 in number, should meet, deliberate, and enact laws for us' without any local voice being heard.[4] In almost every issue of *The Western Echo*, especially between April and August 1886, considerable space was devoted to explaining what was required. The principle of appointing unofficial members of the Legislative Council must be revived; but they must not be government nominees, nor must they be 'swamped' by the *ex officio* members. Regular elections should take place for representatives of every class in the community, including illiterates, and Europeans too. The country would then be virtually ruled by this assembly, the Governor-in-Chief himself being under its control. In a remarkable passage, Brew declared that they did not ask for total separation from the British Empire—'May that never be!'—but for a House of Representatives of every section in the community from the highest to the lowest, 'a white Governor and the Union Jack—but nothing more!' Other aims were also mooted; compensation for emancipated slaves and the reduction of spirit duties doubtless appealed to the Chiefs and traders respectively.[5] But it is clear that Brew and his collaborators had the political acumen to realize that political representation was the master-key. In this they were ahead of their time.

The proposed new technique of protest was obviously difficult and expensive; but a glowing description was given of the advantages of Africans themselves going to Downing Street. A memorial, it was argued, consisted only of its written contents: 'it cannot answer questions, it cannot remove doubts, it cannot argue beyond what it contains'. A deputation, on the other hand, would give the Government 'ocular proof' of the capabilities of the people whom they governed and who were now claiming the right to govern themselves, or at least to have their representatives in the local legislature; 'it will

[1] Confidential Dispatch of 2 Feb. 1886, from Brandford Griffith to Stanley; CO/96/172.
[2] Confidential Dispatch of 10 Apr. 1886, from Brandford Griffith to Granville; CO/96/173.
[3] Confidential Dispatch of 14 June 1886, from Brandford Griffith to Granville; CO/96/174.
[4] *The Western Echo*, 7 Aug. 1886.
[5] Ibid. 31 May and 29 July 1886.

be better able to secure the assistance of powerful friends than tons of memorials, which can be shelved with the greatest facility'.[1] How was the deputation to be chosen and paid for? Brew had his answer ready. The country should be divided into three districts: from Axim to the Sweet River, from there to the Seccum, and from that river to the Volta. In each district there would be meetings of Chiefs, headmen, and educated people; money would be collected, and delegates chosen from as many towns as possible, to meet later at either Anomabu, Winneba, or Accra. There, two representatives would be chosen for the deputation, which was at first optimistically scheduled to sail for England at the beginning of July 1886.[2]

Brew now wrote to selected Chiefs and educated inhabitants outlining his plans. In one message he urged: 'A representative Government the Country must have, come what may, but it is obvious this never can be obtained unless we send the deputation to England.' He was careful to add that any agitation must be conducted on constitutional lines.[3] From the first, a special appeal was made to the educated community to explain to the unlettered masses around them the objects of the deputation. Dark hints were also dropped of a hostile counter-movement, and of a 'system d'espionage' among African civil servants.[4]

Brandford Griffith was unable to take the demand for representative institutions at its face value. He alleged that he did not know of a single native in the Colony, outside government service, who could bring 'clean hands, or an honest and intelligent mind' to the duties of a representative of the people.[5] Working on such assumptions, the Governor and his advisers could only put the worst possible interpretation on the deputation scheme. Brandford Griffith suggested that Brew and Edmund Bannerman simply wished to raise money for a holiday in Europe. He also alleged that 'the intelligent and responsible sections of the native community'—presumably the handful in government service, since he had already denied the existence of any others —were averse to the movement.[6]

But the bitterness with which *The Western Echo* attacked what it called 'the stupid, senseless, and suicidal policy' of the Governor and his officials did not altogether help matters.[7] *The Gold Coast Methodist*,[8] while admitting that many criticisms could be made, disapproved of the disrespectful language and offensive expressions frequently used, and refused to believe that the Governor was entirely to blame. Probably Brew's hard-hitting style cost him the European support that had been forthcoming for earlier constitutional protests. An appeal was made to the merchants, but in terms hardly calculated

[1] *The Western Echo*, 21 May 1886.   [2] Ibid. May and June 1886.
[3] Circular Letter of 15 June 1886, from 'Chief Brew of Dunquah, Editor and Proprietor of *The Western Echo*'; CO/96/175.   [4] *The Western Echo*, 14 July and 7 Aug. 1866.
[5] Confidential Dispatch of 14 June 1886, from Brandford Griffith to Granville; CO/96/174.
[6] Confidential Dispatch of 27 July 1886, from Brandford Griffith to Granville; CO/96/175.
[7] For example, 10 Apr. and 30 June 1886.   [8] Dec. 1886.

to rally them to the cause: 'We are aware that you came here only to make money as rapidly as possible ... Nevertheless you owe a duty to the country in which you seek to accumulate wealth.'[1]

In the main coastal towns popular interest, or at least curiosity, was aroused, and public meetings were called in support of the deputation scheme. The first was held in Cape Coast, and was of course fully reported in *The Western Echo*, especially Brew's own speech. A collection was made, and J. W. Sey, a rising African business man, promised 'if anyone gives three-pence I will give a shilling. Let us help the country. (Loud cheers)'[2] The next protest was held at James Town, Accra, where it was calculated that there were more women than men present. The chair was taken by T. F. Bruce, and Edmund Bannerman, the organizer, 'mounted himself on the top of an empty rum puncheon'; speeches and questions were translated into Gã. But some doubts were expressed about the wisdom of joint action with the Fantis, and it was agreed to await the arrival of delegates from the neighbouring towns before reaching a decision. The proceedings ended with three cheers for the Queen.[3] Other meetings were held at Apam, Dixcove, Ada, and Keta; but it soon became obvious that the majority of the Chiefs were not particularly enthusiastic, and that without them there was no ready organization and little money.

Towards the end of 1886 the Governor appointed two unofficial members to the Legislative Council: C. W. Burnett, who had been on the coast with Swanzy's for fourteen years, and George Cleland, an African merchant and divisional Chief of James Town, who was known to be opposed to the deputation scheme.[4] This move may have been influenced by reports that Brew intended to get questions asked in Parliament about the administration of the Gold Coast; but it was well timed, and calculated to undermine the campaign of *The Western Echo*. Allegations that the nominees had been selected for their pliability could not disguise the fact that unofficial representation had been restored.[5]

But even before these appointments had been approved by the Colonial Office, the growing tension in Accra had erupted into violence. The ostensible reason for this was the conduct of a trial, at which King Tackie had unreasonably been asked to 'lower his cloth'—a mark of deference—when giving evidence in the witness box. This trivial incident precipitated a riot in which some police and townsfolk were injured by stone-throwing.[6] It also encouraged

[1] *The Western Echo*, 30 Dec. 1885.   [2] Ibid. 14 July 1886.

[3] Ibid. 29 July 1886. Also report of meeting at James Town, 24 July 1886, enclosed in Confidential Dispatch of 27 July 1886, from Brandford Griffith to Granville; CO/96/175.

[4] Shortly after his nomination, Cleland informed the Governor that he had advised 'Bannerman & Co.' to present their grievances first to the local Government, and that he had told his own James Town people not to subscribe to the deputation scheme. Enclosure in Dispatch No. 24 of 20 Jan. 1887, from Brandford Griffith to Stanhope; CO/96/179.

[5] *The Western Echo*, 9 Oct. 1886.

[6] Report of Commission of Enquiry into Accra Disturbances, 1886; CO/96/179.

King Tackie to throw in his lot with Bannerman, and to write to the King of Akropong suggesting that Krobo East and West should each raise £360 towards the expenses of the deputation, by means of a tax, just as their friends and countrymen the Fantis, from Axim to Winneba and in the interior, were doing.[1] *The Western Echo*, anxious to guard against any defection by this new ally, published a report that the Governor was trying to win over King Tackie, and commented sharply on 'this outrageous attempt' to sever him from the educated community and above all from the deputation movement. The need was for unity between the educated and illiterate classes, and the Government must not be allowed to play off one against the other.[2]

Owing to the increasing difficulties and opposition, the proposed date of departure of the deputation had been postponed more than once. In addition, the would-be organizers were becoming increasingly alarmed at the Governor's uncompromising attitude. At the turn of the year, King Tackie, Edmund Bannerman, and other Accra citizens affirmed their loyalty, and stated that they had always intended to submit their programme to the Administration first, as they might perhaps thus attain their object without sending a deputation.[3] But they feared that this might not be enough to placate Brandford Griffith, and that he might take steps to prevent the deputation leaving the Gold Coast. So a somewhat injudicious telegram (costing £32) was sent direct to Buckingham Palace. This contained a lengthy recapitulation of their constitutional demands and grievances, and included some melodramatic touches: 'Rumoured Governor contemplates arrest and deportation of Kings and Chiefs and principal men for meeting to raise funds to despatch deputation to Colonial Office. Accra loyal and will remain so though Governor goading them to rebellion but earnestly pray for recall of Governor'.[4] Fortunately this telegram did not provoke Brandford Griffith into making any arrests, as might have happened in earlier days. A curt reply came from the Colonial Office, to the effect that representations must be made in the usual way, through the Governor; and the promoters meekly agreed.[5]

The restraint of the Governor, and the official coolness in London, had chilled the ardour of the movement. *The Western Echo* made a desperate attempt to rally support: 'Now or Never! If this opportunity is let slip . . . we deserve the doom and fate of slaves.' The people of Cape Coast were singled out for reproach, especially 'two or three individuals whose wealth is all they have to boast of'. But the influence of the newspaper was waning.

[1] Letter of 30 Oct. 1886, from King Tackie to King of Akropong, enclosed in Dispatch No. 24 of 20 Jan. 1887, from Brandford Griffith to Stanhope; CO/96/179.

[2] *The Western Echo*, 23 Oct. 1886.

[3] Letter of 29 Dec. 1886, from King Tackie and others to Acting Colonial Secretary; CO/96/179.

[4] Telegram of 9 Jan. 1887, from King, Chiefs and people of Accra to Sir Henry Ponsonby, for Her Majesty the Queen, London; CO/96/187.

[5] Letter of 29 Jan. 1887, from King Tackie and others to Governor; CO/96/180.

In the same issue readers were solemnly admonished:

our staff cannot subsist on the iron, lead and brass of which our plant consists, nor on the ink, paper and the like of which our materials are composed ... Our staff is on the point of being broken up owing to our readers being anxious to read the paper but being without anxiety to pay for the same.[1]

The Governor, who considered *The Western Echo* 'a scurrilous, malignant and mendacious publication', had some justification for thinking that no attention was given locally to anything it published.[2]

In April 1887 King Tackie, Bannerman, and others were called to the Castle to receive a fuller message from the Secretary of State in reply to their telegram. This emphasized that representations made to the Governor in writing would receive full and careful consideration in London; and added that no deputation would be received unless the consent of the Colonial Office had been given before it left the country.[3] Brandford Griffith believed that as a result of this reply the people in Accra became dissatisfied with the 'foolish conduct' in which they had been encouraged by Bannerman and his associates.[4] *The Western Echo* in Cape Coast tried to put a bold face on the situation: if the delegates could not be officially received, so much the better, for then they could appear on public platforms in various towns and plead their cause 'before the British nation. Sir Henry Holland cannot prevent *that*'.[5]

But the *raison d'être* of the deputation was fast disappearing. During 1887–8 fuller expression was given to Cape Coast views in the Legislative Council. On one occasion, three extraordinary members were appointed from that town;[6] and when Cleland died,[7] he was replaced permanently by John Sarbah, 'a merchant of pure African descent, resident at Cape Coast, of good social and commercial repute and independent means'.[8]

If anything more was needed to doom the deputation scheme, it was the financial decline and fall of *The Western Echo*. The paper had been published every ten days in November and December 1885, and once a fortnight during 1886; but thereafter only about once a month. The last issue appeared in December 1887, with a valedictory reproach to the Secretary of State for refusing to receive a deputation, and so providing 'our weak-kneed brethren' with an excuse for not giving more than verbal assistance. The epitaph on

[1] *The Western Echo*, 10–27 Jan. 1887.
[2] Dispatch No. 101 of 1 Apr. 1887, from Brandford Griffith to Holland; CO/96/180.
[3] Dispatch No. 45 of 4 Mar. 1887, from Holland to Brandford Griffith; CO/96/179. Extracts were published in the *Government Gazette*, 6 Apr. 1887.
[4] Dispatch No. 121 of 7 Apr. 1887, from Brandford Griffith to Holland; CO/96/180.
[5] *The Western Echo*, 14–28 Apr. 1887.
[6] These were F. C. Grant, John Sarbah, and W. Hutchison; they were appointed under Section 15 of the Royal Instructions of 13 Jan. 1886, while Brandford Griffith was on leave. Dispatch No. 203 of 9 June 1887, from White to Holland; CO/96/181.
[7] 'Mr. Cleland was one of the few trustworthy natives.' Minute of 28 Dec. 1887, by Hemming; CO/96/185.
[8] Dispatch No. 157 of 12 May 1888, from Brandford Griffith to Knutsford; CO/96/191.

Brew's scheme appeared in *The Gold Coast Echo*, the successor to *The Western Echo*, edited by Casely Hayford. 'A Young Fanti' wrote: 'we are disunited, and . . . selfish in the extreme; patriotism . . . is not known to the majority of us'. He criticized those who had been saying in effect: 'Why should I, A, contribute a penny towards the despatching to England of B, who though he may be an abler man and more fitted to represent the country than myself, yet would never have a chance of visiting England but for my contribution?'[1]

No doubt such remarks encouraged officials to believe that the idea of a deputation had arisen solely from the attractions of a free passage to a land of promise and opportunity. The Colonial Office certainly took this view throughout, calling the scheme a swindle, since a much smaller sum than the £5,400 aimed at would suffice for a bona fide transaction.[2] Brew himself was known to be in debt;[3] and it is almost impossible, at this distance in time, to separate the motives of public and private advantage that prompted him and his friends. The fact that Brew went to London, on his own personal affairs, early in 1888, would suggest, however, that he was not so short of funds that he needed to collect money in this way. His anxiety to present Gold Coast grievances in London cannot entirely be written off as political camouflage.

Initially, a serious grievance had existed concerning the Legislative Council. But the belated grant of additional representation was sufficient to allay the demand for the time being, especially among the merchants; and political representation had not yet become such a burning issue as to touch the ordinary man's pocket. In Ashanti a threat to national independence in 1896 was able quickly to win the powerful backing of the Asantehene for the Ansahs' embassy in London. In the less politically integrated Colony, it was the lands issue, affecting personally a large number of Africans, especially the Chiefs, that aroused the necessary mass indignation to launch a deputation.[4] Nevertheless, the foundered scheme of 1885–7 had charted out some of the straits and barriers of the course ahead.

Municipal Government as a 'Stepping-stone'

Temporarily thwarted in their wider national aspirations, the educated Africans in Cape Coast next turned their attention to conditions within the town, and began to work out a system which, they hoped, would at least give them a voice in municipal government. They felt that in general the Chiefs had little control over the people, that the Asafo companies were frequently on the verge of collision, and that only their own intervention in recent years had prevented bloodshed. In 1887, therefore, a series of local elections was held in Cape Coast, which the organizers described as 'our humble effort to

[1] *The Gold Coast Echo*, 15–29 Feb. 1888.
[2] Minute of 2 Mar. 1887, by R. H. Meade; CO/96/179.
[3] Confidential Dispatch of 30 Sept. 1887, from White to Holland; CO/96/183.
[4] For Brew's connexion with both these issues, see Ch. VII, pp. 286–9, and Ch. IX, pp. 337–8, 344, 347, above.

train up our people in the art of self-government. Since that is professed to be the primary object which the British Government has in view.'[1]

Meetings were convened of the seven Cape Coast companies, each of which proceeded to elect a Chief, to represent them and to be answerable for their good conduct; all then jointly chose one Head Chief, Cudjoe Imbrah, 'known as Master of Arms from time immemorial'. Seven educated councillors were next elected by the companies, to be responsible for maintaining order, taking as their guide Pine's Municipalities Ordinance of 1858. These were F. C. Grant, John Sarbah, James Sago, J. W. Sey, W. E. Pietersen, T. F. E. Jones, and A. Q. Yarquah. Considerable support and publicity was given to the elections by *The Western Echo*.[2]

The organizers now hastened to inform the Government of what they had done and of the reforms they hoped to secure, for which they offered the services of the educated community. But the Administrator, F. B. P. White, did not appreciate this *fait accompli*, and at once summoned the Cape Coast Chiefs, before whom he staged almost a caricature of the paternal colonial attitude, declaring 'I cannot believe that the Chiefs I see with my eyes could have done or written this letter.' He demanded to know 'who is it you want to be the Head Chief in preference to the British Crown and Authority here?' and accused the educated Fantis of misleading the Chiefs:

I don't think you would have dared to write such a letter to the King of Ashantee ... he would have cut off all your heads. But we don't do that in Great Britain, and the Queen is ready to forgive you for having written it, so instead of cutting your heads off I forgive you, I have got your welfare at heart, everyone of you.[3]

The grievances and attempts at municipal self-help of the educated *élite* were given more careful and sympathetic consideration at the Colonial Office, notably in a minute written by Sidney Webb. Their efforts appeared to him worthy of praise, and just what an English town would have done. 'There is practically no Government at Cape Coast: the people take steps to create one ... Surely there never was an opportunity better fitted for trying those Municipalities which we have been professedly pressing on the Governors.'[4] The Secretary of State then suggested to White that this was a favourable opportunity for the creation of a semi-official municipal board.[5] Meanwhile Grant and his friends, including Brew, Timothy Laing, and J. F. Amissah, had proposed a formal scheme for municipal government that left

[1] Letter of 18 May 1887, from F. C. Grant and others (Chiefs, councillors, captains and educated natives of Cape Coast) to White, enclosed in his Dispatch No. 246 of 5 July 1887, to Holland; CO/96/182.

[2] According to Casely Hayford, who was then assisting his uncle to edit *The Western Echo*, the elections were held 'under its auspices'; he also claimed that this form of representation became 'the prototype' of the later Aborigines' Rights Protection Society. *Gold Coast Native Institutions*, pp. 176-7.   [3] Report of meeting at Cape Coast, 13 June 1887; CO/96/182.

[4] Minute of 25 Aug. 1887, by S. Webb; ibid.

[5] Dispatch No. 227 of 5 Sept. 1887, from Holland to White; ibid.

both officials and Chiefs out of account. A council of seven members should be elected, every alternate year, by householders and tenants paying at least £24 per annum in rent; a Mayor, elected annually from among the councillors, should preside over his own court. The crucial point was their request for an annual grant; they suggested that up to £10,000 would be required, but that the municipality might be able to dispense with this later on, once the people were assured of the benefits from paying rates of some kind.[1]

The Administrator and his advisers appear to have disliked this scheme as cordially as they distrusted its authors. An exhaustive account of their characters and morals accompanied the documents to London. Grant was described as a West Indian who possessed no influence over the people, and no claim to represent them.[2] Brew in particular was attacked, as a disbarred solicitor, generally disliked and distrusted, whose real object was 'to obtain a Court where he could practise'. Both were said to be deeply in debt, and to have only managed to keep their creditors quiet by promising to pay once the council was established. The other signatories were dismissed, in this classic example of Secretariat smear, as 'men of straw'. The Chiefs, on the other hand, were alleged to be totally against the plan, on the grounds that its adoption would destroy their power, dignity, and revenue. The educated people—unspecified —who were satisfied with the existing state of affairs were said to be prepared to admit that the Government had done a great deal for the town. White professed himself ready to grant Cape Coast a 'workable' system of municipal institutions, but there must be some local source of revenue.[3] Seasoned opinion at the Colonial Office was at once suspicious: 'Nice "pickings" Messrs. Grant and Brew no doubt anticipate.' Taking the confidential gossip from Cape Coast at its face value, A. W. L. Hemming agreed that the whole scheme was much too ambitious for people who were 'still wholly barbarous and uncivilized';[4] so it was not sanctioned.[5]

It says much for the optimism of the colonial authorities that they now proceeded to prepare legislation which did not even attempt to build upon the foundation of the Cape Coast proposals, and which yet would depend entirely upon the co-operation of the inhabitants for its execution. An elected majority on the town councils was the main bait offered; but there was to be no compromise on the question of finance. The Secretary of State insisted that no grant-in-aid of any kind should be made from the funds of the

[1] Letter of 6 July 1887, from Grant and others to Acting Colonial Secretary, enclosed in Dispatch No. 361 of 30 Sept. 1887, from White to Holland; CO/96/183.

[2] Contrast Pope Hennessy's description of Grant, fifteen years previously; p. 408, above. Only three months earlier White had expressed himself 'pleased with the advice and assistance' given by three extraordinary members of the Legislative Council, one of whom was Grant. Dispatch No. 203 of 9 June 1887, from Administrator to Holland; CO/96/181.

[3] Confidential Minute of 16 Sept. 1887, by P. Hughes, and covering Confidential Dispatch of 30 Sept. 1887, from White to Holland; CO/96/183.

[4] Minute of 6 Nov. 1887, by Hemming; ibid.

[5] Dispatch No. 323 of 11 Nov. 1887, from Holland to Brandford Griffith; ibid.

Colony. The Governor, Brandford Griffith, was pessimistic about the prospects of any scheme which involved the direct payment of rates; but he had a Bill drafted by his son, the Acting Queen's Advocate, on the lines laid down from London.[1]

The draft Municipalities Ordinance, published early in 1888, provided for the establishment of municipal councils as follows:

Membership: a President and three members were to be appointed by the Governor; six others were to be elected.[2]

Voters: an assessment was to be made, every alternate year, of the annual value of houses; owners of houses of an annual value of £2 or more were to be qualified to vote.

Powers of Council: to deal with street sanitation, water supply, general conservancy, and inspection of nuisances; and to levy rates on all houses having an annual value of £2 or more.

As soon as this was published, many editorials and letters on the subject appeared in *The Gold Coast Echo* from August to October 1888. The 'Elected Committee of Cape Coast' discussed the proposals in detail, and produced their own radically amended Bill.[3] The Secretary of State agreed that minor adjustments might be accepted, at the Governor's discretion, and authorized the admission of tenant-occupiers and not just house-owners to the vote;[4] but he continued to insist that finance for the proposed councils must be raised by house rates, so as to relieve the colonial revenue.[5]

The Cape Coast group had not yet given up hope that the Government could be persuaded to make a direct grant. During 1889 they persuaded over 170 inhabitants to sign a petition to the Secretary of State, which went so far as to assert: 'The principle that Representation means taxation cannot be applied to this Colony. For from time immemorial we have enjoyed representative institutions without such direct taxation as is contemplated'. If the Government would not agree to a lump sum, perhaps it could consider specific grants-in-aid. This document was drafted by the recently qualified lawyer, J. Mensah Sarbah—son of John—whose hand can easily be recognized

[1] Memorandum of 7 Feb. 1888, by Acting Queen's Advocate, and covering Dispatch No. 87 of 26 Mar. 1888, from Brandford Griffith to Holland; CO/96/190.

[2] The Secretary of State suggested that the elections should be organized by tribes or companies. Dispatch No. 227 of 5 Sept. 1887, from Holland to White; CO/96/182. But this idea was deliberately omitted, because it would mean that ratepayers and non-ratepayers would vote indiscriminately, and people might even come in from the bush for the purpose; whereas the whole scheme must depend on payment of house rates.

[3] Enclosed in Confidential Dispatch of 5 Nov. 1888, from Brandford Griffith to Knutsford; CO/96/195.

[4] This had been suggested by Sidney Webb, who had criticized the original Bill on the grounds that if most of the occupiers were not also house-owners, there would be 'a mere oligarchic franchise (without popular participation) which would certainly fail'. Minute of 30 Apr. 1888; CO/96/190.

[5] Dispatch No. 175 of 25 May and Confidential Dispatch of 6 Dec. 1888, from Knutsford to Brandford Griffith; ibid. and CO/96/195.

in a lament over the 'great disorganisation of society' and in the demand: 'grant us a Municipality built on our native institutions so adapted, re-organised and reformed as to satisfy our modern wants'.[1] It should be remembered that this was the foundation year of the *Mfantsi Amanbuhu Fékuw*, of which Mensah Sarbah was the prime mover.[2]

The Governor had no sympathy with the views of the petitioners, and forwarded to London the customary critical personal analysis, even more comprehensive, though less scandalous, than usual.[3] The Colonial Office, however, continued to press him for some form of acceptable action. Would there be any objection, he was asked while in London, to setting up a municipality and handing over a sum of money representing the amount voted in the Estimates for certain local services? Then if more funds were needed for special purposes, rates would have to be levied: 'we can say "yes you can have it if you will raise the money"'. But to turn down the petition outright would extinguish any hope of introducing a system which, carefully nursed, might relieve the central Government of much expenditure.[4]

Brandford Griffith was no longer open to argument on this matter. He blustered that it would be injudicious and impolitic to yield to 'the narrow-minded and intensely selfish ideas' of the natives, in their ignorance of 'the broad, enlightened, straightforward and liberal views' of English statesmen.[5] Such strong opinions, coming from a Governor, had to be respected, although not all London officials found his reasoning conclusive.[6] It was small comfort that their gloomy forecast was proved correct. Although the Municipalities Ordinance was enacted, almost in its original form, before the end of 1889, it remained a dead letter. Over two years later Brandford Griffith reported that in no town on the coast had the inhabitants volunteered to put it into force.[7]

Gold Coast Government officials were also dissatisfied with the law as it stood. A. M. Ashmore, Acting Colonial Secretary in 1894, was one of these who felt that it was unworkable, mainly because of too many elected seats on the municipalities, whereas it was difficult enough to find only one or two unofficial members suitable to sit in the Legislative Council. As for the idea of an elected Treasurer, this was in effect 'to proclaim a ballot for the privilege of embezzling the public funds'.[8] He therefore assisted in drafting a new Bill, based largely on his experience in Ceylon, and designed to secure greater

[1] Petition of 5 June 1889, to Secretary of State from principal inhabitants of Cape Coast, enclosed in Dispatch No. 180 of 18 June 1889, from Brandford Griffith to Knutsford; CO/96/202.
[2] Cf. Ch. III, p. 150, above.
[3] Confidential Dispatch of 28 June 1889, from Brandford Griffith to Knutsford; CO/96/202.
[4] Minute of 2 Aug. 1889, Meade; ibid.
[5] Minute of 5 Nov. 1889, by Brandford Griffith; ibid.
[6] Minute of 8 Nov. 1889, by J. Bramston; ibid.
[7] Confidential Dispatch of 7 Jan. 1892, from Brandford Griffith to Knutsford; CO/96/222.
[8] Memorandum on Local Government in Coast Towns by A. M. Ashmore, dated 6 Aug. 1894; CO/96/254.

central control over town councils; these were now to consist half of nominated officials, half of elected unofficials, with an additional casting vote for the District Commissioner as President. At the same time, it was conceded that the yield of house rates could be supplemented from—though not replaced by—the proceeds of general indirect taxation.

The Town Councils Bill reached the Legislative Council in November 1894. The principle of a rate on property remained a major source of objection, but there were also complaints of lack of time for adequate discussion. The measure was pushed through all its stages on the same day, standing orders being suspended for the purpose; the main reason was that Ashmore was just due to go on leave, but the Governor promised to wait two months so as to allow objections to be forwarded to London with the Ordinance.[1] This was something of a tactical error, for opposition was immediately encouraged.

At a public meeting in Accra, a deputation was appointed to meet the Governor and 'impress upon him the opposition of the people' to both the Town Councils Ordinance and the Crown Lands Bill.[2] King Tackie of Ussher Town, King Dowuona of Christiansborg, and Chief Ababio of James Town were accompanied by four young barristers, Charles Bannerman, William Addo, Philip Randolph, and F. H. Fearon, who helped to detail the municipal objections, item by item. Their most unexpected excuse stole the Governor's own argument that they were 'not sufficiently civilized' to submit to such an Ordinance. But he pointedly suggested that the real trouble was that they did not want to put their hands into their pockets.[3]

The Accra opposition continued to grow. A Town Committee was formed, with E. Bannerman as President, Addo as Secretary, and T. Hutton Mills as 'linguist', prominently supported by J. Bright Davies, editor of *The Gold Coast Chronicle*. A printed petition to the Secretary of State revived the old argument that 'taxation and representation should go hand in hand'. In fact, it would appear that neither was wanted at the local level; the petitioners could see no necessity for imposing additional burdens under the pretext of giving them 'municipal rights which they have neither demanded nor required'.[4] The merchants joined in the outcry, and a deputation from the recently formed Accra Chamber of Commerce complained that the Ordinance

[1] *Legislative Council Minutes*, 14 Nov. 1894.

[2] Report of public meeting in Accra, 22 Jan. 1895, enclosed in Dispatch No. 39 of 30 Jan. 1895, from Brandford Griffith to Ripon; CO/96/254.

[3] Report of meeting with deputation, 2 Feb. 1895; CO/96/268. Also Letter of 3 July 1895, from Brandford Griffith to Colonial Office; ibid. The Attorney-General had already warned the Governor: 'Until the people are willing to tax themselves for local purposes, and are sufficiently advanced to be able to take an honest and intelligent interest in their own affairs, I consider such attempts as this will fail.' Memorandum of 12 Jan. 1895, by E. B. Hindle, enclosed in Dispatch No. 39 of 30 Jan. 1895, from Brandford Griffith to Ripon; CO/96/254.

[4] Petition of 30 Mar. 1895, to Secretary of State from Kings of Ussher Town and Christiansborg, Chief Ababio of James Town, and 52 merchants and residents, enclosed in Dispatch No. 140 of 6 Apr. 1895, from Brandford Griffith to Ripon; CO/96/256.

had been passed 'behind their backs'.[1] The Governor, on tour, was lobbied by the King of Akropong and traders in Odumasi; and petitions were organized in Cape Coast, Anomabu, and Winneba.[2]

As a result, the implementation of the Ordinance was delayed until after Brandford Griffith had left; and the next Governor, Sir William Maxwell, waited until after the Ashanti campaign before deciding to apply it to Accra and Christiansborg, in 1896. The limits of the municipality were then defined, and the number of councillors fixed at six.[3] Immediately Kings Tackie and Dowuona secured a public interview with Maxwell, at which they declared their opposition, and soon there were disorderly demonstrations of protest, especially by the women.[4] The organizers later petitioned the Governor, who had declined to receive them, 'on behalf of ourselves and all the women of the lower or illiterate class of Accra';[5] this was followed six months later by a printed petition, drafted with legal advice, which was claimed to be the first direct appeal from the women of the Gold Coast to the Secretary of State.[6]

It is not surprising that no candidates at all were forthcoming for election to the Accra Town Council; and it was not until early 1898 that three Africans —Charles Bannerman, E. Quartey-Papafio, and Chief Ababio—could be persuaded even to accept nomination.[7] The Council's first attempt to collect rates in that year provoked serious resistance, actively encouraged by King Tackie.[8] Noisy meetings were held, the African councillors were intimidated and the town was placed under the Peace Preservation Ordinance. A deputation of educated men met the Governor, who told them, 'There is no crisis. . . . I shall expect you to advise the people to be quiet.' Order was restored after the arrest of King Tackie's linguist and war captain, and a threat to double the unpaid rates.[9] But the Town Council, 'born in an atmosphere of

---

[1] Report of meeting with deputation, 16 May 1895, enclosed in Dispatch No. 211 of 23 May 1895, from Maxwell to Ripon; CO/96/257.

[2] Petitions of 9 Apr. and 9 May 1895, to Secretary of State, enclosed in Dispatches Nos. 196 of 11 May and 219 of 28 May 1895, from Maxwell to Ripon; ibid. A petition of 20 May 1895, from seventy-three Chiefs and others in Winneba to the Secretary of State, did not get beyond Accra, as there was some doubt about the validity of the signatures. Ghartey Papers, G.N. Archives.

[3] Government Gazette, 31 July 1896.

[4] Dispatch No. 2 of 2 Jan. 1897, from Maxwell to Chamberlain; CO/96/288.

[5] Petition of 4 Dec. 1896, to Governor from Akole Ankrah ('her X mark') and other illiterate women, enclosed in Dispatch No. 386 of 4 Sept. 1897, from Maxwell to Chamberlain; CO/96/298.

[6] Petition of 31 May 1897, to Secretary of State from the women of Accra and Christiansborg; ibid. For the 'humble petition of the ladies of the Gold Coast Protectorate' of 1875, see Ch. VIII, p. 304 n., above.

[7] Dispatch No. 282 of 4 July 1898, from Hodgson to Chamberlain; CO/96/318.

[8] The King's annual stipend of £100, first paid in 1893, had been withdrawn in 1897 'until the first year's rates under the Town Council Ordinance, 1894, have been collected'. Secret Dispatch of 9 June 1897, from Maxwell to Chamberlain; CO/96/294. The King had had two of his own houses assessed, to pay rates of 10s. 3d. and 3s.

[9] Dispatch No. 282 of 4 July 1898 and enclosures, from Hodgson to Chamberlain; CO/96/318.

ill-will and sullen resentment',[1] never worked smoothly, mainly owing to the lack of public support.[2]

The conclusion drawn in London was that 'In Africa people object very strongly to being expected to manage their own affairs.'[3] This is hardly supported by the evidence of various unofficial attempts to establish some form of municipal government, and of the considerable amount of organizing ability that was expended upon committees and demonstrations of protest. As the Colonial Office had recognized in 1889, town councils could have won the co-operation of the people, under certain circumstances; and there were several substantial reasons why they did not.

The first, and historically the most important, was the association of municipal government with local rates. This had been one of the main causes of the failure of Pine's progressive scheme in 1858; and ever since the poll tax the people's dislike of any form of direct taxation, central or local, had been almost pathological in its intensity. There was indeed some genuine hardship. The inhabitants of James Town claimed: 'a poorer neighbourhood it would be difficult to find in the Eastern District';[4] and King Tackie complained at the end of 1898 that 'by reason of the hardness of the times many of the houses are without doors and windows'.[5] Although one chairborne official declared, 'There is practically no poverty on the West Coast of Africa',[6] the Ordinance was amended in 1900 to allow rate exemptions in cases of need. But this was not sufficient to endear the councils to the people.

The recalcitrant attitude of the Chiefs was perhaps the second main reason for the widespread opposition. From very early days, the emergence of elected authorities to govern the towns had appeared as a threat to their traditional rights and privileges, especially when it came to the administration of justice. During 1859–1860 the municipal mayor's court had aroused some hostility in Cape Coast.[7] Now the Chiefs, already resenting the loss of their court fees and fines, and the curtailment of their powers by the central administration,[8]

[1] 'Report by the Town Councils Committee on the Constitution and Working of the existing Town Councils in the Colony', Sessional Paper No. XVII of 1922–23.

[2] In 1901 the attractions of office were sufficient for twelve candidates to be nominated for the elected seats; but out of 1,651 qualified electors, only 175 voted, and this remained a record number for nearly twenty years. In 1903 no candidates at all were nominated, 'an unmistakable sign of indifference of the native population to municipal affairs'; so the Governor appointed all the councillors. Accra Town Council, Annual Report, 1901 and 1903. For the similar sequence of protests followed by electoral apathy in Cape Coast and Sekondi, see Ch. X, pp. 360–1, above.

[3] Minute of 14 Nov. 1898; CO/96/318.

[4] Petition of 22 Jan. 1895, to Governor and Legislative Council from King, Chiefs and headmen of James Town, enclosed in Dispatch No. 39 of 30 Jan. 1895, from Brandford Griffith to Ripon; CO/96/254.

[5] Petition of 10 Dec. 1898, from King Tackie and 70 other residents of Accra, enclosed in Confidential Dispatch of 4 Jan. 1899, from Low to Chamberlain; CO/96/337.

[6] Minute of 2 Feb. 1899, by R. L. Antrobus; ibid.

[7] Cf. Ch. IV, p. 186, above.

[8] See Ch. XII, p. 466, below, especially Nathan's comments on the diminution of King Tackie's prestige and powers.

were not even being invited to co-operate in these new forms of town government, although the Government had repeatedly been urged to use traditional native institutions as the model for municipal government.

The latest legislation had, moreover, succeeded in antagonizing not only the Chiefs but the educated townspeople as well. This third source of opposition was partly the cumulative result of past blunders, where the initiative of the educated *élite* in developing their own town committees had been either suppressed or ignored. This had happened in Accra in 1869,[1] as well as in Cape Coast in 1887. Their protests were also invited by the very nature of the 1894 Ordinance. As a later inquiry suggested, this had been modelled on an example from Ceylon without adequate discussion and with little regard to the difference in conditions between the two countries, instead of following the principles of Pine's early experiment, which had given real power and responsibility to elected African councillors.[2]

The principle of an official majority did nothing to arouse public interest in the humdrum tasks of local government. Nor did it offer the educated leaders any incentive by way of increased responsibility to help in overcoming the opposition to taxation.[3] Mensah Sarbah later claimed that they were protesting not so much against the tax as from a desire to participate in the government of their country;[4] but such arguments went unheeded. Small wonder, then, that the growing demand for some degree of self-government found expression in attacks upon the town councils, rather than attempts to enter and reform them from the inside. Election to such bodies carried neither the prestige of membership of the Legislative Council, nor the opportunity for real control at the local level; so after the initial opposition the main problem was the almost complete apathy and indifference of educated Africans, which went far to nullify the whole system.

Prior Claims at the Centre

Meanwhile, the last decade of the nineteenth century saw a considerable increase in the pressure for further unofficial representation in the Legislative Council. John Sarbah continued as the only African member until his death in 1892, when Brandford Griffith expressed regret at the loss of such a loyal and patriotic man, a useful—if not very active—member of the Council. But, as on previous occasions, he could not see any suitable African to fill the vacancy.[5] The Governor could hardly have expected this omission to pass

---

[1] See Ch. VI, pp. 239–40, above.   [2] *Sessional Paper No. XVII of 1922–23.*

[3] In 1913 a European member of the Legislative Council alleged that the town councils were being managed by officials as if they were government departments; that owing to the official majority, 'the native members are ignored, they have little or no influence upon the actions of the Council'; and that there was not even a measure of self-government. W. H. Grey, *Legislative Council Minutes*, 26 Mar. 1913.

[4] *The West African Mail*, 15 Oct. 1905.

[5] Dispatch No. 164 of 7 July 1892, from Brandford Griffith to Knutsford; CO/96/224.

unnoticed. Now, however, it was the merchants who took the initiative in protest, partly because they were dissatisfied over other matters as well. It was at this juncture that W. Waters—a leading agent of Swanzy's, who had been acting as a temporary member of the Legislative Council during the absence of Burnett—produced his memorial from the local merchants, agents, and traders, against the 10 per cent. customs duty.[1] This, in the course of a formidable indictment of Brandford Griffith's long governorship, proclaimed the urgent necessity of securing adequate representation of the general public on the Legislative Council; the trading community, especially, upon which the whole basis of the Government rested, had 'practically no voice whatever' in the administration of the Colony. The single unofficial member, they claimed, had no influence on the Council, and was in a hopeless minority.[2]

As a further protest, Waters himself resigned from the Legislative Council on the grounds that his reasoned objections to a Bill affecting commercial interests had not even been recorded: 'I have long felt that the position of a single Unofficial Member is a mere nonentity and proceedings of Yesterday fully confirm this.'[3] When the Secretary of State heard about this he advised the Governor that there should be a total of three unofficial members.[4] But *The Gold Coast People* had much more drastic proposals. The existing constitution was dismissed as a sham, since the voice of the African members was hardly ever effective, nor their opinion able to influence administrative action, owing to the official majority. The country could provide at least 'six worthy characters to represent its interests in the Council'.[5]

Meanwhile, Brandford Griffith was apparently finding it difficult to suggest even one suitable member either to replace Sarbah, or to act (instead of Waters) for Burnett. 'Mentally, I went over every town in the Colony, but where a name occurred it had to be dropped for some unfitness', he explained to the Colonial Office, pointing out that his difficulty would be even greater if the number of unofficial members were increased.[6] In the end the Governor nominated J. H. Cheetham, an African merchant of Accra; but the Secretary of State requested him to bear in mind the importance of finding another suitable mercantile representative.[7]

In the middle of 1893 Brandford Griffith produced his voluminous reply to the merchants' memorial, which had taken him many months to prepare. He had thought out carefully all the problems in the way of unofficial African

[1] See Ch. VIII, pp. 309–11, above.
[2] *Despatch from Governor Sir W. Brandford Griffith, K.C.M.G., forwarding a Memorial from Merchants, Agents, and Traders of the Gold Coast Colony, with his Observations and the Secretary of State's Reply* (London, 1893), C. 7225.
[3] Letter of 1 Nov. 1892, from Waters to Brandford Griffith, enclosed in his Dispatch No. 339 of 26 Nov. 1892, to Ripon; CO/96/226.
[4] Confidential Dispatch of 12 Jan. 1893, from Ripon to Brandford Griffith; ibid.
[5] *The Gold Coast People*, 14 Jan. 1893.
[6] Confidential Dispatch of 6 Mar. 1893, from Brandford Griffith to Ripon; CO/96/232.
[7] Confidential Dispatch of 24 Apr. 1893, from Ripon to Brandford Griffith; ibid.

representation, such as tribal antipathies, and the difficulties of finding English-speaking, cultured Africans of some substance, with a respected position, integrity and independence of character. On the other hand, he explained, European agents had not the time to fulfil properly their duties on the Legislative Council.[1] The truth was that the Governor did not want any of them; he complained that their usefulness was greatly reduced by their necessary lack of acquaintance with official matters; while their views often appeared to him to be so short-sighted, and restricted by motives of self-interest, as to deprive their speeches of 'any real legislative value'.[2]

The Governor was now nearly seventy years old, and although he was still held in high regard by the Colonial Office, it was known there that he was an increasingly difficult man to work either with or for.[3] Brandford Griffith complained that he and his officials were overworked, although this was partly due to excessive centralization and attention to minutiae at headquarters.[4] Because of petty jealousy he stubbornly delayed implementing several major schemes of reform proposed by his energetic Colonial Secretary, F. M. Hodgson. He alleged that the European merchants were trying to obstruct the efforts of the Government and its officers 'by both aggressive and passive means', and carried his feud with them to the extent of forbidding them to stay at Aburi sanatorium.[5]

While the Governor was away on leave, Hodgson reported that Waters was willing to resume his seat, in the continued absence of Burnett. Although the Colonial Office realized that Brandford Griffith might be extremely indignant, they agreed to this reappointment because Hodgson was unable to recommend anyone else.[6] But early in 1894 he found an African merchant to act as the third unofficial member of the Legislative Council: John Vanderpuiye, the educated divisional Chief of Ussher Town, who lived comfortably in European style. The fact that there was no scandal known about him seems to have been an important consideration at this time. Hodgson refused to consider Edmund Bannerman, 'whose periodic fits of insobriety render him unfitted for the honourable position', while F. H. Fearon and E. Quartey-Papafio, although more influential in Accra than Vanderpuiye, were ruled out

---

[1] Even when Burnett had been in the Gold Coast, he had seldom bothered to attend the Legislative Council; from Dec. 1889 until June 1893 he had been present at only three out of seventy-five possible sittings.

[2] Dispatch No. 171 of 12 June 1893, from Brandford Griffith to Ripon; C. 7225.

[3] While Brandford Griffith was on leave in England during 1893–4 the Colonial Office suggested that he should retire. But it was eventually agreed that he could wait until the completion of a particularly personal project, the Anglican Church in Accra, in 1895. CO/96/237 and 247.

[4] One head of department complained privately to the Colonial Office: 'I cannot order a new washhand basin without the Governor's written authority—and then have to answer a string of enquiries as to the breakage of the old one!' Quoted in Minute of 18 Apr. 1893, by Hemming; CO/96/232.

[5] Dispatch No. 209 of 5 July 1893, from Brandford Griffith to Ripon; CO/96/235.

[6] Minute of 28 Oct. 1893, by Hemming, and Telegram of 1 Nov. 1893, from Ripon to Hodgson; CO/96/237.

—one was a native of Sierra Leone, and the other had a record which was 'not . . . altogether untarnished'.[1]

In 1895 Sir William Maxwell, the new Governor, secured permission from the Colonial Office to appoint a fourth unofficial member to the Legislative Council. He argued that as Burnett lived at Cape Coast, and as the other members concerned themselves little with public affairs, except when African interests, of a more or less personal nature, were under consideration, another European should be appointed.[2] The pattern of two European and two African unofficial members of the Legislative Council was to last for the next twenty years.[3]

The introduction of unpopular land legislation during 1894–7 at once brought the composition of the Legislative Council under strong African criticism. The Chiefs of Elmina and of other former Dutch settlements complained of having lost under the British Government the privilege of representation which they had formerly enjoyed.[4] In 1897 some Fanti Chiefs, claiming the right to be represented by counsel against the Lands Bill, agreed that they had no member of their own to give them any control over or voice in matters before the Legislative Council.[5] Cape Coast, in particular, had had no representative since the death of John Sarbah in 1892. When the Cape Coast leaders of the Lands Bill protest organized a parallel petition for a radical alteration in the constitution, they seemed to be under the misapprehension that 'the natives have no independent representation whatever in the Council'. Perhaps they meant the natives of Cape Coast.

This 1898 petition is worthy of study, since it was the first time that a major constitutional proposal had accepted the Legislative Council as the basis for further advance. Political power was now clearly seen to lie at the centre, with the law-making body, as the number of Ordinances and their influence on the development of the Colony increased. British-style parliamentary government was henceforward assumed to be the goal; the demand was therefore made for elected representatives:

Your Petitioners respectfully suggest as a first step . . . the Kings and Chiefs of the Colony and the Protectorate to elect to the Legislative Council eight additional members, of whom three shall also be members of the Executive Council . . . for the

[1] Confidential Dispatch of 27 Feb. 1894, from Hodgson to Ripon; CO/96/243. The Government never nominated any other than Gold Coast Africans to the Legislative Council. But in 1930 G. J. Christian, who had come from the West Indies, was elected by the ratepayers of Sekondi, and was returned unopposed until his death in 1941.
[2] Confidential Dispatch of 19 Nov. 1895, from Maxwell to Ripon; CO/96/262.
[3] A full list of African unofficial members is given at the end of this chapter.
[4] Memorial of 29 Apr. 1895, to Secretary of State from Kings, Chiefs and headmen of Elmina, Shama, Sekondi, Adjua, Axim, Apollonia, and including Eastern and Western Wassaw, enclosed in Dispatch No. 196 of 11 May 1895, from Maxwell to Ripon; CO/96/257.
[5] Petition of 23 June 1897, to Governor and Legislative Council from Head Chief of Gomua, and Chiefs of Egimaku and Winneba, enclosed in Dispatch No. 306 of 15 July 1897, from Maxwell to Chamberlain; CO/96/295.

purpose of the election . . . the Gold Coast Colony and the Protectorate [shall] be divided into four Provinces, viz:

(A) From the River Volta to the River Seccum:
(B) From the River Seccum to the Sweet River:
(C) From the Sweet River to Dixcove:
(D) From Dixcove to Half Assinnee:[1]

and that each Province [shall] have the right of electing two members to the Legislative Council, the members thus elected themselves electing from amongst themselves the three members of the Executive Council.

It was assumed that these eight elected Africans would sit beside the existing nine nominated members (seven officials, including the Governor, and two European unofficials).[2]

When this petition was examined at the Colonial Office it was feared that the nominated majority would be too narrow, and that occasionally the Government might be outvoted, especially if some members were absent. The scheme was described as 'an ingenious and insidious way of placing great obstacles in the way of Govt. control, while nominally preserving the numerical majority of the Govt.'[3] The Permanent Under-Secretary of State wondered how many of the Kings and Chiefs 'in whose name this Petition purports to be signed by Messrs. Sey, Jones & Hughes' had the slightest idea of what it meant.[4] So the London deputation was not even allowed to discuss 'this grotesque petition'[5] for constitutional reform at their interview with Chamberlain in 1898. The solicitors were officially informed that it would have been turned down, even if transmitted properly through the Governor, in view of the many grave objections to the proposed changes.[6]

An important factor that weighed against the petition in London was the belief that Africans required 'preparation by municipal work for the larger duties of colonial government'.[7] Such an opportunity had, it was felt, been offered in the recent Town Councils Ordinance of 1894, and the fierce opposition that had greeted this was taken to prove the unfitness of the Gold Coast for any major constitutional advance. There was indeed some inconsistency in the plea of the Accra inhabitants that they were 'not sufficiently

---

[1] Cf. Brew's proposals (p. 414, above) for raising money for the earlier deputation scheme, in almost the same territorial divisions. He was currently in London, and added his signature to this petition.

[2] Petition of 13 July 1898, to Queen in Council from Kings of Anomabu, Abura, Nkusukum, Ahanta, Dixcove, Eastern and Western Wassaw, Axim, Eastern and Western Apollonia, Denkyira, Ekumfi, Elmina, Adjumakum, and Ayan; also signed by over 65 Head Chiefs, Chiefs and headmen, and by J. H. Brew, J. W. Sey, T. F. E. Jones, and George Hughes. *Report of the Proceedings of the Deputation from the Kings and Chiefs of the Western Province of the Gold Coast* (London, 1898).   [3] Minute of 16 July 1898, by W. A. M.; CO/96/333.

[4] Minute of 19 July 1898, by E. Wingfield; ibid.

[5] Minute of 20 July 1898, by Selbourne; ibid.

[6] Letter of 3 Aug. 1898, from Colonial Office to Ashurst, Morris, Crisp & Co.; ibid.

[7] Minute of 19 July 1898, by Wingfield; ibid.

civilised' to have a municipality, set beside the latest demand for representation in the Legislative Council.[1] Nevertheless, the demand for constitutional reform continued to centre upon the Legislative Council as the focus of nationalist aspirations; and the unanswered proposals of the 1898 A.R.P.S. petition remained the basis of African political demands until the 1920's.

The effectiveness of the Legislative Council was improved in 1898 when T. Hutton Mills replaced Cheetham, whose 'deficient knowledge of the English language' had prevented him from taking a serious part in the proceedings. This was a significant change; Hutton Mills, who had already appeared as counsel for the Lands Bill petitioners, was the first African barrister to be appointed. The Governor considered him a useful man to have in the Council, because he was in touch with African opinion.[2] When the Concessions Bill was considered in 1900, four extraordinary members were appointed, including J. Mensah Sarbah.[3] Hutton Mills shortly afterwards resigned, and was replaced permanently by Mensah Sarbah in 1901;[4] and the A.R.P.S. was well represented when he was joined by J. P. Brown (then President) in 1904, in place of Chief J. Vanderpuiye.

Up till 1901 the authority of the Legislative Council had been conterminous with the extent of British jurisdiction. When the annexation and protection Orders in Council of that year extended and defined that jurisdiction up to the northernmost boundary, it might have been expected that the powers of the central legislature would have been similarly enlarged, following the precedent of 1874. Yet it was the Governor who was now given sole legislative authority over Ashanti and the Northern Territories.[5] This was due partly to the belief that representative government would be meaningless for such undeveloped areas—certainly official members would have been hard to spare and literate unofficials impossible to find, in the early years—and perhaps partly to the desire to keep them in isolation from political trends in the south. The most serious results of this policy were to encourage southern politicians to think in terms of the interests of the Colony, or even of Cape Coast, instead of the country as a whole, and to divert public attention from the uneven rate of social, economic and political development as between the three major territorial divisions.

During the first decade of the new century, the A.R.P.S., holding a virtual monopoly of the African unofficial seats, saw no particularly urgent need to demand a remodelled Legislative Council. During this period Casely Hayford

---

[1] Report of Governor's meeting with Accra deputation, led by Kings of Ussher Town and Christiansborg, and Chief Ababio of James Town, 2 Feb. 1895; CO/96/268.

[2] Confidential Dispatch of 25 June 1898, from Hodgson to Chamberlain; CO/96/317.

[3] Dispatch No. 95 of 5 Mar. 1900, from Hodgson to Chamberlain; CO/96/358.

[4] Confidential Dispatch of 20 Apr. 1901, from Nathan to Chamberlain; CO/96/379.

[5] 'The dependencies in which the governor ordains laws form the lowest group in the gradations of crown colony government.' M. Wight, *British Colonial Constitutions 1947* (Oxford, 1952), p. 20.

kept alive the tradition of criticism from outside the Council, and developed a new line of argument concerning the fitness of Africans for direct representation. He contended that 'you are not dealing with a savage people without a past, who are merely striving to copy or imitate foreign Institutions'; on the contrary, he boasted, the people of the Gold Coast had already evolved a system of self-government 'as perfect and efficient as the most forward nations of the earth to-day can possibly conceive'. The non-official element in the Legislative Council was farcical, especially since the members were supposed to support the Government, and were put there 'as an apology for the denial of proper representation'. Casely Hayford claimed that if the 1898 constitutional proposals had been accepted, and the eight representatives of the people from the Volta to Assini had been sitting in the Legislative Council, the Golden Stool fiasco—'the greatest blunder of the last decade'—could have been avoided.[1]

A new departure was the appointment of a paramount Chief, Nene Mate Kole, Konor of Manya Krobo, a former Basel Mission schoolmaster, to the Council; he took the seat of Mensah Sarbah, who died in 1911. The principle was not immediately challenged, though it was later to become acutely controversial. More important in the eyes of the A.R.P.S. was the fact that, J. P. Brown having been replaced by Hutton Mills of Accra in 1909, Cape Coast was again left without representation. The proposals for forest legislation during 1910–11 took the Society by surprise, and sharpened their feeling of exclusion from the legislative process. Casely Hayford complained that they had no means of effective criticism, owing to the official majority in the Legislative Council: 'What passes for public opinion has often, with difficulty, to filter its way to the surface.'[2] They soon organized a protest, and persuaded Hutton Mills to lay on the table of the Legislative Council—together with their appeal against the Forest Bill—two petitions from the Chiefs of the Central and Western Provinces, praying for (1) fuller representation of the people in the Legislative and Executive Councils, and (2) an opportunity to study draft legislation of special interest, before the Bills were read a first time and published in the *Gazette*.[3] The 1912 A.R.P.S. deputation to London also took the opportunity to present a constitutional petition to the King praying for the opportunity to 'elect the Unofficial African Members to the Legislative Council'.[4] They became more anxious for reform during 1913, when the Palm Oil Ordinance was passed against strong opposition from the unofficial members.[5] The next constitutional advance, however, was to be made on the initiative of the Governor, and not as a direct result of any political pressure from below.

[1] *Gold Coast Native Institutions*, pp. 123–9 and 268.
[2] J. E. Casely Hayford, *Gold Coast Land Tenure and the Forest Bill* (London, 1911).
[3] *Legislative Council Minutes*, 13 Sept. 1911.
[4] Quoted in 'Correspondence relating to the National Congress of British West Africa', *Sessional Paper No. VII of 1919–20*, p. 23.   [5] See Ch. I, pp. 46–47, above.

Clifford's Enlargement of the Legislative Council, 1916

Sir Hugh Clifford made his own assessment of the situation soon after his arrival as Governor in 1915. He found a Legislative Council consisting of nine nominated members. In addition to himself as President, there were four officials; and of the four unofficial members, two were Europeans (for the mercantile and mining interests) and two Africans (one representing the educated class, and one Chief). He was impressed by the tremendous social revolution now in progress, brought about by the phenomenal development of the cocoa industry, and as he travelled through the Gold Coast he became convinced that the existing machinery of government was inadequate for modern requirements.[1] He contended that one of the most severe disabilities of the Government was the absence of any efficient means whereby policies affecting African interests could be explained and made widely known to those most vitally concerned.

Clifford had had previous experience of a much more representative and useful Legislative Council in Ceylon, where non-Europeans had been elected since 1910. But, as may be seen from the analysis he sent to the Secretary of State, he did not think the Gold Coast was yet ready for elections:

a few of the educated natives at Cape Coast have from time to time agitated for the recognition of the elective principle; but I am convinced that the vast majority of the general public of this Colony has not yet reached such a stage of intellectual development as would enable them to exercise the franchise with wisdom and discrimination and in the best interests of the community as a whole.

He said that the ratepayers of Accra, Cape Coast, and Sekondi had hitherto made little real use of their franchise, and suggested that in Legislative Council elections racial and tribal animosities and rivalries would probably be excited.

Having decided that further nomination was inevitable, Clifford proposed to depart from the practice whereby the African members had usually been 'drawn exclusively from the ranks of the local barristers', and to develop the 'innovation' of 1911, when a Chief had been appointed to the Legislative Council.[2] The Governor considered that, as far as possible, the Africans nominated should be paramount Chiefs—as the natural leaders of the people, they were intimately acquainted with their needs and interests.[3] He was willing to concede that one nominated African should represent the Western Province, but only until such time as a suitable literate Chief was available for the purpose. He also felt that Cape Coast and Accra should have their own specific

---

[1] Clifford, *Legislative Council Debates*, 25 Sept. 1916.

[2] Clifford's analysis was not altogether accurate, for in fact only two African barristers, Mensah Sarbah and Hutton Mills, had served on the Legislative Council to date; and Nene Mate Kole, although the first paramount Chief, had been preceded by two divisional Chiefs.

[3] For some account of the development of indirect rule through the Chiefs, especially under Clifford and Guggisberg, see Ch. XII, below.

F f

representatives, to give a fair balance to different sections of the community; then the new Council would not afford plausible grounds for discontent to any section represented on it.[1]

The Colonial Office was not anxious to have too large a Legislative Council, and suggested that the maximum size should be eight officials, including the Governor, and seven unofficials (i.e. four Africans and three Europeans).[2] But Clifford preferred a more substantial increase, while retaining the official majority. His aim was to achieve both 'direct tribal representation' through paramount Chiefs belonging to each main group of tribes, and for 'those sections of the native population who have obtained a European education', direct representation on their own behalf.[3]

The Governor pressed his case successfully; and in 1916 the Legislative Council was enlarged to twenty-one members, 'to enable the Government of the Colony to obtain advice from as many varied quarters as possible'.[4] On the official side, there were seven additions—the Secretary for Native Affairs, the Comptroller of Customs, the Director of Public Works, the General Manager of the Railways, and the three Provincial Commissioners—making twelve officials in all. On the unofficial side, five additions made a total of nine. The convention was established of nominating three Europeans, three paramount Chiefs, and three educated Africans.[5] In 1916 these were as follows:

European member for the mercantile community
European member for the mining industry
European member (initially, from the Bank of B.W.A.)
Omanhene of Akim Abuakwa: for Twi-speaking people
Omanhene of Anomabu: for Fante-speaking people
Fia of Awunaga: for Ewe-speaking people
J. E. Casely Hayford (Western Province)
E. J. P. Brown (Cape Coast)
T. Hutton Mills (Accra)

Clifford believed that now, for the first time, an institution which might be regarded as really representative of the people had been established. But he made no secret of his conviction that it was not yet time to change the method of appointment to, or procedure in, the Council. It might be possible, as

[1] Dispatch of 15 Apr. 1915, from Clifford to Harcourt; 'Correspondence with the Secretary of State for the Colonies on the subject of the Constitution of the Executive and the Legislative Councils', *Sessional Paper No. VII of 1916–17*.

[2] Dispatch of 30 Oct. 1915, from Bonar Law to Clifford; ibid.

[3] Dispatch of 25 Nov. 1915, from Clifford to Bonar Law; ibid.

[4] Clifford, *Legislative Council Debates*, 25 Sept. 1916.

[5] The Royal Instructions of 20 Sept. 1916, specified the twelve *ex officio* members, but referred only in general terms to such non-officials 'as may from time to time be appointed'. The A.R.P.S. draft petition of 1918 complained that 'the increase being proportional, leaves them where they were before as regards effective representation'. In fact, *African* representation had slightly increased in proportion, from 2/9 to 6/21, although the proportion of *unofficials* had fallen.

education spread among the masses, to give the people a greater measure of self-government: 'But I am firmly convinced that the time for any such development has not yet come.' He considered that Crown Colony government, being of a paternal rather than a democratic character, was the most suitable form for the immediate development of the Gold Coast. Clifford emphasized the essential difference between a Legislative Council and a Parliament:

in no circumstances whatever can the unofficial members displace the official members and take over their duties from them ... There is no such thing in such an Assembly as a Government and an Opposition ... we form a single corporate Body all of whose members are working equally for the attainment of a single end—the prosperity of the Gold Coast Colony.[1]

Although the Governor found it satisfactory, this was precisely the aspect of the Council upon which demands for reform were to concentrate, and which was least likely to endure.

The Gold Coast Nation made it clear that Clifford's action was not to be accepted passively, with grateful thanks. Strong exception was taken to his view that the enlarged Legislative Council should be regarded by the people of the Colony as 'a gift from Her Majesty in person'. The editor expressed surprise at such a remark, and criticized Hutton Mills, E. J. P. Brown, and Casely Hayford for not at once correcting the Governor.[2] As on so many other occasions, reference was made to the Fanti Confederation scheme of 1872, which had asked for five elected members. The good intentions of the Governor were dismissed in an editorial on 'Camouflage', and readers were asked emotionally, 'Shall we ever be emancipated from the shackles of disenfranchisement?'[3] Some journalists looked even farther back: 'the machinery really exists although 67 years old'. They demanded the restoration of the Poll Tax Agreement of 1852 constituting a Legislative Assembly—in which 'the Chiefs, the educated elements and other elected representatives of the people' should now have seats—to control legislation and finance. They wanted 'not an enlarged Legislative Council, but a Legislative Assembly, a kind of House of Commons in miniature ... this is the only way we may be educated in the art of self-government'.[4]

The Idea of Elective Representation, 1918–23

The changes made by Clifford were thus not likely to satisfy public opinion for long. It was ironical that soon after the Governor had given fuller scope to the expression of African views, he was forced by Colonial Office policy

[1] *Legislative Council Debates*, 25 Sept. 1916.
[2] *The Gold Coast Nation*, 28 July and 4 Aug. 1917.
[3] Ibid. 21 July and 24 Nov. 1917.
[4] *The Gold Coast Independent*, 12 July and 1 Nov. 1919.

to provoke a head-on collision between the official and unofficial members, over the London-sponsored Palm Kernels Export Duty Bill.[1] The overruling of a unanimous unofficial vote on this occasion sharpened the demand for some form of representation that would give greater weight to the views of African members. Even some of the Europeans foresaw the need for further changes. Major-General W. H. Grey said openly in the Legislative Council in 1918 that the time was bound to come when there would be 'a very loud cry for elective representation'. He thought it was the duty of the Government to allow that demand, when the time came, by taking the necessary steps to have some, if not all, unofficial members elected.[2]

Soon after his arrival, F. G. Guggisberg met the executive of the A.R.P.S. at Cape Coast. J. P. Brown was the main spokesman and, among other matters, asked for elective representation.[3] Now, for the first time, an inkling was given of what some of the Society's leaders were really seeking—the recognition of the A.R.P.S. as the electoral body to return unofficial members. An attack on the system of nomination was launched at the next meeting of the Legislative Council. Casely Hayford pointed out that election would not be a new idea to Gold Coast Africans: 'From the man who carries the message stick right up to the Paramount Chief, our system of choice is elective.' He was supported by Dr. B. W. Quartey-Papafio, who claimed that formerly the people had had a full share in government, no laws being passed without their consent. They would continue to harp on the matter, promised the doctor, until some form of election was granted. Guggisberg immediately repeated an offer previously made by Clifford to consider carefully any scheme put forward, and said he only wanted breathing-space to take the matter up. He was waiting for some well-considered plan which could then be thrashed out at a future conference.[4]

Both the A.R.P.S. and the National Congress were considering detailed proposals between 1918 and 1921; but these did not immediately reach Guggisberg. The petition drafted for the Society in 1918 was shelved owing to the disagreement between E. J. P. Brown and Casely Hayford;[5] and the 1920 Congress resolutions by-passed the Governor completely, being taken straight to London. In 1921 the Society produced an elaborate scheme for turning itself into an electoral college. The details of these three unsuccessful plans may be compared more easily if tabulated as follows:

1918 A.R.P.S. draft petition[6]
(produced by E. J. P. Brown and Casely Hayford)

   Executive Council: [no reference]

   [1] See Ch. I, pp. 51–55, above.
   [2] W. H. Grey, *Legislative Council Debates*, 2 Nov. 1918.
   [3] *The Gold Coast Nation*, 8–15 Nov. 1919.
   [4] *Legislative Council Debates*, 26 Nov. 1919.   [5] See Ch. X, p. 377, above.
   [6] A.R.P.S. draft petition of 12 May 1918; quoted by E. J. P. Brown and Casely Hayford, *Legislative Council Debates*, 25 and 27 Apr. 1921.

PLATE 5

a. The 1920 Inaugural Conference at the Rodger Club, Accra, of the National Congress of British West Africa

From left to right, seated: A. B. Quartey-Papafio, H. Van Hein, Dr. H. C. Bankole-Bright, F. W. Dove, Gã Manche, T. Hutton Mills, Manche Kojo Ababio, J. E. Casely Hayford, Prince Bassey, Duke Ephraim, Patriarch J. G. Campbell.

Standing: E. E. Offiong, Rev. M. C. Hayford, A. Newton, E. Ofori, S. R. Wood, W. G. Essien, C. J. Bannerman, S. A. Quagraine, Adeniji Olugbile, Adeoye Deniga, S. D. Bervell, J. B. Nelson, W. Ward Brew, Akilagpa Sawyerr, J. E. Eminsang, F. Arkhurst.

Balcony: J. Kitson Mills, L. E. V. M'Carthy, J. H. Coussey, J. M. de Santana, C. A. Barnes, Dr. F. V. Nanka-Bruce, J. T. Addy, C. J. Reindorf, W. E. G. Sekyi, H. Quartey-Papafio, A. Vanderpuye, Dr. C. E. Reindorf, Prince K. Atta Amonu, K. Quartey-Papafio, H. R. Ribeiro, J. Glover Addo, J. M. Opong, R. S. Sackey.

b. The 1920 London Deputation of the National Congress

From left to right, seated: Dr. H. C. Bankole-Bright (Sierra Leone), T. Hutton Mills (Gold Coast, President of the Congress and of the London Committee), Chief Oluwa (Nigeria), J. E. Casely Hayford (Gold Coast), H. Van Hein (Gold Coast).

Standing: J. Egerton Shyngle (Nigeria), H. M. Jones (Gambia), Herbert Macauley (Chief Oluwa's Private Secretary), T. M. Oluwa (son of Chief Oluwa), F. W. Dove (Sierra Leone), E. F. Small (Gambia).

Legislative Council: the Government to nominate 'the present number of official and unofficial members'; 'at least fifteen members' to be elected, five from each of the three provinces in the Colony.

Method of election: by 'your petitioners'.

Financial control: a court of Policy 'with financial control as obtains in . . . the West Indies'.

1920–1 Congress demands[1]

(resolved at the 1920 inaugural Conference and put forward by the deputation to London)

Executive Council: 'as at present composed' [i.e. the Governor and five officials].

Legislative Council: 'one-half shall be nominated by the Crown and the other half elected by the people'.

Method of election: 'through such local groups as may be found most convenient and expedient and . . . where indigenous institutions do not provide a ready means of ascertaining the will of the people, other qualifying methods for voting, such as property or an educational standard, shall be resorted to'.

Financial control: 'A House of Assembly, composed of the members of the Legislative Council together with six other financial representatives elected by the people, who shall have the power of imposing all taxes and of discussing . . . the Annual Estimates of Revenue and Expenditure prepared by the Governor in the Executive Council and approving of them' [i.e. African control of finance, again on West Indian lines].

1920–1 A.R.P.S. proposals[2]

(prepared by Brown and circulated as 'the outcome of the Aboriginal unofficial members' conference' in Accra, in the absence of Casely Hayford)

Executive Council: three elected representatives (including one European).

Legislative Council: twelve elected representatives (four, including one European, from each Province). In addition, the present eleven officials and the Governor, who should have a second or casting vote.[3]

Method of election: the A.R.P.S. to be 'constituted into an Electoral College', in which 'ten Kings and Chiefs in each Province shall form a quorum' to elect their four members, every five years. Three of the elected representatives should then be 'chosen by the Society' to sit on the Executive Council.

Financial control: 'a House of Assembly composed of the Governor as President and the present number of official members of the Executive Council and nine elected unofficial members of whom six shall be aboriginal natives and three Europeans to be elected by the Society, shall be established for the administration of the Public Funds and other financial matters and also for the discussion of the general policy of the Government'.

---

[1] *Resolutions of the Conference of Africans of British West Africa* (London, 1920).

[2] Quoted by Casely Hayford, *Legislative Council Debates*, 25 Apr. 1921.

[3] Guggisberg commented that the long-promised scheme of the A.R.P.S. 'does not at present contemplate an unofficial majority'. Ibid. 27 Feb. 1922. Contrast the 1918 draft, which had clearly implied a majority of unofficials.

Within the Council itself, since the 1916 enlargement, there had been for the most part harmonious co-operation between the official and unofficial members. The latter had been particularly gratified when the war bonus payments were increased in response to their strong representations, although they were not empowered to move a financial resolution themselves.[1] Brown went out of his way in 1921 to say that the old idea of unofficial members as 'mere puppets sitting here to respond to the ayes and noes of the Administration' had been exploded. Guggisberg was equally pleased with the working of the system; with the sole exception of the palm kernels episode, he said, on every occasion when the unofficials had objected to a Bill, it had been withdrawn for further discussion and amendment, and had then usually received universal approval.[2]

But some of the nominated members of the Legislative Council felt themselves to be in an invidious position. Hutton Mills confessed publicly that people sometimes looked upon him as a favourite of the Governor.[3] In fact, Guggisberg had already realized that a wholly nominated Council was not going to satisfy the country for much longer, and had started to think out a possible line of advance. His problem was to introduce some form of franchise without thereby undermining the authority of the Chiefs, which the Government was committed to uphold.

When the A.R.P.S. scheme of 1921 reached Guggisberg, it was rejected as 'an attempt to transfer the Government of the Colony from the Governor and the Legislative Council' to the executive committee of the Society.[4] But in any case it was soon supplanted by a new plan put forward in 1922, again in the name of the A.R.P.S. but this time sponsored by Casely Hayford and the new office-holders. These latest proposals were more complicated. They included a Legislative Council and House of Assembly on the lines of the earlier Congress petition; but they also provided for three preliminary stages of indirect elections, starting with heads of families in village groups and working upwards to three provincial electoral assemblies, which would return members directly to both the Council and the Assembly.[5]

Perhaps the very intricacy of this scheme saved it from being rejected out of hand. Certainly the Governor was not in favour of direct elections. He had been advised earlier in the year by Winston Churchill, as Secretary of State, that the grant of the franchise to the 'ordinary native, living under the tribal system', would necessarily tend to break down the authority of the Chiefs

---

[1] See Ch. II, pp. 102–3, above.

[2] E. J. P. Brown and Guggisberg, *Legislative Council Debates*, 4 Feb. 1921.

[3] Speech at inaugural conference of the National Congress, Accra, 15 Mar. 1920; *Sessional Paper No. VII of 1919–20*, exhibit D.

[4] Confidential Memorandum of May 1922, by J. Maxwell, Acting Colonial Secretary; G.N. Archives.

[5] Memorial by certain Head Chiefs in conference with the A.R.P.S., enclosed in Confidential Letter of 11 Oct. 1922, from Colonial Secretary to Central Province Commissioner; ibid.

and destroy the tribal organization, which it was essential to preserve for a long time to come, until the spread of education had rendered the people 'ripe for a more advanced type of national organisation'.[1] But Guggisberg was certainly not thinking in terms of self-government, at least for many years to come. He expressed the fear in Manchester that some day the idealists might get a little power in England and would then turn round and say to the Gold Coast, 'You are men, and brothers with us. Some of you are very finely educated. We will give you self-government and see how you can govern yourselves.' If that moment were to come 'within the next 100 years . . . Manchester merchants would be wise to cut their losses and start trade with some other part of the world'.[2]

Government officials were not at all enthusiastic about either the role of the African politician or the technique of the ballot box. It was argued that the influence of the educated minority was disproportionate to their numbers, and that their political views carried weight only because less than half the Chiefs and only a small fraction of the people were literate. If all were literate, the threat to the Chiefs would vanish, because the people would not tolerate any attack on their political institutions. But under existing circumstances, the educated African, who could find few political opportunities within his own local State, was likely to be attracted by 'the strange but convenient doctrine of the equality of men', and to seek representative institutions on the European model. If he succeeded, the Chiefs would be reduced to the position of mere puppets, who could then have no more influence on the government of the native State than the humblest of their subjects through the ballot box; and this would mean the destruction of the traditional system of government.[3] From this point of view, the problem seemed intractable.

Guggisberg, however, was prepared to consider the idea of election by heads of families, and he spent some time sounding leaders of African opinion about their views on electoral techniques.[4] He called a semi-official conference in March 1923 to discuss the latest A.R.P.S. petition.[5] But the majority of Chiefs seemed to find the scheme too complicated and likely to lessen their own authority. H. Van Hien and W. Ward Brew, for the A.R.P.S. executive, therefore agreed that the electors should be the Head Chiefs of each Province rather than the heads of families; but they maintained that it should not be

[1] Confidential Dispatch of 4 Apr. 1922, from Churchill to Guggisberg; ibid.

[2] *West Africa*, 9 June 1923.

[3] These were the views of H. S. Newlands, later quoted by Guggisberg in *The Gold Coast; a Review of the Events of 1920–1926 and the Prospects of 1927–1928* (Accra, 1927). Another official, W. J. A. Jones, also quoted by Guggisberg, said: 'Foreign political organisation and methods of representation . . . must lead to the destruction of these native institutions.' Cf. F. G. Guggisberg and A. G. Fraser, *The Future of the Negro* (London, 1929), p. 68: 'the ballot box is not compatible with native institutions'.

[4] Notes of interviews in S.N.A. 793, Case 39/1920, G.N. Archives.

[5] Memorandum of 8 Mar. 1923, by Guggisberg; No. 6751 Confidential M.P. 15103/1923, G.N. Archives.

compulsory for the Head Chiefs to elect one of themselves to the Legislative Council.[1]

Thus the Governor was now able to accept the A.R.P.S. proposals in principle, while insisting that the Head Chiefs should be strengthened and intimately associated with the new machinery of government. He was convinced that any electoral system must 'support the power of the Oman, and not lead to the Oman being overrun by the young educated people of the coastal towns, such as are commonly styled the intelligentsia'. He was prepared to recommend direct elections for the inhabitants of those large towns already possessing municipal government, but the provincial members of the future Legislative Council should be elected or chosen from the paramount Chiefs.[2] How was this election or choice to be organized? Fortunately for Guggisberg, the Head Chiefs in the Eastern Province were themselves developing a system of mutual consultation which was to offer him a ready-made solution.

It was in March 1918 that Nana Ofori Atta had first persuaded most of the principal Chiefs of the Eastern Province to meet together in Accra. They then presented a petition and memorandum to Clifford, who gave them an interview, at which he welcomed their spontaneous joint action, remarking, 'except when some great danger like an Ashanti invasion was imminent it has never before been possible'. The Chiefs asked particularly that they should be given sufficient time to express their opinion on proposed measures before their introduction into the Legislative Council. They also pointed out the disadvantage of waiting for the Governor to visit each of them in turn.[3]

J. B. Danquah, looking back, saw in this meeting the first germ of the Provincial Council system.[4] However that may be, in 1923 several similar meetings were held, and began to acquire some official standing; the Provincial Commissioner referred to the 'Head Chiefs' Council' as a useful means of settling inter-tribal disputes and removing personal animosities.[5] By 1924 the Head Chiefs in the Eastern Province were pressing for the foundation of an officially recognized Council.[6] It was at this point that Guggisberg decided to set up three Provincial Councils of Head Chiefs, as an integral part of the proposed new constitution, and a means by which the existing form of native

---

[1] They also proposed that European members of the Legislative Council should have had at least five years' residence in the Gold Coast. This was the last occasion when the A.R.P.S. was officially consulted by the Government.

[2] Guggisberg, *Legislative Council Debates*, 21 Mar. 1923.

[3] Notes of interview at Government House, 5 Mar. 1918; S.N.A. 892, Case 33/1918, G.N. Archives.

[4] 'Without doubt this conference sowed the seed which has grown to become the Provincial Council of Chiefs'. J. B. Danquah, *The Akim Abuakwa Handbook* (London, 1928), p. 118. But the idea might be traced even farther back, to Clifford's suggestion that there should be 'a series of durbars to be attended by the principal Chiefs in each Province, at which important matters of interest to the native communities can be freely debated'. *Legislative Council Debates*, 3 Oct. 1913.

[5] *Departmental Reports*, Eastern Province, 1923–4.   [6] Ibid. 1924–5.

administration might be preserved and strengthened. But he still set his face against an 'indiscriminate application of the franchise to the totally illiterate who form ninety *per centum* of the population'.[1]

The 1925 Constitution and Its Reception

The constitutional instruments took some time to prepare; during the interval, although no details were available concerning the composition of the Legislative Council, the forthcoming creation of Provincial Councils became common knowledge. Casely Hayford said that he would welcome them as electoral bodies, although he hoped the Chiefs would not use them to put forward policies not sanctioned by their people. He and Van Hien urged that it would be better to get all the Chiefs of the country together, instead of grouping them by Provinces, in order to promote 'unity of action towards nationhood'; and they suggested that the A.R.P.S. was ready to hand as an organizing body.[2]

Eventually the new constitution was published in the *Gold Coast Gazette* at the end of 1925;[3] and it was announced that the old Legislative Council would cease to exist in April 1926.[4] The new Council was to consist of thirty members; there were to be sixteen officials, including the Governor as President, and of the fourteen unofficials, it was clear that five would be Europeans, and nine elected Africans.[5] The methods of election were the most interesting and the most controversial points in the new constitution. Three municipal members were to be directly elected, one from each of the main coastal towns (Accra, Cape Coast, and Sekondi), when new municipal corporations had been set up under an Ordinance of 1924. The franchise in these towns was to be open to all persons over twenty-one years of age in occupation of a house with a rateable value of at least £8 per annum.[6]

The remaining six provincial members were to be elected by three Provincial Councils of Chiefs, now officially introduced and defined; each would consist of the Head Chiefs whose headquarters were situated within the Province, and would elect one or more representatives from among its members. Seats in the Legislative Council being allotted on the basis of population, the Western Province was to be represented by one member, the Central Province by two, and the Eastern Province was to have three, one from each of

---

[1] Confidential Dispatch of 4 Mar. 1924, from Guggisberg to J. H. Thomas; G.N. Archives.

[2] Casely Hayford and Van Hien, *Legislative Council Debates*, 24 Feb. 1925.

[3] Order in Council of 8 Apr. 1925, and Letters Patent and Royal Instructions of 23 May 1925; *Gold Coast Gazette*, 10 Dec. 1925.

[4] Ibid. 9 Jan. 1926.

[5] For a full account of the nature and working of the new Legislative Council, see M. Wight, *The Gold Coast Legislative Council* (London, 1947), chs. iii and iv.

[6] 1925 Order in Council, Sections XX and XXIII, and Legislative Council Electoral Regulations, Sections 39–51. In theory Europeans might thus be elected as well as Africans; but in practice this was hardly likely.

the main language groups, Gã–Adangme, Ewe, and Akan.[1] Head Chiefs were defined as those who, in the opinion of the Governor, were not subordinate in their ordinary jurisdiction to any other Chief, and whom the Governor declared to be recognized Head Chiefs for the purpose of the Order.[2]

Guggisberg himself regarded the Provincial Councils as the outstanding feature of the constitution of 1925. What was the theory behind their formation? He claimed that what the Government had done was not to invent Provincial Councils, but to recognize the principle adopted by the people themselves.[3] In support of this thesis, a copy of the District Assemblies Ordinance of 1858 was forwarded to each Provincial Commissioner, with the somewhat fanciful statement that Provincial Councils 'were actually constituted 67 years ago'.[4] (No reference was made to the fact that this Ordinance had been disallowed by the Colonial Office the following year.)

In 1926 the Acting Secretary for Native Affairs delved farther into the past, claiming that the first Provincial Council had been held on 4 August 1826, at the village of Oyeadufo in the Accra district, when the Ashantis invaded the Eastern Province: 'the result was the Battle of Dodowa'. Again, it was now said to have been a Provincial Council that assembled at Cape Coast in 1852 and passed the Poll Tax Ordinance.[5] This official even claimed that the Fanti Confederation of 1871 was a Provincial Council, and that it was only destroyed because educated members had 'appointed themselves' to its executive council.[6] He referred to the 'very similar' system of election for the United States President, and described how each Chief would now carry with him to the Provincial Council the instructions of his State Council concerning the policy—and even the vote—expected of him: 'Could anything be more democratic or more representative of the wishes of a people?'[7] The official theory was that the Provincial Councils were thus to be the channels through which Government for the first time could become acquainted with the views of the people as a whole.[8]

[1] The Provincial Councils were created mainly on a basis of historical alignments and administrative convenience. R. L. Buell thought they should have been based on ethnic principles: 'It would seem to an outsider that if native institutions are really to be utilized, an effort should be made to organize councils upon a real tribal basis.' Buell complained that representation was 'controlled merely by geography'; but if a failing, this is one common to democracy. *The Native Problem in Africa* (New York, 1928), vol. i, pp. 841–2.

[2] 1925 Order in Council, Sections XVI and XVII.

[3] Guggisberg, *Legislative Council Debates*, 3 Mar. 1927.

[4] S.N.A. 921, G.N. Archives.

[5] Notes on the 1926 A.R.P.S. Petition by H. S. Newlands; S.N.A. Acc. No. 1503, G.N. Archives.

[6] This interpretation of history was an interesting contrast to the version offered by *The Gold Coast Leader* of 10 July 1926: 'We cannot too often remind our people that the Gold Coast Aborigines' Rights Protection Society took up the work just where the Fanti Confederation left it; and, whereas in the Confederation days the assembly at Mankessim was the national assembly of the people, so is the assembly today of the Aborigines' Society at Cape Coast the national assembly of the people.'

[7] Newlands, quoted by Guggisberg, *Legislative Council Debates*, 3 Mar. 1927.

[8] *Departmental Reports*, Eastern Province, 1926–7.

A lone educated voice was raised—from London—on behalf of those professional Africans whose sympathies and aspirations inclined towards strengthening the authority of their Natural Rulers. This belonged to the young half-brother of Nana Ofori Atta, J. B. Danquah, who welcomed the new constitution as 'a splendid advance on the old'.[1] But in the Gold Coast, opposition began to mount early in 1926. J. E. K. Aggrey of Achimota commented shrewdly on the situation, in a private letter:

> The new Order in Council concerning the new Legislative Council has stirred up a hornets' nest . . .Wish I had known about the whole thing before it was promulgated . . . I tried to point out some of the parts of the Order that seemed to conflict with our native constitution. Sir Gordon is the best British Governor that has been sent here lately . . . I am not sure that all his advisers are so genuine . . . Some seem to dislike the educated class.[2]

Mass meetings of protest were held in Cape Coast, Sekondi, and Elmina The opposition viewpoint was generally expressed cautiously, to avoid offending the Chiefs. A favourite argument was that it was contrary to native custom for the Natural Rulers to attend Provincial Councils at all, much less to be allowed to represent the people in the Legislative Council. Many speakers promised that every effort would be made to co-operate, if the Government would allow the Oman Councils to elect suitable and progressive men other than, or in addition to, the Chiefs.[3]

The new Provincial Councils were not intended simply as a piece of electoral machinery. The Order in Council laid down that they might also discharge such other functions as might from time to time be assigned to them by Ordinance;[4] and from the start, the Chiefs were encouraged to take this opportunity of consulting together on subjects concerning the common welfare of their peoples, and of advising Government on any proposed legislation. To Guggisberg, the Provincial Councils were 'the chief means by which the nationality of the Africans of the Gold Coast will be built up out of many scattered tribes'.[5] Surely, the Governor must have thought, this was an appeal that would awaken a response in Chiefs and educated Africans alike.

---

[1] *West Africa*, 2 Jan. 1926. Evidently Danquah had not then seen the full text of the Order in Council, since he asked 'Would it be a breach of the new Constitution were the Provincial Council to elect a lawyer-politician as its representative on the Legislative Council?'

[2] Letter of 24 Apr. 1926, from Aggrey to T. Jesse Jones; E. W. Smith, *Aggrey of Africa* (London, 1929), pp. 259–60.

[3] *West Africa*, 10 Apr. 1926. *The Gold Coast Leader* later summed up the view of the opposition on this point in its issue of 26 Mar. 1927: 'We and others have pointed out over and over again that the root objection to the present Provincial Councils lies in its being restricted to the Amanhin who have the right to vote for members to the Legislative Council from their ranks *only*. In other words . . . freedom of choice as to the persons to serve in the Legislative Council would remove all the difficulties.' But this reform was not secured until 1940, when the constitution was amended to allow Provincial Councils to elect non-Chiefs; and in practice they did not do so before 1946, when Danquah was one of the first two to be elected.

[4] 1925 Order in Council, Section XVII.

[5] *Events, 1920–1926, and Prospects, 1927–1928.*

In fact Casely Hayford, the champion of national unity, had suggested Provincial Councils as early as 1903. He had outlined a system of local discussion working upwards from village communities to district councils: 'Next, each district would send its representatives with the Head Linguists to the Provincial Council. Lastly, the several Head-Chiefs of the provinces would attend the State Council in great state . . . and finally dispose of the matter, such *plebiscite*, of course, binding the entire State.' Although officials were apparently unaware of this early suggestion, the new constitution appeared to its creators to have done exactly what Casely Hayford had advocated: taking the native State system, developing and improving it 'on aboriginal lines, and on scientific principles'. But the crucial point in his argument, and in nearly all subsequent demands for electoral reform, had been the leadership of the non-traditional *élite*: 'It must be the work of the educated Native, if the British Government will trust him to do it.'[1] Now, a generation later, educated Africans were more articulate, more confident— and there were many more of them. This had already led to the open clash between the National Congress leaders and Nana Ofori Atta in 1920 over the question whether the Chiefs or the educated class had the better claim to represent 'the bulk of the inhabitants'.

It was therefore a serious blow to Casely Hayford and his supporters to find that under the long-awaited constitution it was the Head Chiefs who were to double their representation, since only they were eligible for election, as provincial members, to the Legislative Council. There were still only three seats open to other educated Africans, who were thus offered no increase on 1916. Small wonder that some protested vigorously at being outpaced, and outnumbered, by the Chiefs.

There was an educational qualification for all members, who had to be able to read and write English sufficiently well to take an active and intelligent part in the proceedings.[2] But as far as the Chiefs were concerned this merely served to restrict the choice still further. As *The Gold Coast Leader* complained, the Chiefs qualified by education to sit in the Legislative Council could almost be numbered on the fingers of one hand. And it was feared that even they would become tools in the experienced grip of British officials.[3] Other critics accused the Government of deliberately creating a division between the Chiefs, as 'the true and accredited representatives of the illiterate masses', and the educated classes, as if they were some 'foreign breeds imported into the Colony!' By contrast, only thirty years earlier, 'the Gold Coast nation' had opposed the Lands Bill, 'as one mass—literates and illiterates working together with Paramount and Sub-Chiefs as one people'.[4]

[1] Casely Hayford, *Gold Coast Native Institutions*, pp. 250 and 253–4.
[2] 1925 Order in Council, Section XVIII.
[3] *The Gold Coast Leader*, 26 Mar. and 22 May 1926.
[4] *The Gold Coast Independent*, 7 Aug. 1926.

The immediate reaction of the A.R.P.S. was an absolute refusal to co-operate in what they regarded as a distortion of their careful electoral proposals. In March 1926 a conference of the Society at Cape Coast expressed the fear that the whole scheme was designed to do away with the A.R.P.S. and to create a division between the Natural Rulers and the educated inhabitants. They asked the Government to suspend the new constitution, pending detailed objections to the King; meanwhile, emergency steps were to be taken to prevent the most objectionable features being put into operation. It was resolved that no Head Chief should attend any of the Provincial Councils or accept nomination to the Legislative Council, since his presence would involve 'a breach of the Native Constitution'.[1] More constructively, they resolved that there should be equal representation as between Europeans and Africans, and that they should be allowed to elect their own members in their own way.

The attendance of Chiefs was not encouraging to the organizers of the conference, but it was uniquely decided 'That these resolutions are binding not only on the Natural Rulers present at this Conference but also on those who are not present'—even if they no longer supported the Society. The A.R.P.S. lawyers promised to help to defend any Chief who might now get into difficulties with the Government. The lay members of the Society's executive were bound by a further resolution not to accept nomination themselves.[2] But events were to show that the attractions of membership of the Provincial and Legislative Councils were too great for these self-denying resolutions to be implemented for long. More important still, there were prominent Chiefs and educated Africans who were already prepared to seek the prestige and responsibility involved, and some of them, led by Nana Ofori Atta, genuinely believed that this was both in the best tradition and in the public interest.

The task of getting the Head Chiefs to attend the new Provincial Councils, and to elect their own members to the Legislative Council, did not prove easy. Electoral regulations were published in April 1926, and the three Councils first met the following month, with varying degrees of success. In the Western Province there was such apathy and opposition to the idea of a Council of Head Chiefs, that only eight out of twenty met at Tarkwa in May 1926, and no provincial member was elected. The A.R.P.S. opposition was concentrated in the Central Province; they sent supporters to interview all the Chiefs and to persuade them to have nothing to do with the Provincial Council.[3] Less than half the Head Chiefs attended any of the first four sessions; but the inaugural attendance was just sufficient for the immediate purpose of electing two members to the Legislative Council: Nana Otu

[1] Cf. their resolution of 1922, which sought to deprive any Chief, 'whilst in attendance' at the Legislative Council, of 'his natural or customary functions, rights and privileges, which shall thereupon devolve upon the Oman', or such person(s) as they should appoint.

[2] Records of the A.R.P.S. shown to me by the late W. E. G. Sekyi of Cape Coast.

[3] *Departmental Reports*, Central Province, 1926-7.

Ababio II (Omanhene of Abura) and Nana Ayirebi Acquah III (Omanhene of Winneba).

In the Eastern Province, where there had already grown up a tradition of unofficial joint meetings, all the Head Chiefs but one came to the inaugural session at Nsawam. The Gã Mantse—who must have inherited some of the pertinacity of his predecessor, King Tackie—remained at home and complained that it was against custom for him to travel from Accra to hold meetings with other Head Chiefs, or to go to the Legislative Council.[1] The following were chosen as provincial members: Nene Mate Kole (Gã–Adangme), Togbui Sri III (Ewe), and Nana Kwesi Akuffo, Omanhene of Akwapim (Akan).[2] At the end of the meeting the Chiefs recorded their deep sense of gratitude for this opportunity for united discussion of matters affecting the welfare of the country.[3] By September 1926 it could at least be officially claimed that 'Provincial Councils have been established. They are in existence.'[4]

It was not possible, however, even to hold elections for the municipal members of the Legislative Council during 1926, because the three towns had not yet agreed to operate the associated Municipal Corporations Ordinance of 1924. This had been introduced as a deliberate 'experiment in the practical political education of the African',[5] with elected town council majorities as a long-overdue reform; other provisions included the replacement of the official President by an African Mayor, a graduated rating scheme, with total exemption for property of an annual value up to £5, and the continuance of official grants-in-aid. Guggisberg believed that the Ordinance practically conferred self-government upon the citizens of the main towns and would be 'the biggest step in political advancement ever taken by the inhabitants of this country'.[6]

But he had reckoned without the stock response of the people of Accra, in particular, to any proposals involving direct taxation. They—and their fathers before them—had had closed minds on the subject ever since the 1854

---

[1] The Mantsemei of Gbese, Asere, Sempe, and Akumanji (four of the seven subdivisions of Accra) protested to the District Commissioner that the Gã Mantse had not sought their consent to such a message, which had been prompted by his association with the intelligentsia, with their own 'axes of self-aggrandisement to grind'. S.N.A. 925, Case 28/1925, G.N. Archives. These four sub-Chiefs were already bitter enemies of the G~ Mantse, and had in 1921 and 1924 tried very hard to destool him, so their attitude was discounted as being 'rather anti-Gã Mantse than pro-Constitution'. Minute of 10 June 1926, by C. W. Welman; ibid.

[2] It is surprising that Nana Ofori Atta was not chosen for the Akan area, in spite of his prestige and experience as a member of the Legislative Council since 1916. He was later nominated to fill the vacancy for the Western Provincial Council member, and this appointment was criticized in the press; e.g. The Gold Coast Leader, 14 Aug. 1926.

[3] Departmental Reports, Eastern Province, 1926–7.

[4] Memorandum of 13 Sept. 1926, by Acting Attorney-General; S.N.A. 793 Case 59/1920, G.N. Archives.

[5] Sessional Paper No. XVII of 1922–23.

[6] Legislative Council Debates, Governor's Annual Address, 6 Mar. 1924.

bombardment of Christiansborg.[1] The finer points of increased responsibility and the grant of an elected Mayor, for which the educated leaders had been pressing, were entirely lost on them. There had been considerable unrest during 1924, including a personal campaign against the Gã Mantse, largely for having failed to lead the opposition to the Ordinance; but the Government refused to recognize his alleged destoolment, on the grounds that it was 'irregular and not in accordance with native custom'.[2]

The operation of the Ordinance—which had only been intended for Accra, initially—had been suspended after an official inquiry had revealed the intensity of public feeling on the matter.[3] But the Governor now felt that he might win the support, at least of the educated and politically ambitious, by so framing the 1925 constitution that only those towns to which the Ordinance had been applied could elect a municipal member for the new Legislative Council. Representation at the centre was thus offered as a bait for the acceptance of the Municipal Corporations Ordinance, to encourage budding politicians 'to devote a part of their time to the service of their fellow townspeople'.[4] In the event, this condition simply proved an additional obstacle to the formation of the new Legislative Council. The mere hint of a revision of rating assessments in Accra during 1925–6 brought a deputation of protest, led by the Gã Mantse and several spokesmen, including Hutton Mills and Dr. F. V. Nanka-Bruce.[5] Guggisberg, who said he had never intended to make it impossible for the people to enjoy the benefits of the new constitution, reluctantly decided in 1926 to remove the limiting condition.[6] The constitution was accordingly amended by an Imperial Order in Council the following

[1] The Osu Mantse and his followers gave evidence at an inquiry into the objections to the Ordinance:

A FOLLOWER: Through the Town Council taxation my mother died . . .

MANCHE: We have seen the whole thing and found that it is not good so we do not want to go further.

COMMISSIONER: Why do you not like to listen to my explanations of the Ordinance? I should like to tell you of the things in the Ordinance which will be better for your town and people.

MANCHE: Through this Ordinance we would die more than as before . . . If our representative in the Council says they like it we people do not like the Ordinance.

A FOLLOWER: If our Manche says that we should have this Ordinance, then we people, knowing that it will not be good, we will destool him.

'Report on the Objections Lodged with the Colonial Secretary against the Application of the Municipal Corporations Ordinance, 1924, to the Town of Accra, with Minutes of Evidence', *Sessional Paper No. I of 1925–26.*

[2] 'Report of an Inquiry held by the Honourable C. W. Welman, Secretary for Native Affairs, on a Commission by His Excellency the Governor issued under the Commissions of Inquiry Ordinance and dated 26th February, 1925', *Sessional Paper No. X of 1925–26.*

[3] *Sessional Paper No. I of 1925–26*, and *Departmental Reports*, Native Affairs, 1924–5.

[4] Guggisberg, *Legislative Council Debates*, 3 Feb. 1925.

[5] Notes of meeting with Committee of Protest against the Accra (Special Assessment of Assessable Premises) Ordinance, 1925; S.N.A. 889, Case 37/1924, G.N. Archives.

[6] Notes of interview between Gã Chiefs and Welman, 14 July 1926; S.N.A. 925, Case 28/1925, G.N. Archives.

year;[1] at the same time, the 1924 Ordinance was withdrawn, and that of 1894 was amended,[2] so that the existing town councils could continue to function with some minor improvements.

Guggisberg confessed that the failure to make municipal self-government for the coast towns a 'stepping-stone' to elective representation on the Legislative Council had been his only real disappointment as Governor.[3] Permanent officials were not so much disappointed, as confirmed in their misgivings over constitutional advance. It was noted that the unanimous and energetic opposition ceased as soon as the Government decided to continue the official majority on the existing town councils; this was held to prove that both the educated and uneducated classes were 'clearly quite unprepared to shoulder the elementary responsibilities of local government'.[4]

But meanwhile the municipal members for the Legislative Council had to be found somehow, and the Government therefore decided in 1926 to nominate one person for each town for a year. The idea of nomination immediately strengthened the opposition to the constitution as a whole, especially among the townspeople.

At first all those invited refused nomination—including Casely Hayford, Van Hien, and Glover-Addo, even though they had been members previously. The Government then tried to persuade the Gã Chiefs to suggest somebody who might be nominated to represent Accra. The Osu Mantse wrote declining to suggest anyone; the Gã Mantse said that he had called a meeting and that no educated person would accept nomination. But the Mantsemei of Gbese, Asere, Sempe, and Akumanji, who were pursuing a long-standing feud with the Gã Mantse, submitted the name of A. W. Kojo Thompson,[5] who was formally introduced to the public at a mass meeting in Bukom Square. In Cape Coast, E. J. P. Brown surprisingly agreed to resume his seat on the Legislative Council; and in Sekondi George Grant, a merchant of Axim, was eventually nominated.[6]

---

[1] Gold Coast Colony (Legislative Council) Order in Council, dated 7 Feb. 1927, and effective from 27 July 1927.

[2] By the Town Councils Law Amendment Ordinance of 1927.

[3] Guggisberg, *Legislative Council Debates*, 3 Mar. 1927. *The Gold Coast Independent*, 20 July 1918, had ridiculed the theory of town councils as an education in self-governing institutions: 'after nearly twenty years working, we have not come across that peripatetical graduate in the science of municipal elections'. In fact, during the period 1898–1928, six town councillors—C. J. Bannerman, Dr. B. W. Quartey-Papafio, E. C. Quist, E. J. P. Brown, J. E. Casely Hayford, and J. Glover-Addo—'graduated' to membership of the Legislative Council. On the other hand, six members of the Legislative Council—J. Vanderpuiye, T. Hutton Mills, J. Mensah Sarbah, J. P. Brown, A. W. Kojo Thompson, and H. Van Hien—later became town councillors. This proves little more than that able men were in demand for both fields of public service.

[4] Notes on the 1926 A.R.P.S. Petition by Newlands; S.N.A. Acc. No. 1503, G.N. Archives.

[5] Letter of 17 July 1926, from Mantsemei to Welman; S.N.A. 925, Case 28/1925, G.N. Archives.

[6] A telegram to the Colonial Secretary protested that the Chiefs and people of Sekondi 'do not know the said George A. Grant', and that he had never lived in the town. *The Gold Coast Leader*, 2 Oct. 1926. 'Pa' Grant, as he was later known, became President of the United Gold Coast Convention in 1947.

The A.R.P.S. Petition of 1926

The new Legislative Council first met in August 1926. The A.R.P.S. had failed in their immediate object of preventing any Africans from taking seats on the Council; but they had already decided to appeal once more to London.

A petition against the new constitution was drawn up by the Society and forwarded to the Colonial Office in September; but it was returned to their solicitors for submission through the proper channels, and the Governor then referred it back to the A.R.P.S. at Cape Coast 'for authentication', since it bore only the signature of Casely Hayford. All this meant considerable delay before it reached the Secretary of State. Meanwhile, money was being collected for a deputation to England, although the Government was doing its best to discredit the campaign. The following statement from the headman of a town illustrates well some of the less inhibited techniques of rural fund-raising:

The Head-Chief sent his linguist to me about 3½ months ago to collect £10. When asked what it was for, the linguist who had the Head Chief's Messenger Stick stated that the Queen of England had sent a law stating that if a man had two children the Queen took one and the father took one. Further that the Queen had taken all our lands together with our cocoa. Further that another law was to be made that if a wife had a little child on her back she must not sleep in one room with her husband.

The Head-Chief's message was that all these laws were placed before them at Cape Coast and they needed money to send a deputation to England to oppose these laws. We paid the £10 then.

Wider circulation was achieved by the more subtle story that the Government intended to create one or more 'super Amanhene' and so reduce the powers and authority of the other Head Chiefs.[1] The total collected is not on record; but towards the end of 1926 Casely Hayford arrived in London as the A.R.P.S. delegate.

The Society's petition opened as usual with a historical résumé, this time starting with the Bond of 1844 and the Fanti Confederation, and dwelling on each successive landmark: Lands, Forests, and Native Jurisdiction.[2] Turning to the 1925 Order in Council, the petition declaimed, with mounting fervour, that this was conceived in a most illiberal spirit; that it conferred only a restricted measure of elective representation; that it struck a deadly blow at 'the federal union of the Native States' and at the independence of the Chiefs; that it violated customary law in its most vital particulars; that it promoted friction, by attempting to divide the Head Chiefs from their sub-Chiefs, linguists, councillors, and the general mass of their people; and that, if unamended, it would soon result in 'the disintegration of the Native States'.[3]

[1] J. C. Maxwell, *Legislative Council Debates*, 30 Aug. 1926.

[2] For successive government attempts to amend or bring up to date the 1883 Native Jurisdiction Ordinance, and the attitude of the A.R.P.S. between 1906 and 1924, see Ch. XII, below.

[3] A.R.P.S., *Petition for the Amendment of the Gold Coast Colony (Legislative Council) Order in Council, 1925* (London, 1926).

G g

The task of demolishing the A.R.P.S. case fell to the Acting Secretary of Native Affairs, H. S. Newlands, who seems to have relished the opportunity to discredit its claim to be 'a national movement'. He repeated the stock charge that the petition expressed merely the views of the executive committee of the Cape Coast section of the Aborigines' Society, which represented only the educated communities of the coast towns. He complained that the Society was directed, managed, and controlled by its executive officers, and not by the Head Chiefs themselves; and that the Society's delegate was apparently regarded as 'being competent under native customary law' to speak not merely for the various Divisions of the Colony, but also on behalf of the people living in Ashanti and the Northern Territories. He claimed that the A.R.P.S. had never been recognized as coming between the Government and the Chiefs, and that it was the most important Chiefs themselves who had, despite the strenuous efforts of the Society, made two of the Provincial Councils 'an unqualified success'. But Newlands was too anxious to prove his case. The thirty-four Head Chiefs who had so far abstained from support in the Western and Central Provinces—all of them members of the A.R.P.S.— ruled over '495,000 people only'.

In answer to the argument that the Provincial Council system was un- customary, Newlands emphatically affirmed that there was no question of a Head Chief himself making laws. Native custom with all its safeguards was to be scrupulously observed throughout, and the function of those who were members of the Legislative Council was 'to represent the views of the Pro- vincial Council as a whole', but not (oddly enough) 'to make laws'. Newlands went on to assert that the only political institution infringing native custom was the A.R.P.S. itself, which by its 'interference with, and assertion of authority over, the prerogative of the Head-Chiefs' was seeking to stifle their free and unfettered deliberations.

Several other arguments were adduced against the A.R.P.S. For example, that the support for it, in terms of the number of names appended to its documents, was dwindling; that many of these names were represented by 'marks', rather than signatures, which showed that it appealed mainly to the uneducated Chiefs (who might not even know what they had thus marked); and that the Cape Coast leaders often revealed their ignorance of native con- stitutions, especially those of the Eastern Province. In view of all this, New- lands was convinced that the petition was not a spontaneous expression of the independent opinion of the Head Chiefs.[1] Thus heavily discounted, it could not hope to find favour at the Colonial Office.

In London Casely Hayford sought to create the impression of nation-wide support by claiming that the Society was a national assembly, and that among the Chiefs supporting this latest move were even some who had opposed the National Congress. He was also reported as saying that Africans had not

[1] Notes on the 1926 A.R.P.S. Petition by Newlands; S.N.A. Acc. No. 1503, G.N. Archives.

been sufficiently consulted by the Government in drawing up the new constitution.[1] But he was a general without an army. The new Legislative Council having just been inaugurated, it was clearer than ever before that the A.R.P.S. was not in a position to present 'the case of the Gold Coast', or even of the majority of Chiefs. Casely Hayford did not remain long in London, and returned in December 1926.

Once the A.R.P.S. petition had been set aside, it looked as if the new constitution was beginning to work; Guggisberg had great hopes that it might 'develop into something bigger and wider than any mushroom constitution based on the ballot-box and the eloquence of politicians over whom the people have no control except at election time'.[2] He attached great importance to the fact that the Provincial Councils could look beyond the tribe to the nation. No doubt they did help to break down tribal barriers—at least among the Chiefs. But, ironically enough, their initial contribution to national unity was the opposition aroused by their creation.[3]

Municipal Elections and Politics, 1927–8

The introduction of elected members for municipal councils on the one hand, and for the central legislature on the other, had both been greeted with strong criticisms and petitions of protest, though for very different reasons. But there could hardly be a greater contrast than between the continued apathy and indifference throughout many years of town council elections, and the growing interest that followed the establishment of the new Legislative Council from 1927 onwards. Only at the centre was there some chance of influencing government policy, and possibly demanding further reform. Although it had fallen so far short of African demands, the new electoral system was recognized as a first step towards the fuller representation that had been sought; and it soon called into being a Western-type electoral machinery of rudimentary parties and propaganda.

Election for municipal members of the Legislative Council became possible in 1927 with the removal of the restrictive condition concerning the abortive Municipal Corporations Ordinance. In spite of the earlier opposition to the new constitution, there were now signs of a change of heart—or at least of tactics. Early in the year an open split developed between two factions within the A.R.P.S., and soon Casely Hayford severed his connexion with the diehards at Cape Coast, rejecting their policy of boycott, which he had decided was fruitless. He and his associates could see—once the new Legislative Council was functioning, and the Provincial Councils at least initiated—that if they themselves did not stand for election, sooner or later other Africans would.

[1] *West Africa*, 20 Nov. 1926.
[2] *Events, 1920–1926, and Prospects, 1927–1928.*
[3] See Ch. XII, pp. 491–505, below, for the subsequent controversy over the Provincial Councils.

In June 1927 Casely Hayford addressed a meeting of the National Congress in Accra; he mentioned that their members had captured Legislative Council seats in both Sierra Leone and Nigeria. It would be a sad reflection on the Gold Coast if they allowed the new seats here to go to those who had been 'supine' in the days when Congress was striving for their liberties.[1] Soon afterwards election campaigning started in earnest. Perhaps the most interesting feature was the formation of new associations specifically for the occasion.[2] The National Congress of British West Africa, almost by definition, was not a suitable body to organize canvassing, so its leaders proceeded to form *ad hoc* voters' associations.

The inaugural meeting of the Accra Ratepayers' Association was addressed by Casely Hayford, Nanka-Bruce, and Glover-Addo, who was adopted as candidate.[3] Their main rival was the Manbii Party, a body resuscitated by Kojo Thompson to secure his own return to the Legislative Council as an elected member. This claimed to be the mouthpiece of the *manbii*, or townspeople, especially the illiterates; it owed its origin to the agitation over the Municipal Corporations Ordinance of 1924. K. Quartey-Papafio also stood for election, and felt bound to claim the support of an organized group, which he called the Independent Party. All three candidates were lawyers. Kojo Thompson still suffered from the unpopularity he had incurred through accepting official nomination in 1926; neither he nor Quartey-Papafio presented a serious challenge to Glover-Addo, who won the Accra election with an absolute majority in August 1927. Out of 1,816 registered electors, 780 voted; but it was officially estimated that about 60 per cent. of these were illiterates, and that few of the intelligentsia took part.[4]

The Sekondi campaign was more colourful, though less closely contested. The Municipal Electors' Association started advertising itself in June 1927, and soon afterwards declared that its main aim was 'to educate the community in the proper exercise of the privilege of electing representatives' to the town and Legislative Councils. It would also 'consider, discuss, accept and endorse or oppose, entirely or partly', Government measures affecting Sekondi.[5] Casely Hayford—the moving spirit behind this organization, together

[1] *The Gold Coast Leader*, 18 June 1927. During the same month Glover-Addo and Van Hien reversed their previous attitude, and accepted nomination as extraordinary members of the new Legislative Council.

[2] Cf. M. Duverger, *Political Parties, Their Organisation and Activity in the Modern State* (London, 1954), pp. xxvii–xxviii: 'The emergence of local electoral committees is directly linked with the extension of popular suffrage . . . Sometimes it is the candidate himself who gathers around him a few faithful friends in order to ensure his election . . . Sometimes, on the other hand, a few men form a group to launch a candidate and help him in his campaign . . . Very often some previously existing society . . . [or] newspapers bring about the creation of electoral committees' Duverger's pioneer study of the electoral and parliamentary origin of parties provides an illuminating background to the following brief account of early municipal politics in the Gold Coast.

[3] *The Gold Coast Leader*, 9 July 1927.

[4] Dispatch No. 691 of 3 Sept. 1927, from Slater to Amery; Adm. 1/622, G.N. Archives.

[5] *The Gold Coast Leader*, 16 July 1927.

with A. Essien and other close friends—was adopted as candidate for the election. Rival groups put forward other names; but after several withdrawals, the electors' choice lay between Casely Hayford and G. J. Christian, a West Indian lawyer, who relied on his personal reputation, unbacked by an organization—'Christian in name, Christian in sympathy and Christian in attitude'. His propaganda was enterprising: 'To whom do you turn when in trouble? Who will help you to maintain your citadels? Whose interests are identical with yours? Vote for Mr. G. J. Christian. For 15 years Liberian Consul— Approved by His Majesty King George V.' Casely Hayford countered this with: 'If you want better economic conditions, respect of your rights, cheaper living, educational advantages, opportunities for earning £. s. d. Higher appointments and the 1001 Blessings of this life, Vote for Casely Hayford.'[1]

There were scenes of crowded excitement in Sekondi on election day, with cars, lorries, posters, and flags out for the occasion; but the poll was very small—about one-quarter of the registered electors voted—and Casely Hayford easily defeated his rival by 146 votes to 25. The results in Accra and Sekondi were hailed by *The Gold Coast Leader* as 'The Triumph of Common Sense', and a rebuke was offered to those who had tried 'to pitch their claims for recognition against those of such a veteran as the Honourable J. E. Casely Hayford'.[2]

In Cape Coast alone, the A.R.P.S. was still influential enough to ensure that no candidate should stand for the Legislative Council elections. A meeting was held in August 1927, but no one at that time, however personally ambitious, dared to risk public disapproval. The European President of the Town Council attempted to persuade Van Hien to stand, having secured a promise from Nana Mbra III, Omanhene of Cape Coast, that he would not actively interfere with any individual candidate. Van Hien at first agreed; but he discovered that the voters who had promised to sign his nomination paper had 'received instructions' not to do so, and after discussing the matter with W. Ward Brew and others he 'decided not to offer himself'.[3]

Towards the end of the year the new Governor, Sir Ransford Slater, met the Chiefs and people in Cape Coast, and tried to persuade them that they needed a spokesman in the Legislative Council on such questions as the water rate and the proposed closing of the local port.[4] Although Slater had put a finger on two sore points, it was not until 1928 that a move was made to break the boycott. A Ratepayers' Association was then quietly formed, supported by several prominent citizens and some of the Asafo leaders; Van Hien led a deputation to ask for an interview with Nana Mbra III, but this was refused. The Oman Council voted to fix a date for an election, but the Omanhene,

---

[1] Ibid. 24 Sept. 1927.

[2] Ibid. 3 and 10 Sept. 1927.

[3] Letter of 8 Aug. 1927, from Bleasdell to Colonial Secretary, enclosed in Dispatch No. 691 of 3 Sept. 1927, from Slater to Amery; Adm. 1/622, G.N. Archives.

[4] Report of meeting at Cape Coast, 15 Nov. 1927; *The Gold Coast Leader,* 17 Dec. 1927.

supported by several of his councillors, including W. E. G. Sekyi, refused to forward the application to the Government. The Acting Governor came to Cape Coast in June 1928, and appealed to the 'youngmen' to reject their traditional leaders rather than 'commit constitutional suicide'. A few of the Omanhene's councillors were wavering, and were restrained only by the oath they had sworn; as Tufuhene Coker explained, 'If we do not respect it, our youngmen will always break it and our Chiefs will not be able to sit over a matter because the oaths that are attached to the Stool have been broken.'[1]

But the Cape Coast Ratepayers' Association was no longer prepared to wait for the Omanhene and the A.R.P.S. to do nothing. As a result of their pressure, the District Commissioner called together the leaders of the other main organizations, including the Literary and Social Club, the Chamber of Commerce, and the Eureka Club. He explained the details of electoral procedure, and made it clear that it was not necessary to wait for the traditional leaders to act. Those present then formally requested a proclamation of the election date.[2] A full meeting of the Ratepayers' Association was next convened, attended by Casely Hayford, D. Sackey, Ward Brew, and others; Tufuhene Coker had by now been won over, and agreed to become President. K. A. Korsah, a young barrister, was put forward as their candidate for the Legislative Council.[3] An interesting account has survived of how various names were considered, including that of Sekyi, who was turned down with the excuse that he was 'too stiff on Europeans, and officials don't like him'.[4] Clearly the emphasis was now on co-operation with the Government. A few months later *The Gold Coast Leader* denounced destructive criticism which could not help 'the promotion of Gold Coast nationhood'.[5]

There had been another significant shift of power within the A.R.P.S. following their petition against the 1927 Native Administrative Ordinance.[6] Casely Hayford had left the executive of the Society for a period,[7] and Van Hien had resigned from office as President early in 1928; Glover-Addo and Korsah had also resigned. The diehards—though of a younger generation than before—were now regaining control, and the Society continued to prompt the Omanhene of Cape Coast in his obstructive attitude. Tufuhene Coker was declared destooled, and all the leaders of the Ratepayers' Association were attacked in *The Gold Coast Times*. The Omanhene unsuccessfully attempted to secure the postponement of the election, and gong-gong was beaten to warn electors not to vote. There was a good deal of excitement

---

[1] Report of meeting at Cape Coast, 23 June 1928; *The Gold Coast Leader*, 25 July 1928.

[2] Coker, 'The Truth about Cape Coast Municipal Election'; ibid. 19 Sept. 1928.

[3] Sir Arku Korsah later became Chief Justice of Ghana.

[4] *The Gold Coast Leader*, 2 Jan. 1929. Cf. Ch. XIII, p. 547, below,

[5] 'The Dangers of Extremism'; ibid. 24 Oct. 1928.   [6] See Ch. XII, pp. 497–8, below.

[7] Afterwards Casely Hayford continued to hold the nominal office of Vice-President. But *The Gold Coast Leader*, 21 Nov. 1928—probably at his instigation—attacked 'the nonsense and dictatorship of the extreme group of the Central Executive', and urged the need for reconstruction of the Society if it were not able to 'die a natural death'.

and intimidation. An anxious official telegram was dispatched to Accra: 'News cried by linguist Kwami Hendrick as follows: if anyone will go to Accra on his arrival his family may go to the lorry station with his coffin to bury the party who went to the Council. Members of Ratepayers Association to take warning. The crier swore by Oguaa Wukuda.'[1] By contrast, Korsah's propaganda was decorous and restrained in the extreme. One placard ran: 'Self-injurious conservatism has ruined Cape Coast. It requires a man of great tact, integrity and ability to save the present situation.'[2]

Some of the sting was taken out of the campaign by the lack of any rival to Korsah, who was returned unopposed in August 1928. He took his seat in the Legislative Council in October. But the tension mounted again in Cape Coast when the Omanhene tried to have the result set aside by legal action. Eventually the petitioners, led by Sekyi, were non-suited, and the Judge criticized them for introducing a mass of irrelevant matter and unduly prolonging a 'frivolous and vexatious' case, which he said should never have been brought to court.[3] Casely Hayford represented Korsah in this case, and the remnant of the A.R.P.S. at Cape Coast never forgave him for his part in their final discomfiture.[4]

Thus from 1928 onwards, Accra, Sekondi, and Cape Coast were represented in the Legislative Council by three elected Africans. They made full use of their opportunities for constructive criticism, and soon showed themselves willing to co-operate with the Chiefs, in spite of past differences. In March 1929 Casely Hayford effected a reconciliation of his quarrel with Nana Ofori Atta,[5] which dated back to the early days of the National Congress; and the three municipal members thenceforward joined the six provincial members in their unofficial consultations in Accra during sessions of the Legislative Council. As Danquah wrote in 1928, 'We have here a form of responsible government literally thrust upon us. It is for us to seize it and make it a polished and refined form of government.'[6]

*   *   *   *   *   *

AFRICAN UNOFFICIAL MEMBERS OF THE LEGISLATIVE COUNCIL, 1850-1926

James BANNERMAN	1850-6
merchant, Accra	
George BLANKSON	1861-73
merchant, Anomabu	

[1] Telegram of 3 Aug. 1928, from Deputy Provincial Commissioner to Colonial Secretary; S.N.A. 925, Case 28/1925, G.N. Archives.   [2] *The Gold Coast Leader*, 12 Sept. 1928.

[3] Judgement of 28 Nov. 1928, by C. E. Woolhouse Bannerman; ibid. 12 Dec. 1928.

[4] Casely Hayford's death in 1930 was almost completely ignored by the Cape Coast newspaper, *The Gold Coast Times*.

[5] For an account of this important development, see Wight, *The Gold Coast Legislative Council* pp. 73-74.

[6] J. B. Danquah, *An Epistle to the Educated Youngman in Akim Abuakwa* (Accra, 1928).

Robert HUTCHISON 1861–3
    merchant, Cape Coast
F. C. GRANT 1863–6, 1869, 1871, 1873, 1887[1]
    merchant, Cape Coast
S. C. BREW 1864–6
    merchant, Anomabu
G. F. CLELAND 1886–7
    merchant, divisional Chief, Accra
W. HUTCHISON 1887[1]
    merchant, Cape Coast
John SARBAH 1887,[1] 1888–92
    merchant, Anomabu and Cape Coast
J. H. CHEETHAM 1893–8
    merchant, Accra
J. VANDERPUIYE 1894–1904
    merchant, divisional Chief, Accra
T. HUTTON MILLS 1898–1900, 1909–18
    barrister, Accra
J. MENSAH SARBAH 1900,[1] 1901–10
    barrister, Cape Coast
J. P. BROWN 1904–9
    teacher, Cape Coast
Nene MATE KOLE 1911–16, 1921–26
    paramount Chief, Manya Krobo
Nana AMONOO V 1916–21
    paramount Chief, Anomabu
Togbui SRI II 1916–21
    paramount Chief, Awunaga
Nana OFORI ATTA 1916–26
    paramount Chief, Akim Abuakwa
E. J. P. BROWN 1916–26
    barrister, Cape Coast
J. E. CASELY HAYFORD 1916–26
    barrister, Sekondi
Dr. B. W. QUARTEY-PAPAFIO 1919–24
    medical practitioner, Accra
C. J. BANNERMAN 1921[1]
    barrister, Accra
Nana ESSANDOH III 1921–6
    paramount Chief, Nkusukum
J. GLOVER-ADDO 1924–6
    barrister, Accra
H. VAN HIEN 1924–6[1]
    merchant, Cape Coast and Elmina
E. C. QUIST 1925[1]
    barrister, Accra

[1] Extraordinary members.

XII

THE CHIEFS AND THE GOVERNMENT
1871–1928

THE Chief, as the traditional leader of his people, might have been expected to be in the forefront of the Gold Coast national movement. This was to some extent true of King Aggery, and later of the Fanti Confederation. But both these examples revealed inherent weaknesses in the structure of chieftaincy that prevented any similar movement developing on a national scale.

Aggery's challenge to British jurisdiction in Cape Coast was ineffective partly because the area of his own inherited jurisdiction was too small; and the later Confederation broke down largely because the fatal inability of the Chiefs to agree among themselves prevented their effective combination over a wider area. The only place where the traditional unit of government was powerful enough to build up anything approaching a nation out of a large number of different tribes was Ashanti[1]—and here, when the British eventually recognized a barrier to the extension of their own authority, the Asantehene was removed. This ensured both the continuance of national feeling and the lack of any traditional outlet for its expression.

South of Ashanti, however, the Government was from the time of the Fanti Confederation onwards endeavouring to find means whereby British rule could be exercised through—rather than in spite of—the Chiefs. Increasingly the Chiefs were made responsible for enforcing central decisions at the local level; and this practice encouraged opposition to them as mere agents of colonial rule without effectively strengthening their authority. At the same time, however, the earlier form of negotiation with the Chiefs—as in the Bonds of 1844—was being replaced by the direct proclamation of authority as a means of extending British jurisdiction; the culmination of this process may be seen in 1901.

The Annexation and Protection Orders in Council, although unexceptionable according to English law, were unacceptable to Gold Coast politicians because they appeared to ride roughshod over the traditional system of jurisdiction. Endless arguments were provoked; for example, did the Chiefs possess inherent jurisdiction, or was it derived from the Crown? or, as some extremists urged even after 1901, were the powers of the Crown derived only from the voluntary consent of the Chiefs, as expressed in bonds and treaties? Similarly, the official theory that the central Government had the power to

[1] Cf. the view of the Chief Commissioner in 1920: 'we have in Ashanti the nearest approach to a nation on the Gold Coast'. Letter from Harper to Guggisberg, enclosed in his Confidential Dispatch of 1 Nov. 1920, to Milner; G.N. Archives.

dismiss a Chief aroused the most vehement opposition, and repeatedly frustrated attempts to define and regulate the powers of the Chiefs by Ordinance.

Although growing national sentiment often found expression in a spirited defence of the traditional status and powers of the Chiefs, the institution of chieftaincy was becoming too closely interwoven with the pattern of British authority for them to make any effective protest themselves. In addition, the social and economic structure of the country was changing too fast for them to retain adequate control by traditional means—especially where they were faced with a challenge from educated young men in their own States who felt that the old apparatus of government was out of date.[1]

A few outstanding personalities—notably Nana Ofori Atta—were able to rise to the status of national figures during the latter part of the period. But it is significant that they did so by accepting and working within the new framework of national government, and that their very status on the Legislative Council was fiercely challenged for many years. The introduction of Provincial Councils by Sir Gordon Guggisberg in the 1920's was a serious attempt to bridge the gap between the multiplicity of local units and the concentration of power at the centre, without violating traditional institutions. This aroused even more controversy than usual; it marked, however, a fresh determination on the part of the Government to work with and through the Chiefs, and opened the way to some renewal of their influence and authority during the 1930's.

Official Attitudes to the Chiefs, 1871–82

During the 1870's there was considerable heart-searching, both in the Colonial Office and among Gold Coast administrators, concerning the proper relationship between the Chiefs and the Government. The summary treatment of Aggery, though it had emphasized that the British were not prepared to tolerate any local challenge to their authority, had left the jurisdiction of the Chiefs still undefined, and had certainly not solved the problem of how to secure their voluntary co-operation in the new order. In 1871 the Administrator-in-Chief at Freetown recommended the payment of permanent stipends, as the cheapest and most efficient system, which had already been proved in Sierra Leone; and he suggested that the very fact of bringing the Chiefs or their messengers face to face with the Queen's representative, once or twice a year, to receive their pay, would have 'the best moral effect'.[2]

---

[1] Cf. the view that 'the Stool authorities were not adapted, and are perhaps now inadaptable, as instruments for carrying out such measures of social reconstruction as are pre-eminently the problem to-day.' C. K. Meek, W. M. Macmillan, and E. R. J. Hussey, *Europe and West Africa* (London, 1940), p. 98.

[2] Dispatch No. 108 of 8 Nov. 1871, from Kennedy to Kimberley; CO/96/89. Perhaps the first such stipend paid in the Gold Coast had been the £50 per annum granted by the Council of Merchants to an earlier King Aggery in 1780, in return for bringing about peace and reconciling

H. T. Ussher, the Gold Coast Administrator, agreed with this suggestion; after the dispute over the Fanti Confederation, he was anxious to play down the influence of the 'scholars', and to bring the Chiefs together in such a way that they would be directly amenable to government influence.[1]

A comprehensive scheme for 'utilizing, regulating and controlling' the power of the Chiefs was soon afterwards outlined by D. Chalmers, the Chief Magistrate, who was the first to describe the existing system as one of grada- tion of authority. He admitted that a King possessed little real power over his 'subordinate Chiefs'; nevertheless, assuming that this was the basis of the system, it was the best foundation on which to build. He therefore suggested that the most reliable Chiefs should be directly recognized and assisted by a stipend, and should have their own courts of first instance. They would be held responsible for the behaviour of lesser Chiefs, whose position would not be affected, except that complaints from their areas could be heard in British courts. Unfortunately it would be impracticable to appoint magistrates in every district to work together with the Chiefs. But in view of their lack of education, the Government should appoint a clerk to each Chief, and if they were young they should be taught to read and write in their own language; their recognized successors should be fully educated.[2]

The Ashanti war of 1873-4 delayed further thought and action on the position of the Chiefs in the Protectorate, besides revealing the crippling lack of unity among them in the face of an outside threat. After the Orders in Council of 1874, the first act of the Gold Coast Government was to emanci- pate all slaves and abolish internal slave-dealing, thereby seriously weakening the power of the Chiefs. The Supreme Court Ordinance of 1876 further com- plicated matters for them, by introducing an alien judicial system based on the English model. The application of the Ordinance varied in towns and rural districts, and there was considerable uncertainty as to the extent of jurisdiction left to the Chiefs.[3] Many had come to rely on the Government as their source of authority, and they began to complain increasingly that their subjects would not obey them and that officials would not tell them what powers they had. They asked with some force 'how they can know what is lawful and what is not if they are not told'.[4]

The alienation of land in the developing Tarkwa gold-mining area intensified doubts about the ability of the Chiefs to cope with modern conditions. In 1877 the Governor, S. Freeling, took the view that their authority must be upheld as much as possible, both to reduce the cost of government and to avoid

the factions in Cape Coast. J. J. Crooks, *Records relating to the Gold Coast Settlements from 1750 to 1874* (Dublin, 1923), p. 42.

[1] Confidential Letter of 4 May 1872, from Ussher to Pope Hennessy, enclosed in his Dispatch No. 93 of 29 Oct. 1872, to Kimberley; CO/96/94.

[2] Letter of 6 June 1872, from Chalmers to Pope Hennessy; ibid.

[3] See Ch. VIII, pp. 304-6, above.

[4] Dispatch No. 189 of 26 July 1877, from Freeling to Carnarvon; CO/96/121.

influential discontent. He considered it a matter not only of policy, but of justice, 'to effect reforms by as slight a disruption of long-cherished powers and customs as possible'.[1] This view, which prevailed in subsequent legislation, kept alive the tradition of 1844, by which the Government 'treated the States as independent authorities over whom control could only be secured by their individual agreement'.[2]

Thus the first Native Jurisdiction Ordinance, enacted in 1878, was considerably milder than Chalmers's original suggestions; it omitted all reference to stipends or government control, and simply set out 'to facilitate and regulate the exercise in the Protected Territories of certain powers and jurisdiction by Native Authorities'. In fact, this represented the first public statement of the jurisdiction of the Government *vis-à-vis* the Chiefs of the Protectorate, although the main object was to define the powers of the Chiefs themselves.

Kings were now to be officially termed 'Head Chiefs'; within their States, divisions were to be created, with villages grouped in further subdivisions. Head Chiefs and minor Chiefs were to be both empowered and enjoined to establish tribunals; Head Chiefs, with the assent of their councillors, might make by-laws on a list of prescribed subjects, with the Governor's approval. The 1878 Ordinance did not claim to bestow any jurisdiction on the Chiefs, but to define it, in both civil and criminal matters. Nevertheless, this definition, by non-traditional legislative process, was the first step towards making the British Government the source of the Chiefs' authority. The tendency was emphasized by one major innovation—the power now explicitly given to the Government to 'dismiss' a Chief. The Secretary of State felt that this might be somewhat more than was justified by existing relations with the Protected Territories; and therefore he laid down the proviso that such power should never be exercised without prior reference to London.[3]

The Ordinance received the Queen's assent; and it was to have been implemented by proclamation in various places from time to time. But there was considerable delay, mainly because the Lieutenant-Governor, C. Lees, was doubtful about its likely reception. Several important Kings were known to be against the Ordinance, and he suggested that twenty-six of them should be given £40 per annum each, since the expectation of such stipends should favourably influence their reactions.[4] When Ussher returned as the new Governor in 1879, the whole problem, including the possibility of some associated scheme of taxation, was referred to him.

As a result, the 1878 Ordinance was never implemented. Ussher now thought even less of the Chiefs than he had before and was opposed to working through them in any way; for example, he wished to remove King Tackie

---

[1] Dispatch No. 143 of 29 May 1877, from Freeling to Carnarvon; CO/96/121.

[2] Lord Hailey, *Native Administration in the British African Territories* (London, 1951), pt. iii, p. 201.

[3] Dispatch No. 137 of 30 Sept. 1878, from Hicks Beach to Lees; CO/96/124.

[4] Dispatch No. 230 of 18 Nov. 1878, from Lees to Hicks Beach; CO/96/125.

of Accra, because of his ineffectiveness in general and the state of his prison in particular. Ussher criticized the sudden abolition of slavery, which he felt had been a hasty and ill-advised concession to agitation in Britain. But he had no sympathy with the Chiefs' complaints, nor did he think that they were entitled to much consideration in any scheme for the better government of 'their wretched people'; their protests against each step of reform should even be regarded with satisfaction, as a direct index of its value.[1]

Ussher also made some practical suggestions for bringing Europeans into immediate contact with the inhabitants, by the appointment of District Commissioners who should live in the rural areas and rule in conjunction with the Chiefs. But in London there was alarm at the prospect of having to recruit for such posts:

What man of integrity and ability, unless imbued with the zeal for the secular welfare of the negro which animates the missionary for his religious conversion, would be willing, or could be tempted by any conceivable remuneration, to undertake such a duty? The horror of such a life is appalling to contemplate—the isolation and absence of society or companionship; the constant prospect of sickness and death far from friends or medical assistance; being ever surrounded by foul sights and fouler sounds and smells; the monotony and weariness! If, as we so often hear, officers stationed in coast towns take to drink to drown their cares and discomfort, what would be the temptation to such a course to the man in Akim or Wassaw?[2]

These objections did not apply so strongly to the appointment of a few travelling officers to visit Chiefs, hear complaints, receive taxes, and report on what was going on. But that should be all; and caution prevailed, the Colonial Office disclaiming any intention of entering upon a crusade to reform native customs, or to abolish the power of the Chiefs simply because they might not always administer justice in accordance with English ideas. In some respects, they should even be strengthened, since the Government was not in a position to substitute its own authority in 'the inaccessible wilds and impenetrable forests of the interior'.[3]

The real issue for the authorities to decide was whether the country was to be governed through the Chiefs, with only general supervision and control by the British; or whether all power and authority was to be taken out of traditional hands and exercised instead by white officials stationed in different parts of the Protectorate, making its position similar to that of a Colony.[4] Ussher, who believed that the Chiefs were useless, tyrannical, and not to be trusted to administer justice, would clearly have preferred the latter solution.[5] When given grudging permission in 1880 to increase his staff, he appointed two Civil Commissioners, at Odumase, near the Volta, and Tarkwa, the

---

[1] Dispatch No. 24 of 26 Jan. 1880, from Ussher to Hicks Beach; CO/96/130.
[2] Minute of 9 Mar. 1880, by A. W. L. Hemming; ibid.   [3] Ibid.
[4] Ibid. 18 June 1880; CO/96/131.
[5] Dispatch No. 151 of 11 May 1880, from Ussher to Kimberley; ibid.

mining centre, and urged the need for at least one more.[1] The Secretary of State, who had previously avoided a clear choice between the two alternatives, was now persuaded by his officials to 'Apply the drag'; and Ussher was told to continue to leave local administration as far as possible in the hands of the Chiefs.[2]

Ussher died only a month later. His successor, Sir Samuel Rowe, held very different views about the traditional rulers, and stated categorically, 'I think the proper way to administer the Gold Coast Colony is by acting through the Chiefs.'[3] He described them as the most respectable persons in the community and 'the expression of the native mind in favour of social order and the rights of property'. Some had a certain amount of education, and most of them, he thought, compared favourably with the mass of the community whose opinion supported them in office. They appeared essential for the supervision of local affairs, and for the maintenance of social organization in most parts of the Protectorate; Rowe was therefore anxious to do all in his power to encourage them to work with the Government.[4] This was directly in line with the Colonial Office belief that it was impossible, even if desirable, to introduce all the forms and procedures of English law in these outlying districts.[5] But it also illustrates once again the importance of the man on the spot, who could either implement or effectively block the policy laid down in London.

The Native Jurisdiction Ordinance, 1883

When Rowe went to London on leave in 1882, he urged the need for a clear-cut system of administration, especially in the increasingly important Tarkwa area. He was anxious to improve and enforce the existing law, and was confident that the Chiefs would listen to advice if it came from the Governor.[6] Soon after he returned to the Gold Coast the 1878 Ordinance was repealed and re-enacted, with one major modification, by which decisions of native tribunals were made subject to appeal to the British courts.[7] This seemed a logical further step in the integration of the two judicial systems; but in practice it increased the pre-eminence of the British courts, upon which the Chiefs came to depend for confirmation of their judicial authority.

The 1883 Native Jurisdiction Ordinance was applied initially only to six Head Chiefs, and later extended to other divisions of the Protectorate.[8] Many criticisms of it were made, by successive Governors, by educated Africans, and sometimes by the Chiefs themselves. Numerous attempts to improve or

[1] Dispatch No. 243 of 25 Sept. 1880, from Ussher to Kimberley; CO/96/131.
[2] Minute of 12 Nov. 1880, by Kimberley, and his Dispatch No. 170 of 19 Nov. 1880, to Ussher; ibid.   [3] Letter of 31 Aug. 1882, from Rowe to Colonial Office; CO/96/147.
[4] Dispatch No. 68 of 6 Mar. 1882, from Rowe to Kimberley; CO/96/138.
[5] Minute of 25 Apr. 1882, by Hemming; ibid.
[6] Minute of 4 Oct. 1882, by Rowe; CO/96/147.
[7] Dispatch No. 37 of 30 Jan. 1883, from Rowe to Derby; CO/96/149.
[8] It was applied to one more division in 1889, and then not again until 1898; by 1909 it had been extended to over forty. Brandford Griffith C.J., *Legislative Council Minutes*, 2 July 1910.

modify the law invariably aroused immediate, and often confused opposition. Nevertheless, this Ordinance remained the basis of native jurisdiction up to 1927, and through it the administration of justice by the Chiefs gradually became interwoven with the English system.[1]

The immediate reaction in Cape Coast was unfavourable, and there was some press abuse of the Governor.[2] One extreme, though untypical protest reached the Secretary of State from J. Renner Maxwell, the first graduate African lawyer in the Gold Coast. He considered himself emancipated from the jurisdiction of 'uneducated and savage' Chiefs, and complained that the Ordinance preferred 'Ignorance and Barbarism to Education and Civilisation'.[3] But this legislation also prompted the first serious discussion among the educated community of the nature of the Chiefs' jurisdiction. Several Africans began to study and interpret their own institutions, and to resist interference with them. They argued, in particular, that the Governor should not have the power to suspend or dismiss Chiefs, 'on sufficient cause', without referring to the Oman Council or the people.[4] It was feared that dismissals might take place on any pretext whatsoever; and here the Chiefs themselves realized that their own interests were affected. To some extent, therefore, this Ordinance might be said to have laid the foundation for the co-operation of the Chiefs and the intelligentsia when the A.R.P.S. came to be formed.

[1] For an interesting account of traditional procedure in native courts, see B. Cruickshank, *Eighteen Years on the Gold Coast of Africa* (London, 1853), vol. i, ch. x. This may be compared with a later memorandum by Brandford Griffith C.J., published in *Report of the Gold Coast Local Committee of the Society of Comparative Legislation* (Accra), for the quarter ending 31 Dec. 1904.

[2] For example, 'Governor Rowe ... is pre-eminently the worst, most unfit, and most objectionable ruler that the Gold Coast has ever been afflicted with'. *The Gold Coast Times*, 18 Aug. 1883.

[3] Renner Maxwell was particularly worried by the domestic consequences of the Ordinance: 'my present cook is a son-in-law of and captain to the chief of the district in which I live, and if the Ordinance is ever made to apply to Cape Coast, which I pray God and your Lordship will forbid, I may become the victim of a great deal of annoyance from my own cook'. Letter of 23 Aug. 1883, from Renner Maxwell to Secretary of State, enclosed in Dispatch No. 420 of 4 Dec. 1883, from Rowe to Derby; CO/96/153.

[4] The Government had never explicitly claimed this right before 1878, but had often dealt in summary fashion with troublesome Chiefs.

In 1848 Lieutenant-Governor Winniett had sent an expedition to Apollonia to avenge the murder of the French Commandant of Assini. Lord Grey, the Secretary of State, entirely disapproved; but the King was captured and imprisoned in Cape Coast Castle until his death in 1851. Crooks, *Records*, pp. 312–14.

In 1852 Governor Hill had deposed the King of Assin with 'the unanimous consent of the Chiefs, Magistrates, and in accordance with my own opinion', and had imprisoned him 'for life', for taking a bribe from the Asantehene and declaring his intention 'to throw off his allegiance to the English'. Four days later the King was restored to his position, after the Assin Chiefs and captains had given an undertaking for future good conduct. Dispatches of 23 and 27 Oct. 1852, from Hill to Pakington; CO/96/25.

In 1879 the Colonial Office admitted that it had long been 'a common practice to deport Kings who stirred up disturbances or otherwise made themselves troublesome', including King Aggery (1867), the King of Elmina, and two of his Chiefs (1873), followed soon by the two Kings of Sekondi, and the King of Juaben with some of his Chiefs (1878). Minute of 17 Mar. 1879, by Hemming; CO/96/126.

The argument persisted for many years. J. Mensah Sarbah, for example, claimed in 1906 that 'The right of dismissal is in the people, not in the Crown', and declared that the Government had abused its powers in the case of the Chief of Tarkwa and Awudua.[1] Over twenty years later, J. W. de Graft Johnson was still concerned to argue the case against this provision of the 1883 Ordinance.[2]

Attempts to Improve the Ordinance, 1887-1910

In 1887 a legal decision raised again the whole question of Chiefs and their courts. For some years the Government under Sir William Brandford Griffith had been discouraging native courts—and especially their severe punishments for debtors, which were considered a 'remnant of barbarism'—without actually attempting to suppress them. But the Full Court now decided that the Supreme Court Ordinance of 1876 had not impaired the judicial powers of Chiefs in the Protected Territories; and it was further held that in certain circumstances they had the right to imprison their subjects.[3]

This decision provoked further local discussion, since officials were by no means agreed over the future of the Chiefs. One extreme view was taken by W. Brandford Griffith jun., the Acting Queen's Advocate, who looked forward to the day when 'The Chiefs will lose their power and we shall rule through the District Commissioners as on the Coast instead of depending on the tottering and uncertain power of the Chiefs.' He recommended legislation aimed at the gradual extinction of native prisons, and thereby the Chiefs' courts as well. The latter should certainly be suppressed in towns where there was a District Commissioner; even those subject to the Native Jurisdiction Ordinance were liable to abuses and corruption, their decision being based 'as much on fetish as on facts'.[4]

But other officials took the more practical view, which found support in London, that the Colony could not afford either the District Commissioners or the police necessary to keep the people of the interior 'in hand', to clear the roads, and to prevent slavery; and that there was no hope of doing all this if the Chiefs were not respected and obeyed by their own subjects. Therefore they must retain the power to fine and imprison.[5] The legislation which emerged from this controversy was intended as a compromise. The Native Prisons Ordinance of 1888 empowered the Governor to regulate and, if necessary, to close village prisons, and prohibited imprisonment in them for longer than one month.

[1] *Fanti National Constitution* (London, 1906), pp. 134-5.

[2] *Towards Nationhood in West Africa* (London, 1928), pp. 37-38.

[3] Oppon *v.* Ackinnie; J. Mensah Sarbah, *Fanti Customary Laws* (London, 2nd edn. 1904), p. 232. Cf. Ord's denial of this right, before the 1865 Committee; see Ch. V, p. 202, above.

[4] Memorandum of 3 Dec. 1887, by W. Brandford Griffith jun., on Native Prisons, enclosed in his father's Dispatch No. 116 of 10 Apr. 1888, to Knutsford; CO/96/191.

[5] Memorandum of 22 Jan. 1888, by Acting Colonial Secretary; ibid.

At last the dream of Colonel Ord, to shield all the inhabitants of the Protectorate from imprisonment 'at the hands of their masters', had been fulfilled. This was the logical consequence of British policy, whereby the traditional sanctions in the hands of the Chiefs had one by one been removed— powers over life and death, enslavement and pawning, physical punishment such as chaining 'in log' and, now, all but the minimum term of imprisonment.[1] Each restriction had had the best of humanitarian motives; but their cumulative effect was such as to weaken considerably the judicial authority of the Chiefs and to substitute for it the central, impersonal machinery of the British courts. Serious offences could no longer be punished within the community in which they arose, and the Chief was no longer able to express the collective judgement of his people on such matters. The advantage of a uniform legal system enforced at the national level by the Supreme Court gradually became apparent; but so did the potentialities of friction between the Chiefs and their subjects at the local level.

The Government was at this stage concerned mainly to secure further definition and control of the powers of the Chiefs. In 1894 an amending Bill was introduced; but this hung fire while a commission inquired into the constitution, jurisdiction, and procedure of native courts.[2] They reported the following year that the proposed amendments were on the right lines;[3] but when Sir William Maxwell arrived he found that the problem had been shelved in Accra while Brandford Griffith had been preoccupied with Ashanti affairs. The new Governor soon decided that the Bill did not go far enough; further definition was needed. He himself could not be certain who were the Chiefs of particular districts, towns, and villages; what were their customary powers, duties, and relative importance; or which of them were recognized by, and how far these were held responsible to, the central Government. Maxwell tried, somewhat inaccurately, to classify the Chiefs into three categories; and he had no hesitation in recommending that their position should be 'improved', while making them more directly responsible to the Government for the proper performance of their functions. Further, he suggested that elections of Chiefs according to native custom should require official sanction.[4]

Another new Bill was therefore drafted 'to define and regulate the power of Native Chiefs and Tribunals', and this was gazetted in 1896. The Secretary

---

[1] Cf. the considered view, expressed twenty years later, that the 1888 Ordinance 'practically took away from the Native Tribunals their effective power of punishment by imprisonment'. Attorney-General, *Legislative Council Minutes*, 2 Sept. 1907.

[2] The Chairman of the Native Courts Commission was the Chief Justice, Sir John Hutchinson; members included J. H. Cheetham and J. Vanderpuiye, the two African members of the Legislative Council.

[3] Report of the Native Courts Commission, dated 12 Jan. 1895; J. Mensah Sarbah, *Fanti Law Report* (London, 1904), pp. 171–83.

[4] Dispatch No. 131 of 15 Apr. 1896, from Maxwell to Chamberlain; CO/96/272.

of State deferred consideration until the effect of its publication was seen;[1] then, with the embarrassment of the Lands Bill affair, the Government did not consider it wise to press this controversial legislation, which was quietly dropped. The drawbacks of the 1883 Ordinance remained. For the Chiefs the crucial question was: 'Will the Government enforce their orders or shall they be allowed to enforce them themselves?'[2]

The position of some of the older Chiefs had changed almost beyond recognition in their own lifetime.[3] They were now increasingly being expected to act as agents of the central Government, in such unpopular and untraditional tasks as the maintenance of roads and telegraph lines.[4] A particularly harassing burden was imposed by the Compulsory Labour Ordinance of 1895, which required them to provide workers demanded by the Government. It was under this Ordinance, initially designed to secure carriers for the Ashanti expedition, that the newly installed Omanhene of Cape Coast was imprisoned, 'his hair clipped, and made to don prison clothes'. J. E. Casely Hayford succeeded in getting the conviction quashed on appeal, but later wrote bitterly: 'what of the indignity?'[5] More often, however, it was the unfortunate labourers who suffered severe penalties under the Ordinance, which seems to have been harshly applied;[6] and their natural resentment was directed primarily against the Chiefs as the immediate source of this unwelcome pressure.

The new pattern of British authority imposed at the turn of the century was bound to involve the Chiefs still further in the network of central government. A Native Affairs Department was founded in 1902 to secure greater continuity in administration, and to assist in providing information about many of the finer points of African customs. This was the beginning of a more consistent policy, designed to strengthen the hands of the leading Chiefs, and to support their dignity and authority: 'Recognition is given of their position; communications to their subordinates are sent through them; the Government, when it is considered desirable, enforce their proper orders.'[7] In addition, under the provisions of the 1883 Ordinance, they were encouraged to enact by-laws with the advice of their councillors.

---

[1] Dispatch of 3 June 1896, from Chamberlain to Maxwell; CO/96/272.

[2] Chief Justice, 1901, quoted by Attorney-General, *Legislative Council Minutes*, 2 July 1910.

[3] It was said of King Tackie: 'He no longer has a Court in which to sell justice at Accra and so has no revenue. He has also no powers of punishment and so no means of making his nominal subjects obey him. He is an old man with the recollection of great former importance and of an influence extending over all the Gā-talking people and he naturally resents the new order of things and is not inclined to assist the Government that has brought it about.' Confidential Dispatch of 10 Mar. 1901, from Nathan to Chamberlain; CO/96/378.

[4] Under the Trade Roads Ordinance of 1894 (cf. Ch. I, p. 26, above) and the Telegraph Ordinance of 1896.

[5] J. E. Casely Hayford, *Gold Coast Native Institutions* (London, 1903), p. 260.

[6] Letter of 24 Feb. 1898, from Brandford Griffith C.J. to Hodgson, enclosed in his Confidential Dispatch of 18 Apr. 1898, to Chamberlain; CO/96/314.

[7] *Departmental Reports*, Native Affairs, 1903.

In 1904 the Chiefs Ordinance was enacted, despite the opposition of Mensah Sarbah and J. P. Brown in the Legislative Council.[1] Whenever the election or deposition of a Chief was questioned, the Governor's decision was now to be final, and not subject to challenge in the courts, although he must satisfy himself that his verdict was in accordance with native custom. The associated Stool Property Detention Ordinance enabled a District Commissioner to compel an ex-Chief to hand over the stool and other symbolic paraphernalia. At the end of the year, the Native Affairs Department claimed that the Government was not encroaching on traditional rights, but preventing discredit being brought on some of the most time-hallowed institutions of the country; and was satisfied that the general public thought so too. But it was suggested that the Chiefs needed further powers to enforce their own judgements and the wishes of the Government.[2]

Mensah Sarbah's *Fanti National Constitution* (1906) was a more reliable indication of the attitude of the educated community, and their growing inclination to defend the original status of the Chiefs. He repeated the claim of the Lands Bill petitioners that the Gold Coast had not been conquered, and argued that British influence and jurisdiction had only been acquired in special circumstances, by treaties with existing tribal governments who had their own rights of sovereignty.[3] To some extent, of course, this argument was supported by the wording of the 1878 Ordinance, as well as by the Bonds of 1844, although it conveniently ignored the effect of the 1901 Orders in Council. But in a judgement of 1907, the Chief Justice, Sir William Brandford Griffith, held that Chiefs exercised their jurisdiction in native courts only with the consent of the Crown, which had been implied in the Orders in Council.[4]

In the same year a new Bill was introduced to define more clearly the powers and duties of Chiefs, to provide machinery for enforcing their lawful orders, and also to repeal the Native Jurisdiction Ordinance of 1883. These proposals aroused some concern, especially among the A.R.P.S. leaders; and during the debate on the second reading J. P. Brown tabled a memorial of protest from the Society. The Governor, Sir John Rodger, was anxious to reach agreement, so the Bill was referred to a special committee of the Legislative Council (including both the African members), empowered to suggest amendments.[5] Unfortunately their report was not unanimous; both the Chief Justice and Attorney-General registered objections to the majority findings, although they did not even see eye to eye with each other. A year later, in 1909, the Governor was unable to settle the question, and could only report that it was still under consideration.[6] There seemed to be no urgency; the

---

[1] *Legislative Council Minutes*, Jan. 1904.

[2] *Departmental Reports*, Native Affairs, 1904.   [3] *Fanti National Constitution*, ch. iii.

[4] Judgement by W. Brandford Griffith, 9 Dec. 1907, *in re* Mutchi v. Kobina Annan, Kobina Inketsia; and Mutchi v. Kudo. *Report of the Gold Coast Local Committee of the Society of Comparative Legislation* (Accra), for the quarter ending 30 Sept. 1907.

[5] *Legislative Council Minutes*, 2 Sept. 1907.   [6] Ibid. 28 Oct. 1909.

Native Affairs Department commented on the entire absence of unrest, and the great prosperity arising from the development of commercial agriculture.[1]

Rodger made his next attempt in 1910, this time introducing amending legislation only, instead of repealing and re-enacting that of 1883; the advantage was that every clause need not then be open to discussion. The new proposals applied the provisions of 1883 to all the divisions of the Colony, thus providing more native courts to deal with minor, everyday cases, and machinery for enforcing their judgements. In the Legislative Council many doubts and queries were expressed; and an unexpected feature of the debate was the unrelenting opposition of the Chief Justice, who claimed that he had earned for himself the title of 'member for the Natives'.[2] He was opposed to the universal application of the Bill, and thought that many illiterate Chiefs and their unskilled clerks would be hard put to it if they all had to set up courts—quite apart from the risk of abuses.[3] He complained that the Bill had been gazetted only one week in advance, with no statement of reasons or objects, and that very few copies were available. He alleged, with some justice, that it had been hurriedly rushed through the committee stage without giving the members or the public sufficient opportunity for useful criticism; and finally, that the proposed changes in the law were not only unnecessary but prejudicial to the interests of the Colony.[4] He even petitioned the Secretary of State against it.[5]

Mensah Sarbah took an important part in this debate, pointing out that the A.R.P.S. had been discussing the matter since the 1906 proposal had been withdrawn. He objected to several points in the present Bill, especially the procedure for referring appeals from Head Chiefs' courts to District Commissioners, and repeated his earlier suggestion that the services of educated Africans should be used in the dispensation of justice, to visit native tribunals and assist the Chiefs generally in the hearing of cases. He also proposed, with the support of Hutton Mills, that the suspension or dismissal of Chiefs should be carried out by resolution of the Legislative Council, instead of by Order in Council, so that the question could be publicly considered. Their motion to this effect was defeated, but they managed to get the words

[1] *Departmental Reports*, Native Affairs, 1909.

[2] Brandford Griffith, *Legislative Council Minutes*, 2 July 1910.

[3] Local action was sometimes effectively taken to check such abuses. For example, in Okwawu the 'mmeranti', consisting of practically the whole of the non-official male population, i.e. those who were neither Chiefs nor members of their courts, combined to prevent 'abnormal fines and extortion in those courts'. *Departmental Reports*, Native Affairs, 1905.

[4] *Legislative Council Minutes*, 26 Aug. 1910. The Chief Justice revived this issue many years later in his memoirs, alleging that Rodger was 'a tired and exhausted man and should have gone home months before, and his anxiety to get what he considered a valuable measure passed, outran wisdom...The next Governor, Thorburn, said openly that he could not understand how such a Bill ever came to be passed!' W. Brandford Griffith, *The Far Horizon* (Ilfracombe, 1951), pp. 96–97.

[5] Petition of 2 Sept. 1910, from Brandford Griffith C.J. to Crewe, referred to by Casely Hayford, *Legislative Council Debates*, 30 Nov. 1922.

'dismiss' and 'dismissal' changed to 'depose' and 'deposition'.[1] The Native Jurisdiction Amendment Bill then became law in August 1910.

It was unfortunate for Mensah Sarbah's reputation that the details of this debate did not become generally known for a long time. Stones were thrown into his house at Cape Coast after the Ordinance was passed. He died a few months later, and was consequently unable to rebut the criticisms which persisted for many years, and which were probably sharpened by the fact that he had received the C.M.G.[2] As late as 1925, J. W. de Graft Johnson accused him of inconsistency and compromise, and compared his published views of 1906 with his apparent acceptance of the 1910 Ordinance.[3] And J. B. Danquah wrote in 1932 that the episode 'clouded Sarbah's name in the political estimation of his countrymen'.[4] Such was the strength of feeling on the matter.

The Chiefs Under Pressure

When Sir Hugh Clifford arrived in the Gold Coast in 1913, he found the Chiefs suspicious of government intentions towards them, and smarting under real or imagined slights. For example, the Chiefs of Sekondi complained that they were made to lower their dress to the waist before the District Commissioner, a mark of humiliation which aroused some feeling.[5] The new Governor lost no time in making clear his attitude: 'it is my earnest wish to see the authority of the Chiefs supported by all Government officers, and the Chiefs and their principal advisers taken into the confidence of the Government, and habitually consulted when any matter affecting them and their people is under consideration.' Clifford believed in the 'tribal system' as the natural machinery of administration.[6] The Chiefs were encouraged to approach him during his travels and to explain their views, in a way that had been impossible in the past.[7] It was ironical that just at the time when the Government was disposed to support them more whole-heartedly than ever before, the Chiefs were suffering from a loss of prestige and influence in their own States, and on a wider national scale, for a variety of reasons.

An unsettling influence on stool affairs in some States, especially between

[1] *Legislative Council Minutes*, 2 and 4 July 1910.

[2] Cf. an editorial in *The Times of West Africa*, 18 Apr. 1933: 'There seems to be abroad the very ignorant and superstitious belief that to receive an honour . . . is proof positive that that person so honoured has sold his country.'

[3] E. W. Adjaye, J. Buckman, and J. W. de Graft Johnson, *Three Sons of the Gold Coast* (London, 1925), p. 25. Later, after reading the report of the debate, de Graft Johnson retracted this criticism. *Towards Nationhood*, pp. 39–40.

[4] Introduction (written in 1932) to M. J. Sampson's *Gold Coast Men of Affairs* (London, 1937), p. 20.

[5] Address to Clifford from the Amanhin of Dutch and English Sekondi and others, presented on his visit in May 1913. J. E. Casely Hayford, *The Truth about the West African Land Question* (London, 1913), app. B. 5. Cf. Ch. XI, p. 415, above.

[6] *Legislative Council Debates*, 3 Oct. 1913.   [7] W. H. Grey, ibid. 1 May 1914.

1913 and 1919, had been the rise—or revival—of the traditional Asafo organizations. These seem to have been on some occasions a useful safety-valve, on others a menace to internal peace and order. The system was of ancient origin among the Fantis; and during the nineteenth century—at the time of King Aggery, for example—the Asafo companies were constantly giving trouble by their habit of flaunting rival, insulting emblems, which often led to pitched battles.[1] The 1892 Native Customs Ordinance had given District Commissioners power to prohibit company meetings if they seemed likely to lead to a breach of the peace. But as late as 1909 the Government was complaining of constant threats to the tranquillity of Cape Coast due to Asafo disputes. The Provincial Commissioner then arranged the voluntary surrender of all 'objectionable and unwarranted flags and emblems', and printed a list of those authorised for each company to use.[2]

The renewed importance of the Asafo arose partly from the lack of education among the Chiefs themselves, which emphasized their isolation from the younger generation. In 1913, for example, it was officially reported that administration in the Western Province was hampered by the fact that not one of the nineteen Head Chiefs was educated; this was regarded as of the greatest importance, since they could not always appreciate the true motives of the Government, and were liable to be misinformed, often unintentionally, by the educated community.[3] The following year the first analysis of its kind showed twenty-four literate Chiefs in the Colony, as against ninety-five illiterate, although no attempt was made to define the term 'literate'.[4]

In 1915 the 'youngmen' of Kwahu decided to make use of the traditional form of organization as an outlet for their economic grievances, and founded their own Asafo 'with the object to protest and resist against the imposition of heavy fines for breach of oaths, because nothing worthy . . . was left as a result'.[5] By 1919 the Asafo was reported to be a dangerous and most undesir-

---

[1] Cf. Ch. III, pp. 127 and 142–3, and Ch. V, p. 210, above.
[2] *A Guide to Cape Coast Company Emblems, and Notes as to Customs, etc.* (Accra, 1909).
[3] *Departmental Reports*, Western Province, 1913.
[4] The details were as follows:

| | Chiefs | | |
Province	Literate	Illiterate	Total
Eastern	16	26	42
Central	7	23	30
Western	1	46	47
Colony total	24	95	119

'Chiefs' were those presiding over tribunals under the amended Native Jurisdiction Ordinance of 1910. S.N.A. 498, Case No. 73/1913, G.N. Archives.

[5] 'New Orders and Regulations inaugurated by the whole Kwahu Asafos', Dec. 1915; S.N.A. 738, Case 11/1919, G.N. Archives.

able element in the politics of Kwahu, undermining all established authority.[1] The Omanhene complained to the District Commissioner of 'the growing power of these youngmen which is breaking the powers of the Chiefs'.[2] In fact, the new power nexus, symbolized by the very presence of the District Commissioner, was disrupting the old relationship between the Chief and his people. Fines, which injured the economic rather than the social status of the offender, were resented most by the individualistic, wealth-conscious, younger members of the community; yet they were the only effective sanction left to the Chief in his judicial capacity.

From 1913 onwards the Asafo in Akim Abuakwa had also been showing increased opposition to the Chiefs. In this State they had long been part of the traditional order; but the Chiefs now accused them of usurping powers they were never intended to possess, and of attempting to destroy the existing form of government by the introduction of mob law. It was claimed that the Asafoatse, or leader, ought to be appointed—or dismissed—by the Chief and elders, whose orders he was supposed to convey to the people in time of war. The District Commissioner reported that at no period in the history of Akim Abuakwa had the Asafo been recognized as a separate political organization capable of acting independently of the elders.[3]

But times were changing. As Clifford pointed out, the 'youngmen' might often be wealthy and successful cocoa farmers: 'Riches mean power all the world over, but individual affluence is as new a thing in the Gold Coast as permanent cultivation itself.' He suggested that a system which permitted the legal deposition of a Chief at the dictates of the popular will placed in their hands an extraordinarily strong weapon of offence.[4] This outlet for popular dissatisfaction had, however, formed an essential part of the traditional system of checks and balances upon the authority of the Chief. His powers had now been circumscribed and delimited by the British, to whom he looked for support; the Asafo, on the other hand, continued to enjoy their traditional freedom of expression, which thus constituted a relatively greater threat to the authority of the Chief. If they succeeded in destooling him, this represented a further source of instability in the system of dual authority which it was Clifford's professed aim to build up.

Only the more powerful Chiefs were able to withstand such a challenge without appealing to the Government for assistance. In Akim Abuakwa, for example, during 1918, the Asafo took part in several attempted destoolments, culminating in an attack on the position of the Omanhene himself, for which they were severely punished. From the end of that year, the Asafo were allowed to send representatives to the Council of every Chief in the State.

[1] Report by District Commissioner, Kwahu, for quarter ending 30 Sept. 1919; ibid.
[2] Letter of 6 Apr. 1920, from Eastern Province Commissioner to Secretary for Native Affairs; ibid.
[3] 1922 Memorandum by District Commissioner, Kibi, on the Asafo in Akim Abuakwa; ibid.
[4] H. Clifford, 'The Gold Coast', in *Blackwoods Magazine* (London, 1918), vol. cciii.

This was intended to disarm critics who alleged that the 'youngmen' were not consulted over important measures; but the concession was more apparent than real, as the Chiefs reserved the right to disband the Asafo and dismiss a troublesome Asafoatse.[1]

A related problem was the growing friction between the Chiefs and the educated *élite*. In 1919 the Akim Abuakwa Chiefs and their followers presented a petition to the Governor, urging that every educated African, whether he be a lawyer, doctor, surveyor, engineer, or any other professional man, should be made to realize that he was still bound by traditional loyalties. They argued that those who, by the accident of wealth or other advantages, had obtained a higher education should not be allowed to 'trample upon' the native authority: 'It does not seem to us that education in the proper sense of the word implies a contempt of the existing authority.' It was absurd for an educated man to refuse to go before his natural court of justice because the president or councillors were not equally educated: 'we beg to sound a warning'.[2]

In 1920 Nana Ofori Atta managed to resolve his conflict with the Akim Abuakwa Scholars' Union; but he quoted this example as a fearful warning to other Chiefs.[3] It was in the same year that he complained that educated Africans would not whole-heartedly respect and comply with traditional institutions: 'There is a loose talk at some quarters that the educated African becomes the natural leader of the country irrespective of any other consideration.' This fear dominated his uncompromising attitude to the West African National Congress; and he recommended two lines of action: the formal study of native customs and institutions, and as much education as possible for future Chiefs, 'willingly or unwillingly'.[4]

Further contemporary evidence of conflict between the Chiefs and the emergent educated—or semi-educated—group was provided by the Commissioner for the Western Province: 'Everywhere is to be found a spirit of impatience and intolerance among the younger men. The latter, with a mere smattering of education, resent, and impede the authority of the Chiefs and elder men, few of whom can either read or write.' He commented gloomily on the frequent destoolment of 'strong' Chiefs, which meant that already few remained with any strength of character; but he hoped for 'a strong counterblast of Education on scientific lines'.[5] By 1922 it was thought that the 'revolutionary spirit' had died out in Akim Abuakwa;[6] but the Asafo remained understandably unpopular with many Chiefs and administrators.[7]

[1] Report by District Commissioner, Birrim, for quarter ending 30 Sept. 1918; S.N.A. 738, Case 11/1919, G.N. Archives.   [2] Quoted by Nana Ofori Atta, *Legislative Council Debates*, 4 Feb. 1921.

[3] See Ch. X, pp. 390–1 and 394–5, above.

[4] Letter from Nana Ofori Atta published in 'Report of the Educationists' Committee . . .', *Sessional Paper No. IV of 1919–20*, app. vi.

[5] *Departmental Reports*, Western Province, 1921.

[6] 1922 Memorandum by District Commissioner, Kibi; S.N.A. 738, Case 11/1919, G.N. Archives.

[7] In 1930 their abolition throughout the Colony was considered, as a result of serious rioting in Apam. But J. C. de Graft Johnson, the Assistant Secretary for Native Affairs, submitted a con-

The following exchange in the Legislative Council illustrates the bewilder-
ment of the Chiefs and the somewhat limited purview of the Government
during this period:

Nana Amonoo V

Can you please explain why during the last few years there have arisen so many
disputes between divisions and within divisions, (a) Whether such disputes were as
numerous, frequent, and serious in the days of the Native Jurisdiction Ordinance of
1883, as it was before it was amended by the Native Jurisdiction Amendment
Ordinance of 1910, (b) Whether this condition of unrest and rivalry is due to the
advance of civilisation in this country, (c) Whether matters are thus in civilized
countries, and (d) What steps the Government are taking or can take to establish
better harmony among the various divisions and within each division?

The Secretary for Native Affairs

The underlying cause of these disputes vary according to local circumstances . . .
there is no doubt that the failure of the Native Jurisdiction Ordinance of 1883, both
before and since its amendment in 1910, to differentiate sufficiently between the
powers and jurisdiction of paramount Chiefs and those of lesser degree has been
responsible for some of the disputes which have arisen in more recent years.[1]

The underlying social and economic causes of friction went deeper than this
reply suggested.

Further Government Proposals, 1916–24

Against such a background of unrest and mutual suspicion, official attempts
to strengthen and systematize the institution of chieftaincy were bound to
identify the Chiefs more and more with an alien system of rule. The Government was attacked for interfering with native institutions, and the Chiefs for
usurping greater powers than were traditionally theirs, although they themselves believed that the main problem was to restore their declining authority.
The resulting clash of opinions and interests, inside and outside the Legislative Council, continued to obstruct successive well-meaning attempts to
draft legislation that would please everybody.

Under Clifford the official habit grew up of consulting the leading Chiefs
in advance over Bills that affected them. In 1916, for example, a draft to
amend further the Native Jurisdiction Ordinance was circulated for their
views;[2] but nothing more was heard of it for over a year. The three Head
Chiefs—of Akim Abuakwa, Anomabu, and Awunaga—who had been
appointed to the enlarged Legislative Council in 1916 inquired what had

---

fidential report advising against such a drastic step. 'The Asafu Organisation of the Gold Coast',
Sessional Paper No. XII of 1931–32. This was not published, although de Graft Johnson made use
of his material for an article on 'The Fanti Asafu', in *Africa* (London, 1932), vol. ii, no. 3.
[1] *Legislative Council Debates*, 25 May 1920.
[2] Clifford, ibid. 23 Oct. 1916.

happened to the proposed Bill,[1] but this remained obstinately under official consideration. The Head Chiefs outside the Council were also becoming impatient, especially in the Eastern Province. At the Accra meetings arranged by Nana Ofori Atta in 1918, they agreed upon the urgent necessity for amending the 1883 Ordinance, and complained of interference by District Commissioners. In reply to their memorandum, Clifford said that he hoped, before relinquishing the Government, to set native jurisdiction upon a sound legal foundation once for all, and thus to consolidate the tribal system and government of the Colony.[2]

The Governor evidently decided that it was impracticable merely to amend further the existing Ordinance, and in February 1919 it was a new Native Jurisdiction Bill that was at length introduced.[3] This attempted to define more closely the distinction between Head Chiefs and other Chiefs,[4] to state clearly the extent of their jurisdiction in land cases, to alter the procedure on appeal, and to give Provincial Commissioners more effective control over the proceedings of tribunals.

At once there was remarkably strong opposition. Clifford was accused of attempting to discredit educated Africans by advising the Chiefs not to show the draft Bill to them, least of all to any lawyer. *The Gold Coast Independent* suspected the Head Chiefs of collusion with a Government which was trying to place them on a level with the Sultan of Sokoto and the Emir of Kano. The whole principle of their participation in central government was challenged:

> They are members of the Legislative Council . . . They act as judges to interpret the laws which they assist to bring into being, and are now being coerced to become autocrats and to exercise sovereign rights (Executive) which they never possessed at any time . . . Is it any wonder that selfish and avaricious Chiefs who have greedily drunk of this new wine, have become intoxicated and are being destooled by the people? (1–8 March, 1919.)

Since the proposals dealt partly with procedure in land cases, the same newspaper did not hesitate to raise the alarm that this was intended to transfer the land rights of the Chiefs to 'the British hegemony'.[5] A protest meeting was held in Accra, and after an appropriately hostile resolution had been unanimously carried, a committee of thirty-four educated Africans was appointed to oppose the Bill.[6] Feeling was running high against individual

---

[1] *Legislative Council Debates*, 21 Nov. 1917.

[2] Notes of interview at Government House, Accra, 5 Mar. 1918; S.N.A. 692, Case 30/1918, G.N. Archives.   [3] *Government Gazette (Extraordinary)*, 15 Feb. 1919.

[4] The Head Chiefs themselves were becoming anxious about this distinction. Nana Amonoo V asked what steps could be taken by the Government to define their respective rights and privileges, 'there being at present little or no distinction in this respect for example, Kweku Atta of Asin Apimenyim has handcuffs and prison whilst his Paramount Chief also has handcuffs and prison'. *Legislative Council Debates*, 25 May 1920.   [5] Quoted in *West Africa*, 19 Apr. 1919.

[6] Hutton Mills, *Legislative Council Debates*, 28 Nov. 1922.

Head Chiefs. It was alleged, for instance, that the Konor of Manya Krobo had ruled that any sub-Chief coming before him must take off his sandals; 'I suppose people will have to take off their boots next when they go before the District Commissioner', jibed a newspaper correspondent.[1]

The leaders of the A.R.P.S. had to be more diplomatic in their approach. Whatever their private views, they could hardly subscribe publicly to the view that ignorant Chiefs would 'become pawns and puppets in the hands of Provincial and District Commissioners in the deft art of the so-called indirect rule'.[2] The Society's newspaper, *The Gold Coast Nation*, urged the Chiefs to study carefully a Bill which so much affected their vital interests; in order to understand thoroughly 'every part, every section, every line', they should employ not merely 'scholars', but really well-educated men.[3] The Government was accused of approaching the Chiefs separately, instead of consulting the A.R.P.S., which proceeded to discuss the Bill in angry detail at an emergency conference in Cape Coast. But the Society did little beyond standing on its constitutional dignity to remind the Acting Governor of the way in which he should have approached them officially.[4]

It was left to the Accra protest committee to marshal the main objections to the latest Native Jurisdiction Bill in a petition to the Secretary of State in September 1919, which clearly grasped the fundamental issue concerning the source of the Chiefs' authority and jurisdiction. They argued that the clause authorizing the Governor to confirm stool elections and installations virtually constituted him the maker and unmaker of Chiefs. Since the judicial powers of a Chief could be extended or curtailed at will, he would soon become 'a Government creature, a quasi-official', bound to act with servility and subservience; to ensure official support and favour, he would have to 'palter with opinions which he knows not to be true, and refrain from speaking his whole mind'. In particular, the provision that a Chief's destoolment might have to be confirmed by the Government would take away from the people their safeguard against tyranny and unconstitutional acts.[5]

In a rather belated reply, the Government denied any intention of refusing to recognize the election or destoolment of any Chief, if this had been carried out in accordance with native customary law; and the Bill would be amended

---

[1] *The Gold Coast Independent*, 19 Apr. 1919.

[2] Ibid. 15 Mar. 1919. The theory of indirect rule had been evolving gradually over many years, although it was given widest publicity by F. D. Lugard, who put it forward as the best means by which the colonial Power could fulfil *The Dual Mandate in British Tropical Africa* (Edinburgh, 1922). Examples of early references are: Freeling writing in 1877 (see pp. 459–60, above); Chamberlain before 1900, impressing the maxim 'Rule through the Chiefs' on officials sent out to the colonies (Confidential Dispatch of 10 Mar. 1901, from Nathan to Chamberlain); and the Native Affairs Department in 1909, reporting 'the gradual extension of the policy of the Government of governing the native through his own institutions'.

[3] *The Gold Coast Nation*, 1 Mar. 1919.

[4] Ibid. 12–19 Apr. 1919.

[5] Petition of Sept. 1919, to Secretary of State from Gã Mantse, eight barristers, and other inhabitants of Accra; quoted by Hutton Mills, *Legislative Council Debates*, 28 Nov. 1922.

to make these points perfectly clear.[1] Meanwhile Clifford had moved on to Nigeria, leaving the Gordian knot still uncut, and the new Governor, F. G. Guggisberg, was anxious to weigh up the views of all sections of the community before proceeding. By the 1920's many Head Chiefs were longing to check the increasing number of stool disputes; they feared that their authority would be weakened by the pending Bill and were unwilling to be convinced by official assurances to the contrary.[2] While the Government continued to ponder and procrastinate, the storm over the National Congress of British West Africa served only to widen the gulf between the Chiefs and the educated *élite*.

It was a different Native Jurisdiction Bill that eventually saw the legislative light of day in 1922.[3] The Government professed to regard this as 'little more than a consolidation' of existing laws—those of 1883, 1888, and especially of 1904.[4] But, in addition, the Bill still attempted to distinguish clearly between Head Chiefs and Chiefs, and to define their jurisdiction; it also made the Provincial Commissioner's decision final, on appeal in land cases, which meant that counsel could not be heard. Neither the Chiefs nor the lawyers were happy about this.

The Government faced a dilemma. Clearly it was impossible—and, some argued, undesirable—to appoint professional European Judges to every provincial court. But if justice was to be administered by political officers, how could African lawyers be admitted to plead before them? The executive officer would know none of the finer points of English law or of cases familiar to the barristers. 'He might even lose his temper with an African barrister who attempted to cite precedents to him.' So argued the American writer, R. L. Buell; he thought it had been wise to exclude appeals from these courts, because Africans did not understand the principle of separation of powers, and being used to the single authority of a Chief they might not respect an administrative officer whose decisions could be reversed by judicial magistrates. Litigants would also be protected from the expense of unnecessary appeals to the Supreme Court, often made purely for the sake of prestige, and they might even receive better justice in a provincial court, acquainted with local issues and personalities.[5]

This reasoning overlooked the change in the climate of opinion. As one of the European unofficial members said: 'the native is not incapable of making a proper choice . . . the people of this country do not require a great deal of protection, either against counsel or against anything else'. Petitions of protest were received against the Bill from the new executive of the

[1] Letter of 10 Mar. 1920, from Acting Colonial Secretary to 'Eastern Province Native Jurisdiction Bill Opposition Committee, Accra'; G.N. Archives.

[2] *Legislative Council Debates*, 21 Jan. 1921.

[3] *Gold Coast Gazette Extraordinary* (*Legislation*), 18 Sept. 1922.

[4] Attorney-General, *Legislative Council Debates*, 27 Nov. 1922.

[5] R. L. Buell, *The Native Problem in Africa* (New York, 1928), vol. i, p. 808.

A.R.P.S. and from the Bar Association; African counsel, T. Hutton Mills and P. Awooner Renner, were permitted to appear on behalf of each before the Legislative Council, prior to the second reading in November 1922. Hutton Mills emphasized that he was speaking for the Chiefs, and not for the lawyers; but they both objected most strongly to the exclusion of lawyers in land cases and to the fact that British subjects were losing their right to appeal to the Privy Council. Some play was also made with the argument that Provincial Commissioners were already heavily overburdened with administrative work; was this fair to them? kindly inquired Casely Hayford.

The most general argument against this Bill, used by Chiefs, lawyers, and journalists alike, was that the Government was encroaching upon native institutions.[1] Particular objection was taken to clause 42, which excluded native tribunals from exercising any jurisdiction 'except as provided by and in accordance with, the provisions of this or some other Ordinance'. It was held that in view of the Bond of 1844,[2] and other treaties, the Government could not curtail the power of the Natural Rulers without their consent. The A.R.P.S. put forward a long series of detailed amendments; but the key to them all was contained in the suggestion that the title of the Bill should be 'An Ordinance to facilitate and regulate the exercise by Native Authorities of certain powers and jurisdiction inherent in them'.[3] Casely Hayford went so far as to argue that the jurisdiction of the Crown was derived from the Chiefs as representing the people, instead of vice versa.

The Government could not accept such a claim; and the Attorney-General reminded speakers of the strict legal position, that since the Annexation Orders in Council of 1901 no courts could exercise jurisdiction except under the direct authority of the Crown, or by virtue of British recognition. Nevertheless there remained serious objections to the Bill; and the fact that it was little more than a consolidation of the existing law did not make it any the more acceptable.[4] As Nene Mate Kole said: 'in 1883, there were no scholars to interpret the law. Now . . . there are more intelligent men among us and we can read and if we do not understand anything we have Counsel to read for us.' E. J. P. Brown threatened that it might be necessary to send a deputation

[1] Dr. B. W. Quartey-Papafio, for example, moved the rejection of the Bill on the grounds that it weakened 'the inherent rights, and powers of the Chiefs', and sought to create 'new native authorities not racy of the soil'. *Legislative Council Debates*, 29 Nov. 1922.

[2] The original Bond was quoted in full by Casely Hayford; E. J. P. Brown capped this by listing the signatories of all the subsequent Bonds. Ibid.

[3] The Government had called it 'An Ordinance to make better Provision for the Regulation and Exercise of certain Powers and Jurisdiction by Native Authorities'. Cf. J. W. de Graft Johnson's claim: 'the British Government during the whole of its connection with the Gold Coast never conferred jurisdiction on Native Government . . . the jurisdiction exercised by these is inherent in the system'. *Towards Nationhood*, p. 36. As D. E. Apter has put it: 'The most disruptive element of all was introduced by transmuting traditional legitimacy into legitimacy derived from Great Britain.' *The Gold Coast in Transition* (Princeton, 1955), p. 123.

[4] Awoonor Renner claimed that so far from being a consolidating Bill, it was 'creative, constructive, oppressive, if not unconstitutional'. *Legislative Council Debates*, 28 Nov. 1922.

to England; but it was the attitude of the Head Chiefs in the Legislative Council that finally convinced Guggisberg that the Bill would have to be withdrawn. Their lack of support was a serious set-back to a Government which set great store by their opinion. Nana Ofori Atta said that they and their councillors had discussed the Bill constructively, and he urged the Government to consider their suggestions and criticisms seriously, especially the view that 'the inherent powers, jurisdiction and rights of the Chiefs and people should not be disturbed'.[1]

Guggisberg was surprised at the unanimity of opposition, however mistaken it might be on strictly legal grounds. He complained that there had been a complete change in the attitude of the Head Chiefs to the Provincial Commissioners, and that they had suddenly veered round on a clause which they themselves had originally introduced, concerning the differentiation between Head Chiefs and other Chiefs. He did, however, congratulate the African members of the Council on the way in which they had come together and put forward their case. The amendment (supported by all the unofficial members) against the second reading was lost; but the Bill was then withdrawn, for further consideration.[2] Later the A.R.P.S. was to claim that it had been withdrawn as the result of their action, but this was certainly not the only reason.[3]

For the third time since 1907 the Government had deferred to public criticism, in spite of its obvious anxiety to remove the defects of the 1883 Ordinance. Throughout this period, as Hailey points out, the Government had concentrated on attempts to improve the system of native justice; and as a result there had been a tendency to forget the need for better agencies of local administration.[4] But now, partly as a result of R. S. Rattray's work on native institutions, the Government was beginning to see more clearly how the existing system might be used and adapted. Some officials developed theories of the nature of tribal government which even out-praised earlier expositions by educated Africans.[5] Policy in the 1920's was also bound to be influenced by the development of indirect rule in Nigeria; certainly Guggisberg was disposed to consider carefully the views of the few articulate Chiefs in devising a system under which they would co-operate with the Government.

In 1924 a stop-gap Bill was introduced, to improve the 41-year-old Native Jurisdiction Ordinance by means of minor amendments.[6] This move

---

[1] *Legislative Council Debates*, 28–30 Nov. and 1 Dec. 1922.   [2] Ibid. 5 Dec. 1922.

[3] Guggisberg said on another occasion: 'I found that the Bill had not been sufficiently thrashed out between the Political Officers and the Chiefs concerned; and that was the long and the short of why the Bill was withdrawn'. Ibid. 7 Mar. 1924.

[4] Hailey, *Native Administration*, pt. iii, p. 202.

[5] See pp. 485–7 and Ch. XIII, pp. 523–4, below.

[6] These amendments—which had formed part of the proposed 1922 Bill—empowered the Native Authority, or in certain cases the Governor, to prohibit a deposed Chief from entering any specified area where he had formerly ruled. The Colonial Secretary claimed that the Ordinance

aroused the usual protests, and Casely Hayford presented the by now customary petition from the A.R.P.S.; but counsel were not again allowed to appear before the Legislative Council. Guggisberg argued that this practice was a survival from the days when 'the nation was voiceless', and that in any case there were now three African barristers on the Council. The Bill was passed, although all the African members (except Nana Ofori Atta) voted against the second reading; while the Government felt that a totally new and more drastic approach was needed.[1]

Developments in Ashanti and the Return of Prempeh

The year 1924 marked an important event for the Chiefs and people of Ashanti, namely, the return of Prempeh from exile in the Seychelles. The institution of chieftaincy had been going through some difficult years since the 1900 rising, quite apart from the numbing effect of the removal of the Asantehene. The question whether or not the Chiefs possessed inherent jurisdiction could not arise in Ashanti, which had been declared a conquered territory. It was categorically stated in 1902 that 'It shall not be lawful for any headchief to exercise any powers as headchief until he shall have been recognised as such by the Governor'.[2] The powers and prestige of the Chiefs inevitably suffered a decline. Kumasi was no longer the centre of a kingdom, but was reduced to the status of a town governed by a small council of Chiefs. Those who had been deported were replaced by nominees qualified rather by their loyalty to the British Government than by their connexion with the stool family. Several of these new Chiefs were, in fact, aliens to the tribes they were called upon to rule.

The inevitable reaction set in, and during 1904–5 several tribes in and around Kumasi displayed a concerted determination to get rid of their unpopular incumbents. Even though it proved possible to restore the links with the past through more suitable Chiefs, the chain of tradition itself was becoming weakened through other causes. By 1909 it was reported of Ashanti, 'with the spread of Western civilization and more liberal ideas, the inevitable conflict between youth and authority has already commenced . . . It is the duty of the Administration to check this tendency.' Such a task proved no easier than in the Colony, although in the view of the Chief Commissioner, F. Fuller, relationships between the Ashanti Chiefs and the Government continued as cordial as ever.[3]

The advent of the railway had encouraged the introduction of cocoa; and

---

raised an important principle, and that central control and supervision was essential before the Government could delegate powers to the Native Authorities; he urged that this system would not work if they were to take their stand on 'what they called their immemorial rights and principles'. *Legislative Council Debates*, 6–8 Mar. 1924.

[1] Ibid.   [2] Ashanti Administration Ordinance, 1902.
[3] *Departmental Reports*, Ashanti, 1905, 1909, and 1913.

by 1907 planting was proceeding over a widespread area. The Kumasi Agricultural Show at the end of the following year brought visitors and exhibits from many parts of the country. During 1913–14 the production of cocoa increased by over one-third; it was officially reported that Ashanti was prosperous, and money was plentiful. In 1918 a sign of the changing times was the drawing up of a 'Magna Carta' by the 'youngmen' of Bompata; this sought to reduce native court fees and fines, and to grant them some minor privileges. The Omanhene and elders were wise enough to accept these terms, and peace was restored throughout the division; similar agreements were successfully concluded in Juaben and Obogu.[1]

But the spirit of unrest went deeper than this. The new generation was less inclined to support the power and prestige of the Chiefs. The progress of trade, education, and Christianity had all tended to enhance the importance of the individual, and to introduce the new doctrines of personal reward, of private property, and of the right of bequest. Destoolments were now very frequent; although they were officially described as 'rather a symptom of the vitality than of the decay of native institutions',[2] it is doubtful whether the Chiefs themselves were able to take such a detached view. By 1924 officials in Ashanti noted a gradual change coming over the Chiefs' relationships with their people:

blind obedience is no longer the order of the day. The 'Youngmen' are no longer ignorant; they do not fear torture or death at the hands of a more or less barbaric tyrant. That former fear has been displaced by a feeling of independence and safety which gives vent to criticism of their elders, and a desire, when dissatisfied, to take the law into their own hands.

If the Chiefs wanted money, then those who were asked to contribute wanted to know for what purpose it was needed and how much was required. When they had paid, they wished to be told that it had been used for the purpose for which it was ostensibly collected; and a number of minor disturbances had arisen where the people were not satisfied with the answers they were given.[3]

The growth of a money economy was bound to cause some unrest of this kind; but it also stimulated constructive development. Officials found that people were now only too willing to turn out with pick and shovel for road construction, due to their business sense in realizing that a motor road meant a new market, or a higher price for their cocoa. As the roads pushed outwards from Kumasi,[4] so did the motor lorries, which quickly came to represent one of the most lucrative forms of business in Ashanti; retail stores followed, and the large European firms opened branches in small towns that only a few

[1] *Departmental Reports*, Ashanti, 1907, 1913, 1914, and 1918.
[2] Ibid. 1920.   [3] Ibid. 1923–4.
[4] In 1921–2 there were 500 miles of motor roads in Ashanti, which had increased to 1,157 by 1928–9. Slater, *Legislative Council Debates*, 17 Feb. 1930.

years earlier had been considered far too remote. During 1923–4 trunk telephone lines were opened from Kumasi to both Accra and Sekondi.[1]

In spite of these changes there was still a prejudice against the election of
a literate man as a Chief. But the clash between the old and the new, between
educated youth and traditional authority, did not break out into open conflict in Ashanti as in the Colony. One of the most important restraining
influences was the Asante Kotoko Union Society,[2] founded in 1916 by a group
of educated Ashantis who were in close touch with the traditional leaders, and
were concerned to make the best of both worlds.[3] The main aims of the Society
were:

> To diffuse by inculcating on its members and the rising generation of Asante
> generally the importance of nursing and advancing their loyalty to the British Crown
> and to their Natural Rulers.
>
> To promote a sound National Educational Policy with particular attention to
> Agricultural, Scientific and Industrial Training in the whole country.
>
> To encourage its members and the rising generation with a knowledge of their
> historical past, and the study of the Laws, Customs and Institutions of their country,
> and to disseminate the Christian Religion among its members.
>
> To train its members to be unselfish, helpful, patriotic and reverent to themselves
> and to the country at large, and to render every possible assistance to their Natural
> Rulers, when necessary.

In addition the members were exhorted to aim at moral and intellectual
improvement, and to encourage the virtues of patriotism, thrift, mutual aid,
and the 'spirit of sports'.[4]

There were in this statement some echoes of the published aims of the
A.R.P.S., although there was a stronger emphasis on loyalty to the Chiefs.
The Kotoko Society did not claim to lead so much as to follow the Chiefs,
and any influence they may have exerted in practice, especially at first, was
strictly behind the scenes. The Society planned, for example, to study Ashanti
festivals and to consider how they might be modified to suit modern conditions. All the members were educated, and it was laid down that the English
language should 'prevail' at all meetings. Apart from this, and the requirement
of good moral character, there was no restriction on membership, and they
specifically set themselves to avoid 'All personalities and vain shows of
knowledge'. There was, however, an absolute ban on resignation; if a member
persisted in 'threatening the Society with resignation' he was to be brought

---

[1] *Departmental Reports*, Ashanti, 1920, 1923–4, and 1924–5.

[2] The Ashanti porcupine, *Kotoko*, had long been an important symbol of power, and this was
originally the title of the ruling Council; see Ch. VII, p. 266, above.

[3] Among the foundation members was E. P. Owusu, then a storekeeper, and now the ruling
Asantehene, Otumfuo Sir Agyeman Prempeh II. Others were: J. Adjaye-Kyem, S. T. A. Affainie,
J. W. K. Appiah, I. K. Agyeman, O. S. Agyeman, J. E. Bandoh, Mensah Bonsu, Kodjo Jantuah,
J. S. Kankam, Kobena Mensah, Henry Owusu, Kofi Sraha, and A. B. Thompson. I am indebted
to I. K. Agyeman, who became Secretary, and later President, of the Society, for this information.

[4] *Rules and Bye-Laws of the Asante-Kotoko-Union Society* (Cape Coast, 1923), Article 2.

to order by the President, and in the last resort allowed to go after paying a fine of £5.[1]

This was for many years the nearest approach to a political organization in Ashanti; but its political activities were not welcomed by some administrators, and were initially kept as quiet as possible. After the First World War the demand for the return of Prempeh became increasingly insistent, and the Society played a leading part. This campaign well illustrates the unity and strength of Ashanti tradition, in spite of all the disintegrating effects of conquest and commerce; and its eventual success marked a rallying point in the prestige of the Chiefs and their hopes of a future restoration.

Not all the political prisoners of the 1900 rising had been sent to the Seychelles; the majority had been held in Elmina Castle. These were released in 1908, and a few of them were allowed to return to Ashanti, the others remaining in exile in Accra.[2] In 1914 Clifford authorized the return to Ashanti of three more; but he made it clear to the Chiefs in Kumasi that this was the last request of the kind which he would grant, or even consider.[3] The Government did not wish this concession to be the thin end of the return wedge from the Seychelles. But a few years later there came news of the death in exile of Prempeh's mother, Yaa Kyia, and his brother, Agyeman Badu. The prospect that Prempeh himself might die on foreign soil seriously alarmed the Ashantis, and a petition for his return was sent to the Secretary of State from numerous Chiefs in February 1919.[4] This request was declined, although Clifford relented sufficiently to release all the remaining exiles in Accra.

Hopes were revived the following year, when Guggisberg arrived, and visited Ashanti almost immediately. He met the Kumasi Council of Chiefs, and they again begged for Prempeh's release and promised that it would cause no trouble. But the Chief Commissioner had already told them that they must first give up the Golden Stool; and Guggisberg was unable to hold out any alternative hope, although he expressed his regret.[5] On the Governor's return to Accra a resolution was moved in the Legislative Council, praying for the royal clemency on behalf of Prempeh. The Government did not wish to appear too sensitive to pressure; and the time seemed particularly inopportune, as the experienced Chief Commissioner was soon due to leave Ashanti. 'We must wait a little longer', declared Guggisberg; but he was obviously impressed by the unanimity and sincerity of the African members, none of them Ashantis, who pleaded Prempeh's cause.[6]

---

[1] Articles 8, 22, 26, and 31. There seems to have been some secrecy over the proceedings of the Society, and even now it has proved impossible to trace the minute books and records.

[2] *Departmental Reports*, Ashanti, 1909.

[3] Dispatch of 23 Mar. 1914, from Clifford to Harcourt; S.N.A. 624, Case 13/1916, G.N. Archives.

[4] 'Petition to the Secretary of State by certain Ashanti Chiefs Praying for the Return of Ex-King Prempeh, and the Secretary of State's Reply thereto', *Sessional Paper No. VIII of 1918–19.*

[5] Report of meeting between Kumasi Council of Chiefs and Guggisberg, 30 Oct. 1919, enclosed in his Confidential Dispatch of 15 Feb. 1921, to Milner; G.N. Archives.

[6] *Legislative Council Debates*, 26 Nov. 1919. See Ch. XIII, p. 531, below.

Early in 1920 Guggisberg met the Chiefs in Kumasi again, and made his last stand on the old policy of attempting to secure the Golden Stool, which had remained hidden for twenty years; the second condition for the return of Prempeh was that he must come back as a private individual, and not interfere in political matters in any way. The Chiefs protested that the Stool was not the private property of Prempeh, but belonged to Ashanti, and they begged that this question should not be mixed up with that of his return. But Guggisberg replied:

The Stool belongs to the Ashantis. Prempeh sat on the Stool. The Government must have that Stool before Prempeh comes back to the country . . . I will say to the Secretary of State that I think that after Prempeh is dead, we should then consider whether we should give the Stool back again, or perhaps before he is dead if all is well . . . What the Government will do with the Stool I cannot say now, but I repeat that it is always *generous* and *just*. That is my answer. Think it over well.[1]

But before the year was out the Golden Stool itself had come to light, robbed, and desecrated; and in an astonishing volte-face the Government not only refrained from seizing the Stool but assisted in arranging an unusual compromise, whereby the offenders were brought before the traditional full council of Ashanti Chiefs (except that the Mamponghene presided in the Asantehene's place), for an inquiry conducted 'according to the principles of British justice'. The six men concerned were found guilty of exposing and unlawfully dealing with the Golden Stool, 'thereby betraying the said Ashanti nation and laying it open to disgrace and ridicule, and debasing the name and fame of Ashanti, much to the annoyance and provocation of all people, young and old, thereby giving occasion for disturbance and bloodshed, but for the intervention of Government.'[2] Such desecration was in Ashanti law a capital offence, more serious than murder; but in British eyes the crime was stealing, and the death sentence passed by the court could not be confirmed. Instead, the guilty men were deported for life.[3] What the Chiefs and people regarded as a national council was to the Government only an *ad hoc* committee of inquiry; and the overruling of its verdict brought home as nothing else had done 'the fact that Ashanti was not a sovereign nation'.[4]

On the other hand, the official attitude was that the Ashantis could now if they wished keep open custody of the Stool instead of concealing it, and that there would be no interference unless it was used for seditious purposes.[5]

[1] Report of meeting between Kumasi Council of Chiefs and Guggisberg, 27 Apr. 1920, enclosed in his Confidential Dispatch of 15 Feb. 1921, to Milner; G.N. Archives.
[2] E. W. Smith, *The Golden Stool* (London, 1926), p. 11.
[3] Eight others had been found guilty of buying the gold ornaments; but the Chief Commissioner acquitted them for lack of corroborating evidence. For further details of this incident, see K. A. Busia, *The Position of the Chief in the Modern Political System of Ashanti* (Oxford, 1951), pp. 114–17. Seniagya, the last survivor of those deported, was permitted to return from Nigeria by The Golden Stool of Ashanti (Detention and Deportation of Desecrators) Repeal Act, 1957.
[4] Ibid. p. 117.   [5] *Departmental Reports*, Ashanti, 1921.

Members of the Kotoko Society acted as peace officers during the trial; and the amicable outcome of the affair helped to prepare the way for Prempeh's return, although Guggisberg felt it necessary to move cautiously.[1] Further representations were made by Casely Hayford and other non-Ashantis, and in 1923 by the National Congress meeting in Freetown. Nana Ofori Atta returned to the attack in the Legislative Council, quoting a pathetic letter from Prempeh: 'During this time I have lost my mother, father, brother, and almost all my chiefs. Now there remain six chiefs, and out of the six one is blind, the remaining are old and are ill.'[2] This appeal, made by such an influential Colony Chief, gave greater weight to yet another petition from Ashanti presented at the end of 1923.[3]

Guggisberg had great hopes for the future development of Ashanti, for since the people had turned themselves from warriors into farmers, their large tribal divisions were eminently suitable for the development of native rule, while the accumulation of wealth from cocoa offered opportunities for progress that had previously been lacking.[4] By 1924 he was prepared to take the risk, and Prempeh was allowed to return, as a private citizen, after twenty-eight years in exile. His arrival at Takoradi was deliberately kept as quiet as possible, so that the first welcome on a large scale might take place in Ashanti. But in Kumasi an outbreak of plague was at its height, so even there the Chiefs had to promise not to call public gatherings; the sale of wines and spirits was also prohibited for a week. The ex-Asantehene and his party left the train two miles south of Kumasi, and entered by car in an attempt to avoid large crowds. But inevitably there was great national rejoicing among the Ashantis:

As Prempeh started to make his way through the crowd, the Christians present broke forth into the 'Auld Hundredth' in which all the people joined although they did not know the words. The scene presented by the huge assembly of Ashantis with their white head bands signifying rejoicing or victory, some laughing and cheering, while others wept with emotion, was a most moving and never-to-be-forgotten sight.[5]

Prempeh returned as a Christian, educated and attuned to European ways. He wisely remained in the background at first, renewing his acquaintance with tradition, and ranking as a 'youngman'. The Omanhene of Mampong was still the official paramount Chief of Ashanti, and Prempeh attended the great durbar for the Prince of Wales in 1925 only in his capacity as 'ex-King'—

[1] Confidential Dispatch of 15 Feb. 1921, from Guggisberg to Milner; G.N. Archives.
[2] Legislative Council Debates, 2 July 1923.
[3] Published in The Gold Coast Leader, 26 Jan. 1924. Illustrations of the pro-Prempeh campaign of this Cape Coast newspaper are given by W. Tordoff, 'The Exile and Repatriation of Nana Prempeh I', in Transactions of the Historical Society of Ghana (Legow, 1960), vol. iv, pt. 2.
[4] F. G. Guggisberg, The Post-War Gold Coast (Accra, 1924).
[5] Departmental Reports, Ashanti, 1924–5.

and in European dress.[1] When the Kumasi Public Health Board was formed the same year, Prempeh was one of its first members. In 1926 Guggisberg was petitioned by the Chiefs of the Kumasi Division to allow him to be re-elected as their Omanhene, and the Secretary of State agreed. In November, on the second anniversary of his return from exile, Prempeh was enstooled as Kumasihene before an estimated crowd of 100,000.[2] The Kumasi Council of Chiefs, which had helped the Chief Commissioner to govern the town since 1905, was then dissolved.

The Chiefs rallied round Prempeh, but not in any spirit of defiance; they were for the most part prepared to co-operate with the Government. Relationships between the Chiefs and their subjects were much less satisfactory;[3] but the strong personal loyalty felt towards Prempeh, coupled—ironically enough —with the fact that he was unable to assert any strong central authority, meant some voluntary increase in the respect shown towards Ashanti traditional rulers.[4]

The Official Revival of 'Native Institutions'

The tactful handling of the Golden Stool episode and the sympathetic treatment of the requests for Prempeh's return were indicative of a new government policy towards the Chiefs, and towards native institutions generally. They were now treated with considerable respect by the Administration, mainly as a result of closer study and understanding. There had been an almost complete reversal of nineteenth-century official attitudes. Indeed, Clifford seemed to have accepted the A.R.P.S. idealized view of the past, when he said in the Legislative Council in 1916 that the 'essentially democratic' nature of the native constitutions differentiated them abruptly from all other indigenous systems of government in tropical lands.[5] Every effort was being made to abide by traditional customs and procedure in all internal tribal matters; and Clifford blamed those who had had a European education for any tendency to weaken the tribal authorities. He suggested that 'the Native of the Gold Coast to-day is very largely self-governed', and with this *The Gold Coast Nation* heartily agreed.[6]

Guggisberg was the first Governor to be convinced of the need for systematic research, which had been urged by anthropologists and others in Europe for some time. On the most practical grounds, it was clear that 'An accurate acquaintance with the nature, habits and customs of alien

---

[1] *Visit of His Royal Highness The Prince of Wales to the Gold Coast Colony 1925* (Accra, 1925), illustrated.

[2] *West Africa*, Dec. 1926.   [3] *Departmental Reports*, Ashanti, 1925–6.

[4] Prempeh died in 1931, and when the ceremonial rites took place a year later, 'Every Omanhene and every Ohene of note in Ashanti was in attendance.' This was clearly more than a Kumasihene's funeral. See *Report on the Observance of the Funeral Custom of the Late Kumasihene* (Accra, 1933).

[5] *Legislative Council Debates*, 23 Oct. 1916.   [6] 12 July 1916.

populations is necessary to all who have to live and work amongst them in any official capacity.'[1] The new approach was illustrated by the decision in 1922 that all Assistant District Commissioners in the Eastern Province were to be asked to write essays on local history and customs. This was later extended to other Provinces, and several interesting studies were produced, in a virtually untouched field.[2] It was also discovered that much useful material had been accumulating in Government files; the Secretary for Native Affairs now planned to publish a series on the history and constitution of various tribes, and himself wrote the first two volumes.[3]

The most important development, however, was the formation of an Anthropological Department in Ashanti in 1921. This was under the direction of R. S. Rattray, who had spent several years in West Africa, initially among the Hausas.[4] He had already published a collection of Ashanti proverbs, which he regarded as 'the very soul' of a people; he warned his readers against undue astonishment at the words of wisdom that could spring from those hitherto regarded as savage or primitive.[5] In his first book on *Ashanti*, Rattray stressed the need to appeal to Africans 'not as denationalized Ashanti, but as an African People who . . . have not bartered the wealth of their past, metaphorically and not infrequently in reality, for a coat, a collar, or a tie'.[6] In *Religion and Art in Ashanti* he presented the results of further research with almost missionary fervour: 'Guard the national soul of your race and never be tempted to despise your past. Therein I believe lies the sure hope that your sons and daughters will one day make their own original contributions to knowledge and progress.'[7] He was able to confirm the existence of a widespread and well-based democratic element in their political structure, and his *Ashanti Law and Constitution* laid the foundation for a new respect for what he called 'this wonderful people'.[8] Rattray was well qualified to win the confidence of the older generation, and to tap their stores of tradition, which were gradually being forgotten and overlaid by Western education. As a result,

---

[1] *Report of Royal Commission on University Education* (London, 1913). The pioneer work of the Basel missionaries in the field of African studies should not be forgotten; see Ch. III, p. 159, above. The above quotation sums up the guiding principles of their Mission during the nineteenth and early twentieth centuries.

[2] For example, J. K. G. Syme on the Kusasis, R. G. Cooper on the Krachis, L. J. Mothersill on the Ho Division, W. A. S. Cole on the people of Dadiaso in the Aowin District, D. S. Sutherland on Manya Krobo. S.N.A. 824, Case No. 9/1923, G.N. Archives.

[3] C. W. Welman's *The Native States of the Gold Coast: I. Peki* (London, 1925), was introduced as the department's first publication of any importance. The material was not confined to Peki alone, but contained, for example, a detailed account of the swearing of State oaths as generally practised among the Akan peoples and those who had come under their influence. Welman followed this up with *The Native States of the Gold Coast: II. Ahanta* (London, 1930).

[4] *Hausa Folk-Lore, Customs, Proverbs, etc.* (Oxford, 1913).

[5] *Ashanti Proverbs* (Oxford, 1916). Rattray drew largely on J. G. Christaller's *Twi Mmebusem*, 'A Collection of Three Thousand and Six Hundred Tshi Proverbs' (Basel, 1879), and was also familiar with R. F. Burton's *Wit and Wisdom from West Africa* (London, 1865), which included over 200 proverbs.   [6] Oxford, 1923, preface.

[7] Oxford, 1927, preface.   [8] Oxford, 1929.

his publications on Ashanti represent an unrivalled source of information on African institutions, social organization, and the religious beliefs in which they were rooted.[1]

At first Rattray concentrated on the Ashantis as a nation in themselves. But after transferring his anthropological studies to the Colony, he reported in 1928 the far-reaching and important conclusion that Ashanti and Akan institutions—at least in the area under observation—showed no striking dissimilarities, so that most, if not all, of what he had written concerning Ashanti could be applied generally to the Akan-speaking peoples.[2] This conclusion was not new to Africans such as Casely Hayford or de Graft Johnson; but it carried some official weight.

The renewed interest in customs and institutions fitted in well with the policy of indirect rule. As Guggisberg and Fraser put it: 'We must aim at the development of the people along their own racial lines, and not at the whole-sale replacement of their ancient civilizations by our own.'[3] Guggisberg felt that his Provincial Councils could usefully link traditional forms of government with the central legislature; he even called them 'the breakwaters defending our native constitutions, institutions and customs against the disintegrating waves of Western civilization'.[4] Yet it should be remembered that Rattray himself gave a warning against the contradictions inherent in the principle of indirect rule:

we would therefore appear to be encouraging on the one hand an institution which draws its inspiration and validity from the indigenous religious beliefs, while on the other we are systematically destroying the very foundation upon which the structure that we are striving to perpetuate stands. Its shell and outward form might remain, but it would seem too much to expect that its vital energy could survive such a process.[5]

Chiefs in the Northern Territories

In the north the Government had from the beginning been attempting to work through the Chiefs, not so much out of respect for native institutions as for the sake of administrative convenience. Their functions had never been clearly defined. The Administration Ordinance of 1902 had simply empowered native tribunals, in an inspired piece of gobbledygook, to 'exercise the jurisdiction heretofore exercised by them in the same measure as such jurisdiction has been heretofore exercised'. In practice, the Chiefs were expected to keep

[1] Rattray regarded his *Akan–Ashanti Folk-Tales* (Oxford, 1930), as finally completing his survey of 'the soul of an African people'.

[2] *Departmental Reports*, Special Commissioner for Anthropology, 1927–8. The term 'Akan' is now normally extended to cover Ashanti; see Ch. XIII, p. 509, above. Rattray was using it simply for the Twi–Fanti group of peoples.

[3] F. G. Guggisberg and A. G. Fraser, *The Future of the Negro: Some Chapters in the Development of a Race* (London, 1929), p. 65.   [4] *Legislative Council Debates*, 3 Mar. 1927.

[5] Rattray, *Ashanti Law and Constitution*, p. ix.

order according to British notions, while themselves obeying the orders of District Officers; as in the south, the fact that they were forced to look to an outside source of power weakened their own traditional authority. Where the Chief was a government nominee his difficulties were all the greater.[1]

In some areas the system of chieftaincy was rudimentary or non-existent; for example, among the Lobi-Dagarti and Fra-Fra, each cluster of compounds was said to be a small kingdom, of which one might be friendly, the next hostile.[2] Here, such ruling authorities as could be found had greater responsibilities thrust upon them than their own customs could sanction; the resulting social tensions were not conducive to harmonious rule.

An official report of 1907 recognized that the major problem was the absence of any 'really big Chiefs'; this was ascribed partly to the Muslim conquests of Samory and Barbatu, which had disintegrated former kingdoms. Other difficulties were caused by the lack of any common laws concerning land, matrimony, and so on, even among tribes speaking one language; and by the constant stream of traders passing through the country, who preferred 'to bring their small native matters to the white man rather than take them to the local chief'. In this the traders were probably encouraged by Commissioners who shared the views expressed in this same report concerning the 'absolute imbecility of 60 per cent of the present elected Chiefs'.[3]

Perhaps the greatest obstacle to securing smooth collaboration with the Chiefs was the official ignorance of local traditions and customs. District Commissioners were encouraged to furnish reports on various tribes,[4] and during the 1920's a few informative essays were produced, including R. A. Irvine's *Morals and Manners of the Dagombas*. But for many years little was known, for example, about the mystical functions of the *Ten'dana*, or priest-king, and his powers over land. As late as 1924 an official questionnaire was circulated to all districts, which included such elementary but fundamental points as: 'Is the Tindana hereditary, or can he be elected? . . . How long can a man leave his farm fallow, and still retain possession . . . ? Are all the . . . *Dawa-dawa* trees owned . . . ? Can a man give a friend who is not a native a piece of his land? . . . In short, who is really the owner of the land, or is anybody?'[5] It was the French and Germans who were the pioneers of detailed research into the sociology of the northern peoples.[6] Some interest was aroused

---

[1] Cf. the Chief Commissioner's attitude: 'When at Navarro I appointed the Chief of Sandema Paramount Chief of Kanjarga, and if Adachuro gives any more trouble he must be destooled altogether and deported.' Letter of 27 Aug. 1912, from Armitage to Acting Commissioner, NE. Province; 1953 Acc. No. 1297, G.N. Archives.

[2] Confidential Letter of 16 Apr. 1904, from Morris to Governor; 1953 Acc. No. 1289, G.N. Archives.   [3] *Departmental Reports*, Northern Territories, 1907.

[4] For example, 1953 Acc. No. 1388, Case No. 87/14, G.N. Archives.

[5] Questionnaire enclosed in Letter of 15 July 1924, from Acting Chief Commissioner to Commissioner, N. Province; 1953 Acc. No. 1375, Case No. 8/1911, G.N. Archives.

[6] Especially L. Tauxier, *Le Noir du Soudan* (Paris, 1912), *Le Noir de Bondoukou* (Paris, 1921), and *Études soudanaises: nouvelles notes sur le Mossi et le Gourounsi* (Paris, 1924). Other works

by A. W. Cardinall's *The Natives of the Northern Territories of the Gold Coast* (London, 1920), and *In Ashanti and Beyond* (London, 1927), although the latter was largely a travelogue of his 'Arduous and Dangerous Treks'. In 1927 he drew up a correlated report on native customs from official reports and other material available, but realized that it was far from complete.[1]

A considerable task awaited Rattray when at last he turned his attention from Ashanti to study the peculiar character of chieftaincy in the north. In spite of some official scepticism,[2] he was able to reveal much new information about the dual origins of the system, which derived partly from the priest-kings of the indigenous inhabitants, and partly from the invading warrior bands from farther north with their secular rulers, who had assumed control in many areas before the Europeans came. The new, foreign Chief had nominal authority over the *Ten'dana*, the former ruler, who nevertheless continued to conduct all 'religious or magico-religious concerns'. Rattray often heard a secular Chief say: 'The people belong to me, the land belongs to the *Ten'dana*.'[3] The pattern was not uniform throughout the Northern Territories, and Rattray also showed that the old way of life under the priest-kings had continued undisturbed in many areas, until the more revolutionary invasion of the white man with his preconceived ideas. When he asked to see the King, some unimportant individual was often put forward, who in course of time might become more confident in his new-found authority, and even act despotically.

For the most part, therefore, it was not surprising that administrators had found 'these petty unconstitutional European-made Chiefs', as Rattray called them, lacking in power and prestige. Many of them depended heavily on the local Commissioner for support and guidance, and would often go out of their way to prove themselves loyal subjects.[4] This policy had not always been successful. In 1916 one of them gave evidence at an inquiry into a riot:

> Before I was made a Chief, the people around here used to say—'When the Whiteman goes away, we will teach the Chiefs some sense . . .'—it is only because there has been no Whiteman stationed in Zouaragu that the people have started to go against their Chiefs . . . They disobeyed their Chiefs when the latter had not the direct support of a Commissioner.[5]

were published in German by J. G. von Zech and Z. Mischlich on the Kagbanye, Dagbambas, Moshis, and Hausas.

[1] 1953 Acc. No. 1413, Case No. 27/1923, G.N. Archives. Also A. W. Cardinall, 'The State of our Present Ethnographical Knowledge of the Gold Coast Peoples', in *Africa* (London 1929), vol. ii, no. 4.

[2] 1953 Acc. No. 1421, Case No. 58/1925, G.N. Archives.

[3] R. S. Rattray, *The Tribes of the Ashanti Hinterland* (Oxford, 1932), vol. i, p. xv. Cf. a recent analysis of the functions of the *Ten'dana* by R. J. H. Pogucki, *Gold Coast Land Tenure*, vol. i, 'A Survey of Land Tenure in Customary Law of the Protectorate of the Northern Territories' (Accra, 1955). On p. 15 he shows that 'The religious relationship between the people and the land still exists.'

[4] For example, 'Festivities in honour of His Majesty's Coronation were held at all Stations where the Chiefs assembled in full force and displayed the greatest loyalty and enthusiasm'. *Departmental Reports*, Northern Territories, 1911.   [5] Ibid. 1916.

Soon afterwards it was reported that the old men would still do anything in their power to counteract the growing authority of the Chiefs, for whom they retained a 'fanatical hatred'.[1]

Thus the difficulties of using the Chiefs as agents of local administration were especially acute in the north. But in spite of the essential dualism of chieftaincy there, Rattray found much to confirm his belief that many of the tribal constitutions functioned on similar lines to those of the Akan;[2] and his researches were closely linked in his mind with the aim to build up a system of native administration which should be a model to other territories.[3] The first positive steps towards this, after many years of fruitless effort by the authorities, were at last taken during the 1920's by the Chiefs in the Colony; only later was a similar system introduced in the north.[4]

The Colony Chiefs Take the Initiative, 1925–7

During the early years of Guggisberg's administration the Head Chiefs of the Colony remained increasingly anxious about their relationship with the Government on the one hand and their subjects on the other. There was a growing tendency among sub-Chiefs to break off their allegiance;[5] and, as Nana Ofori Atta later complained, 'There is nothing more ruinous to a State.'[6] They also wanted to systematize the process of dealing with disputes over election and destoolment, thereby removing the growing threat to their position. Destoolments of Head Chiefs had been showing an alarming increase, as follows:[7]

1904–8	.	.	7
1909–13	.	.	23
1914–18	.	.	38
1919–24	.	.	41[8]

[1] *Departmental Reports*, Northern Territories, 1918.
[2] Ibid. Special Commissioner for Anthropology, 1929–30.
[3] Rattray, *The Tribes of the Ashanti Hinterland*, vol. i, preface.
[4] One reason for the delay was the paternalist attitude of northern officials, who had encouraged the people to depend upon them rather than upon the Chiefs. The departure of the Chief Commissioner at the end of 1929 marked the end of an era. His parting words were that native administration was impossible for at least a decade. Handing-over Notes by A. H. C. Walker-Leigh, dated 20 Nov. 1929; Acc. No. 1421, Case No. 58/1925, G. N. Archives. But within five years native authorities, courts, and treasuries were set up in many parts of the Northern Territories, and in 1936, when a local tax was collected for the first time, the receipts actually exceeded the estimates. This was officially regarded as 'the greatest advance in native administration so far recorded in the history of the Gold Coast'. *Gold Coast Annual Report*, 1936.
[5] For example, in one Province in one year, four sub-Chiefs approached the Government in the hope of declaring their independence and severing all connexions with their paramount stools. *Departmental Reports*, Eastern Province, 1923–4.
[6] *Legislative Council Debates*, 4 Mar. 1943.
[7] *Gold Coast Gazette*, 25 Apr. 1925.
[8] The increase may have been due partly to the fact that records were by then more fully kept, and destoolments more carefully noted. Guggisberg claimed, after the introduction of the new constitution, that only one Head Chief was destooled in 1925, and two in 1926.

In the Eastern Province the custom of destoolment was thought to be spreading from one tribe to another, to the extent that Chiefs might be threatened for the smallest indiscretion on their part.[1]

The most obvious example of this was the Gã Mantse, who had had to rely on government support to protect him from destoolment during 1924–5. The Secretary for Native Affairs admitted that the Government had taken out of the hands of the Chiefs the power to deal with disorder by force, so that the Gã Mantse had been unable to handle the situation as his ancestors would have done; this would have spared him much humiliation and distress, and the Gã community much entirely unprofitable convulsion'. He pointed out, accurately enough, that 'When we speak of native custom these days, we mean such native custom as is countenanced by the Government.' He concluded, however, that the Chiefs were now to be regarded as part of the administrative system, so that the Government had an additional responsibility to protect them, by force if necessary, from the effects of disorder and from irregular declarations of destoolment.[2] But such a policy inevitably tended to associate the Chiefs with unpopular government measures, in the public mind.

The official analysis of the situation was opportunely echoed by the Parliamentary Under-Secretary of State for the Colonies, on his visit in 1926. He was impressed by the 'considerable decay in the power, influence and prestige of the Head Chiefs', but could see no alternative to the government policy of ruling through the tribal authorities. He thought that it was only a few Africans in the coast towns who were really detached from their Chiefs, and that the majority were in no way ready for a change.[3] His criticisms of 'detribalized' Africans were, however, strongly resented.[4]

The growing cleavage between the Head Chiefs and the more politically minded section of the A.R.P.S. was emphasized by the establishment of Provincial Councils under the 1925 constitution. The energetic opposition of the Society led the Chiefs to suspect that some of the lawyers would not be sorry to see native tribunals done away with altogether. They were therefore only too willing to act when Guggisberg made it clear, early in 1925, that he intended to wait for them to make the next move themselves. He complained that previous legislation had usually met with firm opposition from the very native rulers that it was intended to help.[5] The Chiefs therefore 'set to work very earnestly', having first ascertained that the Government would

[1] *Departmental Reports*, Eastern Province, 1924–5.

[2] 'Report on an Inquiry held by the Honourable C. W. Welman on a Commission by His Excellency the Governor issued under the Commissions of Inquiry Ordinance and dated 26th February, 1925', *Sessional Paper No. X of 1925–26*.

[3] *Report by the Hon. W. G. A. Ormsby-Gore, M.P. (Parliamentary Under-Secretary of State for the Colonies), on his Visit to West Africa during the Year 1926* (London, 1926), Cmd. 2744, p. 135.

[4] For example, *The Gold Coast Leader*, 4, 11, and 18 Dec. 1926.

[5] *Legislative Council Debates*, 3 Feb. 1925.

agree to the introduction of a Bill by an unofficial member.[1] Many of them assembled in Accra for an official reception to the Prince of Wales, and the opportunity was taken to arrange a conference in May 1925, at Nsawam. There they drew up proposals for legislation, which were printed and circulated.[2]

The genesis of this Bill is of interest, as bringing the Chiefs into closer association than ever before with the legislative process. Describing this many years later, Nana Ofori Atta claimed that there was no section of the African community which was not invited to co-operate, but that no help whatsoever came from the A.R.P.S. On the contrary, it was in Cape Coast that the strongest opposition developed, because the Society's leaders thought that their functions were being usurped, and that the Chiefs were not the proper people to discuss such matters, especially when they met at Nsawam. 'In the opinion of the critics, the Aborigines' Rights Protection Society should have been the proper body to formulate proposals concerning Native Administration.'[3]

The Chiefs moved slowly in this unaccustomed world. They next consulted their State Councils, and discussed the proposals again at the inaugural meeting of the Eastern Provincial Council in May 1926.[4] Then Nana Ofori Atta was 'charged with the consolidation of the views that had been expressed'; and with the assistance of the Attorney-General for the legal phraseology he produced a new draft. This was considered first by the Chiefs of the Eastern Province at Bososo, then sent to the Central Provincial Council, but to individual Chiefs in the Western Province, since that Provincial Council was not yet functioning. Eventually a draft Bill was forwarded to the Government, and was given its final shape at joint discussions between officials and leading Chiefs. The Acting Secretary for Native Affairs later paid tribute to the Chiefs on this occasion for their breadth of view and willingness to accept reasonable compromise, 'which would have done credit to the statesmen of any country'. Nana Ofori Atta claimed that throughout the whole lengthy process the Bill received a warm welcome from all the Chiefs, except two who asked him to refer it to the A.R.P.S.[5]

The Native Administration Ordinance, 1927

The Native Administration Bill was gazetted in February 1927, and had its second reading proposed by Nana Ofori Atta in April. Despite all the elaborate care that had gone into its gestation, the Chiefs were unable to call down the blessings of the press and the politicians; A. W. Kojo Thompson, for example, alleged that it was 'a Government Bill indirectly introduced'.[6]

[1] Question by Nana Ofori Atta, and reply by Colonial Secretary, *Legislative Council Debates*, 4 Feb. 1925.   [2] Nana Ofori Atta, ibid. 19 Apr. 1927.
[3] Ibid. 4 Mar. 1943.   [4] *Minutes of the 1st Session of the Eastern Provincial Council*, 1926.
[5] Nana Ofori Atta and C. W. Welman, *Legislative Council Debates*, 19 and 20 Apr. 1927.
[6] Kojo Thompson, ibid. 19 Apr. 1927.

The main purpose of the Bill was to give a firmer foundation to the power of the Chiefs, and in some respects to extend it, notably in judicial matters. The Oman Council was recognized as the highest authority within each State, responsible for deciding stool disputes. The Provincial Councils, which had initially appeared simply as a piece of electoral machinery, were now given formal administrative and judicial powers, including the right to hear appeals in stool disputes; they were also to adjudicate on the demands of sub-Chiefs for independence and, if so requested by the Government, on inter-tribal disputes. But the Governor was to be the final arbiter on all stool disputes and matters affecting native custom,[1] and Provincial Council decisions were to be subject to review. The working of the Head Chiefs' tribunals was also regulated more carefully to prevent abuses, their jurisdiction was extended in civil matters, and their decisions could now be enforced by the right to seize property.

Hailey takes the view that this Bill fell short of any effective measure of reform, because it 'did nothing to show that a State Council, as such, could exercise powers only when so authorised by the Government, and only to the extent of that authorization'; also because it did nothing to control the use of stool resources or set up native treasuries.[2] Nevertheless, the Bill took a firm stand on the old stumbling-block of inherent versus derived jurisdiction, since it set out 'to assign certain functions to the Provincial Councils'.[3]

Even this limited measure aroused vehement protests. As soon as the details became known, the latent opposition to the 1925 constitution—and especially to the Provincial Councils, its 'most objectionable feature'[4]—was revived. The main newspaper attack on these lines came from *The Gold Coast Times*:

> These paramount Chiefs got to the Legislature by the backgate, by the dubious method of constituting themselves into Provincial Councils and electing some of their number to the Legislature. They were not elected to the Legislature by the votes of the people, nor would our people be so imprudent as to take such a step and violate their own institutions.[5]

The Chiefs, it was alleged, were now about to increase their privileges even further, at the expense of the people. Suspicions were raised that the Provincial Council system was part of a deliberate campaign to extend their authority beyond the limits prescribed by customary law, and not merely to preserve them against the impact of Western civilization, as the Government had claimed.[6]

The detailed proposals of the Bill were also attacked, including those that formed part of the existing law. For example, the Governor's power to withhold

---

[1] The Oman Council could lay down what it considered to be customary law, but this could only be given binding force in native courts by the sanction of the Governor.

[2] Hailey, *Native Administration*, pt. iii, p. 203.

[3] Contrast the tentative phraseology of the 1878 (and the 1883) Ordinance, quoted on p. 460, above.   [4] *The Gold Coast Times*, 6 Feb. 1927.   [5] Ibid. 15 Mar. 1927.

[6] Ibid. 19 Mar. 1927.

recognition of the destoolment of a Chief was singled out for special abuse: 'The time is coming when a Chief once installed will sit firmly on the neck of the people, like the old man of the sea, and rule them in his own way without any lawful means of getting rid of him.'[1] *The Gold Coast Leader* feared that complaints, legitimate under the old system, would now be prematurely 'gagged', and attributed ulterior motives to the Chiefs, as well as accusing the Government of insidious plans for 'denationalising' the people.[2] The press examined the proposed Bill week by week, item by item, often going over the same ground, and occasionally finding fresh objections. Perhaps the most damaging allegation was that it was nothing more nor less than the system of indirect rule already obtaining in the Northern Provinces of Nigeria. Kojo Thompson organized a public meeting in Accra, at which lengthy resolutions of protest were drawn up for expensive transmission to the Colonial Office. *The Vox Populi* offered the Government its only support, claiming that there was nothing new in the Bill, and ascribing the opposition in Cape Coast to the A.R.P.S. faction, and in Accra to the unsettled state of native administration.[3]

The Government was anxious to ensure as representative a debate as possible, and to bring out all the criticisms before, instead of after, the Ordinance was enacted. But at the time the A.R.P.S. was observing its boycott of the new Legislative Council; so an attempt was made to end this with a direct invitation to Nana Hima Dekyi XII of Upper Dixcove, Casely Hayford, and J. Glover-Addo to become extraordinary members when the Bill was due to be debated.

Meanwhile, the Sekondi and Accra sections of the A.R.P.S. were anxious to find some more direct means of influencing government policy. At their request, Casely Hayford, Glover-Addo, and Nanka-Bruce went to see the Governor in March 1927, and learnt that he was prepared to make a useful concession concerning the newly established Provincial Councils; instead of four unspecified 'followers', a Chief would now be required to take with him eight Oman councillors.[4] Casely Hayford considered that this would enable some of the educated men to take their proper place beside the Chiefs. The three politicians returned pleased from their interview; but soon afterwards the Cape Coast A.R.P.S. called upon the Sekondi section to explain this departure from their policy of non-co-operation. The uncompromising W. E. G. Sekyi published attacks on 'Our Defective Leaders' in *The Gold*

---

[1] *The Gold Coast Times*, 19 Mar. 1927.

[2] *The Gold Coast Leader*, 26 Mar. 1927.

[3] *The Vox Populi*, 26 Mar. 1927. The next year the Eastern and Central Provincial Councils agreed to give £50 and £100 respectively as a subsidy to T. K. Orgle, the owner of this Accra newspaper, in return for support and the publication of their news.

[4] Casely Hayford later claimed that their interview had 'effected the change', and also made possible the concession concerning the election of municipal members to the Legislative Council. *Minutes of the 3rd Session of the Western Provincial Council*, Jan. 1929. But the latter decision had been announced to the Gã Chiefs as early as July 1926; see Ch. XI, p. 447, above.

Coast Times, criticizing them for their servile habit of mind in even associating with the Government during what he considered a state of war.[1]

The summons from Cape Coast was disregarded; both the Sekondi and Accra sections were showing signs of growing dissatisfaction at this inflexible attitude. But for the time being they followed the official A.R.P.S. line; Casely Hayford turned down the invitation to sit as an extraordinary member, and Glover-Addo reversed his initial acceptance.[2] The Society simply sent a brief petition which was laid on the table for them by E. J. P. Brown. They counted on being able once again to present their case fully through counsel; but this request, like that of 1924, was firmly refused. The Governor was annoyed that his invitations to sit in the Council had been declined, especially by two former members, and he felt that the blame for lack of representation could now fairly be laid on the increasingly obstructive attitude taken up by the A.R.P.S.[3]

Nana Ofori Atta, introducing the second reading of the Native Administration Bill, put up a staunch defence against his critics. He considered that those who called it unconstitutional were simply ignorant of what their own institutions had been, long before the Ordinances of 1883 and 1910. He reminded them that the Chiefs had once had power over life and death; why then cavil at raising the limits of their jurisdiction to cases involving £100? The claim of the A.R.P.S. to be 'the custodians of the native customary laws and procedure written and unwritten in this country'[4] was repudiated by Nana Ofori Atta, who claimed that it was the Chiefs who should codify customary law. He emphasized that it was they themselves who wanted the advice of the District Commissioners in the administration of justice, after trying it out in practice: 'an ounce of experience is worth a ton of theory'. The Chiefs wanted legal recognition for their Oman Councils; and he saw nothing wrong about their being given power to accumulate revenue, since it was for the benefit of the stool and the State.

As for the Provincial Councils, Nana Ofori Atta failed to understand why anyone should object to these. In particular, he defended them against the argument that it was unconstitutional for Chiefs to make laws:

Since the Divisional Chief as President of Council of his own division, becomes a member of the State Council which is representative of the particular Oman when

[1] *The Gold Coast Times*, 30 Apr. and 14 May 1927.

[2] Nana Hima Dekyi XII accepted, and so became the first Chief from the Western Province to sit in the Legislative Council.

[3] Dispatch No. 389 of 19 May 1927, from Maxwell to Amery, in 'Despatches relating to the Native Administration Ordinance', *Sessional Paper No. XIII of 1927–28*. Petitions were also received from R. Crowther Nicol and a group of non-Gold Coast West Africans, and from the lawyers G. J. Christian and E. M. Abbensetts on behalf of West Indians living in the Gold Coast, protesting against the terms of the Ordinance being applied to them, since they did not consider themselves 'natives'. They felt that in all other respects they were treated as strangers, and were unable to take any part in political movements, including the A.R.P.S.

[4] H. Van Hien, *Legislative Council Debates*, 23 Feb. 1925.

dealing with an affair concerning the whole Oman, so do the Paramount Chiefs who, in their individual capacities, are Presidents of their respective States or Oman Council become members of the Gold Coast (Oman) Council when they meet to deal with matters affecting the whole country.

Although this analysis showed considerable flexibility and willingness to experiment within the traditional framework, Nana Ofori Atta expressed certain views that were bound to be unacceptable to nationalist politicians. For example, he commended the Bill because it enabled a native tribunal to 'close its eyes and stop its ears' in any political matter. He said the Chiefs preferred to leave politics to the central Government: 'the worst democracy consists of a large class of citizens who have very little or nothing to do, and who have full leisure for politics . . . Let us leave politics to those who understand them, and let no one think because he is a native, he is a politician.'[1] Kojo Thompson spoke up for the politicians, complaining that Chiefs could not be legislators and judges at the same time. He challenged their right to introduce such a Bill, when they should have been criticizing and opposing it on behalf of their people, who he claimed were against it.[2] He thought that the public—as opposed to the Chiefs—had not had sufficient notice; but his motion for the rejection of the Bill could not even find a seconder.[3]

Thus the Native Administration Ordinance (N.A.O.) was enacted in April 1927, after more than forty years' delay and opposition to government attempts to revise the 1883 Ordinance. Meanwhile, the official emphasis had changed from defining and controlling the power of the Chiefs to bolstering up an institution that now seemed an essential adjunct to the central Administration and a defence against too rapid social change. In the process the nature of chieftaincy itself was being considerably modified; a form of government adapted to small local communities was being brought into a new relationship with a wider national system. This meant that the flexibility appropriate to direct democracy at village level must be replaced by the stability required of agents of the colonial Government—hence the controversy over official control of destoolments. It also meant that the Chiefs had to be given a voice at the centre; and from this sprang many further arguments. There was the obvious, if negative, criticism that the presence of Chiefs in the Legislative Council was against tradition; and those few capable of rising to the status of national figures laid themselves open to the charge of exceed-

[1] Nana Ofori Atta, *Legislative Council Debates*, 19 Apr. 1927.

[2] Cf. J. W. de Graft Johnson, who stated in 1928 that the Bill should have been introduced by the Attorney-General: 'That would have avoided the clash between the people and certain of the Chiefs, since in that way the Chiefs would not have been privy to its passage and could therefore appeal on behalf of the people for any amendments in the legislation . . . the enactment was largely to extend their jurisdiction . . . It was a case of making the accuser the judge in his own cause'. *Towards Nationhood*, p. 86 n.

[3] E. J. P. Brown, who had promised to support the amendment, failed to appear on the second day of the debate owing to illness. *Legislative Council Debates*, 19–20 Apr. 1927. He did not take his seat again.

ing their constitutional functions and seeking power at the expense of their subjects. The educated politicians felt that they alone were free to assume leadership on a national scale, and to offer a central point of convergence for the local interests and views which each individual Chief was bound to represent.

The Chiefs were now faced with a clear choice: on the one hand, alliance with the nationalist leaders, who would have relegated them to a strictly local sphere as the price of an independence from the colonial authorities which would have been hard to assert in practice; on the other hand, closer collaboration with the British Government in return for a definite increase in prestige and responsibility. Nana Ofori Atta and his paramount peers almost inevitably chose the latter. The resulting conflicts, of principles and personalities, were bitter and often prolonged; but it is difficult to see what other temporary solution could have been found.

Even the nationalist leaders were uncertain over what tactics to adopt. Casely Hayford came to regret having declined nomination, and criticized the A.R.P.S. for bringing about the humiliating position whereby the only voice raised against the Bill in the Legislative Council was that of Kojo Thompson, whose very nomination had been severely criticized in 1926.[1] Casely Hayford now decided that more progress might be made by compromise, by accepting the new constitution sufficiently to attempt alterations from the inside. He and Glover-Addo hastily re-entered the political arena, and were elected to the Legislative Council as municipal members for Sekondi and Accra later in 1927.[2] They lost little time in asking critical questions about the new Ordinance, and unsuccessfully demanded first its postponement and then an official inquiry into the protests already lodged.[3] Casely Hayford still continued his newspaper attacks on the Provincial Council system as unworkable.[4]

Controversy over the Role of the Chiefs

The A.R.P.S., now under the leadership of Sekyi, persisted in their campaign of unremitting opposition from Cape Coast.[5] Many educated Africans, and some of the Chiefs themselves, felt they were on strong traditional ground in seeking to curb the increased powers and influence of the Head Chiefs. The main objections to the N.A.O. were eventually marshalled by the Society in a petition to the Governor in February 1928. Their arguments may be summarized as follows:

1. That the Ordinance placed Head Chiefs beyond the control of their sub-Chiefs and peoples, contrary to native custom.

[1] *The Gold Coast Leader*, 12 Sept. 1928.   [2] See Ch. XI, pp. 451–3, above.
[3] *Legislative Council Debates*, 24 Oct. 1927, and 1 Mar. 1928.
[4] For example, *The Gold Coast Leader*, editorial of 26 Nov. 1927.
[5] After the resignation of Van Hien early in 1928 (he died the same year), 'Father' J. P. Brown, then well over eighty, was recalled to act as President. But his function was largely nominal, and in practice it was Sekyi who controlled the policy of the Society.

K k

2. That it sought to alter the constitutional position of the Head Chief; formerly '*primus inter pares* among the greater *Ahinfu* of the State', he now became the absolute ruler; whilst the greater sub-Chiefs, or *Apakanmfu*, became mere provincial heads under him. This was sure to bring about internal discord within the State.

3. That it conferred judicial powers on executive officers, from the Governor down to District Commissioners.

4. That it was against custom for Chiefs to frame laws for their own subjects, let alone for those of other Chiefs.

5. That not all the Head Chiefs had been consulted, and that, even in the twenty-four States which initially supported Nana Ofori Atta, the people had not been consulted.[1]

But this document was presented almost a year after the Ordinance had been enacted; like the Society's petition against the 1925 constitution, it was a year too late to be seriously considered.

The controversy over the Provincial Councils was taken up by some of the younger African intellectuals and writers. J. W. de Graft Johnson was one who wanted to preserve the authority and dignity of the Chiefs; but believing that the Government had not set about this the right way, he strongly attacked the Provincial Councils. Speaking in London, he argued that the people traditionally exercised jurisdiction over the Chiefs, that the Chief or Oman-hene could not be separated from his Oman Council, and that the creation of a new electoral body could mean the annihilation of African democratic government.[2] In his book, *Towards Nationhood in West Africa*, published in 1928, de Graft Johnson attacked the position of the Chiefs in the central legislature, which he said was not at all the same as that of a divisional Chief in his Oman Council. The Legislative Council was not the national assembly of the people, from its very nature and composition, and hence the Chiefs sitting there should not be empowered to legislate for them.

de Graft Johnson believed, with the A.R.P.S. leaders, that the trouble had started with the 1883 Ordinance, which he alleged had conferred privileges on the Chiefs as a class distinct from the people who had elected them. This tendency had been consolidated by the 1927 N.A.O., and carried great danger of a clash of interests between the two: 'Herein lies the possibility in the last analysis of the abolition of the office of Chief.' The disintegration of traditional authority should be prevented by reinforcing not the Chief, but the Oman Council, the most effective form of representation of the people, and this would be in line with modern thought on kingship. de Graft Johnson was the son of one of the founders of the A.R.P.S., and regarded it as 'the heart of the body politic, because it connotes all the members of the great family, Chiefs and people together'. But he complained of a great deal of idle

[1] Petition of 13 Feb. 1928, to Slater; *Gold Coast Aborigines' Rights Protection Society, 1934 Petition* (London, 1934), annex F.

[2] Speech at Union of Students of African Descent; *West Africa*, 14 Jan. 1928.

and unnecessary criticism emanating from Cape Coast against all government measures.

In place of the negative sniping of the A.R.P.S., de Graft Johnson had some detailed proposals of his own to offer. He suggested, for the first time, the creation of an Upper House of Chiefs, or Council of *Nanamu*, composed of 'the venerable fathers of the State', with advisory, amending, and delaying powers. The three existing Provincial Councils would then act as sections of the Upper House. To counterbalance this, provincial Assemblies of *Begwafu* (Councillors) should also be set up, each of which would elect two representatives (not Chiefs) to the Legislative Council; the present six Head Chiefs there should immediately vacate their seats, and revert to their original function as administrators. Once established, the Council of *Nanamu* and Assembly of *Begwafu*,[1] fully recognized by Government, would 'automatically relieve the Aborigines' Society of political duties and make room for the furtherance of its social objects'.[2]

The Government case found a supporter in J. B. Danquah, a young paternal brother of Nana Ofori Atta, who had welcomed the new constitution while he was studying in London. He returned to the Gold Coast in 1927, after six years' absence, to become a State councillor of Akim Abuakwa and a close associate of his brother in upholding the value of tradition.[3] He took the view that there was much work before the educated members of the community in tactfully instructing the Chiefs in the value of reform, and in volunteering to serve under their orders. He also carried on the tradition of Mensah Sarbah and Casely Hayford by interpreting the heritage and problems of the Chiefs to a new generation of educated readers, in a series of books dealing mainly with the affairs of Akim Abuakwa.[4]

Danquah's basic position was clear: 'We in Abuakwaland are prepared to accept the conditions of advance imposed upon us by enlightened culture, but we are not prepared for a wholesale sacrifice or disregard of the basic principles of our traditional form of rule.' He was wholly in favour of the principles underlying the N.A.O., which he felt admirably fulfilled these conditions. His reasoned defence merits careful examination, since he dealt in turn with the main objections made by the A.R.P.S. On the question of

[1] At this point (p. 110) de Graft Johnson seems to be thinking of the latter as one central Assembly; but the scheme is not always clear in detail.

[2] J. W. de Graft Johnson, *Towards Nationhood*, chs. xv, xvi, and xvii.

[3] Danquah accompanied the Omanhene on a trip to London in 1928 to receive his knighthood, and wrote of the occasion: 'Ofori Atta's triumph in England is one that should be the pride of every Gold Coast man, woman and child.' *West Africa*, 22 Sept. 1928.

[4] J. B. Danquah, *Gold Coast: Akan Laws and Customs and the Akim Abuakwa Constitution* (London, 1928), claimed that Nana Ofori Atta was 'moulding our ancient laws and customs into accord with modern exigencies', but at the same time preserving undisturbed the best of them. *Cases in Akan Law* (London, 1928) made available some important judgements delivered by the Omanhene. *The Akim Abuakwa Handbook* (London, 1928) offered an outline of the history and customs of the State. Finally came *An Epistle to the Educated Youngman in Akim Abuakwa* (Accra, 1929).

extending the power of the Chiefs, he appealed unanswerably to the distant past, before custom had been codified—which in any case no one could remember clearly—claiming that they had not now been given any more power than they had been entitled to before the advent of European governments. He pointed out that the Ordinance had not given authority to Chiefs as such, but had rightly taken cognizance of their councils and councillors.

Another objection concerned the position of the Head Chiefs in the Legislative Council. Danquah developed Nana Ofori Atta's analogy of the Ohene who was a Chief in his own town, but became at times a councillor to the Omanhene and helped to make laws for him; 'so the Omanhene becomes a mere member, a Councillor in the Central Legislative or other assembly'. Here Danquah was at his most realistic, pointing out that the supremacy of the British Government, though unpalatable, was nevertheless a fact, which meant that a Head Chief was not the absolute sovereign of his State. In other words, 'The Paramount Chiefs assembled in Council do not legislate for the country as Paramount Chiefs but as Councillors of His Majesty the King'; and each was thus acting as the representative of an electorate in his own State. This remained true, whether a Chief went to the Legislative Council himself or whether he sent instead an ordinary member of his State. Although this argument represented a departure from traditional custom, it opened the way towards a more national outlook on the part of the Chiefs.

There was no object in labelling the Provincial Councils unconstitutional, Danquah further explained, since there was no written constitution. This was not the way to organize opposition, even if an Ordinance was found to be bad and to require repeal. He himself remained convinced that the N.A.O. was a good law in principle, and made some practical suggestions for improving it in detail, through the proper channels: on the platform, in the newspapers, by pamphlets, by appeals to representatives in the Legislative Council and to the Chiefs.[1]

But these arguments and proposals were unlikely to convert the rearguard of the A.R.P.S., who concentrated their efforts during 1927-8 on an attempt to wreck the operation of the Provincial Councils; for if these could yet be made to fail, so might the 1925 constitution and the hated N.A.O.

Provincial Councils: the Critical Years

The A.R.P.S. campaign, although based on a reasoned case, was carried on largely by rumour and exaggeration in the rural areas. According to Nana Ofori Atta, messengers were sent 'all over the country' making deliberate misrepresentations of the motives of the Head Chiefs, and accusing them of wanting to deprive the people of their rights and property.[2] Rumour

[1] Danquah, *An Epistle to the Educated Youngman in Akim Abuakwa*, passim.
[2] *Legislative Council Debates*, 4 Mar. 1943.

gave a fantastic twist to prosaic details of the Ordinance. For example, section 32—'Any Native not being a Chief or Headman and not having authority to act as such who usurps the position of a Chief or Headman shall be guilty of an offence'—was interpreted to mean that for the future only Chiefs would be permitted to wear silk cloths or gold ornaments. Another widespread and effective technique was the swearing of local oaths, forbidding recognition of the Provincial Councils; around Cape Coast, for example, some such oaths had to be formally dissolved in 1929.[1]

Until the passing of the N.A.O., it had been believed that the Central Provincial Council was firmly established, and that the States which had stood out would soon be converted. In fact, less than half of the Head Chiefs had been attending the Council, and the situation quickly deteriorated as suspicions were revived by their opponents, who gained a marked success in their campaign.[2] An opportunity for propaganda was offered by section 129, which made it lawful (but not obligatory) for the Governor in Council not to apply the Ordinance to any State whose Head Chief was not attending the Provincial Council. It was therefore spread abroad that if you wished to avoid coming under the N.A.O. you had only to stop your Chief attending the Provincial Council. This ingenious misapplication of the law led to a number of threats of destoolment; so the Ordinance was applied, as from 1 January 1928, to all States in the Colony, irrespective of the attendance of Chiefs at the Provincial Councils.[3]

At the end of 1927 Nana Amanfi III of Asebu was forced to resign his membership of the Central Provincial Council under pressure from his own State. Nana Otu Ababio II of Abura similarly withdrew; and his fellow member of the Legislative Council, Nana Ayirebi Acquah III of Winneba, had his car destroyed by fire, although it had, ironically enough, been presented by his people in honour of his election. It was claimed locally that he had been destooled, although this action was not recognized by the Government; by January 1928 there appeared to be little prospect of the Central Provincial Council surviving the onslaught.[4] The following month the Provincial Council had to elect a new member to the legislature in place of the Omanhene of Abura, who had suddenly died. Only ten State Councils were represented. But the President gave a strong lead, and said that no attention should be paid to the 'STUPID LIES intentionally invented by the Aborigines' Society at Cape Coast and its Emissaries all over the Country'.[5] The voting resulted in the election of Nana Aduku III, Omanhene of Mankessim, the ancient stronghold of the Fanti Confederation.

This was the turning-point in the Central Province. At the next meeting the

---

[1] *Departmental Reports*, Central Province, 1927–8 and 1928–9, and Eastern Province, 1927–8.
[2] Ibid. Central Province, 1927–8.
[3] Slater, *Legislative Council Debates*, 1 Mar. 1928.
[4] *Departmental Reports*, Central Province, 1927–8.
[5] *Minutes of the 8th Session of the Central Provincial Council*, 1928.

President welcomed back several members who had been obliged to keep away by their State Councils, under pressure of the violent agitation against the N.A.O.[1] No doubt an important factor in swaying local public opinion was the personal contact of government political officers with Chiefs and individually influential Africans.[2] Several other State Councils now reconsidered their decision to abstain from membership of the Provincial Council, and at the tenth meeting (held shortly afterwards) the attendance for the first time reached substantial proportions.[3]

The sequence of events in the Eastern Province was similar, although the pendulum swung more gradually. During 1927 there arose decided opposition in several States; in Kwahu the Asafo even tried to prevent the Omanhene by force from meeting the Governor at Mpraeso.[4] The two main complaints were that while the position of the Head Chiefs had been strengthened, no improvement had been offered to other Chiefs; and that many small tribunals, set up under the old Native Jurisdiction Ordinance, had now been closed. Officials explained, however, that the Governor in Council was still empowered to add to the list of authorized tribunals, on the recommendation of the Provincial Council.[5] This reassured several Chiefs, who now cherished the hope that they might be able to satisfy the Provincial Council with a good case for their own tribunal. In 1928 representatives from only two States in the Eastern Province—Akwapim and New Juaben—signed the belated A.R.P.S. petition against the N.A.O., and although another attempt was made to destool the Gã Mantse, this time he refused to be deterred from attending the Provincial Council. At the seventh session the Chiefs present recorded their full appreciation of the N.A.O. as 'the first solid step in their political advancement'.[6]

In the Western Province an unsuccessful attempt had been made to inaugurate the Provincial Council at Tarkwa in 1926. At the end of the following year the new Governor, A. R. Slater, tried personally to convince the Chiefs in the Sekondi–Dixcove area of the value of the system. He stressed the limited powers of interference in tribal affairs by the Provincial Councils, and asked why, if the A.R.P.S. could call Chiefs together to discuss common problems—and primarily to criticize the Government—it was wrong for the Chiefs themselves to meet and discuss constructive proposals. But he received the familiar reply that the A.R.P.S. was a body constituted by popular consent, and already possessing many advantages claimed by the new Councils, which were merely institutions established by the Government.[7]

---

[1] *Minutes of the 9th Session of the Central Provincial Council*, 1928.
[2] *Departmental Reports*, Central Province, 1927–8.
[3] See Table on p. 504, below.
[4] Dispatch No. 827 of 20 Oct. 1927, from Slater to Amery; Adm. 1/622, G.N. Archives.
[5] *Departmental Reports*, Eastern Province, 1927–8.
[6] *Minutes of the 7th Session of the Eastern Provincial Council*, 1928.
[7] S.N.A. 921, Case No. 24/1925, G.N. Archives.

There were other difficulties. The Acting Provincial Commissioner was at some loss for a topic to be discussed, and gloomily predicted that there would be no Head Chief really suitable for election to the Legislative Council, even if they all met together.[1] In spite of these official doubts, and a further campaign of opposition from the Axim section of the A.R.P.S., the inaugural meeting of the Western Provincial Council was eventually held at Dunkwa in April 1928 (immediately after the opening of the deep-water harbour at Takoradi). It was attended by thirteen Head Chiefs, who elected Nana Annor Adjaye, Omanhene of Western Nzima, as their member in the Legislative Council.[2] He had been one of those members of the A.R.P.S. who had signed the 1926 resolution forbidding Chiefs to attend either the Provincial or the Legislative Councils.[3] Afterwards he had wavered, and consulted his elders and councillors, who told him that since his brother Chiefs had now requested him to go, he could not refuse, But Nana Annor Adjaye still felt uncertain of his position, and was pleased to find that some of his educated friends endorsed his decision.[4]

Once the Western Provincial Council had been inaugurated, steady progress was made. At the third session in January 1929, seventeen State Councils were represented at Axim, the heart of the A.R.P.S. opposition in this Province. It was here that the most significant number of educated Africans participated; the Omanhene of Dutch Sekondi was accompanied by J. E. Casely Hayford and his son, and by D. W. Gwira and F. Awoonor Williams, all lawyers. Casely Hayford emphasized his volte-face by publicly calling the Provincial Councils 'a useful institution', and remarking how the system had come to be considerably amended and 'made workable'.[5]

An important contribution towards making the system workable was the liberal scale of cash payments for time spent at meetings and in travelling. Many of the Head Chiefs came from poor States, and they saw the financial advantage of attending meetings.[6] In 1928 the Central Provincial Council

[1] Ibid.

[2] Nana Ofori Atta, who had been nominated to the Legislative Council, resigned his seat so that this election could be held. Soon afterwards he was elected for the Akan section of the Eastern Province, to replace Nana Kwesi Akuffo, who died in 1927.

[3] Cf. Ch. XI, p. 445, above.

[4] Nana Annor Adjaye later quoted their letters; for example, 'I am glad to find that wiser counsel has now prevailed so as to make it possible for you to attend the Provincial Council... How can you effectively criticise the arrangement of furniture in my sitting room without first coming in?' Another had written, 'there are many things about both the Native Administration Ordinance and the Provincial Council itself which are to be rectified, but how can we legitimately effect it by standing outside and pelting stones at them?... Don't forget, we need Street Lights very badly in Beyin.' *Nzima Land* (London, 1931), pp. 45–47.

[5] *Minutes of the 3rd Session of the Western Provincial Council*, 1929.

[6] There was an even bigger financial inducement not to oppose the N.A.O. Any tribunal which functioned had to be subject to the provisions of this Ordinance, and even its most determined opponents had realized that to possess a regular tribunal was preferable to depriving themselves of the considerable portion of stool revenue derived from tribunal fees and fines. *Departmental Reports*, Central Province, 1928–9.

requested that since the number of followers had been increased from four to eight, the daily allowances for attendance should be raised; the existing rates were £4 per day for each Omanhene, or £2 per day for a representative in his absence.[1] Once assembled, the Chiefs were in no hurry to conclude business and return. The Commissioner for the Western Province reported that one session had cost the Government nearly £1,000, apart from travelling; he anxiously pointed out that they could not afford many more meetings—at this rate—during the remainder of the year.[2] Similarly, in the Central Province the Commissioner complained that one session had cost about £1,800, nearly exhausting the year's vote; and that during a fortnight's meeting in April and May 1929, nothing definite appeared to have been done, nearly all the important items of business having been merely talked over and postponed. Some of the Chiefs took strong exception to these statements.[3]

Paradoxically enough, it was the slow and unsensational working of the Provincial Councils that helped to make them more acceptable to those who had feared the setting up of a dangerous oligarchy of Head Chiefs.[4] The following table gives the attendance at meetings of the Provincial Councils from their birth up to August 1929, and sums up the ebb and flow of support during that critical period.[5]

Eastern Province	13 paramount stools		Central Province	27 paramount stools
1st meeting	11 attended		1st meeting	11 attended
2nd	11		2nd	10
3rd	10		3rd	11
4th	10		4th	13
5th	9		5th	11
6th	5		6th	13
7th	7		7th	11
8th	8		8th	10
			9th	18
			10th	24
			11th	24
Western Province	20 paramount stools		12th	25
1st meeting	13 attended			
2nd	16			
3rd	17			
4th	19			

[1] *Minutes of the 8th Session of the Central Provincial Council*, 1928.

[2] S.N.A. 921, Case No. 24/1925, G.N. Archives.

[3] *Minutes of the 13th Session of the Central Provincial Council*, 1929.

[4] 'The Provincial Councils were for a considerable time after their institution condemned as being oligarchic in nature, as secret conclaves of Paramount Chiefs where matters detrimental to the interest of the people were discussed.' Acting Secretary for Native Affairs, *Legislative Council Debates*, 26 Feb. 1930.

[5] S.N.A. 921, Case No. 24/1925, G.N. Archives.

Casely Hayford's change of heart in deciding to accept the Provincial Councils had an important influence on the outcome. This decision was expressed at the personal level by a full reconciliation with Nana Ofori Atta in March 1929; and the following year he announced in the Legislative Council his complete conversion: 'whatever may have been my views at one time I am a practical man . . . and I desire to say here this afternoon that as at present advised, our practical course of advance is through these Councils'.[1]

But this new approach did not mean any abrogation of the claim of the intelligentsia to national leadership. Nor could it resolve the fundamental contradiction inherent in the very existence of the Provincial Councils. As D. E. Apter points out, an essentially unstable political situation arose from the fact that 'conflicting sources of authority, so different in nature as to be directly contradictory, were procedurally integrated into one system, indirect rule'.[2] The Head Chiefs had improved their status and extended their functions with external official support; but they had not really strengthened their position within their own States, where political instability was still a problem, and where they were most vulnerable to attack as agents of the central Government. The lesser Chiefs found their subordinate role—*vis-à-vis* both the District Commissioner and the paramount Chief—was if anything emphasized under the new system; and they had no compensating increase in prestige or responsibility. The weakening of traditional authority made possible the emergence of new social groupings as a basis for modern nationalism; but it also meant a painful and prolonged process of transition for the Chiefs themselves.

[1] Casely Hayford, *Legislative Council Debates*, 26 Feb. 1930.
[2] *Gold Coast in Transition*, p. 120.

XIII

THE GROWTH OF NATIONAL CONSCIOUSNESS

HANS KOHN has defined nationalism as 'first and foremost a state of mind, an act of consciousness'; and he suggests, further, that 'Nationality is formed by the decision to form a nationality'.[1] This conscious and deliberate process can be seen clearly in the Gold Coast. Through the influence of the new, educated *élite*, the consciousness of a common origin, a common destiny, a common purpose—in a word, a common nationality—was deliberately fostered and gradually evolved.

The process was neither inevitable nor easy. External forces—including the chances of exploration and the whims of European chancelleries—had determined the arbitrary collection of peoples whose 'national' unity was being consciously cultivated. But to say this is not to deny the existence of any common national factors between such peoples. The arrival of Europeans had revealed to Gold Coast Africans—as it might have done to West Africans over a much wider area—how much they had in common concerning religious beliefs, political institutions, social customs, and family traditions. The basic difference of colour, not initially regarded as of fundamental importance, but later exacerbated by false notions of superiority and inferiority—on both sides—did much to awaken national feeling. The very fact of domination by an alien authority, which became more apparent as the complexity and responsibility of government increased, encouraged the nursing of national grievances and the development of counter-claims on a national scale.

But there were other difficulties. As T. L. Hodgkin has pointed out, ex-colonial nations are in fact 'made, not born, and made in the face of strong opposition from elements within the nation, who realise that the strengthening of a national loyalty will mean the weakening of other traditional loyalties'.[2] Indifference and especially ignorance were also serious problems; for, as E. H. Carr reminds us, 'a large numerical majority of the people of the world feel no allegiance to any nation',[3] even in countries where most of them are literate.

The absence of a national language might appear to have been the most obvious difficulty in the way of developing a sense of Gold Coast nationality. In fact, though a fruitful source of controversy, it never proved a major hindrance to the development of national consciousness. This found expression at first through the deliberate revival of native culture, institutions, and history; later came a consciousness of belonging to the African continent and Negro race, and a sense of affinity with national movements in other parts of

[1] H. Kohn, *The Idea of Nationalism* (New York, 1945), pp. 10 and 15.
[2] 'Background to Nigerian Nationalism', in *West Africa*, 4 Aug. 1951.
[3] *Nationalism and After* (London, 1945), p. 39.

the world. Perhaps the most difficult stage was the development of a sense of common cause between the Colony, Ashanti, and the Northern Territories, a major reorientation that was by no means completed by 1928.

The attempt to reinterpret the past in terms of 'national respect and self-confidence' may have had only a slender factual basis; there is indeed an element of myth in the process by which any nation is created. That does not mean that the process is any the less worthy of study; and in the growth of national consciousness in the Gold Coast we find the key to an understanding of the political movements and protests which have already been outlined.

Language and the Nation

Language is known to be an important factor in national sentiment.[1] A group of people are more likely to consider themselves a nation if they have a common cultural heritage, and especially a common language. Sir Ernest Barker has gone as far as to say that 'it is common speech which is still the main cohesive bond of nations and a generally necessary basis for the foundation of an homogeneous national character'.[2] On the other hand, the lack of a common language will not prevent the rise of nationalism, if the political urge is strong enough, although it may cause difficulties of inter-communication within the national boundaries.

As in many other countries, political boundaries in the Gold Coast did not coincide with linguistic boundaries. It was probably inevitable, owing to the manner in which the country took shape, that numerous tribal groupings would be dissected or ignored. Few of them were sufficiently organized to protest; but the division of the Ewes—further complicated by the mandatory partition of Togoland after the First World War—was more strenuously criticized, mainly because they were a distinct, and vocal, language group.

The main problem for the Gold Coast arose from the diversity of languages within its boundaries. Peaceful coexistence of different language groups has been attained in such dissimilar countries as Canada and Switzerland. But there is obviously a limit to the number of different languages which can be officially cultivated within a small community, especially if they have no literature, and if they emphasize minor divisions between peoples in a society where tribalism is breaking down. On the other hand, linguistic unity cannot easily be imposed or dictated; and often the minority is not prepared even to agree to differ. It is therefore not surprising that in the Gold Coast, with its multiplicity of languages and dialects, there has been no strong, united demand for a national language.

[1] An illuminating analysis of this question is given by H. M. Chadwick in *The Nationalities of Europe* (Cambridge, 1945), especially ch. i, 'Nationality and Language', and ch. ii, an historical account of 'The Languages of Europe and the Growth of National Feeling connected with them'.

[2] *National Character and the Factors in its Formation* (London, 1927), p. 12. Cf. D. Westermann's conclusion that 'Nothing binds people more closely together' than a common language. *The African To-day and To-morrow* (Oxford, 3rd edn. 1949), p. 117.

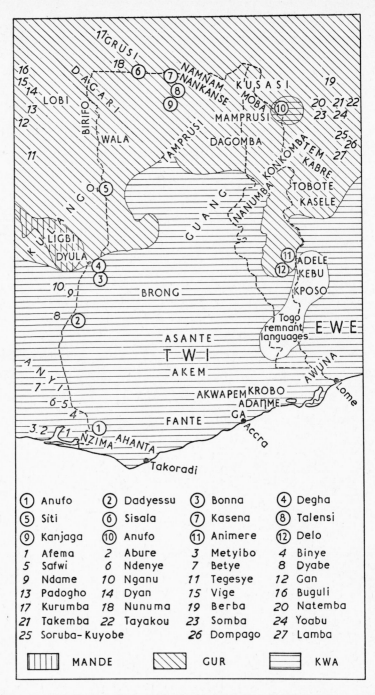

MAP 8. Languages spoken in and around the Gold Coast.
(after Westermann and Bryan)

Classification of Gold Coast Languages [1]

A. KWA LANGUAGES

1. *The* AKAN *language group:*

   a The *Twi–Fante* dialect cluster:
      Twi: Akem, Akwapem, Asante.
      Fante.

   b. Some of the *Anyi–Baule* dialect cluster:
      Anyi: Ahanta, Anufo, Nzima.
      Baule: Bonna, Dadyessu.

   c. Some of the *Guang* dialect cluster:
      Brong, Guang.

2. *The* GÃ–ADANGME *dialect cluster:*
   Gã, Adangme, Krobo.

3. *Some of the* EWE *dialect cluster:*
   Awuna.

B. GUR LANGUAGES

1. *Some of the* LOBI–DOGON *language group:*
   a. Some of the *Lobi* dialect cluster.

2. *Some of the* MOSSI *language group:*

   a. Some of the *Dagomba* dialect cluster:
      Dagomba, Kusasi, Mamprusi, Nanumba.

   b. Some of the *Dagati* dialect cluster.

   c. The *Birifo* language.

   d. The *Namnam* language.

   e. The *Nankanse* language.

   f. The *Talensi* language.

   g. The *Wala* language.

3. *Some of the* GRUSI *dialect cluster:*
   Degha, Kanjaga, Kasena, Sisala, Siti, Tamprusi.

4. *Some of the* GURMA *dialect cluster:*
   Konkomba, Moba.

5. *Some of the associated dialects of the* TEM *language:*
   Animere, Delo.

C. ISOLATED LANGUAGE GROUP

Some of the TOGO *remnant languages:*

Adele, Ahlo, Akpafu, Avatime, Bowili, Lefano, Likpe, Logba, Lolobi, Nyang-bo, Santrokofi, Tafi.

---

[1] From D. Westermann and M. A. Bryan, *The Languages of West Africa* (Oxford, 1952). J. H. Greenberg, who has promised 'a complete reclassification of African languages on genetic and historical rather than structural principles', has reached substantially the same conclusions as Westermann concerning the Kwa and Gur languages, which he places within a yet wider Niger–Congo Family. See his *Studies in African Linguistic Classification* (New Haven, 1955).

The situation has been further complicated by the intrusion of foreign tongues. From the earliest days of European exploration and expansion, the traders brought their languages as well as their goods to the Gold Coast. Where administration developed, those in authority seldom troubled to learn the unwritten languages of the country. When they needed Africans as clerks, messengers, or assistants, they first taught them Portuguese (some words have survived as many centuries as their fortresses); later, Dutch, Danish, or English. This Babel was gradually reduced as British influence came to predominate.

English became the language of government, of overseas trade, and, in particular, of the schools. Education, to many people, came to mean simply the ability to speak and write English. It was both the gateway to opportunity and the main medium of communication between educated Africans of different tribes. As early as 1857 an African news-sheet, *The Accra Herald*, was produced in English, laboriously transcribed by hand; the importation of printing presses increased the influence of newspapers, and of the English language. It was not, however, the language that people spoke at home; it could not arouse any national sentiment, nor any of the emotional associations of a mother tongue. Sooner or later, a reaction against the language of the ruling race was inevitable; but the effects of this were delayed until the local languages were put into writing, and proved to be capable of literary expression.

The missionaries were the first to take an interest in the structure of Gold Coast languages, and to try to give them a written form, for they realized that to reach the majority of the people—and especially to bring Christianity home to them—the local languages must be used. As Sir Ernest Barker puts it, 'You cannot enter the heart and know the mind of a nation unless you know its speech.'[1] A few word-lists and brief translations were published during the seventeenth and eighteenth centuries;[2] but it was the Basel missionaries, arriving in the early nineteenth century, who were the real linguistic pioneers of the Gold Coast. The Rev. J. G. Christaller, in particular, was responsible not only for numerous Biblical and devotional translations, but also for a grammar and dictionary of Twi, two remarkable works which are still unsur-

---

[1] *National Character*, p. 13.

[2] The earliest word-list seems to have been made by a Dutch navigator and trader, Pieter de Marees, *Beschryvinge ende historische verhael vant' Gout Koninckrijk van Guinea, anders de Gout-Custe de Mina* (Amsterdam, 1601). W. J. Müller's *Die Africanische auf der Guineische Goldküste gelegene landschafft Fetu* (Hamburg, 1673), contains a vocabulary of about 500 words in the Afutu dialect, by a former Chaplain to the Danes at Frederiksberg, near Cape Coast. In 1744 an African, J. E. J. Capitein, published a Fante translation of the Lord's Prayer, the Creed, and the Ten Commandments; see R. Eckhof, *Nederlandsch Archief voor Kerkgeschiedenis* (The Hague, 1916). Charles Protten, a mulatto of Christiansborg who had been educated in Denmark, produced a brief grammar of the Fante and Akra languages, *En nyttig Grammaticalsk Indledelse til Tvende hidindtil gandske ubekiendte Sprog, Fanteisk og Acraisk* (Copenhagen, 1764).

passed in their field.[1] His researches resulted in a spate of prayers, hymns, Bible stories, and translations into Twi, including the four Gospels (London, 1859), the Acts of the Apostles (Basel, 1859), Genesis, Revelation, and a selection from the Epistles (Stuttgart, 1861–2). The complete Bible (Basel, 1870–1) was translated with the help of David Asante and Jonathan Bekoe, two of the Basel Mission's earliest students.

This new approach came as a liberating influence to the older generation of educated Africans, who had received all their schooling in English, with nothing at all that they could read in their mother tongue. In 1853 Brodie Cruickshank had declared that 'the sooner their own language gives place to the English, which is rapidly spreading among them, the better will it be for their progress in knowledge and civilization'.[2] But the vernacular textbooks produced by the Basel Mission won the admiration of both the Government and the Wesleyan General Superintendent, who agreed that 'Education will never be appreciated by the natives of the *interior* until it is imparted in their own language.'[3] The African writer, Dr. J. A. B. Horton, commented in 1868 that the Basel Mission had 'established the literature of the language', and helped 'the rising generations to feel the beauty and pathos of their mother tongue when reduced to writing'.[4]

Christaller was the first to state clearly the main linguistic problem: 'The chief language of the Gold Coast stands not only in want of a generic name universally recognized; the question *which dialect is to have mastery in its literature* too is to be solved.' And it was to remain unsolved for over eighty years, although Christaller himself had no hesitation about choosing Akwapim Twi as his standard for 'a common book-language'.[5]

Meanwhile, the Wesleyans had been working along different lines in Cape Coast, among Fante speakers.[6] Although they could not attempt to rival the wealth of scholarship from Basel brought to bear upon the Twi language, their work was notable for the contribution made by Africans themselves. The first primer appears to have been produced in 1837 by William de Graft,[7] who had been responsible for bringing Wesleyan missionaries to the coast, and had been left in charge when they died; he also compiled a short Fante–English vocabulary.[8] Several Biblical translations, and a brief Fante grammar,[9]

---

[1] *A Grammar of the Asante and Fante Language called Tshi* (Basel, 1875), and *A Dictionary of the Asante and Fante Language called Tshi* (Basel, 1881).

[2] *Eighteen Years on the Gold Coast of Africa* (London, 1853), vol. ii, p. 262.

[3] Dispatch No. 43 of 11 July 1859 from Bird to Bulwer Lytton; CO/96/45.

[4] *West African Countries and Peoples* (London, 1868), p. 144.

[5] Christaller, *A Grammar of . . . Tshi*, Introductory Notes, pp. xviii–xix.

[6] The spelling 'Fante' has here been adopted for the language, as opposed to the people, since it is most commonly used by linguistic writers.

[7] Listed by F. W. H. Migeod, *The Languages of West Africa*, vol. ii (London, 1913), p. 264.

[8] Published in J. Beecham's *Ashantee and the Gold Coast* (London, 1841); see pp. 167 and 359–76.

[9] R. Brooking, *Nucleus of a Grammar of the Fanti Language: with a Vocabulary* (1843).

were prepared after 1840 by Wesleyan missionaries from England;[1] but they seem to have made little attempt themselves to conduct services in the vernacular.[2]

Among the next generation of educated Africans, the Rev. Timothy Laing wrote a small *Fante Primer* (Cape Coast, 1864), and D. L. Carr and J. P. Brown collaborated in producing the more ambitious *Mfantsi Grammar* (Cape Coast, 1868). The aim of this book was 'to confer upon the Nation the rights of having its languages added to the catalogue of written languages'; and the motto on its title-page ran, 'Let every foreign tongue alone, till you can read or write your own'. Carr and Brown attempted to provide one standard system of spelling and usage for all the various dialects of Fante, using as a basis that of Cape Coast. Christaller criticized their orthography, based on the English alphabet; and claimed that his system of transliteration would have suited Fante and Asante as well as Akwapim Twi; but no attempt was made to work out an agreed written form. It was unfortunate that the two Missions, by working along independent lines, crystallized, and sometimes unwittingly exaggered, minor dialectal differences, even before the end of the nineteenth century.

English-speaking Africans, outside the Missions, long showed little interest in their mother tongue. In 1888, however, a writer in *The Gold Coast Echo* called upon the educated community to take in hand 'the great AKAN language' and reduce to a minimum the many impurities and imperfections of its present written state. He suggested that it was 'destined to be the medium through which Science, Literature, Art, etc., may be eventually disseminated and recorded' amongst Akan-speaking tribes, including the Fantis, Ashantis, Akims, Denkeras, Wassaws, Akwapims, and Akwamus. As with customs and culture, so with language, the earlier attraction of everything European was now being countered by a revival of pride in all things 'racy of the soil'.[3] This was a cause dear to the editorial heart of *The Gold Coast Methodist Times*, which launched a campaign against 'the admixture of English words', in order to preserve the purity of the Fante language, and defended its 'wonderful vitality' in expressing abstract and modern ideas.[4] The Rev. S. R. B. Attoh Ahuma did not forsake these principles when he had to give up editing the newspaper. In a pamphlet published in 1911 he discussed the potential unifying force of a common tongue, claiming that the Akan language

[1] In Dec. 1842 the Rev. S. A. Shipman wrote: 'I am endeavouring to compile a vocabulary of the Fanti language, and have also got translations made of the Commandments, the Lord's Prayer, and part of the Catechism.' T. B. Freeman, *Journal of Various Visits to the Kingdoms of Ashanti, Aku, and Dahomi* (London, 1844 edn.), p. 281.
[2] A member of the Wesleyan Missionary Society Committee who visited the Gold Coast expressed surprise at their failure 'to acquire and speak the languages of the country . . . a matter of paramount importance'. *The Life and Journals of the Rev. Daniel West*, ed. by T. West (London, 1857), entry for 19 Nov. 1856.
[3] *The Gold Coast Echo*, 15–29 Feb. 1888.   [4] 15 Jan. 1897.

extended along a seaboard of 350 miles, and over an area of more than 100,000 square miles; its subdivisions were not themselves languages, but simply 'so many dialects, often mere Provincialisms'.[1] Not long afterwards, J. P. Brown expressed the hope that Mfantsi-speaking people would take a pride in their own tongue; and remarked that it was 'humiliating to hear a native speaker or a preacher inflicting English on his audience', regardless of the fact that he was quite unintelligible to most of his hearers.[2]

In 1914 *The Gold Coast Nation* also accused the Churches of 'dragging poor souls along the path of a strange tongue to do homage to the Great King without the heart and mind in tow with the lips'.[3] This was accompanied by significant comments upon the change in educated attitudes:

A hopeful sign of racial advancement is the tendency of native scholars to appreciate their mother tongue and the evincement of natural thirstiness after native literature. A short while ago the majority of our scholars thought it most detractory from their training to be heard speaking their mother tongue in public. Some went to the extreme of thinking it a 'grand' thing to affect gross ignorance of the vernacular and would not so much as listen when accosted in it . . . Now there is no scholar but holds the vernacular to be as good as the most elegant foreign language.[4]

This restoration of the prestige of the vernacular did not mean that it was universally adopted for practical purposes. English was still the lingua franca for educated men, not only in the Gold Coast but in the other British West African territories. This was a great convenience for the organizers of the National Congress, which was almost entirely a movement of the English-speaking intellectuals.

In the government schools the emphasis had been on English for many years, with some vernacular work for the very youngest children. Indeed, the first Inspector of Schools had recommended in 1884 that grants to the Missions for reading in the vernacular should be only temporary, until they were able to replace it by English teaching right from the beginning.[5] He was not untypical in regarding the local languages as 'only interesting to the Comparative Philologist and never likely to become of any practical use in civilization'.[6] But a few years later the Governor began to encourage his

---

[1] *The Gold Coast Nation and National Consciousness* (Liverpool, 1911).

[2] *Mfantsi Grammar* (Cape Coast, 1913 edn.), introduction.

[3] This remark—rather unfair in view of the pioneer work done by the Missions—was mainly aimed at the Wesleyans in Cape Coast, whose translators were then concentrating on the Fante Bible, a labour of many years, rather than on vernacular material for immediate use in the Churches.

[4] *The Gold Coast Nation*, 10 Sept. 1914. Cf. S. H. Brew's *Practical Fanti Course* (Cape Coast, 1917).

[5] Dispatch No. 552 of 9 Apr. 1884, from Derby to Young; CO/96/163.

[6] *General Report on the Results of the First Inspection of Elementary Schools in the Gold Coast Colony and Lagos, 1884* (Accra, 1885).

officers to study Gold Coast languages;[1] and it was a Transport Officer who during 1911–13 produced the first major linguistic study of West Africa, declaring that 'without learning a native language, no European can hope to understand the black man's mind'.[2]

J. E. Casely Hayford was probably the first African—in a letter to *The Weekly News* of 5 May 1908—to criticize publicly the practice of starting children's education with the English language, to which he attributed later inconsistencies of character. But it was not until 1920 that the supremacy of English in the school system was seriously challenged, by the Educationists' Committee, which recommended strongly that although the acquisition of English was essential, 'the Vernacular should be the *medium* of instruction'. English should be a *subject* of instruction, as early as possible, and opportunities should be taken to combine both, particularly in games. They aimed thus to avoid the meaningless repetition of sounds in a foreign language. Guggisberg thought that this emphasis on the vernacular was probably the most important of all their recommendations;[3] and special attention was paid to the study and teaching of local languages at Achimota during subsequent years.[4]

Nana Ofori Atta also urged on the 1920 Committee 'the necessity for an early standardization of the Fante and Akan languages'.[5] By this time the problem had become acute. The Wesleyans were now anxious for a uniform system of transliteration, because some Ministers who could read the Fante Scriptures could not read the Twi Bible, and vice versa. There was even a difference in script between earlier and later editions of the Twi Bible; in Aburi, for example, the two were in use side by side, because the older people preferred to keep the one with which they grew up. But it was easier to recognize the problem than to agree on a solution. In 1924 representatives of the Government and the Missions decided that it was impracticable then to standardize the Fante and Akan 'languages', although the natural process of assimilation might bring this about in course of time. They did, however, consider a common script to be feasible.[6]

Meanwhile, the increasing interest of government officers in local customs and institutions had led to detailed study of smaller language groups,

[1] In 1889 the Colonial Office agreed to a suggestion by Brandford Griffith that gratuities should be paid to European officers for proficiency in Fante, Twi, and Gã. CO/96/195. In 1907, however, the Chief Commissioner of the Northern Territories felt strongly that 'the pushing of the English language in the country is of more lasting benefit than forcing Commissioners to learn one of the many languages'. *Departmental Reports*, Northern Territories, 1907.

[2] F. W. H. Migeod, *The Languages of West Africa*, vol. i (London, 1911), p. 76.

[3] 'Report of the Educationists' Committee appointed by His Excellency the Governor on 5th March, 1920, to advise the Government on Educational Matters', *Sessional Paper No. IV of 1919–20*.

[4] Cf. J. B. Anaman, *The Gold Coast Vernaculars and the Prince of Wales College, Achimota* (Cape Coast, 1928).   [5] *Sessional Paper No. IV of 1919–20*, app. vi.

[6] 'Report on a Conference of Representatives of the Government and the Missions on the subject of the Adoption of a Common Script for Gold Coast Languages', *Sessional Paper No. V of 1925–26*.

especially during the 1920's; and this in turn probably encouraged increasing linguistic fragmentation, helping to perpetuate a number of dialect forms.[1] The first grammatical studies of northern languages for English readers had been published towards the end of the First World War,[2] and soon afterwards A. W. Cardinall provided a general survey.[3] In 1927, however, an official memorandum admitted that 'The study of native languages in the Gold Coast, too long neglected, is in its infancy', and that facilities for research had been meagre.[4] The pendulum was now swinging the other way; in that same year the Colonial Office published *The Place of the Vernacular in Native Education*, and Professor D. Westermann visited the Gold Coast, at the invitation of the Government, to study language problems.

Westermann's Report on 'A Common Script for Twi, Fante, Gã and Ewe' proposed the adoption of a new, phonetic script; linked with this, but not essential to it, was a proposal for the unified spelling of Twi and Fante words, even where they were pronounced differently.[5] The phonetic script was welcomed by representatives of Government and the Missions,[6] and by some influential Africans; for example, J. W. de Graft Johnson considered a uniform script a definite advance towards the creation of 'a lingua franca and literature African in character and spirit'. But although he himself admitted that some tribal pride would have to be sacrificed in order to arrive at this desirable goal,[7] it soon became clear that the minor modifications necessary in practice were not going to be generally acceptable.

As the scheme became more widely known among the general public, deep-seated prejudices were aroused. Confusion of the principles of the Westermann script with those of the unified Akan spelling resulted in opposition to both;[8] and although some vernacular textbooks had begun to appear, further

[1] For example, C. W. Welman in *A Preliminary Study of the Nzima Language* (London, *c.* 1925) deplored the lack, and the inaccuracy, of knowledge about languages and dialects allied to Akan. The Rev. J. B. Anaman quickly followed up Welman's work with *Standard Nzima* (Accra, 1926) and *English and Nzima Key Book* (Accra, 1927).

[2] J. O. Okraku, *Dagomba Grammar* (Oxford, 1917), and R. S. Rattray, *An Elementary Mole Grammar* (Oxford, 1918). Some earlier studies of Moshi and Dagbani had been made by French and German writers, working mainly on the other side of the political boundary; the White Fathers at Navrongo were probably the first Europeans to learn the Kassena tongue.

[3] In *The Natives of the Northern Territories of the Gold Coast* (London, 1920), Cardinall indicated both the diversity of tongues and the similarity of many of those related to Moshi.

[4] 1927 Memorandum on Native Language Study; S.N.A. 1927, G.N. Archives.

[5] 'A Common Script for Twi, Fante, Gã and Ewe. Report by Professor Diedrich Westermann of Berlin University at the conclusion of his visit to the Gold Coast in March and April, 1927, together with a Memorandum on School Textbooks in Vernaculars, and a Note on Language Conditions North of Ashanti', *Sessional Paper No. V of 1927–28*. See also Westermann, 'A Visit to the Gold Coast', in *Africa* (London, 1928), vol. i, no. 1; and 'The Linguistic Situation and Vernacular Literature in British West Africa', in *Africa* (London, 1929), vol. ii, no. 4.

[6] Minute of 17 May 1927, by Acting Secretary for Native Affairs, printed with Westermann's Report.

[7] *Towards Nationhood in West Africa* (London, 1928), p. 88.

[8] Later, an Akan Language Association was formed, with the Rev. E. D. Martinson as President, 'to protect the purity of the spoken and written language'; it declared from its inception

publications were delayed by the controversy.[1] Eventually, however, the phonetic script was adopted for use in government and Mission schools and publications;[2] but the proposed unification of Twi and Fante spelling was not achieved. Thus tribal and conservative loyalties triumphed, in face of the growing pressure for national unity.

Westermann himself has commented, speaking of Africa generally, on the opposition aroused by any attempt to use, in one language area, even a neighbouring dialect in school and literature; 'This is partly due to tribal jealousy, but also the feeling that language is a valuable possession the loss of which would impair the individuality and integrity of the group.'[3] In the Gold Coast it was not only one language group, but several, who were faced with linguistic modifications for the purpose of unification, and who resisted the challenge to their group identity. As a result, in spite of the efforts made at standardization, none of the Gold Coast languages was able to offer an acceptable alternative to English.[4] They had been subjected to foreign competition at such an early stage that they could hardly be expected to hold their own; the process of amalgamation of cognate dialects had not gone far enough, and their cultural background was too narrow.

English remained the language of government and of all official documents, even of Native Authority minutes. It was spoken at Legislative Council and town council meetings.[5] English became a practical necessity for anyone wishing—without the aid of an interpreter or letter-writer—to apply for a driving licence, write to a government department, deposit money in the Post Office Savings Bank, give evidence in a Magistrate's Court, consult a telephone directory, or manage a retail store; and in many other walks of everyday life. Newspapers, if they were to sell enough copies to survive commercially, let alone reach a national audience, had to choose English.[6] A few missionary

that the new Westermann script was unacceptable. *The Times of West Africa*, 18 Mar. and 21 May 1932.

[1] *Departmental Reports*, Education, 1929–30 and 1931–2.

[2] Not least among the temporary inconveniences caused was the fact that the Wesleyan Fante Bible translation, then almost completed, had to be rewritten in the phonetic script, and revised all over again, so that final publication was delayed for over twenty years. Ida Ward said in her *Report on an Investigation of some Gold Coast Language Problems* (London, 1945), 'The actual letter-forms no longer present any contentious questions, though not all the spelling suggestions and conventions recommended by Westermann . . . were accepted and tried out.'

[3] *The African To-day and To-morrow*, p. 121.

[4] Twi has recently shown some signs of becoming a lingua franca among illiterates, spreading even into the north via the seasonal migrant labourers.

[5] English automatically became the language of Ghana's Parliament in 1957; this may be contrasted with the use of both English and Hausa as official languages of the Regional Assembly in Northern Nigeria.

[6] This was true even of *The Christian Messenger and Examiner* (founded in Cape Coast in 1859 by the Rev. T. B. Freeman and the Rev. H. Wharton), which extolled—albeit in English—the virtues of African languages, and urged that 'the riches of classic and foreign literature' should be translated. Compare the contemporary *Iwe Irohin*, published in Yoruba at Abeokuta; in spite of the advantages of serving a bigger language-group, this was soon forced to carry an English supplement.

news-sheets and periodicals were published in the vernacular;[1] but their subject-matter as well as their circulation was limited. Those Africans who wanted to read for themselves what was being said about current events and mundane issues were probably already literate in English. After the First World War *The Gold Coast Independent* experimented with a smaller, cheaper edition in Twi, and for a brief period in Gã as well; but neither of these was commercially successful.

English was the common language of the educated *élite*, and inevitably became the main medium of expression for nationalism.[2] The knowledge of English opened up a new world of political ideas, facilitated inter-tribal as well as international contacts, and provided a more effective outlet for grievances. J. B. Danquah might write (in 1928) of the Akan tribes 'as one racial stock bound together in one common language, and the sentiment of a common tradition and ancestry'.[3] Yet the fact remains that even the Akans were divided by linguistic rivalries, and that none of the local languages could provide a common medium of expression for the whole country.

The Beginnings of Cultural Nationalism

The predominance of the English language was only one aspect of the acquisition of European culture and social habits by educated Africans. During the nineteenth century the tendency to imitation was strong,[4] and a conscious effort was necessary if they were to retain or recapture anything of value from the older ways of life. It was not long, however, before such an effort was made by those members of the new *élite* who realized the importance of national customs and institutions in the formation of national character.[5]

In 1884 a reader of *The Gold Coast Times*[6] had suggested a series of articles on the manners and customs of the Accras.[7] The following year James Brew

[1] The Basel Mission, for example, published *Sika Nsona Sanegbalo*, and E. W. Quartey-Papafio was editing *Hogba Skul Ngmalo*, a Gã paper, for the Methodists, before the turn of the century. Ewe readers were comparatively well catered for by the Bremen Mission. The quarterly *Ewe Hame Gbele* was produced at Amedzofe from 1896 to 1902, and the following year *Nutifafa Na Mi* commenced publication—initially in Germany, and later at Lome. This periodical continued through the 1920's, in company with the Catholic *Mia Xole*.

[2] By the time that national political parties were being organized, from 1948 onwards, it was clear to the organizers that to press the claims of any one vernacular for general acceptance would immediately antagonize the other main language groups, and that the feelings of Ewes and northerners, in particular, had to be respected.

[3] *The Akim Abuakwa Handbook* (London, 1928), p. 12.

[4] Cf. Ch. III, pp. 133–4, above.

[5] This change seems to have come about earlier in the Gold Coast than, for example, in Nigeria. J. S. Coleman shows how cultural nationalism developed among the second generation of educated Nigerians in the late 1930's and early 1940's. *Nigeria: Background to Nationalism* (Los Angeles, 1958), pp. 147 and 327–8.   [6] 9 Sept. 1884.

[7] Cf. later articles on 'The Homowo Festival', *The Gold Coast Independent*, 29 Aug. 1896, and on 'The Hooting Away of Famine', ibid. 17 Aug. 1918. Educated Africans retained a particular interest in this important festival; M. A. Barnor produced a pamphlet, *An Explanation of Gã Homowo* (Accra, 1924), in which he compared it with the Jewish Passover.

introduced a regular folk-lore column in *The Western Echo*, and soon Casely Hayford was stressing the significance of national language and dress, in *The Gold Coast Echo*. As one writer put it: 'The fact is we have been born and bred Pseudo Englishmen, and the result will soon be the entire loss of race characteristics.' He urged his readers to 'cultivate a deep reverence for what God has been pleased to give us'.[1] And another, more practical-minded, suggested the adoption of some convenient 'natural' dress: 'How we dress at present is, surely, a great evil, inasmuch as it would appear it injures our health in some degree'.[2]

It was partly to counteract excessive Western influence that in 1889 the *Mfantsi Amanbuhu Fékuw* was formed in Cape Coast.[3] Mensah Sarbah later summed up the significance of the *Fékuw* and its leaders, who had been shrugged off and ridiculed by some Europeans as having 'gone Fantee'. Their guiding principles were, he said, that it was better to be called by one's own name than be known by a foreign one, that it was possible to acquire Western learning and be expert in scientific attainments without neglecting one's mother tongue, and that African dress, closely resembling 'the garb of the Grecian and Roman', should not lightly be cast aside. Japan had shown that it was possible 'to retain one's national costume and yet excel in wisdom and knowledge'.[4] A sense of release was experienced by those who had the courage of their convictions:

I failed not to be present at the second concert presided over by Mr. J. Mensah Sarbah, who in his native cloth looked like a Roman in toga garb at the Forum. Let us be thankful Fantis are proud to be Fantis and are not ashamed to be known by their native names, heard speaking their liquid language, and seen arrayed in their flowing robes . . . I am sorry I did not wear my cloth on that warm night, I had the misfortune to wear the alien badge of coat and trousers.[5]

Another growing fashion was to discard European in favour of African names. One of the first recorded instances must be a newspaper advertisement published in 1892:

To all whom it may concern!! Two gentlemen of intelligence having pluckily dropped their foreign names, have encouraged me to do the same . . . I am no slave, so nobody must call me *Ebenezer* Weldu *Cole* Eshun any more. My real name is Esuon Weldu.[6]

A socio-theological controversy developed in 1897, when the Rev. S. R. B. Solomon wrote to several of his Wesleyan colleagues, asking them: 'Do you see the advisability of a general resumption of Native Names in the case of persons baptized or not who had assumed European Names?' He even

---

[1] *The Gold Coast Echo*, 19 Nov. 1888.　　　　　　　　[2] Ibid. 14 Feb. 1889.
[3] See Ch. III, p. 150, above.
[4] J. Mensah Sarbah, *Fanti National Constitution* (London, 1906), pp. xvii–xviii.
[5] *The Gold Coast People*, 30 Nov. 1893.　　　　　　　[6] Ibid. 15 Aug. 1892.

raised the question of a second baptism. The replies were published in *The Gold Coast Methodist Times*, which Solomon was then editing, and they showed great variation in outlook, among both Europeans and Africans. For example:

The Resumption of Native Names is unadvisable ... on Religious grounds:— because a rejection of the names given to persons at Baptism in preference to heathen ones, looks as if they were ashamed of Christ and His Cause.

I am glad you have commenced baptising with the native names only.

I have never believed in the anglicising of our people ... I should like to see more true patriotism. Perhaps the movement you imply would bring about such a desirable end.

On national and racial ground, I consider a change, on such lines as hereunder indicated, desirable.

1. All anglicised native names should be dropped: Mends should be Mensah, Hackman, Akuma &c.

2. All English names fancifully adopted should also be dropped for native ancestra names, Instance: Solomon, Ellis &c. &c.

3. I do not think however, that the change should extend to the Christian names.

Already almost every native scholar has two names by both of which he is known. To instance myself: I am known by the names of 'Kweku Anamua'—this is my native name—amongst my family as well as by several persons outside it. Then I am also known as Isaac Anaman ... But there are also several natives who cannot conscientiously do away with their foreign names. These are persons descended from foreign ancestors. Instance, Grants, the Laings, the Fergusons, the Bannermans, the Minnows and a host of others—particularly mulattoes. I would also remark that in adopting foreign names—Christian names in particular—we have precedent from other nations. Such names as Nehemiah ... Job ... Mary ... came originally from the Hebrews . . . On the whole it is my opinion the whole thing may be left optional.

A budding poet was inspired by the new trend to write:

> Hie hence! Remains of slavish day,
> When we were chattels—nothing more;
> And like some tamed beasts of prey,
> Were hailed by names our *captors* bore.
>
> O let us wear the Sacred badge
> Of honour that makes not asham'd;
> Our Land's our own, a royal catch,
> So be the names, that we are named.[1]

It was not long after this that Solomon changed his own name to Attoh Ahuma.

[1] *The Gold Coast Methodist Times*, 30 Sept. 1897. The practice of reverting to native names became more widespread in subsequent years, and such changes were often publicly announced in the *Government Gazette*, as well as in the local newspapers. Some of the educated Chiefs also took an interest: e.g. the ex-Omanhene of Akwapim wrote on 'The Necessity for

In this revivalist atmosphere the new Lands Bill of 1897 resounded like a blasphemy. The *Fékuw* was immediately translated into the Aborigines' Rights Protection Society, and became an active political force. This is perhaps the clearest illustration of the relation between the cultural renaissance and the rise of nationalism. The crucial issue of land touched economic interests as well as sentiment, and brought about a unity of opposition to the Government that was to prove a permanent factor in Gold Coast nationalist politics. Land was the touchstone of national solidarity, according to J. B. Danquah: 'It and it alone can and always does bring all States and all the peoples together to act as one man, to act with the will and purport of a nation.'[1]

But Attoh Ahuma remained vigilant to remind the A.R.P.S. that it had a social and cultural as well as a political mission:

We have fought valiantly for what we deemed were our Ancestral Rights in the past . . . but the greatest calamity of West Africa that must be combated tooth and nail, we feel, is the imminent Loss of Ourselves . . . Rather let me rob our lands if possible, but let us see that they do not rob us of ourselves. They do so when we are taught to despise our own Names, Institutions, Customs and Laws, even when these do not in any way conflict with the Christian faith and European civilization.

He suggested that those who had 'gone Fantee' had found the key to 'national salvation'; yet there was no exclusiveness about his ideal. The Gold Coast man must return to 'the simplicity of his forbears, sobered and matured with all that is excellent in Western civilization and religion'.[2] Here seemed to be a prospect of reconciling the individualist European way of life with the communal forms of African society.

'We have a Past'

The A.R.P.S. leaders were determined to retain the links with the past that had been the inspiration of the *Fékuw*. The first issue of their newspaper, *The Gold Coast Aborigines*,[3] declared that the rising generation must be instructed in the history of their country: 'we do not know of a better weapon to be wielding in any political struggle for existence than a smart acquaintance with the history of a country, backed by a clear intelligence of the laws of the land'.[4]

Africans to Prefer Ancestral or Native Names to European Names'. *The Gold Coast Nation*, 2 Dec. 1915. Cf. Nana Annor Adjaye, *Nzima Land* (London, 1931), p. 158: 'why should the European missionary wish to see Kwesi Mensa in Heaven as John Menson?'

[1] *Liberty of the Subject* (Kibi, 1937). Cf. J. E. Casely Hayford, in *Gold Coast Native Institutions* (London, 1903), p. 4: 'There is a keen pleasure in the sense of possession. *My* land, *my* house, as contradistinguished from *your* land, *your* house, will remain, till the end of time, worthy objects of ambition. As with the individual man, so with the individual nation.'

[2] S. R. B. Attoh Ahuma, review of Casely Hayford's *Gold Coast Native Institutions*, reprinted in app. to *Memoirs of West African Celebrities* (Liverpool, 1905).   [3] 1 Jan. 1898.

[4] Cf. the first published constitution of the A.R.P.S.; one of their stated aims was 'To foster in

At the time there were very few books on the history of the Gold Coast. The Rev. J. B. Anaman was the first to compile a brief historical summary of local events, in his annual *Gold Coast Almanack*, which he began to publish in 1888;[1] this was later expanded into *The Gold Coast Guide* (London, 1895).[2] J. Mensah Sarbah also published a brief list of 'Notable Events', as well as a selection of constitutional documents, in his *Fanti Customary Laws* (London, 1897). But the first African historian was the Rev. C. C. Reindorf, a Basel Mission pastor of Gã and Danish descent, who in 1889 made a remarkable attempt to preserve oral tradition in written form in his *History of the Gold Coast and Asante* (eventually published at Basel, 1895). He was conscious of the need to write with 'true native patriotism', and thought of his work not only as a 'methodical narration of events', but as the 'history of a nation'.[3] Although often overloaded with unimportant detail, and somewhat lacking in general perspective, the book preserved many valuable records, especially of affairs in the Gã State.[4]

Extracts from early publications were occasionally serialized by a few enterprising journalists.[5] But apart from Reindorf, the only nineteenth-century writers of Gold Coast history were Europeans. None of them were academic historians; it was a few missionaries, soldiers, administrators, and traders who kept alive the record of the past. Naturally this history was written from a European point of view, from outside, and the argument of Empire runs through it. There is an interesting contrast between the approach of Reindorf, and that of the British officer A. B. Ellis in *A History of the Gold Coast of West Africa* (London, 1893). Both start with the Phoenicians; but whereas Reindorf then proceeds to the origins of the Gold Coast tribes, Ellis turns to

the rising generation a knowledge of their historical past, and to encourage the study of the laws, customs and institutions of their country.' *Bye-Laws, Rules and Regulations* (Cape Coast, 1907).

[1] Anaman had been inspired by *Payne's Lagos and West African Almanack and Diary*, which had been published annually since 1873.

[2] The material ranged from memorable personalities to parochial minutiae. For example:

1890 The Great Rev. T. B. Freeman d. Accra, August 12.
   Gold Coast Chronicle newspaper published September 25.
1891 West Indian troops removed from the Gold Coast, June.
   Father E. Granier, Catholic Mission, d. Elmina, June 30.
   Fosu pond at C.C.C. opened into the sea, July.
   Hon. C. Pike, C.M.G., d. at Accra, August 9.

J. B. Anaman, *The Gold Coast Guide* (London, 1902 edn.), p. 171.

[3] Thirty-five years later J. B. Danquah told students in London: 'Reindorf has been dead for some years now . . . not a single voice has been raised to recall our inestimable debt to this most admirable prophet of Gold Coast nationality.' *West Africa*, 8 Mar. 1930.

[4] The Rev. E. Samson, another Basel Mission pastor, produced in 1908 *A Short History of Akuapim and Akropong*, intended to supplement Reindorf, and urged other writers to complete the history of their own country 'for the welfare of their fatherland'.

[5] For example, in 1885 the English editor of *The Gold Coast News* started to serialize T. B. Freeman's 'Life and Travels on the Gold Coast' (1840). This was sufficiently popular to be continued in the African-edited *The Western Echo* (1885–7) and *The Gold Coast Echo* (1888–90). The following year Mensah Sarbah began to publish in *The Gold Coast People* excerpts from Bosman's *New and Accurate Description of the Coast of Guinea* (1705).

European discoveries in West Africa in the fourteenth century. His book was the first comprehensive account of 600 years of Gold Coast history.

At the turn of the century Mary Kingsley wrote a history of West Africa for English schools. Although unusually sympathetic to African aspirations, she could not see history through their eyes; she assumed that 'The moulding of that history is in the hands of the European whose superior activity and superior power in arts and crafts gives the mastery.'[1] Yet the A.R.P.S. was just at this time beginning to express the desire of educated Africans to mould their own history; and they looked upon the study of the past primarily as a means of equipping themselves for this practical task. Mensah Sarbah had already undertaken some research at the suggestion of the *Fékuw*, and had published the result as *Fanti Customary Laws* (London, 1897). This was followed by *Fanti Law Report* (London, 1904), which made available to the public further important judgements, and helped to establish a uniform interpretation of traditional law.

During this formative period African scholars were mainly interested in descriptive studies of legal and political institutions, rather than historical accounts of how they had developed. With this approach, Mary Kingsley had much sympathy; she encouraged Mensah Sarbah in work that would bear out her own attempts to prove to the British public that Africans were not 'living as a mere horde'.[2] Since the white race had claimed a desire to improve the natives as their justification for interference in Africa, she blamed them for

proceeding to alter African institutions without in the least understanding them;[3] while the African is to blame for not placing clearly before the Anglo-Saxon what African institutions really are . . .

There are thousands of Englishmen . . . who would not destroy native independence and institutions if they but knew what those things really were; who would respect native law if they knew what it was, and who would give over sneering at the African and respect him if they knew him as he is . . .[4]

Thus, she felt, true friendship would be possible, on the basis of acknowledged differences.

[1] Mary Kingsley, *The Story of West Africa* (London, 1900), p. 19.

[2] Letter of 5 July 1898, from Mary Kingsley to Mensah Sarbah; quoted in his *Fanti National Constitution*, pp. 259–60.

[3] This process is best illustrated in Mary Kingsley's inimitable style, by 'that improving fable of the kind-hearted she-elephant, who, while walking out one day, inadvertently trod upon a partridge and killed it, and observing near at hand the bird's nest full of callow fledglings, dropped a tear, and saying "I have the feelings of a mother myself", sat down upon the brood. This is precisely what England representing the nineteenth century is doing in West Africa. She destroys the guardian institutions, drops a tear and sits upon the brood with motherly intentions; and pesky warm sitting she finds it.' *West African Studies* (London, 1899, 2nd edn.), pp. 326–7.

[4] Letter (*c.* 1899) from Mary Kingsley to Editor, *New Africa*, Monrovia; ibid. pp. 261–5. Cf. the earlier appeal made by the Aborigines' Protection Society of London in their Memorial to Chamberlain of 28 Mar. 1896, for a 'rigid avoidance of meddling with native institutions, even if they are objectionable in themselves, unless and until they can be replaced by or gradually developed into something manifestly better'. CO/96/284.

Mary Kingsley's main interest in the study of native institutions was for the purpose of improving the methods of imperial rule; she urged Europeans to 'master the knowledge of the Native and his country'. But Mensah Sarbah and his associates were anxious to promote an understanding of African institutions among their own people, because they might thereby be enabled to achieve a greater control of their own affairs. For example, Casely Hayford's *Gold Coast Native Institutions* (London, 1903) arose out of research on an A.R.P.S. brief for the Lands Bill deputation, which had convinced him of the need for 'an intelligent and scientific study of Native Institutions', as a basis for 'the revival of representative government on native lines'.[1] This book was the first full analysis of the apparatus of Akan government and the organization of society, including the functions of traditional office-holders.

Soon afterwards, Mensah Sarbah produced a complementary work, *Fanti National Constitution* (London, 1906). He quoted Gladstone as saying, 'Unhappy are the people who cut themselves from their past', and claimed that 'The study of their own ancient as well as modern history has been shamefully neglected by the educated inhabitants of the Gold Coast.' His aim was now to demonstrate 'the existence of an African State, to trace the broad outlines of Akan-Fanti communities, and to explain the principles controlling and regulating the government thereof'.[2] A few years later, Mensah Sarbah was still concerned to challenge 'the idea that aboriginal administration is hopelessly saturated with cruelty and inextricably permeated with corruption, and therefore should be destroyed'.[3] He did, however, suggest that the energy and enthusiasm shown in company fights should be diverted to proper use.[4]

Thus the awakening of national consciousness was partly responsible for —and partly stimulated by—the revival of interest in the past. Both Mensah Sarbah and Casely Hayford, by taking a pride in their early history and forms of government, encouraged their countrymen to strike down roots into the past. Perhaps they tended to rationalize and idealize the tribal past, forgetting how often practice might fall short of theory. But they tried to show, to the British as well as to educated Africans, that their ancient institutions had adequate rhyme and reason and were essentially democratic; and that their own customs, ways of life, and ideas were a sufficient basis for educational and constitutional advancement: 'Allow us to make use of our own Native Institutions, which we understand, and which from experience are adapted to us.' They believed that it was both possible and essential to rule the people through their Chiefs, with the co-operation and enlightened guidance of the

[1] pp. 15 and 128.
[2] p. 71.
[3] Cf. Ch. III, p. 131, above.
[4] Preface to H. W. Hayes Redwar's *Comments on Some Ordinances of the Gold Coast Colony* (London, 1909), pp. v–xix.

educated African, if only the British Government would trust him to take the Native State system, 'and develop and improve it on aboriginal lines, and on scientific principles'.[1]

During subsequent years this educated leadership had a strong traditionalist bias. By 1911 Attoh Ahuma was even hoping for 'an era of Backward Movement' among 'all cultural West Africans . . . Intelligent Retrogression is the only Progression that will save our beloved country.' He urged the need 'to rid ourselves of foreign accretions and excrescences' as an indispensable condition of 'National Resurrection and National Prosperity'. More positively, he declared: 'We have a nation, and what is more, we have a Past—"though ungraced in story". We own a Political Constitution, a concentric system of government, of one Race, born and bred upon our own soil.'

The very title of Attoh Ahuma's pamphlet—*The Gold Coast Nation and National Consciousness*—was a declaration of faith. Although he admitted that some 'rash and irresponsible literalists' would not grant the title of nation to the Gold Coast, with its numerous independent States, complex political institutions, laws, customs, and variety of languages, he dismissed such objections as 'academic': 'In spite therefore of the dogmas and *ipse dixits* of those wiseacres who would fain deny to us, as a people, the unalienable heritage of nationality, we dare affirm, with sanctity of reason and with the emphasis of conviction, that—WE ARE A NATION.' This claim was not to be forgotten, though it was not yet politically important. 'The Difficult Art of Thinking Nationally', the subject of one of Attoh Ahuma's chapters, had still to be learnt.

It was in the same year that Casely Hayford produced his *Ethiopia Unbound* (London, 1911), a book of sundry reflections on race relations, cast loosely in the form of a novel. He stressed the need for the African to cherish 'the good things of the treasure house of his own nationality', including language, manners, customs, religion, and household gods. Such matters were the basis of African self-respect, including 'the sober garb in which the Romans conquered the material world, and in which we may conquer the spiritual world'.[2] The adoption of a distinctive dress for the educated African, therefore, would be 'a gain to the cause of Ethiopian progress and advancement'. Casely Hayford claimed that the African in America had committed 'national suicide'. In particular, he cherished a dream of a 'national University for the Gold Coast and for Ashanti', with its own Chair of History: 'and the kind of history that I would teach would be universal history with particular reference to the part Ethiopia has played in the affairs of the world . . . Africa

[1] Casely Hayford, *Gold Coast Native Institutions*, pp. 127–8 and 250, and Mensah Sarbah, *Fanti National Constitution*, ch. vi.
[2] Cf. a comment in *The Gold Coast Leader*, 24 Feb. 1907, on the occasion of the enstoolment of the Gã Mantse: 'The "scholars" looked quite noble and full of dignity in the native dress.' The writer recommended them to take 'a few lessons' from 'the sartorial simplicity and elegance of their forebears',

was the cradle of the world's systems and philosophies, and the nursing mother of its religions.'[1]

Some Europeans in the Gold Coast were beginning to recognize the African's claim to re-inherit his own past; and the aims of the A.R.P.S. in this sphere were admirably summed up for them by an expatriate school-master at their banquet for Clifford in 1913:

It is a grand thing when a people recognises that it has a heritage of ancestral rights; when it feels that the past is not a nameless, shameful shadow, and realises that its forefathers have in the long, long years evolved a system of customs and usages which are trustworthy, practicable, and expedient in the economy and policy of the present . . . Tribes and factions can only be transformed into a nation from within.[2]

These words may have had some influence on Casely Hayford's next project, the Gold Coast National Research Association, which he founded in Sekondi. The movement was later extended to Accra and Cape Coast, under the leadership of J. C. de Graft Johnson and W. E. G. Sekyi respectively. The Cape Coast branch held their first public meeting—conducted entirely in Fante—in November 1915, and adopted as their Sisyphean object 'the elimi-nation of the white man's standpoint from the black man's outlook'. They were even more backward-looking than Attoh Ahuma, aiming to restore 'national respect and self-confidence' by observing native custom alone, without European intrusions, and by reconstructing 'on paper' the native State 'before the disintegrating foreign element intruded, or insinuated itself, into it'.[3]

Yet one should not forget that it was Casely Hayford and his associates who were pressing most strongly for the reform of the Legislative Council, who demanded political, educational, and social reform on modern, Western lines, and who were to be condemned by the Chiefs for undermining the authority of their 'Natural Rulers' when they came to form the National Congress of British West Africa. It is impossible, during this period at least, to draw a clear-cut distinction between the 'traditionalist' and the 'modernist' leaders of the national movement, as some have tried to do. It was inevitably the more highly educated Africans who felt cut off from their own history; but the re-establishment of links with the past did not cause them to lose sight of future political progress.

The teaching of history is in most countries, whether or not by design, one of the most important sources of 'national respect and self-confidence'. But in the Gold Coast such studies had long been almost entirely centred on Britain; any reference to West Africa was likely to relate to European ventures

---

[1] *Ethiopia Unbound*, pp. 170–4 and 194–7.

[2] The Rev. S. J. Gibson, Acting Principal of Mfantsipim, proposing the toast of the A.R.P.S.; J. E. Casely Hayford, *The Truth about the West African Land Question* (London, 1913), app. B.

[3] *The Gold Coast Independent*, 2 Dec. 1915.

overseas.[1] In 1910 the Education Department reported: 'The lack of a suitable text book on the History of the Gold Coast is largely responsible for this subject being deleted from the school timetables.'[2] The most then offered was 'Twelve simple lessons in the form of stories from the History of the Gold Coast', for Standard III.[3] In 1915 *The Gold Coast Nation* complained that children were not being brought up as 'the units of a NATION'. Any schoolboy could answer questions on English history or the geography of Europe; 'but ask him about the battle of Katamansu or the course of the River Prah or Volta and he is a perfect blank'. The article summed up the growing dissatisfaction of the intelligentsia in the Colony with the narrow and uninspired routine of many schools: 'Education that fails to recall and install into the minds of the children the wisdom, brave deeds and civilization of the past is bound to produce an educated class of indigenes prone to foreign customs and ideals which will make them a soulless people in the land of their birth.'[4]

It was in the same year that Dr. W. W. Claridge published *A History of the Gold Coast and Ashanti from the Earliest Times to the Commencement of the Twentieth Century*, a monumental two-volume work which is still a standard authority. Claridge drew heavily and often uncritically upon Ellis, and displayed a marked bias in favour of the Ashantis, 'the most powerful and in fact the only really important kingdom and empire that the Gold Coast has ever seen'. His own interest was clearly excited most by the battles he described so vividly, in ever greater detail towards the turn of the century; the siege and the relief of Kumasi Fort were for him the crisis and the resolution of his story. The defect of Claridge's method was that little attention was given to African opinions and activities, or to the social and political background. For example, out of the 100 pages devoted to the last ten years of the nineteenth century, only one paragraph was given to the A.R.P.S. and the Lands Bill agitation. He did, however, take the trouble to distinguish educated Africans from bogus 'scholars', and remarked that the former constituted 'an increasing, useful, and honourable section of the community on the Gold Coast'.[5]

So far there had been no attempt to meet the needs of the schools. In 1920 the Educationists' Committee proposed new readers and textbooks, and Guggisberg himself made a list of suggestions for infant and primary schools, on such subjects as local geography and history.[6] A useful aid to secondary school teachers was *A History of the Akan Peoples of the Gold Coast* (London, 1925), by the Rev. W. T. Balmer, a former headmaster of Mfantsipim. This

---

[1] In 1905 the examination for junior civil service clerkships included the following questions: 'Give a short account of the history of any castle or fort in the Gold Coast . . . What European countries have had settlements on the Gold Coast? Name the towns occupied by each at different times and if possible give the dates when they fell into the hands of the British.' *Departmental Reports*, Education, 1905.   [2] Ibid. 1910.
[3] Ibid. 1912.   [4] *The Gold Coast Nation*, 2 Sept. 1915.
[5] Vol. i, pp. 182–3, and vol. ii, p. 185.   [6] *Sessional Paper No. IV of 1919–20*.

was given a prefatory welcome for its 'notable impartiality' by the Secretary for Native Affairs: 'It is refreshing to find an English writer at last saying a good word for the Fantis.' He considered the book particularly opportune 'at the present rather critical moment in the growth of a national consciousness in the people of the Gold Coast'. Balmer himself wrote: 'The goal for which one should hope and strive is surely that these people be moulded into a real unity.' Not even the most fervent nationalist could have quarrelled with the Hegelian words he quoted in his preface: 'It will always make for better history to generalise the soul of a people and regard it as a uniform striving towards self-realisation amid continual change of circumstance, than to detail the endless circumstances without reference to the controlling purpose that utilises or resists them.'

But national sentiment could hardly be satisfied with a history written almost entirely by foreigners. Africans were less interested in the quality of the research than in the attitude of the writer; they did not like to be called 'these people', and they resented the general impression of the Gold Coast as simply 'the land of fever, palm oil and trade rum'.[1] They particularly resented the failure to give due weight to African tradition. As J. C. de Graft Johnson put it, 'any people who disregard their customs and ignore their past history will soon cease to be a people'.[2]

The first African attempts to introduce school-children to their own national history were not made until shortly after the First World War. The Rev. J. B. Anaman's two small booklets of *Simple Stories from Gold Coast History* (Cape Coast, 1919) were commented upon favourably by the local newspapers,[3] and soon afterwards E. J. P. Brown started to write his two-volume *Gold Coast and Asianti Reader* (London, 1929). This miscellany, dedicated to the A.R.P.S., consisted of a brief outline of the Gold Coast and Ashanti 'from the earliest times to the Early Native States of the eighteenth century', with brief stories from traditional history. A closer view of the history of one State was given by J. B. Danquah in the course of his *Akim Abuakwa Handbook* (London, 1928). The local historical material was, however, related to the wider story of the development of the Akan people, whose 'fine political institutions' were regarded as a legitimate source of national pride. The book occasionally reveals a tendency towards conjecture and wishful thinking: 'From 1742 till 1822 these inter-tribal wars disturbed the desirable peace that otherwise could have enabled the Akan people to develop the noble arts of peace: to invent writing, to create a high religion, to institute schools, and to build roads and townships' (p. 19). Such statements were, however, an inevitable reaction to the many disparaging accounts that had been produced by Europeans.

[1] A. B. Ellis, *West African Sketches* (London, 1881), p. 1.
[2] 'Interim Report of the Educationists' Committee, 1922', *Sessional Paper No. 1 of 1924–25*, evidence given on 3 Aug. 1922.   [3] For example, *The Gold Coast Nation*, 6–13 Dec. 1919.

About the same time, J. W. de Graft Johnson produced an *Historical Geography of the Gold Coast* (London, 1929), based on his teaching notes as headmaster of the Wesleyan School, Cape Coast, some ten years previously. He brought his history right up to date with four chapters on 'The Nationalist Movement' (perhaps the first public use of the phrase by a Gold Coast African), which dealt with such items as the Fanti Bond of 1844, the Poll Tax, the 1865 Parliamentary Committee, the Fanti Confederation, the A.R.P.S., and the National Congress of British West Africa.[1] It is noteworthy that the book included one short chapter on 'The Protectorate of the Northern Territories'; little was then known about the region, although a few tribal histories had been published in English in the 1920's.[2] But de Graft Johnson was more concerned with his politically conscious readers than with the tribes of the hinterland. He offered a clear challenge to the future:

The leaders [of the National Congress] knew that without a strenuous and serious fight no political good would ever accrue to the people. England did not obtain her present form of government by the mere asking. King John did not beam with smiles and congratulate himself over his gracious act when he signed the Magna Charta.[3]

Thus de Graft Johnson subscribed to the belief of his elder brother that 'it is a far greater pleasure helping to build up a tradition than being obliged to live on the memory of one'.[4] But the desire to explore and re-create the past remained strong. As a leading West African historian has more recently pointed out: 'Every nation builds its future on its past; so the African must not only instinctively have faith in his own inheritance, but must also satisfy himself by scientific inquiry that it exists. West African history remains largely unexplored.'[5] The feeling persists that it is West Africans who have to undertake their own explorations.

Colony–Ashanti Rapprochement

Well into the twentieth century the revival of interest in the past was largely Fanti in origin, though it brought members of various Colony tribes to realize their common meeting-points of history and culture. Meanwhile, both the improvement of communications and the centralization of British administration made it easier to think of the Colony as a unit. The newspapers also played an important part. As early as 17 November 1877 *The Gold Coast*

---

[1] An interesting contrast to the official examination questions of 1905, quoted above, is afforded by de Graft Johnson's topics for discussion, presumably based on his own class work. For example: 'What steps has the Government taken to meet the legitimate aspirations of the people as interpreted by the Congress?... Mention the chief causes of misgovernment that led to the creation of the Fanti Confederation.' *Historical Geography*, pp. 207 and 225.

[2] For example, three brief Hausa manuscripts translated by J. Withers Gill: *A Short History of Salaga* (Accra, 1924), *A Short History of the Dagomba Tribe* (Accra, n.d.), and *The Moshi Tribe. A Short History* (Accra, 1924).   [3] *Historical Geography*, p. 220.

[4] J. C. de Graft Johnson, 'The Significance of some Akan Titles', in *The Gold Coast Review* (Accra, 1926), vol. ii, no. 2.

[5] Professor K. O. Diké, 'African History and Self-Government', in *West Africa*, 28 Feb. 1953.

Times invited its readers to send in items of local news: 'Is there an event of general interest taking place in your neighbourhood? . . . Thus you will be instrumental in knitting in closer union the various portions of the Colony'. But even such advocates of unity scarcely looked beyond the boundaries of the Colony. The old fear and bitterness between the coastal tribes and the Ashantis was a difficult kernel to crack. The first steps towards a common nationality were, of course, taken not when Ashanti and the Colony became united under the British flag, but when Africans began to think of themselves as one.

There were a few straws in the wind, even during the nineteenth century. A correspondent from Anomabu commented prophetically on the end of the Ashanti war in 1874: 'Providence will yet make the whole Gold Coast, with Ashantees, &c., one country under the British Government; one flag, all brothers—only the wild King to be locked up, and let the people rest.'[1] In 1882 *The Gold Coast Times* commenced to serialize a long article on the 'Future of the Gold Coast', in the course of which it was suggested that Ashanti could fairly be called a Gold Coast country; apart from certain local 'peculiarities', both nations spoke a common language, and sprang from 'one and the same stock or progenitor'.[2] The 'whiteman' was blamed for the loss of African unity; he had found a united people, ruled by their own princes, and had seen that 'to effect his wicked design he must separate them from each other'.[3] In 1895 *The Gold Coast Chronicle* looked forward a little more truculently to the time 'When we have once annexed Ashantee'.[4] The ideal of unity remained, although it now involved a conquered neighbour.

It was Casely Hayford who in 1903, shortly after the annexation, gave this ideal its finest expression. He asked: 'Shall the Ashantis be treated as a conquered people, or as friends and allies? This will be . . . the true test of statesmanship.' He ridiculed the idea that they were 'a barbarous, bloodthirsty people, whose only lot is to be gradually wiped off the face of the earth'. His own answer was clear. The only realistic aim could be 'a prosperous and contented federal Gold Coast and Ashanti'; and this meant

nothing less than the fusion of the Fantis and the Ashantis into one people. Remember that by language, traditions, customs, and laws, they are practically one people. Remember that they are cousins, and that in remote times they lived together in brotherly unity and concord at Takiman, until one day they quarrelled and split . . . when you have two peoples so nearly related as to be, in fact, one people, welded together by a common language, by common customs, common laws, common aims, hopes, and aspirations, it is madness to try and keep them separate.

But the task of bringing about 'this long-wished-for-union' he reserved for the educated African rather than the 'foreign intermeddler'.[5]

---

[1] Letter from John Hammond; *The African Times*, 30 Apr. 1874.
[2] Ibid. 20 May 1882. [3] Ibid. 3 June 1882. [4] 12 Dec. 1895.
[5] Casely Hayford, *Gold Coast Native Institutions*, pp. 131, 241, and 249–50.

Casely Hayford remained a tireless advocate of a united Gold Coast and Ashanti. He even suggested that his proposed national university should be centred on Kumasi, so as to be 'far beyond the reach of the influence of the coast'.[1] But his contemporaries did not immediately respond to this call for unity. Meanwhile, the administration of Ashanti was kept separate from the Colony; and in spite of the opening of the Sekondi–Kumasi railway in 1903, there was little intercommunication of ideas. Even in 1915 *The Gold Coast Nation* found it necessary to apologize for occasional references to affairs in Ashanti; evidently some readers in Cape Coast had criticized the paper for 'overstepping the boundary'.[2]

As a member of the Legislative Council, Casely Hayford lost no opportunity to recur to this favourite theme;[3] but the Council was precluded from discussing Ashanti affairs directly. In 1919 Clifford was impressed by the divisions between the Colony and Ashanti, and within the Colony itself, rather than by their national unity:

> The Gold Coast and Ashanti . . . could not be regarded as a single State . . . Even in the Fanti country many of the peoples were strangers to each other. At Cape Coast and Anamaboe, situated something like Somersetshire and Devonshire, the inhabitants regarded themselves as mutually strangers. Away from the Fanti country, in Ashanti, the difference was greater still; and in the eastern part and in the Volta the people were as widely separated as the French and Italians.[4]

But the epoch of which Clifford spoke was already passing. In the same year *The Gold Coast Independent* hoped that Guggisberg, the new Governor, would be able 'to incorporate Ashanti and the Northern Territories with the Gold Coast into one vast protectorate which should be developed together'. The extension of the railway to the north would be 'one of the greatest achievements of his government'.[5] The following year, the Chief Commissioner of Ashanti suggested that with the extension of railways and motor roads 'the amalgamation of the Gold Coast Colony with Ashanti, or vice versa, will soon become an issue of practical politics'.[6]

The very act of meeting and consulting together in the Legislative Council was encouraging some Chiefs, as well as the urban politicians, to look far beyond their tribal boundaries. For example, in 1921 Nana Ofori Atta of Akim Abuakwa spoke of his friendly relationship with the late Nana Amonoo V of Anomabu, and of how they had regarded their peoples as 'practically

---

[1] *Ethiopia Unbound*, p. 194.   [2] 26 Aug. 1915.

[3] For example, *Legislative Council Debates*, 31 Dec. 1918; commenting on the appointment of a travelling Judge in Ashanti, Casely Hayford expressed the hope that the Gold Coast and Ashanti soon would be 'amalgamated' and always would be 'as one politically and otherwise'.

[4] Clifford, Address at the Royal Colonial Institute; *West Africa*, 31 May 1919. Cf. his remarks about the Colony in 1918, and Nigeria in 1920, Ch. X, p. 390 n., above.

[5] *The Gold Coast Independent*, 18 Oct. 1919.

[6] Letter from C. H. Harper to Guggisberg, enclosed in his Confidential Dispatch of 1 Nov. 1920, to Milner; G.N. Archives.

brothers'.[1] Nana Amonoo had previously asked how soon the administration of Ashanti would be placed 'on the same level' as the Colony, 'in view ... of the fact that even the most backward child must grow somehow'; but the Colonial Secretary, although he repudiated the term 'backward child', said 'No change in the present system of administration is contemplated.'[2]

Soon the demand for the repatriation of Prempeh from the Seychelles became a matter of common concern in both Ashanti and the Colony, submerging if not destroying the old rivalry. Casely Hayford had been retained by the Ashanti Chiefs to prepare a petition for Prempeh's return in 1918;[3] and when the Secretary of State turned this down, the question was taken up on their behalf in the Legislative Council. Nana Ofori Atta argued that this would be an appropriate recognition of the part Ashanti had played in the recent war; although he had not been to Ashanti, he was certain that there would be no opposition to the return of Prempeh. E. J. P. Brown's supporting speech illustrated the remarkably charitable feeling of leading Fantis towards those who had once 'wantonly oppressed' their ancestors. He had visited Ashanti in 1910, being 'curious to see the place as well as the people who had sent invading armies to our country in years gone by', and he now believed that no uprising need be feared. But Prempeh should return only as a private individual: 'We do not ask that he be allowed to ... continue to reign over his people.'

Dr. B. W. Quartey-Papafio, a Gã, made the point which most appealed to all Africans, that Prempeh should be allowed to die in his own land. Casely Hayford, who knew Ashanti better than the other speakers, declared: 'I am quite certain that their desire to live in peace and harmony is as genuine as that of the Gold Coast people.' Guggisberg frankly admitted that these speeches had done more than anything else towards getting the question of Prempeh's repatriation considered. He thought that such remarks came extremely well from 'you who are not Ashantis'.[4] No immediate action was taken, but the African members continued to prod the Government in question and debate.[5]

When Prempeh was eventually allowed to return towards the end of 1924 —as a private citizen—the occasion was celebrated in the Colony in sympathy with the Ashantis.[6] In spite of official precautions, large crowds at Takoradi gave him an enthusiastic welcome,[7] and this was echoed in the Accra and

---

[1] *Legislative Council Debates*, 25 Apr. 1921.   [2] Ibid. 25 May 1920.

[3] 'Petition to the Secretary of State by certain Ashanti Chiefs Praying for the Return of ex-King Prempeh, and the Secretary of State's Reply thereto'; *Sessional Paper No. VIII of 1918–19.*

[4] *Legislative Council Debates*, 26 Nov. 1919.

[5] For example, Casely Hayford, ibid. 18 Oct. 1921; Nana Ofori Atta and others, ibid. 20 Mar. 1922, and 14 Dec. 1923.

[6] The return of Prempeh is dealt with from the Ashanti side in Ch. XII, pp. 479–85, above.

[7] *Departmental Reports*, Western Province, 1924–5. Contrast Claridge's description of Prempeh's arrival at Cape Coast as the prisoner of the British in 1896: 'For days ... people had been pouring into the town ... to see their once dreaded enemy ... As they caught sight of the hammocks with the prisoners, they set up a tremendous shout of mingled triumph and hate ...

Cape Coast press. *The Gold Coast Leader*, in an editorial on 'Nana Prempeh', expressed 'great relief and satisfaction', and urged that 'Ashanti must be fully opened up without delay and linked constitutionally with the Gold Coast'.[1] When Prempeh became Kumasihene in 1926, the same newspaper proclaimed 'the important truth that the Ashantees and the people of the Gold Coast are cousins . . . they are destined in the order of Providence to become welded together in one national unity and entity'.[2] Details of Ashanti affairs also began increasingly to enter the columns of coast newspapers; and in 1931, after Prempeh's death, there were many sympathetic articles and editorials.[3]

But during the 1920's there was no thought of a common political movement. The A.R.P.S. had always won most of their support from Fanti purists, while the Congress leaders were looking beyond the Gold Coast borders to the ideal of West African unity. In any case, travel up-country was still limited, and communications difficult; it was not until 1923 that Accra and Kumasi were linked by railway, and by a trunk telephone line. Even then, there were only a few educated leaders in Ashanti;[4] and intellectual contacts in either direction were not encouraged, to put it mildly, by the Government. The exclusion of barristers from Ashanti courts—which lasted until 1933, despite repeated protests[5]—was only one aspect of this cautious attitude.[6]

There was still a rigid administrative separation between Ashanti and the Colony. The Legislative Council was not allowed to deal with questions of administration in Ashanti or the Northern Territories;[7] and in 1929 the Colonial Secretary insisted that 'The constitution of Ashanti is as separate and distinct from that of the Gold Coast Colony as is, say, the constitution of Sierra Leone.'[8] This extreme claim prompted Casely Hayford to point out

Prempi was completely unnerved by his reception, and cowered back in his litter almost livid with fear. He could have no doubt what his fate would have been but for the strong escort that marched with fixed bayonets on each side of him.' *History*, vol. ii, p. 417.

[1] *The Gold Coast Leader*, 20 Dec. 1924.

[2] Ibid. 27 Nov. 1926. Cf. the report of a debate at the Literary and Social Club, Sekondi, on the question whether Prempeh should re-occupy the Ashanti stool; at the end, 'The whole house, including the members who had argued to the contrary, wholeheartedly voted for the AYES.' Ibid. 29 May 1926.

[3] For example, *West Africa Times*, 13 May 1931.

[4] There was as yet no secondary school in Kumasi, although Wesley College had just been founded for the training of teachers.

[5] For example, E. J. P. Brown, *Legislative Council Debates*, 22 Sept. 1922, and Casely Hayford, ibid. 26 Feb. 1930.

[6] A former Chief Commissioner wrote of Ashanti: 'One of the secrets of their present contented state may be ascribed to this rule.' F. Fuller, *A Vanished Dynasty: Ashanti* (London, 1921), p. 221. Cf. Ch. VIII, p. 325, above.

[7] M. Wight suggests that the restriction was not very irksome in practice, since in the following fifteen years only one member was ruled out of order for attempting to discuss these territories. *The Gold Coast Legislative Council* (London, 1947), pp. 195–6. But of course there is no record of the number who would have liked to discuss them.

[8] Colonial Secretary, *Legislative Council Debates*, 15 Feb. 1929.

its anomalous implications; he complained that members were required to approve the salaries of Ashanti officials, 'yet we are supposed not to have any voice in the Administration'. He then went on to make an important suggestion, for the first time in the Legislative Council, although he had probably been responsible for earlier editorials on the subject.[1] 'The time has come when Ashanti should be represented on this Council . . . so that we may get the information where necessary, and we might also be able to criticise where necessary.'[2] This request was repeated a year later by Nana Ofori Atta, and on that occasion Casely Hayford stressed the developments which had taken place; he saw 'very little difference' between the outlook of life in the Colony and Ashanti.[3] This new approach was to lead to the formation of several joint economic, political, and cultural movements during the 1930's,[4] although Ashanti representation on the Legislative Council was not to be achieved until 1946.

The Isolation of the North

It was much more difficult for nationalist leaders to extend their political thinking to include the Northern Territories. There was no general awareness in the Colony of northern conditions and problems. The geographical features of the dry, orchard–savannah belt—so sharply distinct from the rain-forest area—and the physical conditions of life were sufficient to emphasize the isolation of the region. There was not even the sense of common origin, as among the Akans of Ashanti and much of the Colony. The traditional forms of social organization differed from those in the south, and among themselves, and had been less affected by outside influences. Since 1901 the Northern Territories had been legally as well as territorially attached to the Gold Coast, their trade had been directed towards the sea rather than the desert, they had been governed—at least on paper—from Accra, and they became subject to a similar pattern of British influence. Yet the northern peoples remained physically and psychologically remote; they were in the Gold Coast and yet not of it.

The circumstances in which British influence had been extended over the north encouraged officials to regard it as a 'hinterland' rather than as a component part of the Gold Coast in its own right. The innate poverty of the area and the difficulties of communication offered no immediate returns for Government expenditure; the general policy, foreshadowed by Sir Frederic Hodgson in 1899, seems to have been based mainly on the text 'Unto him that hath . . .':

I cannot too strongly urge the employment of all the available resources of the Government upon the development of the country south of Kintampo . . . I would

---

[1] For example, The Gold Coast Leader, 27 Nov. 1926, and 8 Aug. 1928.
[2] Casely Hayford, Legislative Council Debates, 25 Feb. 1929.
[3] Ibid. 26 Feb. 1930.
[4] For example, the Gold Coast and Ashanti Cocoa Federation of 1930–1, the Central National Committee of 1934, and the Youth Conference.

not at present spend upon the Northern Territories—upon in fact the hinterland of the Colony—a single penny more than is absolutely necessary for their suitable administration and the encouragement of the transit trade.[1]

This penny-wise attitude persisted for many years. In 1912, for example, another Governor, J. J. Thorburn, said, 'until the Colony and Ashanti have been thoroughly opened up and developed, the Northern Territories must be content to await their turn', and any extensive programme designed to render the area more accessible 'must be suffered to stand over' for a long time to come.[2] The outbreak of the First World War made matters worse; the Chief Commissioner was instructed that 'the object of Government in the immediate future must be to reduce not to increase expenditure especially in the Northern Territories'.[3]

More serious than this deliberate official neglect was the lack of exploitable resources which might have attracted private enterprise in the same way as the gold mines and cocoa farms of the Colony and Ashanti. As a result the north, historically an important source of slaves, became in the twentieth century a large-scale supplier of migrant labour to the other regions, contributing substantially to their increasing wealth at the expense of social unbalance in the home villages deprived of their menfolk.[4] By 1918 the old men, especially in the extreme north, were reported to be more than ever intolerant and reactionary, and to dislike their young men coming into contact with civilization.[5] Nevertheless, they were fighting a losing battle; the forces of change, including roads, schools, and the insistent demand for labour in the south, were to prove too strong for them.

It might be supposed that the way in which British authority had been extended piecemeal, in successive stages, over the whole country, was the explanation of the uneven pace of economic and social development. The north, however, came under colonial rule at almost exactly the same time as Ashanti; in neither area had the British acquired any direct influence before the 1890's, and the simultaneous Orders in Council of 1901 were precipitated mainly by the developments of the preceding five years. Yet it was the Northern Territories, far more than Ashanti, that lagged behind the rate of advance of the rest of the country. More important than their date of acquisition was their distance from the coast, from the long-established European trading stations, from the disturbing influences of urbanization and commercialization, while their deliberate isolation from mission education helped to delay there the modern political challenge to the old social order. The disparity between north and south became increasingly marked over the years.

[1] Confidential Dispatch of 20 Dec. 1899, from Hodgson to Chamberlain; CO/96/346.
[2] J. J. Thorburn, quoted in *Departmental Reports*, Northern Territories, 1912.
[3] Letter of 4 Nov. 1914, from Colonial Secretary to Chief Commissioner; 1953 Acc. No. 1303, G.N. Archives.   [4] Ch. I, pp. 41–43, above.
[5] *Departmental Reports*, Northern Territories, 1918.

From the beginning of British administration, all clerical and skilled work had been done by 'foreigners' from the south; but this only served to emphasize the relative backwardness of the north, and these stations remained very unpopular among African civil servants. As early as 1898 they were applying for transfers back to the coast, and the following year field allowances of 30s. per month had to be paid to them as a special inducement. One grievance was the lack of any fixed term of service 'abroad';[1] and although there was some intermarriage with northern women, the little colony must have lived like expatriates, with their own amusements and church services, few of them speaking the local languages.[2] In 1913 the Twi-speaking community at Tamale, then numbering over fifty, formed a kind of friendly society, 'The Foreigners' Arbitration', to hear their own petty cases and to charge fees and fines, in order to avoid being summoned before local Chiefs; but official recognition was refused.[3] The imported craftsmen, for their part, felt no common interest with their fellow workers in the north; in 1914, for the first time, eleven local apprentice masons were employed by the Public Works Department, but they made little progress, since the coast mason was said to be 'in no hurry to impart his knowledge to those who might oust him and his fellows eventually from their jobs'.[4]

Local officials were increasingly anxious to avoid any infiltration of dangerously progressive ideas from the south. As Thorburn himself had noted, the inhabitants of the Northern Territories were 'much more easy to deal with than their compatriots on the coast. They willingly make the most excellent roads, culverts and resthouses for small "dashes".'[5] In 1914 the Chief Commissioner urged his officers to be particularly careful to observe the letter of the law in their courts, reminding them that only the previous year the Secretary of State had suggested that lawyers should be admitted to practise before the courts of Ashanti and the Northern Territories; and that it had only been dropped as a result of the Governor's strong insistence that 'such action would be speedily fatal to the social and economic well-being of the native population'.[6] Sometimes it seemed that British 'protection' was interpreted simply as a jealous defence of the *status quo*.

This was particularly true of educational policy, elsewhere such a potent

[1] Ibid. 1899.

[2] An exception was E. F. Tamakloe, a clerk in Yendi, who had commenced service as a second-class warder. He took the trouble to pass an examination in a local language (intended for Political Officers), and later produced *A Brief History of the Dagbamba People* (Accra, 1931), recording the drum history he had heard. A. W. Cardinall's *Tales Told in Togoland* (London, 1931), included a chapter by Tamakloe on the mythical and traditional history of Dagomba.

[3] Letter of 21 Oct. 1913, from Chief Commissioner to Colonial Secretary, and enclosed petition; 1953 Acc. No. 1301, G.N. Archives.

[4] Letter of 19 Feb. 1914, from Armitage to Colonial Secretary; ibid.

[5] Dispatch No. 380 of 6 June 1912, from Thorburn to Harcourt; 1953 Acc. No. 1390, Case 74/1915, G.N. Archives.

[6] Letter of 16 Apr. 1914, from Chief Commissioner to outstations; 1953 Acc. No. 1302, G.N. Archives.

catalyst of social change.[1] Here, the isolationist policies of Tamale officials, who kept the missionaries at bay as long as they could, meant a protracted delay in the emergence of an indigenous educated *élite*. Meanwhile, Gold Coast political leaders showed little interest in the problems of the Northern Territories, and often it seemed that their mental frontiers were drawn just north of Kumasi. (Few of them had travelled even as far as that, to see the country for themselves.) In 1918 E. J. P. Brown, for example, suggested some retrenchment of expenditure in the Northern Territories; but the Government refused to agree that the area was a financial drain upon the Colony.[2]

In 1927, however, *The Gold Coast Leader* criticized the artificial separation of the country into three administrations, and suggested that the differences between the Gold Coast, Ashanti, and the Northern Territories were 'practically the same' as between the Eastern, Central, and Western Provinces of the Colony.[3] The editor went so far as to say: 'The people of the Northern Territories are now considered the people of the Gold Coast. In any case they form a dependency of this country, and it is our concern to safeguard their interests.'[4] The occasion for this protestation was the Northern Territories Land and Native Rights Ordinance, which had been enacted without reference to the Legislative Council, although it was alleged to be as harmful to African interests as the 1897 Lands Bill.

There was still no constitutional method whereby Northern Territories affairs could be publicly debated.[5] It was not until 1934 that the Chief Commissioner was made a member of the Executive Council, and the Legislative Council was given power to legislate for the Colony, Ashanti, and the Northern Territories as if they were a single territory.[6] This provided an opportunity for some discussion of national affairs, although the north was not directly represented until 1946, when the Chief Commissioner entered the new Legislative Council on behalf of the inhabitants.[7] The first—nominated—northerners took their seats only in 1950; indirect elections were held the following year, direct elections not till 1954. This relatively late constitutional evolution meant that the potential internal stresses that had been building up during the years of social and economic isolation found an outlet only during the last few years of colonial dependence. This added yet a further complication to the problems of achieving national unity.

[1] See Ch. III, pp. 138–40, above.   [2] *Legislative Council Debates*, 29 Oct. 1918.
[3] *The Gold Coast Leader*, 19 Nov. 1927.   [4] Ibid. 24 Dec. 1927.
[5] K. A. Korsah was once ruled out of order for attempting to discuss the Northern Territories Native Rights Ordinance. *Legislative Council Debates*, 8 Mar. 1932.
[6] The Northern Territories Order in Council of 1934, and Additional Instructions of 23 Nov. 1934.
[7] This advance was more apparent than real, since he did not take part in any of the debates. The first time any voice from the north was heard in the Legislative Council was in 1949, when the then Chief Commissioner said: 'My predecessor in office and I have sat in this Chamber for nearly four years; but owing to the peculiar constitutional position of the Protectorate, ours has largely been an inarticulate role.' E. Norton Jones, *Legislative Council Debates*, 13 Dec. 1949.

'African' Consciousness

The gradual extension of 'national' thinking to include Ashanti and the Northern Territories and the breaking down of the old regional barriers of ignorance and fear coincided with an awakening of pride in things African. The very words 'Africa' and 'African' were originally the terminology of those who looked at the continent from outside. It was only after several centuries of European contact with the Gold Coast that any of the inhabitants began to think of themselves as Africans. Up to about the middle of the nineteenth century, neither race nor colour seems to have been regarded as important in the Gold Coast; they were certainly no barrier to social intercourse among the merchants, and since many Africans adopted European names it is sometimes impossible to tell from the records which they were.

But gradually, as more Europeans came to live and work on the coast, they began to take for granted certain African characteristics as being due to innate differences and inequalities.[1] Dr. J. A. B. Horton was the first West African who felt it necessary to challenge, seriously and publicly, the widespread belief in the natural inferiority of Africans. In 1868, while in the Gold Coast, he published *A Vindication of the African Race*; and it is interesting to notice the use he made of European witnesses for the defence, such as Dr. R. R. Madden and other humanitarians and anti-slavers. Horton argued that 'the natural tendency of the now civilised European was exactly the same as the natural tendency of the now uncivilised African', whom he compared with the ancient Briton. In two of his chapters he attacked the 'False Theories of Modern Anthropologists', and as a surgeon gave 'Some Anatomical Accounts of Negro Physique'. His main thesis was 'The Progressive Advancement of the Negro Race under Civilizing Influence', and he evoked the past in terms of which his readers in the Gold Coast could be proud:

Africa, in ages past, was the nursery of science and literature; from thence they were taught in Greece and Rome, so that it was said that the ancient Greeks represented their favourite goddess of Wisdom—Minerva—as an African princess . . . Origen, Tertullian, Augustin, Clemens Alexandrinus, and Cyril, who were fathers and writers of the Primitive Church, were tawny African bishops of Apostolic renown. Many eminent writers and historians agree that these ancient Ethiopians were negroes, but many deny that this was the case . . . Herodotus describes them as '*woolly-haired blacks, with projecting lips*'[2] . . . And why should not the same race who governed Egypt . . . who had her churches, her universities, and her

---

[1] One of the members of the 1865 parliamentary inquiry in London persisted in asking such questions as: 'So that physically and morally your knowledge of the negro would not induce you to say that he was an inferior animal altogether to the white man?' *Report from the Select Committee on Africa* (*Western Coast*) (London, 1865), question 4,832 by Cheetham.

[2] Clemens Alexandrinus was a Greek; the others may well have been of North African birth or descent. But Horton—like some later nationalists who equate 'African' with 'Negro'—here ignores Herodotus' fundamental distinction between the two indigenous races of Africa, namely the Libyans (or Berbers) and the Ethiopians (or Negroes).

repositories of learning and science, once more stand on their legs and endeavour to raise their characters in the scale of the civilised world?[1]

But the work of Dr. E. W. Blyden, from the 1870's onwards, had a much greater influence on West African nationalist thought, especially in Sierra Leone and Nigeria.[2] Some early articles were republished in his major work, *Christianity, Islam and the Negro Race* (London, 1887), which like his pamphlet, *West Africa Before Europe* (London, 1905), became the treasured property of several influential Gold Coast families. Casely Hayford, who wrote an introduction to the latter, subsequently paid tribute to Blyden's efforts 'to reveal everywhere the African unto himself . . . to lead him back into self-respect' and to restore him to 'his true place in creation upon natural and national lines'.[3]

European prejudices, once formed, were slow to change. The work of A. B. Ellis illustrates well the common assumptions of the time about 'the ordinary characteristics of the uncivilized negro':

In early life they evince a degree of intelligence which, compared with that of the European child, appears precocious; and they acquire knowledge with facility till they arrive at the age of puberty, when the physical nature masters the intellect, and frequently completely deadens it. This peculiarity, which has been observed amongst others of what are termed the lower races, has been attributed by some physiologists to the early closing of the sutures of the cranium . . . They can imitate, but they cannot invent, or even apply. They constantly fail to grasp and generalize a notion.[4]

But Ellis also conceded that 'the Caucasian', in similar circumstances, would have been unlikely to reach unaided 'that higher state of civilization from which he now complacently regards the Negro'.[5] Other writers were more extreme and more explicit, even those who claimed to support African interests. The early views of Sir Harry Johnston, a noted campaigner against the cruelties of the slave trade, read strangely today:

the Negro in a primitive state is a born slave. He is possessed of great physical strength, docility, cheerfulness of disposition, a short memory for sorrows and cruelties, and an easily aroused gratitude . . . He does not suffer from homesickness to the over-bearing extent that afflicts other peoples torn from their homes, and, provided he is well fed, he is easily made happy . . . Abominable as the slave trade

[1] Horton, *West African Countries and Peoples . . . and a Vindication of the African Race*, pp. 66–67. Most of these examples and some of the very phrases were probably taken direct from Wilson Armistead's remarkable book, *A Tribute for the Negro: being a Vindication of the Moral, Intellectual and Religious Capabilities of the Coloured Portion of Mankind* (Manchester, 1848). This had, embossed in gold on the cover, the device of the Anti-Slavery Society: a picture of a chained Negro between two palm trees, with the motto, 'Am I not a Man and a Brother'.

[2] See Ch. III, p. 154 n., above. See also Coleman, *Nigeria*, pp. 183–4, and J. D. Hargreaves, *A Life of Sir Samuel Lewis* (Oxford, 1958), pp. 48–50.

[3] Casely Hayford, *Ethiopia Unbound*, pp. 161–6.

[4] *The Ewe-Speaking Peoples of the Slave Coast of West Africa* (London, 1890), pp. 9–10.

[5] *The Tschi-Speaking Peoples of the Gold Coast of West Africa* (London, 1887), p. 8.

has been . . . there is an underlying sense of justice. The White and Yellow peoples have been the unconscious agents of the Power behind Nature in punishing the negro for his lazy backwardness.[1]

Educated Africans were only too anxious to refute such beliefs; but their first task was to convince their own people of the possibilities of advancement. It was Casely Hayford who first started to recall the achievements of outstanding Gold Coast men for the specific purpose of fostering racial and national pride.[2] In 1896 he wrote an appreciation of the life of Hendrick Vroom for *The Gold Coast Independent*, adding this explanation: 'Why do I recount these facts? It is that I may take the liberty of adding another name to the catalogue of great characters that the West Coast of Africa has, can, and will produce. The future of the West African races is sure: they will be a people yet, all pessimistic criticism notwithstanding.'[3] A year later, Casely Hayford followed this up with an account of the life of George Ferguson in *The Gold Coast Chronicle*: 'Once more I take up my self-constituted task of drawing public attention to the careers of distinguished sons of the soil.'[4] In 1898 *The Gold Coast Aborigines* began to publish a series of 'Sketches of the Lives and Labours of our Great Men'.

In 1905 Attoh Ahuma published his *Memoirs of West African Celebrities*, turning, as Horton had done before him, to Wilson Armistead's *Tribute for the Negro*.[5] He drew heavily upon this for the biographies of 'Nineteen Representative Men of culture and renown' who had had some connexion with West Africa, especially the Gold Coast: including Christian Protten of Christiansborg, Philip Quaque of Cape Coast, Attobah Cugoano of Ajumaku, and Anthony William Amo of Axim—the latter a scholar who in the early eighteenth century was made a Doctor of the University of Wittenberg and a Counsellor of State by the Court of Berlin.

These and other West Africans were to acquire a rather shadowy status as national heroes in the Gold Coast mainly as a result of Attoh Ahuma's glowing tributes.[6] He claimed that he had by no means exhausted the list of

---

[1] This is an extract from *A History of the Colonization of Africa by Alien Races* (Cambridge, 1899, 2nd edn. 1913), pp. 151–2. In later years Johnston strongly attacked the theory of white supremacy, and admitted the justice of the African demand for 'a voice in their own taxation and government'. See R. Oliver, *Sir Harry Johnston and the Scramble for Africa* (London, 1957), pp. 351–3.

[2] Some early newspapers had occasionally featured detailed obituaries of leading Africans; e.g. of the Rev. Timothy Laing, b. 1824, in *The Gold Coast Times*, 11 Feb. 1882.

[3] 13 June 1896.   [4] 12 June 1897.

[5] Attoh Ahuma also claimed Abbé Grégoire, *De la littérature des Nègres, ou recherches sur leurs facultés intellectuelles, leurs qualités morales, et leur littérature* (Paris, 1808), as one of his major sources. But nearly all his material came directly from Wilson Armistead, who had drawn extensively on Abbé Grégoire's book, and had noted that this was a 'scarce volume', even in 1848; it seems unlikely that Attoh Ahuma had seen it himself.

[6] For example, E. J. P. Brown gave brief biographies of several of them in his *Gold Coast and Asianti Reader* (London, 1929), bk. ii, pt. iv. Similarly, Nana Annor Adjaye added 'Biographical Sketches of Two Prominent Africans' as app. G to his *Nzima Land* (London, 1931).

'these intellectual giants—sons of Africa—who held their own in Europe and America' in the eighteenth century; but that owing to 'the arbitrary and gratuitous custom of foistering foreign and fanciful names upon our people' it had been impossible to identify them all. He was quite certain, however, that all his 'shining lights' were men of Guinea, 'and that in the land of bondage they successfully vindicated the moral, intellectual and religious capabilities of their race'.[1] Attoh Ahuma's declared purpose was 'to foster in the minds of the young an ardent affection for our motherland, and an intelligent appreciation of her history and destiny. In other words, to lift up our protest and awaken a passionate patriotism, if possible, in the breasts of our fellow-country-men.'[2]

Another strand in twentieth-century African thought was the increasing objection taken to the use of the word 'native'. Mensah Sarbah was one of the first Gold Coast writers, in 1906, to point out that he had deliberately avoided the term; and he quoted an amusing case from his own experience, when he had been examining a European mining expert in the Concessions Court at Axim:

After he had spoken of *native* bush-path, *native* canoe, *native* river, *native* mines, and *native* gold, I asked him to explain to the Court, in what respects *native* gold and the other *native* things particularly differed from those found in other parts of the world, but he could not; for the absurdity of always describing in Africa everything non-European as *native* had dawned on him by that time.[3]

The Gold Coast Nation, commenting in 1914 on 'a much vexed question', suggested that 'the use of the word "Native" in substitution for "African" is bad taste and should be discontinued'.[4] After the war, *The Gold Coast Leader* emphasized the unpleasant associations:

The term 'Native' is a term of exploitation and usurpation. The meaning of the word as applied by the European to the African is—Native: primitive, backward, undeveloped, uncivilised ... If you are speaking of the Gold Coast man, say Gold Coaster, the Fanti man, the Gã man ... Africans consider the word 'Native' as applied to them as an insult; a concerted action on the part of the African press is necessary. In the meanwhile, it is for the Africans to abolish the word amongst themselves before they can succeed anywhere.[5]

[1] Cf. W. H. Ferris, *The African Abroad* (New York, 1913), vol. ii, p. 923: 'Every distinguished colored man sheds the lustre of his achievements over the entire colored race'. His 'Forty Greatest Negroes in History' were headed by Toussaint L'Ouverture of Haiti, whom he ranked with Cromwell and Napoleon as a general, and with Washington and Lincoln as a statesman.
[2] *Memoirs of West African Celebrities*, preface.
[3] *Fanti National Constitution*, p. x.
[4] 3–10 Dec. 1914.
[5] Quoted in *West Africa*, 4 Jan. 1919. This periodical had already suggested that the Colonial Office should make 'a beginning by abolishing, so far as official documents are concerned, the use of the word "native" in its present connotation ... we could refer to him as an African without giving ourselves too much mental trouble, surely?' Ibid. 6 July 1918.

Casely Hayford, when sitting on a government committee in 1920, pointed out that the word 'native' was often strictly inaccurate, and was considered by Africans a slur on their race. A minority recommended that the word 'African' should be used consistently instead of 'native' in the committee's report, 'and that the alteration be preserved and observed in the Civil Service and in all Government publications'.[1]

Originally a neutral, factual term, 'African' soon acquired its own emotional overtones. It became increasingly preferred to 'Negro'. At the inaugural meeting of the African Progress Union in London early in 1919, one speaker was reported as saying:

I am an African, and I am proud of it, and I take exception to the term 'Negro' or the term 'nigger' being applied to me. Why do I take exception? Negro, philologically is incorrect . . . No other race in the world has ever been described by colour . . . You are all aware of the fact that the term 'Negro' means black . . . I take exception to the term 'Negro'.[2]

'Negro' was, of course, standard usage in the United States, where coloured people had long been struggling for racial equality and respect.[3] Negro American nationalism was an important influence in widening West African horizons during the twentieth century. The foundation of the A.M.E. Zion Church of the Gold Coast in 1898 provided some early transatlantic contacts, including the first opportunities for further studies in the United States;[4] a new world of Negro protests and activities was revealed. In 1911, the year of the A.R.P.S. Forest Bill deputation, the First Universal Races Congress was held in London, attended by several Negro American leaders.[5] By 1912 Casely Hayford was writing to Booker T. Washington at Tuskegee, who was then considering how far methods used by Negroes in America might be appropriate for Africa. Soon there was a growing interest in 'Pan-African and 'Back to Africa' movements, on both sides of the Atlantic.[6]

An ambitious scheme for resettlement in the Gold Coast was mooted in 1912. Alfred C. Sam of Oklahoma issued a prospectus in the name of the Akim Trading Company, which claimed to 'own' twenty square miles of

---

[1] 'Report of Committee of Enquiry on the Native Civil Service', *Sessional Paper No. VII of 1920–21*. The views of the minority appear to have been quietly accepted: 'African Civil Service' was the title of *Sessional Paper No. I of 1922–23*.   [2] *West Africa*, 25 Jan. 1919.

[3] One small manifestation of this was the deliberate use of a capital 'N' for Negro, which soon found its way across the Atlantic. *The Gold Coast Leader*, 20 Nov. 1926, criticized a recent Colonial Office report for 'the spelling of the word Negro and Native with a small "n", which was felt to be 'offensive to educated Africans'. The capital letter was officially adopted by the *New York Times*, 7 Mar. 1930, as 'an act in recognition of racial self-respect for those who have been for generations in "the lower case"'. See A. Phelps Stokes and others, *Negro Status and Race Relations in the United States, 1911–1926* (New York, 1948), pp. 38–40: 'Changes in Usage as to Negro Terminology and Courtesy Titles affecting the Negro'.

[4] Cf. Ch. III, p. 163, above.

[5] G. Spiller (ed.), *Papers . . . Communicated to the Universal Races Congress* (London, 1911).

[6] See G. Shepperson, 'Notes on Negro American Influences on the Emergence of African Nationalism', in *The Journal of African History* (London, 1960), vol. i, no. 2.

West Africa, to be developed by joint Afro-American enterprise. Although the Gold Coast Government did its best to discourage several Negroes who wrote to inquire about their prospects, by 1914 Sam had collected 250 emigrants ready to sail for Africa, and had sold each of them a $25 share in return for a passage on the S.S. *Liberia*. The Colonial Office was now alarmed by a Reuter report of the proposed establishment of 'A Negro Kingdom on the Gold Coast of Africa by an Oklahoma Negro named Chief Sam'.[1] As a counter-measure, an Ordinance was enacted empowering the Governor to demand a £25 deposit from any immigrant not born in West Africa.[2]

The first reaction in the local press had been to pour cold water on the project; *The Gold Coast Leader*[3] had warned 'our American brethren who may be led away by Mr. Alfred C. Sam's rose-coloured scheme' of the difficulties of the climate and of competing with experienced Gold Coast farmers. But when the *Liberia* arrived off Cape Coast at the beginning of 1915, after many adventures and delays, *The Gold Coast Nation*[4] decided that the scheme had 'a national object . . . of immense uplifting force to this country', and welcomed the 'Afro-Americans' to 'the home of their ancestors'; they were personally greeted by the A.R.P.S. leaders. But the unexpected demand for deposits, combined with other practical difficulties, including claims by the Portuguese crew for arrears of pay, effectively punctured their inflated hopes of the promised land. After a short stay, the ship moved off towards Liberia.

Gold Coast intellectuals were taking an increasing interest in Negro leaders and movements in the United States. Dr. W. E. B. Du Bois, who founded the National Association for the Advancement of Colored People in 1910, had first attracted public notice by rejecting the 'old attitude of adjustment and submission' among Negro leaders. In particular, he advocated education of a high standard for the 'talented tenth' or *élite*, in place of Booker T. Washington's policy of mass agricultural and vocational training.[5] In 1900 he had attended a Pan-African conference called in London by H. Sylvester Williams, a barrister from Trinidad; those present included Alexander Walters, who in 1910 became the first A.M.E. Zion bishop to visit the Gold Coast.[6] In 1919, with the assistance of M. Blaise Diagne of Senegal, Du Bois organized his first Pan-African Congress in Paris, in order to bring 'all pressure possible on the Delegates at the Peace table in the interest of the coloured peoples of the United States and of the world, and to press the question of the internationalisation of the former German Colonies'.

[1] Reuter report of 26 Feb. 1914.
[2] *Government Gazette*, 11 Apr. 1914; also *Legislative Council Minutes*, 18 Mar. 1914.
[3] 31 Jan. 1914.   [4] 21 Jan. 1915.
[5] Du Bois also attacked Booker T. Washington's so-called Atlantic Compromise, which suggested that Negroes and white Americans could be 'as separate as the five fingers' in purely social matters, so long as they were united 'as one hand' in their material progress. *The Souls of Black Folk* (London, 1905 edn.), ch. iii.   [6] A. Walters, *My Life and Work* (New York, 1917), ch. xx.
[7] *West Africa*, 1 Feb. and 17 May 1919.

The Congress and its resolutions were fully reported in the West African press, and Du Bois is known to have been in touch with Casely Hayford concerning his subsequent plans. Three similar Pan-African Congresses were held during the 1920's, meeting in one European capital after another to secure maximum support from their colonial subjects: the second (1921) met in London, Brussels, and Paris, the third (1923) in London and Lisbon, and the fourth (1927) was held in New York. The movement received considerable publicity in the Gold Coast; some journalists criticized its 'lack of constructive and practical policy',[1] but Du Bois's leadership was destined to have a lasting influence. Gold Coast nationalists found that the Pan-African movement helped them to become aware of problems in other parts of the continent, and to acquire wider techniques of organization; and later they themselves were to take a prominent part.[2]

The most spectacular Negro leader of the post-war years was, of course, Marcus Garvey, a Jamaican who had spent two years in London just before the war, and had then returned home to found the Universal Negro Improvement Association. In 1916 he went to the United States and transformed the U.N.I.A. into a mass movement, which later sent resolutions to the Versailles Peace Conference—at the same time as those from the West African organizers of the embryonic National Congress.[3] *The Gold Coast Independent*, reporting these resolutions by 'Negro Africa and Negro America,' had no doubt about their meaning: 'Negro peoples throughout the world are demanding, not as a favour but as of right, their place among the Nations of the Earth . . . Any one who stands aloof in order to buy the whiteman's favour, betrays his country.' (1–8 March 1919.) Two years later the same Accra newspaper hailed Garvey's U.N.I.A. as the 'most potent organisation in the United States'.[4] It was said to have grown within four years from thirteen members to a total strength of four million, with branches all over the world; in the Gold Coast, in Nigeria, and in Sierra Leone—'even in remote but oppressed South Africa'.

The charismatic appeal of Garvey was to the masses, rather than the intellectuals; and by stressing the superiority of a black skin and Negro features he even managed to depreciate the prestige of lighter-coloured leaders such as Booker T. Washington and Du Bois.[5] His campaign, in spite of its dependence on superficial bombast and showmanship, touched off a response among

[1] For example, *The Gold Coast Independent*, 22 Oct. 1921.
[2] The fifth Pan-African Congress was held in Manchester in 1945, and was attended by K. Nkrumah, J. S. Annan, J. Appiah, R. E. G. Armattoe, Ako Adjei, F. R. Kankam-Boadu, J. C. de Graft Johnson jun., Ashie Nikoi, B. Awoonor Renner, W. J. K. Mould, and E. Kurankyi-Taylor of the Gold Coast, as well as the still-active Du Bois. See G. Padmore (ed.), *History of the Pan-African Congress* (Manchester, 1946).
[3] Cf. Ch. X, p. 379, above.   [4] 22 Oct. 1921.
[5] Garvey's greatest asset was said to be his colour: 'unmistakably black with prominent Negroid features'. Cf. G. Padmore, *Pan-Africanism or Communism?* (London, 1956), pp. 88–89; also Wilson Record, 'The Negro Intellectual and Negro Nationalism', in *Social Forces* (Baltimore, 1954), vol. 33.

black people all over the world, not least in the colonies: 'Up, you Mighty Race', was a favourite theme. 'You can accomplish what you will. It is only a question of a few more years when Africa will be completely colonized by Negroes . . . No one knows when the hour of Africa's redemption cometh.'[1] The first international convention of U.N.I.A., in 1920, adopted a 'Declaration of Rights of the Negro Peoples of the World'.

Garvey did everything in the grand manner; he was elected Provisional President of Africa, and created a nobility with such titles as Earl of the Congo, Viscount of the Niger, and Knight of the Distinguished Service Order of Ashanti. He did not just send one ship to Africa, but founded a Black Star Line, and nearly succeeded in establishing a permanent settlement in Liberia.[2] His African Orthodox Church, founded in 1921, did not attract a large following, either in the United States or elsewhere;[3] but by depicting Christ as a Negro and the devil as white, it provoked sharp reactions on both sides. The fascinating details of Garvey's meteoric career cannot be told here;[4] but his impact was profound, especially his racial theories.

The Gold Coast Leader remarked pointedly of Garvey in 1926 that 'so forceful has he been in racial thought and endeavour that the only place for him was Atlanta gaol, if so be he might be silenced for the moment'.[5] The editor alleged that the Gold Coast authorities had placed an embargo on the free circulation of Garvey's *Philosophy and Opinions*, which ought to be widely read.[6] Casely Hayford considered that the U.N.I.A. had done more than any other agency to bring 'to the notice of world opinion the disabilities of the African race'.[7] The growth of colour consciousness in the Gold Coast owed much to 'this great Negro awakening', which according to *The Gold Coast Independent* brought into being 'not only those American National Organisations, but the National Congress of British West Africa . . . the West Indian Congress, the Grenadian Association, the Trinidad Delegation Committees, and last but not least the new life and activity of the Indian National Congress'.[8] This was written in 1921. For the first time, Gold Coast politicians were seeing themselves in some kind of world perspective.

New sources of information about the outside world were already reaching the country. Occasional copies of Du Bois's *The Crisis*, and later of Garvey's

---

[1] Quoted by Padmore, *Pan-Africanism or Communism?*, p. 95.

[2] J. A. Rogers, *World's Great Men of Color* (New York, 1946), vol. ii, p. 609.

[3] At least one congregation of this Church was established in the Gold Coast, at Larteh in 1936, under the title of *Abibipem*, 'The Thousands of Africa'.

[4] See Marcus Garvey, *Philosophy and Opinions* 'or, Africa for the Africans' (New York, 1923 and 1927), 2 vols.; also E. D. Cronon, *Black Moses* (Wisconsin, 1955).

[5] Garvey had been imprisoned for fraud in 1925, and was deported from the United States two years later.

[6] *The Gold Coast Leader*, 29 May 1926. A full-page advertisement of *Philosophy and Opinions* had described it as 'A Second Uncle Tom's Cabin with the Appeal of a Bunyan's Pilgrim's Progress'. Ibid. 27 Mar. 1926.

[7] *The Disabilities of Black Folk and their Treatment, with an Appeal to the Labour Party* (Accra, 1929).   [8] *The Gold Coast Independent*, 22 Oct. 1921.

The Negro World, found their way across the Atlantic. In London the weekly journal *West Africa* had been refounded in February 1917. This gave both commercial and political news and comments, mainly for the benefit of Europeans, who were often anxious to know 'what Africans think about them and their work';[1] but it also became the intelligent African's guide to current affairs. Extracts were published from British periodicals, parliamentary reports, society proceedings, and many other sources, if they were even remotely connected with West Africa. Articles from African newspapers were sometimes reprinted, and Gold Coast journalists often returned the compliment by reproducing extracts of interest to their own readers.

The direct impact of the war upon the Gold Coast was limited to the fortnight's campaign that led to the surrender of Togoland in 1914; more disturbing, however, were the uncertainties of international trade, the removal of the German missionaries, and the depletion of the civil service. Several thousand Africans were recruited for the forces overseas, and substantial contributions were raised at home for war funds.[2] Many thus became conscious for the first time of international problems; the effects were not comparable to those of the 1939–45 war, but the demand for equal status between the races was certainly encouraged by the sense of a common cause. As *The Gold Coast Independent*[3] put it, 'if they were good enough to fight and die in the Empire's cause, they were good enough . . . to have a share in the Government of their countries'. Sir Harry Johnston even suggested in 1919 that the defeat of Germany had shaken European domination in Africa, arousing a dormant nationalism, and stimulating 'the beginning of revolt against the white man's supremacy'.[4]

There was a notable revival of cultural nationalism during the war and post-war years. W. E. G. Sekyi gave much thought to the whole problem of the African brought up in an alien tradition, and published a significant series of articles on 'The Anglo-Fanti' during 1918. He described the process by which an African boy became gradually but almost irresistibly Europeanized and denationalized, in name, dress, and outlook, at school, games, chapel, and Sunday school; his marriage to a 'frock lady'; and his progressive

[1] *West Africa,* 8 Feb. 1919.

[2] Between 1914 and 1918 over 3,000 men of the Gold Coast Regiment—and more than 1,000 drivers—were dispatched abroad, mainly to the Cameroons and East Africa, where they served with Indian as well as white troops. Recruitment, which was still voluntary, was extended to Ashanti and the Colony, whereas before it had been confined to the north; a number of educated Africans volunteered for service abroad, including one barrister. See C. Lucas, *The Gold Coast and the War* (Oxford, 1920), and H. Clifford, *The Gold Coast Regiment in the East African Campaign* (London, 1920). For details of Gold Coast contributions to war funds, and the influence of President Wilson's doctrine of self-determination, see Ch. X, pp. 376 and 384–5, above.

[3] 22 Oct. 1921.

[4] H. H. Johnston, Address to the African Society, 28 Mar. 1919; *West Africa,* 5 Apr. 1919. Cf. Johnston's earlier warning that the Imperial Government must 'recognise and re-affirm' the rights of black citizens of the Empire, as soon as the war was over. *The Black Man's Part in the War* (London, 1917).

disillusionment in England and on his return home, 'grappling with a problem he cannot yet solve'. The crux of the matter was his renewed desire to live again as a Fanti, instead of as 'a black Englishman'; and in his environment this was a lost cause.[1]

The publication of these articles, and their careful editorial appraisal in *West Africa*,[2] heralded a more general change of outlook among Africans after the war. In 1919 the revival of tradition was sufficiently widespread for W. F. Hutchison to remark, on returning to the Gold Coast after an absence of over twenty years:

A promising sign is the interest taken by the rising generation in their Native language, history, customs, and institutions. In each town clubs have been formed by the young men for the study of these things ... The questions and the discussions which followed my addresses were marked by keen interest, intelligence, and ability. There is a healthy desire to advance along African lines.[3]

West Africa summed up the position on 3 December 1921: 'The day is past when it was supposed that by the simple process of teaching the African to read and write, to sing hymns, and to dress like an Englishman, he could be turned into a black Englishman.'[4]

Although the new 'African' consciousness could thus be expressed constructively, at the same time there was a good deal of bitterness below the surface. Susceptibilities were sharpened during the post-war years, both at home and abroad;[5] Africans began to resent incidents and feel slighted by behaviour that previously they would have accepted as normal from Europeans. For example, one Sunday morning in 1918, when Holy Trinity Church in Accra was crowded, several Africans were placed in a pew reserved for the Governor and his staff; whereupon the two European occupants stepped out, bowed before the altar, and left the Church. *The Gold Coast Independent*[6] reported this episode under the heading 'Officialism or Race Hatred', and commented: 'Surely small as the incident is, its import is great. The writing on some official wall is clear: Should not all West Africans sustain and cherish and build up themselves looking to tomorrow, educating their children to loyalty but resisting oppression!'[7]

---

[1] *West Africa*, from 25 May to 28 Sept. 1918. Sekyi himself tried to get the best of both worlds, for example concerning his name. He pointed out publicly that he was registered with the University of London, the Inner Temple, and the Council of Legal Education as William Essuman-Gwira Sekyi, and that he used the name Kobina Sekyi 'only where there is no need to indicate either my academic or my professional status'. Letter to *The Gold Coast Nation*, 24–31 Aug. 1918.

[2] 28 Sept. 1918.	[3] *West Africa*, 30 Aug. 1919.

[4] Sekyi continued his influential articles: notably a series on 'The Social System of the Peoples of the Gold Coast' in *The Gold Coast Nation* in 1918, and another in *The Gold Coast Times* in 1924, urging the abandonment of the outlook of the 'average whiteman'.

[5] European army officers invented an unfortunate (though affectionate) nickname for West African soldiers, and an article in *Blackwood's Magazine*, entitled 'The Apes at Sea', aroused particular resentment among educated Africans in London. *West Africa*, 6 July 1918.

[6] 16 Nov. 1918.

[7] Under the Holy Trinity Church Accra Ordinance of 1916, the six front pews were reserved

The same newspaper alleged on 11 January 1919 that the Governor and his advisers did not even know who were the leading African figures, apart from the favoured few admitted to dine at Government House; and that this ignorance was due to the 'gulf' which even in West Africa divided black from white. In the same year Casely Hayford raised in the Legislative Council several recent examples of colour discrimination, including the treatment of Africans returning home on board ship. He referred also to an ugly incident in Liverpool, when three Gold Coast Africans had been mobbed;[1] this had been reported in the local newspapers, which frequently took morbid notice of racial violence in the United States, especially lynchings.[2]

Against such a background, the racial theories of Garvey made a strong appeal; and their influence may be seen in a new tendency to single out for special praise those Gold Coast men who were of pure African descent. During the nineteenth century, when mulattoes (many of whom had had special educational advantages) played a leading part in Gold Coast life, it had been believed by some that their achievements were due mainly to the admixture of 'white' blood. Similar theories had been expressed in the United States. But in 1919 Dr. B. W. Quartey-Papafio, who had been the first Gold Coast doctor, was publicly described as 'a thorough Negro, not of the Booker-Washington type', but one like Bishop Crowther, Mensah Sarbah, E. W. Blyden, and Sir Samuel Lewis the lawyer, 'of whom no one dares to say that what they achieved in life was due to mixture of birth with the European race'.[3]

Gold Coast nationalists never accepted such extreme doctrines of racial purity as those propounded by Garvey; nor was racial tension so acute as it was in other parts of Africa, aggravated by problems of white settlement. But undercurrents of suspicion and distrust remained. In 1921 Guggisberg complained that the policies of the National Congress had intensified the bitterness and race consciousness revealed in the press;[4] and a few years later Sekyi took up an uncompromising attitude, at least on paper, in a series of newspaper articles on 'our White Friends', which were republished in *West Africa* during 1925. He gave warning that the white man, in the course of 'a natural transition from his abused position of superiority to the more normal and natural one of equality with other races', was becoming 'decidedly more unscrupulous'. Sekyi therefore suggested that friendship or close alliance with white men, especially officials, ought not to be encouraged.

for the Governor and other Europeans. (This was not repealed until 1958.) In 1911 Casely Hay-ford had complained of such petty discrimination as in the segregated cemetery at Sekondi: 'a path, thirty-six feet wide, was marked between the European and native cemeteries, and the former beautifully fenced in with money mostly contributed by the black folk.' *Ethiopia Unbound*, p. 84.   [1] *Legislative Council Debates*, 20 Oct. 1919.

[2] For example, *The Gold Coast Nation*, 5 July 1919, and *The Gold Coast Independent*, 18 Oct. 1919.

[3] Letter published in *West Africa*, 31 May 1919.

[4] See Ch. X, p. 395, above.

In complete contrast with this was J. E. K. Aggrey's ideal of racial co-operation, as expressed in his work at Achimota and in his famous simile of the black and white piano keys. Many of Aggrey's other sayings gained widespread currency:

> If I went to heaven, and God said, 'Aggrey, I am going to send you back, would you like to go as a white man?' I should reply, 'No, send me back as a black man, yes, completely black.' And if God should ask, 'Why?' I would reply, 'Because I have a work to do as a black man that no white man can do. Please send me back as black as you can make me.'[1]
>
> No first-class educated African wants to be a white man . . . Every educated Negro wants to be a first-class Negro, not a third-class European . . . The superiority complex is doing a tremendous lot of mischief in Africa.'
>
> I am proud of my colour: whoever is not proud of his colour is not fit to live.[2]

It is the more remarkable that Aggrey spent many years in America, and worked in the southern States, yet managed to avoid the bitterness characteristic of many African students returning from abroad. His eloquence and his international reputation did much to raise Africans' opinion of their own race and potentialities, and helped to encourage pride, rather than prejudice, in the matter of colour. But to some extent Aggrey's reputation stood higher among Europeans than among African politicians, who were less willing to compromise or co-operate.

Credit must also be given to Guggisberg for a certain improvement in race relations within the Gold Coast during the post-war decade. According to an African commentator: 'his white enemies call him the "Niggers' friend". . . . Have you not noticed the great change in the treatment you receive from Europeans out here today?'[3] After Guggisberg's death Glover-Addo recalled an episode which may be contrasted with the 1918 incident: 'in the service of the English Church Mission it was arranged that he should be the first to receive communion but when the time came he sat down in his pew and allowed the Africans to go first and then joined them. He thereby showed that in the presence of God all men are equal'.[4]

---

[1] Aggrey's vivid speeches did much to encourage the conscious rehabilitation of the word 'black', which had become so debased during the nineteenth century (see Ch. II, p. 89, above). Cf. a lecture entitled 'Thinking Black' by the first A.M.E. Zion resident Bishop in Cape Coast: 'I think of God as African; he loves black colour so . . . Black preachers who . . . invite black men to be washed "whiter than snow" are merely parrot-like, repeating stereotyped platitudes. The Bible has never once referred to sin as being black. It speaks of it as being like scarlet and crimson in colour.' *The Gold Coast Leader*, 12 June 1926.

[2] Quoted by E. W. Smith, *Aggrey of Africa* (London, 1929), pp. 2, 4, and 231. Contrast the extraordinary attitude taken up by J. Renner Maxwell, thirty years earlier; as 'a Negro of pure descent' he asked, 'Why is the Negro so despised? Let the truth be told. It is because he is ugly . . . uglier than the other races of mankind.' *The Negro Question, or Hints for the Physical Improvement of the Negro Race, with special reference to West Africa* (London, 1892), pp. 10 and 40.

[3] Pamphlet by Eldred Taylor (Accra, 1921).

[4] *Legislative Council Debates*, 19 June 1930.

A sense of African solidarity was already strong among the increasing number of students in London, and several organizations were active during the early post-war years. There was, for example, the Union of Students of African Descent, founded in 1917 to provide 'young men and women of African race and heritage, resident in London for educational purposes', with opportunities for social and intellectual contact. The Coterie of Friends, a club for 'young men of colour' from Africa, the West Indies, and America, was meeting in London during 1919; also the African Progress Union, an amalgamation of the Union of African Peoples and the Society of Peoples of African Origin.[1] West Africans had their own Gold Coast Students' Union and Nigerian Progress Union; an important step was taken when in 1925 these two were combined to form the nucleus of the West African Students' Union.[2]

W.A.S.U. set out to discuss all matters affecting West Africa 'educationally, commercially, economically and politically', and in particular to cooperate with the National Congress of British West Africa. The moving spirit—and the first Secretary—was Ladipo Solanke, a Nigerian, who received some assistance from Casely Hayford. J. B. Danquah was among the ten founder members; and an early President was E. O. Asafu-Adjaye from Kumasi, who asked rhetorically in the first issue of their magazine, 'Should West Africans Co-operate?'[3] It is no exaggeration to say that almost every Gold Coast politician of note who has studied in London since 1925 has held office in W.A.S.U. Its impact on the growth of nationalism has therefore been at one remove, as each generation of students returned; the increased racial awareness of these post-war years found its fullest expression in the Gold Coast during the 1930's.

Of some significance was the fact that in 1928 the Sixth World Congress in Moscow initiated a policy of encouraging Negro nationalism. Among those invited to the Soviet Union were two journalists who had been contributing to the Gold Coast press from Europe: George Padmore, a West Indian, and Wallace Johnson, a Sierra Leonean. Both of these were later to play an important part in arousing a more militant nationalism in the Gold Coast.[4]

But during the post-war decade the dominant influence was that of Casely Hayford, and although the problem of race and colour was never far from his mind, he did not use it as a political weapon within the Gold Coast. His speeches were notable for their lack of personal bitterness, in spite of his repeated denunciation of what he called 'African disabilities' from the platform of the National Congress. He reminded his audiences of their 'brethren

---

[1] *West Africa*, 1917–20 *passim*. [2] Ibid. 31 Oct. 1925.
[3] *WASU* (London, 1926), no. 1.
[4] Another sign of the new Soviet policy was the increasing number of publications reaching the Gold Coast from 1930 onwards which were considered seditious. The Colonial Secretary, introducing the 1934 'Sedition Bill', complained of those who were seeking 'to poison ... the relations between class and class, between race and race, between colour and colour'. *Legislative Council Debates*, 21 Mar. 1934.

in distress' in the four corners of the earth.[1] There must be 'an international feeling among all black folk', just as there was among white or yellow men; already (at the end of 1925) 'where two or three of our race are gathered together, the thought uppermost in their minds is how to attain African emancipation and redemption'.[2] By 1929 Casely Hayford was even more specific in his suggestions: 'while propagandists of another race are spreading abroad doctrines which may submerge our continent and make the black man perpetually a hewer of wood and drawer of water, it will be criminal for us to remain silent, and to pretend that these matters do not concern us'. West Africans, he declared, must give a lead in making constructive proposals; they must not stop at West African unity, but must pursue 'an African nationality which will tend to focus world opinion upon African interests generally'.[3]

Self-government as the Test of Nationhood

Perhaps one reason for the relative lack of racial bitterness in the Gold Coast was that nationalist aspirations were so consistently expressed in the form of constitutional demands. There developed what might be called 'institutional nationalism'—the demand for free and representative institutions—rather than racial nationalism. Although tribal, cultural, and racial factors all played their part, the awakening of national consciousness was accompanied, from the very earliest days, by a demand for self-government, within an ever-widening area. 'The true policy I believe to be . . . the formation of a regular government on the European model . . . so that the interference and assistance of the British authorities may be less and less required.' This was written of the Gold Coast, not by a nationalist, but by Lord Grey in 1853,[4] probably before any African had begun to think in such terms.[5]

The idea of self-government—which was to some extent supported by the 1865 Select Committee, mainly on the grounds of economy—was soon taken up by Africans themselves. King Aggery was the first to come into serious conflict with the British authorities on this issue. But to Africanus Horton belongs the credit of having been the first to voice national aspirations in the Gold Coast. 'Nations rise and fall', he wrote. 'Such being the tendency of all

[1] Presidential address, 2nd session of the National Congress, Freetown, Jan. 1923; M. J· Sampson (ed.), *West African Leadership* (Ilfracombe, 1950), pp. 67–76.

[2] Presidential address, 3rd session of the National Congress, Bathurst, Dec. 1925; ibid. pp. 77–85. *West Africa*, 6 Mar. 1926, commented that it would be disastrous if British West Africa were to become united 'not by nationality but by a sense of common racial grievance'.

[3] Presidential address, 4th session of the National Congress, Lagos, Dec. 1929; *West African Leadership*, pp. 86–91.

[4] *The Colonial Policy of Lord John Russell's Administration* (London, 1853), vol. ii, p. 286.

[5] The Chairman of the 1865 Select Committee later commented, 'I am quite sure that no miracle can set up the European model in Africa.' C. B. Adderley, *A Review of 'The Colonial Policy of Lord John Russell's Administration', by Earl Grey, 1853; and of subsequent colonial history* (London, 1869).

national greatness, the nations of Western Africa must live in the hope, that in process of time their turn will come, when they will occupy a prominent position in the world's history, and when they will command a voice in the council of nations.' Like Aggery and his advisers, however, Horton read too much into the Parliamentary Report: 'the House of Commons Committee has now set on foot by resolution (and we hope it will soon be by actual practice) that great principle of establishing independent African nationalities'.[1]

In fact, the famous 'self-government' Resolution of 1865 did not contain any reference to West African 'nations', only to tribes.[2] Horton himself was well aware of the disunity among the peoples of the Gold Coast, and of the need to form 'a strong, compact native Government'. He adumbrated two major units, the Kingdom of Fantee and the Republic of Accra, only as 'provisional and tentative experiments'.[3] In Liberia, however, 'the first self-governing civilised black community on the West Coast of Africa', he considered that the transfer of all authority to the inhabitants had virtually given them a 'nationality'.[4] In other words, nationality in the full sense to Horton implied self-government. His ideas had a strong influence on the founders of the Fanti Confederation, whose ambitious scheme of 1872 represented the first detailed proposals for internal self-government. Their ambitions were dashed when it became clear, from 1874 onwards, that Britain had no intention of withdrawing from West Africa, and doubted the capacity of Africans to manage their own affairs. But the demand for representative institutions was not forgotten, as shown by the deputation scheme of 1885–7; although this achieved nothing, it marked the first attempt to organize a united 'national' demand from both the Fanti and the Accra areas.

Ashanti, however, was still a 'foreign' country, desperately struggling to preserve its own national identity, whether by the Ansahs' ill-fated mission to London, or the last revolt of 1900. All the more remarkable, therefore, was Casely Hayford's vision, as early as 1903, of a federal union which should include both the Colony and Ashanti: 'with the same laws, the same customs, the same hopes, and the same aspirations . . . all flying the Union Jack, not by coercion in any shape or form, but by free choice, as becomes a free people'. To Casely Hayford, self-government was the necessary key to open the door wide to unlimited progress in all directions:

If the Gold Coast were a country with free institutions, free from the trammels of Downing Street red-tapism, we should soon have good wharves and harbours, gas

---

[1] Horton, *West African Countries and Peoples*, pp. 67–68 and 73–74.
[2] *1865 Report*, Resolution No. 3.   [3] Cf. Ch. VI, pp. 230–2, above.
[4] Horton, *West African Countries and Peoples*, chs. ix–xi. He had been influenced by E. W. Blyden's pamphlet about Liberia, *Our Origins, Dangers and Duties* (Monrovia, 1865). This republic was to become an important symbol of the possibility of independent African self-government, especially through the later publications of Blyden; e.g. *The Significance of Liberia* (1906). See also G. W. Ellis, 'Liberia in the Political Psychology of West Africa', in *Journal of the Royal African Society* (London, 1912), vol. xii.

works, water works, and railway communication all over the country. Prosperous cities would grow up, and knowledge would spread among all classes of the people, producing a willing and an efficient body of workmen for the material development of the vast wealth and resources of the country.[1]

From 1898 onwards the A.R.P.S., having rallied mass support to protect land rights, became the self-appointed mouthpiece for constitutional demands, accepting the Legislative Council as the main instrument for advance towards self-government, but always hoping to strengthen the influence of the Society. Later, the National Congress captured the political initiative, and for a time proclaimed the wider ideal of a united West Africa. But its main achievement was probably to crystallize the demand for political reform, in the years immediately preceding the 1925 constitution. The Congress leaders eventually disclaimed any demand for complete self-government; but their clash with the 'Natural Rulers' gave the new constitution a bad start in an atmosphere of suspicion and mutual distrust between the Chiefs and the educated leaders.

Out of this tension there emerged fresh proposals for constitutional advance, notably J. W. de Graft Johnson's *Towards Nationhood in West Africa*, although this lay unheeded by Government for many years. In his own way, de Graft Johnson was just as strongly convinced as Guggisberg of the need to avoid the misapplication of European ideas and institutions. But this led him to take a new approach to nationhood, and to disclaim Western theories of nationality as he saw them:

What is the criterion by which nations are adjudged as such? The Western idea of a nation denotes the possession of military, naval, and air power; capital, wealth and population; industries, trade, and commerce. Of these qualifications great emphasis is laid on the first three, for it is chiefly on them that the 'nations' of the world are so regarded. But such an interpretation of the term deprives many groups and communities of people, principally coloured, of the privilege of the status of nationhood (pp. 97–98).

To de Graft Johnson, the crucial question was 'Should there be an African State Government on the Gold Coast under the aegis of the British?' This was the test of nationhood. He was ready to welcome Ashanti as 'an integral part of the Native Self-Government'; and, like Casely Hayford, he stressed the cultural affinities between Ashanti and the Colony: 'There is unity of race, language, religion, customs and laws as well as common ancestry.' Soon, there must be a unified administration: 'When that auspicious moment arrives, Ashantees, Akims, Akwapims, Fantees, Gas, Ahantas, and all, would be drawn together in one great Akan organisation', which de Graft Johnson claimed would have evolved naturally, 'if Britain had not intervened too early in the history of the Gold Coast and Ashanti.' He looked forward to the

---

[1] *Gold Coast Native Institutions*, pp. 130 and 254–5.

day when 'In due time the Northern Territories may stretch out their hands and join the group.'[1]

In the tradition of Africanus Horton, James Brew, Mensah Sarbah, Casely Hayford, and many others, de Graft Johnson specifically wished to preserve the British connexion; his ultimate goal was Dominion status. 'Under the tutelage of Britain therefore, the inhabitants hope to realise their dreams of a nation within the Commonwealth; they wish to be not only "civilised into an orderly community", but "welded into a Nation".'[2] And he made the significant claim, later to become a sacred text of Gold Coast nationalism: 'good government is no substitute for self-government'.[3] This was the tradition in which Kwame Nkrumah's 'Seek ye first the political kingdom' was to find mass support.

[1] *Towards Nationhood*, pp. 79 and 127.
[2] Cf. *The Gold Coast Leader*, 10 Apr. 1929: 'men are asking the question, "What shall we do to become a nation?"'
[3] *Towards Nationhood*, pp. 100 and 125. Cf. E. Barker: 'The energy of a nation in its own self-government may be a greater thing than the efficiency with which a nation is governed.' *National Character*, p. 169.

RETROSPECT

A SURVEY of Gold Coast nationalism that closes with the year 1928, on the threshold of a period of more intensive nationalist agitation, permits of only tentative and provisional conclusions. It is evident, in any case, that the words 'nation' or 'national' have meant very different things at different times; hence our study, like that of radioactive isotopes, is concerned with a constantly changing phenomenon. Yet there was an essential continuity of development, as the centre of loyalty shifted from the small independent State (e.g. Adansi) or the tribe (e.g. the Fantis), to the confederacy of States (e.g. Ashanti) or the wider ethnic or linguistic group (e.g. the Akans). Each in turn was credited with the title of nation; but eventually, after many vicissitudes and internal rivalries, it became possible to think of 'the Gold Coast nation' as a unit, and to demand for it the status appropriate to a modern nation-state. Similarly, the name 'Gold Coast', originally applied literally to the handful of scattered forts, was gradually extended up to the borders of a sizeable Colony, so that even the creation of the Northern Territories of the Gold Coast seemed a logical extension of the term.

It is important to realize that this synthesis could have taken place for almost any combination of West African peoples who might have been arbitrarily united under imperial rule. It was the existence from 1902 onwards of a common territory, with clearly defined boundaries, governed by a single British authority, that provided the physical framework within which the claim to Gold Coast nationhood could develop. There were formidable obstacles to the growth of a sense of a common national cause: not least being the old military hostility between Ashanti and the south, besides the rigid tripartite division of the Administration and the deliberate attempt to isolate the Northern Territories from the twentieth century. But the rise of nationalism does not wait for a fixed, final definition of the 'nation'. For its origins in the Gold Coast we must go back at least as far as Hill's gatherings of Chiefs in 1852, which touched off the first supra-tribal protest movement, or perhaps rather to the inauguration of a Legislative Council in 1850, which increasingly provided a focus for nationalist demands for representative government.

One conclusion that emerges from this detailed study is the essential continuity of the nationalist tradition, extending backwards much farther than had previously been suspected. The record of Gold Coast nationalism has hitherto appeared as a series of isolated episodes, which nearly always took officials by surprise, especially in the intensity of the protests registered. These include the resistance to the poll tax, King Aggery's challenge to British jurisdiction in Cape Coast, the opposition to every variety of land and forest

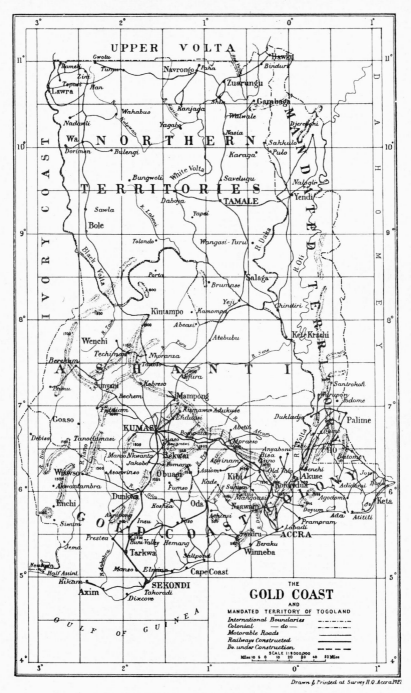

MAP 9. The Gold Coast, 1927—published by the Survey Department, Accra.

legislation, the hitherto unexplained dislike of municipal government, and the growing demand for elective representation at the centre. Peering over the rim of the nationalist crater, however, we can now see that in between these major eruptions the heated lava remained as an ever-present threat of disturbance, and often gave warning of severe internal pressures. Elaborate metaphors are notoriously misleading. The point is that there was a continuously growing volume of resentment and criticism against various aspects of colonial rule. The specific protests which from time to time emerged must be considered a connected series, in the sense in which the participants regarded them.

An important link was the influence of the Press. The spontaneous expression of grievances, against this tax or that bureaucratic decision, was built up by a handful of Cape Coast and Accra journalists into a generalized protest against the fact of British authority. They began to create the stereotype of a harmful, inefficient, unsympathetic colonial government, thus providing a coherent and consistent explanation for everything that went wrong; and gradually there emerged a desire for some alternative to the authority, the paternalism, and the prejudices of the white man. By recalling past protests and offering future targets, the struggling newspapers encouraged the sense of a continuing campaign; and their grandiloquent phrases, depicting everything including the 'national' cause as a little larger than life, offered a splendid spur to action without the sobering prospect of responsibility.

At the grass-roots level, there was constant improvement in the techniques of organization and joint action, to be attributed largely to the experience gained in a multitude of voluntary associations. Ephemeral as many of these were, they offered a means of adjustment to the social structure of the towns, a form of training for leadership, especially for the office-holders, and a novel source of status and prestige. Although largely non-political, these multifarious groups helped to build up something of an African body politic. Even the Temperance Society of Anomabu had an honourable part to play in the establishment of a sense of community and common purpose. More spectacular in their effect, however, were those organizations, such as the combination of Chiefs in the Fanti Confederation, the Aborigines' Rights Protection Society, or the National Congress of British West Africa, which attempted to assert positive national claims *vis-à-vis* the colonial régime.

The underlying unity of purpose is further stressed when we take a closer look at the personalities involved. In the small world of the nineteenth-century Gold Coast, where literate society was limited to the even smaller confines of the coastal towns, it is not surprising that the names of a few persistent individuals or dominant families tend to recur again and again in connexion with widely separated causes. The nationalist politician in his time played many parts; as newspaper editor, lay preacher, platform orator, or petition drafter: as the champion of native customs, electoral reform, or higher pay: defending the Chiefs' jurisdiction in their own domain, or attacking their enhanced status in the new Provincial Councils. A direct tactical success, such as the withdrawal of a Bill under fire, was relatively rare; but each concession became the basis for further demands, and a closed door might stimulate a fresh push in another direction. Thus the supporters of the abortive deputation scheme of 1885–7, far from being discouraged by that fiasco, took up other issues as they arose; fuller representation in the Legislative Council or the protection of land rights were only various aspects of an overriding cause.

Articulate Africans never stopped to query this step-by-jerk advance as anything but just, natural, or inevitable. But how can we explain the existence of a national movement at all? It is true that social and economic changes were producing an environment in which it was possible for nationalism to develop. The growth and differentiation of trade, for example, encouraged people to look outside the small, traditional community for their economic requirements. It created new demands, new opportunities for satisfying them, and new social relationships; it enriched some individuals and left others dissatisfied. At the most homely level, the replacement of the sun-baked clay pot by the cheap imported basin, of the laboriously woven strips of cloth by the gay Manchester substitute, left a kind of cultural vacuum, which the general European disdain for African customs served only to confirm.

Meanwhile, the expanding network of communications made possible the interchange not only of goods but also of ideas over a wider area. The accumulation of capital, further encouraged by the commercialization of land values, and especially by the development of cocoa as a cash crop, introduced private wealth as another claim to social status; it also enabled wealthy families to educate their sons for a new role in the community. The rise of a non-traditional *élite*, the growth of towns with social patterns differing from those of the villages, and the emergence of an employed labour force, all tended to loosen the bonds of clan, lineage, and birthplace, to weaken the authority of the Chiefs, and to produce a power vacuum not altogether filled by outside authority.

It cannot, however, be assumed that such environmental factors led inevitably to the rise of nationalism. They simply created the conditions within which new ideas, new loyalties, new forms of association could develop. It was the colonial situation—the super-imposition of an external, centralized bureaucracy, which involved the political as well as the economic and cultural subordination of African groups and interests—that precipitated the nationalist reaction. The colonial situation is not, of course, a static condition. Imperialism is a dynamic movement which involves expansion and advance on several fronts. In the Gold Coast, at least in the early stages, political control was patchy and uneven in its application, exerted most strongly where urbanization, for example, demanded firmer measures, where the

Chiefs were more compliant, or where District Commissioners were more conveniently stationed. Eventually the influence of the imported oligarchy made itself felt right up to the furthest borders of the territory, once these were stabilized. As the roads and expatriates fanned out from the coast, with them went consumer goods, Bibles, law courts, schools, and all the contents of Pandora's box to disintegrate the old society. In short, the imposition of European authority facilitated and hastened the economic and social changes already inexorably under way. And it is not simply the process of change, but its speed and consequent unevenness of impact that produce discontent and problems of adjustment.

Nationalism must be regarded primarily as a reaction, not as a spontaneous political force. As a reaction to colonialism, it does not require any special explanation, if we assume that men have a universal preference to manage their own affairs. But its character and intensity depend very largely upon the nature of the colonial impact. A harshly authoritarian form of government, decisively overruling local Chiefs, actively imposing its own language and culture-patterns, and effectively denying economic opportunities to the inhabitants, may build up deep resentment; and tension will be exacerbated where race and colour play an important part. On the other hand, a more liberal régime may encourage clearer visions of the political freedom desired, and be more prepared to offer concessions along the road. Most colonial governments in practice generate an explosive mixture of frustration and expectancy.

Imperial rule may be exercised to secure certain strategic or economic advantages, often summed up in the blanket term 'exploitation'. It has to be maintained by varying degrees of military power, political repression, or superior administrative efficiency. In modern times it has commonly been buttressed by claiming various respectable motives, such as the suppression of slavery, the establishment and protection of legitimate trade, or the incapacity of Africans to govern themselves. But these have a way of fading over the years. The colonial situation tends to be of its very nature transitory. The British form of imperialism, more surely than most, might be said to have carried the seeds of its own decay. In comparison with other European powers, their régime could hardly be called repressive, since they allowed liberty of speech, of movement, of organization, and tolerated a considerable degree of abuse from Press and public platform. There is no suggestion that Africans in the Gold Coast enjoyed untrammelled freedom; there were sufficient 'disabilities' inherent in their subordinate position to arouse resentment, but the difference lies in their relative freedom to object publicly in an organized fashion. Recent developments in French Africa and the Belgian Congo, however, suggest that policies of assimilation or repression may be only a means of delaying rather than avoiding or diverting the rise of nationalism.

It looks as if nationalism is the logical outcome of colonialism, given a context of rapid social and economic change. But how do we explain its particular strength and persistence, not to mention its long, almost respectable history, in the Gold Coast? Part of the explanation lies in the long period of contact with Europe which had prepared the way for the increasing momentum of the late nineteenth century. The colonial status of the Gold Coast, and the earliest nationalist reactions, were established before much of East and Central Africa had been explored or annexed. Another important factor, common to West Africa generally, was the absence of a white settler community to confuse the demand for self-government or to offer a counter-claim of tutelage. Furthermore, the way in which British jurisdiction had initially been acquired, largely by negotiation, agreement, and 'tacit assent', encouraged the belief that the refusal of African consent could bring about a change in policy, and that the authorities were open to argument and persuasion, if not in Cape Coast or Accra, then at least in London.

How significant was the indirect influence of British political ideas? Even if thoughtful Africans did not see these applied in practice, they could hardly fail to be aware of the theories of parliamentary democracy, of the liberty of the subject, of national self-determination. British colonial policy was never so single-minded as to still the voice of opposition at home; and the views of the liberal democrats, the Little Englanders, the humanitarians, and the champions of African rights were given wide publicity in 1865, and thereafter remained in the Cape Coast air, to reappear in petition after petition, not to mention schoolboys' essays. Ideals of the brotherhood of man provided a ready yardstick against which to measure acts of injustice or discrimination by local officials; the ultimate prospect of redress and constitutional advance soon became a nationalist article of faith.

Another important reason for the early rise of nationalism in the Gold Coast was the early start of education, and its special encouragement—or at least freedom from interference—under the British. Colonial Governors needed local talent to assist in the lesser tasks of administration, and this provided the main *raison d'être* for the Castle schools which appeared under the Portuguese, Danish, Dutch, and British. But a thoroughgoing imperial policy involves close official control of the aims and methods of education, whereas under British rule—whether by merchants or government officials—the main expansive and directive force came from the Missions, who were allowed a relatively free hand. There was little attempt to inculcate colonial assumptions and attitudes, and every opportunity for such subversive doctrines as the equality of men before God. The administrators of the Northern Territories who attempted to exclude missionaries altogether were at least consistent in their colonial philosophy, if out of step with developments farther south. The predominance of Protestants, with their emphasis on individual responsibility rather than ecclesiastical authority, offers another suggestive contrast between the Gold Coast and the colonies of other European nations.

The schools offered an English-style education, though the metropolitan model was not so closely followed as in the neighbouring French territories. Very occasionally young Africans were officially selected for study in Europe —a tradition dating back to the Portuguese—but these were few and far between. The cost for private students was almost prohibitive, although a handful of lawyers and doctors managed to qualify abroad during the nineteenth century. Africans were certainly not prevented from seeking higher opportunities overseas, nor even limited to the mother country, as witness the first of the few who sailed for America in 1897. For many years postelementary education in the Gold Coast was left mainly to missionary enterprise, fitfully supplemented by a few optimistic Africans. Increasingly, however, the Government was drawn into the regulation and expansion of the educational system, and eventually took a jump ahead of public opinion with the establishment of the school at Achimota. Here a deliberate attempt was made—although it was currently attacked as retrogressive—to maintain African traditions in the curriculum and outlook of this *élite*-producing institution; the students were certainly not expected to become 'black Englishmen'. This was in contrast to the policy of assimilation which was developing elsewhere.[1]

But the lack of any English equivalent term for *évolués* or *assimilados* indicates the absence of any officially recognized role for the products of the school system. In the early 1850's educated Africans were few enough to be accepted on their merits. But as their numbers increased, far from receiving any official recognition of their emancipation they were made more sharply aware of the social gulf between themselves and Europeans. After 1900 there were new barriers to promotion and various attempts were made to edge Africans farther down the social scale. Whether highly or partially educated, they were equally distrusted by administrators, and all alike disparaged as 'scholars' with audible quotation marks. Where their activities were not directly suppressed they were left to their own nationalist devices, instead of being carefully led to participate in a colonial system regarded as fundamentally stable and permanent. As a result, the unsatisfied demand for personal status, social acceptance, and racial equality added a sharper cutting edge to nationalism in the Gold Coast.

We have been considering economic and social change as the necessary environment, and the colonial situation as the necessary precipitant, of modern nationalism. Some forms of colonialism may have been more conducive to its development than others; but perhaps the crucial determinant has been the emergence of the educated *élite*, whose leadership gave direction

---

[1] A recent survey speaks of 'the duplication in Angola and Moçambique of the metropolitan primary and secondary school system'; this follows from the conception of 'the overseas provinces as an integral part of the Portuguese state', which is written into the constitution. J. Duffy, *Portuguese Africa* (Oxford, 1959), pp. 312 and 280.

and impetus as well as continuity to the national movement. Why were they increasingly acknowledged as leaders by their own people? Education had been presented by the missionaries as a means of civilization and advance, of emancipation from 'primitive' standards. The school door appeared as a gateway to progress of all kinds as well as to personal betterment. Even elementary schooling offered a recognizable economic status in the white-collared world of regular jobs and salaries; and in spite of the patronizing attitude of most Europeans to their imitators, there was some compensation in that they themselves were respected and envied by other Africans. The charge that they were unrepresentative misleaders of the masses was particularly resented, and was almost as undiscriminating a misjudgement as the uncritical claim that all educated Africans were *ipso facto* equipped for leadership.

It was the educated *élite* who had to act as mediators and interpreters of Western culture and ideas, and who had the uncomfortable task of working out in everyday life some compromise between—for example—the obligations due to their extended family and the individual responsibility demanded by European employers, between traditional living arrangements and foreign notions of sanitation, between customary observances and the religious requirements of Christianity. Later, with the awakening of what has here been called cultural nationalism, it was still they who set the fashion in an attempt to revive respect for the old civilization, while retaining the conveniences of the new. But why was it that their undoubted influence and prestige were exerted so notably in the political field? What brought them to the forefront of the nationalist movement?

Educated Africans had a multiple role to play in the uncertain world of Afro-European relations. They were often called upon to act as negotiators between the traditional authorities and the Government. When letters were written on behalf of Chiefs, it was often difficult to tell how far the writers had dictated the sentiments; when documents and official policy had to be translated and explained in vernaculars singularly innocent of abstract concepts, it was easy to add their own interpretative slant. From here it was only a small step to initiating and negotiating political claims on behalf of the Chiefs and people. It was the Europeanized Africans who had sufficient economic independence to desire political emancipation, and they alone were articulate enough to demand it. Since their aspirations were higher, they felt grievances the more keenly; they were more alive than others to the inconsistencies of colonial policy, more active in defence of African rights, and more receptive to external stimuli. Even in Gold Coast schools, the study of European history and geography introduced the idea of a world organized into nation-states. Those who travelled abroad were inevitably influenced by nationalist thought and activity in other countries, and especially by the post-war doctrine of national self-determination. Student organizations in London and contacts with American Negro movements also helped to stimulate colour consciousness, spilling over colonial boundaries into a more general 'African' awareness.

Thus it was the educated *élite* who took the lead not only in forming public opinion but also in formulating political objectives: in books, pamphlets, newspapers, and petitions, from the platform and even the pulpit—and almost exclusively in English, the language in which they were administered and in which they had been made aware of other possible forms of government. They were able to recognize the existence of common interests and aspirations over a wider area than that covered by the archaic State system; and this led naturally to the deliberate cultivation of a sense of national consciousness. They had first to create the nation, in a sense, before they could demand political autonomy.

The concept of leadership must not be exaggerated. There was no such thing as a homogeneous public opinion, even among the educated, and attempts to organize and direct it were beset by conflicts of personality rather than principle. The outlook of the leaders was recusant and largely opportunist; their parish was small, their following divided, and their aims were shifting and often confused. Nevertheless, they were to be invoked as the heroes of a later generation, and their tentative but persistent efforts helped to inspire a more militant leadership and a more coherent philosophy of African nationalism. Meanwhile, as the demand for self-government on a national scale emerged, it was the new *élite*, not the old, who were the chief claimants to power.

This claim brought them into open collision with the Chiefs. The possibility of such a clash had always been inherent in the changing social order, but it had been disguised partly as a result of British policy. Any colonial threat to native jurisdiction was regarded as an infringement of African rights, and the educated were quick to react by rallying popular support. In the early days, they had been content to seek power through the Chiefs whom they advised, as in the Fanti Confederation, or to use their 'Natural Rulers' as figureheads, as during most of the history of the A.R.P.S. But it soon became clear that the structure of chieftaincy could support little more than either a very localized form of self-government, or a modified form of indirect rule responsible to an alien authority. Later, as non-traditional functions began to be written into Bills and even into the constitution, the fear that the Chiefs were becoming part of the apparatus of colonial government provoked some sharp attacks.

In the Gold Coast the traditional system did not succeed in absorbing the allegiance, ambitions, and activities of the 'youngmen', to the extent that it did for example in Buganda or in Northern Nigeria, where British protection reinforced instead of disturbing a strong pre-existing unit of government. But in 1928 there was nothing that could yet be called a popular anti-Chief movement. Even the dramatic personal split between Casely Hayford and Nana Ofori Atta was patched up, and during the 1930's Chiefs and intelligentsia were still capable of making common cause, as during the cocoa holdups or in forming a Central National Committee. The conflict was to sharpen after the Second World War, when it became possible to harness sporadic local discontent with the Chiefs into a general upsurge of feeling against authority of all kinds. But it is important to notice that the latent struggle for status and power had already begun to emerge in the early inter-war period.

The situation in 1928 offers no clear pointers to the future, except that the bitterness of the 1930's and the rapid progress towards self-government in the 1940's are now perhaps more readily explained in the light of all that had gone before. Histories of European conquest and administration, of the metropolitan connexion, of 'Africa before the white man', do little to prepare us for the sudden take-over bids issued by African politicians during recent years. An attempt has here been made to recount Gold Coast history from the other end, as it appeared to the subjects of imperial rule, to give full weight to their point of view—without necessarily sharing it—and to explain the emergence of patterns of thought and activity that became almost second nature to many educated Africans. Colonial officials have therefore appeared mainly in a somewhat negative role, in so far as their actions and decisions provoked African protests, or as they were concerned to counter political agitation. This is not intended to deny or ignore the contribution of British administrators in the progress of the Gold Coast towards independence. Nevertheless, British policy was then still based on the assumption that the colonial relationship would continue for many years to come, as Guggisberg put it; and it is the nationalist pressures designed to challenge or change that relationship which have formed the main subject matter of this study.

Many questions remain unanswered. More details are needed about the origins of nationalism in other African territories, if we are to ask what were the common underlying causes and, perhaps more important, what have been the factors responsible for delay or acceleration. Again, how far can we usefully compare the situation in different colonies at different points in time? However tempting it may be to conclude with a flourish of doubtful generalizations, the history of one territory can be taken as proving only the complexity of the forces governing modern nationalism and the pressing need for further study.

INDEX

A Mina, 15 n., 151. *See also* Elmina.
Ababio, Chief of James Town, 336 n., 381 n., 423, 423 n., 424, 431 n.
Ababio II, Nana Otu, 398, 445–6, 501.
Abaddo, D. M., 292 n.
Abadoo, J. M. (1871), 249.
Abadoo, J. M. (1920), 136 n.
Abbarsen and Eyen, Chief of, 173 n.
Abbontiakoon, 43.
Abetifi, 26, 85 n., 281.
Aboasi, 15.
Abodoom, 298.
Abokobi, 179 n.
Aborigines' Protection Society, London, 53 n., 330, 330 n., 331, 344, 352 n., 372, 452, 522 n.
Aborigines' Rights Protection Society, 53 n., 57, 86, 100, 150, 167, 263, 313, 327, 330–1, 436–56, 463, 467, 468, 475–505 *passim*, 520, 520 n., 522, 525–8 *passim*, 532, 552.
Abosso, 43.
Abraham, Chief J. D., 341, 373 n.
Abrobi, 15.
Abura (or Abrah), 378 n.; Chiefs of, 173 n., 335, 336 n., 344, 345, 347, 355 n., 360, 369, 371, 398, 445–6, 501. *See also* Otoo.
Aburi, 9, 26, 27, 32, 34, 49, 71, 85; sanatorium, 14 n., 428.
abusa system, 19, 19 n., 36, 40.
Abyssinia, 166 n.
Accra, *passim*, especially Chs. X and XI.
Accra Herald, The, 182, 182 n., 510.
Achimota, xvii, 56, 58, 109, 111–12, 114–17, 120 n., 121, 123, 124, 401, 402, 402 n., 443, 548, 559.
Achiriboanda, Yaw, 278, 278 n., 279, 283 n., 284, 294, 295, 317.
Acquaah, Rev. G. R., 87 n.
Acquah, Ioné, *Accra Survey*, 164 n.
Acquah III, Nana Ayirebi, 446, 501.
Ada, 27, 32, 94 n., 169, 174, 178, 309, 415.
Adafia, 12.
Adangme, 16 n., 18 n., 19 n., 20, 174, 230.
Adansi, 23, 265 n., 272, 275, 278, 291–2, 297, 319, 322 n., 343; Chiefs of, 17–18, 24, 24 n., 272 n.
Adderley, C. B., 205; *Review of . . . 'Colonial Policy'*, 208 n., 550 n.
Addo, W. (c. 1860), 6.
Addo, William (1895), 423.
Addy, W., 185 n.

Adjaye, E. W., *Three Sons of the Gold Coast* (with J. Buckman and J. W. de Graft Johnson), 469 n.
Adjaye, Nana Annor, Omanhene of Western Nzima, 160, 393, 503; *Nzima Land*, 61 n., 154 n., 160 n., 503 n., 539 n.
Adjaye-Kyem, J., 481 n.
Adjei, Ako, 543 n.
Adjiempon, Chief, 241, 241 n., 255, 255 n., 256, 269, 270.
Adjin, W. A., 120 n.
Adjuah (or Ajua), 27; Chiefs of, 337 n., 429 n.
Aduku III, Nana, Omanhene of Mankessim, 501.
Advisory Committee on Native Education, 114.
Affainie, S. T. A., 481 n.
Afilfa, Chief Kwami, 297, 319 n.
Aflao, 12 n., 13 n.
African-Aid Society, 192 n.
African Association, 48.
African and Eastern Trading Corporation, 48.
African Gold Coast Company, 16 n.
African Interpreter and Advocate, The, 220.
African Mail, The, 93 n.
African Methodist Episcopal Zion Church, 86, 163, 163 n., 164, 541, 548 n.
African Orthodox Church, 544.
African Progress Union, 392 n., 541, 549.
African Steamship Company, 5.
African Times, The, 5, 8, 9, 22, 26, 27 n., 28 n., 38 n., 68 n., 69, 72, 75 n., 89, 90, 100 n., 146 n., 147 n., 192–217 *passim*, 222–63 *passim*, 273 n., 304 n., 331 n., 407 n., 529 n.
African World, The, 122 n.
Agah, Chief of, 173 n.
Agbosome, 12 n., 13 n.
Aggery, George Fynn, Chief of Cape Coast, 173.
Aggery, John, King of Cape Coast, 68, 88, 135, 167, 192–221, 222, 225, 228, 231, 232, 407, 457, 458, 463 n., 470, 550, 551.
Aggery, Joseph, King of Cape Coast, 65 n., 194 n., 197 n., 204.
Aggery, King of Cape Coast (1780), 458 n.
Aggrey, J. E. K., xvii, 113, 113 n., 115, 115 n., 117, 118 n., 148, 163, 163 n., 342 n.
Agogo, 281, 322 n.
Agona, Ashanti, 265 n.; Chief of, 319.

Pp

PRINTED IN GREAT BRITAIN
AT THE UNIVERSITY PRESS, OXFORD
BY VIVIAN RIDLER
PRINTER TO THE UNIVERSITY

WESTMAR COLLEGE LIBRARY